POLITICAL THOUGHT

(Modern, Recent and Contemporary)

Our other books by the same author

1. Political Thought (Ancient and Medieval)
2. Masters of Political Thought
3. Indian Parliament

POLITICAL THOUGHT

(Modern, Recent and Contemporary)

J.C. JOHARI

M.A., LL.B., Ph.D.

Seventh Edition

Volume II

METROPOLITAN BOOK COMPANY PVT. LTD.
NEW DELHI-110002
INDIA

Published by :

Vivek Gupta, Jt. Managing Director
Metropolitan Book Company Pvt. Ltd.
4273/3, Ansari Road, Daryaganj, New Delhi-110 002
Phones: 23271661, 23255914
Fax: 011-23272497
Email: metrobks@vsnl.com

First Edition	:	1965 - 66 (Two Volumes)
Second Edition	:	1972 - 73 (Two Volumes)
Third Edition	:	1981 (Combined)
Fourth Edition	:	1985 (Two Volumes)
Fifth Edition	:	1995 (Two Volumes)
Reprint	:	1999 (Two Volumes)
Sixth Edition	:	2006 (Two Volumes)
Seventh Edition	:	2012 (Two Volumes)
Reprint	:	2014, 2016 (Two Volumes)
Reprint (Edited)	:	2017 (Two Volumes)

ISBN : 978-81-200-0442-9
ISBN : 978-81-200-0443-6 (Set 2 Volumes)

Printed & Typeset by:
Nirula Printers
New Delhi

PREFACE TO THE SEVENTH EDITION

I feel pleasure in placing the seventh edition of this book in the hands of my readers. Once again, for certain pertinent reasons, I have divided the book into separate volumes. While first volume covers the period of ancient and middle ages, study of modern, recent and contemporary political thought has been included in the second one. All chapters have been thoroughly revised and suitably enlarged so as to meet the long-felt requirement of the readers offering this course at the degree and post-graduate levels as well as preparing for some competitive examinations. Once again, I desire to take the opportunity of thanking my eminent friends who conveyed their critical comments and suggestions to me from time to time in the light of which necessary changes and improvements have been made in this edition. In this regard, I wish to count on the gracious co-operation and indulgence of my readers.

– **J.C. Johari**

PREFACE TO THE FIRST EDITION

This work is mainly intended to cater to the requirements of the students preparing this course for the degree of various universities as well as preparing for competitive examinations. Herein a consistent attempt has been made to arrange and present the material in a way conveniently and interestingly intelligible to the readers. Realising that the subject of political thought is too complex and amenable to controversies, debates, discussions and interpretations of a diverse variety, I have throughout been guided by the consideration of removing such difficulties of the students as well as of the general readers. I have, therefore, endeavoured to present the matter in a very simple and lucid manner trying to give no place, as far as possible, to controversial analyses causing confusion. However, I have left it to my readers to make their own assessment in regard to the usefulness of this work. It shall be very obliging if my readers take the trouble of sending me their valuable suggestions in the light of which necessary changes may be introduced in the next print or edition of this book.

In the preparation of this book, I have taken great help from published literature. In particular, I owe much to the text-books and general commentaries written by Western scholars whom I offer my deep regard and appreciation. Hence, I do not claim any originality as such. At every place I have acknowledged these sources, but the arrangement and presentation of the subject-matter is entirely a work of my own scheme.

I am thankful to my publishers, particularly their Managing Director, Shri B. V. Gupta, who took great interest in accepting the manuscript and expediting the work of its publication.

J. C. Johari

CONTENTS

12

MODERN POLITICAL THOUGHT

The central political problem of the transitional period was the position of the new national state and its secularised government in respect of the old cosmopolitan authorities, and in relation to the Christian principles which had so long dominated Western affairs. The central social problem was how to restrain and limit the dangerous liberty of the emancipated individual, and how to turn to the advantage of the community the experience of his egoistic activity.

— **F.J.C. Hearnshaw**[1]

A period of 'strange interlude' took place between the death of Marsiglio of Padua in 1323 and the birth of Niccolo Machiavelli in 1469. Of course, it constituted one of the most momentous epochs of change in the history of Western civilisation and also marked a time of momentous beginnings and of equally momentous endings of much that had been counted fundamental since the end of classical civilisation. Remarkable developments in the art of printing, the discovery of America by Columbus, the opening of unknown continents, the rise of unforeseen possibilities of commerce, the growing shift in the

1. Hearnshaw: *The Social and Political Ideas of Some Great Thinkers of the Sixteenth and Seventeenth Centuries,* p.10.

theatre of world events from the Mediterranean to the Atlantic, were the significant events of this changing span of time. Men like Copernicus and Galileo did a lot of spadework in effecting revolution in the sciences of alchemy, astronomy and numbers. The capture of Constantinople by the Turks in 1453 marked the fall of the Byzantine Empire. By this time the feudal society also hastened to ruin and, after the Conciliar Movement, it clearly appeared that the Roman Catholic Church had ceased, except in name, to be either Catholic or Roman.[2]

CHARACTERISTICS OF MODERN POLITICAL THOUGHT : EMPHASIS ON NATIONALISM, SECULARISM AND SOVEREIGNTY

In this remarkable changing span of time the European mind, once and for all, rendered itself free from the shackles of medievalism and derived inspiration from the great models of the pagan antiquity. It witnessed intellectual emancipation, because people abandoned their faith in the dogmatic absolutes and made many adventurous expeditions, explorations and experimentations in the fields of art, literature and science. As in other fields, so in the realm of political thought, the birth of intellectual activity was marked by the germination and growth of new trends and tendencies. While, on the one hand, these developments indicated a sharp decline of the theories of strong papacy or weak empire; on the other, they harbinged the genesis and growth of an intellectual and spiritual revolution demanding a new state based on the ideals of secularism, nationalism and sovereignty. In a word, these trends and tendencies revealed the breaking of the last bond between the polities and the politics of the medieval and modern ages. They, in other words, testified to the existence of a new outlook which, in the manner of Plato and Aristotle, sought to lay stress on the self-sufficiency of the politically organised community and emphasised its independence of the church. In popular parlance, they formed part of a new movement, called the Renaissance, whose hallmark was admiration for the antiquity and whose triumph meant the termination of medieval tendencies of universalism, feudalism and scholasticism and the emergence of a new world with its emphasis on the spirit of nationalism, secularism and independence of the individual.

2. C.C. Maxey: *Political Philosophies*, pp. 125-26.

The political thought that developed after the medieval period came to have its central concepts much different from those of the ancient and medieval ages. They may be discussed as under:

1. Modern political thought witnessed the rise and growth of nationalism. The national character of the state signified that the citizens of every state were bound to each other by the tie of national unity and not by their membership of a Christian commonwealth. It was on account of this national character that each state became separate and distinct from the other. As a result of the Renaissance, a new tendency developed which insisted that every group of sufficient permanence and with enough of a distinct tradition to have a national character should have an opportunity for developing its own forms of law and government.[3]
2. It witnessed the rise of secular state. It signified the separation of politics from religion and complete independence of the state from the control of the church. By adopting and following a 'policy of blood and iron' and depending on the use of force, the state brought under its control even the monasteries and the church. The secular state superseded the authority of the church to the extent that even the religious heads became subject to royal dominance. The result was that the church lost its prestige and authority and "became what it had never before been for Christian thought–either a voluntary association or a partner of national government."[4]
3. It centred its attention on the existence of a sovereign state. In the medieval period there was no state as such, because Church acted like the state in itself. The state was not an independent unit, rather it constituted a police department of the church.[5] Contrary to the medieval hierarchical set-up

---

3. According to C. D. Burns, "Out of the confused units of the Middle Ages came the definite separations of the renaissance and men began first to feel what we now call their nationality." *Political Ideals*, p.140.
4. G.H. Sabine: *A History of Political Theory*, pp. 333-34.
5. Ernest Troeltsch says that, speaking generally of the Middle Ages, there was then "no feeling for the state: no common and uniform dependence on a central power, no abstract basis of association in formal and legal rules-or at any rate, so far as anything of the sort was present, it was a matter only for the Church and in no wise for the state." See E Barker: "Unity in the Middle Ages" in F.S. Marvin (ed.): *The Unity of Western Civilisation*, p.116.

with a Pope sitting at the top, it saw the rise of strong and powerful monarchies in the western part of Europe, particularly in England, France and Spain. The result was a revolution in the nature of political authority as well as in men's minds about it. Of course, in distinct opposition to medieval Empire and Papacy, the conception of a sovereign as the fountain-head of all political power "became in the sixteenth century a common form of political thought."[6]

4. As a corollary to the above, it may be pointed out that modern political thought found its another outstanding feature in monarchical despotism. When both the Papacy and the so-called Roman Empire lost their prestige and authority, strong national monarchies developed. This marked a great political upheaval, because the national monarchs ruthlessly usurped the power of feudal lords and corporations and concentrated all powers of their respective kingdoms in their own hands. They shook of the Papacy. Besides, inventions of the means of transport and communication enabled them to exercise strong control over all persons living within their kingdoms. The growth of commerce and industry necessitated their further intervention even in the economic sphere of the society. In this way, not only political but economic changes also greatly facilitated the abandonment of the medieval idea of weak and limited royal government and prepared the way for the rise of strong and unlimited monarchies. It may be pointed out that by the sixteenth century all the royal governments "had adopted a conscious policy of exploiting national resources of encouraging trade both at home and abroad and of developing national power."[7]

5. Modern political thought gathered material from the struggle for the cause of individual liberty and democracy. In the sixteenth and first-half of the seventeenth centuries, monarchy moved towards absolutism. But it could not remain unchallenged for long. With the growth of enlighten-

---

6. Sabine, *op.cit.*, p.311. Allen says: "A crash became inevitable and in the sixteenth century the Church was torn to pieces." *A History of Political Thought in the Sixteenth Century*, p.xiii. M. Ruthnaswamy thus points out: "The personality of the state was absorbed in the personality of the ruler. The enlightened despots of the eighteenth century in Prussia, France and Russia stood out as the sole representatives of the State." *The Making of the State,* p. 46.
7. Sabine, *op. cit.*, p. 318.

ment and understanding and the realisation of their power and importance, the people began to question their duty of passive obedience to absolute royal control and to demand more and more their political rights and privileges. The result was a prolonged fight between obstinate royal absolutism on the one side and common people imbued with new confidence in themselves on the other. The people realised that royal absolutism was undoubtedly necessary to weld them together and bring order and unity out of feudal disorder and anarchy. As such, when the purpose was achieved, the continuance of royal despotism became intolerable. This tendency grew particularly manifest in England in the conflict between early Stuart kings and their Parliaments which culminated in the Glorious Revolution of 1688. However, in France, it took a violent turn and ensued in the Great Revolution of 1789.

In short, modern political thought has its central characteristics in nationalism, secularism, sovereignty and royal absolutism substituted by representative government. It may, however, be noted that all these trends and tendencies did not develop simultaneously in the fifteenth or sixteenth centuries, nor did their appearance and growth mark a sudden and complete breakdown of the chain of medieval political ideas.[8] Rather, they developed incessantly till they testified to the existence of strong national, secular and sovereign states and thereby marked complete disappearance of the medieval and final emergence of the modern ages. In particular, the trend of nationalism attained visible maturity in the later part of the eighteenth century. But the movement in the directions of secularism, nationalism, sovereignty and democracy took such deep roots and worked so irresistibly that secular, sovereign, democratic and national state became the fundamental subject of modern political thought.

8. Allen says: It is an error to suppose that the sixteenth century saw the development of much that was strikingly new in political philosophy. Controversy was, of course, mainly concerned with questions men were forced, by what was happening, to consider. Many old questions were, therefore, stated in new terms. But all through the century, except at least in Italy, political thought remained essentially medieval in character. All through the century the main division of late medieval opinion was expressed." *Op. cit.*, p. xiv.

RENAISSANCE : EMERGENCE OF A SCIENTIFIC OUTLOOK

The medieval world came to an end 'with the pestilance of the Black Death of the fourteenth century'.[9] In this direction, Renaissance and Reformation were the two great movements which contributed to the transformation of the medieval into modern period.

Renaissance means new life or revival of old knowledge or learning. In this sense, Europe had to pass through three Renaissances–first in the eighth century when introduction of the old Roman education and learning took place; second in the thirteenth century when the ideas of Aristotle and the Arabs were rediscovered; third, in the fifteenth century when there occurred a resuscitation of the whole culture of the classical world. The first prepared the way for the second, and the second did the same for the third. Here we are concerned only with the third one which had its germination in later part of the fourteenth century and was roughly extended to the sixteenth : and since its rise and growth occurred mainly in Italy, it is also known as the Italian Renaissance.

Renaissance marked the re-emergence of a humanistic and a scientific outlook. It indicated that the European people had developed a new consciousness of life and a new sense of liberty. Achievements in the fields of art, literature and science threw off medieval forms and looked for new values. Inspiration was derived from the models of classical world. Platonic societies were formed and Plato was found to be a theologian and a prophet. The result was that medievalism receded into the background and antiquity came on the front pedestal. In this way, by the end of the fifteenth century, a new world opened 'before the staggered gaze of man already eager to explore, already intoxicated with the intellectual stimulants they had received from their study of antiquity.'[10] Allen aptly says: "What is here meant by the Renaissance is that shift of the point of view which brought earth into the foreground istead of heaven and hell, and partially, at least released men from preoccupation with a life hereafter. The period of the Renaissance was one in which men were falling more and more deeply in love with life as they knew it in everyday experience. Human

9. R.H. Murray: *The History of Political Science from Plato to the Present,* p. 104.
10. P. Doyle: *A History of Political Thought,* p.127.

relations became more interesting than man's relation to God."[11] Similarly, Mayers describes it as that march of a new spirit which finally shattered the medieval order, laid the foundations of a new spirit of a new world of the seventeenth century–the world, in essentials, put an end to the Middle Ages one and for all."[12]

Renaissance informed that 'man is the measure of all things', or 'the proper study mankind is man.' It rejected the whim of 'otherworldliness' of the medieval period and developed interest in studying man's relation with his own fellow beings. Humanism and naturalism superseded the place of celestialism and supernaturalism. Interest in and pre-occupation with human problems and efforts to find out their solutions dispelled the superstitions of supernatural authority and inspired the lay mind to revolt against the control of ecclesiastical authority. In short, Renaissance adhered to the worth and significance of man by making him 'once more a man in the fathomless universe."[13] According to William Ebenstein, "The most important discovery of the Renaissance–more significant than the single work of art or and one genius–was the discovery of man."[14]

Finally, it should be remembered that while Renaissance was the birth of emotions and scientific outlook which had remained dormant during the last one thousand years or so, it was something more than a mere resuscitation of the antiquity. Of course, antiquity dominated, but medievalism was also accepted to the extent it could maintain its congruity with it. The whole history of the New Learning forms a commentary on the wise and unwise use of the classics. While the wise used the past knowledge in order to think for themselves, the unwise did the same to have their thinking done for them. Undoubtedly, the Renaissance transferred interest from the form to the matter, or from the supernatural to the natural, and dominated the thought of men, yet it never really made classical ideas as exclusive part and parcel of the mental furniture of their system of thought. Plato and Cicero were frequently read and invoked, but John of Salisbury and St. Thomas Aquinas were not wholly ignored. Rather, the fashion of the Renaissance was to accept

11. Allen, *op. cit.*, pp.78-79.
12. Mayers: *Political Thought:* The European Tradition, p.107.
13. R.H. Murray, *op. cit.*, p.106.
14. Ebenstein: *Great Political Thinkers*, p.278.

classical truths in a pupil-like manner. In this way, the acceptance of the past was purely mechanical and if the people had any interest in medievalism, they maintained it 'with a veneer of classical learning.'[15]

REFORMATION : TRIUMPH OF SECULARISM

Like Renaissance, another movement that brought the Middle Ages to an end was the Reformation. Indeed these two great movements destroyed the medieval concepts of universalism and scholasticism and supplemented the work of each other by creating modern sovereign, secular and national states. Indeed, they gave such a rude setback to the medieval notions of universal church and Holy Roman Empire that they could never recover.[16] In this way, they did the remarkable work of transforming Europe from its medieval into modern existence. Ebenstein correctly observes: "Renaissance and Reformation are inextricably inter-woven with the birth and growth of the modern national-state. In the field of secular thought and experience, the Renaissance brought about the rediscovery of the ancient world and witnessed the immense broadening of man's horizon through the discovery of the New World. In the field of religious thought and experience, the Renaissance opened the gates to a new religious world through the Protestant Reformation."[17]

In a way, the Reformation was a part of the general process of rebirth of the religious aspect of the Renaissance. Its early leaders denied any revolutionary intention and merely wanted a return to the early sources of Christianity like faith in the scriptures. Prior to the fourteenth century, the Roman Church acted ruthlessly in checking, even destroying, its critics or opponents by means of persuasion, winning over, or burning

15. Murray, *op. cit.*, p.105.
16. According to Adams, "It was the most important positive work of the sixteenth century to bring the national church under the same degree of parliamentary control which had been at that date established over the monarchy." *Constitutional History of England,* p.224. Similarly Hallam remarks: "No Revolution has ever been more gradually prepared than that which separated almost one half of Europe from the communion of the Roman see, nor were Luther and Zwingli any more than occasional instruments of the things which, had they never existed, would at no great distance of time have been effected under the names of some other reformers." See Taswell-Langmead: *English Constitutional History,* pp.385-98.
17. Ebenstein, *op. cit.,* p. 298.

alive at the stake. But after the notorious event of Babylonish captivity, papacy became the object of frank condemnation in the name of its having lost the original ideals of the faith and grown corrupt by the earthly ambition of lust, wealth and power. Although the Conciliar Movement failed owing to several weaknesses of its own and the Papacy became once again dominant, yet papal obstinacy drove the reformist tendencies into a revolution which in the next century successfully destroyed the power of the church never to revive again.

The history of the Reformation movement dates from October 1517 when Martin Luther pasted his ninety five theses on the church door at Wittenberg. Soon this movement spread from Germany to the rest of the continent. It rented in twain the unity of the medieval church and menaced the very existence of Roman Catholicism. At first, the French monarch welcomed this movement, because Luther and his followers paralysed the arms of his enemy *i.e.,* the German Emperor, and it was, indeed, owing to the fostering support of Francis I that they could successfully defy the authority of Charles V and ultimately compel him to make with them the famous Peace of Augsburg in 1555 which recognised the two 'religions' and left the princes of the Empire free to choose either of them. Thus, the movement gained enormous progress throughout Europe and its pioneers were full of hope that their cause would triumph in no distant future.

As a result, Protestantism developed rapidly and it appeared that in Germany itself, apart from the three ecclesiastical electorates, little remained to be captured from Catholicism except Austria, Bavaria and Palatinate. In Switzerland, the followers of Zwingli and Calvin held the field who were more virulent and more actively opposed to the old creed of Christianity. In the reign of Gustavus Vasa, Sweden adopted the new creed to inspire with religious zeal her natural revolt against the overlordship of Denmark. In the days of Henry VIII, England threw off her allegiance to Rome and subsequently in the time of Edward VI drifted towards extreme anti-papalism that received further accentuation in the brief but bloody reign of Queen Mary. The religious fanaticism of Philip II of Spain marked an inquisitorial rule in the Netherlands and roused a vehement passion of protest that was destined soon to break out in an open revolt. Similarly, in Scotland, the flame kindled by John Knox consummated the fire of patriotic Calvinism.

As a matter of fact, the Reformation marked a religious upheaval. Its pioneers like Luther, Calvin, Melanchthon and Zwingli and their followers attacked the system of Roman Catholicism and justified the supremacy of nation-states. Hence, its description forms part of modern European history. But in politics its importance is due to the fact the it did set in motion the chain of events and let loose a tide of ideas that was destined to shape the political thinking and influence the political behaviour of all succeeding generations. True it is that its pioneers as well as their followers were no political theorists of first rank, but they started a movement that turned out in the end to be almost as much a political as a religious rebellion and the flow of their political ideas shaped the course of human events to the extent that in the end it appeared as much a political as a religious upheaval.[18]

The political doctrines of Reformation which appeared more important than its religious counterpart had their important effects. They may be discussed as under :

1. The Reformation completed the work of the Conciliar Movement. In the fifteenth century the Conciliar Movement had attempted to reform the church from within, but it failed. However, its failure revived the important conception of the congregational character of church authority with its corollarly that an office was in the nature of a trusteeship rather than an inalienable power. When reform from within failed, revolution from without in the shape of religious upheaval took place. The Reformists assailed the papacy for having lost the original ideals of the Christian faith and for having become currupt by the worldly ambitions of lust, wealth and power. Thus, the Reformists accomplished the unfinished

18. According to Maxey, the Reformation 'turned out in the end to be almost as much political as religious, and the political doctrines to which it gave currency have shaped the course of human events even more than its religious ideology. Religiously it divided the Western world into two never friendly and often bitterly hostile camps, brought to life the seeds of sectarianism which had lain dormant since the Nicene creed received the cachet of Roman officialdom in 1361 and wrecked for ever the spiritual and temporal hegemony of the Roman Pope. Politically, it completed the dissolution of the Holy Roman Empire, hastened the proliferation of independent national state, fanned up furious conflagration of warfare and persecution which gutted the entire structure of feudal society and released a torrent of radical ideas that have defied the most strenuous effort of constituted authority to choke them down.' *Op. cit.,* p. 154.

task of the Conciliarists and the movement thus represented a continuation of the conciliar tendency.[19]

2. The Reformation supplemented the work of the Renaissance. The movement of New Learning influenced all spheres of life, including the Roman church, that still adhered to the traditions of primitive Christianity and, what more, "was determined to remain unchanged."[20] The Reformation influenced the church to the extent that medieval concepts of universalism, scholasticism and Christian commonwealth were destroyed. In this way, this religious movement marked an end of that period in which Papacy was regarded as the indispensable condition of individual and corporate life and the church regulated the relationship between the rulers and the ruled and thereby stood as the highest court of appeal on all matters concerning life. Thus, while the Renaissance left the religious field, the Reformation covered it.
3. The Reformation led to the transference of a good deal of authority to the state which in the Middle Ages belonged to the church. Together with Renaissance it broke the superstition of a universal society with a Pope sitting at the top and fragmented Christian society into many territorial units (nations) partaking more of the nature of a state than that of the church. Its assertions subordinated religious authority to the secular one and distinctly brought it under the control of a 'godly prince'.
4. The Reformation led to the growth of absolute monarchy. In their rejection of papal dominance, the Reformers got the support of kings and princes who were anxious and ambitious to save themselves and their people from papal exploitation. As a result of this movement, the kings consolidated their power and position by suppressing disorderly elements living within their territories. They also confiscated clerical property and frankly flouted the jurisdiction of the Pope. In this way, the Reformation led to the emergence of sovereign nation-states.
5. The Reformation led to the growth of marked individualism by resenting the practice of religious persecution and advocating the notion of 'justification of faith'. The Reformers

19. Ebenstein, *op. cit.*, pp. 288-89.
20. Adams : *Civilisation During the Middle Ages*, p. 406.

denounced the intermediary role of the church and justified man's direct relationship with God. As a result, freedom of conscience received recognition and, from a political standpoint, it led to the growth of individual liberty and political democracy.

6. The Reformation had its economic repercussions as well. Already there was a reaction against the enormous wealth belonging to a thoroughly degenerate church. The Reformers by their doctrines helped the princes to aggrandise their powers by confiscating the property and encroaching upon the jurisdiction of the church. As a result, their teachings led to communistic disorders and revolts of the peasants.
7. From one point of view, unlike Renaissance, the Reformation indicated a tinge of medievalism. The teachings of the Reformers decidedly did much to counteract the radicalising non-moral and non-religious trend of Machiavellianism. Of course, this movement rejected the notions of medieval universalism and scholasticism and aligned itself with the concepts of nationalism and sovereignty, yet in its doctrines the union of religion and ethics with politics was distinctly medieval. This union which characterised the Middle Ages but which had temporarily been sundered by Machiavelli was once again resolved in the doctrines of the Reformists.

In a word, the political teaching of the great Reformers created a set of important ideas in the sixteenth century. Although in certain respects they borrowed from the medieval traditions, they were also radical in other directions. For example, on the question of relationship between church and state and the moral basis of political obligation, they followed and developed the medieval doctrines. As already pointed out, they did much to counteract the non–moral and non–religious spirit of Machiavellianism. Their frank rejection of the medieval notion of universalism allied itself with the idea of modern nationalism. In particular, the political thought of Reformation exalted the status of secular authority by propounding the doctrine of divine character of temporal government. As a result, the case of emerging national monarchies grew strong more and more and when the kings began to exercise their powers in an absolute manner, a reaction was set in which formed the political thought of counter–Reformation or anti–monarchism. Dunning well points out that the effect of the Reformation was "to strengthen absolutism in the political sovereign."[21]

CONTRIBUTIONS OF MODERN POLITICAL THOUGHT: VALUES OF LIBERALISM, SECULARISM, NATIONALISM AND INTER-NATIONALISM

If a startling break in the continuity of the history of European political thought occurred after the death of Aristotle, another, though not equally startling, found its expression after the death of Marsiglio of Padua. As between the times of Aristotle and Cicero, so in the interval between Marsiglio and Machiavelli, a sort of void happened to take place that marked a genuine break in the running tradition. After the fourteenth century, geographical discoveries and scientific inventions so fundamentally altered the shape of conditions that a real break was inevitable. The result was that the great medieval Church-State, *Respublica Christiana* or Christian Commonwealth, established upon the ruins of Caesarian Rome by the prudence of Emperor Constantine, the genius of St. Augustine and the statesmanship of a long line of powerful Popes passed into the hands of secular and national kingdoms.

Obviously, the difference between medieval and modern political thought is quite sharp. The central problem of medieval political thought was the problem of Two Powers, the Spiritual and the Temporal, or the Ecclesiastical and the Secular, or the *Sacerdotium* and the *Regnum,* or the Papacy and the Empire, or, in modern phraseology, the Church and the State. But after the fourteenth century, the central problem was the emancipation of the slave, the elevation of the serf, the edification of the free man, and, in general, the establishment of conditions which would render possible the liberation and the realisation of individual soul. Hence, while the medieval period witnessed the rise and fall of the Christendom, the growth and decay of the Holy Roman Empire, the progress and degradation of the papal monarchy and the development and disappearance of the ideal unity of the Faith, the modern period displayed the formation of national states, the rise of strong dynastic kingships, the advent of the middle class of prominence and power, the revolution in the art of war due to the introduction of gunpowder and fireams and the emergence of a man together with the moral and intellectual transforma-

21. W.A. Dunning: *A History of Political Theories,* Vol. II, p. 24.

tion which was effected by the Renaissance and Reformation movements.

It all leads us to say that like the political thought of ancient and medieval periods, modern political thought has its own salient contributions which may be enumerated as under:

1. Its secularism solved the problem of religious faith. Upto the times of Emperor Constantine it was recognised that every individual was free to choose any religion. But the great persecutions of Holy Rome marked the abandonment of the policy of religious toleration. Within eighty years of Constantine's edict of toleration, paganism had been proscribed and orthodox Christianity established as the sole legal religion of the Empire. As a result, heresy became a treason and ex-communication meant ostracism, infidelity, even death. But the Reformation Movement brought religion out of the world of politics and re-established its long-sundered alliance with ethics. The new tendency demanded that the state should tolerate all religions and that the believers of various religions or creeds should live together in peace and harmony with each other. Hence, Bodin insisted that it was not advisable to interfere in the matters of faith, because none could be forced to believe against his will. Milton contended that the interests of truth demanded freedom of expression. Similarly, Oliver Cromwell, John Locke, Roger Williams of Connecticut and Benedict Spinoza demanded freedom for the individual in matters of faith and suggested that the state should not interfere in the sphere of religion until its own security was menaced. It is true that even in the sixteenth and seventeenth centuries the states took part in activities of religious persecution, yet gradually the coincidence of political necessity with philosophical conviction led to the abandonment of the worst forms of persecution and to the wide establishment of religious toleration in some form or other.

2. It solved the question of relationship between church and state. The tendency of secularism did not simply separate politics from religion, rather it placed church under the control of the state. It rejected the medieval theory of divine origin of state and treated political institutions as mere human contrivances. National monarchs like Henry VIII of England, Philip II of Spain and Louis XIV of France refuted the argument of the Calvinists that ecclesiastical authority

was superior to political and, in stead, strongly emphasised royal supremacy even over the class of the ecclesiasts. Likewise, Hooker, Hobbes and Barcley lent support to the view of erastianism and rejected the contention of the Jesuit Publicists (like Mariana, Bellarmine and Suarez) who emphasised that church had a divine character, while state had a human origin deriving only that authority from the people as it possessed from the sanction of sinful men.

3. The trend of democracy finally solved the problem of nature and source of political authority. In the beginning, when national consciousness was weak and immature, people favoured a strong monarchical set up and the supporters of the state exalted kingship and justified royal supremacy in the name of Divine Rights of Kings. As a measure of defence not only against Papalists but also against Calvinistic rebels, common lawyers, recalcitrant parliamentarians and social revolutionaries, the supporters of state sought to justify royal absolutism in the name of king's being a vicar of God on earth. In the seventeenth century, however, Hobbes did the same by adopting the framework of social contract. He set a new tradition which was subsequently followed by the defenders of state sovereignty like Spinoza, Hume, Austin and Hegel. But this tradition witnessed its gradual repudiation when people began to question the scope and legitimacy of political obligation. Like John of Salisbury, Catholic Mariana and Calvinist Beza justified tyrannicide and John Locke held that people could depose their sovereign if he violated the terms of social compact. Against this newer tendency, the royal despotism out of its stubbornness resorted to the arbitrament of sword. However, when popular resentment was successful in threatening, deposing and executing some of the obstinate rulers, the gateway for the emergence of representative government was finally opened.

4. The establishment of secular nation-states with strong monarchies claiming sovereignty and repudiating the cosmopolitan authority of both the Pope and the Emperor opened the field of international politics. Wars between powerful monarchs for the sake of some religious truth or for extending territory to exploit natural and economic resources, or for establishing mastery over the newly discovered parts of the globe created the need for formulating a law of

universal validity. On the basis of this realisation, men like Suarez and Grotius built up the magnificent fabric of what is now commonly known as the International Law.

5. Among others, it brought about a great change in the world of law–its nature, variety, sanction and classification. The medieval superstitions of Law of Nature and Law of God were abandoned. There happened a striking change in the socio-economic set-up and in response to them several thinkers and publicists like Sir Thomas More, Bacon, Campanella and Harrington drew pictures of ideal commonwealths. The decline of feudalism and the rise of capitalism over its debris created a pauper proletariat whose miserable plight supplied abundant material to the political ideas of socialism.

In short, modern political thought is the thought of secularism, nationalism, sovereignty, democracy, liberalism, socialism and internationalism. Its various trends and tendencies arose and developed as the newer conditions demanded from time to time. Representative government came as a revolt against unlimited monarchy; *laissez faire* arose as a reaction against paternalism; pluralism came as a challenge to monism; socialism appeared as a panacea for social ills engendered by free competition and private economy. In many ways, various thinkers and their doctrines contributed to the fundamental question of proper reconciliation between the nature and scope of political authotiry and individual liberty.[22]

---

22. See R.G. Gettell: *Introduction to Political Science,* pp. 66-67.

13

MACHIAVELLI

Machiavelli is sometimes called the first modern political philosopher. It is quite as accurate to say that he ends the medieval era as that he begins the modern. Great as was his influence in stimulating reflection, it was not by his radical rejection of all the characteristics of medieval political theory that the modern era was introduced.

— **W.A. Dunning**[1]

No political thinker has probably been 'so persistently abused and so little understood' as Niccolo Machiavelli (1469-1527) whose enigmatic figure stood in the porch of the sixteenth century as 'a sinister rock of offence'.[2] Born in a noble family of Florence, he had the privilege of being widely read in the Latin and Roman classics. However, what came to him as an event of great fortune was the establishment of the Republic in Florence in 1494 wherein he had his great friend and intimate counseller in Piero Soderini–an association for which a number of aristocrats characterised Machiavelli as "Soderini's lackey'. Thus, he joined the Government of Florence as the Secretary of the Ten–a body responsible for war and interior affairs. His ambassadorial assignments to the courts of Louis XII of France,

1. Dunning: *A History of Political Theories,* Vol.I, p.326.
2. Allen: *A History of Political Thought in the Sixteenth Century,* p. 447.

Maximilian of Germany and, most important of all, Caesar Borgia of Romagna imparted him a first-hand knowledge of the statecraft. This career is very important in the life of Machiavelli as he had the practical experience of administration, diplomacy and warfare. However, what impressed him most was the career of Caesar Borgia, son of Pope Leo III, who in his region torn by the chaos of tyranny and bringindage managed "to establish order and security by the most ruthless methods, by accurate judgment and unfailing energy, by daring, treachery and murder."[3] Machiavelli took it for granted by the career of this ruler of Romagna that "only by such methods he could have succeeded. Scruples or hesitations or any failure of will would have ruined his work."[4] However, more important than all this was the event of 1512 when the Republic was terminated and Machiavelli had to suffer the torment of forced exile owing to the coming into power of Lorenzo de Medici.[5] It much hardened his views about human nature. From now onwards till the end of his life, Machiavelli had ample time to ponder and contemplate and then express his views in his great works on politics that subjected him to 'a chorus of denunciation'.[6]

ENVIRONMENT : MACHIAVELLI AS A CHILD OF HIS OWN TIMES

Machiavelli has rightly been called 'a child of his own times'. As the period of his life and work coincided with the glorious days of the Renaissance and as he vigorously represented the shade of New Learning in his writings, he is also known as the 'Child of the Renaissance'. Of course, the political ideas of Machiavelli were coloured by the conditions of his own days. The period of the first quarter of the sixteenth century

---

3. *Ibid.*, p. 449.
4. *Ibid.* It is certain that in the initial stage Machiavelli "had bitterly protested his assignment to the camp of Caesar Borgia, but the longer he watched the manoeuvring of that cold-blooded schemer the more impressed he became." See M. Judd Harmon: *Political Thought from Plato to the Present*, p.156.
5. Owing to this, it is said that the 'most famous victims of the restoration of the Medici rule was Machiavelli.' Felix Gilbert thus says: "The circumstances of Machiavelli's life were drastically altered after the return of Medici to Florence. Indeed, the year 1511 is generally considered to have been the turning point in his life: from a *vita active* of practical politics he turned to a *vita contemplativa* of writing". *Machiavelli and Guicciardini: Politics and History in Sixteenth Century Florence,* p.160.
6. Allen, *op. cit.*, p. 447.

coincided with the period of his maturity. This was the period when movement for limited government in the church, that had attained a definite achievement in the Conciliar Movement, had largely disappeared. It was a period of strange interlude witnessing the decline of Papacy and the rise of modern nation-states. So while the Popes still acted in clear contravention of the decisions taken at various Church Councils, (including the Constance Council),[7] several ambitious monarchs like Henry VII of England, Ferdinand of Spain and Louis XI of France immensely increased their power in their respective kingdoms by ruthlessly crushing the institutions of feudalism and repudiating the hold of the Papacy.

However, to Machiavelli, the most shocking factor was the unfortunate conditions of his beloved Italian peninsula where none of the rulers of Venice, Florence, Naples, Milan and Papal States was able to consolidate her strength. Not only this, Italy was the battleground of intriguing and ambitious potentates, local as well as foreign, who had very little capacity to preserve or protect the integrity and independence of Italy from the aggressions of the belligerent neighbours. Machiavelli cautiously noted the tragic fact that for the last twenty years his beloved country "had been oppressed by foreign dominations and distracted by the wars of aliens within her border. The entry of Charles VIII into Naples had heralded a struggle between France and Spain for dominance in the peninsula. In 1513 the Spaniards were at Naples, the Swiss in Lombardy and the French, in the background, were about to set on foot a new invasion."[8]

Machiavelli also noted the unfortunate fact that during the period of constant disorder and internecine warfare, public leadership was actuated more by selfish gain than by public interest. Public morality was deplorably low and an unscientific statecraft had become the sole arm of defence. The norms of public conduct declined so precipitously that the old institutions of the church and the empire were no longer able to evoke a spirit of unity and to simulate an interest in private and public morals. As Sabine says: "Cruelty and murder had become normal agencies of government; good faith and truthfulness had become childish scruples to which an enlightened man would hardly give lip service; force and craft had become too frequent to need comment; and selfishness, naked and un-

7. See Creighton: *History of the Papacy*, p. 234.
8. Allen, *op. cit.*, p. 461.

adorned, need only succeed in order to supply its own justification. It was a period truly called the age of the 'bastards and adventurers', a society created as if to illustrate Aristotle's saying that 'man when separated from law and justice, is the worst of all animals."[9]

The tragic facts of the period of extra-ordinary political turbulence had their indelible impact upon the mind of Machiavelli. "Frustrated personal ambition, humiliation at the sight of country's domination by foreign armies, resulting from the weakness and instability of her governments, and cynical disillusionment in the moral authorities of the time–such was Machiavelli's experience."[10] It was, however, during the period of his forced retirement of the last 14 years of his life that he pondered over the miserable conditions of his beloved country with a firm resolve to suggest the ways to seek their eradication. "He set himself, therefore, to find out what are the causes of the greatness and decline of states, what are the factors of political success, how a state may attain stability and, above all, what is needed in Italy to secure the expulsion of the barbarians."[11]

It is obvious that the political ideas of Machiavelli constitute a faithful reflection of his observations and conclusions based on his wide personal and practical experiences. Moreover, the contributions of Machiavelli in the form of specific counsels to the rulers to commit and omit certain things made him much more than a political philosopher; he became not a mere theorist but also a realist and not a mere political philosopher but also a policy scientist. It appears that the fundamental purpose of Machiavelli is not to enunciate the philosophy of state as such but to solve the master problems of concrete statecraft. But the dominant force is the environment–contemporary conditions of his beloved country: it is rightly pointed out that 'in no system of political philosophy is the influence of environment more manifest than in that of Machiavelli.'[12]

WORKS : VOYAGE OF DISCOVERY TO A NEW SCIENCE OF POLITICS

The political philosophy of Machiavelli comes to us from his several works in which the *Prince* occupies the most im-

9. Sabine: *A History of Political Theory,* pp. 337-38.
10. William T. Bluhm: *Theories of the Political System,* p. 249.
11. Allen, *op. cit.,* p. 449.
12. Dunning, *op. cit.,* p. 285.

portant place, His *Art of War* is but an expression of one of the favourite themes of his patriotism–unification of Italy under a powerful central government. His *Florentine History* does little but confirm and illustrate a similar impression. However, his *Discourses on the First Ten Books of Titus Livius* is also important inasmuch as it reveals his whole mind on the subject of state and its life. The *Prince* and the *Discourses,* though they deal with two different forms of polities–the former with the subject of absolute monarchy and the latter with that of republic–that makes the issue of his real preference for a particular form of political system a matter of academic controversy, it should be noted here that the two works are 'companion pieces' each of the two "is a 'how to' book; a set of rules for the construction of a strong and stable political order."[13]

The most important work that gives Machiavelli a notorious distinction is the *Prince* that has been characterised as a hand-book for a successful Caesar. Discarding all canons of logic and morality, here Machiavelli lays bare the springs of human motivation with ruthless and consummate insight. It contains 26 chapters which lend themselves to three divisions. Its first part (Chapters 1 to 11) gives a general introduction and deals with various forms of absolute government. Its second part (Chapters 12 to 14) denounces contemporary practice of engaging mercenary troops and emphasises the need for and significance of keeping national standing armies. Its last part (Chapter 15 to 26) offers a very valuable set of counsels to the ruler for establishing a strong and big state. This part constitutes Machiavelli's monumental contribution to the science of statecraft. In a real sense, it is nothing but a memorandum on the art of government and political success. For this reason, it is said that the political philosophy of the *Prince* "is a study of the art of government rather than a theory of the state."[14]

The study of this important work on the master-science of concrete statecraft should be made with two essential considerations in mind. First, what motivated Machiavelli to write so authoritatively on the science of statecraft was his appreciation of the wicked and ruthless practices of Caesar Borgia for the sole reason of having a capable and powerful ruler who would make his beloved country united and strong. Thus Caesar Borgia has been described as the 'model' of Machiavelli's

13. Bluhm, *op. cit.,* p. 253.
14. Dunning, *op. cit.,* p. 293.

Prince. It well obviates the point that what really motivated Machiavelli was a sense of staunch patriotism. Second, Machiavelli's effort in this direction started in 1513 (after the restoration of the Medici rule in the revolution of 1512 causing his forced banishment from a distinguished service) reveals that it was written for presentation to the new rulers in the hope that such a gesture 'would cause them to look favourably upon his aspirations for employment.'[15]

The central idea of the *Discourses* is the prerequisite for the establishment of a good republic. It contains 142 chapters some of which are exceedingly short like that of a single paragraph in length. However, the rationale of their organisation is a matter of controversy. In his 'Introduction' to Machiavelli's *Discourses,* Leslie Walker holds the view that the work 'is arranged in terms of the things which made Rome great'–her constitution, her military organisation and skill, and, prowess and finally, the virtues of long succession of outstanding men.'[16] Strauss considers the work as having three parts–first dealing with the internal affairs of Rome that were transacted on the basis of public counsel, second being a study of the foreign affairs of Rome that were transacted on the same basis, and the last showing an analysis of both private and public affairs of the Romans that were transacted on the basis of private counsel.[17] With a view to present a simplified analysis, it may be said that the *Discourses* seems to have three broad parts–the first apparently designed to deal with the constitution of states and the factors conducing to vigour, public spirit, stability and expansion of state and liberty of the people, the second mainly dealing with the methods of expansion of the dominion and thus embodying a great deal about military matters, and the last apparently planned to deal with the causes of revolution and destruction and the devices of their prevention.

The real value of this work is, therefore, a matter of difference of opinion among important commentators. For example, Bluhm holds: "Whatever the ambiguities concerning the threefold arrangement of the book, however its main themes are clear. It deals with the social and political conditions under which republican virtue is generated and destroyed, the proce-

15. F.J.C. Hearnshaw (ed.) : *The Social and Political Ideas of Some Great Thinkers of the Renaissance and Reformation,* p. 108.
16. Leslie Walker: *Discourses,* Vol. I, p. 60.
17. Leo Strauss: *Thoughts on Machiavelli,* p. 97.

dures which statesmen may take for cheating, maintaining and renovating the republics, and the procedure for destroying republics."[18] Opposed to this, Allen remarks: "But the rough plan is so roughly adhered to that, looked at closely, the book appears as disorderly medley of reflections on various, slightly connected, subjects. Often there is no apparent connection between the subject of a chapter and that of those preceding and following it. Often a chapter is unconnected with what appears to be the subject of the 'book' it stands in. Reflections on war are scattered about in the second and third books, as though, as new points occurred to the writer they were set down at once without reference to what preceded or followed. Insertions made, almost at random, after the first draft of the book was completed, might account for much of this patchwork."[19]

Despite these points of weaknesses in the rationale of the two important works of Machiavelli, it is certain that they are tied to the issues of political immediacy and to questions that were being discussed by the people of his times. Machiavelli took up the specific issues which mirrored the political experiences of the Florentines during the days of extraordinary political turbulence. Truly speaking, the two works of Machiavelli–*Prince* and *Discourses–are sister treatises on the subject of 'new politics' discovered by the 'child of the Florentine Renaissance'. As Gilbert says: "These two treatises signify the beginning of a new stage–one might say, on the modern stage–in the development of political thought. Machiavelli wrote the Prince* and the *Discourses* in the years immediately following his removal from office. As he declared in the dedication of the *Prince,* he wanted to impart to others 'the knowledge which he had acquired through a long experience of modern events and a constant study of the past.' One might say that the *Prince* and the *Discourses* are the works of a defeated politician who reflects on the mistakes which brought about the failure of his cause. The dominating idea in these two works is an appeal to recognise the crucial importance of force in politics."[20]

METHOD : A PERCEPTIVE USE OF HISTORY

One of the most original features of Machiavelli's political philosophy is his method or manner of approaching the problems of politics. Sharply distinguished from the approach

18. Bluhm, *op. cit.,* pp. 253-54.
19. Allen, *op. cit.,* p. 450.
20. Gilbert, *op. cit.,* pp. 153-154.

of the medieval thinkers, he abandons the path of deductive reasoning and, instead of taking start from the abstract principles of religion, justice and morality, he adopts a method that is often described as historical, inductive, empirical. Discarding the medieval tradition of invoking the revealed will of God or deriving arguments from the interpretations of scriptures, he refers to historical evidences and appeals to human reason. Representing the tendency of the Renaissance, he denounces the sanctity behind the authority of some mystical subject like Law of Nature or Law of God and deprecates their venerable axioms as practically misleading and theoretically unsound. Hence, contrary to the tradition of medievalism, Machiavelli believes that the true method of investigation for the science of politics is the use of historical and empirical investigations. His theory of human nature informs him that as in all ages and places human nature has been influenced by some motives and called upon to find solutions to the same problems with the same means, a study of the past throws full light on the needs of the present and also makes future predictions possible.

In the case of Machiavelli, the adoption of historical method has a definite purpose in the background. We have seen that the fundamental purpose of Machiavelli was to secure the unification of the Italian peninsula under a strong central government potent enough to maintain internal peace and resist foreign aggressions. For this he turned to the glorious past when Roman genius, patriotism and statesmanship had established a big and powerful empire. As he himself records: "The wise are wont to say, and not at random or without foundation, that he who desires to foresee what is going to take place, should consider what has taken place; because all the things in the world, at all periods have an essential correspondence with past times. This arises because as they are the marks of men, who have and have always been, had the same passions, they must of necessity produce the same effects. In all cities and among all people there exist the same appetites and the same dispositions that have always existed."[21]

It may, however, be pointed out that Machiavelli in a distinctive manner combines his knowledge of history with his own hard experiences and impressions borne out of contemporary conditions. His belief in the innate and thorough badness of man, his faith in the stability of the political order, his

21. See Coker : *Readings in Political Philosophy.*

realisation of the paramount need for public spirit and his view of politics as entirely independent of ethics were all evidently derived from his own experiences; they also coincided with the characteristics of his temperamental limitations. The essential point to be remembered is that these impressions were adequately strengthened by his selected historical references of the past particularly relating to religion, republican organisation, patriotism, military genius and political methods of ancient Rome. It follows that Machiavelli makes a perceptive use of historical evidences. While his method is truly unmedieval, it is not purely empirical or historical for the simple reason that the observations of Machiavelli are supported by a shrewd selection of the material. He confines his attention to the days when Rome had a glorious empire. He deliberately ignores the facts of history occurred after the disintegration of the great Roman empire and triumph of the new religion of Christianity.

A very startling aspect of Machiavelli's so-called historical method finds place in the fact that the influence of contemporary conditions far outweighs his knowledge of the historical references. It will not be out of place to assert that the actual source of his inspiration was his interest in the contemporary conditions and, for this reason, whatever parallel he could find in the history of the past were only those which deemed congruous to his impressions or which seized upon him as revelations of essential truth. Truly speaking, Machiavelli is a most acute analyst and a most correct observer of the conditions and circumstances of his own age. In fine, the method of Machiavelli stands on the perceptive use of history and to call it historical, in a true sense, "seems a little grandiloquent."[22]

In a true sense, the use of historical method requires a thorough examination of all historical evidences and a proper evalution of them before making their utilisation. It is not difficult to prove that human history has as much evidence of human goodness as of wickedness. It is a matter of personal philosophy of history whether one is more impressed by the essentially good or bad aspects of human personality. Thus, it "is not a sound philosophy of history, and still less is it a sound science of politics, to reduce all history to one common denominator, be it goodness or badness."[23] Likewise, it "is misleading to say, as has been done, that Machiavelli followed his-

22. Allen, *op. cit.,* p. 487.
23. Ebenstein: *Great Political Thinkers,* p. 285.

torical method, because his examples were often drawn from the past. He used history exactly as he used his own observation to illustrate or suggest a conclusion that he had reached quite without reference to history. In one sense, he was very unhistorical."[24] In fact, Machiavelli's method "was historical rather in appearance than in reality. The actual source of his speculation was the interest he felt in the men and conditions of his own time."[25]

HUMAN NATURE: PESSIMISTIC AND CYNICAL PSYCHOLOGY

The political ideas of Machiavelli are the outcome of his grossly pessimistic conception of human nature.[26] In his view, man is a strange mixture of weakness, folly and knavery: he is fit only to be hoodwinked and ruled over. Selfishness and egoism are the cardinal motivating forces of human conduct. Deceitfulness, cowardice, avarice, fickleness and ungratefulness are the chief qualities of his personality. Like beasts, man is driven away by the forces of fear, lust for power, avarice and cunningness. Man is more prone to evil than to good and, as such, whenever a choice is given to him to pick and choose between good and bad, he resorts to the later. In his *Discourses,* Machiavelli endorses: "The people often deceived by an illusive good, desire their own ruin... Those who have been present at any deliberative assemblies of man will have observed how erroneous their opinions often are; and, in fact, unless they are directed by superior men, they are apt to be contrary to all reasons."[27]

It is clear that Machiavelli presents a very dismal and contemptuous picture of human nature. He, in very forceful terms, tells us that one must take it for granted that all men are wicked and that they always give vent to the malignity that

24. Sabine, *op. cit.,* 341.
25. Dunning, *op. cit.,* p. 293.
26. We have already seen that Machiavelli's understanding of human nature is based on his hard personal experiences. According to W.T. Jones, Machiavelli nowhere "works out a detailed and formal psychological doctrine as Hobbes, for instance, was later to do. But over and over again in his comments on the conduct of men of his own time, we find the same black view of human nature which all of his contemporaries seemed to share, and for which, indeed, there was ample evidence in the lives of Caesar Borgia and the other Italian princes whose careers Machiavelli had studied." *Masters of Political Thought,* Vol. II, p. 29.
27. Cited *Ibid.,* p. 30.

is in their minds whenever opportunity so offers. It is a matter of ordinary prudence, he carries his point further, that men never do good unless necessity drives them to do. At one place in the *Discourses,* he says: "Those who have discussed the problems of civic life demonstrate that whoever organises a state and arranges laws for the government of it must presuppose that all men are wicked and that they will not fail to show their natural depravity whenever they have a clear opportunity, though possibly it may lie concealed for a while."[28]

Similar approach of Machiavelli is contained in his *Prince* where he says that men "are ungrateful, voluble dissemblers, anxious to avoid danger and covetous of gain."[29] It becomes clear from the tenor of his approach that, in Machiavelli's firm view, men are animals motivated primarily by self-interest, personal aggrandisement, fear, vanity and the lust for power. Only by shrewdness and a calculating ruthlessness can the individual hope to cope with his environment and satisfy his appetites and instincts. In a penetrating analysis of Machiavelli's pessimistic psychology, McCoy suggests that the 'Florentine' considers the animal and rational nature of man as two unrelated principles of action. By his animal nature man acts like a beast and by his rational nature he acts like a man. Moreover, for a man to act like a beast, it requires intelligence and demands the exercise of rational principles on behalf of the animal nature. The lion can never act as a fox, but man precisely because of his rational nature is able to assume the character and qualities of several different beasts as the occasion demands. By failing to perceive that man is essentially a rational being, Machiavelli also fails to see that the animal passions and appetites in men are ordered under the rational principle and that there is a right desire, a right fear, and a right use of force which are properly attributable to man as man.[30]

The essential point to be remembered at this stage is not the dismal picture of human psychology as portrayed by Machiavelli but the fact that it becomes the main sanction behind the existence of political authority in the system of the Florentine. Not will but this 'contemptuous nature' of man is

---

28. *Ibid.,*
29. *The Prince,* p.61. (Modern Lib. Ed., New York, 1940).
30. Charles N.R. McCoy: "The Place of Machiavelli in the History of Political Thought" in *American Political Science Review* (Aug. 1943). p. 633.

the basis of the state. All these bad qualities of human nature constitute the factor of self-preservation or security for which political authority is needed. As Allen observes: "Man, he (Machiavelli) thought, cares for nothing but himself; he is a rascally mean, greedy, sensual creature, more ready to forgive the murder of his father than the sizure of his property: gratitude for him is but the hope of benefits to come and what he calls his love is but love of himself. But the selfish will is a will to order and security, and all men, therefore, may see the general interest as their own. Man wills government and the state for this own profit and protection."[31]

Such a study of Machiavelli's theory of human nature leads to following important conclusions. First, the cause of the origin of society, state and government lays embedded in the need for security against aggressions of the strong over the weak. Second, the success and failure of a ruler should be measured in the light of security arrangements afforded by the state. Third, the motives behind the sanction of political authority are selfishness and egoism and, as such, the ruler must care for the ends, while means are always honourable. Fourth, politics cannot be aligned with ethics or religion; when the people cannot do any good unless they are forced to do so, the ruler need not count on the social and moral virtues of the people. Finally, force should be used by the state in a ruthless manner as it is only through its application that the evil propensities of the people can be placed under effective control.

It is clear that the approach of Machiavelli is basically different from that of Plato, Aristotle and Christian thinkers of the Middle Ages. In this direction, he is perfectly unmedieval and his approach foreshadows the thought of Hobbes. Moreover, the conclusions made by Machiavelli on the basis of this approach indicate that he is not so much a general theorist as he is a political model builder on the basis of realistic foundations of human psychology. Indeed, it is on account of this theory of human nature that Machiavelli's realism "has been called pessimism, his science cynicism."[32] The fact that Machiavelli has ever been misunderstood by his readers has its source in his presentation of the human nature. However, a correct appreciation of his system requires that his approach to human nature must be studied in the light of all that

31. Allen, *op. cit.*, p. 454.
32. Andrew Hacker: *Political Theory, Philosophy, Ideology, Science,* p.166.

prompted him to deal with the affairs of politics. As Allen says: "It must never be forgotten that Machiavelli referred all political action to public welfare. It is only the promotion of public welfare that justifies. It must be remembered too that what he desired above all was to revive public spirit in Italy. If to him the state was an expression of the purely selfish will in man, yet its health and strength depended, for him, on a patriot's devotion that could not be merely self-regarding. He was in a way a moralist, but he was a moralist without any sense of the beauty of goodness or of the horror of evil."[33]

THE PRINCE: A PRACTICAL HANDBOOK ON STATECRAFT

Machiavelli's work titled *The Prince* assigns to him the title of being the maker of a new Political Science as Galileo is known for being the founder of a new science of physics. Herein we find the picture of a Prince–a despot–capable of disciplining his subjects in a strong political organisation under his perfect leadership. Herein we find his dismal picture of the human nature that serves the very purpose of having an absolute ruler in the state. Most important of all, herein we find a set of specific injunctions that the Prince must observe for the consolidation of his power. It is this part of the *Prince* that assigns to him the credit of being a great scholar on the subject of statecraft. However, the underlying point ought to be borne in mind that all is written for the sake of his beloved country. "It is an essay on what makes for success in Italy from the point of view of a Prince. It is an endeavour to show what a Prince must understand, what he must do and be, and what he must not do, in order to consolidate and extend his dominion. It has reference throughout to Italian conditions of the moment."[34]

The subject matter of the *Prince,* for the sake of a convenient study, may be classified into three heads–organisation of a strong central government, territorial expansion of the empire, and a passionate appeal to the ruler of Italy to make his country powerful and great. In the first place, the organization of a strong central government is the *sine qua non* of restoring unity and strength in the state. For this sake, Machiavelli advises his ruler to destroy completely the customs and institutions of a free people in order that he may begin again to create

---

33. Allen, *op. cit.,* p. 74.
34. *Ibid.,* p. 466.

a new community not infected with the virus of freedom. Though the people are generally conservative, they admire great renovators like Moses, Curus, Theseus and Romulus if the reformers succeed in altering the shape of a society by their tough endeavours.[35] The ruler may make use of sheer treachery and brutality and other perfidious methods by his demonstrable skill.[36] However, the use of such methods should run for a very short duration, as it is the affection of the people that has a long-term effect and the ruler ought to win it as a remedial measure to surmount the impending crises.[37]

Machiavelli also advocates the doctrine of divide and rule for the use of the Prince in regard to consolidating his power. Feuds among the people and the nobility have always been there and it is for the ruler to consolidate his power by playing off one against the other. The ruler must maintain his own strong army to beat the invaders. In settlement of disputes among his rivals and opponents, the ruler must possess and exercise the talents of the lion and the fox. As he says: "A prince being thus obliged to know all how to act as a beast must imitate the fox and the lion, for the lion cannot protect himself from the traps, and the fox cannot defend himself from the wolves. One must, therefore, be a fox to recognise traps, and a lion to frighten wolves. Those that wish to be only lions do not understand this. Therefore, a prudent ruler ought not to keep faith when by so doing it would be against his interest, and when the reasons which made him bind himself no longer exist. If men were all good, this precept would not be a good one; but as they are bad, and would not observe their faith with you, so you are not bound to keep faith with them."[38]

The element of *fortune* is elaborately discussed by Machiavelli who compares it with a woman and for that reason advises the ruler to keep it under his strong control. Machiavelli admits the hand of accident in the rise and fall of the rulers; at the same time, he cautions his Prince against the insidious tendency of depending upon the element of chance without making use of critical commonsense. Thus, he solves the traditional controversy between fixed fate and free will. As he says: "Fortune is a woman and it is necessary, if you wish to master

---

35. *Prince,* Ch. 5.
36. *Ibid.,* Ch. 8.
37. *Ibid.,* Ch. 9.
38. *Ibid.,* Ch.12.

her, to conquer her by force; and it can be seen that she lets herself be overcome by the bold rather than by those who proceed coldly."[39] Allen makes the point more clear thus: "The Prince who has grown great by audacity breaks down when circumstances imperatively demand caution; he whose caution was his strength, fails when the moment absolutely requires audacity... What is required for success is just two things : will and intelligence, a ruthless will and an intelligence that sees things as they are."[40]

The second important part of the *Prince* may be said to find expression in Machiavelli's advice for the ruler to seek territorial expansion of his empire. The state should expand or perish. War gives a natural outlet to the ebullient energy of the people; it also manifests a mark of patriotism in the hearts of the people. Security is impossible unless a state is stronger than its neighbours and, more than that, to be securely stronger, it must dominate, better conquer others. In foreign affairs the ruler should make treaties and agreements but abrogate them if ever so required in the national interest. If there is a war, the state should never remain neutral. It is always wiser to take sides in a war. Thus, the Prince should join hands preferably with a weaker party and win after conducting an honest struggle. A strategy of coalitions is better than a policy of letting alone in foreign policy situations, both offensive and defensive. Thus, the foreign policy of the state must be framed and practised in sheer consonance with the national interest.[41]

The last part of the *Prince* seems to be like a passionate appeal to the ruler (Lorenzo do Medici) of Florence in particular to restore national unity and power. The author makes a bold proof of his patriotism by desiring his rule, to expel all aggressors and barbarians from the soil of his beloved country. In a roundabout reference to Medici, he issues a powerful appeal: "You see how she prays to God daily to send someone to deliver her from the cruelty and insolence of the barbarians. You see how fain and ready she is to follow the banner if only it were set up."[42] A strong leader and a powerful army of the natives was the need of the hour and the gate was opened for one to

39. *Ibid.*, Ch. 25.
40. Allen, *op. cit.*, pp. 468-469.
41. *Prince*, Ch. 21.
42. *Ibid.*, Ch. 25.

win the title of being the deliverer of Italy. For this he wrote: "I am not able to express with what love he would be welcomed in all the provinces that have suffered from this alien inundation, with what a thirst or vengeance, with what stubborn fidelity, with what devotion, with what tears?"[43].

A word of caution may be given at this stage. The *Prince* does not at all reveal the real preference of Machiavelli for any particular form of government. It appears from the general tenor of the discussion that this small book on the science of statecraft signifies Machiavelli's real preference for the rule of an absolute monarch. It is not so. The real purpose of the *Prince* is to make specific counsels for the ruler to consolidate his power with a resolve to establish a stable and strong state. The Prince of Machiavelli means the government whether in the hands of one, or few, or many. Allen well observes: "Though it tends to leave an impression that Machiavelli considered despotism the most effective form of rule, there is really nothing in the book from which such a conclusion can logically be drawn."[44]

THE DISCOURSES : IDEALISATION OF A FREE REPUBLIC

Machiavelli's *Discourses*, a longer and more discursive work than the *Prince,* contains a very large number of observations on the excellence of a strong republican government. Rambling from one subject to another and then trekking back, it does represent an integral part of the general theory of state as given by the Florentine what he lauded as 'a new route which had not yet been followed by anyone'. The central theme of this work, though shrouded in the mass of miscellaneous reflections, is contained in all that has a direct as well as indirect bearing on what "constitutes political strength and stability."[45] For this very sake, Machiavelli looked into the history of the great Romans and then placed great emphasis on five cardinal qualities–virtue, religion, liberty, patriotism and maintenance of citizen-solidery–that form the subject matter of this great work of the Florentine.

In attempting to solve every problem relating to the instability and decline of a political order, Machiavelli comes to the conclusion that the well-being and development of any

43. *Ibid.,*
44. Allen, *op. cit.,* p. 470.
45. *Ibid.,* p. 457.

political society depends less on its institutions than on the *spirit* that stands behind them. Machiavelli calls this spirit by the name of *virtus* having its English version in *virtue.* However, the meaning of this term at the hands of Machiavelli "has many facets; basically it was an Italianisation of the Latin word *virtus* and denoted the fundamental quality of man which enables him to achieve great works and deeds."[46] Making the meaning of this term more clear, Allen says: "His virtue is indeed a highly inclusive term. It denotes energy, hardihood, boldness, unflinching will, even intelligence. Yet he seems sometimes to use the word as though it were almost equivalent to public spirit or patriotism; and certainly to him that was an ingredient of the highest virtue."[47]

A study of the glorious Roman history taught Machiavelli that what made his country great in the past was nothing but this great quality of character. Thus, he insists that the determining quality of leadership is virtue. The sole reason for the decline and fall of the Roman glory thus, according to him, should be traced in the absence of the great quality of human character. The Romans, who had established tribunes and censors for the purpose of investigating whether institutions fulfilled their function of preserving the vitality of the political society, lacked this fundamental quality that made them subject to national humiliation. For this he suggested that in Florence officials ought to be created and charged with the duty to undertake such examinations. However, the notable point is that in this connection Machiavelli makes a distinction between the idea of *keeping* and *reviving* the virtue. For this

46. Gilbert, *op. cit.,* p.179.
47. Allen, *op. cit.,* p. 457. The ambiguity of virtue is due to different meanings given by Machiavelli and they cannot be reconciled in a single comprehensive connotation. Sometimes, he uses 'virtue' as anything in opposition to vice and vileness, sometimes he identifies it with moral goodness, goodness and honesty in contrast to badness indolence, fury and wickedness. Occasionally, he adopts the current biological designation of virtue as life–force. Sometimes, it stands for fortune, bravery and valour, manliness. energy of will, excellence good action or quality, even energetic decisiveness. See Neal Wood: "Machiavelli's Concept of Virtue Reconsidered" in *Political Studies,* June, 1967. Fredrick Meinecke says that the concept of virtue shows "a striking mixture of pessimism and idealism, of mechanistic and vitalistic elements'. Refer to his "Machiavelli" in Downtron Jr. and Hart (ed.s): *Perspectives on Political Philosophy,* Vol. I, p.409. But J.H. Whitefield comments that Machiavelli gives to virtue so many meanings that no single one of them can do justice to them all." *Machiavelli,* pp. 29-105.

sake he ardently desires that his people should not only take lessons from the pages of their glorious history, they must rather establish a perfect republic in the form of a unified body that by acting instinctively "generated the strength, single-minded will power, and vitality necessary for political success."[48]

Machiavelli's judgment of religion "is strictly utilitarian."[49] He calls religion, as prevailing in his times, a force of disunity and disruption. In his view, the right kind of religion can be of immense value in creating stability and strength in the state. He says: "As the observance of divine worship is the cause of the greatness of a state, so the contempt of it is the cause of its ruin. For where the fear of God is wanting, either the state must needs be ruined or it must be maintained by the fear of some Prince, supplying the defect." It implies that, according to Machiavelli, religion is not at all a superstition, it has its instrumental value. It should be taken as a useful instrument in keeping good men in the right way and bad men to open shame. "What is needed is a religion after the fashion of old Rome: a religion that teaches that he who best serves the state best serves the gods."[50]

Like virtue, the notion of liberty has a very complex connotation. It seems, to consist essentially not in any mode or form of government but in security for life, honour and property under law. In its widest sense, liberty includes all relating to the rights of the people, freedom from oppression, share in the direction of public affairs, security and discharge of public duties. It should not be incorrect to say that, according to Machiavelli, virtue, liberty and patriotism are interchangeable. Not only that, liberty also infers rule under a Prince of exceptional ability. A corrupt people cannot keep liberty as they lack the quality of public spirit; so liberty cannot be enjoyed by the disunited and insecure people. In fine, men who have security, freedom from oppression and a burning sense of patriotism in their hearts encouraging them to take a positive part in the direction of public affairs, worship the name of liberty.

Integrally allied with virtue and liberty is the notion of patriotism. The public spirit of the citizens rests on the sure

48. Gilbert, *op. cit.*, p. 191.
49. Harmon, *op. cit.*, p.169.
50. Allen, *op. cit.*, p. 459.

foundation of their self-regard. It is the absence of this spirit of true public service that encourages the corrupt rulers to engage mercenary troops for suppressing the freedom of their own people. Similarly, it is the want of this quality that brings disunity and corruption in the society entailing its own decline and fall. Where there is no public spirit, people are divided into hostile classes. The upper classes dominate the lower and, not only that, they strain every nerve to maintain their unpopular rule with all possible means. The inevitable ambitions and animosities of the particular individuals combine with group antagonism to break the regular procedures of the organic life of the people. Nothing but a sharp sense of patriotism is needed to make the state stable and strong. Allen rightly says that the healthy state of Machiavelli "is one animated by strong public spirit and armed with an army of its very own."[51]

The last quality flows from the above: maintetance of a citizen-soldiery. The state must not at all depend upon the support of the mercenary troops as they are never loyal to any particular Prince. Machiavelli strongly enjoins upon the ruler to have a disciplined army of his own people whose hearts are filled with a deep sense of faithfulness to their country. For this sake, he recommends compulsory military training for all youths of the country. Public spirit and appropriate training constitute the real strength of the military forces. Instead of requisitioning the support of the paid mercenary troops, the state must have a well trained militia of its patriotic people in view of the fact that a citizen–army is a natural expression of patriotism. As he warns : "Prince or Republic is much to be blamed if without an army of its own."[52]

If these are the cardinal factors that bring about strength and stability in the state, a republican system of government is decidedly the best form of government where these qualities have their best possible prospect of realisation. Machiavelli elaborately argues that a popular government of the republic is in every respect superior to that of despotism of a single ruler. The worst form of government, according to him, is the rule of a despot. As he says : "The mass is wiser and more constant than a prince."[53] Again : "I affirm that a people is more prudent,

51. *Ibid.*, p. 482.
52. *Discourses,* 1, 21.
53. *Ibid.*, I, 58.

more stable and of better judgment than a Prince. Not without reason is the voice of a people likened to the voice of God."[54]

SEPARATION OF ETHICS AND POLITICS : DISTINCT GROUNDWORK OF MACHIAVELLIANISM

One more important factor that makes Machiavelli a distinctively modern thinker is his complete separation of politics from religion and morals. Unlike the ancient and medieval thinkers, Machiavelli relegates the dictates of religion and morality frankly to a subordinate, even to an insignificant, position. Undoubtedly, herein we find a formal and conscious separation of politics as a science from the realm of ethics. Although the separation of politics from ethics was involved in the work of Aristotle, it was incidental and not an essential feature of his political philosophy. While Aristotle never frankly repudiated the independence of the political from the moral and, in a way, systematically maintained that the latter conditioned the former; on the other hand, Machiavelli refused to consider the excellence of the moral virtues as superior to the political virtues and he studied the phenomena of politics wholly without reference to the priority of the facts of moral existence.[55]

This distinctive aspect of Machiavelli's political philosophy becomes clear from his affirmation that while it is most praiseworthy for a Prince to be good, nevertheless he must remain prepared to set aside all moral considerations and employ every possible method to maintain his power. The employment of the methods of violence, cruelty, bad faith, intrigue and the like in preference to the maxims of religion and morality is thoroughly approved of by Machiavelli in situations calling for the consolidation of power and expansion of the dominion. According to Machiavelli, a discreet ruler should particularly avoid the infamy of those vices which imperil the life of the state and thus be relieved of concern about those that are necessary for the sake of its preservation, consolidation and expansion. In his own words: "Let a prince, therefore, aim at conquering and maintaining the state, and the means will always be judged honourable and praised by everyone, for the

54. *Ibid.*
55. Dunning aptly says: "Machiavelli's political man is entirely dissociated from all standards of conduct save success in the establishment and expansion of governmental power as is the 'economic man' of the orthodox school from all save success in the creation of wealth." *Op. cit.*, p. 289.

vulgar is always taken by appearances and the issue of the event; and the world consists only of the vulgar, and the few who are not vulgar are isolated when the many have a rallying point in the prince."[56]

Obviously, in Machiavelli's system, moral judgments, religious precepts or ethical considerations are frankly subordinated to the exigencies of the political interests. Since the necessity of the existence and the preservation of state are an object of fundamental concern, Machiavelli subordinates every consideration to the interest of the state and expatiates upon the dictates of unscrupulous patriotism. In his *Discourses* he says: "Where the safety of one's country is at stake there must be no consideration of what is just or merciful or cruel, glorious or shameful; on the contrary, everything must be disregarded save the course which will save her life and maintain her independence."[57] Likewise, he continues: "There is no disgrace in not keeping promises that were imposed on you by force and extorted promises that concern public interest will always without shame be broken when the power to enforce them is wanting."[58]

Moreover, Machiavelli not only separates politics from religion and ethics, he also adheres to the latter's instrumental value. He insists that the Prince should employ the norms of religion and ethics to influence his people for the sake of his own interest. The considerations of religion and ethics have no intrinsic or objective value of their own, rather they are valuable instruments of policy and, for this reason, the ruler should utilise them as a tool whenever so necessary. In no way, they are sacrosanct, because if the state were ever to observe them strictly, it would disintegrate owing to the overflow of egotistic and aggressive tendencies of its own people. The science of statecraft thus demands that political authority should pay no regard for the qualms of conscience but adopt all means, even religious and moral, to pursue a policy pertaining to the strength and security of the state. Obviously, neither like St. Thomas Aquinas, Machiavelli justifies the supremacy of religion over politics, nor like Marsiglio of Padua does he the reverse, rather his principles simply recognise the instrumen-

56. *The Prince,* p. 66.
57. *Discourses,* III, 41.
58. *Ibid.*

tal value of anything like religion, ethics and morality for the sake of consolidation and expansion of the power of the state.

Machiavelli's affirmations in this regard lay down his theory of double morality–private and public. He clearly suggests that the conduct of the people and the state cannot be properly judged by the same canons of morality. It is wrong if one man kills another; but even the massacre is justified if by such action the state tends to promote public good. It follows that for the sake of public welfare the ruler should always be ready to do dishonourable things. As the state is the highest form of social organisation and the most necessary element of all social institutions meant for the protection of the people and the promotion of their welfare, it should not be placed on a pedestal of equality with its own people and be governed by the same standards of morality by which their actions are examined. In this way, Machiavelli insists that the norms of private morality do not apply to the action of the state.

It may, however, be pointed out that Machiavelli maintains separation of politics from religion and ethics consciously as a sequel to his conviction that it corresponds most closely to the facts of human existence. It should still be remembered that the real purpose of Machiavelli is to get back to the very truth of things in this world and so he seeks to determine the working of a real and not a hypothetical political life. Keeping in view the bold facts that his times made the moral and religious emotions practically extinct and a calculating self-interest served for a practical standard of conduct, Machiavelli formulates his political philosophy independently of medieval ethical and theological influences. In this way, he represents the tradition of the Renaissance and corrects the medieval tendency of making politics a mere congeries of moral and religious precepts. It made him, in the fullest sense, the student of modern politics.

In fine, Machiavelli's total separation of politics from religion and ethics signifies his advocacy of the doctrine that end determines the means : nothing but consolidation of power ought to be the aim of the ruler; nothing but the realisation of this aim ought to be his commitment. As Allen says: "To be successful in politics, he asserts, you must be ever ready to deceive or to slaughter and, in fact, to commit any atrocity; and whether you call the doing of such things good or bad, does not alter the fact that the doing of them may, and often does, conduce to the general welfare of a political society."[59] Dunning evaluates the approach of Machiavelli thus : "He is not immoral but unmoral in politics. And the same attitude appears in relation to religion. He is not irreligious but unreligious. So far as religious practices involve operation of forces above the influence of human reason, they are entirely out of this sphere, but so far as religion is operative in determining relations to the state and the trend of political development it is subjected to the same cold-blooded analysis as appears in his treatment of morality."[60]

STATECRAFT : PRESCRIPTION FOR POWERFUL STATE-BUILDING

We have already seen that Machiavelli's political theory relating to the master-science of concrete statecraft finds place in his fundamental search to provide a solvent for the wretched conditions of his beloved country. In his firm view, it was the result of gross misrule and improvidence that many of the disasters took place that made Italy a chosen arena of conflict and the coveted prize of foreign nations. Obviously, the essence of his teachings was the demonstration of a scientific statecraft; in his works he made it quite clear that his objective was to write in order to produce actual changes in the practice of his days. Villari has rightly commented that the real aim of Machiavelli's researches and science "was the demonstration of precepts relating to political action."[61]

The theory of statecraft, as given by Machiavelli, shows his keen interest in the subject of pathology of states, the seamy side of politics and the conduct of government under emergency conditions. His observations, maxims and conclusions are addressed primarily to a ruler caught in an anomalous situation rather than to a Prince ruling safely in an established position. Indeed, he has little to say about normal governments inasmuch as for them no problem, as such, exits at all. He cites the cases of the Roman Emperors who had no need either for the Praetorian bands or a multitude of legions to defend them, for their own goodness and the affection of the people were like a sufficient defence. In his *Discourses* Machiavelli says: "For when people are well governed, they neither see nor welcome any change of government."[62]

59. Allen, *op. cit.,* p. 479.
60. Dunning *op. cit.,* pp. 299-300.
61. Cited in H. Butterfield: *The Statecraft of Machiavelli,* p. 14.
62. Cited *Ibid.,* pp. 90-91.

Machiavelli warns that if one weak prince succeeds another, it is impossible to maintain the state unless it is supported by the virtue of its ancient rulers and fundamental laws of the constitution. As he says in the *Prince:* "I say therefore, that in hereditary states, accustomed to their reigning family, the difficulty of maintaining them is far less than in few monarchies; for it is sufficient not to exceed the ancestral usages and to accommodate oneself to accidental circumstances so that a prince of this kind, if of ordinary ability, will always be able to maintain his position in a state, unless some very exceptional and overwhelming force deprives him of it; and even if he is thus deprived of it, as soon as the new occupier comes into any kind of difficulty, he will be able to regain it."[63]

Hence, Machiavelli's theory of statecraft finds expression in both of his great works. Although his *Discourses* contains a large number of observations and reflections on several different subjects and of which even necessary connection is missing at some stage, yet the mass of the miscellaneous reflections seems to bear directly or indirectly on the question of what constitutes political strength and stability. His reflections on religion and liberty, his stress on the need for native armies, his emphasis on the importance of strict and impartial administration of law and maintenance of security for life and property, his realisation of the importance of a large population, his observations on the dangers and difficulties attendant on the introduction of the changes in law or institutions, his warning against the menace of arbitrary and tyrannical action or against excessive reliance on the power of money–all have a direct and indirect bearing on the question relating to the strength and stability of the state.

According to Machiavelli, the stability and strength of a state depends upon several factors in which public spirit connected with religion and liberty plays the most important part. Lack of public spirit breeds corruption, while it is fostered in the conduct of administration without fear or favour, caution in making changes, adherence to law, necessity of securing and respecting life and liberty of the people and the like. Hence, public spirit procreates energy, boldness, courage, hardihood, unfinching will, intelligence and all such qualities essential for bringing strength and stability in the state. It is true that Machiavelli separates politics from religion, but, as a matter of

63. Cited *Ibid.,* p. 91.

fact, he makes religion a tool in the hands of the state. Instead of treating religion as a mode of social philosophy or a way of life, he considers it as a factor of social make-up. In his view, the misuse of religion manifests wickedness and lack of patriotism in the hearts of the people. Thus, the ruler should use religion as a tool and favour or augment it in the interest of his power.

Another essential factor is liberty which, according to Machiavelli, consists not in the conferment of rights on the individuals by any form of government but in security of honour, life and property. The state should protect liberty of its people for the very sake of its own stability. A wise ruler should respect law and establish good government, for when the people are well governed, they neither seek nor wish for anything else than liberty. Machiavelli's explanation of liberty also includes share in the direction of public affairs. It inculcates patriotism. It is understandable that Machiavelli prefers a republican system. Moreover, he warns that a corrupt people cannot maintain liberty as they lack the virtue of patriotism; for such a people there is no escape from servitude and their state can be maintained only by the terror of some powerful ruler.

Although the *Discourses* contains a mass of miscellaneous reflections on the subject of statecraft, it is the *Prince* that should be treated as a representative work of Machiavelli in this direction. Here Machiavelli's objective is to show what a ruler should unfailingly do in order to consolidate his power and extend his dominion. The reference to the conditions of Italy persists through, but the general tenor of his argument constitutes a very serious endeavour to lay down what the ruler should invariably omit or commit for the said purpose. Hence, from one point of view, the *Prince* is 'a handbook for a tyrant'. Allen well says that it "was written of a Prince, for a Prince, and for no one else; it was certainly not written for the general public."[64]

It is indisputable that the *Prince* contains a comprehensive code of specific counsels as well as warnings to a ruler who is committed to the cause of establishing his big and powerful dominion. Butterfield thus sums up the purpose of Machiavelli: "It should be noted that Machiavelli's intention was not the study or the creation of that particular science which we today

64. Allen, *op. cit.*, p. 466.

call political science; and it is important that we should come to his works as historians, not as theorists who hanker after synthesis. The science, which he is regarded as having invented, has indeed no point save in its detail. It was always a particular policy or expedient that he was commanding for adoption by the practical statesman; or it was an element conditioning political action that he was subjecting to analysis. His teaching is a collection of concrete maxims, warnings and injunctions in regard to certain points of policy, rules of conduct for specified emergencies, and exposition of tactical moves. He gives up the principles to observe if we wish to retain a foreign conquest or to found a new state that is intended for aggrandisement; the conduct to pursue when our neighbours are at war, or when a subject is becoming dangerous, or when institutions are to be altered; the ruses to be employed when besieging a city or dealing with conspirators or handling a refractory people."[65]

The leading principles of statecraft, as propounded by Machiavelli, may be thus summed up :

1. The ruler should regard public welfare as his chief concern, or he would lose the affection of his people and have no effective remedy to deal with the moments of crisis. He should never take the risk of unpopularity or general opposition, or the enmity of a small faction of the nobles would assume formidable proportions.
2. The ruler should win the affection of the people; or, in its absence, create an air of terror, but it is ruinous to be hated. To avoid the possibility of being hated by the subjects he may even commit an outrage on the property or person of his people with or without plausible pretexts and thus suppress the element of popular contempt by generating the sense of fear.
3. The ruler should well protect the person and property of his subjects as it inculcates the feelings of loyalty and promotes patriotism.
4. The ruler should be very ambitious in expanding his dominion. The security of the state is not possible unless the perpetually unsatisfied souls of the people are given to dominate, if not outrightly conquer, the neighbours. However, Machiavelli disfavours the idea of indiscriminate ex-

65. Butterfield, *op. cit.*, p.19-20.

pansion; he desires that only those newly acquired territories should be placed under the rule of the prince where the people speak the same language and observe same principles of religion and culture.

5. The ruler should be blamed if he is without an army of his own. Machiavelli rejects the use of mercenary troops as they lack the sense of loyalty to the land. He even sanctions compulsory military training for all youths (males) of the country.
6. Machiavelli advises that the ruler should use force ruthlessly, exercise persuasion skilfully and act decisively. Mere force is not enough and, for this reason, he should use devices for lulling his people into peace but without making any real concession for them. The ruler must possess the qualities of both the lion and the fox.

It is obvious that Machiavelli's theory of statecraft embodies a code of many important principle which a wise ruler should follow in order to preserve and consolidate his power. The real purpose of Machiavelli, as already suggested, is to show that if these principles are strictly observed, they will decidedly make a new prince look like a hereditary ruler and render him at once secure and firm in the state than if he were established there of old. Undoubtedly, he is writing for the ruler of Italy, but his principles are of general application and they constitute a solid insurance against the future. As Butterfield observes: "It is not strange, therefore, that in a certain aspect his new statecraft was regarded as an insurance against the future. And since most of these discussions have been referred to the downfall of Italy, and particularly the invasion of 1494, it was an insurance against the very kind of misfortune which the Italians of the kind seemed so ready to complain."[66]

In fine, by offering specific notes of counsel and caution to his ruler with regard to various important acts of commission and omission, Machiavelli makes his significant contribution to the science of statecraft that is now treated as a branch of policy science. By separating politics from morals, Machiavelli suggests that political device need not contain a moral content. And assuming the role of a professional specialist, he counsels that if these were the objects and purposes and such happened to be the conditions and circumstances, then acts of commission

66. *Ibid.*, p.19.

and omission required this or that. It may be said that here Machiavelli follows into the tradition of Aristotle who advised his rulers to prevent the outbreak of revolutions in order to maintain stability in the state. However, Machiavelli's total separation of politics from ethics takes him much beyond the Aristotelian line. His conclusions based on the inductive study centre round the facts of political life and his fundamental objective seems to be guiding those who wish to wield power effectively. Whether he wrote on democracy or monarchy, free societies or oppressed communities, his attention was directed every time toward the central point of political survival and greatness.

In a word, the sole concern of Machiavelli was to porpound a doctrine of the stability and greatness of the state. As Hacker well understands: "Political survival of men and government becomes Machiavelli's ultimate test. The aim of the state is not to promote freedom or virtue or the good life for its citizens. Its goal is to stay in operation. If its survival value is increased by its being a free state, then it should be free. But it might just as easily be oppressive by the same token. Machiavelli believes in human liberty and the rule of law. But he adheres to these values because they are conducive to political stability and survival. If he talks the language of political philosophy on occasion, it is only because he has first laid the groundwork of a political science."[67] As Pollock comments: "The modern study of politics, however, begins with Machiavelli. Not that he made any definite or permanent contribution to political theory which can be laid hold of as a principle fertile of new consequences. His works are more concerned with the details of statecraft than with the analysis of State...Machiavelli does not approve or advise fraud and treachery, as he has been charged with doing...He only points out that power gained in certain ways must be maintained, if at all, by corresponding means...Therefore, even Machiavelli, full as he is of observation and practical wisdom, is only on the threshold of political science. His doctrine is a theory of the preservation of States rather than a theory of the State."[68]

---

67. Hacker, *op. cit.*, p.166. According to M.B. Foster, Machiavelli's most famous book *The Prince* consists mainly of such rules and counsels, addressed particularly to one in position of political power and this is what is popularly known as 'Machiavellianism.' *Masters of Political Thought*, Vol. I, p. 272.
68. Pollock: *An Introduction to the History of the Science of Politics*,

FORMS OF GOVERNMENT : EXCELLENCE OF THE REPUBLICAN SYSTEM

Like Aristotle, Machiavelli presents a sixfold classification of governments, namely, monarchy, aristocracy and constitutional democracy with their corresponding perversions in tyranny, oligarchy and democracy. However, like Polybius and Cicero, he prefers mixed form of government as the best of all in having stability and strength of the state. While the line of typological illustration is not followed in detail, serious attention is given to the relative merits and demerits of two forms of governments, viz, monarchy or Princedom and republic or popular government. The *Prince* "is essentially a study of monarchy in relation to the extension of political dominion, and the *Discourses* is in the like manner a study of popular government, in relation to the same end."[69]

According to Machiavelli, the republican form of government is the best for a community in which general economic equality prevails and the people, as a whole, happen to be wiser and no more vacillating than a single ruler and their judgment in legislative, deliberative and administrative matters is in general sound and unimpeachable. Such a government is best qualified to maintain the establishment of legal and political institutions. Likewise, a republic is less likely to be corrupt because the masses are less corruptible than a single prince. Finally, such a system is better than that of a monarchical government owing to its adaptations to times and circumstances essential to the success of any policy.

At the same time, Machiavelli recognises the usefulness of the monarchical system. In his view, only a strong monarchical government can arrest the disintegrating forces particularly rampant in the Italian states of his days. For this purpose, he even idealises absolute monarchy in his *Prince*. Only a strong and unscrupulous despot can fulfil the task of unifying the country and manage all public affairs with or without any consideration of justice or injustice, humanity or cruelty, shame or glory as the circumstances require. Strong monarchy is the most effective instrument for establishment and maintenance of the independence of the state and the safety of its citizens. It is on account of this that Machiavelli's political theory appears "not very different from that of Thrasymachus."[70]

---

pp.43,45,47.

69. Dunning, *op. cit.*, p. 307.

70. Foster, *op. cit.*, p. 278.

However, two points should carefully be noted in this connection. First, Machiavelli fully realises that different conditions and circumstances require different types of government for different times and different places and he is chiefly concerned with the question as to what system of political organisation is best suited to his beloved country. Second, he nowhere prefers despotism, no matter it so infers from the general tenor of the argument of the *Prince* looking like a great work on tyranny. Machiavelli is far from being a thoroughgoing advocate of a despotic rule and whatever idealisation of the absolute monarchy we find in the *Prince,* it is not at all akin to that of Hobbes as given in his *Leviathan*; it is rather a result of his fundamental endeavour to provide a solvent to the wretched conditions of his beloved country. Correctly understood, Machiavelli prefers republican system in the light of its possibility and a monarchical system in the light of its necessity. "We are bound to conclude that Machiavelli conceived of the popular government as a character of the healthiest, most vigorous and lasting type of state and of the arbitrary government of a Prince as a desperate temedy for corruption. This was not a sentiment merely but a deliberate judgment."[71]

INCONSISTENCIES : UNITY IN THE GENERAL VISION OF POLITICS

One difficulty in understanding the political philosophy of Machiavelli lies in his different, sometimes contradictory, references and interpretations that appear in the course of his subsidiary argumentations. For example, he speaks of the King of France as being both all-powerful and limited by law. At one place in the *Discourses* he states that the people of the Roman republic had been poor, while at another place he declares that they had been wealthy. With many examples drawn from the events of history he tells that the Roman people elected right men for right jobs, while at other places he also asserts that the Florentines elected wrong men to work as military commissioners.

Then, Machiavelli's theory of universal egoism of the human nature and his theory of state do not cohere with each other. If man is inherently selfish and he cannot do any good unless forced upon, it is inferrable that he cannot live in association with others which is always a condition precedent for

71. Allen, *op. cit.,* p. 465.

the making of a state. Moreover, if the man is driven away by the sense of security and for this establishes the state, in that case despotic monarchy is the only possible and desirable form of government. If such is the base, obviously Machiavelli commits another inconsistency by preferring the republican system of government that demands sacrifice to the selfish ends for the good of the community. Again, if the state arises out of man's search for security, and security is obtained when the people join together as members of a group, the very *raison d'etre* of the existence of the state disappears. How is it possible that the men with mischief-ingrained hearts would join together to form a nation and live under the authority of a prince?

Similarly, Machiavelli is inconsistent when the lauds absolute monarchy in his *Prince* and a republican system in the *Discourses.* His meaning of the word 'virtue' change from one system to another. When he speaks as a monarchist, he means by it the capacity of a man enabling him to achieve success and fame for himself as an individual. As a republican, he sees that free states possess a virtue which the monarchical states do not; here implications of vitue include the possession of vigour, power of endurance and the capacity of growth. This virtue of a free state must be derived from some quality residing in the character of its individual citizens. At the same time, he insists that his virtue which is presupposed in the citizen of a free state must be something very different from that combination of intellect and force directed to the end of the individual preeminence to which he gives the name of virtue elsewhere. Obviously, Machiavelli's meaning of virtue contains various implications which make his fundamental meaning of the term quite ambiguous.

Finally, Machiavelli's theory of double morality embodies a point of inconsistency. It is true that the standards of private morality cannot be equally applicable to political sphere and the necessity or expediency of state knows no laws or norms of private ethics, still it is hard to believe that men are always good when the end is successfully accomplished. Besides, if the end is the only factor that justifies the means, there can be no clear distinction between the standards of private and public morality and, hence, there can be no civil society in which the standards of public morality are founded on the premises of self-interest and expediency.

In brief, Machiavelli's assertion of different examples and precepts at different places creates a case of self-contradiction that makes his political ideas inconsistent with each other. A community in which the people are determined on doing mischief and, more than that, they are inherently selfish and wicked, can have no state that is stable and secure. If so, the existence of the community itself will become a transient phenomenon. Likewise, a state of which all the citizens are endowed with the quality of egoism would not be a free, strong and vigorous state. Indeed, it would hardly subsist as a state at all, for it would have no bond of coherence. According to Foster, "In order that a state may be vigorous, it is necessary that its members should possess a different virtue from this. It is necessary that they should be possessed of public spirit, of willingness to sacrifice their private advantage to the public good, of patriotism: in a word, of those qualities which were designated by the ancient Roman term *virtue*."[72]

As a word of caution, however, it should be taken note of that Machiavelli is not a literary figure, he is a practical politician and, for this reason, he is far less concerned with the explanation of facts than with making an impressive argument. There is no place for these points of inconsistency in an over-all study in understanding the meaning of Machiavellian politics. Gilbert well understands this point when he says: "However, these inconsistencies appear only in his subsidiary argumentations; unity is provided by his general vision of politics. He was eager to state as forcefully as possible the ideas which he thought important and necessary to impress upon his readers. But he was not a man who builds a system in which every detail has an appointed spot and forms part of a whole."[73]

THE MACHIAVELIAN STATE : NEW SCIENCE OF AUTONOMOUS POLITICS

What Machiavelli asserts in the preface to his *Discourses* that his object 'is the discovery of new ways and methods' and likens his work to 'a search for new seas and unknown lands' has been a matter of interesting debate in the history of political thought. We find that even today scholars "are engaged in hot debate over the value of the continent he discovered. To some it is the promised land of an exact science, to other a sub-

72. Foster, *op. cit.*, p. 284.
73. Gilbert, *op. cit.*, p.167.

moral continent not fit for human habitation."[74] Max Lerner tells us that it is unfair to malign Machiavelli as 'the father of power politics' as it is like speaking of Harvey as 'the father of the circulation of blood'.[75] Allen says: "But, in the main, Machiavelli expressed ideas about the states of his own time rather than about the state."[76] A plausible point is made by Bluhm who holds: "But whatever its value, there is no disagreement that Machiavelli discovered something strikingly new. The movement is sharply away from tradition."[77]

The general view that Machiavelli contributed to the cause of modern state–a secular, sovereign, and national organisation–is supported by all that he gives in his *Prince* and *Discourses.* Let us examine the salient features of the Machiavellian state that ascribe him the title of being the first modern political thinker. First, the Machiavallian state is a secular organisation. It has no relation to the church, God or any other thing pertaining to the cosmic order. The place of religion is very much there in the system of Machiavelli, but as we have already seen, it is all for serving like an instrument. The state is not under the control of the religion, rather the latter is in the hands of the former to be used like a tool for the purpose of consolidation of power and extension of the dominion. The bishop, Pope, Church and all incidental institutions of the Middle Ages belonging to the world of theology and scholasticism "are eliminated from Machiavelli's system as unknown or unknowable or non-existent, or simply perhaps as irrelevant."[78]

The secular state of Machiavelli is a morally isolated entity. It has no obligations to anything outside itself. Machiavelli's complete separation of politics from religion and ethics informs him that the business of the prince is to do all for the sake of his power without circumscribing his authority by the norms of morals. End justifies the means and, as such, the ruler should have his concern alone with the realisaion of his objectives. No promise or commitment or even the terms of a treaty stand in the way of the prince if he is to maintain and increase his power. He sets forth the sound maxim: "All

74. Bluhm, *op. cit.*, p. 247.
75. Max Lerner: 'Introduction' to the *Prince and* Discourses, p. xiii.
76. Allen, *op. cit.*, 479.
77. Bluhm, *op. cit.*, p. 247.
78. Allen, *op. cit.*, pp. 480-81.

reprehensible actions may be justified by their effects and that when the effect is good, as it was in the case of Romulus, it always justifies the action.' Thus, Machiavelli "divorced politics from ethics in the same sense every science divorces itself from ethics. Scientific descriptions and theories must be based upon the facts, the evidence, not upon the supposed demands of some ethical system."[79]

Machiavelli's state is a central authority. It has all powers in its hands. The state in the system of Machiavelli has no principalities with powers divided among themselves like the component units of a federal state. What he really desires is the unification of all principalities under a powerful ruler so that Italy is once again a strong state. In a way, Machiavelli lays down the doctrine of monarchical sovereignty by arming his prince with the absolute authority to finish his rivals. However, Machiavelli's endeavour for making Italy a national state creates a point of controversy whether his state is a national entity or not. Allen is of the view that the concept of the formation of a national state, as such, "was foreign to his mode of thinking."[80] We may not agree with such an extreme view and, instead, appreciate the observation that the continuing relevance of Machiavelli's advice to the problems of contemporary politics—even his argument for the superiority of conscripted citizen armies over mercenaries— "is a testament both to his perception and to the national orientation of modern life."[81]

The dominant characteristic of the Machiavellian state lies in its being an organisation of force for the maintenance of security of possessions. But as men desire something more than mere security after they have it, the state should expand for giving additional satisfaction to the appetites of its people. As such, the Machiavellian state is an instrument of power for subduing and conquering the neighbours. By virtue of its inherent tendency of passing from revolution to revolution and, in the long run, falling prey to destruction, the state must thrive on the spirit of patriotism as the only effective way to escape the application of the inevitable law of politics. It should have a regular army of its own natives; it must increase its power more and more. It should also give a large amount of share in

79. James Burnham: *The Machiavellians,* p. 38.
80. Allen, *op. cit.,* p. 483.
81. Lee Cameron McDonald: *Western Political Theory: The Modern Age,* p.14.

its affairs to its people. "Other things equal, that state of all will be that which includes the largest number of people, similar in language and usage, and animated by patriotism. The ruin of such a state may be long in coming."[82]

A study of the Machiavellian state should not involve the debatable issue of his being a monarchist or an absolutist and the like. The general impression of a student of political philosophy informs him that the Machiavellian state is an instrument of power and that Machiavelli's prince is a perfect tyrant. For this reason, it appears that "even the *Prince* is interpreted within the framework of the *Discourses*, the anti-democratic character of Machiavelli's thinking still remains unmistakably evident."[83] Some commentators are of the view that to speak of Machiavelli as a champion of democratic government, as Gentili spoke of him, is nearer the truth. However, neither view reveals the real character of Machiavelli's approach. The truth is that what he "really cared about was the establishment of orderly government and general security. What he, above all, hoped was to see Italy so strengthened that she should be able to rid herself of foreign domination."[84]

The net conclusion of the entire study of Machiavelli under this head is that his works signify politics as a new science having an autonomous place of its own. Politics is thus freed from the shackles of religion, ethics and theology. The Florentine clings to the idea that politics has its own laws and therefore it is, or ought to be, a science with its purpose to keep the society alive in the ever moving stream of history. "To Machiavelli, politics is an exacting mistress; man's whole behaviour must be adjusted to her commands. Man ought to be purely *homo politicus*. It was not a weakness, but a matter of pride to Machiavelli that he could not reason about the production of silk or wool, or about gains and losses, but that it was his lot to reason about politics."[85] Again, "In placing politics in the stream of history, in demonstrating that every situation is unique and requires man to use his forces to probe all the potentialities of the moment, Machiavelli has revealed–more than anyone before or after him–that, at any time, politics is choice and decision."[86]

82. Allen, *op. cit.*, p. 481.
83. Henry J. Schmandt: *A History of Political Philosophy*, p. 201.
84. Allen, *op. cit.*, p. 465.
85. Gilbert, *op. cit.*, p. 176.
86. *Ibid.*, p. 200.

CRITICAL ESTIMATE : MACHIAVELLI AS FIRST MODERN POLITICAL PHILOSOPHER

The political philosophy of Machiavelli has ever been a great subject of abhorrence mainly to those who disfavour complete separation of politics from religion and ethics that takes it to the extent of its total vulgarisation. We have already hinted at the points of weaknesses in the political philosophy of Machiavelli. However, some general lines of criticism may be enumerated as under :

1. Machiavelli is not a systematic political philosopher. His purpose is not to write on the state as such as on the state of Italy which, in his firm view, was badly torn by the factors of disunity and corruption. Like Plato and Aristotle, he does not expound any system of an ideal nature or a practical one of lasting significance, rather he responds to the call of his own age that was nicknamed as 'an age of bastards and adventurers,' or, in Aristotelian phrase, an age in which man was separated from the bonds of law and justice. For this reason, Machiavelli failed to take any interest in any question whether religious, economic or political, unless it had a bearing upon the politics of his beloved country. In a peculiar sense, he propounded a theory of the 'masterless prince' ruling a community in which the members had no motives except those informed by their egoism and wickedness. Sabine is thus of the view that Machiavelli "writes about nothing except politics, statecraft and the art of war."[87]

   It follows from the above that, in a real sense, Machiavelli was not a system-builder and, whatever he wrote, it was a reflection of his hard personal impressions. Not only that, he wrote with such a strong sense of conviction and that he showed his so much concern with the fact of making an impressive argumentation that he cared very little for being thoroughly consistent as well as clear. Owing to this, his *Prince* as well as *Discourses* have been described by the critics as 'misleading' and 'unfinished' works. It is also said, that apart from facing the crisis of his days like a true patriot, Machiavelli exposed himself to cheap ideals in influencing the new ruler of Florence in an indirect way so that his high position in the government might be restored. The cumulative effect of all this was that his political philosophy

87. Sabine, *op. cit.,* p. 352.

became inconsistent in the face of his being a man of extremely acute perceptions capable of subtle and searching analysis of the concrete situation. "The elusive quality of his writings, which account for a great deal of the disagreement about him, arises from the fact that in spite of the sharpness of his vision of the actual, his thought was at bottom confused."[88]

2. Machiavelli's theory of human nature is extremely pernicious. His political philosophy based on the principles of universal egoism and wickedness made his name an anathema. It is certain that he took a thoroughly wrong view of human nature; he was unmindful of the fact that if a man is not wholly good, he is not wholly bad either. Man has a social aspect of personality that brings him in natural association with other human beings and thereby seeks his co-operation in the pursuit of a common good. The result is that Machiavelli's thoroughly inaccurate judgment of human nature made him the propounder of an immoral and inaccurate doctrine. According to Prof. Jaszi, "At the same time by the passionate and enthusiastic glorification of political crime he must bear the responsibility of having made from the diffused crimes of isolated princely criminal a compact philosophical doctrine which corrupted public opinion in many parts of the world and which envenomed still more an unscrupulous political practice.

3. Machiavelli's total divorce of politics from religion and morals deprives the sphere of secular authority of many fundamental virtues. His naked secularism looks barren and pernicious. Politics wholly deprived of the canons of religion and morality is a death–trap that kills the conscience of the civilised people. Naturally, the secular authority cannot be divorced from the disciplines of ethics in entirety. Thus, Machiavelli is accused of corrupting and demoralising the sphere of politics. As Allen says: "But what most of all shocked most people and made him seem to some terrible and to some contemptible, was that he seemed to teach that reasons of state might justify every degree of treachery and brutality. To many he seemed to go further and to imply that the highest virtue was that quality which

88. Allen, *op. cit.,* p. 452.
89. Geisar and Jaszi: *Political Philosophy from Plato to Jeremy Bentham,* p.119.

enabled a man, without fear or scruple, to deceive and assassinate, whenever he could gain a desired end by so doing. He seems to have taken evil for good and to ask admiration for the worst deeds of the worst men."[90]

4. Machiavelli's theory of statecraft is very dangerous. If the state, in a correct sense, is the first condition of a civilised life, it can never be treated as a machine of violence and coercion for the sake of fulfilling certain egoistic and wicked purposes of a man in power. Machiavelli thus ruthlessly ignored the aspect of noble statesmanship. He spent his power of writing on making the state strong and great by all possible means whether good or bad. Murray thus remarks: "In truth he committed the fundamental blunder of a low-strung mind; he mistook cunning for the craft of the statesman in the large sense of the terms. C. J. Fox reached the statesman–like standpoint when he enunciated the maxim that 'what is morally wrong can never be politically right', an axiom that eternally condemns the Florentine."[91]

5. Machiavelli wrote handbooks for the 'tyrants' with a view to please his new ruler of Florence in particular. In general, both the *Prince* and *Discourses* were intended to reveal the laws for the benefit of the usurpers and conspirators. In particular, the ambition of the younger Medici, first Giuliano and then Lorenzo, for founding a dynasty "stimulated Machiavelli to prepare a treatise on the policy to be followed by a new prince."[92] Summing up the general approach of Machiavelli, Butterfield points out: "His maxims were written for princes, usurpers, conspirators, soldiers and citizens in turn: for princes rather than for the states, for princes even when their interests are not those of the state. Machiavelli is willing to tell the tyrant how to move if he wishes to increase his power or to destroy free institutions At the crucial points his statecraft, in the *Discourses,* at any rate, cannot take shelter behind a doctrine which judges conduct by reference to public good."[93]

In spite of this, Machiavelli is remembered for exercising great influence both on the political philosophy and the science of statesmanship and diplomacy. His use of empirical method,

---

90. Allen, *op. cit.,* p. 471.
91. Murry: *History of Political Science from Plato to the Present,* pp.128-29.
92. Gilbert, *op. cit.,* p. 161.
93. Butterfield, *op. cit.,* pp. 108-9.

his separation of politics from ethics and, above all, his alignment of political theory with political practice made his political philosophy realistic. Moreover, his doctrine of a secular, sovereign and national unitary state gave him the title of being the first modern political thinker. For this reason, Machiavelli is admired as "the first writer to embark on the express task of describing the world of politics as it actually operates."[94] It is also commented: "Niccolo Machiavelli is perhaps the most universally reprobated figure in the history of political literature. The man whose precepts are universally disavowed in principle, but regularly followed in practice."[95] Beard pays his tribute in these words : "Living at a time when the old political order in Europe was collapsing and new problems, both in state and society, were arising with dazzling rapidity, he endeavoured to interpret the logical meaning of events, to forecast the inevitable issues and to elicit and formulate the rules which, destined henceforth to dominate political action, were often taking shapes among the fresh forming conditions of national life."[96]

---

94. Hacker, *op. cit.*, p.159.
95. Maxey, *op. cit.*, p.126.
96. L.A. Beard in *Cambridge Modern History,* Vol. I,.

14

BODIN

Bodin fabricates no ideal commonwealth, offers no panacea for the ills of the body politic, advances no dogma to prop up existing political structures. His quest is for a scientific explanation of the phenomena of politics and for a system of policy constructed in the light of this knowledge and in conformity with its principles.

— C.C. Maxey[1]

Jean Bodin, 'the most powerful of all French political thinkers of the sixteenth century', appeared as the most outstanding figure in the group of French moderates called the Politiques.[2] Born in 1530 and died in 1596, he is known as the most important thinker of the century as well as the pioneer of modernity. His vast knowledge of several European languages

1. Maxey: *Political Philosophies,* p.164.
2. The word 'Politique' was first applied by the critics who alleged that this group consisted of those who set their own case before their duty to God and peace and quiet above religion. One of the critics signified them as those who preferred the kingdom of their own homes to the salvation of their souls; who would rather want that the kingdom remained at peace without God than at war with him. The fact is that the members of this group denounced the raging civil war in France, detested policy of religious persecution and in stead desired toleration and supported the cause of strong monarchy in France. See Allen: *A History of Political Thought in the Sixteenth Century,* pp.370-77.

like Greek, Latin and French enabled him to acquire a first-hand acquaintance with the Greek and Roman writers and his attachment to the court of Henry III gave him the training of politics as well as law. In 1571 he acquired a place of trust in the household of the Duke of Alecon, but his official connection with the Duke seems to have ceased before 1576. Moreover, this connection was certainly not such as to injure his terms with Henry III, who showed him his marked favour. Another important event of his life took place in 1576 when he attended the assembly of Estates at Blois and was elected as deputy for Vermandois. The following year he acquired a post in the magistracy of Laon. He repudiated the League in 1593 and died three years after at Laon. However, not these events of his career as his erudite scholarship immortalised his name. Besides politics, he wrote on history, economics, jurisprudence, public finance, education, religion, astrology, ecology and witchcraft. Bodin is, for this reason, known for being "a scholar who strove to be a thinker, a lawyer who was interested in the origin of the legal rules as in the rules themselves, a man of the world who brought all the resources of his shrewd common-sense to the investigation of political problems; a sociologist who neither dealt in names nor played with words.[3]

TIMES AND WORKS : BODIN AS A PIONEER OF MODERNITY

Like Machiavelli, Bodin's political ideas were greatly influenced by the conditions of his own age. He lived in the sixteenth century when the unsuccessful efforts of the Protestant rulers to stamp out Catholicism and, in turn, of the Catholics to root out the power of the Protestants convinced every sane mind that religious fanaticism on the part of the state was detrimental to the cause of national peace, security and progress. It was thus keenly felt that religious toleration was the best way. Besides, papal intervention in secular matters was also denounced and, as an alternative measure, the need for strong monarchical rule was ardently realised. Finally, the tendency of anti-absolutism and counter-reformation as developed in Scotland, Holland, Spain, Italy and France revealed the dangers of unrestrained loyalty for absolute kingship drawing inspiration from the dogma of divine right of kings. Bodin thus found that his France was torn by religious

3. Murray: *History of Political Science from Plato to the Present,* p.172.

feuds and political strifes and the need of the time was unity of the people under a strong secular ruler.

It is obvious that the conditions of the age had their definite impact upon the mind of Bodin. He understood the call of the time more than anyone of his contemporaries and thus laid stress on two counts–religious toleration or complete secularisation of France and a strong national monarchy. He denounced religious fanaticism and advocated the policy of religious toleration on the ground that the function of the state was to promote common welfare. Condemning the notion and practice of religious partisanship, he held that the maintenance of any particular religion, faith or doctrine was no concern of the state. In this direction, he went so far that his profoundly religious attitude was dubbed by his critics as his being an infidel, a Jew, or a pagan. Jacques Gillot, writing to Scaligar in 1607, said that Bodin died like a dog, neither Jew, nor Christian, nor Turk.[4] However, Bodin's advocacy of the policy of religious toleration and his emphatic assertion of strong national monarchy gave to his political philosophy a practical character.

The political philosophy of Bodin comes to us from his several writings where the influence of Neo-Platonism and also of the Old Testament is discernible on his mind. In 1569 he published his *Response aux Paradoxes de M. Malestroit* which dealt with the subject of political economy. Herein he explained the revolution in prices of the sixteenth century, advocated free trade and pointed out the economic factors that underlay the relations among states. His another work *A Method for the Easy Understanding of History* is important as it contains an account of the historical method which Bodin considered as novel and which he largely employed in his political speculations. His another work *Heptaplomeres* shows his attack on the orthodox form of Christianity and his preference for the policy of religious toleration to be pursued by the state. His small work titled *Demonomanie des Sorciers* is a peculiar contribution to the subject of sorcery and witchcraft; it also provides a practical manual of legal procedures for the use of magistrates. But, for our purpose, the most important work of Bodin is his *Six Livres de la Republique* published in 1576-77. Known in English by the title of the *Republic*, it consists of six books dealing with the subject of origin and basis of state,

4. See Allen, *op. cit.*, p.400 n.

citizenship, climatic conditions and, most important of all, sovereignty for which he is known as the father of the new concept.

It is said that Bodin's *Republic,* like Machiavelli's *Prince,* was written with a definite purpose: if the latter wrote for the ruler of Italy, the former did the same for the ruler of France. This view may be correct but not to the extent as it is ascribed to the case of the Florentine. Bodin had his own times the most important characteristic of which was a terrible civil war going on in the country centred on the principle of religious persecution. Bodin wrote with a dispassionate approach, as much as possible, and for this reason his work was accepted as well as rejected by his people at one and the same time in varying degrees. The real purpose of Bodin was to write with a patriotic mind of a practical reformer. Thus, the *Republic* was written by Bodin to serve the interest of his country.

However, like Aristotle's *Politics,* the order of the chapters and the matter discussed in Bodin's *Republic* has been criticised for being a chaotic collection of miscellaneous ideas. The whole plan of the book covering his interest from state and its power (sovereignty) in the first three books to his emphasis on the effect of climatic conditions on the life of the people having their concurrent effect on the political make-up of the community in the fifth book suffers from several serious lacunae. Allen thus observes: "The plan of the *Republic* is so confused that one wonders, in reading it, what he thought he was writing about. He could never keep to one point at a time. In the first three books of the *Republic* the arrangement, in which he seems to be guided by Aristotle, is tolerable, orderly and logical; the rest is chaos. All the later books are miscellanies; even the chapters tend to be miscellaneous. He goes back and forth and back again in the same chapter; he turns from ideal considerations to actual France without seeming aware of the change of subject; he discusses the means of guarding against revolution in one chapter and the question whether the property of condemned felons should go to the treasury in the next; he repeats himself constantly and from book to book of the *Republic*; he overwhelms the reader with illustrations that do not illustrate, with irrelevant references and with remarks on events of Roman and other history; he interlards the discussion with disquisitions on astrology and the magic of numbers. It is as though he felt that every scrap of the information, he had collected, bearing even remotely on any of his miscellaneous subjects of discussion, must be crammed into his book. His verbosity, his enormous prolixity, his utter lack of any sense of humour, reduce the reader to something like despair. Powerful and original thinker as he was, he was yet in the highest degree a bore."[5]

The works of Bodin ascribe to him the title of being the pioneer of modernity. Some critics have gone to the extent of ascribing this title to Bodin and not to Machiavelli, while others have discovered a peculiar mixture of medievalism and modernity in his political writings.[6] For instance, Sabine says that Bodin's political philosophy "was a singular mixture of the old and the new, as all philosophical thought in the sixteenth century was. He had ceased to be medieval without becoming modern."[7] The truth is that in Bodin there is a peculiar blending of the old and the new elements although the latter has a far weightier part. His emphatic affirmation of the laws of God and nature, his faith in astrological devices and planetary influences, and his recognition of sorcery and witchcraft intended to be used by the magistrates in the detention and trial of the culprits indicate his interest in antiquarianism and medievalism. On the other hand, his use of the historical method, his doctrine of sovereignty and his preference for a strog national - monarchical system and his differentation between state and government broadly suggest the reflections of modernism in his political writings. Nevertheless, it may be said that Bodin is a modern thinker and his faith in certain medieval notions was just owing to the conditions of his own age that had their definite impact upon his mind.

5. *Ibid.*, p.404.
6. Two eminent writers include Machiavelli in the study of medieval political thought. See Dunning: *A History of Political Theories,* Vol. I and R.W. Carlyle and A.J. Carlyle: *A History of Medieval Political Theory in the West,* Vol. VI. Sabine has his own misgiving in this regard, though he includes Machiavelli in the class of modern political thinkers. The reason that informs Sabine to hold his judgment lies in his discovery of the influence of Machiavelli's political ideas after a long gap of scores of years supervened by the movements of Reformation and Counter–Reformation. Thus, he says: "Machiavelli's indifference to the truth of religion became in the end a common characteristic of modern thought, but it was emphatically not true of the two centuries after he wrote. In this sense, his philosophy was both narrowly local and narrowly dated." *Op. cit.*, p.352.
7. Sabine, *op. cit.*, p. 400.

METHOD : HISTORY AS THE HANDMAID OF POLITICS

Like Aristotle and Machiavelli, Bodin is known for his method. By 1566 he had grown convinced that the way of solving the problems of practical politics existed in the study of history. However, to Bodin history has three forms–Divine History dealing with God and His dealing with human beings, Natural History dealing with the things of the world of sense distinct from man, and Human History dealing with the human beings alone. In his view, all forms of study are inseparable, because divine history is connected through religion with human history and, through geography, human history is connected with natural history. But he urges that the understanding of human history must begin with and be based on the knowledge of ourselves, far from the knowledge of the elements of the human nature we may move to the study of the primary and natural form of the association called the family.

In Bodin's view, the chief use of the study of history is to subserve politics; to help us to understand the meaning and the function of the state, its need and its structure, the causes of its prosperity or decline. So the business of the historian is to explain the revolutions, the profound and radical changes through which human societies have to pass. According to him, only from a sufficiently wide study of history it should be possible to draw accurate conclusions as to the laws governing human society and to determine the best form of government as well as law under the given conditions.

The Roman legal system is denounced by Bodin. He believes that the study of the history of human society should primary be a study of the systems of law. The manners and character of a people, the nature of their society and co-operation, the form of government and their changes etc. are embodied in the history of its laws. Thus, a comparative study of all legal systems with constant reference to the natural law is needed. Moreover, he insists that the geographical and climatic conditions must also be explained with reference to these permanent factors, because they play a great part in determining the character of the people and their laws and institutions. In his view, the complete understanding of human history should involve knowledge not only of the origin of society but also of the origin of man. He also believes that there exists a mysterious correlation of human history with planetary movements and positions and with numerical and proportional relations.

In his quest for a scientific explanation of the phenomenon of politics, Bodin discards the superstition of a golden age believed to be once existed in antiquity. Rather, he asserts that if the human races were degenerating, we should long since have reached the lowest depths of degradation. Contrary to this, he holds that the sixteenth century was more civilised than the earlier ones. So he seeks to give reasoned answers to his contemporary questions. Generally he deals with the questions of policy and method in relation to circumstances and warns of actual and immediate dangers and for them suggests positive remedies and reforms. He also holds that the foundations of a well-ordered state should be dug deep and for this it is essential that an understanding of the nature of political authority be acquired. He tries to show that the nature and extent of such authority lay embedded in the history of the structure and the end of political association. In this direction, he also endeavours to discover some principles of order and unity that should reconcile liberty and subjection, define political obligation and satisfy reason and conscience. Hence, it has been commented that, like medieval schoolmen, he advocates the synthesisation of all human knowledge.

STATE : ORIGIN AND BASIS OF POLITICAL COMMUNITY

Bodin's theory of the origin and basis of state represents a crude mixture of ancient concept of Aristotelianism and modern notion of the social contract, while a passing reference is made to the idea of force as well. In this regard, Bodin at first deals with the origin of state and tries to find out its basis but fails to formulate a clear theory of its end or ultimate *raison d'etre.* His theory may be explained with the help of following features:

Firstly, Bodin defines the state as an association of families and their common possessions, governed by supreme power and reason based on force. Clearly, the starting point of Bodin is much akin to that of Aristotle. In his view, the individual is related to the state through the membership of his family. The family essentially consists of man, his wife and children with such other things as are necessary for its maintenance. Besides, it is natural, because it necessarily arises out of the nature of man. To him it is not merely the primary but an inevitable form of human association. It does not include slaves, the 'living instruments', but does keep property for the sake of its existence. Moreover, the family founded on the indispensable association of man and woman involves in the nature of things not only children and property but rightful authority and government also. In a family, man is the master of his wife and children because of his reason, intellectual superiority and greater strength and he has the power to force his wife into obedience or to divorce her as well as to kill or throw his children. His authority is therefore natural, because without him the family cannot exist.

Secondly, although the conception of the family is so fundamental in Bodin's system, he does not regard state as the natural development of the family and the spontaneous expression of the natural sociability of man. Now he ascribes its origin to force. It is in the order of time that the formation of civil societies preceded the formation of the state. For the purposes of defence and common worship the families were drawn into groups and in the process of this amalgamation war and conquest played a large part. When the number of such loose unions was limited, different groups fought against each other for their possession in which the stronger groups conquered and dominated the weaker ones. The victors tried to establish their permanent control over the defeated and, in the process, themselves came under the control of the chiefs whom they had chosen to lead them in war.

It may, however, be pointed out that Bodin's affirmation is different from the view of traditional exponents of force theory. He does not mean that the state was created merely by force. The human exercise of force can be nothing but an expression of will. He simply means that where there is a powerful chief, there is the state and since the recognition of his authority may be imposed by fear, the state may be or may have been established by force[8]. In the words of Bodin: "Indeed a citizen is no other than a free man who is bound by the supreme power of another. For before any state or commonwealth took form, each *pater familias* had final power of life and death over his children and wives. Afterwards strength and desire to rule, as well as avarice and the passion of revenge, armed one against the other, and the issue of war forced the conquered to serve the pleasure of the more powerful. He who showed him-

8. See Coker : *Readings in Political Philosophy*, pp. 371-74.

self a valiant leader ruled then not only over his household but also over his enemies and allies–the latter as conquered friend, to each of whom was given freedom to give as he pleased, the former (his enemies) as slaves. Thus, that complete liberty, which is derived from the nature, was taken away, even from the victors, by him whom the latter had chosen as their leader at least their liberty was diminished, for each in his private capacity, had to recognise the supreme authority of another. Thus, we see the origin of slaves and subjects, citizens and foreigners, prince and tyrant."

Thirdly, the state is governed by a supreme power called sovereignty. It is the most essential element without which the state is bound to go into its disintegration. Only this element distinguishes it from other associations. This power possesses right to make peace or declare war, to appoint magistrates, to grant pardons and amnesties and to decide all causes in the last resort. Law is nothing else but its command. The customary law can derive authority only from its sanction. Hence, this power is absolute, unlimited, indivisible and permanent. However, Bodin asserts, it is subject to the law of God, law of nature, and law of nations.

Finally, Bodin believes that the state has its own end. It is governed by reason also and is thus quite different from a band of robbers. He emphatically declares that its end is not mere happiness or unity or communism, rather upon the recognition of private property and the natural inequality of man the state rests absolutely. Its end thus cannot be stated as anything else than the realisation of all that is good for mind and body. A state that lacks means of subsistence has no care for moral or intellectual values. He strongly asserts that in a well-ordered state, the government must concern itself first with justice, defence and economics and then with the realisation of virtue of moral and intellectual values, for virtue includes knowledge and it is the final justifying end.

Thus, Bodin traces the origin of state in family and comes to formulate his doctrine of sovereignty. It is surprising that while, to him, the family is natural, the state is not and he tries to cover up this inconsistency by responding to the call of his times. From a philosophical or logical point of view, his theory of family on which he places so much reliance has no connection with his theory of state and sovereignty. The result is that in the end he neither remains an Aristotelian advocating the naturalness of state nor a Stoic believing in the artificial character of political authority. Sabine rightly says: "Bodin's theory of the family is a distinctive part of his work, but it is too hard to relate it to the theory of sovereignty."[9]

SOVEREIGNTY : SUPREME POWER ACTUALISED IN A LEGAL AUTHORITY

But the important feature of Bodin's political philosophy is his doctrine of sovereignty. Indeed, it is not merely the fundamental part of his political philosophy, it is his unique contribution to the subject of political science. Bodin rightly claims that no philosopher or jurist before him could propound this concept. The 'supreme power' of Aristotle cannot be identified with the concept of sovereignty, because the Greek philosopher confined its scope by the bonds of law which had its source in reason. Likewise, the Romans and the medievalists failed to propound the doctrine of sovereignty. Living in a period of political chaos and conceiving that religious and other disturbances of the time were attributable in the last analysis to impotence of political authority, Bodin naturally arrived at a view of the state which exalted its unity and power.

According to Bodin, "sovereignty is supreme power over citizens and subjects unrestrained by law."[10] He argues that this power is not only supreme but perpetual; for, if it be limited as to time or so to scope, it cannot be supreme. It is a power which has its origin in the people acting as a corporality, and orginates in the will of the people who may themselves retain it. It is customary, however, to commit this power in whole or in part, temporarily or permanently, to the custody of prince and other functionaries of government. He further argues that if it is bestowed, for any term of years, at the pleasure of anyone or in any form so that the possessor is not the supreme legislator–unrestrained by laws–that functionary, no matter how great the power he enjoys, does not possess sovereignty, for only he has sovereignty who after God acknowledges no one greater than himself."[11]

It implies that sovereign being the creator of law cannot be subject to law. Law is the command of the sovereign. Bodin very carefully rules out the considerations of metaphysical and

9. Sabine, *op. cit.*, p.403.
10. See Coker, *op. cit.*, p.374.
11. *Ibid.*, p.375.

theological elements by explicitly pointing out that when he speaks of 'supreme power' (*legibus solutus*), he regards it unrestrained by civil laws. He says: "As for the laws of God and of nature, princes and people are equally bound by them, so that no one who attempts to abrogate or weaken them can escape the judgment of divine sovereignty. What we have said as to the freedom of sovereignty from the binding force of law does not have reference to divine or natural law."[12] He clearly insists that the law which has its origin in definite human sources and is executed by human agencies does not come within these categories and such law sovereignty necessarily transcends. Sovereignty alone is the supreme legislative authority and its first and foremost function "is to give laws to citizens generally and individually, and, it must be added, not necessarily with the consent of superiors, equals or inferiors."[13]

Besides, in Bodin's view, sovereignty is the highest will that can exist in a society. The human society consists of individuals associated in groups each having a capacity for ultimate and indefeasible volition with respect to the affairs of that group. But the state being an all inclusive entity possesses such a volitional capacity that it overmatches all other groups of the society. Thus, sovereignty represents the human will at its highest point of development. It is the unity which stands above all diversity in human society, the centripetal force which exceeds any countervailing centrifugal force.

Hence, according to Bodin, sovereignty has the traits of being absolute, perpetual and unrestrained by laws. On account of being absolute, it is supreme both internally and externally and so it does not recognise the authority of any external power like the Pope or the Holy Roman Emperor or any internal force like feudal lords and corporations. Similarly, on account of being perpetual, it cannot be limited by the duration of time and so it does not inhere in regents, viceroys and dictators vested with temporary powers. Finally, its characteristics of legislative supremacy or legal omnicompetence manifests the peculiar position of the state in relation to its subjects and other associations. By virtue of it the state is excepted from all sorts of legal compulsion, owes obedience to no earthly superior and can be subjected to no will but of its own. Without its own consent it may not be used or made responsive

12. *Ibid.*, p.376.
13. *Ibid.*, p.379.

to any legal process whatsoever, internal or external, because its fiat is law, binding upon all subjects under its jurisdiction regardless of ethical or any other consideration.[14]

Again, while the sovereign is the creator of every positive law, he is not bound by them either enacted by him or by his predecessors. He is hardly bound to observe them even if he has taken an oath to that effect or given any specific condition or commitment or made some such contract with his people. The sovereign must rule with reason in the interest of justice. Bodin says: "A state is an association of families and their common possessions, governed by a supreme power and by reason."[15] Again, in his own words: "We must not confuse laws and contracts. Law depends upon the will of him who holds supreme power in the state and who can bind subjects of law, but cannot bind himself. A contract between a prince and his subject has mutual binding force, so that it cannot be departed from save with the consent of both parties; in this the prince seems to have nothing above his subject, except that the purpose of a law to which he has sworn having ceased to exist, he is no longer bound either by the law or the oath which he took with regard to that law. A well-advised prince will not suffer himself to be bound by oath to observe the laws, for in such case he does not possess the supreme authority in the commonwealth."[16]

One noteworthy aspect of Bodin's theory of sovereignty is that he points out some restrictions on the scope of the sovereignty. Although the sovereign is the creator of the laws and, as such, he stands above all laws, he is bound by the laws of God, the laws of nature and the laws of nations. The sovereign must respect the law of private property, because without a good cause no citizen can be deprived of his natural rights. Property is very essential for the maintenance of the family and even any taxation over it without the consent of the people is not justified. If the sovereign violates the laws of God and of nature, he becomes a tyrant. Likewise, the sovereign

14. Sir F. Pollock thus summarises Bodin's view: "In every independent community governed by law there must be some authority whether residing in one person or several whereby the laws themselves are established and from which they proceed. And this power, being the source of law, must itself be above the law". *An Introduction to the History of the Science of Politics,* p.47.
15. See Coker, *op. cit.,* p.370.
16. *Ibid.,* p.377.

must respect the laws of the constitution which determine the very existence of the state.

It is quite clear that the enumeration of above restrictions reduces the real value of Bodin's theory of sovereignty. The limitations of divine law, natural law and constitutional law make his theory full of contradictions, confusions and inconsistencies. The inalienable right of the family to property, the superiority of the law of the constitution and the sanctity of divine law and natural law clearly contradict the salient traits of sovereign with the laws of God and nature, by observing fidelity to the constitutional law of France and by asserting inviolability of private property, Bodin makes his whole theory confusing and inconsistent and it remained for later philosophers, like Hobbes, to formulate a correct theory of sovereignty. W.T. Jones thus comments: "Hence, Bodin does not make his sovereign supreme in the Hobbesian sense that whatever he does is right simply because he wills it. Rather, in the ultimate analysis, the supreme sovereign's decisions are not absolutely final, since they are subject to divine law. But how this restriction is to be effective or who is to recognise it and put it into operation. Bodin does'nt tell us."[17] Coker, similarly, says: "Bodin was not thoroughly clear and consistent in the matter. Apparently he was, on the one hand, attempting to establish the doctrine that there were laws of an ordinary and 'civil' character which became laws only by command of the political sovereign and which did not bind the sovereign himself, and, on the other hand, insisting upon the older idea that every political ruler is subject to customary laws which he cannot lawfully change. In other words although the powers of the sovereign are not legally unlimited, there are no institutions independent of the state or ultimately independent of control by the state sovereign, to tell him what the laws that limit him are."[18]

As Bodin imposes certain restrictions on his sovereign, some critics feel that he stands at the cross-roads between the medieval notion of the ruler as subject to the directive although not to the coercive power of human law and the modern notion of the sovereign as completely free from any law on earth.[19]

17. Jones: *Masters of Political Thought,* Vol. II, p.62.
18. Coker: *Recent Political Thought,* pp.500-1.
19. See M.A. Shepard: "Sovereignty at the Cross-Roads: A Study of Bodin" in *Political Science Quarterly,* 1930, pp.580-603. Also see Schmandt: *A*

Contrary to this, Maritain contends that Bodin may rightly be considered as 'the father of the modern theory of sovereignty'. While constructing Bodin's definition to mean freedom of the sovereign from the human law, he asserts that this is the essence of the absolute rule and absolutism is alien to medieval political thought. In his view: "Yet the fact remains that Bodin's sovereign was subject only to natural law, and to human law whatesover, as distinct from natural law, and that is the core of political absolutism."[20]

CITIZENSHIP : AN ARISTOCRATIC PRIVILEGE

Bodin's definition of citizenship is necessarily allied with his theory of family and state. In his view, when family represents the primary unit of the state, it is its head who is the citizen. However, in this regard, he specifically adheres to two things. Firstly, all citizens have but one thing in common and that is their common subjection to a sovereign authority. While the Greeks and the Romans usually regarded citizens as the favoured associates of a fellowship devoted to the commonwealth, to Bodin citizens are subjects and nothing more having no right of participation in government and no power or immunities whatever. He argues that what makes a citizen is not the enjoyment of rights and privileges generally associated with the conception of citizenship in ancient Greece and Rome but the fact of submission to the sovereign authority of the state. Secondly, Bodin allows a special and political status to the class of the nobility and thus rejects the principle of equality of rights and privileges among all citizens. Discarding the principles of communism and slavery, he believes that different classes have different rights and privileges although all are alike under the regulation and unifying power of the sovereign.

According to Bodin, "If citizens all insist on being equal and having equal rights and privileges, how many disturbances and civil wars we will see. It is important, therefore, to remember that it is not equality of rights that makes men equal citizens... A citizen is a free subject under the sovereignty of another... But neither is a slave a citizen... A slave has no rights: he counts for nothing... But a citizen, on the one hand, is free because he has certain rights and privileges, and, on the other, subject because his liberty is diminished by the majority of him

History of Political Philosophy, p.216.

20. Jacques Maritain: "The Concept of Sovereignty" in *American Political Science Review* (June, 1950), p.344.

to whom he owes obedience... Every citizen, even the meanest, has some rights. Every citizen, even the noblest has some duties. There is not a state anywhere in which those with the greatest rights and privileges are not subject in some respects. Thus, with us, the nobility is exempt from taxes but are bound to take up arms for the defence of the state upon the pain of losing their property and lives... Thus, once more, it is not equality of rights that makes men citizens. It is a mutual obligation of sovereign and subject; for the good faith and obedience which the one receives, he owes justice, counsel, comfort, aid and protection to other."[21]

From this statement it infers that the concepts of law and sovereignty exist together. Bodin's citizen is quite different from a man living in a stateless stage enjoying unrestrained freedom as well as from a slave who has no freedom at all. The freedom of a citizen is restricted only by the bond of law. And, since it is the law that restricts, the sovereign too is not completely free and his command is not coterminus with his power to command. It involves duties which are as real as those of the most insignificant citizen. Everyone, from the lowest to the highest, has a station which entails certain corresponding duties and obligations. He believes that the good state is simply one in which everyone from the king to an ordinary citizen knows his station and lives upto its duties; and the essence of good government consists in finding the means for maintaining this structure.

REVOLUTION : PROBLEM OF THE CONSERVATION OF STATE

Like Aristotle, Bodin takes up the subject of revolution. In this connection, he deals in detail with the causes of revolutions in each type of state and suggests specific means for preventing them. According to him, "However states be established–whether by the violent act of some strong men or by the consent of all subjecting themselves freely to a sovereign–and however long they endure, none lasts for ever, so changeable and uncertain are human affairs. Some states rise slowly to a great height and then fall at once of their own weight; others are destroyed by the attack of enemies from without when they think them-

21. See Jones, *op. cit.*, pp.72-3. Hence, Jones says: "Thus, though Bodin's state is in some respects the opposite of equalitarian, though, there are the great possible differences in rank, there is one sense in which all are equal." *Ibid.*, p.73.

selves safest; still others by interior maladies... Hence, there is great need that this whole matter be studied and that we come to some conclusion about what exactly are the causes the change and overthrow of states. Let me say first that by a change of state, I mean a change of the seat of sovereignty...Anything else, such as a change of law, of customs, or of religion, is but an alteration...Changes are most frequently involuntary, though they may be voluntary, as when one sovereign prince willingly submits to the sovereignty of an over-lord...whether voluntary or involuntary changes may be either natural or violent, so the change of a state may be either so slow and gradual that one scarcely notices it, a kind of growing old, or it may happen all at once, as a consequence of a sudden, violent blow...[22]

Like Aristotle, Bodin takes a very comprehensive view of the meaning of the term 'revolution'. To him every event amounts to a revolution if it signifies displacement, transfer or destruction of the sovereign power of the state. According to him, all such events mean the end of one and beginning of another state. That is, any event showing alteration in the sovereign power of the state becomes a 'revolution' in the view of Bodin. True that Bodin is preoccupied with the conditions of France, he also endeavours to make use of his knowledge of history in generalising the meaning of this term. Thus, revolution means any event from the displacement to the destruction of the sovereign power of the state. Keeping it in view Allen says: "He was trying to discover all the factors that make from social disturbance and civil war for the condition that Aristotle called 'stasis'.[23]

In dealing with the causes of revolution, Bodin takes into account both the incalculable will of man and the mysterious and inexplicable part of the stars and planetary positions. The surprising part of the study of Bodin is that he places his reliance so much on the part of the planetary influences that the role of man's incalculable will recedes into the background. It, however, does not imply that Bodin indirectly dismisses the role of man's will in bringing about a change in the sovereign power of the state. What he really means is that though human prudence can do much for the occurrence of a revolution, the superiority of the invisible hand of the mysterious stars should

22. Cited *ibid.*, pp.74-5.
23. Allen, *op. cit.*, p.526.

well be taken note of in understanding the causes of revolution and in seeking devices to prevent them. He thus broadens the scope of his ruler's concern in removing, or mitigating, the causes that shake the stability of the political order.

Some important points should be noted in this regard. Firstly, Bodin, unlike Aristotle, believes that the transformation of state is inevitable and that men should direct their attention to the regulation of the way of the change and not to the prevention of change itself. Secondly, a revolution may be slow or sudden, and violent or peaceful, but the essential thing is shift in the possession or location of sovereignty. Thirdly, the revolutions are caused by human factors like unrestricted freedom of speech and bearing of arms as well as by natural and divine factors like climatic and topographical conditions or influence of physical environment on the temperament of the people. Fourthly, among all forms of government, monarchy is best while democracy most liable to the occurrence of revolutions.

In addition to this, Bodin also suggests some specific remedies. He insists that inequality of wealth and 'usury' (including every form of profiteering) should be curbed and removed. Whatever be the form of government, a senate or an advisory council should invariably be set up. Not a body like the parliament but the senate should share the sovereign power. Then, in order to give an idea of the numerical and economic strength of a nation, censorship should be exercised. Bodin holds that the king should not ally himself with any faction but follow a policy of conciliation using repression cautiously and only where there is a strong probability of success. The policy of religious toleration should be pursued and the monarch should discourage the elements of fanaticism. He also suggests the use of astrological methods. Finally, he believes that national temperament should have a middle course involving the vigour of northern races and intellectual make–up of the southerners.

BEST STATE : PROFILE OF A WELL-ORDERED COMMUNITY

Bodin's theory of the best state finds place in his views on the forms of state and government. At first, he makes a clear distinction between state and government by pointing out that while the possession of power determines the form of state, the system and method through which this power is exercised determine the forms of government. That is, while the form of state is determined by the residence of sovereignty in it, that of government depends upon the manner and framework in which sovereignty is exercised. Hence, he urges that there are several forms of state and government.

As regards the forms of state, Bodin believes that if the sovereign authority is possessed by a single individual, the state is called monarchy; if it resides in a small number of individuals, it is aristocracy. It is obvious that in Bodin's view the number of persons holding supreme power determines the various forms of state. However, since sovereignty is indivisible between the various elements, he rejects the idea of a mixed state calling it nothing but a state of anarchy.

Then, Bodin makes it clear that the forms of state and government do not depend upon each other, rather they may exist differently in different cases. That is, a monarchical state may have an aristocratic government (in which the offices and honours are conferred upon a small class of society to the exclusion of many) or a democratic government (in which they are conferred upon all alike on the basis of merit). Hence, he argues that the principle of the form of government is different from the form of state which is sovereign. The collective participation of different elements is possible in the government, not in the state.

In addition to giving a typological version of the forms of state and government, Bodin takes up the question of best state. Very summarily he dismisses the case of aristocracy. He doubts its stability and fears that it reaches the extreme of distress and ruin by the feuds and jealousies of its members. Likewise, he dismisses the case of democracy. He demolishes the view that it is consonant with the law of nature, allows no privilege or legal superiority and gives equal justice to all without respect for the talents of the persons. According to him, in a democracy, the sovereignty is vested in a majority which is ignorant, foolish, emotional and shifty. Finally, he takes up the case of monarchy and admires its excellence in the name of its stable and satisfactory character. But, in his view, monarchy is of three types–despotism, tyranny and royalty. He distrusts the depotic and tyrannical forms and recognises the excellence of the monarchy alone, because in it the people feel secure in their rights of person and property and they respect and obey their ruler who observes the laws of God and nature.

The whole idea becomes clear from Bodin's own statement. As he says: "The place in which sovereignty resides determines what sort of state we have. If sovereignty resides in a single prince, we call the state a monarchy; if the people have a share in the sovereign power, we call it a popular state, if only a part of the people have the supreme power we call it an aristocracy. Now monarchy itself is divided into three sub-types, for it may be lordly, royal or tyrannical. In a legitimate or royal monarchy, the subjects are obedient to their prince's law, while he in turn obeys the laws of nature. In this kind of monarchy the subjects enjoy their natural liberty and the possession of their property. Monarchy is tyrannical when the prince scorns the laws of nature and treats his free subjects as if they were mere slaves and their property as if it were his own. It is then a true mark of a royal monarchy that the prince himself is just as obedient to the laws of nature as he desires his subjects to be to him. Further marks of royal monarchy are that the prince fears God above all, that he is pitiful towards the afflicted, prudent in business, brave in exploits, modest in prosperity, constant in adversity, faithful to his promises, wise in counsel, helpful to his friends, terrible to his enemies, charitable to men of goodwill, dreadful to evil-doers, and just to all."[24]

Bodin's preference for monarchy seems to have rested above all on his conviction that only in monarchy can the conception of sovereignty be completely realised. The essential feature of the state (sovereignty) cannot exist except in a monarchy. Only in a single will can sovereignty actually exist. The sovereignty attributed to an aristocracy or to a whole people is necessarily fictitious. In an aristocratic or democratic state, the majority may at any moment be sovereign, but this majority is a shifting phenomenon that changes from day to day. A majority of wills has neither any definite form nor any constant substance. A group is always divided and it has no will at all. Its actions are distorted by the compromise and disordered by the faction. Above all, a monarch alone can give real unity to the society and establish definitely the distinction between sovereign and subject.[25]

24. See Jones, *op. cit.*, pp.65-66.
25. It is necessary to note that Bodin's theory of sovereignty mainly implies royal and not popular sovereignty. In his view, the sovereign power may

INFLUENCE OF CLIMATE : RELATIONSHIP OF ECOLOGY AND POLITICS

The effects of the environmental conditions, what Bodin calls 'climate' in the penultimate part (Book V) of his *Republic*, on the political make-up of a people constitutes an essential element of his political philosophy. It appears that Bodin finds a natural relationship between the healthy life of the people and the stable conditions of their state. Moreover, the factors contributing to the physical health of the people, according to Bodin, are unalterable and their effect on the bodies of the people has a concurrent effect upon the composition of the political system. "Behind all policies and constitutions lie those fundamental facts which are permanent or are hardly alterable. It is these that determine, within limits the characters and potentialities of peoples and therefore they are forms of government and law. It is these permanent factors that give stability to human institutions in this world of continuous change. Failure to understand the limitations they impose may result in the ruin of the state."[26]

If climate means the unalterable factors of nature that create permanent differences among the people of world, it will be worthwhile to see as to what, in Bodin's view, is meant by it. Bodin makes a very comprehensive meaning of the word 'climate'. He uses it "to include all those conditions of man's life which, though practically permanent for any one area, vary from part to part of the earth's surface. It includes heat and cold, humidity and dryness, sun, rain, and wind; it includes topographical permanencies, mountains and marsh and plain, proximity to or distance from the sea; it includes the character of the soil and its products. It include also starry influence mysterious and diverse; for different people live under different stars."[27]

On the basis of such an ecological examination, Bodin classifies the world into three zones–southern, nothern and middle. In his view, while the people of the southern zone are

be vested in one, few or many, but his own preference is for the one like that of Hobbes. He is definitely opposed to the mixed form. He does not regard the state as a whole as sovereign but one element thereof is the bearer of the supreme power and the object is the object against which the power is directed". C.E. Marriam: *History of the Theory of Sovereignty Since Rousseau,* p.16.

26. Allen, *op. cit.,* p.413.
27. *Ibid.*

subtle and contemplative, inclined to philosophy and religion, relatively feeble in body unpractical and sometimes averse to action; the people of the nothern zone are physically strong, energetic, turbulent and restless, and rather stupid. Bodin admires the people of the middle zone (covering Mediterranean region and France) who go to neither extremes and possess the good qualities of both. "They are better balanced, more active and practical than the southerners, more intellectual, less violently egotistic, more disciplined than the northerners. If from the north come the great armies and the great invasions, the people of the middle zone are more apt for war, since war demands intelligence and discipline rather than mere brute force and courage. Still greater is the superiority of the middle people in all the arts of government and it is by them that all the great empires have been established. The southerners have led the way in philosophy and mathematics and all occult knowledge; but it is the middle peoples who have developed law and jurisprudence and political science."[28]

Bodin thus advises a political scientist to take note of the ecological factors in understanding the psychology of the people that acts as an important factor in the right conduct of a government. He also counsels his rulers to take note of this dominant fact of a people's life. A further examination of the views of Bodin in this regard, however, leads a critic of his political philosophy to say that while one may not disagree with the effect of the environmental conditions on the life of a people having their concurrent effect on the political make-up of their community, he may well disagree with the threefold climatic classification as given by him (Bodin) that, in a real sense, signifies his appreciation of the people of France. Moreover, one may also differ from his views that the people of the southern zone tend to theocracy, of the north to democracy, and of the middle to monarchy.

CRITICAL ESTIMATE : BODIN AS THE FATHER OF THE DOCTRINE OF SOVEREIGN STATE

The real place of Bodin in the history of Western political thought, though recognised for the single-most important reason of his being the 'father of the modern doctrine of sovereignty', has been a subject of debate in the sense that his critics have regarded him as "less a mere polemicist than a

28. *Ibid.*, p.432.

philosopher."[29] It is also commented that Bodin "was more a jurist than a philosopher, perhaps; but he was far more a philosopher than a party politician."[30] Again, Bodin's political philosophy "is an astonishing jumble. Critical acumen and extreme credulity went to the making of it; logical method, the crudest speculation and the wildest guessing went hand in hand to its construction."[31]

In spite of the fact that Bodin's political philosophy embodies a blending of superstition, rationalism, mysticism, utilitarianism and antiquarianism, his importance is great. He is regarded as the father of the doctrine of sovereignty–a doctrine which established the school of monism and which was further developed by Hobbes, Hegel and Austin.[32] His method of historical research and contemporary observation was certainly much refined and more genuine than of Machiavelli. Like Machiavelli, he did not keep his concern only with the subject of statecraft, rather he wrote both on political science and political practice. He brought out a clear distinction between state and government and by ascribing sovereignty to the state he contributed a very important idea to the subject of political theory. Hence, he exerted considerable influence on his contemporaries as well as successors chiefly as Hobbes, Filmer and Locke. Owing to this, various laudatory phrases have been used by the writers to admire his contributions. For instance, Dunning says: "Bodin brought back political theory to the form and method from which it had gone far astray since Aristotle and gave to it again the externals, at least, of a science."[33]

29. M. Judd Harmon: *Political Thought from Plato to Present,* p.208.
30. Allen, *op. cit.,* p.396.
31. *Ibid.,* p.398.
32. Pollock comments that in Bodin "we get for the first time the definite enunciation of at least one capital point of modern political doctrine." *An Introduction to the History of the Science of Politics,* p.87.
33. Dunning *op. cit.,* p.120. The main point of emphasis in this regard is his theory of sovereignty that furnished the basis of seventeenth century absolutism and laid the founations of the modern doctrine of sovereignty. Murray specifically comments: "The history of the seventeenth century centres around that problem of sovereignty that Bodin was first to state with any measure of preciseness." *Op. cit.,* p.186.

15

GROTIUS

It is this analysis of the rights and duties of states, in attempting to decode when one state has a just claim against another, that constitutes the main contribution of Grotius to the sciences of international law...Grotius was not the first to discuss the many particular problems that fill the pages of his great treatise; but he was the first to bring all of them together in systematic form, and to combine in a single co-ordinated treatise the most progressive thought of the century in which he lived.

— **C.G. Fenwick**[1]

Hugo Grotius, the celebrated 'Father of International Law', was born in 1583 in the Van Groot family of Leyden in Holland. In a very short time he earned renown for his learning and scholarship. At the age of 15 he got an assignment in the Dutch embassy in Paris. At the age of 16 he became the Doctor of Law. For some time he served as the official historiographer of the province of Holland and thereafter as a practitioner of law. However, his appointment as the magistrate of Rotterdam at the age of 30 proved unfortunate in the sense that it dragged him in a political controversy between the two sects of Arminism and Gomarism. Owing to the successful prosecution of

1. Fenwick : *International Law*, p. 53.

Prince Maurice of Orange (who supported the Gomarists), Grotius was arrested and held guilty of sedition. The trial finally resulted in the life imprisonment of Grotius. However, with the help of his spirited and ingenious mind, he managed to escape from the jail and therafter lived in poverty and exile. It was during this period that he wrote his immortal work *De Jure Belli ac Pacis* or *The Laws of War and Peace* that entitled him to be known as the Father of International Law. He died in 1603.

ENVIRONMENT AND WORKS

Like Machiavelli, the writings of Grotius were profoundly influenced by the circumstances of his own age. Already the unity of Christendom and the superstition of *respublica christiana* or Christian Commonwealth had broken down and several nation-states appeared each claiming to be independent in its own sphere. The strong national monarchies repudiated the superior control of papacy and by reaping full advantage of the newly-established freedom they converted Europe into swamp of warfare. The Catholic League and the Calvinistic Confederation raged internecine warfare till it finally came to blows in the horrible and inhumanly conducted Thiry Years War. At the same time, several important thinkers contributed to the literature of anti-absolutism and several events marked reaction against the tyranny of great monarch. The publication of *De Reeget Regis* in 1599 synchronised with a systematic campaign of tyrannicide. In 1705 the Gunpowder Plot was hatched in England. In 1610 Henry IV was assassinated in France. Likewise, protest came against the arbitrary warfares conducted by strong monarchs. Francisco Vitoria, Professor of Theology at Salamanca, inquired into the just causes of waging war. Francisco Suarez insisted upon the existence of a law of nature which all nations must obey. Gentili, an Italian refugee and later a Professor of Civil Law at Oxford, discussed the nature of just and unjust wars. The Protestant jurists like Winkler and Melanchthon similarly discussed the law of nature and found its content in right reason supplemented with and directed by the explicit injunctions of God. They stressed that natural rights were based on the law of nature.

All these events had their cumulative effect on Grotius. To him, the great truths of his religion held in common by Catholics, Lutheran Calvinists and Armenians were much more significant and essential than petty differences. The diabolical cruelty and folly of a war of Christian against Christian troubled him and so he desired peace in the interest of Christianity and the comity of European nations. This fact is evident from his own words thus: "I saw prevailing throughout Christian world a licence in making war, recourse being had to arms for slight reasons or for no reason and when arms were taken, all reverence for divine and human laws were lost, just as if men were henceforth authorised to commit all crimes without restraint."[2] He saw that the churches were powerless to stop war and to restrain its horror; moral considerations were usually thrown to the winds by the contestants. Grotius aspired to remedy this state of affairs and with a view to obviating or at least checking the situation, he set out to discover a philosophy that would provide a standard for the conducting of war in terms of social and earthly objectives.

The political philosophy of Grotius comes to us from his several writings. In 1604 he wrote *De Jure Proedoe* to defend the Dutch East India Company in conflict with other peninsular Powers. In 1609 he wrote *Mare Liberum* in which he developed the doctrine of freedom of the seas. But his most important work is *De Jure Beli ac Pacis* or *The Laws of War and Peace* published in 1621. The work was completed when he received a pension from Louis XIII and was settled in France. In this classical work he presented a code of international morality and custom and discussed in detail the laws of war embodying moral and customary limits which the belligerents must observe. Regarding the importance of this work, Hearnshaw says: "The very fact that it contained no startling novelties commended it to the conscience of the age. It summed up the accepted wisdom of the ancients and applied it to the unprecedented conditions of the Renaissance and Reformation world; it epitomised all that had been written by Stoic philosophers, Roman Lawyers, Scholastic theologians, Jesuitical Causists concerning the Laws of Nature and the Laws of Nations and combined it into a solid foundation for an incalculably valuable superstructure of international morality and custom. *The De Jure belli ac Pacis* won instant recognition not only by reason of its vast learning, its methodical arrangement, and its admirable style but also because of its European reputa-

2. Cited in Cook: *History of Political Philosophy from Plato to Burke,* p.428.

tion of its author and because of its own amazing oppositeness to the circumstances of the age in which it appeared."[3]

STATE AND SOVEREIGNTY

Like Aristotle, Grotius treats man as a social and political animal and finds the cause of the origin of society in the gregarious instincts of mankind. Hence, he believes in the natural character of society. But, unlike Aristotle, he distinguishes between the society and state. To him, state is not natural, it is artificial and its origin is founded on social instinct as well as in a deliberate contract based on self-interest. In his own words: "Man is an animal indeed, but an animal of excellent kind differing much more from all other tribes than they differ from one another...and among those properties which are peculiar to man is a desire for society, that is, a desire for life spent in common with fellowmen, and not merely spent somehow, spent out tranquilly and in a manner corresponding to the character of his intellect. This desire the Stoics call the domestic instinct, or feeling of kindred."[4]

In the view of Grotius, the society thus comes into being naturally and instinctively as a result of the operation of man's gregarious impulse. The state, however, is different from society. It is both more and less. Numerically it is less, because it consists of but a fragment of the whole community of mankind, the great society. Functionally it is more because it exists for the work of defence against external foes, the maintenance of law and order against internal disorders and the promotion of the general welfare of its constituent members. The state is the perfect union of a body of free men joined together for the purpose of enjoying the protection of the law and of promoting the common interest. In short, the state is a section of society organised for a specific purpose. It is, therefore, not a product of nature in the same sense as the society. It involves a perception of utility and also an element of mutual consent or even contract. It may be remembered here that although Grotius clearly recognises the existence of an agreement of wills beneath the structure of the state, he does not emphasise or develop the social contract theory as it is emphasised by his contemporaries like the monarchomachs or his successors like the Republicans.

3. Hearnshaw (ed.): *The Social and Political Ideas of Some Great Thinkers of the Sixteenth and Seventeenth Centuries,* p.137.
4. *Ibid.,* p.138.

Grotius also differentiates between state and government. He does not regard government as based on contract. He looks upon it as human in origin and legal in character. Nor does he know anything like the divine right of kings. In his view, the social contract simply produced the state, because originally men, not by the command of God but by their own accord, after learning by experience that isolated families could not secure themselves against violence, united in civil society out of which act sprang governmental power.

On the subject of sovereignty, like Bodin, Grotius represents the tendency of the Politiques. But while Bodin securely laid the foundations of national sovereignty and described it as the indispensable foundations of peace and progress in a well-established state, Grotius develops the theory of an international order consisting of independent nation-states as members and thus he "no less securely laid the foundations of the international sovereignty."[5] Hence, the quest of Grotius is quite different. While Bodin purposely wrote for the sake of his French monarchy, Grotius has no purpose as such. Obviously, while Bodin propounded the theory of sovereignty with a deliberate purpose, Grotius had to say about it in the context of his approach to the questions of war and peace. His attention is primarily engaged in the questions of international relations. But it was in his attempt to define and locate social authority competent to sanction the use of force that he felt compelled to introduce the doctrine of sovereignty.

Grotius defines sovereignty as that power whose actions "are not subject to the legal control of another, so that they cannot be rendered void by the operation of another human will."[6] Its essential features may be enumerated as under:

1. Political sovereignty is human in origin. In the view of Grotius, originally the people united in a civil society out of their own accord when they learnt by experience that isolated existence could not secure against violence and aggression. Out of this governmental power arose. Hence, with the establishment of civil society entire responsibility for maintaining peace and order devolved on the state.
2. Sovereignty is originally vested in the people who can delegate it conditionally or unconditionally. By social con-

5. Murray, *op. cit.*, p.186.
6. Kelsen's Eng. Trans. of *De Jure Belli* ac *Pacis*, p.102.

tract they may retain it in their own hands or transfer it to the king who may exercise it as he thinks fit. Generally, the people vest it in the king who exercises supreme political authority as their sole representative.

3. Grotius accepts the possibility of a divided and limited sovereignty. It is like 'a piece of land or a right of way, either in full ownership, or in usufruct or for a limited term only.' In his view, it is distinctly limited by the bonds of international relations and customs. The authority of the monarch is subject to canons of Divine Law, constitutional law, international law and law of nature.
4. Each sovereign has supreme authority over all persons and matters, whether secular or ecclesiastical. Each is completely independent of the other sovereign or any supra-national authority.In this way, each sovereign state is on terms of complete equality with other states as such from a legal and diplomatic point of view. However, it is essential that for the sake of equality each sovereign state must have a civilization similar to that of European Christian powers, a fixed territory under complete control, an organised government capable of concluding and maintaining honourable agreement and stable foundation.
5. The sovereignty of state is not incompatible with compliance of international law and morality. Drawing an analogy between the individual and state, Grotius holds that just as each individual citizen is subject to the control of his state for his own good, so every state should respect and obey the principles of international law and morality for the good of international society. While the law of the state represents the will of the community, the international law represents the will of the community of nations.
6. Sovereignty of the people is not inalienable but when once delegated to a king, its transfer becomes irrevocable. Thus, the people have no right to resist the superior power of their sovereign. The supreme power of the monarch is subject to no rights and not revocable by human will. So the people must remain completely subject to their sovereign. The supreme authority is independent of the interests and judgment of the subjects and any protest or rebellion against it is wrong in spite of the fact that it deprives the subjects of their liberty.

7. It may be noted that Grotius is concerned with describing the state and defining its sovereignty not as a political philosopher but as an international lawyer. His task consists in framing a code of rules applicable to the relations between states and their governments. Therefore, it is imperative for him to classify his ideas and to give the precise connotation of his terms. All this work of definition and classification is, however, preliminary in its nature.

No doubt, none but Bodin's name comes after Machiavelli among the important political thinkers of the modern period and in this chain Bodin's name is followed by the Dutch jurist–Grotius. The concept of sovereignty occupies a significant place in the political philosophy of both inasmuch as while the former immortalised himself 'by being first to employ the term, the latter did the same for himself by buiding up a system of law regulating the relationship between sovereign states.[7] This point of basic difference between Bodin and Grotius is sometimes lost sight of in the apparent examination of their notions. For instance, while Bodin defines sovereignty as 'supreme power of the state over citizens and subjects unrestrained by law', Grotius calls it 'supreme political power vested in him whose acts are not subject to any other and whose will cannot be over-ridden.'

JURISPRUDENCE : MODERNISATION OF HIGHER LAW

In the history of jurisprudence, the importance of Grotius rests not upon his theory of the state or upon anything that he had to say about constitutional law but, upon the conception of a law regulating the relations between states. However, he employs the phrase *jus naturale* to designate the law of nature rather than the phrase *lex naturalis* as was done by Suarez. In other words, he selects a term which connotes right irrespective of its origin and rejects one which suggests statutory enactment. Its simple reason lies in his awareness of the thing that Suarez's interpretation had not found favour with the Protestants, because by calling it the command of God, he (Suarez) had given to theologians the exclusive privileges of defining it. Hence, Grotius prefers the term *jus* and insists that it is not the expression of will, but it is rational in nature that even God cannot change it.

7. See Sabine : *A History of Political Theory*, p.421.

Grotius comes to the conclusion that there is a body of universal law–the universal law of nature, or right reason which is uniformly applicable to all peoples, and is authoritative and also pure as supreme reason itself. He says: "The law of nature, again is unchangeable even in the sense that it cannot be changed by God. Measureless as is the power of God, nevertheless, it can be said that there are certain things over which the power does not extend. Just as even God, then, cannot cause that two times should not make four, so he cannot cause that which is intrinsically evil be not evil...Furthermore, some things belong to the law of nature not through simple relation but as a result of a particular combination of circumstances. Thus, the use of things in common was in accordance with the law of nature so long as ownership by individual was not introduced; and the right to use force in obtaining one's own existed before laws were promulgated."[8]

Following implications may be derived from the definitions of law of nature as given by Grotius:

1. It is eternal and immutable like the arithmetical truth.
2. It is rational in nature and so it can be known to all rational beings without the need for any priestly interpretation.
3. It is uniformly applicable to all men and all states not because of any divine fear, expediency or perception of unity but due to its absoluteness and authoritativeness like the Supreme Reason itself.
4. It impresses upon the reason of man to do good and refrain from evil and thus enjoins upon security of property, good faith, fair dealing and general agreement between the consequences of men's conduct and their desires.
5. It is independent of divine guidance and power because even if there were no God, man would be guided by his rational nature.
6. As civil law is rooted in the law of nature, so the practice of the most civilised peoples of the world is confirmed by it.

As a jurist, Grotius believes that this natural law gives rise to the positive law of states which depends for its validity upon the underlying ground of all social obligations and especially upon that of good faith in keeping covenants. In his own words, "For those who had associated themselves with one

8. Kelsen, *op. cit.*, p.40.

group, or had subjected themselves to a man or to men had either expressly promised, or from the nature of the transaction must be understood impliedly to that which should have been determined in the one case by the majority, in the other by those upon whom authority had been conferred."[9]

According to Grotius, there exists another law by the side of the law of nature called the *Jus Gentium* or law of nations. This law includes those practices which the civilised nations observe in their dealings with one another. He devotes much space and energy in giving to it an objective existence and in placing it in its proper position in the category of laws. However, he differentiates the *Jus Naturale* from *Jus Gentium* by arguing that the latter presenting a code of precepts is of lower authority yet immensely valuable. It provides a body of international custom which in a most serviceable way can supplement the universal morality of the law of nature. According to him, "The distinction between these kinds of law is not to be drawn from the testimonies themselves...but from the character of the matter. For whatever cannot be deduced from certain principles by a sure process of reasoning, and yet is clearly observed everywhere, must have its origin in the free will of man."[10] The latter type which Grotius calls 'volitional' law is based not upon absolute reason but upon mutual consent evidenced by unbroken custom and the testimony of those who "are skilled in it."[11]

In the view of Grotius, *Jus Naturale* is sub-divisible into three varieties—*Jus Divinum* or law of God, *Jus Civile* or law of the state and *Jus Gentium* or the law of nations, the last variety governs the intercourse between nations and represents a human and volitional law. It embodies those principles that have been accepted as obligatory by the consent of all or of many nations. As such, it represents the body of rights for their welfare, although it is not welfare alone but also the social instinct which is its source. Hence, while the principles of natural law are of an abstract and general nature, not always directly and readily applicable to the concrete and complex situations in life and express what is abstractly desirable with regard to which most men agree and as there may not be the same measure of agreement and understanding in regard to

9. See Sabine, *op. cit.*, p.423.
10. Kelsen, *op. cit.*, pp. 23-24.
11. *Ibid.*, p.40.

their application, it is the *Jus Gentium* which regulates the mutual intercourse of nations. The relationship between the two is thus obvious. While the *Jus Naturale* provides the foundations on which the nations should regulate their dealings, *Jus Gentium* constitutes the code of precepts on which their intercourse is actually based. As the latter has lower authority, it should not contravene the fundamental principles of the former.

CRITICAL ESTIMATE : GROTIUS AS THE FATHER OF INTERNATIONAL LAW

The political philosophy of Grotious may be criticised on certain grounds as given below:

1. Grotius's theory of sovereignty takes a very awkward turn when he puts it under external limitations. By calling sovereignty as supreme authority at one place and by placing it under the yoke of external factors at another, he actually commits an act of inconsistency. If sovereignty means supreme authority, so far at least as external relations are concerned, how can a sovereign state be subject to international law? Maxey thus comments that on this point Grotius "ran into heavy seas."[12]

2. Grotius's theories of *Jus Naturale* and *Jus Gentium* have also been criticised from different points of view. His idea of an international community of states bound by voluntary subjection to the principles of natural reason and justice does not correspond to the facts of the international situation in the seventeenth century and has not been realised to an appreciable extent till today. His theory of *Jus Gentium* is not free from its inherent defects. It included only some powerful nations of Europe. The very expression of *Jus Gentium* remained ambiguous and Grotius could not make it thoroughly clear that whether it meant law common to the people of all nations or law which regulated the mutual relations of states. Summing up this view, Hearnshaw says: "The weakness of so-called International Law has always been the absence of any extraneous standard. The *Jus Naturale* has no objective existence and the *Jus Gentium* is a mere code of custom devoid of moral quality. Thus, International Law lacks determinate source, lacks precise formulation, lacks sanction, lacks effective tribunal."[13]

.2. Maxey: *Political Philosophies,* p.182.
.3. Hearnshaw, *op. cit.,* p.151.

3. It has also been doubted that the great work of Grotius on International Law had really great value. In his careful and scholarly study, Dr. T.A. Walker says that there "was little novel in the legal system of Grotius, and there was equally but little original in either the arrangement or the matter of his work."[14] A great jurist like Holland commented that the first step towards making International Law, what it is, was taken not by Grotius but by Gentili.

Nevertheless, Grotius is important for making his own contributions. He formulated a scheme of rights and duties applicable to the mutual relations of sovereign states. He set limits to the unfettered predominance of state as stressed by thinkers like Machiavelli to flout the dictates of international morality. His theories of the state of nature and the implied contractual origin of political society put him in line with the anti-royalist writers. he introduced a normative element in his conception of natural law in the shape of values like justice, good faith and fair dealing by which the positive law of a state could be judged. However, his real importance lies in the field of international law and jurisprudence. By predicating International Law upon a hypothetical community of nations, he not only gave a tremendous impetus to juridical thought which treats the usage of international life as though they were the law of a community of nations, but also traced out the only path by which a world of independent sovereign states may move in the direction of order and integration. From his inspiration, several thinkers and lawyers like Hobbes, Spinoza, Descartes, Leibnitz, Vattel and Gentili tried to make further elaborations and give a more demonstrative shape to their systems. It is owing to his great contributions to the subject of International Law and jurisprudence that he has been widely acclaimed as the 'Father of International Law.' A well known writer, C.G. Fenwick thus observes: "The *De Jure Belli ac Pacis* is not merely an effort to put restraints upon the conduct of war, to which Book III of the treatise is devoted, it is an effort guided by moral idealism and an exhaustive knowledge of the civil law, to determine specifically the rights and duties of states as the basis of peaceful relations between them."[15]

14. Walker: *History of the Law of Nations,* Vol. I., p.333.
15. Fenwick: *International Law,* p.53.

16

HOBBES

.......his principles are pernicious both to piety and policy and destructive to all relations of mankind, between prince and subject, father and child, master and servant, husband and wife: and.... they who maintain them obstinately, are fitter to live in hollow trees among wild beasts, than in any Christian or political society.

— **Bishop Bramhall**[1]

The most important place in the history of modern English political thought is occupied by Thomas Hobbes who is rightly regarded as 'the originator of modern political philosophy'.[2] His life, particularly its main part, passed through a very crucial period of English political history. Born in 1588 and died in 1679, he closely watched the events that witnessed the decline of absolute monarchy and the rise of constitutional government as a result of war between the king and his people in the middle of the seventeenth century. He was the son of an English vicar whose stormy career forced him to keep

1. Cited in Howard Warrender: *The Philosophy of Hobbes: His Theory of Obligation*, p.1.
2. Leo Strauss: *The Political Philosophy of Hobbes: Its Basis and its Genesis* (Translated from German into English by Elsa M. Sinclair), p. xv. Sir Fredrick Pollock says that with Hobbes "modern school of political theory begins". *An Introduction to the History of the Science of Politics*, p.58.

his children under the care of one of his elder brothers who was a prosperous glove-maker of Malmesbury. Hobbes received his education mainly at Oxford. At the age of 20 he became a tutor in the family of William Cavendish, Baron Hardwick and later Lord Devonshire. This event is very important in his life as it opened his contact with eminent figures like Bacon and Ben Johnson. The more important event in his life, however, was his 'eye-opening' Europoean tour with his family that brought him in touch with prominent figures like Galileo and Mersenne. It enabled him to acquire a good knowledge of the Italian and French languages and, more important than that, inculcated his interest in the principles of natural sciences. However, the story of his political career begins from 1637 when he returned to England and started supporting the royalist cause in his occasional papers the most important of which is a pamphlet titled *The Elements of Law, Natural and Politique.* When Hobbes found that the Long Parliament had sent Laud and Stafford to the Tower, he escaped to France for the safety of his person. In 1642 he published a pamphlet in Latin titled *De Cive* which was later published in English under the title of *Philosophical Rudiments Concerning Government and Society.* However, the work that immortalised his name is the *Leviathan* that appeared in 1651 and soon became the most controversial book of the day. Once more a turning point in the life of Hobbes took place in 1660 when monarchy was restored in England under Charles II who granted a life pension to him and made him a regular attache to his court. After this Hobbes passed a life of ease and retirement writing some minor papers till he died of brief illness leaving a host of his critics till this day like Anthony Wood who accuses him of being the 'corrupter of half the gentry of the nation'[3] and his great admirers like Wayper who says: "Succeeding generations have usually disagreed with him, but it is no exaggeration to say that they have found in him a mine well worth their while to work for the riches of the ore that it yields."[4]

LEVIATHAN : A MASTER-PIECE WORK ON POLITICAL PHILOSOPHY

As already pointed out, the *Leviathan* is the greatest work of this English philosopher; it is also one of the greatest

3. Remark of Anthony A. Wood cited by C.B. Macpherson: 'Introduction' to his edited work *Leviathan,* p.23.
4. C.L. Wayper: *Political Thought,* p.65.

works on the subject of political thought. For the first time appeared in 1651, it saw its several editions during the time of Hobbes himself who is said to have made some corrections by his own hands in the subsequent prints of this controversial work. In our times, this work has seen several editions in the English language with important 'Introductions' added to the text along with editorial touches given by eminent commentators like Michael Oakeshott, A.D. Lindsay, E. Rhys, Pogson-Smith and C.B. Macpherson. It is a different matter, however, that the commentators have variously evaluated these words of Hobbes that it 'was occasioned by the disorders of the present time' and that it 'is without partiality, without application, and without other design, than to set before man's eyes the mutual relation between Protection and Obedience.'[5]

The long text of the *Leviathan,* in addition to a letter written by Hobbes to his most honoured friend (Francis Godolphin) dated Paris, 15-25 April, 1651 and a brief 'Introduction' in the beginning and in the end 'A Review, and a Conclusion', has four parts. Part I captioned 'Of Man' has 16 chapters dealing with his views on Sense, Imagination, Speech, Reason and Science, Motions and Passions, Knowledge, Power, Worth, Dignity, Honour, Worthiness, Manners, Religion, Felicity, Misery, Natural Laws, Contract and Persons. Part II captioned 'Of Commonwealth' has 15 chapters (17 to 31) showing the view of the author on the Causes, Generation and Definition of Commonwealth, Sovereignty, Government, Liberty, Political System, Civil Law, Crimes, Rewards, Punishments and the Kingdom of God by Nature. Part III captioned 'Of A Christian Commonwealth' has 12 chapters (32 to 43) relating to the erastianism of the author. It shows his views on the Religious Scriptures, God and His Prophets, Eternal Life, Miracles, Hell and Heaven and Ecclesiastical Power. The last Part title 'Of the Kingdom of Darkness' having 4 chapters (44 to 47) shows his radical views on Spiritual Darkness flowing from the Misinterpretation of the Scriptures, Demonology, Vain Philosophy and Fabulous Traditions, and the Benefits accruing from Supernatural Agencies.

---

5. See Hobbes: *Leviathan,* 'A Review and A Conclusion.' I wish to make it clear for the information of my readers that I have tried to put the words of Hobbes in modern English usage fearing that the original style of Hobbes touching the world of Latin language and having the form of very old English may be a source of some difficulty to them.

A deeper study of the text of this great work of Hobbes enables a student of political thought to take it as having four distinct parts dealing with four important subjects–Psychology, Politics, Religion and Philosophy. It may be understood without any great difficulty that what must have really made Hobbes a very 'dangerous man' is his view of religion that constitutes his erastian outlook. The subject-matter of the Third Part naturally incurred the wrath and resentment of the Godmen. However, what assigned a place of unprecedented significance to Hobbes in the history of modern political thought is his views contained in the First and Second Parts that show how he reacted to the raging controversy revolving around the struggle for power between the Rex and the Lex–the King and Parliament. Thus, what really concerns a student of political thought is the study of the first two parts of the *Leviathan* where Hobbes repudiates the traditional doctrine of the divine right of kings and establishes the rule of a man-made absolute sovereign as the only guarantee against the lawless conditions of life existing in a supposed pre-political stage of human life.

The outstanding fact of history stands that the political philosophy of Hobbes as contained his master-piece work is certainly a product of the conditions of his own age. Hobbes cautiously noted that the conflict between the first two Stuart Kings and their Parliaments brought England on the verge of a bloody civil war as a result of which anarchy prevailed throughout the country and King Charles I was beheaded in 1649–a most revolutionary event of English history that led to the establishment of a form of military dictatorship until monarchy was restored in 1660 under Charles II. This period boldly indicated that little respect "was shown to the civil law; crime and violence had increased steadily, murder, arson and highway robbery were common events of daily life."[6] It is owing to this indubitable fact that the *Leviathan* represented the fundamental search of Hobbes for establishing a balance between the obdurate claims of the absolute monarchy and an equally obdurate stand of the fighting people claiming themselves as the real makers of the political community. Hence, Hobbes conceived his new design of bringing all his powers of thought and expression to bear upon the production of an English book that should set forth his whole theory of civil

6. Terry: *The History of England,* p.265.

government in relation to the political crisis resulting from the war.[7]

Though a product of the historical circumstances, the *Leviathan* of Hobbes did not appear as a cheap exercise of literary authorship made to win the favour of the new ruler. It was taken by different sections of the people in different ways for the simple reason that it hit hard at the root of every mentality standing on the fundamental premise of self-interest. Curiously,it confirmed what Hobbes really wanted to prove. It was owing to this that the *Leviathan* became a most controversial work of the day. While, on the one hand, the Royalists said that it "was an endorsement of the Cromwellian *status quo,* some even claimed that it was but a deceitful expression of supporters of the Commonwealth did not like his apparent irreligion and his association with monarchists."[8] The truth seems to be that while Hobbes did fail in concealing his personal predilections (appreciation of strong monarchical government) as is natural with every philosopher, he did take the care of saving his skin from the feared hands of the Cromwellians. However, it is wholly incorrect to say that the *Leviathan* became such a controversial work that it resulted in making Hobbes 'an isolated thinker, rejected by his contemporaries, without influence on his own time either on the reading public or on other political writers, and thus outside the main stream of political thought in the seventeenth century.'[9]

This master-piece work of Hobbes, despite its being the most controversial book of the day and despite its being vehemently hated and condemned by the class of the Godmen, witnessed its proper evaluation in due course. Michael Oakeshott has described it as "the greatest, perhaps the sole, master-piece of philosophy written in the English language."[10] Macpherson says that it "still stands as the crowning achievement of his political science."[11] The profound hopes of Hobbes have now

7. Refer to " Thomas Hobbes" in *Encyclopaedia Britannica,* Vol. XIII, p.547.

8. Le Cameron McDonald: *Western Political Theory: The Modern Age,* p.75.
9. See Quintin Skinner: "The Ideological Context of Hobbes's Political Thought" in *Historical Journal,* Vol. IX, No. 2 (1966), pp.316-317.
10. See Oakeshott: 'Introduction' in his (ed.) : *Leviathan,* p.viii. Further, "And the history of our civilisation can provide only a few works of similar scope and achievement to set beside it. Consequently, it must be judged by none but the highest standards and must be considered only in the widest contest." *Ibid.*
11. Macpherson, *op. cit.,* p.22.

been realised that his work shall be taught 'in the Universities from where the preachers and the Gentry, drawing such water as they find, use to sprinkle the same (both from the Pulpit and in their Conversation) upon the people."[12]

METHODOLOGY : HOBBESISM AS A NEW TRADITION OF MECHANISTIC DETERMINISM

One important feature of Hobbes's political philosophy should be discovered in his method of study that indicates a startling break with the tradition; instead of taking the help of history and empiricism as was done by Machiavelli and Bodin, he takes the help of physics and mathematics. Thus, we are struck to note that Hobbes constructs his political philosophy on the basis of his postulates derived from the principles of a natural science. It is found that after his 'discovery of Euclid,' he became clearly aware of the need for a new political philosophy. It taught him that the necessity and possibility of treating politics as a science was a matter of course. One may call it a big reform made by Hobbes in the sense that he showed the possibilities of presenting a social study like a 'demonstrable science'. Let us see the elements of physics (motion) and mathematics (numbers and figures) in the methodology of Hobbes as a result of which he secured the distinction of being a mechanistic materialist and his political philosophy earned the reputation of being systematic, scientific and revolutionary.

The element of physics in the methodology of Hobbes is discoverable in his assertion that everything is to be explained in terms of motion. "The clarity, precision, and simplicity of mechanical explanations appeal to his neat, well-ordered mind."[13] As he says: "For seeing life is but a motion of Limbs, the beginning whereof is in some principal part within; why may we not say that all automata (engines that move themselves by springs and wheels as does a watch) have an artificial life? For what is the heart but a spring and the nerves but so many springs, and the joints, but not so many wheels giving motion to the body, such as was intended by the Artificer.'[14] The explanation of Hobbes centres on the assumption that even the elements of our body that appear to be non-material like hopes,

---

12. Hobbes: *Leviathan*, 'A Review and a Conclusion.'
13. Bluhm: *Theories of the Political System*, p.288.
14. *Leviathan*, Introduction.

ideas, thoughts, fears, loves and hates "can be reduced to mere internal motions brought into play by the stimulus of an external body and eventuating in action on the outside world."[15]

Side by side with the element of physics is the element of mathematics. Hobbes accepts the excellence of geometry as it reaches absolutely demonstrable complex propositions. The science of geometry teaches how to start from self-evident propositions to reach the final point of proving a hypothesis. It is the science of geometry that teaches how to move step by step in the correct direction with the help of numbers to solve a theorem that in the end becomes a conclusive proof. The significance of the mathematical method is also accepted by Hobbes owing to his belief that it is based not on passion but on reason and, owing to this, a study of politics can, in a real sense, be immune from the traditional complexion of being an irrational discipline. That is, in the view of Hobbes, the application of mathematical method to political philosophy 'means that politics is not for the first time raised to the rank of a science, a branch of rational knowledge. The only completely passionless, purely rational science, and therefore, the only science, which is already in existence, is mathematics; thus only by orientating oneself by mathematics, *i.e.,* by progressing as mathematicians do from self-evident principles by means of evident conculsions, can politics be reduced to the rules and infallibility of reason. Political philosophy must be just as exact and accurate as the science of lines and figures."[16]

The essential point to be noted here is that Hobbes integrates the elements of physics and geometry in his study of politics so much so that he looks "passionately devoted to building a political system, one that tied together psysics, psychology, politics and ethics."[17] If everything moves and motion produces nothing but another motion, the essential point to be taken account of is to study by means of a geometrical method how one state of motion passes into another to lay down and sustain the inevitable law of change. We may thus observe the important feature of Hobbes's methodology that the irreducibility of motion and faith in geometry are welded together. As Hobbes confidently asserts: "They that study natural philosophy, study in vain except they begin at

15. Bluhm, *op. cit.,* p.288.
16. Leo Strauss, *op. cit.,* pp.136-137.
17. McDonald, *op. cit.,* p.78.

geometry; and such writers and disputers thereof as are ignorant of geometry do but make their hearers and readers lose their time."[18]

It follows that the system of Hobbesian politics is based on the natural sciences of motion and numbers in view of the fact that what occurred to him was that various forms of matter are distinguishable only by the differences of motion inherent in them and that mathematical method can well be applied to a solution of problem relating to the disciplines of a social science. A study of Hobbes's political philosophy, viewed from the angle of methodology, indicates that it may be called a 'three-part philosophy relating to physical phenomena, knowledge and sensation, and social phenomena.[19] However, a better title that is ascribed to Hobbes's methodology is the 'resolutive-compositive method'. While the resolutive part is the way to reach the required simple basic propositions, the compositive is the way to build the complex ones from those.[20]

The system that Hobbes builds is, therefore, based upon the premises of his mechanistic determinism. To a student of political philosophy, it may, in the first instance of study, seem unintelligible and puzzling. However, the meaning of Hobbes is clear when a student discovers that Hobbes applies the laws of physics and mathematics to the study of politics by telling us that, like every natural object, man moves and the motivating force is his love for life. It has two expressions: negatively, it is his care for avoiding death, positively it is his effort for preserving existence. Thus, the element of fear having its corollary in the element of vanity has its decisive part. It is this factor that creates the feeling of self-interest in man and aspires him to struggle for 'Power' in which he suffers from 'vanity' if he is strong and from fear if he is weak. The way Hobbes moves step by step following the geometrical process from his axiom ultimately shows the creation of the all-powerful state in which man lives for the sake of his self-preservation.

18. Cited in Leslie Stephen: *Hobbes,* p.81.
19. M. Judd Harmon: *Political Thought from Plato to the Present,* p.221.
20. See C.B. Macpherson (ed.): *Leviathan,* 'Introduction', pp.25-26. Macpherson points out that Hobbes took inspiration from a leading mathematician like Descartes and a physicist like Galileo and thus he learnt that the "resolutive stage of the Galilean method, as applied to the political science, consisted in resolving political society into the motions of its individual human beings and resolving their motions in turn into imagined or hypothetical simple forces which, if compounded, could be shown to explain them." *Ibid.,* p.26.

As a result of this, Hobbes confidently feels that "civil philosophy is demonstrable, because we make the commonwealth ourselves."[21]

The system of Hobbes or 'political Hobbesism', as it may be termed, stands on these postulates:[22]

1. God made man such a beast and rascal that he inclines universally to malice and fraud. Man's typical acts, when he is unrestained, are violent and ruthless, savagely disregarding the persons and property of his fellows. His greatest longing is to preserve himself by gaining power over others. And he deems the exercise of power honourable, no matter for what ends it be exercised.
2. There is no real distinction between moral right and moral wrong. Moral distinctions are artificial suppositions foisted upon the generality of men by some superior power; they are arbitrary conventions which rulers impose upon their subjects and have no validity beyond the frontiers within which those rulers exercise control. The state is thus the originator of what men have come to deem virtue; and a part from the state there would be no moral distinctions of principles at all.
3. A *de facto* ruler is always justified in all his ways. Since the distinction between good and bad arises from the dictate of princes, the command of princes are *ispo facto* the criterion of right and wrong for those whom they are strong enough to command. A ruler, being himself the source of morality, cannot be immoral.
4. Appeal to law as a protection of popular rights is essentially invalid. For not simply are there no popular rights, but the passing whims of rulers of more force than what is alleged to be law.
5. Both religion and personal character are to be despised by the discerning. Religion is a sham and a trick whereby shrewd rulers buttress their wills by playing cleverly upon the fears of superstitious men. Character, too, is an idle notion. Men's inner motives are indifferent. What a man really seeks, what he hopes or wishes, what he secretly thinks,

21. Cited *Ibid.*, p.27.
22. See Sterling P. Lamprecht: "Hobbes and Hobbesism" in *The American Political Science Review*, Vol. XXXIV, 1940, pp.31-53.

these are of no consequence provided his outward acts conform to his ruler's will.

However a condensed interpretation of all these postulates irresistibly leads to this conclusion: "It was Machiavelli, that greater Columbus, who had discovered the continent on which Hobbes could erect his structure."[23]

It is well understandable that Hobbes, unlike Machiavelli and Bodin, discards the premises of history as well as of empiricism in his method of study. It is rightly said that if there "was one thing for which Hobbes had neither sympathy, nor even patience, it was experimental science."[24] Hobbes himself is reported to have said: "Experience concludeth nothing universally."[25] It is all owing to his fundamental belief that a science of society "could be developed if, as in mathematics, the simplest propositions could be used as a basis upon which a more complex structure could be built in a step by step procedure. Hobbes repudiated the inductive method and empiricism. The lessons of history were, he thought, largely worthless. To construct a commonwealth required the ascertaining of specific rules and principles that had scientific, and thus eternal, validity."[26] "Mere practice was not enough like a 'tennis-play', reason was a dependable guide than history in the firm view of Hobbes."[27]

For this reason, the method of study, as adopted by Hobbes, is known by the name of mechanistic determinism. In fine, it is based on his fundamental postulate of an innate impulsion that keeps man going and whose form is discernible in the fact that "everyman shuns death and this he does by a certain impulsion of nature, no less than that whereby a stone moves downward."[28] It shows that Hobbes "was convinced that all things were to be explained by motion. He was a thorough-going exponent of the mechanical view of the universe and of man. All science, if properly worked out, will be seen to be mathematical, politics as much as physics. He is, therefore, a determinist. All men are actuated by the same principle."[29]

23. See Leo Strauss: "On the Spirit of Hobbes's Political Philosophy" in Isaac Kramnic (ed.): *Essays in the History of Political Thought,* p.168.
24. W.G. Pogson–Smith: "The Philosophy of Hobbes: An Essay" appended to the text of *Leviathan,* p.vii.
25. See Molesworth (ed.): *English Works of Hobbes,* Vol. II, 18th Ed.
26. Harmon, *op. cit.,* p.221.
27. See Sheldon S. Wolin: *Politics and Vision,* pp.241-42.
28. Hobbes: *Rudiments,* Ch.1, Sec. 7, p.26.
29. A.D. Lindsay: 'Introduction' to *Leviathan,* p.20.

POWER LINEAMENTS : NATURALISTIC CONCEPTION OF HUMAN NATURE

The grandest conclusion of the Hobbesian politics finds place in his clearest and most perfect expression of the naturalistic conception of human nature when he tells us that man "desires power and ever greater power, spontaneously, and continuously, in one set of appetite, and not by reason of a summation of innumerable isolated desires caused by innumerable isolated perceptions."[30] As Hobbes specifically says: "I put for a general inclination of all mankind, a perpetual and restless desire for power, that ceaseth only in death. And the cause of this is not always that a man hopes for a more intensive delight, than he has already attained to; or that he cannot be content with a moderate power; but because he cannot assure the power and means to live well, which he hath present, without the acquisition of more."[31]

While exposing the lineaments of 'power', Hobbes takes the care of defining term in a comprehensive way. To him power means some 'future apparent good'. As he says: "Natural power is the eminence of faculties of body or mind: an extra-ordinary Strength, Form, Prudence, Arts, Eloquence, Liberality. Instrumental are those powers, which acquired by these, or by fortune, are means and instruments to acquire more as Riches, Reputation, Friends, and the secret working of God, which men call Good Luck."[32] A clear inference from this explanation leads Hobbes to admit that search for power is the root cause of competition among the individuals. Interests collide in the race to acquire more and more riches, honours and commands and for this sake the competitors take to the means of killing, subduing, supplanting and repelling their opponents. Though the struggle for power has its incessant play among the competitors, Hobbes further tells us, it is also true that men like to live in peace in order to enjoy the iota of power they possess; it disposes them to live under a Common Power.

It is clear that Hobbes uses the word 'power' in a very comprehensive sense. Power, though identifiable with anything like 'future apparent good' has a very wide connotation. After making a deep study of the political philosophy of the *Leviathan,* Macpherson comes to hold the view that Hobbes defines man's natural power "not as his faculties of body and

30. Leo Strauss, *op. cit.,* p.10.
31. *Leviathan,* Ch. 11.
32. *Ibid.,* Ch.10.

mind, but as the *eminence* of his faculties compared with those of other men, and that his acquired powers are those he has acquired by means of that eminence. A man's power consists of the amount by which his faculties, riches, reputation, and friends exceed those of other men."[33] A proper study of the Hobbesian politics culminating in the construction of the commonwealth under a perfect sovereign ordaining all individuals to live in peace in order to avoid the 'violent fear of death' leads to the conclusion that, in a strict sense, Hobbes's meaning of power "means specifically or only power over other men."[34] Studied thus, one may partly accept the observation of Bluhm when he says that power, according to Hobbes, "does not mean only domination but, more broadly, the ability to secure a good. Wealth is power, friends are power, good luck is power."[35]

Hobbesian politics based on the fundamental concept of power inheres certain salient ingredients:

1. It is power (in the form of desires or appetites) that moves man to play his part in the world. Love and hate, affinity and aversion, hope and despair all arise out of the element of fear in man. These appetites are incessant and operate as long as man lives. But the appetites change continually according to the physiological make-up of man. Man is thus like a machine in motion. He is moved by one force: Desire or Appetite being innate (like the desire for food, warmth and shelter) as well as non-innate one proceeding from his experience and the trial of other effects. It is well evident from Hobbes's own words: "Life itself is but Motion, and can never be without Fear, no more than without Sense."[36]
2. True that the force or Desire of Appetite is the motivating factor, it is equally true that the play of it differs from man to man. Different men have within themselves 'more or less Desire of Power, of Riches, Of Knowledge and of Honour: this Difference of Passions proceedeth partly from the different Constituion of the body, and partly from different education or not only from the difference of men's complexions but also from their difference of customs and education."[37] It follows that while all men incessantly see the

33. Macpherson, *op. cit.*, p.35.
34. Macpherson: *The Political Theory of Possessive Individualism*, p.35.
35. Bluhm: *Theories of the Political System*, p.289.
36. Hobbes: *Leviuthan*, Ch.6.
37. *Ibid.*, Ch.8.

satisfaction of their desires, as the strength of appetite differs from one man to another, different men feel satisfied with different levels of power, riches and honours. "Every man must always seek to have some power, although not every man is self-impelled to seek as much power as others have, or to seek more than he now has."[38]

3. Every man's power resists and hinders the effects of other men's power and that all acquired power consists in command over some of the powers of other men. Since all powers are opposed, the only way to require power is to master the power opposed to one's own. The value of a man in society is determined by the amount of power he wields in relation and comparison to others. The struggle for power has thus both harmful and harmless dimensions. Man who, in the first instance, desires peace in order to avoid the violent fear of death, competes with others for seeking more and more power in the second and, in this way, the harmless dimension of the desires is transormed into the harmful one. "Everyone, those with moderate as well as those with immoderate desires, is necesarily pulled into a constant competitive struggle for power over others, or at least to resist his powers being commanded by others."[39]

The political system of Hobbes is thus based on his fundamental concept of power. It is man's necessarily competitive search for power that ultimately calls for and sees the establishment of the civil society. The drawing on the frontispiece of the *Leviathan* is extremely fascinating as well as descriptive of the general theme of the political philosophy of Hobbes. We find that towering in the background of a neatly arranged town is the upper portion of the figure of a huge giant wearing a crown and holding in the extended hands a sword and crozier, the one is the symbol of the secular and the other of the ecclesiastical office. The waist and the arms of the figure are made up of a small people with their eyes raised towards the face of the king. At the top of the page there is a quotation: "There is no power on earth that can be compared with him who was made to fear no one." On the lower half of the page is the inscription 'Leviathan', or the Matter, Form of a Power of a Commonwealth Ecclesiastical and Civil.' On each side of this title are emblems and scenes representative of temporal and

38. Macpherson: 'Introduction', *op. cit.*, p.33.
39. *Ibid.*, p.37.

spiritual power such as the crown and the miter, and the castle and the church. In a word, power is the central theme of Hobbesian political system. Macpherson well remarks that Hobbes "exposed the lineaments of power more clearly than any one had done since Machiavelli, more systematically than anyone had ever done, and than most have done since."[40]

In appreciation of this, Prof. Oakeshott observes: "It is, indeed, of the greatest importance, for Hobbes' philosophy is, in all its parts, preeminently a philosophy of power precisely because philosophy is reasoning, reasoning the elucidation of mechanism and mechanism essentially the combination, transfer and resolution of forces. The end of philosophy itself is power. Man is a complex of powers; desire is the desire for power, life the unremitting exercise of power and death the absolute loss of power. And the civilised order is conceived as a coherence of powers, not because politics is vulgarly observed to be a competition of powers, or because civil philosophy must take its conception from natural philosophy, but because to subject the civil order to rational enquiry unavoidably turns it into a mechanism."[41]

MATERIALIST-MECHANISTIC METAPHYSICS: POSTULATES OF PEACE, PRIDE AND POWER

A keen student of Hobbes's political philosophy is struck with the fact that this 'maker of the theory of theories' covers up the antithesis of nature and human will in such a way that his model looks complete and systematic entitling him to be the greatest political thinker of England. The postulates of peace, pride and power are so inextricably women into the political system of Hobbes that the dualism of nature and human will becomes a monism that may be described as his materialist-mechanistic metaphysics. It is true that Hobbes found himself forced to adopt this approach simply because he saw no other possibility of escaping from the 'substantialist' conception of mind and, therefore, the kingdom of darkness.[42] It is equally true that he asserted the equal natural rights of man along with exposing the lineaments of power and, more than that, by putting the two things together to get a theory of right and obligation as well as a theory of power.[43]

40. *Ibid.*, p.9.
41. Oakeshott, *op. cit.*, p.xxi.
42. Leo Strauss, *op. cit.*, p.168.
43. Macpherson, *op. cit.*, p.9.

Let us first examine the three fundamental postulates in their details in order to see how Hobbes fuses them in his masterpiece doctrine of politics of power based on the facts of human psychology and experience. The fact of his premature birth owing to the threatened invasion of the Spanish Armada,[44] and the more important fact of his being a cautious witness to the events of the English Civil War made him a staunch seeker of peace–a condition of human existence in which man feels free from the fear of violent death and remains in a position to defend his rights. The first and foremost inference that Hobbes draws from the Law of Nature is the 'first and fundamental Law of Nature' commanding the people 'to seek peace and follow it.' As he says: "That every man ought to endeavour peace, as far as he has hope of obtaining it; and when he cannot obtain it, that he may seek, and use, all helps and advantages of war."[45]

The second postulate, and which also flows from the first, is the pride having its manifestation in the twin elements of fear and vanity. The twin factors of pride or vanity (vainglory) and fear have their effect upon the psychology of man: whereas vanity is the force which makes man blind, fear is the force which makes man see. It is the fear of violent death that makes man clear-sighted; it is the fearlessness of violent death that make man vain and self-conceited. The vain man who in his imagination believes himself superior to others, cannot convince himself of the rightness of his estimate of himself; he requires the recognition of his superiority by others. For this reason, he steps outside his imaginary world. In this situation, either others take his claim seriously or come forward with a challenge and the result is breaking out of war. It settles the relationship between master and servant. "The victor who has safeguarded his honour becomes the master. The vanquished who submits for the fear of death, who admits his weakness and with that has forfeited his honour becomes the servant."[46]

We thus come to find an identification of natural reason with fear that has its meaningful expression in the comparison of life with a race living in the 'state of nature' where force and

---

44. It is said that Hobbes's mother was supposedly fearful of the invasion of her town of Malmesbury by the threatened Spanish Armada and so she gave birth to her son prematurely. He and terror were thus born twins, said Hobbes, See McDonald, *op. cit.*, pp.72-73.
45. *Leviathan,* Ch.14.
46. See Leo Strauss, *op. cit.*, pp.21-22.

fraud are cardinal virtues and man's search for self-preservation leads to the establishment of the civil society under a powerful sovereign. It is inferrable that in this interpretation of Hobbes the factor of fear, that moderates the unchecked race of the state of nature to a reasonnable competition and ultimately to the regulated role of the state, is exalted so much so that it (fear) replaces the factor of reason. The creation of the sovereign authority (that is instituted by man for the sake of preservation of his life) has one end–peace at any price. It is, therefore, not difficult to understand that, according to Hobbes, the postulate of natural reasoning, in conformity with the standard of natural law, is reduced to the principle of self-preservation: since the preservation of life is the *sine qua non* for the satisfaction of any appetite, it is the primary good. As a logical conclusion of this thought, Hobbes "attempts to deduce natural rights, natural law, and all the virtues from the principle of self-preservation."[47]

If the state is established for the sake of self-preservation of life, and if the fundamental postulate of peace leads to the settlement of the claim for power by means of a struggle, it is understandable that state under the perfect authority of a sovereign is a natural institution. The domination of the master over the servant, *i.e.,* of the strong over the weak in the form of a despotic rule is, therefore, a natural phenomenon. As patriarchy in the family, so monarchy in the state, Hobbes construes both as the symbols of natural rule. The basis of the state is not will but mortal fear having its essential manifestation in the element of pride. Thus, the state is compared to a Leviathan as it, and it specially, is the 'King of all the children of pride.' As Hobbes says: "Hitherto I have set forth the Nature of Man, (whose pride and other passions have compelled him to submit himself to Government; together with the great power of his Governor, whom I compared to Leviathan, taking the comparison out of the last two verses of the one and fortieth of Job; where God having set forth the great power of Leviathan, called him king of the proud."[48]

Such a view of Hobbes makes the state an artificial institution and, at the same time, transforms it into a rational and natural organisation. The dualism thus becomes monism. Strauss well observes: "The artificial state which is as much

---

47. *Ibid.,* p.15.
48. *Leviathan,* Ch.28.

more pefrect, arises when the two opponents are both seized with fear of their lives, overcome their vanity and shame of confessing their fear, and recognise as their real enemy not the rival, but that terrible enemy of nature 'death', who, as their common enemy, forces them to mutual understanding, trust and union, and thus procures them the possibility of completing the founding of the state for the purpose of providing safeguards for the longest possible term against the common enemy. And while in the unforeseen life-and-death struggle, in which vanity to grief, the futility of vanity is shown, it is revealed in the concord of living, and for living in common, to which their pre-rational fear of death is appropriate to human conditions, and that it is 'rational'. It is even shown that it is only on the basis of the fear of death that life comes to concord and that the fear of death is the only postulate of natural reason."[49]

SOCIAL CONTRACT : GEOMETRICAL CONSTRUCTION OF COMMONWEALTH

Hobbes's procedure for fashioning the Commonwealth is geometrical in the sense that he takes his start from a blank page what he calls the 'state of nature'–a hypothetical period of human existence without any institution of government. The people living in this state of nature make a contract whereby they establish civil society under the rule of a perfect sovereign. Thus, the geometrical figure is completed. The start of Hobbes from a hypothetical state of nature culminates in the creation of State, Government and Society all identifiable with what he calls the 'Commonwealth'. The use of geometrical procedure looks like the mathematisation of politics at the hands of Hobbes whose intent is evidenced from the admission that the 'skill of making and maintaining Commonwealth consisteth in certain Rules, as both Arithmetique or Geometry, not as Tennis play or Practise only."[50]

It shall be worthwhile to put a word of caution at this stage that while dealing with the picture of the state of nature Hobbes is not at all concerned with some phase of historical development of human life. He is very much concerned with the facts of philosophy of human life as reflected in the physiological postulates and social observations. Hobbes is really concerned

49. Strauss, *op. cit.*, p.22.
50. *Leviathan*, Ch.20.

with the behaviour of practical men living in a condition without government as also after the creation or restoration of political authority. As a matter of fact, while dealing with the construction of the civil society by means of a social contract, he "was not asking his contemporaries to make a contract, but only to acknowledge the same obligation they would have had if they had made such a contract. He was speaking not to men in a state of nature, but to men in an imperfect political society, that is to say, in a society which did not guarantee security of life and commodious living (as witness its tendency to relapse into civil war). He was telling them what they must do to establish a more nearly political society, one that would be permanently free from internal disturbance."[51]

It follows that the state of nature of Hobbes is a pre-political phase just for the reason of his geometrical procedure that informs him to begin with a hypothesis. As an advocate of macabre psychology, Hobbes starts with the axiom that mortal fear is the prime mover that issues in the form of vanity leading to internecine warfare as a result of which the law of struggle for power determines the relationship between master and servant. What strikes Hobbes so forcefully is the equality of men in the faculties of both mind and body, for despite certain obvious differences in physical and mental development, it seems to him that even the weakest "has the strength enough to kill the strongest, either by secret machination or by confederacy with others, that are in the same danger with himself."[52]

In pursuance of his geometrical method, Hobbes supposes the existence of a primitive pre-social and pre-political condition of human existence which he designates as the 'state of nature'. He draws a very dismal picture of this condition of human existence by calling it 'a state of perpetual warfare' where every man is enemy to other man. Being a selfish creature and full of selfish tendencies everyone believes in the 'cardinal virtues' of force and fraud. In this horrible state of war of all against all, man is a ravening beast and his rights are limited only by his physical power. Naturally there is no distinction between right and wrong, just and unjust, moral and

51. Macpherson, *op. cit.,* p.45. Leo Strauss also says: "The state of nature is thus for Hobbes not a historical fact but a necessary construction...Hobbes does not narrate a true history, but he grasps a typical history." *Op. cit.,* p.104.
52. *Leviathan,* Ch.13.

immoral, nor is there anything like art, craft, science, industry, agriculture and private property. The impulses which move man are passions born in him. In man there is no innate desire towards transcendental good or any splendid ideal, rather as a material being he is concerned with his own satisfaction; he is driven by self-interest directed to the fulfiment of his fundamental urges. In short, it is a condition asking every man: 'Kill whom you can and take away what you can and from this spring all possibilities of internecine warfare.'

The ill, unhappy and intolerable condition of the state of nature is thus described by Hobbes: "In it the State of Nature) men live without either security that what their own strength, and their own invention shall furnish them with all. In such condition, there is no place for industry, because the fruit thereof is uncertain, and consequently no Culture of the earth, no Navigation, nor use of the commodities that may be imported by sea: no commodious Building, no Instrument of moving and removing such things as require much force, no Knowledge of the face of the Earth, no account of Time, no Arts, no Letters, no Society, and which is worst of all, Continual Fear, and danger to violent death: and the life of man is solitary, poor, nasty, brutish and short."[53]

The only standard that determines the way of life in this horrible state is the law of nature that means a set of rules based on the principle of expediency for the sake of self-preservation. It lays down that every man should seek peace and preserve it; if he cannot obtain it, he must defend it by all means at his command. It also informs that man must be willing along with others; and in the interest of peace and self-defence he should forswear his right to all things, be contented with as much liberty as he would allow others over himself and transfer some of his rights by a social contract. It enjoins that man should obey a covenant that he makes out of his own choice. Finally, the law of nature informs man to renounce feelings of pride, revenge, cruelty, avarice etc. and fear no harm from the authority in whose favour the surrender of rights is effected. However, in the view of Hobbes, the observance of natural law is based on expediency and utility and, for this reason, the individual should follow its dictates only when his self-interest is thereby secured.

53. *Ibid.*

The law of nature is different from the right of nature in the view of Hobbes. While the former designates a rule found out by reason that forbids any act of commission or omission unfavourable to the man's search for self-preservation, the latter at best implies a treacherous liberty and authorises man to grab everything even at the cost of war for the sake of his self-interest. Defining the right of nature, Hobbes says that it "is the liberty which each man hath to use his own power, as he will himself for the preservation of his own nature, that is to say, of his own life and consequently of doing anything which in his own judgment and reason he shall conceive to be the aptest means thereto."[54] Thus, different from the right of nature, law of nature, for Hobbes, really means a set of rules according to which a practically reasonable man "would pursue his own advantage, if he were perfectly conscious of all the circumstances in which he was acting and was quite unswayed by momentary impulse and prejudice."[55]

The escape from such a horrible state of nature is effected by means of a contract made by the 'ideally reasonable men' when everyone says: *"I authorise and give up my right of governing myself to this man or to this assembly of men on this condition that thou give up thy right to him and authorise all actions in the like manner."*[56] By this contract everyone surrenders all his natural rights to a sovereign (King or Assembly) and thereby State, Government and Society are established. The person or the assembly of persons to whom the rights are surrendered becomes the sovereign and the covenanting individuals who agree to submit to the authority of the sovereign become the subjects. The sovereign is no party to this contract and the people take it upon themselves to render him their unquestioned obedience. With this there comes into being a society having state and government. As Hobbes says: "This is the generation of the great Leviathan, or rather (to speak more reverently) of that Mortal God to which we owe under the immortal God, our peace and defence."[57]

The construction of the Commonwealth is thus done with the help of several postulates each following the other like a corollary. The development from the first axiom to the last point

54. *Ibid.*
55. Sabine, *op. cit.,* p.461.
56. *Leviathan*, Ch. 77.
57. *Ibid.,*

of demonstration is done with the help of 'theorems'. Here is the story of the generation of the state commencing from the first postulate of mortal fear to the last point of living under the aegis of a perfect sovereign whose essential function is to keep peace at any price. In this way, the ring of inference from the basic rule is completed. "We have the full set of rules of peaceful behaviour. Our model world is complete. Out of the single obligation of the individual to preserve himself we have constructed a whole set of social obligations, linking the individual to his fellows and to his sovereign in an orderly pattern of rules."[58]

A critical study of Hobbes's theory of social contract shows that it is false and absurd from the standpoint of history, philosophy and logic. The whole explanation is nothing but a fiction from the viewpoint of history. It is said that the state of nature presents a thoroughly wrong picture of man's primitive life. It also ignores the facts of sociology and anthropology which, as Cook says, reveal that men have always lived und some form of authority in a social organisation. This line of criticism on the historical ground is not tenable in view of the fact that Hobbes takes his start from a supposed point for the very sake of following his geometrical method in the construction of the Commonwealth. The other points of attack are, indeed, very weighty. It is surprising to see how the ravening beasts living in a state of nature could think in terms of establishing a civil and political authority in order to terminate that horrible condition of continual warfare. It is never possible that a series of discrete individuals living in a state of perfect anarchy could be brought under an organised society with a despot sitting at the head. It can never be taken into conviction that the same individuals who at one moment were rushing to each other's throat, should fly into each other's arms with equal eagerness the following moment. The whole story looks like based on a legendary conversion. Thus Vaughan says: "But if *Laviathan* is useless as a key to history, it is also fruitless as a theory of the state. The society called together by the covenant is no society at all. The result is that so far as the vital development of political thought is conerned, the *Leviathan* has remained without fruit, a fantastic hybrid incapable of propagating its kind."[59]

---

58. Bluhm, *op. cit.*, p.299.
59. C.E. Vaughan: *Studies in the History of Political Philosophy*, Vol. 1, p.54.

LAW OF NATURE : TECHNICAL INJUNCTION OF SELF – PRESERVATION

A clear understanding of the political philosophy of Hobbes leaves a striking impression on the mind of a precocious student that what he (Hobbes) means by the term 'Law of Nature' is nothing but a technical rule of the civil society. The remarkable thing about the implication of the Law of Nature is that it, in spite of having any content of morality or legality in the pre- and post- stage of the creation of the Leviathan, (a point of controversy among the critics and commentators) assumes the inexorable character of a definite law like that of the law of gravitation. Superficially, it appears that Hobbes's Law of Nature is a set of precepts, that should be observed by man; in a real sense, the inexorability of this law cannot be refuted if this dominant fact of human psychology is recognised that "if a man does not preserve himself, he ceases to exist."[60]

Keeping this fundamental fact of human psychology in his mind, Hobbes defines the Law of Nature as 'a precept or general rule, found out by reason, by which a man is forbidden to do that which is destructive of his life, or takes away the means of preserving the same, and to omit that by which he thinks it may be best preserved."[61] More than this, with a view to make the implications of the Law of Nature more clear, Hobbes differentiatates it with 'liberty' and 'right of nature'. "By liberty is understood, according to the proper significance of the word, the absence of external impediments: which impediments may take away part of a man's power to do what he would, but cannot hinder him from using the power left him, according to his judgment , and reason shall dictate to him."[62] Then, according to Hobbes, the Right of Nature "is the liberty each man has to use his own power as he will himself for the preservation of his own Nature; that is to say of his own life; and consequently of doing anything which in his own judgment and Reason, he shall conceive to be the aptest means thereunto."[63]

True that Hobbes makes a distinction of his Law of Nature with the Right of Nature and Liberty by adding: "For though they that speak of this subject, use to confound Jus and Lex, Right and Law: yet they ought to be distinguished, because

60. McDonald, *op. cit.*, p.86.
61. *Leviathan*, Ch.14.
62. *Ibid.*
63. *Ibid.*

Right consists in liberty to do forbear, whereas Law determines and binds to one of them: so that Law and Right differ as much as Obligation and Liberty: which in one and the same matter are inconsistent."[64] However, a deeper examination of the study of Hobbes reveals an underlying fact that in the long run both Law of Nature and Right of nature become analogous in veering round to the fundamental premise that a man shall not like to do what is destructive of his existence in the world. At the most, the two may be distinguished as the two sides of a coin or positive and negative corollaries of the same golden rule of man's being inherently selfish and wicked resolving to enter into the commonwealth for the sake of self-preservation.

The comprehensive implications of the Law of Nature look like contained in the 10 Commandments that Hobbes issues in the form of essential prescriptions. These may be described as 'should', 'dos' and 'donots', or 'injunctions', or 'an easy sum intelligible even to the meanest capacity'. These are:[65]

1. Fear: Man is a creature of his passions that make him afraid of others in the struggle for existence.
2. Peace: Man wants peace, peace at any price and follow it both for saving his life from the horrors of the state of nature and to play his part in the struggle for power.
3. Defence: Individually as well as in confederation with others, man endeavours for the maintenance of defence of his realm from foreign aggressors and internal disrupters.
4. Performance: Man should perform actions that maintain and defend the terms of the covenant.
5. Gratitude: Man should show gratitude for the gifts that are bestowed upon him from others.
6. Compleasance: Every man should strive to accommodate himself to the rest.
7. Pardon: Man should pardon all offences done by him before the establishment of the civil society.
8. Non-Vindictiveness: In a situation returning evil for evil, man should look to the good that will follow his action rather than to the evil that was essential in the state of nature.
9. Contumation: No man by his deed, word, or countenance should declare hatred or contempt of another.

---

64. *Ibid.*
65. *Ibid.* Ch.15.

10. Surrender: After joining the commonwealth, man should surrender all his powers to the state with a resolve to obey the sovereign.

All these commandments issued by Hobbes are consistent as they are grounded upon the dictate of reason concerning what conduces to the conservation and defence of the lives of the people. It is, for this reason, incorrect to say that Hobbes commits an act of self-contradiction by describing the Law of Nature as justifying the principle of 'might is right' in the state of nature and laying down the iron law of political obligation after the creation of the civil society. The two dimensions of the Law of Nature are integrally connected, though their essential meaning differs from the conditions in which human life is led. So realistic is the approach of Hobbes that he specifically excludes covenants with God from his discourse as they cannot be identified with the Conclusions and Theorems concerning what conduceth to the conservation and defence of themselves..."[66]

LEVIATHAN : PERFECT EMBODIMENT OF LEGAL SOVEREIGNTY

Undoubtedly, Hobbes's theory of sovereignty is his greatest contribution to the subject of Political Science. His affirmation of the headship of a masterless man–'an artificial person who personates, not impersonates, every member of the Commonwealth who formerly made up the headless multitude'[67] makes a distinct improvement upon the theory of Bodin who subjected his sovereign to the Law of Nature, Law of Nations and Law of God and thereby, for any reason whatsoever, committed a serious contradiction in the doctrine of sovereignty. For this reason, even his great critic like Vaughan has admired him in these words: "In spite of so many perversions, he must take the credit of being first to see that the idea of sovereignty lies at the very root of the whole theory of state and first to realise the necessity of fixing precisely where it lies and what are limitations."[68]

Hobbes's sovereign called the Leviathan is the creation of the social contract whereby the people enter into an agreement and thus terminate that dreadful condition of the state of na-

66. *Ibid.*, Ch.12.
67. McDonald, *op. cit.*, p.89
68. Vaughan, *op. cit.*, p.55.

ture by surrendering their entire powers to no particular man (or an assembly of men). The making of the contract signifies that there is set up a sovereign with a single will to govern society–the will that takes the place of individual wills and, at the same time, represents them in accordance with the terms of the contract. In fact, this is the substitution of one will for many wills for the paramount sake of securing peace at any price. For this reason, the sovereign whom the people institute must have resources sufficient for the provisions of peace and security. It implies that the sovereign must be absolute and powerful. Merriam well points out that the sovereign of Hobbes "is the judge of the means necessary for the defence of the state; he has the right to decide what doctrine shall be taught among the subjects, the law-making power, the judicial power, the right to carry on war; the right to appoint officers; the rewarding and punishing power."[69]

According to Hobbes, the powers of the sovereign over all governmental functions are absolute. He is the sole legislator, principal executive, and chief judicial officer. He hears and decides all controversies and makes determination of facts and laws, controls the defence and levies taxes to support his administration, chooses his own ministers and counsellors who are like his agents responsible to him alone. Besides, he has the power to reward and punish his subjects. The very creation of the institution of sovereignty makes it evident that, according to Hobbes, authority "must belong to the sovereign, for if his is the responsibility for governing and keeping the peace, which is the chief end of the state, he must control the means to that end."[70] Hobbes thus affirms: "By the authority given him by every particular man in the commonwealth, he has the use of so much power and strength conferred on him that by terror thereof, he is enabled to form the wills of them all to peace at home, and mutual aid against their enemies abroad. And in him consisteth the essence of the commonwealth; which (to define it) is one person, of whose acts a great multitude by mutual covenants with one another, have made themselves everyone the author, to the end he may use the strength and means for them all, as he shall think expedient, for their peace and common defence. From his institution of commonwealth are derived all the rights and faculties of him, or them, on whom

---

69. C.E. Merriam: *History of the Theory of Sovereignty Since Rousseau,* p.26.
70. M. Judd Harmon, *op. cit.*, p. 229.

the sovereign power is conferred by the consent of the people assembled."[71]

It should be noted here that for Hobbes social contract which creates the civil society "is not agreement to abide by the principles of the Laws of Nature but an agreement by mutual alienation of Natural Right, to create a sovereign power."[72] The sovereign of Hobbes with his plenitude of powers is thus a representative of the people who are a party to the contract having these prerogatives–maintenance of social peace and defence of the state against foreign aggression, enforcement of property rights, maintenance of law courts, making of war and peace, appointing civil and military officers, rewarding and punishing the members of the commonwealth. A study of Ch. 18 of the *Leviathan* titled 'Of the Rights of the Sovereign by Institution' shows that Hobbes issues Twelve Commandments in defence of his perfect theory of sovereignty. These are:

1. As the people have made a covenant to terminate the dreadful state of nature by their consent, they should not break it, otherwise it will mean the return of the confusion of a disunited multitude.
2. Whereas the people enter into a compact and thereby establish the rule of a strong monarch, the sovereign is no party to the agreement and, as such, he is under no commitment whatsoever.
3. The minority cannot resist sovereign's authority on the plea that it is no party to the contract as the voice of the majority can coerce the will of the minority in the interest of all the members of the commonwealth.
4. As sovereign's office is based on the consent of all for the peace and security of all, there can be no cause for injustice at his hands whatsoever he does.
5. The sovereign cannot be punished or executed by the subjects, as he is instituted by them with their consent and any move in the direction of terminating his authority will mean a return of the horrible state of nature after the breach of contract.
6. The sovereign is the sole judge to decide matters relating to the maintenance of peace and making of war for the preservation of life of the commonwealth.

---

71. *Leviathan,* Ch.18.
72. Bluhm, *op. cit.,* p.300.

7. It is the business of the sovereign to make and enforce rules for the enjoyment and maintenance of right to property.
8. Matters relating to the adjudication of civil disputes lie within the judicial authority of the sovereign.
9. It is annexed to the power of the sovereign to maintain sufficient armed forces for the defence of realm and to impose taxation for their support.
10. Matters relating to the choosing of public ministers, magistrates and officers in times of war as well as peace belong to the jurisdiction of the sovereign authority.
11. The sovereign has the power to confer titles and honours on his good subjects and punishing those who try to render any disservice to the state.
12. The sovereign has the right to distribute rewards and to determine what order of place and dignity each man shall hold and what signs of respect in public or private meetings the people shall give to one another.

All these attributes of sovereign authority justify the case of royal absolutism. The making of the contract reduces the multitude to a community under the strong and unchallengeable hold of a sovereign whose authority and will reign supreme and unchecked. In the words of Dunning, the sovereign of Hobbes "is the individual or an assembly who, by the terms of the contract, on which the commonwealth rests, is authorised to will in stead of every party to the end of a peaceful life."[73] The most formidable aspect of the affirmations of Hobbes in regard to the powers of the sovereign finds place not in the exhaustive list of commandments as in his bold warning that the people should never think in terms of violating the covenant, otherwise it will mean return of the dreadful state of nature signifying individual as "a masterless man without subjection to law and a coercive power to tie their hands from rapine and revenge."[74]

Hobbes's theory of sovereignty may be criticised on several grounds. First, his theory of the rule of a masterless man is a clear attempt to justify the case of royal absolutism like that of Charles I whose obduracy led to the outbreak of the Civil War in England. Strangely enough, by means of his affir-

73. Dunning: *A History of Political Theories,* Vol. II, p.281.
74. Vaughan, *op. cit.*

mations, Hobbes cuts across the very spirit of social contractualism. The state under the authority of a Leviathan cannot reconcile itself with the fundamental principle of the theory of social contract signifying that state is based on the free consent of the people. The result is that the people, in spite of being the maker of the sovereign authority, are reduced to the status of dumb-driven cattle in the system of Hobbes. The social contract of Hobbes reveals the substitution of one will for many wills and not a transformation and transmission of many wills into a common will what Rousseau called the general will. The result is, as Vaughan says, the society called together by the covenant is no society at all, because all the life "is gathered in one man at the head of it, the rest of the body is a dead weight, a mere unprofitable mass."[75]

Second, the attributes of the sovereign power, as so exhaustively described by Hobbes, are applicable to the government of an absolute monarch the model of which may be seen in the first two Stuart kings. It is certainly not applicable to the case of an aristocratic government or a government of the elite that came into being after the execution of Charles I. Hence, the admission that even an 'Assembly' of men may have the sovereign power is a clear contradiction in the Hobbesian system of sovereignty. What Hobbes says in Ch. 18 of the *Leviathan* is amply contradicted by what he says in the following, that the sovereign power may reside even in an 'assembly of men' whatsoever, an assembly of all that will come together into which everyone has right to enter (which he calls democracy) or an assembly of a party only into which not everyone but certain men distinguished from the rest have the right to enter (which he calls aristocracy).[76] Hobbes even designates as aristocracy a government by an assembly into which anyone could enter by the people's election. It is obvious that such a description of Hobbes "does not seem strictly consistent

---

75. *Ibid.*, p. 54. Warrender disagrees with this situation when he afirms: "It may be remarked, however, that so far as Hobbes's account of authority of the civil sovereign is concerned, this authority is explained as deriving neither from the civil law, nor from sovereign command, but from authorisation of the actions of the sovereign by each citizen, and it is in virtue of this fact that Hobbes is able to say that all forms of government are ultimately democratic. Political authority in Hobbes doctrine is not absolute. It is authority only for and over some person, and here where that person has authorised it or for so much as he has authorised". *Op. cit.*, p.111

76. See *Leviathan*, Ch. 19.

with his concept of sovereignty, for in the case the sovereign power would strictly be in the electors, not in the assembly."[77]

Third, Hobbes's theory of sovereignty has a strictly legal complexion whereby the fact of political sovereignty is altogether dismissed. It is pointed out that Hobbes dismisses the case of political sovereignty as advocated by Locke and of popular sovereignty as asserted by Rousseau. To a student of political theory it seems surprising that Hobbes ignores the case of political sovereignty that lies behind the facade of legal sovereignty. If sovereign is the fountain-head of law and justice and if his command becomes the law of the land, it cannot be denied that there does exist something ulterior and superior to his authority in the form of the will of the people who make the legislative department of their government. Laski has thus justifiably pointed out that the individual "is ultimately the supreme arbiter of his behaviour and if the state is to be a moral entity, it must be built upon the organised acquiescence of its members."[78] So says Gilchrist that political sovereignty "lies behind and conditions and thus limits the legal sovereign, though, legally speaking, the legal sovereign is omnipotent".[79]

Fourth, Hobbes's theory of sovereignty amounts to the case of monism inviting reaction against itself in the doctrine of pluralism–a theory that discredits the omnipotent state by contending that the loyalty of the subjects may and should be shared among various organisations of the community rather than devoted entirely to the state. Thus, Hobbesian theory of sovereignty has also been denounced by modern pluralists whose contention is based on the factor of real worth and personality of social groups and associations entitling them for the due share of sovereignty. The sovereign authority, in the view of the pluralists, is really limited by the sphere of various social groups and organisations that play no less an important part in the life of the individuals. It follows that the case of legal sovereignty is nothing more than a fiction and even a body like the English Parliament is not at all sovereign in the strict sense of the term. A great pluralist like Laski thus contends that legally the King-in-Parliament "may outrage public opinion; particularly it can do so only on the limited condition that it ceases, as a consequence, to be the King-in Parliament."[80]

---

77. Macpherson, *op. cit.*, p.56.
78. H.J. Laski: *A Grammar of Politics*, pp.62-63.
79. R.N. Gilchrist: *Principles of Political Science*, p.94.
80. Laski, *op. cit.*, p.58.

Last, Hobbes's theory of sovereignty has been a subject of abhorrence to the advocates of internationalism. It is said that Hobbes formulates a very dangerous doctrine of state absolutism whereby states become 'enemies' by their very nature. He makes the state absolute to the extent that there remains no room for international law and morality. He seems to be so completely indifferent to the sphere of international law that he does not bother to make his theory of sovereign state square with the framework of international organisation. It certainly does a lot of damage to the cause of internationalism. Bluntschli is right in asserting that the state as a whole is not almighty, because it is limited externally by the rights of other states. R.M. MacIver well evaluates that the relations between sovereign states "demand their regulation in the same way as man subjects himself to certain rules of conduct in his dealings with his fellow citizens."[81]

GOVERNMENT : JUSTIFICATION OF THE EXCELLENCE OF ABSOLUTE MONARCHY

Hobbes's theory of sovereignty provides a key to the proper understanding of his theory of government. In this direction, his view may be thus summed up:

1. Hobbes finds no line of distinction between state and government. Both are the creation of a single contract and, as such, both have their simultaneous dissolution in the breach of the terms of the covenant. Similarly, he finds no distinction between *de facto* and *de jure* authorities.
2. Hobbes prefers unlimited monarchy. He gives absolute powers to the government. The monarch is a perfect sovereign. The monarch of Hobbes is the chief legislator, chief administrator and chief judicial officer. That is, Hobbes discards the theory of the separation of powers. True that he classifies governments according to the number of persons constituting sovereign authority as monarchy, aristocracy and democracy, his final preference is for a monarchy where sovereign holds absolute and unlimited power

81. MacIver: *The Modern State*, p.282. Leslie Stephen finds another fault with Hobbes when he says that such a treatment of political obligation "is to be regarded as a subterfuge or a piece of refined propaganda used in order to induce men to obey the civil law without giving real reasons why they should, or it is a device designed to avoid public outrage or 'religious persecution, or alternatively it is the product of complete mis-understanding by Hobbes and sheer confusion." *Hobbes*, pp.156-57.

and who can bring harmony between private and public interests and well maintain order and security. Nothing but an absolute monarch can pursue a strong policy and show favours to a lesser number of persons than is possible in an aristocracy or a democracy.

3. Hobbes enumerates certain specific advantages which make unlimited monarchy better than any other form of government. In the first place, in such a government the public and private interests are most closely identified and advanced. The riches, power and honour of such a monarch arise only from the riches, strength and the reputation of his subjects. Then, the monarch receives counsels of the people when and where he so pleases. He may seek wise advices only in matters which he deliberates upon. Further, the resolutions of a monarch are subject to no other inconstancy than that of human nature. In democracies, even in aristocracies, this inconstancy comes not only from human nature but also from the number. Again, the monarch cannot disagree with himself out of envy or interest, while bodies (big or small) produce the conditions of civil war. Finally, even if it is said that the rule of one despot may bring destruction to the antagonist or prosperity to the protagonist, such possibilities of gain through flattery or ruin due to personal wrath are lesser in a monarchy than in other government.

Hobbes's theory of government may be criticised for two reasons. Firstly, the government cannot be identified with the state and the society. More upright is the conclusion of Locke and Rousseau who differentiate government with state and society. The change or dissolution of the government never amounts to a corresponding change or dissolution of the state or society. Merriam aptly puts that with Hobbes the government "swallowed up the state and became the sole representative of its personality."[82] Secondly, Hobbes's preference for absolute monarchy is not an admirable contribution. In an age of democracy, the type of government preferred by Hobbes incurs popular disavowal. The entire justification is based on a wrong understanding of human psychology. It is true that the absolute monarchies of the seventeenth and eighteenth centuries "saw many reforms in European countries, which no force less than that of a strong monarchy would have carried

82. Merriam, *op. cit.*, pp.37-8.

through."[83] But when the age of democracy started, it became a matter of popular conviction that no government which does not rest upon the affection of the people, which does not stimulate among them an interest in public affairs and create an active, intelligent and alert citizenship, can be called ideal, and, certainly no government from which the participation of the people in some form is included will ever be able to produce such a body of citizens. The American leader Jefferson even went to the extent of saying that no race of kings "has ever presented above one man of commonsense in twenty generations."[84]

POSITIVE LAW : COMMAND OF THE SOVEREIGN

Hobbes's theory of law is a corollary to his theory of sovereignty and, as such, it precurses the analytical jurisprudence of John Austin. In this direction, Hobbes frankly repudiates Coke's elaborate conception of law as the artificial perception of reason suggested by the lawyers and jurists and declares that the only test is sovereign's reason as embodied in his will. In other words, Hobbes asserts the same thing what Austin said afterwards that law is nothing but the command of the sovereign. Hobbes's theory of law bears the following salient characteristics:

Firstly, law is the command of the sovereign. The sovereign can alone make it, although he is above it. Naturally nothing but the command of the sovereign can have the force of law. Custom is no law unless it becomes sovereign's command. Properly speaking, Hobbes asserts, law is the word of him that by right has command over others. Obviously, sovereign alone is the author of civil law. According to Hobbes, "Civil law is to every subject those rules which the commonwealth has commanded him by word, writing or other sufficient sign of the will, to make use of, for the distinction of right and wrong; that is to say, of what is contrary, and what is not con-

83. Bryce: *Modern Democracies,* Vol. II, p.536.
84. Cited in Garner: *Political Science and Government,* p.378. Lord Brougham declared: "The tendency of all monarchies is towards despotism and its evil; and a constitutional monarchy which provides no checks, that is, a pure monarchy, has enormous defects. It leaves too great scope to the sovereign's interests or passions, benefits the people very little by the alliance he always forms with the nobles, gives facilities to humour his ambition by wars, allows reckless extravagance of every kind, encourages habits of costly ostentation and of pride towards inferiors, and begets a spirit of fawning and truckling towards those in authority" *Ibid.* p.373 n.

trary to the rule."[85] Secondly, with characteristic definiteness, Hobbes distinguishes between several kinds of law. He dismisses the concept of law of nature by saying that its precepts are mere theorems and not laws. All laws (including natural and divine) need sovereign's interpretation which is final and binding on the subjects. Hobbes thus asserts that the sovereign is a determinate superior whose command is law and whose disobedience is accompanied with punishment. Thirdly, this theory emphasises that law must be rational, and the sovereign's reason alone, as expressed in the sovereign's will, is the sole standard of reason. Finally, Hobbes emphasises that although the sovereign is above civil law, he is accountable only to God under the law of nature. Hence, sovereign's rights cannot be abrogated by human beings and any attempt to enforce civil law against him is to deny the existence of sovereignty and undermine the cornerstone of the commonwealth.

On the whole, the imperative jurisprudence of Hobbes seeks to justify the absolute character of sovereignty. The entire analysis is based on the assumption that sovereign is the supreme law-maker who cannot do any injustice to his subjects, because he represents them. The sovereign may commit moral wrong, but he cannot do any legal injustice and he is responsible for his actions to God alone. This is very much like the doctrine that king can do no wrong. In the words of Hobbes: "Covenants, without sword, are but words, and of no strength to secure a man at all."[86]

Hobbes's theory of law has been denounced by the advocates of historical, philosophical and sociological schools. Both Savigny and Maine contend that the people themselves have been law-makers through the formation of habit and custom. Its sanction is not the coercive authority of the sovereign but a general sense of the right of the society. According to Zane, the government "may superficially appear to make law as Hobbes and Austin mistakenly suppossed, but it is the acceptance of the rulers by society that makes law and government."[87] Duguit goes to the extent of saying that "it is not state which creates laws, but it is the laws which create the state."[88] The

85. *Leviathan,* Ch.17.
86. *Ibid.* Sabine thus notes that in substance Hobbes's theory "amounted to identifying government with force; at least, the force must always be present in the background whether it has to be applied or not." *Op. cit.*, p.468.
87. Zane: *The Story of Law,* p.271.
88. Even the sovereign Parliament of England cannot exercise its legislative

truth is that even an absolute state cannot thoroughly kick off the standards of morality, culture and social behaviour. Law is not the only force, among other things, custom does have an important part. Recognising this fact, Maine says: "State has little power to make custom and perhaps even less to destroy it, although indirectly it influences the customs by changing the conditions out of which they spring."[89]

REVOLUTION : CONTINGENT RIGHT TO RESISTANCE

Of course, Hobbes holds his sovereign's authority absolute and unlimited, but he recognises only one condition in which resistance to state authority is justified. He recognises that every man has a right to disobey the sovereign, if he is commanded to kill, wound or maim himself or not to resist those that assault him; or to abstain from the use of food, air, medicine, or any other thing, without which he cannot live..." Hobbes gives the reason that since men contract together to institute a sovereign only in order to save their lives, it cannot be maintained that they grant to the sovereign (to whom they set up) the right to take away their lives. It would be hopelessly inconsistent to claim that in the contract which they make together, by that they agree to love that for which they really did so. Moreover, the right to protect one's life against one's sovereign applies, clearly enough, not only in the case of a subject against whom criminal proceedings are threatened, but whenever any act of the sovereign endangers the life of one of his subjects. Thus, one may refuse to serve as a soldier to kill another or fight against his enemy. The obligation of the subjects to their sovereign is understood to last as long as the power exists by which he is able to protect them.

The right to resistance, as recognised by Hobbes in one exceptional situation, is equally applicable to the cases of sovereignty by 'institution' as well as by 'acquisition' the distinction between two forms of sovereignty is made by Hobbes on the ground that while, in the former, men come together and

---

authority in an absolute manner. Thus, Leslie Stephen rightly said: "If a legislature decided that all blue-eyed babies should be murdered, the preservation of blue-eyed babies would be illegal; but legislatures must go mad before they could pass such a law and subjects be idiotic before they would submit to it." *Science of Ethics*, p.144.

89. Maine : *Ancient Law*, p.160. Likewise, MacIver asserts: "For custom, when attacked, attacks law in turn, attacks not only the particular law which opposes it, but what is more vital, the spirit of law-abidingness., *Op. cit.*" p.161.

establish the sovereign power by means of a social contract; in the latter, the sovereign acquires authority by conquest. Thus, there is a basic difference between the two forms of sovereignty in the sense that while in the former men choose thier sovereign for fear of one another and not of him to whom they institute, in the latter case they subject themselves to the new sovereign after feeling afraid of his coercive power. But the common point is that in both cases the motivating force is 'fear'. 'Whatever the method of establishment, afterward the power and authority of the sovereign is identical."[90]

It may be pointed out that Hobbes indirectly sanctions the case of an inevitable revolution. The very pretext of 'doing it for the sake of self-preservation' is a sufficient excuse at the hands of the rebels to justify their move against the sovereign. If ever such a situation were created, it would appear that Hobbes, though quite unintentionally, invited the very revolution that he so strongly detested. Thus, it is said; "Although revolution was forbidden by Hobbes's interpretation of natural right by giving 'sovereignty by institution' and 'sovereignty by acquisition' equal standing and by giving the subject no voice in the determination of the lines of succession, Hobbes would seem to have made revolution virtually inevitable."[91]

Hobbes's theory of right to resistance brings about an element of contradiction and confusion in his general theory of sovereignty and government. If the sovereign has actual power to govern the state, as Hobbes thinks it requires to be governed, it is clear that people's right to resist is non-existent. On the other hand, the sovereign has no valid title to live in power in case he is too weak to be an efficient instrument of government. It follows that either the right which Hobbes assigns to the subjects is insignificant and meaningless, or the relation between sovereign and subjects is to result in chaos and anarchy. If right means power (as it is in Hobbes's view) the subject has no right in either case whether the sovereign be strong or weak. If the sovereign is strong, the subjects clearly have no right to rebel and, on the contrary, if he is weak he is no sovereign at all and society thereby relapses into state of nature in which no one has adequate means of protecting his life. W.T. Jones thus admirably observes: "Either the subject has a right against his sovereign or he has not. If he has not, Hobbes cer-

90. McDonald, *op. cit.*, p.101.
91. *Ibid.*

tainly should not say that he has the right. On the other hand, if he does have the right, Hobbes's major thesis–that the sovereign's power is, and must be, absolute–is false. Hobbes cannot have it both ways at once. If the sovereign's power is absolute, it cannot be conditioned in any way; and if there is any sort of restriction or limitation on his power, its power is not absolute."[92]

INDIVIDUALISM : ATOMISTIC CONCEPTION OF STATE

Although Hobbes's social contract finally ends in the justification of state absolutism, it is certain that the general tenor of his argument is individualistic. His theory of absolute and unlimited sovereignty is a necessary complement of his individualism. Realising that the rationale of his theory is individualistic, Vaughan remarks: "The whole work of Hobbes breathes the bitterest hatreds not only of the individualism as a theory but even of those elementary rights which none but the most backward nations now deny to the individual in practice, yet this preposterous system rests not only on assumption representing an extreme form of individualism, an individualism uncompromising than that of Wilkes himself, as it rests upon the idea of a contract, the only possible foundation of a civil state."[93]

The state of nature represents man as a selfish being concerned only with his material needs who becomes a party to the social contract purely for the sake of his self-preservation. However, the powers are surrendered not to the entire community but to a particular man (or assembly of men) with the consideration that the advantages of state and government would accrue tangibly to the individuals in the form of peace, comfort and security of individual person and property. The self-inter-

92. Jones: *Masters of Political Thought,* Vol. II, p.125. Thus, Warrender says that Hobbes's use of the term obligation with regard to civil disobedience is illegitimate and his political theory, properly appreciated, becomes, say an analysis of power relationshps more or less effectively exploited in which the citizen will obey the sovereign or rebel as the case may be." *Op. cit.,* p.4.

93. Vaughan, *op. cit.,* Catlin also notes: "Indeed, the famous frontispiece of *Leviathan* displays the body politic composed of human beings as corpuscles wielding in either hand a scepter and bishop's crook and crowned with the head of Charles II." Refer to his *A History of the Political Philosophers.* Similarly, Hacker expresses: "With Hobbes there comes a new departure in political theory: the politics of individualism." *Op. cit.,* p.201.

est of the individual thus constitutes the ground on which the existence of political authority may legitimately be justified. Sabine observes that general or public good, like a public will, "is a figment of the imagination: there are merely individuals who desire to live and to enjoy protection for the means of life."[94]

It is obvious that even after the making of the contract, the society does not have an organic character. It remains a multitude consisting of atoms each having its separate and distinct identity. In spite of living in the society, man is actuated only by his selfish good. The state lives like an outside power holding him precariously together by the sanctions with which it supplements individual motives. The existence of any group or association is scorched by the brilliance of the sun of the state. Everything goes to the absolute state which takes ever possible care to maintain the means of self-preservation.

If Hobbes's atomistic conception treats society as an aggregate of individuals each of whom seeks his own advantage and does so at the expense of other individuals when such aggressiveness seems necessary, his atomistc conception of state signifies that the end of political authritiy is to ensure the safety of the people. The essential nature of man makes him self-seeking, fearful and competitive to the point of combativenes. It thus enjoins upon the sovereign to provide for all 'contentments of life which everyman 'by lawful industry, without danger to hurt to the commonwealth, shall acquire to himself."[95] As Hobbes asserts: "And this is intended should be done, not by care applied to individuals further, than protection from injuries when they shall complain; but by a general Providence, contained in Public Instruction, both of doctrine, and Example; and in the making, and executing of good Laws, to which individual persons may apply their own cases."[96] A deeper scrutiny of Hobbes's views on the fundamental principle of state activity in this regard reveals the dominant fact that there "is no thought here of a Welfare State. It is thoroughly individualist."[97]

This fact is further corrobrated when Hobbes makes his sovereign absolute and enjoins upon the people to render him

94. Sabine, *op. cit.*, p.475.
95. *Leviathan*, Ch.30.
96. *Ibid.*
97. Macpherson, *op. cit.*, p.48.

unquestioned obedience and, at the same time, sanctions right of revolution in one respect. He frankly insists that the people should not resist sovereign's authority, otherwise civil society will be substituted by the dreadful state of nature. But when the sovereign endangers the life of the people, resistance becomes justified. The interest of the individual thus reigns supreme and even the very existence of the Leviathan depends upon it.

The trend of individualism is also evident in Hobbes' theory of natural equality of mankind. Unlike Plato, Aristotle and St. Thomas, Hobbes firmly adheres to the principle of natural equality of mankind. He asserts that nature has made men so equal in the faculties of the body and mind, as that though there may be found one man sometimes manifestly stronger in body, or quicker in mind than the other: yet when all is reckoned together the difference between man and man is not considerable as that one man can thereupon claim to himself any benefit to which the other may not pretend. It follows that privilege must give way to equal treatment, because personal claims to superiority have little basis in political practice to the strength of body, "the weakest has strength enough to kill the strongest either by secret machination, or by confederacy with others."

It is thus evident that Hobbes's political theory is thoroughly influenced by the factor of individual's self-interest. Dunning says: "But notwithstanding his exaltation of the power of the state, his theory was in its foundations wholly individualistic and rested on as complete a recognition of the natural equality of all men as was ever asserted by Milton or any of the other revolutionary theorists. His omnipotent state developed a most distinctive innovation, a contract of individual with the individual through which alone the state could come into being."[98]

ISSUE OF OBLIGATION : RELATIONSHIP OF LAW AND MORALITY

The social contractualism of Hobbes signifying the creation of the civil society under a perfect sovereign as a result of free agreement made by the people to terminate the horrible state of nature creates the controversial issue of his views on the relationship between morality and law. Sometimes it ap-

98. Dunning, *op. cit.*, p.302.

pears that there is no room for morality in the entire political system of Hobbes; sometimes, it seems that morality comes to have its place after the erection of the commonwealth. However, a very interesting study of Howard Warrender presents a thorough illustration of the point that morality as an essential attribute of human character pervades the entire system of Hobbesian politics whether it relates to the pre- or post-political stage of man's existence.[99] Thus, for the sake of a clear study of the political system of Hobbes, it shall be worthwhile to examine the three different standpoints that "most divide contemporary Hobbes scholars."[100]

The first extreme position is taken by those critics of Hobbes who find no element of morality in his systme whether it relates to the period of the state of nature or to the new phase of human existence beginning with the creation of the civil society. For instance, Sir Leslie Stephen in his work *Hobbes* holds the view that whenever Hobbes uses the term obligation, he assumes a very 'descriptive', even 'deceptive', postures.[101] What Stephen really means to say is that Hobbes is nowhere concerned with truly moral connotations. Then, Sabine is another great critic who is of the firm view that on this issue Hobbes "is saying merely that in order to co-operate men must do what they dislike to do on pain of consequences which they dislike still more. In no other sense is there logically any obligation whatever in Hobbes's system."[102] Likewise, Bertrand de Jouvenel affirms that the fear of violent death, that leads to the creation of the state, is replaced by the fear of punishment after the creation of the civil society and, as such, morality has no place in the face of man's selfish interest. As he says: "This desire to avoid punishment forms by degrees good habits, with the result that the punishment becomes no longer present to the mind and the law comes to be obeyed from a respect, now second nature. Let us note that this is to assimilate the training of citizens to the training of dogs."[103]

99. See Warrender: *The Political Philosophy of Hobbes: His Theory of Obligations,* p.6. Similarly, A.E. Taylor holds that Hobbes regards man as subject to moral obligations both in the state of nature and civil society. But the peculiar aspect of obligations in the state of nature is attributable to the fact that these obligations are reciprocal in character and are dependent upon the guarantees that others will perfom also. "The Ethical Doctrine of Hobbes" in *Philosophy,* Vol. XIII, 1938, p.411.

100. McDonald, *op. cit.,* p.90.

101. *Ibid.*

102. Sabine, *op. cit.,* p.469.

103. Bertrand de Jouvenel: *Sovereignty* (Translated from French into English

The second and a moderate view is that morality in the system of Hobbes comes to have its play after the establishment of the civil society. There is no place for it in the state of nature as there is no authority to keep the distinction between right and wrong. It implies that morality is not a natural but a conventional affair coming into existence after the establishment of the state as a result of social compact. This view is also taken by Sterling Lamprecht who holds that, according to Hobbes, morality has a 'social character' and is subject to 'regularised procedures' laid down by the sovereign authority over men. It implies that in the system of Hobbes morality "is not significantly present when men are considered in their separateness as atomic individuals."[104] However, the most important name is that of Michael Oakeshott who forcefully asserts that "the only sort of action to which the term moral obligation is applicable is obedience to the commands of an authority authorised by the voluntary act of him who is bound."[105]

The third and another extreme view is shared by some other critics who are very firm in their convictions that morality pervades the entire system of Hobbes whether it relates to the pre-political stage or to the period following the establishment of the Leviathan. The only point of difference pertains to man's 'first nature' in the state of nature and his 'second nature' after the erection of the civil society. A.E. Taylor is one such critic in whose judgment Hobbes's meaning of the law of nature changes its content from 'first' to the 'second' nature of man. That is, while the Law of Nature makes a man 'moral' by asking him to do what he ought to do for the sake of his preservation in the state of nature, it makes him more moral, rather really moral, in the civil society by asking him to obey the laws of the state. In this way, Hobbes's law of nature has the same kind of obligatory character as Kant's doctrine of self-imposed imperative of duty.[106] This point is very emphatically asserted by Warrender in his 'tightly reasoned book' wherein he declares that a moral obligation to obey the civil law "cannot logically be ex-

by J.E. Huttington), p.242.

104. Cited in McDonald, *op. cit.*, p.90.

105. Oakeshott, *op. cit.*, pp.Iix-Ix. Hobbes regards pre-political obligations as *rational* obligations and these are to be set apart from the moral obligations which hold in civil society. A rational obligation is said to arise when a man is prevented from willing a certain action, because he perceives that its probable consequences are damaging to himself." *Ibid.*

106. Cited in McDonald, *op. cit.*, p.91.

tracted from a system in which man has no moral obligations before or apart from the institution of that law."[107] Morality is based on reason that bids men to enter into social agreement to erect a civil society; it also commands them not to break the terms of the contract. Warrender calls the former as 'physical' and the latter as 'moral' or 'political' obligation.

In an attempt to present a summarised version of the various positions on the issue of 'obligation' in the system of Hobbes, McDonald, instead of concurring with either of the three diverse standpoints or adding his fourth one to the stock, draws four points to elucidate the meaning of the term obligation as possibly given, expressly or tacitly, by Hobbes. First, Hobbes is not a might-makes right man. The good motives of man in the civil society are the externalised forms of the bad motives in him in the state of nature. Second, the fear of violent death is not a despicable human motive but rather a motive of some moral significance. A man can seek the preservation of life with some dignity and rationality by terminating the dreadful state of nature. Third, obedience to the sovereign is morally as well as legally necessary to prevent the return of man to the pre-political stage. Last, the wise sovereign would not do anything to harm his subjects.[108]

Our conclusion should be that Hobbes is not an ethicist like Plato and Aristotle, nor is he a metaphysical idealist like Kant and Green. He is a realist and an individualist whose "major purpose seems to be to establish conditions for the safe pursuit of individual end."[109] Thus, the real meaning of the term morality and its relationship with law should be discussed in the context of the very purpose that Hobbes has in his mind. As Bluhm says: "Let us pause for a moment to ask what the word 'obligation' must mean for the radically selfish men of Hobbes's nominalistic world. It can never signify something accepted as abstractly and inherently good and proper, which one ought to do simply because it is right. The acceptance of obligation is always prompted by the desire of good to himself by the person obliged, and its only sanction is fear. Obligation can never be imposed, but it is always the product of free consent and contract. Thus, by the social contract, one accepts an obligation to live in peace and respect the life of others from a

107. Warrender, *op. cit.*, p.6.
108. See McDonald, *op. cit.*, pp.93-94.
109. *Ibid.*, p.94.

desire for the contentment of a peaceful life and from fear of the consequences of continued existence in a state of nature...In short, he keeps the concept of obligation throughout confined to things which a perfectly selfish but rational person will feel compelled to accept in the way of self-limitations, through hopes of gain to himself and fear of the consequence of disobedience."[110]

BOURGEOIS ORDER : JUSTICE OF THE MARKET SOCIETY

A thorough-going defence of the bourgeois politics and economics is traceable in the social and political philosophy of Hobbes curiously behind his disdain for the middle class citizenry and the affluent sections of the society that, in his firm view, had brought about the conditions of civil war in England. That is, a celebrated acceptance of the principles of bourgeois morality is discoverable in the political ideas of Hobbes and a reader should, therefore, not at all be misled by his superficial condemnation of the ways of the affluent inhabitants of the market-towns. The essential point of study is, for this reason, not the apparent denunciation at the hands of Hobbes of the merchants indulging in 'feigning, lying, cozening, hypocrisy, or other uncharitable ways' and whose only glory is to grow excessively rich by the wisdom of buying and selling' and also 'by making people sell their labour to them at their own prices' but the examination of the lines of 'new morality' laid down by him for the interest and guidance of the bourgeois class of society. For this sake, let us look into the political and economic foundations of his social and political philosophy.

As already pointed out, the politics of Hobbes is an out and out defence of the interest of the bourgeois class. It is evident in three directions–creation of the sovereign authority, maintenance of law and order, and composition of the legislative body. The creation of the Leviathan signifies the termination of that horrible state of human life in which there is no room for science, agriculture, industry, arts and crafts and the like. There is no property in the state of nature. However, as the civil society is established, all these things are available to man. It follows that, according to Hobbes, the creation of a civil society is necesary for leading a life of peace in which alone maintenance of private property is possible. The duty of the sovereign is to keep peace–peace at any price–so that free com-

110. Bluhm, *op. cit.,* pp.299-300.

petition is made possible whereby sale and purchase of labour takes place and the sovereign is there to enforce the terms of the contract. It shows that the sovereign state of Hobbes "is designed not to deny men a life of competition and acquisition, but to ensure that they could have it; it was designed to provide the conditions in which they could go on with the life securely, without endangering civil peace...It was the sort of long-term contract that a businessman could be expected to understand and to enter into with a view to his own advantage."[111]

The making of the social contract signifying termination of the horrible state of nature and the establishment of the civil society does not imply that a perfect sovereign would be entitled for using his absolute authority in any way he so chooses; it implies that both the individuals and their sovereign are bound by the terms of the contract whereby the former would pay the price by rendering him their unquestioned obedience and the latter would make and enforce laws enabling the former to lead a life of 'self-enrichment' by means of buying and selling their labour like any marketable commodity. In this way, the real relationship between the Leviathan and his subjects undergoes a basic transformation. It appears that the sovereign power is the hireling of the individuals, who apply themselves to just and modest self-enrichment, who buy and sell labour like any other commodity, and who also can pay for the work of their defence. As he says: "...the impositions that are laid on the people by the Sovereign Power, are nothing else but the Wages, due to them that hold the Public Sword, to defend private men in the exercise of several Trades and Callings."[112]

A peculiar feature of the bourgeois order finds place in Hobbes's assertion of equality and justice for all people. Formal recognition of equality for all in the name of law, adequate police to keep law and order, and a well-organised judicial system to enforce contracts all these institutions are demanded by the bourgeois order for the sake of having free competition under a free economy that facilitates the affluent class to seek its 'self-enrichment' as much as possible. The duty of the sovereign is thus to maintain the conditions of civil peace and social justice so that the free play of free competition is not hindered even by the proud and presumptuous class of the aristctocrats. It is owing to this that the sovereign of Hobbes

111. Macpherson, *op. cit.,* p.54.
112. *Leviathan,* Ch.30.

"exercises his sovereign right in the spirit and in the interest of the bourgeoisie; he provides for equality before law and for legal security; he chooses his counsellers in consideration not of hereditary privilege but of personal capacity; he opposes the pride and presumption of the aristocracy."[113]

If Hobbes had a strong disdain for the middle class on account of its role in the civil war of England, he had a like distrust in the rule of the aristocrats who misruled England after the execution of Charles I in 1649. True that Hobbes personally esteemed the qualities of aristocracy, he had his disdain for the reason of its pride and presumptions. For this reason, Hobbes desired that the Parliament should be an elected body signifying no place for aristocracy in the legislative composition of the government. However, his real preference for bourgeois morality has its inevitable manifestation when we find him suggesting that the assembly should not continue to be dependent upon the shifty and transient will of the electorate, but it must have the power to perpetuate itself by filling vacancies in its own membership. As he says: "...when any of the Assembly dies, the election of another into his room belongs to the Assembly, as the Sovereign...And though the Sovereign Assembly may give Power to others, to elect new men, for supply of their Court, yet it is still by their Authority that the election is made and by the same it may (when the Public shall require it) be recalled."[114]

A better and more powerful exposition of the bourgeois morality is visible in the economics of Hobbes where justice of the market society covers the issues of labour power, property and taxation. The central criterion of bourgeois tendency is contained in the dictum of Hobbes that 'labour is a commodity exchangeable for benefit as well as for other things."[115] It is further supported with the assumption that the value of everything, including human beings, is determined by the market. Herein we find the principle of market determination of value. For the value of all things contracted for "is measured by the Appetite of the Contracts: and therefre the just value is that which they be contented to give."[116] In this way, Hobbes refutes the principle of commutative justice. It means that in any ex-

113. Leo Strauss, *op. cit.,* p.120.
114. *Leviathan,* Ch.19.
115. *Ibid.,* Ch.24.
116. *Ibid.,* Ch.15.

change or contract the things contracted for should be of equal value, otherwise the ideal is unjust to one of the parties. Hobbes also rejects the idea of distributive justice that means that in the distribution of any benefit among a number of people the rule should be of equal benefit to men of equal merit. Both the old principles of social justice are, therefore, dismissed by Hobbes in view of the justice of the market society that holds that the value of a man is simply his price so much so as would be given for the use of his power.

A bold idealisation of the private property system provides another salient feature of Hobbes's deference for the bourgeois order. In his view, everyone has a property in his own person and the business of the sovereign is to provide conditions in which each man can make the fullest use of it. As he says: "Of all things held in property those that are dearest to a man are own Life and Limbs: and in the next degree (in most men) those that conjugal affection, and after them means and riches of life."[117] Elsewhere he says: "For maintaining of peace at home, there be so many things necessarily to be considered, and taken order in, as there be several causes concurring to sedition. And first, it is necessary to set out to every subject his property, and distinct lands and goods, upon which he may exercise and have the benefit of his own industry, and without which men would fall out amongst themselves, as did the herdsmen of Abraham and Lot, everyman encroaching and usurping as much of the common benefit as he can, which tends to quarrel and sedition."[118]

Above all, there is the issue of taxation where "the picture that emerges is more nearly that of a bourgeois state."[119] In the view of Hobbes, taxes are the payments that a man must make for the protection of his life and the security of his labour. He takes the position that taxes should be equal to the benefits received. Herein we find three approximations of Hobbes. First, everyman should pay the same amount as the benefit that everyman receives thereby is the enjoyment of life which is equally dear to all. Second, a tax should be proportional to wealth as wealth is the measure of the amount of labour commanded. This approximation is integrally connected with the one where we find that, according to Hobbes, taxes should be

117. *Leviathan,* Ch.30.
118. *Elements,* Pt. II, Ch.9.
119. Macpherson, *op. cit.,* p. 48.

in proportion to the amount a man spends on goods for consumption. It would make the taxes in proportion not to the whole benefit that different men receive from the state on account of the protection of their life but to that part of which they consume. Thus, Macpherson points out: "Hobbes's concept of taxation is bourgeois through and through. Taxes were justified only because they needed to enable men to get on with their private enterprises. taxes should be apportioned in a way that makes everybody pay his fair share, so far as this is consistent with encouraging industriousness and accumulation. This is a concept of taxation appropriate to an early stage of capitalism, when the encouragement of labour and thrift are primary objectives of state policy."[120]

A study of Hobbes in this direction should, however, be made with two considerations in mind. First, the appreciation of the bourgeois order finds place behind the facade of his bold denunciation of the ways of the members of this community that contributed to the horrible conditions of civil war. One may say that here is a clear case of inconsistency. Hobbes should be accused of making a self-contradiction by denouncing the ways of the bourgeoisie in one place and exposing the lineaments of a bourgeois order at another. Such a criticism is entirely misleading in view of the fact that real motive of Hobbes is not to debunk the practices of the mercantile class but to enlighten it with the existence of better conditions of social life more suitable to its economic and political interests. Hobbes is, for this reason, a corrector and not a critic of the politics and economics of a bourgeois state. It is well observed: "His morality is the morality of the bourgeois world. Even his sharp criticism of the bourgeoisie has, at bottom, no other aim than to remind the bourgeoisie of the elementary conditions for its existence."[121]

Second, the picture of a bourgeois order exists behind the facade of a liberal state sketched by Hobbes. The sovereign's job is to ensure the 'safety of the people'. The word 'safety' means not a bare preservation of life but also all other Contentments of which everyman by Lawful Industry, without danger or hurt to the Commonwealth, shall acquire to himself."[122] Again, as Hobbes says: "And this is intended should be done,

120. *Ibid.*, pp.49-50.
121. Leo Strauss, *op. cit.*, p.121.
122. *Leviathan*, Ch.30.

not, by care applied to the Individuals, further than their protection from injuries, when they shall complain, but by a general Providence contained in Public Instructions, both of Doctrine and Example, and in the making and executing of good Laws to which individual persons may apply their own cases."[123] The fact is that there is nothing like the exposition of a soft-state or a social service state; here is the case of a liberal state standing for the interest and welfare of the bourgeois class. In fine, Hobbes's superficial disdain for the affluent few should be read with his real dislike for the numerous many who are poor and have neither 'leisure' nor 'curiousity' to find out the 'cause of the Commonwealth' and, as such, the 'Common People are not of capacity enough to be made to understand them."[124]

True that Hobbes covers up the lacuna of being inconsistent in the light of the two points of considerations, it is equally true that here does remain one serious inadequacy in the model if we look into the fact that his lines drawn for the good of the bourgeoisie are not as 'scientific' as he conceived. For instance, Hobbes issues a clear warning that the commonwealth should not be dissolved, otherwise it would mean the return of the horrible conditions of the state of nature. But he forgets that the class of the bourgeoisie may adopt some other effective way or ways of challenging the authority of the sovereign without having the dissolution of the commonwealth. That is, Hobbes 'failed to take into account the possibility that there might be a substantial group or class, such as the bourgeoisie itself, with a sufficient sense of its common interest that it could make the recurrent new choice of members of the legally supreme body without the Commonwealth being dissolved and everyone being thrown into open struggle with everyone else."[125]

Apart from this, Hobbes should be accused of forgetting the point that every society has its own forms of class differentiation and class cohesion. If he failed to convince the bourgeois class that the only alternative to his prescription was the return of the horrible state of nature, he also failed to take note of the fact that with the advancement of social life there does occur a change in the form of differentiation and cohesion in the classes. The factor that informed Hobbes was the fear of the

123. *Ibid.*
124. *Ibid.*
125. Macpherson, *op. cit.*, p.55.

civil war and he remained so much horrified with the events of 1640-48 that he failed to take note of the fact that the class of the bourgeoisie had considerably consolidated in the changed political conditions of England. Macpherson says: "He saw classes, but did not see politically important class cohesion...He saw the first feature of the bourgeois order: its operative need for legal equality and its justificatory need for a postulate of moral equality. He did not see the consequent feature of the bourgeois order: that it necessarily led to class differentiation and class cohesiveness."[126]

ERASTIANISM : THOROUGH SECULARISATION OF POLITICS

Religion in general, but more particularly religion as advocated by the fanatics of the Roman Catholic Church being one of the chief causes of conflict between the Stuart Kings and their Parliaments in England, that ultimately led to the execution of Charles I and more than that being the source of trouble in France as a result of which King Henry IV was assassinated, became a subject of special concern for Hobbes. Thus, we find the views of Hobbes on religion in his three works–*De Cive, Elements of Law* and the *Leviathan.* However, the notable point is the paradox that greeater is his attention on this subject the more secular his thought appears to be. The detailed study of Hobbes in this direction shows that his treatment of religion in 4 chapters of the *De Cive,* 3 chapters of the *Elements of Law* and 17 chapters of the *Leviathan* bears the surprising trend that "is consistently towards greater but more critical attention to the Scriptures, away from 'natural theology' (i.e. discovery of God's will through reason) toward revealed theology, and toward a more rigid political absolutism."[127]

The erstianism of Hobbes has three dimensions. First, he is a champion of the freedom of conscience. Religion is a private matter and the state has no right to interfere in the domain of personal belief.[128] It appears that by advocating the doctrine of religion as a matter of personal belief, Hobbes supports the English Puritans and Presbyterians. However, the real case is quite different. Hobbes has a motive of his own in twisting his

126. *Ibid.,* p.60.
127. McDonald, *op. cit.,* p.99.
128. *Leviathan,* Ch.44.

argument to mean that whenever religion as a personal affair assumes the shape of an organised institution, it presents a serious problem and thereby opens the way for state intervention. An organisation is a material phenomenon that makes the way for keeping it under the unchallengeable control of the sovereign.

Second, Hobbes is the most vehement critic of the priestly class and he contemptuously designates its leaders as 'children of the kingdom of darkness.' To this end he discusses angels, miracles, sacraments, redemption, the 'office of our blessed saviour' and 'power ecclesiastical.' He makes a biting indictment of the "confederacy of deceivers that obtain dominion over men in the present world endeavour by dark and erroneous doctrines to extinguish in them the light both by nature and by the gospel and so to disprepare them for Kingdom of God to come."[129] The 'savage indictment' of Hobbes goes to the extent of comparing the leaders of the priestly class with fairies that "inhabit darkness, solitudes and graves. What kind of money is current in the kingdom of fairies is not recorded...But the ecclesiastics in their receipts accept the same money that we do."[130] In this way, Hobbes subverts what he says in the beginning on the subject of religion as a matter of personal belief. "The scripture vouches for priestly rule is from now on not an argument for priestly rule but an argument against scriptures."[131]

The erastianism of Hobbes does not lie in his biting indictment of the priestly class as such as in his bold advocacy of keeping religion as a tool in the hand of the state. It may be said to be the final dimension of his erastian politics. Here we find Hobbes going a step beyond Machiavelli. While the latter desired secularisation of politics so that religion could not dominate politics and it might be used by the Prince as a tool implementing his science of the statecraft, the former makes his Monarch the head of the church as he is the head of the state. As Hobbes says: "Fear of power invisible, feigned by the mind, or imagined from tales publicly allowed, Religion: not allowed supersition."[132] According to this version, church is a company of men professing Christian religion, united in the

---

129. *Ibid.*, Ch.47.
130. Leo Strauss, *op. cit.*, p.74.
131. *Leviathan,* Ch.6.
132. William Ebenstein: *Great Political Thinkers,* p.340.

person of one sovereign at whose command alone they ought to assemble.

Thus, Hobbes dismisses the contention of the leaders of the Roman Catholic Church as 'nothing else than an earthly manifestation of the Kingdom of Darkness."[133] Herein we find the doctrine of the establishment of the state church where the sovereign "is also the head of the religious community, no conflict can arise between the commands of state and church authorities, for they are one and the same. The citizen is never placed on the horns of the cruel dilemma that compels him to choose between sovereign and God. Moreover, the direction of the sovereign in spiritual affairs will probably accord as well with God's word as would the clerics' direction if they had the responsibility of interpreting and handling on that word."[134]

CRITICAL ESTIMATE : HOBBES AS A SYSTEM–BUILDER

The real contribution of Hobbes to the stock of Western political thought has been variously studied by his admirers and critics. While Joseph Vialatoux calls him 'first theorist of totalitarianism', Laird remarks that 'both his voices and head are medieval'. Bowle accuses him of holding 'a Machiavellian view of human nature.' On the other side, the admirers of Hobbes adulate him as a 'founder of the new science of politics'. McDonald is of the view that Hobbes "is a master political theorist by almost universal agreement."[135] Highlighting the depth of the empirical character of his political philosophy, Leo Strauss comments: "Thus, Hobbes's political philosophy is directed not only against the political science of tradition, but against all norms and values which are based on opinion, against any and every system of morals which is popular and pre-scientific."[136]

---

133. *Ibid.*
134. M. Judd Harmon, *op. cit.*, pp.234-35.
135. McDonald, *op. cit.*, p.72.
136. Leo Strauss, *op. cit.*, p.138. A great defender of Hobbes like Oakeshott comments that the philosophy of Hobbes rubs off the old and writes a new thing in stead. For this reason, it 'is in the nature of a palimpsest'. The system of Hobbes 'is not the plan of or key to the labyrinth of the philosophy; it is rather a guiding clue, like the thread of Adriane. It is like the music that gives meaning to the movement of dancers, or the law of evidence to the practice of a court. And the thread, the hidden thought, is the continuous application of a doctrine about the nature of philosophy." *Op. cit.*, pp.xvii and xix.

Let us examine the areas where Hobbes's political philosophy has been a subject of acute criticism:

1. It is said that Hobbes is a poor psychologist inasmuch as he dwells on the single factor of self-interest that moves an individual to do or refrain from doing anything in the world. If man is bad, he is also good and, for this reason, any theory based on the one side of human psychology is bound to be misleading. Thus, Hobbes's attribution to man as a bundle of self-interest "shows him to be a poor psychologist, a man of study, not of the world" whose "dogmatic materialism and anthropocentric outlook and whose disparagement of human nature found closely connected with his metaphysical and religious scepticism belittles mankind."[137] Rosse, for this reason, regards Hobbes as 'an obscene insect'. Men do not deal so maliciously for delectation. The Hobbesian nature of man, says Bramhall, is a libel on human nature worse than the nature of the bears and wolves'. According to Hobbes, says Eachard, 'man is an errant wolf'. But this is contrary to experience. Mankind, he insists, "is tolerably tame."[138]
2. Hobbes's axiom of self-interest as the motivating factor of human conduct precursed the doctrine of later utilitarians who treated man as a creature seeking pleasure and avoiding pain. One may ask: if man is nothing more than a utilitarian automation led by the single consideration of his pleasure and pain, how he can have the sense of pathos and irony that have their part in the struggle for power. This point is very ably argued by Macpherson: "If the obligation of the individuals to the state is based only on the calculation of their own self-interest, how can it be sufficient to hold a society together, since the same self-interest can be expected to dictate a breach of that obligation whenever changed circumstances would seem to make that profitable?.. But quite apart from the extreme case of civil war, it may still be argued that individual self-interest, however rational or however long run, is not a sufficient cement to hold a society together. The rational self-interest of Hobbes's appetitive, calculating individuals, it may be ob-

137. John Bowle: *Hobbes and His Critics : A Study in Seventeenth Century Constitutionalism*, p. 193
138. *Ibid.*

jected, is bound to set up a perennial disposition to neglect or deny obligation to the sovereign."[139]

3. Hobbes's view of society as a purely contractual and utilitarian entity is wrong. That there is no society before the installation of an absolute monarch and that there will be no such thing after the repudiation of his authority is altogether a misjudgement of human nature. For this we appreciate Locke who took the view of society's being political and differed from Hobbes in giving any warning to his people that the breach of the original contract would mean return of the non-political as well as non-social stage of human existence. Thus, a critic of Hobbes (Lucy), like Burke, declares that institutions "have their own sanctity: that men are born into a commonwealth, which is organic and not supeficially contrived."[140]

4. The political system of Hobbes signifies the enthronement of a dangerous and arbitrary power. The sum and substance of his political theory "is the vindication of the absolute rights of whatever government happens to be in power, not one to suit with the Divine Right of Kings under the Commonwealth."[141] The law is the command of the sovereign and, therefore, nothing but law is enforceable by the government. Hobbes thus lays down his imperative theory of jurisprudence. The command of the sovereign, or positive law of the state, cannot be disobeyed by the subjects even if it were in conflict with the norms of some higher law like law of nature. According to Hobbes, it is the business of the sovereign alone to see what law should be promulgated and also whether a law is in tune with the law of nature. It is only by virtue of having this prerogative that the king is enabled to maintain conditions conducive to the security of the life of the people. Hobbes issues a word of caution: "If the king violates a law of nature, and Hobbes is quite prepared to admit that he probably will, we may not, therefore, disobey him. For though the king by so doing will diminish security, our disobedience will only make matter worse."[142] It may be understood without any difficulty that herein lies a thorough-going defence of monarchical absolutism. None

139. Macpherson, *op. cit.,* p.61-62.
140. Bowle, *op. cit.,* p.196.
141. A.D. Lindsay: 'Introduction' in his (ed.) : *Leviathan,* p.xiv.
142. *Ibid.*

can deny the truth of this political axiom that there ought to be some restrictions on the legislative authority of the government. When Hobbes declares that if a man "denies his subjection, he can be destroyed by the sovereign as an enemy of the commonwealth. Whitehall insists that this 'circumvents the law of treason and brings in arbitrary punishment'. Lawson and Whitehall are both emphatic on this point that the power of the rulers "must be bounded by law, or they will little usurp it."[143]

5. Above all, it may be said against Hobbes that he is not a social contractualist in the correct sense of the term. If state is a creation of social contract, it is a partnership implying residence of sovereignty in the hands of the partners living under the aegies of their 'limited' government. In stead, in the political system of Hobbes the partners are reduced to the status of 'dumb driven cattle' moving at the behest of the rod of the shepherd who may freely choose to behave like a butcher. Sir William Temple rightly questioned that if men "are like sheep, why they need any government: or if they are like wolves, how can they suffer it?" A critic of Hobbes (Rosse) also rightly feels that such a government "is a mere slavery, which is the condition of those who live under the Turk, the Muscovite, Prester John and the Mongol. It would have such power and authority, says Clarendon, as the Great Turk hath not yet appeared to affect. It would not endure; for posterity unbound by such an unthrifty condition of their parents would call God's lieutenant the Vizier Pasha and act accordingly...this is to think that men are not foolish that they take care to avoid what mischief may be done to them by polecarts and foxes, but are content, may think it safely, to be devoured by the lions."[144]

The real weight of the above lines of criticism directed against Hobbes cannot be overlooked. However, it should also be borne in mind that the political theory of Hobbes is a product of history. Contemporary conditions had their abiding impact upon his sensitive mind so much so that it became a matter of conviction for him to say that nature has made man a passionate creature desirous not of pleasure but of power, the passions themselves are not simple emotion, but charged with and mastered by the appetite for power; honour consists only in the

143. Bowle, *op. cit.*, p.199.
144. *Ibid.*, p.202.

opinion of power; the worth of a man is, and of all other things, his price; that is to say, so much as would be given for the use of his power; the public worth of a man, which is the value set on him by the commonwealth, is that which men commonly call dignity. Leave men to themselves, they struggle for power; competition, diffidence, vainglory driving them."[145]

Hobbes may be wrong in various directions of psychology, philosophy, history, economics and politics; to a student of political theory he is certainly right in maintaining that without a supreme authority there can be no state. As a matter of fact, Hobbes's conception of sovereignty is the final improvement upon what Bodin gave to us about a century earlier. A student of sovereignty goes to the extent of admiring Hobbes in these words: "If man is really as Hobbes described him, some form of absolutism is inevitable."[146] The truth is that Hobbes corrected what Bodin left contradicted under the force of historical conditions. It is a misleading assessment that Bodin's theory of sovereignty was 'built upon disjointed and rotten foundations' and in consequence it "tended from the first to disintegrate, crumble into ruin and disappear."[147] However, this part of the same author's assessment is plausible that Bodin "probably assisted Hobbes to reach conclusions totally irreconciliable with his own."[148]

True that one is bound to appreciate the contributions of Hobbes so far as the subject of sovereignty is concerned, he may find fault with his (Hobbes's) estimate of the use of this supreme authority by the absolute monarch. We know that even Plato commanded his all-wise philosopher-king to maintain four cardinal principles, namely, just size and composition of the state, normal economic condition of the people, rule of justice, and educational system. Whereas we find that Hobbes neither places any effective restraint on the supreme power of his all-powerful monarch, nor does he give recognition to the factor of the will of the all-powerless people despite their being the makers of the commonwealth. Hobbes is, therefore, accused of forgetting that "the power of the sovereign, though legally unlimited, actually depends upon the skill with which it gives expression to the general will and that if the sovereign dis-

145. Pogson-Smith, *op. cit.,* pp-ix-x.
146. Bertrand de Jouvenel: *Sovereignty,* pp.239-40.
147. Allen: *A History of Political Thought in the Sixteenth Century,* p.444.
148. *Ibid.,* p.443.

regards the general will, there will come a point at which no amount of legal or constitutional machinery will avert disaster. Spinoza stated this clearly in criticism of Hobbes when he declared that a sovereign has right insofar as he has might and he has might insofar as he rules in such a way that his subjects regard rebellion as a greater evil than obedience."[149]

In a word, the political philosophy of Hobbes has been differently studied by the critics and commentators of Western political thought. The whole of his doctrine "doubtless had its main lines fixed when he was still a mere observer of men and manners and not yet a mechanical philosopher."[150] It is also said: "His whole philosophical system is very near to that of Machiavelli; he may be regarded as an ethical materialist who reduces all the aspirations of human nature to a brutal egoism and, for the most part, the satisfaction of animal appetites."[151] What becomes the point of severest onslaught is Hobbes's defence of state absolutism in regard to which it is observed that he "has the dogmatic arrogance of the theorist: he should remember that it is a very hard matter for an architect in state and policy, who doth despise all precedent, and will not observe any rule or practice, to make such a model of government as will be in any degree pleasant to the governor or governed, or secure for either. Whitehall's whole argument turns on the outrageous impracticability of the Leviathan. It is like nothing on earth–in no relation to the realities of government–the work either of a misguided or an interested theorist, either of a fool or a knave."[152]

If these are the weaknesses where Hobbes has been accused of being a Machiavellian thinker, there are some points of strength as well that entitle him for being the founder of the prudential science of politics. Hobbes deeply influneced his successors like Locke and Rousseau who rendered their further contributions to the school of social contractualism. His theory of sovereignty indicated definitive improvement upon the con-

149. Lindsay, *op. cit.,* p.xxiv. So Warrender feels: "Leviathan is terrible and so Hobbes portrays its terror in a few striking metaphors, but it is also feeble and most of his agreement is really concerned with this aspect, for apart from a few colourful phrases what emerges most strongly from his account is the appalling weakness of the sovereign." *op. cit.,* p.317.
150. G.C. Robertson: *Hobbes,* p.57.
151. Geiser and Jaszi: *Political Philosophy from Plato to Jeremy Bentham,* p.732.
152. Bowle, *op. cit.,* pp.200-01.

tribution of Bodin and thereby presented the complete picture of monistic doctrine. His theory of law precursed positive jurisprudence of the analytical school of Austin. Besides, his stern emphasis on the selfish nature of man had its influence on the hedonistic philosophy of the utilitarians like Hume and Bentham. In fine, Hobbes turned the theory of social contract, an instrument of early liberalism, into the defence of state absolutism at a time when divine right dogma was losing its ground owing to the resurgence of the popular movement. It will hardly be just to call Hobbes the 'Monster' or the 'Sage' of Melmesbury; it will be fair to say: "A great partisan by nature, Hobbes became by the sheer force of his force concentrated intellect a master-builder in philosophy."[153] The contradiction in the evaluation of the critics of Hobbes is well resolved by Leo Strauss in these words: "It is true that every reader of Hobbes is struck by the clarity, rigour and decision of his thought. But every student of Hobbes is also amazed by the numerous contradictions which occur in his writing."[154] In a word, Hobbes is a system-builder. He "stands out, not only among his contemporaries but also in the history of English philosophy, as the creator of a system. And he conceived this system with such imaginative power that in spite of its relatively simple character, it bears comparison with even the grand and subtle creation of Hegel."[155]

153. Pogson-Smith, *op. cit.,* p.xxxi.
154. Leo Strauss, *op. cit.,* p.x.
155. Oakeshott, *op. cit.,* p.xv.

17

LOCKE

Locke lacks the colour and the sparkle and the power of Hobbes. His prose has none of the richness of texture that is Hobbes's, as his mind has none of Hobbes's penetration and profundity. Yet his appeal is a considerable one. He is decently and decorously dignified, but he is never stilled.....Above all, he is a mirror in which Englishmen may find themselves faithfully reflected.

— **C. L. Wayper**[1]

Neither Hobbes nor Rousseau but John Locke is the representative thinker of the social contract school for the simple reason that he keeps the sovereign power of the state with those who institute it and thereby saves the partners of a joint stock company from the totalitarian hold of their chosen manager. Born in 1632 in the town of Wrington (Somersetshire), he was the son of an attorney and a landowner of modest means who in 1642 listed himself in the army of the Parliament and served as the captain of a company of volunteers. He received his education at Oxford and then became a tutor there. However, a turning point came in 1666 when he became a private physician of and confidential secretary to Lord Ashley Cooper (Early of Shaftesbury) who had already made his name in the

1. Wayper: *Political Thought*, pp.67-68.

contemporary history of England. This great event brought Locke into contact with several distinguished personalities of his time. When Lord Ahsley was dismissed from the office of the Lord Chancellor in 1673, Locke also gave up his association with him and escaped to France for the sake of safety. In 1679 he returned to England when King Charles II restored the office of Lord Ashley. Two years later, when Lord Ashley was prosecuted for playing intrigues against the King, Locke feared his own imprisonment and thus he sought asylum in Holland in 1683. During this period of retirement, or virtual concealment, he gave the proof of his intellectual and literary fecundity. The Glorious Revolution of 1688 rejoiced him to the extent that he hurried back to England. The new government was particularly kind to him as he had his every sympathy and support for Mary and William of Orange. He refused the distinguished assignment of British ambassadorship to Brandenburg in the name of his 'inability to bear diplomatic drinking', though he accepted the job of the Commissioner of Appeals that he relinquished some time after owing to ill-health. In 1696 he was persuaded to accept the commissionership of the Board of Trade, but he could not retain it due to travelling strain. Thus, he left it four years after and owing to deteriorating health expired in 1704.[2]

WORKS : TRACTS FOR THE TIMES

The political writings of Locke, in a sense, should be read as 'companion pieces' to those of Hobbes inasmuch as they were inspired by the same historical conditions and shared by the same rationalistic and mechanistic point of view.[3] It is a different matter that Locke differed from Hobbes both in letter and spirit and, despite his drawing heavily from the storehouse of the *Leviathan,* he 'never acknowledged his debt to Hobbes; in fact, he even denied it on at least one occasion, perhaps to avoid the distasteful label 'Hobbist'.[4] The fact is that, like Hobbes, Locke wrote against a background of hectic political activity with the avowed purpose of presenting a sensible defence of the 'reasonable' revolution of 1688 that witnessed the voluntary abdication of James II and the accession of William and

2. The most authentic account of the life of Locke appearing in the form of his best historical biography is that of Maurice Cranston titled *John Locke: A Biography,* New York: Macmillan, 1957.
3. Se Bluhm: *Theories of the Political System,* p.328.
4. McDonald: *Western Political Theory: The Modern Age,* p.106.

Marry as joint sovereign to the throne of England. Thus, it is well said: "The theorist of the Revolution is Locke; and it was his conscious effort to justify the innovation of 1688."[5]

Locke wrote profusely on various subjects like politics, economics, theology and philosophy. To a student of political thought Locke is important for his *Two Treatises, of Civil Government* appeared in 1689. The *First Treatise.* for our purpose, is not important as it is a rejection of all what Sir Robert Filmer had said in his *Patriarchia* in defence of absolute monarchy resting on the foundations of the doctrine of divine origin of state. The influence of Filmer's book as a handle of potential defence of what King Charles II and his supporters were saying had got to be repudiated. For this sake, Locke wrote his *First Treatise* with a sub-title *The False Principles and Foundations of Sir Robert Filmer and His Followers Are Detected and Overthrown.* Locke attacked Filmer's thesis of taking the holy Bible as a piece of reliable anthropological evidence in justifying the principle of royal prerogatives. With cutting polemical skill, he dissected Filmer's claim that the authority of a king could be traced to the primeval authority of Adam and thence to God. Thus, he attacked the unsound testimony employing a rational and commonsense interpretation of the Scriptures in point-by-point refutation. In this direction, Locke succeeded and the demolition of Filmer's work "was so complete that for centuries Filmer had the disadvantage of being known principally through Locke's criticism of him."[6]

The *Second Treatise* is a constructive work of Locke to explain the origin, authority and purpose of civil government. Here one may find the 'heart of Locke's political theory.'[7] It contains 19 chapters showing the views of the author on the state of nature, slavery, property, political and civil societies, ends of government, forms of commonwealth, extent of legislative power, executive tyranny and dissolution of government. The central theme of this work, and also its connection with the *First Treatise,* is evidenced by these words of Locke: "All these premises having, as I think, been clearly made out, it is impossible that the rulers now on earth should make any benefit, or derive any the least shadow of authority from that which is to be the foundation of all power, *Adam's private dominion and*

5. Laski: *Political Thought in England: From Locke to Bentham,* p.28.
6. McDonald, *op. cit.,* p.113.
7. M. Judd Harmon: *Political Thought from Plato to the Present,* p.246.

paternal jurisdiction: so that he will not give just occasion to think that all government in the world is the product only of force and violence, and that men live together by no other rules but that of the beasts, where the strongest carries it, and so lay a foundation for perpetual disorder and mischief, tumult, sedition, and rebellion (things that the followers of that hypothesis so loudly cry out against), must of necessity find out another rise of government, another origin of political power, and another way of designing and knowing the persons that have it, than what Sir Robert Filmer hath taught us."[8]

One notable point about the two treatises of Locke is that he, as a matter of fact, began the second one before taking up the first as his real purpose was to present 'an essay concerning the true origin, extent and end of civil government'. However, as he was confronted with the situation of repudiating the influence of Filmer, he saw it worthwhile to first overthrow what he ought to do in order to clear his way for the second one. The real point of hitch in his way was a lurking fear as to how the people would react to his attack on Filmer as he was well aware of the tragic event of Algernon Sidney's death who had paid with his life in 1683 despite his having a far more moderate view of 'republicanism'. Locke thus took up the job perhaps with a mind to publish his works under fake authorship. However, the Bloodless Revolution of 1688 cleared the way for him to write the *First Treatise* before taking up the *Second Treatise* with a view "to cut the ground from under the opposition before offering a more positive theory of his own."[9]

Apart from the *Two Treatises* appeared in 1689, Locke wrote some pamphlets that give an indication of his views on psychology, epistemology and religion and which have their incidental relationship with his political philosophy as contained in the *Second Treatise.* For this we may take the names of his *Essay Concerning Human Understanding* and his *Letter on Toleration* that appeared a year after or so of the publication of his great work, though under *nom de plume,* as perhaps he was stil afraid of the hostile opposition from some quarters. In 1695 he published his another small work called *The Reasonableness of Christianity* in which he tried to show that the religion of Christ presented the necessary code of moral

8. See *Second Treatise, Ch. 1, Sec. 1.*
9. See Peter Laslett (ed.): *John Locke: Two Treatises of Government,* p.59.

behaviour expressed in terms which the people, in general, may easily grasp.

By virtue of his great works Locke is ranked after Hobbes among the eminent English political thinkers. However, it is said that the works of the former are no match to the qualitative depth of the latter. "Certainly the *Second Treatise* has none of the logical cohesion of the *Leviathan.* It is only a tract for the times, perhaps we should leave it to the historian of ideas and not bother to seek profound political theory in it."[10] It is also said that the writings of Locke are so full of contradictions and inconsistencies that they "have been a great puzzle to scholars until very recently."[11] Different are the observations of others who have sought to discover the real value of the works of Locke not only in the light of historical conditions but also in view of the English traditions of liberalism and their consonance with the framework of a modern representative government, Thus, it is said that Locke "twisted his fingers around the haft of English intellectual life and got so firm a grasp that it pointed at least in the direction which he had chosen."[12] The renowned Scottish logician, A.C. Fraser, regarded the principal work of Locke as the 'most far-reaching of his contributions to social polity.'[13]

POWER FOR PUBLIC GOOD : POSTULATES OF A POPULAR GOVERNMENT

The *Second Treatise* of Locke begins not merely with a hint on the refutation of Filmer's thesis already done by him in the *First Treatise,* it immediately thereafter indicates his attention confined to the problem of finding out 'another rise of government, another origin of political power.' That the whole theory of Locke as contained in this small book embodies the fundamental postulates of popular government is evident from these words of him: "Political power, then, I take to be a right of making laws with panalties of death, and consequently all less penalties, for the regulating and preserving of property,and of employing the force of the community in the execution of such laws, and in the defence of the commonwealth from foreign injury; and all this only for the public good."[14]

10. McDonald, *op. cit.,* pp.111-12.
11. Bluhm, *op. cit.,* p.829.
12. Leslett, *op. cit.,* p.37.
13. Cited in Maxey: *Political Philosophies,* p.250.
14. *Second Treatise,* Ch.1, Sec.3.

The first postulate of Locke that flows from his first affirmation is that if there is anything that he grossly detests, it is the existence of an arbitrary government. The measuring rod is the public good in the light of which the validity of the laws of the state should be examined. It follows that the laws of the state, as important as those laying down the provision of capital punishment, and enforced without any regard to the good of the public "would not only be a bad exercise of power but no power at all a definition that seems to bring true power close to justice."[15] The fact that arbitrary power of the state is *bete noire* of Locke is traceable in his words when he asserts that "freedom from arbitrary power is so necessary to, and closely joined with, a man's preservation, that he cannot part with it but by what forfeits his preservation and life together."[16]

In order to build up a political theory of popular government in opposition to a doctrine of arbitrary government, as given by Filmer and Hobbes, Locke hinges it on the factor of 'consent' that may be regarded as the second postulate of his theory of a popular government. It is consent that makes a man ready to live in the society (under the state of nature) and then in the state established after the making of the contract. The existence of the element of consent "is assumed when the individual remains in the society, takes advantage of the protection and service that society offers him, and obeys the laws of the community."[17] However, the postulate of consent, as understood by Locke, has three characteristics. In the first place, it may be 'express' or 'tacit'. The former case is understandable when the people support the government in the form of great movements with their non-opposition to what the government does on a particular occasion. It implies that a rebellion is the only bold proof of peoples' withdrawal of consent. Second, the giving of consent does not mean complete alienation of man's powers, it relates to a restricted purpose only. It is clear from the nature of the social contract that people surrender just a part of their power to the political authority and thereby establish a limited government. It thus makes the state bound to decide as to what things it ought to do and the way it ought to do them. Finally, the giving of consent in an open or implied form does not mean that the principle of equality should be

15. McDonald, *op. cit.,* p.114.
16. *Second Treatise,* Ch.4 Sec.22.
17. Judd Harmon, *op. cit.,* p.250.

studied in a literal sense in the political theory of Locke. "Age or virtue may give man a just precedency. Excellency of parts and merit may place others above the common level."[18] An examination of Locke's affirmation in this regard infers: "Not *all* persons are equal and persons are equal and therefore not all persons are consent-givers."[19]

The next postulate of Locke's popular government is his sanction for a limited and energetic government. He makes the authority of the government limited by laying it down that it cannot break the terms of a great declaration in the form of a bill of rights; it cannot take away the property of the people without their consent; the legislature should be periodically elected; the powers of the three organs of government should not be fused; there should be no delegation of power by one organ of government to another; the verdict of the referendum should be respected. The limited government of Locke is also energetic as, in a positive sense, it is required in order to ensure peace, order and security of property. The law of nature "stands as an eternal rule to all men, legislators as well as others...and the fundamental law of nature being preservation of mankind, no human sanction can be good or valid against it."[20]

If the government is required to secure peace and order, it is mainly for the sake of the preservation of property. Thus, the postulate of 'property comes to occupy' a prominent position in the forefront of his political system.[21] A most thorough–going defence of this institution is hardly available in the words of Locke's predecessors or contemporaries seeing which it may be said that herein we find the portrait of an economic leviathan. A reader of Locke is surprised by his bold affirmation that property, which is something more than a mere physical estate, is at the heart of his conception of good life and the good state, 'the great end of man's entering into society being the enjoyment of their properties in peace and safety."[22] The most striking feature of Locke's theory of property is that 'property' being an extraneous subject in a work on politics is deeply intruded into his entire political system so much so that it determines man's life in the state of nature and his readiness to join the

18. *Second Treatise,* Ch. 6, Sec. 135.
19. McDonald, *op. cit.,* p.119.
20. *Second Treatise,* Ch.11, Sec.135.
21. J.W. Gough: *John Locke's Political Philosophy* , p.71.
22. *Second Treatise,* Ch.11 Sec.134.

social contract. Thus, Locke's ideas on the state of nature, social contract, creation of political authority, nature and end of state are all governed by his theory of property.

The last postulate of Locke's political theory should be studied in his affirmation of an utilitarian government. Not merely the authority of the government is taken as negatively limited or positively energetic, it is required to be exercised for the sake of public good. The power of the government is in the hands of the majority, but the majority is not entitled for using its power in an arbitrary manner. "For that which acts any community, being only the consent of the individuals of it, and it being one body, must move one way, it is necessary that the body should move that way whether the greatest force carries it, which is the consent of the majority, or else it is impossible it should act or continue as one body, one community which the consent of every individual that united into it and agreed that it should; and so every individual that united into consent to be concluded by the majority."[23] All organs of the government are therefore enjoined upon to serve the good of the public; at the same time, Locke sanctions an 'appeal to the heaven' which means that the people "reserve the right of revolution, and the government is 'dissolved' by any of the foregoing act" at the hands of the people who take up arms to bring about a change in the order of the day.[24]

From a critical point of view, it may, however, be added that Locke's picture of popular government is not as clear as that given by his successors like John Stuart Mill or criticised by others like Sir Henry Maine. What really pertains to the world of popular government in the system of Locke is his assertion that the sovereign power rests with the community and the government should exercise its authority for the public good. It is the extreme case when we find that Locke empowers his people to hold arms in their hands to overthrow an arbitrary government what he curiously calls 'appeal to the heaven.' Either the government is expected to live and work within limits, or the Parliament (being representative of the people) can fairly be assumed to keep the situation under control. In a word, the popular government of Locke stands on the single factor of people's being the judge, in an ultimate sense, of deciding a question relating to the validity of government's action.

23. *Ibid.*, Ch.4, Sec.99.
24. Bluhm, *op. cit.*, p.346.

What is further advisable is that this point should not be studied in the light of the highly unrepresentative character of the Parliament of the days of Locke in view of the fact that what he "was really doing under the guise of erecting a form of government on the basis of freely consenting individuals, was to describe the operation of the traditional English constitution in terms of political philosophy current in his age."[25]

HUMAN NATURE : PSYCHOLOGICAL-EGOISTIC HEDONISM

Locke's view of human nature indicating his psychological egotistic hedonism is contained not in his two treatises on civil government but in another small work titled *An Essay Concerning Human Understanding* where he takes 'desire' as the spring of all human actions making a man aware of the feelings of pleasure and pain. As he says: "What has an aptness to produce pleasure in us is that we call good, and what is apt to produce pain in us, we call evil; for no other reason but for its aptness to produce pleasure and pain in us, wherein consists our happiness and misery."[26] One may find herein what was, later on, copied by Jeremy Bentham and that became known to the world by the name of his utilitarianism.

If desire is the spring of all human actions that makes man aware of the feelings of good and bad, naturally the association of our pleasures and pains with the rule of our behaviour lay down the norms of morality. What gives pleasure, or satisfaction, or delight, or happiness, becomes morally binding; conversely, what gives pain, or anguish, or misery, or torment, or uneasiness, or trouble, become morally unbinding on the people. A trace of Locke's theory of 'sensation' and 'reflection' is visible here when we find that pleasures and pains "arise from sensation and from reflection and 'join themselves to' nearly all other simple ideas, even underpinning concepts of morality."[27]

The idea of our moral relationships and moral duties is thus explained by Locke: "Morally good and evil behaviour, then, is only the conformity or disagreement of our voluntary actions to some law, whereby good or evil is drawn on us from

25. Gough, *op. cit.*, p.71.
26. A.S. Pringle-Pattison (ed.): *An Essay Concerning Human Understanding*, Book I, Ch.21, Sec.41.
27. Bluhm, *op. cit.*, p.334.

the will and power of the law-maker; which good and evil, pleasure or pain, attending on our observance or breach of the law, are the decrees of the law-maker, is that we call reward and punishment...That God has given a rule whereby men should govern themselves. I think there is nobody so brutish as to deny. He has a right to do it; we are his creatures. He has goodness and wisdom to direct our actions to that which is best; and he has power to enforce it by rewards and punishment, of infinite weight and duration in another life; for nobody can take us out of his hands. This is the only true touchstone of moral rectitude."[28]

Locke's theory of morality as flowing from his views constituting his psychological-egotistic hedonism embody certain characteristics. First, he says that there are no universally binding moral laws in man-made spheres. That is, morality of one society may not apply to another. 'The saints who are canonised among the Turks lead lives which cannot with modesty relate.' Second, more laws emanating from the hands of God and Nature are universally binding. Locke tells us that the premises of Divine Law laying down principles of universal morality should be discovered in the holy books of religion, while the premises of the Law of Nature are discoverable by human reason. Finally, man's search for seeking pleasures and avoiding pains should be subject to the law of public happiness in general. Epicurean hedonism is thus transformed into enlightened utilitarianism.

A study of Locke's psychological hedonism creates the problem of his being inconsistent with regard to his notion of rationalist epistemology. The problem arises how Locke's hedonistic ethics can be reconciled with his rationalist theology. If men is a seeker of worldly pleasures, how can he make use of his rational judgment reducing himself to the mundane life of a creature who is just a bundle of earthly pleasures and pains? It is thus remarked by Bluhm that Calvinism and hedonism "are ingeniously joined together in (unholy ?) matrimony."[29] It is also commented: "It must, then, be obvious that Locke's view of human nature is nothing like so profound, and certainly nothing like as consistent, as that of Hobbes."[30] This amount of contradiction may, however, be resolved by

28. Cited *Ibid.*, pp.334-35.
29. *Ibid.*, p.335.
30. Wayper, *op. cit.*, p.70.

studying Locke in the light of the conditions under which he lived and wrote and the problem which he was really confronted with. By making search for earthly pleasures subject to the norm of general happiness, Locke did a great service in giving a humanistic shape to the unsocial doctrine of Epicurean hedonism and thereby made it a workable creed at the hands of his successoss like Hume and Bentham. At the same time, by making man-made laws of morality subject to the norms of public happiness he made political authority consonant with his fundamental postulate of popular government. It strengthened his hands to offer a plausible justification which Hobbes "would have regarded as anarchic and deplorable in the extreme."[31]

EPISTEMOLOGY : FAITH, REASON, SENSE-PERCEPTION

The philosophical foundation of Locke's political philosophy, as contained in his *Essay Concerning Human Understanding* and the *Two Treaties of Civil Government,* present a confusing spectacle of his epistemology that looks like rationalist, nominalist, atomist, empiricist and hedonist. For this, Locke has been criticised, whereas some of his defenders have made serious efforts to establish some form of synthesis between his diverse, and rather antagonistic views in the light of the historical conditions in which he lived and wrote for the justification of the Whig Revolution. The result of diverse interpretations of the commentator of Locke is that he is treated as a refuter of the doctrine of innate ideas as well as the layer of the groundwork of English empiricist thought; he is also regarded as a Thomist drawing inspiration from the tenets of the Scriptures and placing them before his people with a view to give a rationalist justification of the existence of God and His Divine Law as well as a precursor of Benthamite utilitarianism who would dismiss every law and institution if it lacked substitution in the name of its 'utility' to the general public.

The element of faith in the epistemology of Locke is traceable in his axioms–an approach that takes him very close to the geometrical approach of Hobbes. His unshakable faith in the existence of a hypothetical state of nature, natural rights of man, consent as the maker of political authority, sacrosanct character of private property, excellence of the majority rule and the like indicate that Locke's theory of knowledge is condi-

31. *Ibid.*

tioned by his innate faith in certain axioms and it is obvious that this feature of his epistemology leaves no room for the principles of empiricism and utilitarianism. However, a student of Locke having some knowledge of this philosopher's contribution to the stock of empiricism and rationalism is struck with the fact that he (Locke) identifies God with reason in an attempt to give a rationalist orientation to the Law of Nature. It is evident from the assertion of Locke that the certainty of the Law of Nature "is not really, as he tried to maintain, a question of mathematical demonstrability, but a matter of faith. It is part of the nature of the world that He created. It is a law of reason, because God Himself is reasonable, and reason is faculty given to man by God as a means of recognising His will."[32]

As a cautious man and a shrewd philosopher, Locke makes a very intelligent effort to reconcile his epistemology of faith with his epistemology of reason and experience. He coins a key-term 'Right of Nature' (understandable to man by virtue of his faculty of reason and perception) in place of his Law of Nature having the character of being 'innate'. One may understand that Locke makes a shift in his stand for the sake of avoiding the charge of being inconsistent. A defender of Locke thus carries the point that by the 'light of nature', he "did not mean any inner light, placed in men by nature to teach them their duty and lead them constantly without error in the right path. The Law of Nature is not innate; what is knowable by the light of nature is the kind of truth at which a man may arrive, by himself and without extraneous help, through the right use of faculties with which he was endowed by nature. Since the light of nature, he now proceeds, is neither a tradition nor a practical principle inscribed by nature in our minds, there remains only reason and sensation to account for it. These two faculties alone instruct and teach a man, and perform what is appropriate to light: that is, they present to the mind things otherwise unknown and lying in drakness so that they can be known and, as it were, perceived."[33]

We may notice that this is a shrewd interpretation of the philosophy of Locke in telling us that, in effect, there is a 'combination of the interdependent faculties of sense-perception and reason."[34] Here is an explanation of the term Law of Na-

32. Gough, *op. cit.,* p.10.
33. *Ibid.,* p.14.
34. *Ibid.*

ture quite different from the traditional exposition coming since the times of the Stoics. Well says McDonald: "There is little doubt that by themselves, men can arrive at a kind of truth and can base legitimate claims–natural rights–upon it; but insofar as this represents the operation of a law of nature, such a law appears to be almost procedural in character, *i.e.,* without a universal content that specifically commands certain acts. This position is a departure from traditional forms of natural law, which assume a universal, *objective,* moral order discoverable by the right use of reason."[35]

Locke's further movement in this direction leads him to lay down his groundwork of empiricist epistemology. He undercuts the argument of 'innate ideas'–universal principles in the mind of man discoverable by *a priori* reasoning. He cites the actual cases of great man like Newton to reject the doctrine of innate ideas and thereby support his argument that ambition and hard labour are the effective means to 'produce such masters'. Thus he dwells, and dwells heavily, on the factor of self-perception and experience. As he says: "All ideas come from sensation or reflection. Let us then suppose the mind to be, as we say, white paper, void of all characters without any ideas: how comes it to be furnished ? Whence comes it by that vast store which the busy and boundless fancy of man has painted on it with an almost endless variety ? Whence has it all the materials of reason and knowledge. To this I answer, in one word, from experience."[36]

The way is now cleared for the psychological-egoistic hedonism of Locke. Self-interest is the sole governing factor of human behaviour and, as such, a man, making use of his faculties of sense–perception as well as experience, is allowed to seek pleasure and avoid pain. At the same time, Locke's hedonism takes a wise turn toward enlightened utilitarianism when he, further, says that man, as a creature having the faculty of reason, should seek pleasure and avoid pain in a way conducive to the general happiness of the people. It follows that in the rejection of the doctrine of innate ideas, both Hobbes and Locke can be called 'empiricists'; in the acceptance of man's right to seek pleasure and avoid pain in a way that is in consonance with the general happiness of public, both Locke and Bentham can be described as 'utilitarians'.

---

35. McDonald, *op. cit.,* p.128.
36. *Essay,* Book II, Ch.1, Sec.2.

True that Locke succeeded in establishing a superficial connection between the elements of faith, on the one side, and reason, perception and experience on the other, it remains to be pointed out that the elements of confusion and illogical reconciliation are very much present in his epistemological system. His argument for a distinction between the 'law of works' (Scriptures as revealed to the saints) which he calls the Law of Nature knowable by reason and the 'law of faith' (complete faith in God) cannot be validated by reason. It is rightly said: "But Locke was not really a thorough-going rationalist, any more than he was a thorough-going hedonist. Loooked at purely rationally, his argument may seem to form a closed circle, but he would not find it closed, because the existence of God was to him a certainty which could be proved by reason. If his proofs do not convince us, we may say that it was faith and not reason that really provided the escape from the circle; but granted the presuppositions of that faith, the whole hung together without inconsistency."[37]

LAW OF NATURE : SANCTION OF CONSTITUTIONAL GOVERNMENT

As in the case of Hobbes, so in the case of Locke we find that law of nature looks like the 'foundation of his political philosophy.'[38] However, there is a basic difference between the two insofar as the meaning and premises of the law of nature are concerned. According to Locke, it does not imply that a man should do what he likes in the state of nature for the sake of his preservation and submit himself meekly to the command of the sovereign after the installation of the commonwealth (as we saw in the case of Hobbes); rather it has its moral principles governing the form of a civilised social life whether in the pre-political stage or after the creation of political authority by means of a social compact. The actual contents of law of nature, as taken by Locke, may be pointed out in the following manner:

1. The law of nature implies a law of equality. It tells us that all men are equal. There are no privileges in the state of nature which is a state of perfect freedom for men 'to order their actions and dispose of their possessions and person as they think fit, within the bounds of the law of nature.' It wills the preservation of all mankind and teaches that all

---

37. Gough, *op. cit.,* p.17.
38. *Ibid.*, p. 1.

mankind being equal and independent, no one ought to harm another in his life, liberty and posessions. Locke, however, makes a special exception in the case of right to property and tells us that the principle of equality does not apply where a man earns more property by virtue of his hard labour.

2. The law of nature embodies the principle of self-interest. Locke goes so far as to declare that natural reason tells us that men being once born have a right to their preservation and consequently 'to meat and drink and such other things as nature affords for their subsistence.' This content of the law of nature stands as a backbone of his psychological-egoistic hedonism informing man to seek pleasure and avoid pain. However, Locke gives an altruistic orientation to this principle of law of nature by qualifying man's right to seek pleasure and avoid pain with an accompanying consideration for the general happiness of the society. This striking qualification enthuses one of his admirers to interpret that Locke's law of nature is more socialistic and less individualistic than is sometimes supposed.[39]

3. The law of nature sanctifies man's right to property. It ordains that anything which is removed by labour from the common state in which nature left it becomes private property. It is the law of reason that 'makes the deer the Indian's who hath killed it'. Herein we find Locke's labour theory of property having a sacrosanct character. None, even the state, can take away man's property without his consent, Locke warns. However, here again, we find a qualifying provision. According to Locke, if the law of nature sanctions right to property, it also enjoins that a man should keep as much property as he can make use of it properly. It follows that right to property has its bounds and while a man has right to earn and keep his property, he has no right to thrive on its spoils. Once again, Kendall gets a handle to say that Locke's theory of property is collectivist rather than individualist.[40]

4. The law of nature enjoins truth and the keeping of faith and the obligations of this law 'are great and so strong in the case of promises that omnipotency itself can be tied by them.

39. Willmore Kendall: *John Locke and the Doctrine of Majority Rule,* referred to *Ibid.*, p.19.
40. *Ibid.*, p.79.

'Grants, promises and oaths are bonds that hold the Almighty.' In order to corroborate this point with the help of some scriptural argument, Locke cites the case of Adam and Eve and their descendents who 'are under an obligation to preserve, nourish and educate their children' and the children in turn 'are bound to pay honour to their parents'. However, here again, we find a qualifying provision that Locke adds to this content of the law of nature. He is very specific in pointing out that there can be no obligation to keep promises or honour commitments in case of force or coercion. Even the posterity is not bound to honour the promises of its earlier generations as 'nobody can be under a law which is not promulgated to him'.

5. The law of nature is rational. It is pre-eminently a 'law of reason'. Reason, moreover, is the human faculty, which man shares with God, and which has been given to him by God 'to be the rule betwixt man and man'. The law of nature may thus be called the 'law of God'. It also becomes 'an ultimate moral law'. Viewed thus, the certainty of this law is not really a question of mathematical demonstrability, but a matter of faith."[41]

The implications of the law of nature with their qualifying provisions demonstrate the striking fact of Locke's being coherent and consistent, as far as possible, in the light of the conditions of his time; they also reveal his firm resolve to lay down a theory of constitutional government–a form of political order being the reverse of an arbitrary government as seen by his countrymen under the rule of the Stuart monarch. It informs Gough to say that Locke's whole political theory "is stated in general and abstract terms, but the concrete reality lying behind it is the constitutional practice of England of his day. The law of nature is, for him, an essentially the moral standard to which all men, including governors themselves, should conform, and his insistence on it is the foundation of his case for limited, constitutional government, in stead of the arbitrary power so dreaded and hated by the contemporary Englishmen."[42]

Though Locke may be admired for being coherent and consistent, as far as possible, in linking up the various contents of his law of nature culminating in its being identifiable with the

41. *Ibid.*, p.10.
42. *Ibid.*, pp.22-23.

law of God (as mainly contained in the scriptures) with his earthly issues of government by consent and rule of the majority, yet he may be criticised for creating 'confusion' and 'ineptness'. The question arises as to how obedience to 'the law of works' can necessarily be rewarded with political success? "How many successful political–or other–leaders can consistently 'turn the other cheek', 'walk the second mile', 'take no thought of their lives', 'judge not' etc.? In the end, he was left with fidelism rather than the 'reasonableness of Christianity."[43] A leading critic of Locke like Leo Strauss, therefore, calls his law of nature as 'partial law of nature' closer to Hobbes's ideal of self-preservation than to the New Testament's command of self-sacrifice and comes to the conclusion that the inconsistencies of Locke "are so obvious that they cannot have escaped the notice of a man of his rank and his sobriety."[44]

CREATION OF CIVIL SOCIETY : EXPRESS AND TACIT SOCIAL CONTRACTS

In common with other thinkers of his age, Locke seeks to explain the origin and nature of political authority within the framework of social contractualism. Hence, he starts with a hypothetical state of nature–a pre-political stage which "was a state of perfect freedom to order their actions, and dispose of their persons and possessions as they think fit, within the law of nature without asking leave or depending upon the will of any other man."[45] Obviously, it is not a state of perpetual warfare, as Hobbes tells us, rather it is a state of equality wherein all the power of jurisdiction "is reciprocal , no one having more than another."[46]

Locke points out that the state of nature is a state of liberty and not of license. Although in this pre-political stage man has full liberty to dispose of his possessions, yet he has no freedom to destroy himself or his neighbour. The law of nature prevails which obliges and teaches everyone that none has a right to harm another's person or goods. It sanctions that when all men are equal and independent and possess rights to life, liberty and property, none has the exceptional right to encroach upon the freedom of another. The observance of this law re-

43. McDonald, *op. cit.*, p.129.
44. *Ibid.*, For a proper study of this critic's observations see his *Natural Right and History,* Chicago, 1953, pp.330 ff.
45. Locke: *Second Treatise,* Ch.II.
46. *Ibid.*

quires that all men be restrained from invading the rights of others. The law of nature wills the peace and preservation of all mankind and puts into the hand of everyone a right to finish the transgressor to a degree as it might hinder its violation. However, in case of transgression, it sanctions that one man can come by power over another but only "to retribute to him so far as calm reason and conscience dictate, what is proportionate to his transgression, which is so much as may serve for reparation and restraint."[47]

If the state of nature is not a condition of violence and anarchy, it is also not a condition of Arcadian bliss. It is constantly upset by the corruption and viciousness of the degenerate man. "The state of nature had the ill-condition which was full of fear and continual dangers and suffered from three main shortcomings–the non-existence of an established and settled legal system, the absence of an appropriate authority to execute the laws, and the want of an impartial judge to give and endorse just decisions. Hence, in order to escape from this ill-condition and gain certainty and security, men make a contract to terminate the state of nature and enter into the civil society or commonwealth. Thus, the men living in the state of nature voluntarily compacted and agreed to join and unite into a community for their comfortable, safe and peaceable living, one amongst another, in a secure enjoyment of their properties and a greater security against any that are not of it."[48]

In Locke's view, this social contract terminates the era of statelessness and substitutes it by a civil society. Each individual agrees to give up some of the rights he possessed in the pre-political stage. This contract has two main features. Firstly, it is no more than a surrender of some rights and powers so that man's remaining rights remain protected and preserved. Secondly, the contract is concluded for a limited and specific purpose and what is given up is surrendered to the community as a whole and not to a man (or the assembly of

---

47. *Ibid.*
48. *Ibid.* Laski says: "But just as Locke's natural state implies a natural man utterly distinct from Hobbes's gloomy picture, so does Locke's social contract represent rather the triumph of reason than hard necessity. It is a contract of each with all, a surrender by the individual of his personal right to fulfil the commands of law of nature in return for the life guarantee that his rights as nature ordains them–and liberty and property–will be preserved." *Op. cit.*, p.31.

men) as Hobbes had suggested. In this way, Locke holds that people are the real sovereign and state exists for them, not *vice versa.*

Again, unlike Hobbes, Locke supposes the making of two contracts. The first is the *social contract* whereby civil society is established to meet the deficiencies of the state of nature. By it each individual agrees to give up not all of his natural rights but the only one of interpreting and executing the law of nature and redressing his own grievances. Besides, the right is given to the community as a whole and that too on the understanding that the natural rights will be guaranteed and preserved. The second is the *governmental contract.* When civil society (state) is established, another contract is made by community (in a corporate capacity) with a ruler (king) who takes upon himself the responsibilities of removing the 'ill condition' once existing in the state of nature. The second contract is subordinate to the first, because government has only a fiduciary power to act for certain ends and its acts are confined to securing them well. It also implies that if the government fails in this respect, people may dismiss it and substitute it by a new one.

The 'inconveniences' of the state of nature are thus dispensed with by means of a formal or express contract establishing the state and the tacit one setting up the 'government' of a king having limited authority. The basis of the contract, whether express or tacit, is the free consent of the people. As Harmon puts: "Men come to understand that improvement over the natural state may result from the organisation of a civil society and the creation of instruments that will correct the deficiencies indicated above. This systematising of man's affairs is accomplished by the making of a compact in which free and equal men consent to surrender their natural liberty to interpret, judge and enforce the law of nature and 'unite into a community for their comfortable, safe, and peaceable living. One amongst another, in a secure enjoyment to their properties, and a greater security against any that are not of it'. The compact is created by the unanimous consent of those who enter into it. No one is compelled to be a party to it; those who donot wish to form a community simply remain in the state of nature. Those who have entered into the compact, however, agree from this point to be governed by majority decision."[49]

49. Judd Harmon, *op. cit.,* p.242.

Thus, in Locke's view both the state and the government are a consequence of contract which is made by the people living in the state of nature. The peculiar things with Locke are: (1) that law of nature continues to exist even after the making of the contract and thus the rights of the people relating to life, liberty and possessions are not at all destroyed; (2) that the community as a whole becomes the sovereign being both the creator and the beneficiary of the trust; and (3) that government comes after the establishment of the state to accept a unilateral obligation of keeping the trust of the community.

Locke's theory of social contract is unsound from historical, legal, logical and philosophical points of view. It attaches the stigma of 'partnership' and thus reduces the state to a position of limited liability concern. Hence, like Hobbes, Locke has also been criticised for contributing to a 'dangerous', 'absurd, 'fictitious' and 'utterly false' theory of the origin and nature of state. It may be argued that this theory represents a philosophy of propertied and privileged class of which Locke himself was a member. His man living in the state of nature is a propertied gentleman who insists on his own rights and respects the rights of others and he thinks in terms of entering into some contract simply because of his selfish interest. His ultimate preference for constitutional monarchy clearly reveals his happiness over the victory of his class in the Glorious Revolution of 1688. In a word, the artificiality of the system of Locke is evidenced by his assertion that men are isolated individuals bound together just by the thread of a contract made for the sake of their self-interest, that is the adequate protection of their natural rights relating to life, liberty and property. It is all unrealistic and, as Aaron says, it fails to take into consideration the many ties, including race, geography and other things; which hold together the community.[50]

It may also be pointed out that Locke's theory of social contract is not compatible with his theory of natural rights. It is loaded with the interest of a particular class to which he belonged. If the law of nature gives three rights (relating to life, liberty and property) to all, how one (relating to property) as we shall see later, becomes the most important of all for whose protection men enter into the commonwealth. A critic may add that as Plato discards the two elements of courage and appetite and lays all stress on the element of reason in his political

50. See R.I. Aaron: *John Locke*, p.287.

philosophy that culminates in the idealisation of the rule of the philosopher-king, so Locke discards two natural rights relating to life and liberty and places utmost emphasis on the right to property that culminates in the institution of the civil society.[51] "Locke's confusions are the result of honest deduction from a postulate of equal natural rights which contained its own contradiction. The evidence suggests that he did not realise the contradiction in the postulate of equal natural right to unlimited property, but that he simply read into the realm of right (or the state of nature) a social relation which he accepted as normal in civilised society. The source of the contradictions in his theory is his attempt to state in universal (non-class) terms, rights and obligations which necessarily had a class content."[52]

SOVEREIGNTY : CASE OF ACTIVE VERSUS DORMANT MASTERS

Locke's conception of sovereignty is quite different from that of Bodin and Hobbes. To him sovereignty is not absolute and indivisible, rather it seems to be divided between the people on the one hand and the rulers on the other. As already seen, the original contract is an agreement among the people to put an end to the state of nature and substitute it by a civil society. The original contract requires the consent of every member of the society. As a result of the second contract, the rulers are vested with certain powers and if they fail to carry out their requirements, they may be replaced by others without, in any way, affecting the basic character of the society. In practice, this conception means that people have sovereign authority in reserve, while the actual power is exercised by the government and that when the government violates trust, it becomes necessary for the people to overthrow his regime. He says: "Wherever law ends, tyranny begins, if the law be transgressed to another's harm and whosoever in authority exceeds the power given him by law, and makes use of force has under his command that upon the subject which the law allows not, ceases in that to be a magistrate and acting without authority

51. On this point, C.B. Macpherson comments that the postulate of natural rights is turned into, though not displaced by, the postulate of unequal rights and capacities to justify the differentiation of property. *The Political Theory of Possessive Individualism*, pp.231-32.
52. C.B. Macpherson: "The Social Bearing of Locke's Political Theory" in *The Western Political Quarterly*, Vol. VII, 1954 reprinted in Isaac Kramnic (ed.): *Essays in the History of Political Thought*, p.198.

may be opposed, as any other man who by force invades the right of other."[53]

In other words, it implies that Locke makes his people a sleeping sovereign who let the government carry on sovereign authority within certain limits, provided it does not abuse its power, and the moment it does so, the sovereign people wake up from their slumber, overthrow their government and set up a new one in its place. Obviously, Locke's concern is not to exalt political authority but to describe its limitations. He maintains that the people form their government and so their rulers cannot be disobeyed. In case a ruler exercises his powers in a wrong way, he has no right to claim obedience, since he "is not the person the laws have appointed, and consequently, not the person the people have consented to."[54]

Naturally the characteristic of Locke's state is that it is limited, not absolute. It is limited, because it derives powers from the people and because it holds power in trust for the people. It is limited, moreover, by natural law. Civil law is merely the statement of natural law in detail by means of authorised legislation. The true state is a constitutional state in which men acknowledge the rule of law, for there can be no political liberty if man is subject to the inconstant, uncertain, unknown and arbitrary will of another. It should exist for the good of the people and depend upon their consent and should have a limited or constitutional authority, otherwise it loses its *raison d'etre* and can legitimately be overthrown.[55]

It implies that the sovereignty of Locke has two demensions–active and dormant. While the government of the king represents the former, the community of the people indicates the latter. The essential point of distinction between the two lies in the fact that while the king has 'personal' power to rule according to the Law of Nature, the community has the 'real' power to examine and judge the validity of its manager's performance. While studying this essential point of Locke's political theory in the light of the actual conditions of English history and politics, Gough says: "Sovereignty, or majesty (*majestas*) is absolute, arbitrary, *legibus soluta,* but he emphasises the distinction between the 'real' and 'personal' majesty. Real majesty lies in the whole community and is greater than the

53. *Second Treatise,* Ch.II.
54. *Ibid.*
55. See Wayper, *op. cit.,* p.77.

personal majesty which is fixed in certain persons who are 'trusted' with the exercise of it, and may, if they abuse it, forfeit it either to God or to the community. No personal sovereign is free from the obligation of the natural and positive law of God. In England real majesty is in the people, and personal majesty in king and parliament jointly, while the king also has 'a secondary personal majesty, sometimes, greater sometimes less', during the intervals between parliaments. Parliament can do many and great things, but there are some things that it cannot do. It is limited not only by the laws of God, but also by the fundamental laws of the constitution, which it can not alter."[56]

A study of Locke's theory of sovereignty shows that it has these ingredients:

1. The supreme power of the state rests with the community permanently. The community alone is competent to lay down the fundamental law of the land which the government cannot violate.[57]
2. The king as well as the Parliament are chosen by the people and they are like officers on probation to make use of the 'active' sovereignty in the interest of the people. The doors for the entry of an arbitrary rule are thus closed.
3. While the community delegates its power to the government, there can be no further delegation of authority. Thus, all the organs of government, whether executive, or legislature, or judiciary, are required to live and act within the sphere allotted to them by the real, though sleeping, sovereign, that is the community.
4. Locke makes a succinct distinction between legal and political sovereignty by telling us that while the King-in-Parliament is the legal sovereign (which the community is not), the people are the political sovereign who may change their government, but they have no title for framing the laws of the land.
5. The community has no right to censure the conduct of its chosen government exercising active sovereignty unless it is sure that the time has come for making 'an appeal to the

56. Gough, *op. cit.*, p.110.
57. According to J.N. Figgis, "In Locke's theory, sovereignty can exist nowhere except in the community as a whole. This is the original and supreme will which organises the government and defines its powers." *The Divine Right of Kings*, p.242.

heaven'. As Gough says: "The power of the people in his system is exercised at the foundation of the state, but after that it remains dormant unless a revolution become necessary, for the established government is sacrosanct so long as it fulfils its trust."[58]

Locke's theory of sovereignty is erroneous as well as pernicious. The very denial of the absolute and unlimited character of the sovereignty is tentamount to its own negation. Calhoun was right in saying that sovereignty is a whole thing and to divide it means to destroy it.[59] Not only this, Locke's conception bears very dangerous potentialities inasmuch as it opens the doors of rebellion and revolution at every turn of occasion.The sleeping sovereign or the people may break sleep and overthrow their government whenever they are dissatisfied with it. In the last resort, it is just a licence for revolt or rebellion under any form of government. Always there is a residual power in society to overthrow a particular regime and when Locke binds the right to revolution with the decision of the whole community, the position is made much more confused. In such a case, either it will be quite difficult, nay impossible, to determine when it is the act of the whole community, or the residual power in society will go unchecked and declare its act to be valid in the name of its being an act of the whole community. Finally, it has been pointed out that Locke cares little for the fact of legal sovereignty and dwells heavily on the side of political sovereignty. He hardly seems satisfied even with a full-fledged modern representative system of government.[60]

A point of criticism directed against the political philosophy of Locke in this direction is that he "has no far-reaching theory of sovereignty" as suggested by the fact that the term itself "is not used in his systematic work. As the con-

58. *Ibid.*, p.115. J.H. Franklin says that Locke "insists on the right of the people, acting for just cause, not only to replace its governors but to change the form of government itself. By the people, furthermore, he does not mean that Parliament, or even the House of Commons within Parliament, but the general political community considered as a separate legal community." *John Locke and the Theory of Sovereignty,* p.1.
59. See Garner: *Political Science and Government,* p.177.
60. Gilchrist thus remarks that while Hobbes "gives a theory of legal sovereignty without recognising the existence and power of political sovereignty, Locke recognises the force of political sovereignty, but does not give adequate recognition to legal sovereignty." *Principles of Political Science,* p.61.

ventional and indeed strictly official designation of the authority that attaches specifically to a monarch, its implications are, of course, such as the philosopher is careful to avoid."[61] It is by means of drawing implications of what Locke says in regard to the effective exercise of the 'supreme power' that his views on the nature of active and dormant sovereignty are understandable. However, this point should not be carried too far in view of the fact that though Locke deliberately avoids the word 'sovereign' and sanctions the ultimate power of the people behind the 'trusted' and entrusted power of the government, it is not difficult to infer that he knows the real nature of sovereignty and he also knows as to where it should be resided in a system of political theory going to uphold the cause of a constitutional government. Thus, Gough makes a sensible point by adding: "Locke avoided the word sovereign, possibly because of its association with the arbitrary power of Leviathan, but he understood quite well what it meant. His use of the term 'supreme power' may seem confused at first sight, for he applies it to the legislature, and to the 'single person', and may be interpreted thus. The legislature, in the first place, is the legal sovereign. The king is not technically sovereign at all but as a title he is commonly called the sovereign. The people, to whom the legislature is responsible, is political 'sovereign', but this sovereignty he regards as normally in abeyance, and it only takes effect, when the government has been dissolved."[62]

TRUST GOVERNMENT : CASE FOR CONSTITUTIONAL MONARCHY

Locke's political theory favours constitutional or limited monarchy. The government is quite different from state, because it is a consequence of the second contract and its formation or dissolution does not at all affect the life of the state in

61. Dunning: *A History of Political Theories*, Vol. II, pp.359-60.
62. Gough, *op. cit.*, pp.114-15. Lamprecht comments that the most significant thing about Locke's *Civil Government* "is really not what it says but what it avoids saying. Locke's most notable trait is that he could compose an entire treatise on government without so much as mentioning the word of introducing the idea of sovereignty." *Moral and Political Philosophy of John Locke*, p.148. However, while comparing Locke with Rousseau in a way, J.A. Smith holds that Locke "did, to be sure, reject any government which does not rest on the consent of the governed; but he nowhere expounded a doctrine of popular sovereignty." *The Growth and Decadence of Constitutional Government*, p.14.

the like manner. The government is also different from the society or community, because while the latter is really sovereign, the former has a mere fiduciary character. Besides, Locke also differentiates between the *de jure* and *de facto* governments. A *de jure* government is one that comes into being according to the established laws of the state and so its commands should be obeyed. But a *de facto* government is one which is an usurper of authority, or which is not based on the consent of the people, or which has violated the trust of the community and so it should be overthrown.[63]

In the view of Locke, government is not only different from society and state, it holds limited authority. It is made to accomplish certain ends. Locke vests supreme power in the hands of the people to remove or alter the government whenever they find it to have forfeited their trust. It should be noted that Locke assumes the making of a tacit contract by which the government is established and in order to clarify his point yet more he uses the term 'trust' to indicate the real relationship between the people and the government. His ultimate purpose is to justify the sovereign status of the people and so the term 'contract' is not appropriate inasmuch as it implies the standing of two parties at a pedestal of equality. Vaughan thus rightly suggests that by adopting the analogy of a trust rather than that of contract, Locke "makes very fair provision not only for popular control of government, but also–what is yet more improtant–for a progressive extension of that control, as experience may dictate."[64]

It is obvious that in the political system of Locke the position of government is like that of a manager chosen by and accountable to the members of a joint stock company. The servant (government) cannot be treated as equal to that of the master (community) as his fundamental concern is to maintain the 'trust' of his master. As Harmon says: "A contract between the two parties implies their equality and stipulates various rights and obligations pertaining to each. Hobbes rejects the use of contract between people and government, because he

---

63. In this regard, Locke has precursed the utilitarian philosophy by arguing that the government is concerned with the happiness and well-being of the people. According to Dunning, "The happiness and the security of the individual figure not as essential to the perpetuity of a government, but as the end for which alone government is ever called into existence." *Op. cit.*, pp.364-65.
64. Vaughan: *Studies in the History of Political Philosophy*, Vol. I, p.147.

does not wish to imply that people are the equal of government or that government has duties toward people. Locke's reasoning is the reverse of this. Government is not the equal of the people. It must be an agent of the people not a partner....The relationship between the government and the governed is analogous to that which exists between the parties in a legal trust. The government is the trustee who functions for and is responsible to the people who create the trust. Thus, the trustee or government has no rights equal to those held by the people, but only obligations to those for whom it act as an agent."[65]

If the government has constitutional authority, its functions are also limited. According to Locke, its functions are confined to the protection and preservation of the life, liberty and property of the people. In this direction, it has to do three important things. First, it has to establish and make known to all persons the implications of the law of nature and this service is to be rendered by the legislative organ. Second, it has to provide an impartial authority to settle all disputes arising among persons in accordance with the established laws and this business is to be performed by the judicial branch of government. Third, it has to safeguard the interest of its people against aliens and this work is to be done by the executive department.

Another important aspect of Locke's theory of government is that here he throws a faint light on the separation of powers and thus becomes a precursor of Montesquieu. He justifies the separation of legislature from the executive, because he fears that it "may be too great a temptation to human frailty, apt to grasp all power, for the same persons who have the power of making laws to have also in their hands the power to execute them."[66] Hence, he differentiates between the three organs of the government and calls them legislative, judicial and federative (executive) departments. The legislative power is placed in the hands of an assembly that meets periodically, but since the enforcement and administration of law is a continuous task, a power distinct from the legislature must live in ceaseless operation and this Locke decides in favour of the executive.

Although, Locke believes in the tripartite division of governmental organs, he justifies the supremacy of the legislature, for it is the representative of the majority and the ultimate protector of those natural rights for whose security the original

65. Judd Harmon, *op. cit.*, pp.250-51.
66. *Second Treatise*, C. 12.

contract is made. But he also argues that the legislature has to exercise its power only for those needs for which civil society is constituted and for which the government has been established. The powers of the legislature are limited by the law of nature. Moreover, the legislature has no right to delegate its authority to an alien body, for the other organs have a still more limited sphere of authority. In this direction, Locke lays down that while the legislature "is not only the supreme power of the commonwealth but sacred and unalterable in the hands where the community has once placed it,"[67] yet its authority is limited in four ways: First, it "is not, nor can possibly be, absolutely arbitrary over the lives and fortunes of the people."[68] Second, it "cannot assume to itself a power to rule by extemporary arbitrary decrees; but is bound to dispense, and decide the rights of the subject, by promulgating standing laws, and known authorised judges."[69] Third, "the supreme power cannot take from man any part of his property without his own consent."[70] Fourth, the legislature "cannot transfer the power of making laws to any other hands."[71]

Finally, Locke, in a traditional manner, believes in a three-fold classification of governments. In this case, the nature and composition of legislative authority forms the criteria on which one form of government is differentiated from another. Firstly, it is monarchy when the legislative authority is placed in the hands of one man. Secondly, when the community by a majority vote vests this authority in the hands of few selected persons and their successors, it becomes an oligarchy. Finally, when the community retains the legislative power in its own hands and merely appoints magistrates or administrators for the execution of its own laws, it is democracy. However, Locke recognises the excellence of constitutional government in which a powerful legislature lives and works under a sovereign people and the head of the state is merely a nominal king.

It may, however, be pointed out that in the view of Locke, forms of government are of different kinds, but the fundamental principles of all are the same. The legislative power is

67. *Ibid.*, Ch.11.
68. *Ibid.*
69. *Ibid.*
70. *Ibid.*
71. *Ibid.*

supreme, and all members of the state owe obedience to it, but its authority is not arbitrary. He lays down four organic maxims of government:[72]

1. It must be exercised, as it was given, for the good of the subjects.
2. It must dispense with justice by standing laws and authorised judges, for under irregular arbitrary power, the subjects would be worse off than in the state of nature.
3. No man can be deprived of any part of his property without his own consent, given either in person or through his representatives, or they must not raise taxes on property without people's consent given by themselves or by their deputies.
4. The legislature cannot transfer its powers to any other person or body.

Locke's theory of government has been criticised for various reasons. It is said that a government of this type will be no government at all as regards its stability and efficiency. It will merely be a plaything in the hands of some 'mischievous' leaders of the people. Its life will depend on the brink of revolution. Vaughan rightly fears that Locke "formulated not a theory of government but a theory of rebellion."[73] It is good to limit the power of the government, but it is never wise to reduce it to the status of a fiduciary organisation. No government, even a democracy (constitutional government as envisaged by Locke), can ever be in a safe position to discharge its trust in a way that happens to secure general satisfaction. Obviously, Locke has under-rated the importance of political organisation. Sabine aptly observes: "On the whole, Locke regarded the setting up of a government as a much less important even than the original compact that makes a civil society. Once a majority has agreed to form a government, the whole power of the community is naturally in them."[74]

It is also pointed out that the doctrine of separation of powers, as faintly hinted by Locke, is neither a deliberate nor a clear-cut part of his political theory. It has two flaws. First, Locke speaks of the legislative department entrusted with

---

72. Sir Fredrick Pollock: *An Introduction to the History of the Science of Politics*, pp.74-75.
73. Vaughan, *op. cit.*,
74. Sabine, *op. cit.*, p.534.

'sovereign' powers and the executive as the continuous organ of the government. The place of the judicial department is like an adjunct of the executive. Not only that, the separation of the legislative from the executive departments is a matter of 'convenience' and not a 'dogma' emphasised by Locke as 'a vitally important part' of his political philosophy.[75] It is rightly commented that the upshot of Locke's treatment of different organs of government is that his system "contains only two really separate powers the legislative and the combined executive-federative-judicial."[76] Second, any idea of the separation of powers is alien to the very nature of the English political system. Thus, a German writer Carl Ernst Jarcke detected in Locke 'the originator of the doctrine of the saparation and balance of powers', and, regarding this as an absurd and impossible account of the English constitution, branded him as the 'creator of the false theory of the English state.'[77]

CONSENT : LEGITIMATE BASIS OF POLITICAL OBLIGATION

Locke places his main reliance on the element of consent. As nature has made all men free and equal, Locke warns that no one can be deprived of his rights or be made subject to a power without his consent. Men terminate the state of nature and found civil society and thereby convert themselves into citizens, but the element of consent plays its full part behind this all. Locke says: "Men being ...by nature all free, equal and independent, no one can be put out of his estate, and subject to the political power of another, without his own consent."[78]

In the view of Locke, the element of consent has three dimensions. Firstly, consent may be 'express' or 'tacit'. It may either be given expressly as happens in the case of political compact; it may be implied as happens in the case of governmental contract. It follows that both conscious premediation and unconscious acquiescence constitute the element of consent. Secondly, consent of one generation is not binding on the posterity. Hence, a particular thing consented by a man is not binding upon his son or successor and it requires to be renewed by the next generation. In other words, no one can be compelled to accept a particular thing consented by his

75. See Barker's 'Introduction' to *Social Contract,* pp.xxvii-xxxiii.
76. Gough, *op. cit.,* p.97.
77. *Ibid.,* p.94.
78. *Second Treatise,* Ch.11.

predecessors. Finally, consent justifies majority rule. Locke is not in favour of total unanimity or consent of every citizen before anything is actually done by the government. Complete unanimity is desired at the time of social compact. But after the formation of civil society, the implications of consent are changed. That is, a new principle comes into force revealing a form of individual consent to majority rule. Locke says: "It being one body must move one way, it is necessary the body should move that way whither the greater force carries it, which is the consent of the majority."[79]

So strong is the faith of Locke in this regard that he holds no apprehension of majority tyranny. Yet he prescribes four limitations to prevent majority tyranny–first, the government cannot lay arbitrary restrictions over the life, liberty and property of the people; second, it cannot issue arbitrary decrees harming the standards of law and justice; third, the legislature cannot delegate its power to any other body; finally, it "is not, nor can possibly be, absolutely arbitrary over the lives and fortunes of the people."[80]

Locke's theory of consent, as discussed above, suffers from certain weaknesses. For instance, there exists a sort of self-contradiction in his own thesis when we find that the fundamental principle is changed and thus the element of individual consent is substituted by the principle of majority-rule. The result is that the significance of individual consent on which Locke places his main reliance is vitiated and a minority is forced to live under the dictates of the majority even against its own consent. Moreover, Locke's acceptance of majority rule opens the gates for majority tyranny. It is surprising that the champion of individual liberty has no horror of the mob mind or of the tyranny of the crowd drugged by the poison of its ambitions. Coherence and consistency require that Locke should have prevented that form of majority rule that is amenable to majority tyranny. The sacredness of individual liberty, as defended by Locke, requires that even minority should not be coerced by the majority holding contrary views. Hence, far more consistent is the thesis of John Stuart Mill who said that mankind "are greater gainers by suffering each other to live as seems good to themselves, than by compelling each to live as seems good to the rest."[81]

79. *Ibid.*
80. *Ibid.*
81. Cited in Joad: *Modern Political Theory,* p.28

In simple terms, Locke's theory of political obligation begins with the premise that man should obey a government to whose authority he has given his 'personal' consent. If this affirmation is examined in detail, one may ask a relevant question whether it is not a serious distortion both of his (Locke's) aims and achievements. One may understand Locke's point that consent, once given, is not revocable unless the government is dissolved and it is renewed at the time of another contract, he may yet question as to how the passive life of an individual can be identified with his meek submission to the dictates of a government run by a legislature having manufactured majority, or with the demands of a resurgent mob crying for a change in the government in the name of 'breach of trust' just for the sake of its specific interests. It, therefore, appears that in the actual operation of government the element of consent "is relegated to a back seat, and even that it only retains in a shape so modified and reduced as to destroy its original significance."[82]

A critic of Locke is further struck with the great inconsistency of this 'Whig thinker and theoriser' when he finds that whereas the doctrine of consent in its extreme form implies that a man is bound only to what he consents to, yet he can be coerced possibly against his own conscience. Should a man be taught, as Kendall in defence of Locke asserts, that a decision on which all have been consulted and which is supported by a large number is preferable to, and more binding than one; on which nobody has been consulted and which is endorsed or supported only by a few? Then, Locke's affirmation of a tacit consent inferrable from the very fact of a man's residence in a state hardly leaves any defence against the tyrannical rule of the mob. Locke is, therefore, discredited by his critics as 'a loose thinker' who dub his affirmation of the indirect dimensions of the consent (like 'tacit' consent) as a bundle of 'dubious subterfuges' and 'inconsistencies' that may be likened 'with so many nails in the coffin of individualism'. With it they "would gladly bury natural rights, the social contract, and the whole liberal apparatus, leaving the way clear for the idealist doctrine of the absorption of the individual in the social whole under the majestic authority of the state."[83]

82. Gough, *op. cit.*, p.59.
83. *Ibid.*, p.56.

The fact remains that though the term consent literally means voluntary agreement with or acquiescence in what someone desires, in the political system of Locke it has its own implications. It may be 'express' as well as 'tacit', 'individual' as well as 'collective', 'binding' as well as 'revocable', 'a synonym for majority-rule' as well as a bulwark against 'majority-tyranny.' It may also have both moderate and extreme forms. One may rightly find that Locke is highly inconsistent in his treatment of the subject of consent in taking it as the basis of political obligation in his system. However, it should be borne in mind that the element of consent that figures so prominently in the system of Locke beginning from the formal inauguration of the state till the dissolution of the government is nothing else than a yardstick to determine the sanctity of a constitutional government. What he was chiefly concerned with to do "was to refute the claim of absolute monarch to arbitrary power."[84]

NATURAL RIGHTS : KEYNOTE OF LIBERALISM

Locke's liberal theory of individualism is based on his conception of natural rights. Dunning says that the most distinctive contribution of Locke to political theory "is his doctrine of natural rights."[85] His citizen has three rights relating to life, liberty and property; they are natural because they existed even in the pre-political stage. Their possession is enjoyed by the individual both in and out of the government. The individuals have these rights even before the making of the compact and they do not surrender or abandon them even after the formal inauguaration of political authority. Obviously, in contrast to Hobbes and Rousseau, Locke does not write into the social contract that individuals must give up their rights to their sovereign at the time of entering into the community. In his view, the individual fully remains the master of his natural rights as in the state of nature, so by the nature of state.[86]

In this direction, following implications may be drawn from Locke's affirmations:

1. Rights can be ascribed only to the individuals and not to their government and when Locke speaks of the rights of

84. *Ibid.,* p.55.
85. Dunning, *op. cit.,* p.364.
86. Recognising this essential point of Locke's political theory, Prof. Vaughan comments: "Everything in Locke's system is round the individual, everything is disposed so as to ensure the sovereignty of the individual." *Op. cit.*

government or any other body, he simply means by it 'power' to perform a particular function. Indeed, it is the rights of the individuals which bind and limit the power of the government and if there occurs a conflict between the individuals and their rulers, the former are the judges to give a final verdict. If the action of the government is tyrannical, the individuals may either submit to tyranny, or they may overthrow the government and replace it by a new one.

2. When rights are the possession of the individuals, they are held by all without any exception. There is complete equality in this respect. However, right is different from a privilege, because the latter may be granted to a few people due to some superior quality or virtue. There can be no discrimination otherwise on the basis of economic status, sex, qualifications etc. Locke warns that if this basic equality is destroyed, there would be no reason in human relations and no law of nature. It is to preserve this natural and legal equality that each individual must recognise and respect the equality of others and must concede to every man that which he claims for himself.

3. These rights are innate things conferred upon man by God and nature. Individuals continue to have them under any circumstance whatever. They existed in the state of nature, and they exist in the civil society without any reduction or restraint. They specifically call upon the government to refrain from intruding its power into an area where individual claims his personal freedom of action. These rights cannot be surrendered to any alien authority (state or government) and if ever an agreement to this effect is made under duress or through some miscalculation, the very agreement becomes void. The rights are thus an integral part of human personality and if the government ever seeks to encroach upon them, it will entitle the people to rise in open revolt for the sake of the preservation and safety of their natural rights.

4. Locke asserts that the state should use its enforcement action to secure natural rights by giving them an official (legal) protection. By the contract each individual 'has given a right to the commonwealth to employ his force for the execution of the judgments of the commonwealth whenever he

shall be called to it."[87] After the individuals terminate the state of nature, they look to the state to legislate both morally and effectively. It, however, does not mean that in return of official protection there is a surrender of these rights. In a true sense, Locke strives to emphasise that government provides the instrument of protection and meets the deficiency which is not available in the state of nature.

In brief, Locke's theory of natural rights justifies that individual's rights to life, liberty and property are innate and so immutable, inalienable and permanent. The rights form an integral part of his personality and render to the government the character of a manager working with the trust of the people. According to Locke, "Though men when they enter into society, give up the equality, liberty and executive power, they had in the state of nature into the hands of society, to be so far disposed of by the legislative as the good of the society shall require; yet it being only with an intention in every one the better to preserve himself, his liberty and property (for no rational creature can be supposed to change his condition with an intention to be worse), the power of the society, or the legislative constituted by them, can never be supposed to extend further than the common good, but is obliged to secure everyone's property by providing against those...defects...that made the state of nature so unsafe and uneasy."[88]

Locke's theory of natural rights may be criticised on the following grounds:

1. The theory is full of inconsistencies and contradictions. It requires that each individual should have reason to understand the implications of his rights and use them in a temperate and socially benevolent way. If so, it is quite possible that the criteria of Locke would lead to several conflicting interpretations and, in the absence of any superior authority to give a final decision, be liable to upset the established structure of the society. Hacker rightly observes that to endow man with these natural rights "is to open the door to conflict, self-interest and ideology."[89]
2. Locke's theory of natural rights takes a wrong view of social structure. Society is not a sand-heap of individuals but an

87. *Second Treatise*, Ch. 7.
88. *Ibid.*, Ch.9.
89. Hacker, *op. cit.*, pp.271-72.

organic compound in which individual's rights cannot be studied in isolation. Rights have a social content and their legtitimacy should thus be examined from the point of social expediency or interest. They are not based upon personal whims and caprices, rather their existence depends upon the factor of social utility. Obviously, social recognition can be secured only by that individual claim which realises the fact of common consciousness or social welfare. Green's interpretation is thus more judicious and admirable when he says: "It is only a man's consciousness of having an object in common with others, a well-being which is consciously his in being theirs and theirs in being his only the fact that they are recognised by him and he by them as having this object that gives him the claim described. But a claim founded on such a common consciousness is already a claim conceded: already a claim to which reality is given by social recognition and thus implicitly a right."[90]

3. Locke places government in a very awkward position. When the individual is the master and the interpreter of his natural rights and when the government is required to protect them, it is very risky on the part of the administrators to run their office according to the full satisfaction of the people. Obviously, a ruler who fails to attach legal recognition to the natural rights of men, and that too, to the entire satisfaction of his people stands in every chance of being overthrown.

4. Both from the utilitarian and idealistic points of view, it has rightly been said that natural rights are nonsense. Nothing is natural or innate which belongs to a hypothetical state of nature. Rights are the creation of society and state and thus to speak of rights existing in a pre-political stage is absurd. It is from this point of view that thinkers like Hume, Bentham, Kant and Green dismissed the notion of natural rights by calling them 'as nonsense' and 'rhetorical absurdity'.

PROPERTY : PROFILE OF AN ECONOMIC LEVIATHAN

Locke very strongly defends the institution of private property. Plato kept his Guardians aloof from the possession of private property, because it could obscure their reasoning power; Aristotle approved of it but feared that over-wealth

90. R.L. Nettleship (ed.): *Works of Green,* Vol. II, p.450.

could become a cause of threat to political stability. In the Middle Ages, St. Thomas Aquinas refused to assert that private property was sanctioned by the law of nature and claimed that it was an addition enacted by human legislators. Hobbes allowed the people to keep their property but recognised that sovereign had every right to restrict the manner of its use and employment. Different from these standpoints, Locke appears as a powerful defender of the institution of private property. He says: "The great and chief end of men's uniting into commonwealth and putting themselves under government is the preservation of their property."[91]

Locke's defence of private property is based on the following arguments:

1. First, God "has put men on this earth and given them reason"[92] so that they may make use of earthly resources to the best advantage of their life and convenience. The earth and all that is therein "is given to men for the support and comfort of their being."[93] But the best way to accomplish this is to allow individuals to hold possession of the land and materials so that they will have the means and the incentive to turn earth into usable commodities. Locke believes that private ownership is the most appropriate means for turning God-given resources into human benefits. In other words, Locke fears that if this task is left to collective ownership and operation, the resources held in common would be neglected and their potentialities would remain undeveloped.
2. Locke propounds his labour theory of right to property. He asserts that man has a natural right to that with which he has mixed the labour of his body. The right to private property arises, because by labour man extends his own personality into the objects produced. He says: "The labour of his body and the work of his hands we may say are properly his. Whosoever, then he removes out of the state that nature hath provided and left it in, he hath mixed his labour with, and joined it something that is his own, and thereby makes it his property."[94] It simply means that man's enclosing and cultivating a piece of land forms part of his private property.

91. *Second Treatise,* Ch.5.
92. *Ibid.*
93. *Ibid.*
94. *Ibid.*

As much land a man "tills, plants, improves, cultivates and can use the product of, so much is his property,"[95] for by mixing his labour with inert materials he gives them a higher value and a greater usefulness. But the labour need not be physical, it can also be mental concerned with the work of planning and management.

3. Locke justifies private property on the ground of greater productivity. In his view, greater production raises the standard of living of the people and so it is essential that the property-holder must be industrious. When every product is the result of pain, sweat and toil, the owner of the property must intensify his labour to increase yet more its value and usefulness. In his own words: "For it is not barely the polughman's pains, the reaper's and thresher's toil, and the baker's sweet, is to be counted into the bread we eat; the labour of those who broke the oxen, who dug and wrought the iron and stones, who felled and framed the timber employed about the plough, mill oven, or any other utensils, which are a vast number, requisite to this corn, from its sowing to its being made bread, must all be charged on the account of labour and received as an effect of that. Nature and the earth furnished only the almost worthless materials as in themselves."[96]

4. In Locke's view property is based on consent. Division of labour and property was agreed upon when the people lived together and enlarged the use of their resources. It happened before the making of the contract and so when social contract was made, each individual came with his natural right. 'Property is thus without any express compact of the commoners.' Obviously, it emphasises that right to property is prior to the institution of civil government and the right is not at all lost when the government is dissolved or abolished. When the contract is made, and state and government are formed, legal recognition is given not only to private property but also to the pattern of property distribution which existed in the state of nature.

5. Locke's theory contemplates the case of an economic man–a man who will not waste his time and energy in unproductive activities. Expectation of the financial reward is the motivating factor working in the background, because man

95. *Ibid.*
96. *Ibid.*

will not like to undertake a toilsome job where he "had no hopes to commerce with other parts of the world, to draw money to him by the sale of the produce."[97] Property is bound to grow and develop in such a society where men have a material incentive for their pains and where the accumulation of money inculcates their desire to gain more wealth.

6. Locke rejects the notion of acquiring property by means of physical force or conquest of the strong over the weak. He argues: "I may kill a thief that sets on me in the highway, yet I may not take away his money; this would be robbery on my side." He makes it very plain that the most that can be exacted from the land of the conquered is reparation for the damages received and the charges of the war, and that too with reservation of the right of the innocent wife and children. "Consent being the only legitimate basis of government, no right of government can be founded on mere success in unjust and aggressive war; and even in a lawful war the conqueror by virtue of his conquest acquires no rights over his own supporters."[98]

7. Locke urges that the possession of private property should be co-extensive with the capacity of making an use of it. The reward of property-owner is not to be more than what he and his family can actually use. They may live well but they should not make so much that there is cash left over for leading a life of spoilt man. In his own words: "He that gathered a hundered bushels of acorns or apples had thereby a property in them, they were his goods as soon as he gathered. He was only to look that he used them before they spoiled, else he took more than his share and robbed others. And indeed it was a foolish thing as dishonest to hoard up more than he could make use of. If he gave away a part to anybody else, so that it perished not uselessly in his possession, these he also made use of."[99]

In fine, Locke's justification of private property is based on two main planks–divine approval and popular consent. Besides, when Locke combines man's right to property with the reward of his labour, he advances an utilitarian justification. Without property man is insignificant, because the size of

97. *Ibid.*
98. Gough, *op. cit.,* p.86.
99. *Second Treatise,* Ch.5.

private property differentiates between the excellence of men living in the society. The institution of private property impels for the measures of security and holds materials for the advancement of personality. It also gives to its owner a link with the posterity. With it go the laws of inheritance which allow a man to pass on to his children that which he earned and owned in his life time. As it remarks an extension of his personality, it gives him further security by bestowing the knowledge that even the hands of time need not call a halt to the labours he has undertaken.

Locke's justification of private property is not only vague, ambiguous and full of important gaps at various stages, it constitutes an idealisation of the capitalist economy. In other words, it is naked defence of capitalism and, even from a capitalistic point of view, the theory is defective in several respects. He forgets that the interplay of demand and supply amply govern the scope of production and consumption. Moreover, if the owners are only allowed to keep as much in the way of profits as they can use, they will have no surplus cash for capital goods and so there will be no place for the role of investment funds in the productive process. His argument that 'no more property than use' prohibits 'unearned profits' which go to the investors and since modern capitalistic organisation is largely and mainly based on such an investment pattern, it is not difficult to find a place where Locke's thesis is incoherent even with the principles of modern capitalism. According to Hacker, "In Locke, therefore, we see the emergence of the politics of a capitalist society, the state must be strong enough to provide legal underpinnings for private investment and yet not so strong as to interfere with the free decisions of men who wish to risk their money to make a profit for themselves."[100]

Locke's theory of property cuts across his entire thought of social contract. His state or civil society is, in fact, a joint stock company whose shareholders are the men of property. It is evident from the fact that protection of property is the sole end for which they enter into the social compact. If so, how social contract can be an adequate basis of political obligation for those who have no property. C.B. Macpherson points out that while the labouring class is a necessary part of the nation, its members are not, in fact, full members of the *body politic* and have no claim to be so, and that the members of the labour-

100. Hacker, *op. cit.*, p.269.

ing class do not and cannot live a fully rational life. Thus, the working class is in effect in but not of civil society.[101] Again, "Locke's constitutionalism is essentially a defence of the supremacy of property not that of the yeomen only, but more especially that of the men of substance to whom the security of unlimited accumulation was of first importance."[102]

We may hardly admire the ingenuity with which Locke manages to justify an unequal distribution of the world's goods despite his original premise of perfect human equality. The whole case in the end turns out to be far more complicated than he seems to have realised. MacIver calls the whole theory as 'profoundly unrealistic.' He says thus: "A particular government may do little more than uphold an already established system of rights but in the longer perspective it is government that creates property. John Locke went so far as to claim that men set up the state for the preservation of their property, though he sometimes included life and liberty under the rubric of property. So obsessed was he with the motion that he made it a primary maxim of government that it cannot 'take from any man any part of his property without his own consent'–a maxim that, if taken literally, would simply make all government impotent to do anything. It would furthermore make property the eternal master of government...The other idea was that a man made a thing his own–provided it was not yet appropriated by putting his labour into it. But this qualification left the doctrine of property as utterly unrealistic, as remote from the facts of social life, as it was before. It removed none of the hopeless defects of the doctrine. It completely neglected the relation of property to inheritances...The socialist principles of the right to the whole produce of labour is as fallacious as the dogma of the capitalist who claims that a man has the right to do what he pleased with his own."[103]

Commenting on the weak points of Locke's theory of property, Gough thus says: "Locke may more fairly be blamed for the damage he caused to his own reputation by the loose way in which he used the word property. He repeatedly declared

101. Macpherson, *op. cit.*, p. 186.
102. *Ibid.*, p.200. H.J. Laski in support of the same points out that the state of Locke "is not so much as a contract between a group of businessmen who form a limited liability company whose memorandum of association forbids for the directors all those practices of which the Stuarts had, until his time, been guilty." *The Rise of European Liberalism*, p.127.
103. See R.M. MacIver: *The Web of Government*, pp.126-30.

that men entered civil society in order to protect their property, and defined political power...as 'a right of making laws for the regulation and preservation of property.' But he included in the general name 'property' everyman's 'life, liberty and estate,' that is, the whole of natural rights as a human being, and not simply his lands and goods....Locke's error is in failing to differentiate between the right of an individual to his property and the claim of a government to found political power on conquest...His theory of property, like his theory of government, is vitiated by being stated in terms of an antecedent, quasi-historical state of nature, in which men actually enjoyed and exercised their natural rights. It is the quasi-historicity of the state of nature which leads him to base property on appropriation, and to equate this with the exercise of a right."[104]

RIGHT TO REVOLUTION : MAKING AN APPEAL TO THE HEAVEN

In the political theory of Locke, as discussed in the preceding pages, the right to revolution finds a subterraneous manifestation. By strongly advocating the proposition that sovereignty is vested in the community, Locke insists that political authority is a 'trust' which must be directed to the ends for which men abandon the state of nature and establish civil society. It, therefore, follows that if the government belies its trust or overacts its powers, the people have a legitimate right to resist its authority. They have every right to examine and determine if the government is justifying itself or not. Hence, if they find otherwise, they can remove an inefficient or oppressive government and establish a new one in its place. Locke says: "And thus the community perpetually retains a supreme power of saving themselves from the attempts and design of anybody, even if their legislators whenever they shall be so foolish or so wicked as to lay and carry on designs against the liberties and properties of the subjects."[105]

However, the right to resistance is to be exercised by the community or its majority only in the case of specific breach of trust. It has two implications. Firstly, the right should be exercised when the community as a whole or its majority is satisfied with its inevitable need. The revolution should not be an act of the caprice of minority, for the contract is the action of the major

104. See Gough, *op. cit.*, pp.85-88-89.
105. *Second Treatise*, Ch.13.

portion of the people whose consent should likewise call for the dissolution of the covenant. In the second place, there should be a concrete case to justify an invasion by the rulers over the legitimate rights of the people. Locke urges that if the majority of the people 'are persuaded in their consciences that their laws, and with them, their estates, liberties, and lives are in danger," they will have every right to change the government for the sake of their "safety and good."[106] Laski enumerates these contingencies in which revolution will be justified in the Lockean sense. He says: "The substitution of arbitrary will for law, the corruption of Parliament by packing it with the prince's instruments, betrayal to a foreign prince, prevention of the due assemblage of Parliament–all these are a perversion of the trust imposed and operate to effect the dissolution of the contract. The state of nature again supervenes and a new contract may be made with one more fitted to observe it."[107]

As regards the nature and effects of the revolution, Locke says that the dissolution of the government will mean erection of a new legislature based on the confidence of the people. However, he believes that the new legislature may, or may not, have same members or form. The essential thing is that the newly erected body will enjoy full confidence of the community. But as revolution will affect the government alone, state and society will remain untouched by it. It infers that Locke's theory of revolution has two dimensions–one relating to the dissolution of the government in a way that a perverted legislature is replaced by a new one and the other relating to dissolution of the very contract on which the creation of the civil society depends. The former may be taken as an appeal to the electorate, while the latter is like the successful accomplishment of a revolution as happened in England in 1688.

What Locke desires is that the government must honour its trust, or it should be overthrown. The dissolution of the government (legislature) has two aspects–moral as well as legal. The moment a government stops serving the very purpose for which it is created, it amounts to its moral dissolution. It may happen very seldom. However, a government is actually

106. *Ibid.*, Ch.19.

107. Laski, *op. cit.*, p.37. Locke's views in this regard have been differently evaluated. Pollock says that Locke "lays a ferment for frequent rebellion." *Op. cit.*, p.7. Lord treats it as a modified right of revolution. *Principles of Politics*, p.59.

dissolved only when its perversion has reached considerable proportions and affects a large number of the citizens. As Locke says: "The legislative only being a fiduciary power to act for certain ends, there remains still in the people a supreme power to remove or alter the legislative, when they find the legislative act contrary to the trust reposed in them. For all power given with trust for attaining an end, being limited by that end, whenever the end is manifestly neglected or opposed, the trust must necessarily be forfeited and the power devolved into the hands of those that gave it, who may place it anew where they shall think best for their safety and security."[108] In simple terms, it implies that constitutional means "exist, or rather such means ought to exist, for dissolving undesirable governments, and we may suppose that a well-intentioned but incompetent legislature will yield readily to the wishes of the people."[109]

At one place, Locke frankly affirms: "The right of the people to shake off the usurpation of tyranny which the sword has brought in upon them stands till their rulers put them under such a frame of government as they willingly consent to."[110] A commentator may find here that "in the extensive discussion in different parts of his work the causes and consequences of revolt, the correlation so far established between the state of nature, the state of war and political society remains unchanged. No confusion occurs between the hypotheses of a governmentless state of nature and a real situation."[111] Again, "Exactly because Locke upheld the right of revolt, he had to leave the door open for the legitimisation of usurpation."[112] In the same vein, another commentator says that Locke "saw that men need not tolerate despotism for fear that the sole alternative was anarchy. Nor was he afraid that a doctrine of resistance would mean constant instability."[113]

While the process of election is a soft course, revolution is the reverse, and also complementary, side of the supreme power of the people to rid themselves of an erratic political authority.

---

108. *Second Treatise,* Ch.13.
109. W.T. Jones: *Masters of Political Thought,* Vol. II, p.200.
110. *Second Treatise,* Sec.192.
111. M. Seliger: *The Liberal Politics of John Locke,* p.101.
112. *Ibid.,* p.253.
113. T.P. Peardon: "Introduction" to his *John Locke's Second Treatise of Civil Government,* p.xix. Likewise, Lamprecht says that the theory of the state of nature supplies the basis for resistance to arbitrary rule." *Moral and Political Philosophy of John Locke,* p.123.

Locke, well aware of this fact, therefore, prefers that the people "retain final power, but that they exercise it only occasionally in the election process, or, if absolutely necessary, through revolution."[114] Thus, Locke reserves to the community just a conditional right of revolution in case of an unpardonable breach of trust by the government. His pious phrase of 'an appeal to the heaven' does not mean the people passively to wait the operations of divine justice on their behalf. He means that when no earthly judge exists before whom they can take their case, that is, when no constitutional channels of change exist, they must put their trust in heaven and, relieving in the rightness of their case, appeal to arms."[115]

RELIGIOUS FREEDOM : DOCTRINE OF QUALIFIED TOLERATION

The ideas of Locke on the question of relationship between the various religious sects and political authority are contained in his *Letter* on *Toleration*—a work that should be taken as a companion treatise of his *Two Treatises of Civil Government.* Herein we find a sort of solution offered by Locke for the problem that had plagued social and political conditions of England ever since the times of the Tudor monarchs. We may also notice that as a Whig and also as a man subscribing to the religious philosophy of the Protestants, Locke's views have a partisan character. Above all, Locke's rationalism does not make him a non-religious man, rather it takes him to the side of being a profoundly religious man disapproving of atheism and, more than that, desiring their persecution at the hands of the state.

Apparently, Locke is a secularist in the sense that he desires separation of the state from the church. He dismisses the idea that the state has any right to intervene in the affairs of the church relating to the salvation of human soul. The use of force by the state in order to achieve conformity is contrary to Christian morality. Civil magistrates may use 'outward force' only as religion is a matter of 'inward' persuasion. So, the church may not interfere with a civil right or deprive a person of his earthly possessions, though it may resort to exhortations, admonition and advices'. "The greatest punishment the church may properly inflict is that of excommunication, but depriva-

---

114. M. Judd Harmon, *op. cit.,* p.253.

115. Jones, *op. cit.,* p.200. Locke's contribution to the theory of sovereignty was thus to adopt and transmit a principle of resistance consistent with a mixed constitution." See Frankel, *op. cit.,* p.123.

tion of church membership cannot involve any civil consequences. Nor does affiliation of the civil magistrate with the church enhance the power of the church. Within it he is merely another member and cannot carry his civil authority with him into the church organisation."[116]

Locke's doctrine of religious toleration has a qualified character owing to certain essential points. First, be denies the extension of toleration to the atheists as all citizens must take oaths and make promise and agreements in the name of God. Second, Locke holds that certain religious sects as those claiming special 'prerogatives' should be proscribed. Third, no religious order should be allowed to exist whose members are required to pay allegiance to an alien ruler. (Here Locke's reference was distinctly directed towards the Roman Catholics.) Last, Locke disapproves of the right of a state to drive the non-conformists out of the country as such a policy amounts to the loss of native talent and is also likely to result in throwing them underground with a resolve to hatch serious conspiracies.

One may point out that Locke's exceptions to the idea of religious freedom are regrettable and what he has attempted to present is nothing else than what the Whig policies of his days desired. If here is a picture of religious toleration, it is not at all in consonance with the profile of secularism. Thus, Gough observes: "Locke regarded himself as a churchman, but churchmanship was of a very loose and unorthodox kind, in some respects exceeding even the limits of latitudinarianism; and though he never sympathised with sectarian extremism, his conception of the church, and of its relation to the state, was typical of non-conformity. Though not a separatist himself, he championed the right of the separatists to form their own independent churches, and this was the root of his belief in toleration. Even his intolerance of atheism was a consequence of the same belief in the right of free individuals to form voluntary societies by consent; for the atheist, in disbelieving in God, disbelieves in the author of the law of nature. Such disbelief undermines the obligation to keep promises and contracts, which is what holds society together. Atheism, therefore, is potential anarchy."[117]

116. Harmon, *op. cit.,* p.256.
117. Gough, *op. cit.,* p.193.

GOOD STATE : CHARACTERISTICS OF A TRUE POLITICAL SOCIETY

As a matter of fact, the real concern of Locke should be studied not as much with his acceptance of the formal framework of the social contract theory, that was so much like the stock-in-trade in his time, as with formulating the doctrine of a state having certain essential characteristics of a liberal-democratic order. The case of an ideal society living in a pre-political age or the termination of that state of nature by means of a social, really political, compact resulting in the creation of the civil society are just incidental matters. Likewise, Locke's emphasis on 'tacit' contract resulting in the creation of a government running on the 'trust' of the people with its legislative, executive (federative) and judicial departments stands like further incidental affairs in the political system of Locke. What is the real purpose of Locke? The answer is the formulation of a theory of good state–a state having certain essential characteristics making it 'worthy' of being a true or perfect political society. Wayper thus well points out that the form of state "is really for Locke a secondary matter. It may be democracy, an oligarchy, an hereditary or an elective monarchy. Far more important than its form are its characteristics, for unless it can claim certain well-marked characteristics, it is not a Political Society, it is not true State."[118]

The true state or the perfect political society of Locke has following well-marked characteristics:

1. It is a means, not an end, or a machine created for the good of the makers themselves. That is, the state exists for the welfare of the people, for the good of the community. Locke very specifically lays down that the people are not for the state, rather political power–the right of making laws with penalties of death for all acts of commission or omission detrimental to the regulation and preservation of property and defence of the commonwealth–is 'only for the public good'. Thus, the state, in fact, "is a machine which we create for our good and run for our purposes, and it is both dangerous and unnecessary to speak of some supposed mystical good of State or country independent of the lives of individual citizens."[119]

---

118. Wayper, *op. cit.*, p.75.
119. *Ibid.*

2. The state of Locke is founded on the basis of consent. The consent may be either express or tacit. The state is the creation of a social contract that was made by the express consent of the people. Now the will of the representatives occupying seats in the legislative chamber may be taken as a practical manifestation of the consent of the people. The very fact that people obey the laws of the state without staging any revolt or making any serious resistance is a proof of the fact that it stands on the basis of consent. Plamenatz thus makes this point clear that, strictly speaking, he (Locke) argued that a government "governs by consent only when its right to govern is conditional upon those governed having expressed the wish that it should govern them. It does not govern by consent simply because it, in fact, carries out the wishes of its subjects or even when its policy is expressly framed to meet their wishes, or when the fulfilment of their wishes is a necessary condition for its ability to make its rule effective. Consent is essentially the granting of permission to someone to do something which he would not have a right to do without such permission; and government by consent, therefore, implies that the government's right to govern (not its power to do so, nor its actual policy) is created by the expression of the wishes of its subjects."[120]
3. And it also follows from above that the state of Locke is based on permanent sovereignty of the community having a government to discharge its duties in a way that the trust of the people is not forfeited. The people who express their consent also have a legitimate right to withdraw it. He issues a clear warning that if 'you persistently mistreat the people, you must expect trouble'. The people have a right to make 'an appeal to the heaven', that is, to make a revolution to overthrow the government in case it rules arbitrarily. Here lies a very significant affirmation of the doctrine of a constitutional state–a state standing on the basis of the consent of the community. "If it is not for the people's good, if it does not depend on their consent, if it is not constitutional, or if it exceeds its authority, it can, Locke says, be legitimately overthrown."[121]
4. Locke's is a constitutional state with limited authority. It is not an absolute organisation like the Leviathan of Hobbes or

120. Cited in Gough, *op. cit.*, p.45.
121. Wayper, *op. cit.*, p.77.

the Community of Rousseau. It is limited as it derives power from the people and, more than that, it holds power in trust for the people. Its authority is limited by the Law of Nature– a higher law that confers three natural rights on the people and which commands that all civil laws should conform to it for the sake of their validity. The word 'sovereignty' occurs nowhere in the *Second Treatise* that is enough to prove that Locke deliberately avoids every possibility of State's being the wielder of absolute authority over its members. He makes it very plain that being 'only a fiduciary power to act for certain ends', its authority is confined to securing those ends.

5. By virtue of being a constitutional state, it stands for the maintenance of the rule of law. Even if the state is entitled for having certain discretionary powers during emergency periods, it does not imply that it may make use of its extra-ordinary powers during normal times. The State cannot make arbitrary laws. The political authority must rest on the established standing laws promulgated and known to the people and not by extemporary decree. Says Wayper: "This must be the more insisted upon because in every state, Locke realises, the Government must possess discretionary or emergency power. So long as it is understood that this emergency power which in England is called prerogative, is 'nothing but the power of doing public good without a rule', its existence in states will be beneficial and not harmful. But it can only be supplementary to, and never a substitute for, the rule of law. The very necessity for the existence of prerogative is indeed one reason the more why men should never forget that where the law ends, tyranny begins."[122]
6. Locke's state is a tolerant state. It recognises the principle of religious toleration. Horrified by the events of his own times, Locke lays stress on the principle of religious liberty for the people implying that every individual belonging to any sect has a right to interpret scriptures according to his 'rational' approach. An essentially religious question comes to have a political significance for Locke in view of the fact that, while supporting the doctrine of religious freedom, as advocated by the Protestants, he linked the case of freedom of the conscience with the powers of the civil magistrates. As Gough points out: "It was not a question of the freedom of

---

122. *Ibid.*, p.76.

conscience, or of intellectual freedom in the abstract. It was a question of the extent of the power of the civil magistrate in religious affairs. In civil affairs themselves civil magistrate and governments in any case had only limited powers, and they could interfere in religious affairs only insofar as such interference was necessary for civil purposes, such as the preservation of peace and did not go beyond matters 'indifferent."[123]

7. Locke's is not a positive but a negative state in the sense that instead of being an agency of social welfare, its main function is confined to the sphere of protection and preservation of the natural rights of the people. It does not strive to improve the character of its citizens; it merely seeks to maintain their independence. That is, the state of Locke is not concerned with the discharge of socially useful services as advocated by the English Idealist T.H. Green; it is an individualistic state concerned with the protection and not promotion of the lives of its members. One may draw an implication from this that the state of Locke has nothing to do with the eradication of gigantic social ills as those of starvation and unemployment; its area of activity ends with the preservation of security of life, liberty and property of the people.
8. Whereas Locke's is a negative state, it is also a 'transformer' state in the sense that it seeks to transform selfish interests of the individuals into public good. Herein we may study enlightened hedonism of Locke. The individual should seek pleasure and avoid pain in a way conducive to the cause of public happiness. The state is required to lay down conditions, including penalties, for the proper use of the rights of the individual who is a creature of hedonistic tendencies. Though the state "does not change man's character, it nevertheless, makes him behave as God would have him to, for it holds in check his self-interest and is the mechanism whereby men acting as they must in the end are to act as they ought to do–that is, for public happiness...The state thus brings pressure to bear on the individual in such a way that he acts for the public good, and the end–public happiness–is achieved even though the individual's motive–indeed, precisely because the individual's motive is to do good to himself."[124]

123. See Gough, *op. cit.,* p.17.
124. Wayper, *op. cit.,* p.78.

These are the essential characteristics of a true state according to Locke. The worthiness of a perfect political society, according to Locke, is determined by these salient features. Conquest, violence and despotism make the state 'unworthy'; on the contrary, consent, rule of law and limited government giving freedom to the individuals and, at the same time, protecting their natural rights justify its real 'worth'. As Wayper concludes: "But only where these characteristics can be observed, can man be said to have entered Civil Society. And only where Civil Society exists will men understand that "the end of law is not to abolish or restrain, but to preserve and enlarge freedom. Only there will the age-old conflict of authority and freedom be perfectly resolved."[125]

CRITICAL ESTIMATE : LOCKE AS A PROPHET OF LIBERAL-DEMOCRATIC ORDER

Despite being a thinker far less consistent than Hobbes, Locke exercised tremendous influence on the people of his own country as well as on those of France and America. The reason for this should be discovered in his theory's being 'deceptively simple in appearance',[126] or, as Bluhm says, in the nature of its being like a sugar-coated bitter pill. Bluhm rightly says that Locke "intentionally obscured the meaning of his political works. It appears that his purpose was not primarily that of a man who wishes to escape the censor's condemnation, though this was one consideration. More apt is a comparison with a physician who coats a bitter pill with sugar. Perhaps Locke's medical pursuits even suggested an analogous practice for his political teaching. The patient who takes the pill remains unaware of his hidden unpleasantness, and it can quietly work to cure his ill. Without the sugar-coating he might spit it out and remain unaware of his hidden unpleasantness, and it can quietly work to cure his ill. Without the sugar-coating he might spit it out and remain as sick as before. In our analogy, Hobbes is an unwise physician who tried to force the bitter medicine on his unwilling patient and failed. Locke, the wise physician, profited by his example and used the saccharine ruse to get the sick man unknowingly to down the same vile cathartic. The trick was a success. As we have seen, Locke was lionised in his life-time and his work acclaimed to the skies. The fame of the *Essay* and the *Two Treatises* guaranteed the success of all his

125. *Ibid.*
126. Sabine, *op. cit.*, p.539.

later works. In other words, the pill went down whole and stayed down."[127]

It is owing to Locke's deliberate effort to conceal something and present other things to the people of his times in a way justifying the politics of the Whigs that this political theory became a subject of popular interest in spite of being complex and inconsistent at various stages. One may notice the striking fact that he "has so emptied the word 'consent' of meaning that every government that has ever existed, could legitimately claim to have been on consent. It is clear, too, that his social contract has become little better than a farce."[128] Harmon hits at the points of inconsistency in Locke's political theory thus: "In reality it is highly complex. Locke attempted to supply answers to the multitudinous political problems of his time, and analysis demonstrates that the answer to one often detracts from answer to another. Numerous disagreements have arisen with regard to Locke's actual meaning in particular instances. There is, for example, a controversy concerning whether Locke was an individualist or a majority-rule democrat. His support to the rights of individual may lead to one conclusion, and his advocacy of the rights of a majority to determine a minority on the other. The emphasis placed upon property rights also seems to obscure those references revealed through a more careful reading, to the permission of the regulation of property in the public interest. At one point it appears that Locke's proposals dealing with executive prerogative contravene his insistence on legislative supremacy. And although Locke has often been cited as a philosopher of and an apologist for revolution, such an interpretation can only be inferred from his philosophy, for Locke himself, a moderate and prudent man, is loath to incite through the use of inflammatory phrases and does not do so."[129]

---

127. Bluhm, *op. cit.,* p.330. It should be pointed out that Bluhm's analogy of a patient and a sugar-coated pill administered by a physician is based on Locke's similar analogy drawn with a view to attack the doctrine of Filmer in his *First Treatise of Civil Government.* As Locke says: "Like a wary physician when he (Filmer) would have his patient swallow so harsh or corrosive liquor, he mingles it with a large quantity of that which may dilute it that the scattered parts may go down with less feelings and cause less aversion."
128. Wayper, *op. cit.*, p.79.
129. Judd Harmon, *op. cit.,* pp.258-59. The subject of 'inconsistencies' in Locke's political theory is a matter of academic debate. While Leo Strauss and Richard H. Cox hold that Locke did it all deliberately to cloak his real

True that Locke, like every political thinker, may be criticised for being 'complex' or 'inconsistent' in several respects, it is equally true that he deserves the real admiration of the people for giving ideas of lasting value in the sphere of representative government and the rule of law. In France his ideas were popularised by Voltaire and Rousseau and through them deeply influenced the revolutionary leaders of 1789. In America his ideas became the text-book of a revolution. Alfred Cobban says that Locke was a writer whose influence "pervades the eighteenth century with almost scriptural authority." The political thought of modern democracy highlighting constitutional limitations on sovereign power, legal safeguards on individual liberty, security accorded to private property, fundamental rights emanating from the Law of Nature are all predicated largely upon the contributions of Locke. It is thus commented that the great debate "inaugurated by the Reformation ceased when Locke had outlined an intelligent basis for parliamentary government."[130]

meaning from one work to another, Walter M. Simon is of a different view that there is no inherent inconsistency in the works of Locke produced at different times and if there is any, it may be discoverable within the body of a particular work flowing from his attempt to combine the radical empiricism of Bacon and the new rationalism of Descartes." See Bluhm, *op. cit.*, p.380 n.

130. Laski: *Political Thought in England*, p. 61.

18

ROUSSEAU

Rousseau seeks a 'rule' which is simultaneously 'legitimate' and 'solid' because without a legitimate reason for obedience human society only reveals 'the violence of powerful men and the oppression of the weak', and without a solid reason for obedience, the laws of justice are vain among men'. To be reliable, the rules of political justice must begin with the certitude than men, 'as they are', concerned only with their own interests: laws should conform to the nature of man (i.e. to a man who is not naturally just), because right merely 'permits' and interest 'prescribes'. Political right can only replace the important traditional natural law teaching if utility can be combined with justice'.

— Roger D. Masters[1]

Jean Jacques Rousseau (1712-1778) "still holds his place as one of the most stimulating and controversial of political theorists."[2] He was born in the city of Geneva in Switzerland. He belonged to a rich French family that had taken refuge in Switzerland durig the days of the persecution of the Huguenots. Although the city of Geneva was infused with the stern

1. Masters: *The Political Philosophy of Rousseau*, p.303.
2. Fredrick Watkins: *Rousseau: Political Writings*, p.ix (Abridged Ed., Nelson, New York, 1953).

morality of the Calvinist influence, yet it had little impact upon Rousseau. He passed his early life under the supervision of his father, but he refused to apprentice himself to a particular profession. At the age of 16 he ran away from his home city and took to an unending series of wandering to several European countries in a state of poverty and degradation. Curiously, he sized the fate of a political theorist at the age of 37 when he gained distinction in an essay contest conducted by the Dijon Academy on the subject: 'Has the revival of the sciences and arts helped to purify or to corrupt morals?' In this maiden contribution Rousseau stressed the point that all 'artificial' civilizational advancements had "served to suppress all that was good, noble and creative in man."[3] This great event proved a real turning point in his life, because it changed him from a vegabond to a philosopher. The subject-matter of this paper reveals that the mind of Rousseau was seething with new ideas. Henceforth, he vehemently attacked the institution of private property, system of laws and administration and the autocratic rule of the king till he apprehended his arrest and sought safety in living like a fugitive. In 1762 he left Paris and once again returned to the life of a vegabond. For some time he lived in England with Hume and Burke, but when he suspected Hume's motive of plotting against his life, he secretly escaped to France and shortly after expired leaving several important writings that give the 'most constant impresion' of his being 'a man in revolt.'[4]

WORKS : LITERATURE OF REVOLT AND REGENERATION

The political philosophy of Rousseau comes to us from his several important works that reveal his immortal contributions to the age of romanticism in literature and reason and reconstruction in the history of social and political ideas. His *Discourse on the Moral Effects of Arts and Sciences* shows his vehement reaction against the artifical patterns of social life created by the so-called advancement of civilisation. His *Dis-*

3. It is widely acclaimed that this paper of Rousseau created a great sensation in the artificial society of the Age of Reason inasmuch as it 'was the first rumble of the revolution.' See F.J.C. Hearnshaw: "Rousseau" in his *Social and Political Ideas of the French Thinkers of the Age of Reason,* p.179.
4. See J.H. Broome: *Rousseau: A Study of His Thought.* Rousseau's name occupies a very particular place in revolutionary lore. He was regarded by the (French) revolutionaries as their prophet and patron; his life was sometimes pictured as a martyrdom to the cause of the on-coming Revolution." See Joan McDonald: *Rousseau of the French Revolution,* p.3.

course on the Origin and Foundation of Inequality Among Men shows his ideas on the golden age of the primitive times when man led a life of idyllic happiness and pristine simplicity that was vitiated by the origin of the institution of private property. It also shows how the division of society into the classes of the rich and the poor created savage conditions of war and thereby necessitated the creation of political authority. In 1755, he contributed a paper on the subject of Political Economy to the French *Encyclopaedia* wherein he emphasised the point of individual freedom for his economic happiness. In 1761, he published *La Nauvella Heloisie.* His novel-cum-narrative, the *Emile,* appeared in the following year. In this romantic work Rousseau discussed the stages of development of man's personality and presented his views on the system of education with a line of attack on the hold of the clergymen over the imparting of instructions to the children. During the last days of his life he wrote three pamphlets, viz., *Confessions, Dialogues* and the *Reveries.*

The most important work of Rousseau, however, is his *Social Contract* that, according to Rene Hubert, "is the very centre and keystone to the whole structure of political fabric."[5] This work having its sub-title in *The Principles of Political Right* has Four Books each having several chapters that may be counted as 48 in all. This work may be described as Rousseau's noble endeavour for giving us a design of the politics of regeneration. In this respect, Rousseau's *Social Contract* may well be likened with Plato's *Republic.* The fundamental idea of this work of Rousseau signifies his object 'to enquire if, in the civil order, there can be any sure and certain rule of administration, taking men as they are and laws as they might be.'[6] As Wright says: "A society of free consent and not of force; a union of each with all on equal terms for common good; a sovereignty vested in all and voiced by the general will for the maintenance of liberty in law; this is the heart of the *Social Contract.* All else, whether represented or omitted here, is contingent, variable, precautionary. So much is the abstract necessity for the right state; or since it is derived in reason from the very nature of our species, for the natural society."[7]

5. Cited in Hearnshaw, *op. cit.,* p.185.
6. See G.D.H. Cole: 'Introduction' to *The Social Contract and Discourses,* p.xvi.
7. Wright: *The Meaning of Rousseau,* p.90.

The real significance of the *Social Contract* of Rousseau has been differently evaluated. While its critics have undermined it as 'a propylaeum which leads into nothing'[8], others have admired it as 'still by far the best of all text-books of political philosophy.'[9] The way Rousseau brings about an ideal reconciliation of liberty and authority has left a big handle in the hands of his critics as well as admirers to dub him either as a 'liberal' or as a 'totalitarian'. Disagreeing with either of the two extreme viewpoints, Wright holds that this work of Rousseau has a great message of peace and liberty. As he says: "The book is meant for neither individualist nor absolutist. In the struggle between state and individual which has been the torment of political philosophy from Aristotle down, it offers a proposal for a peace...The individual must have liberty for progress, but the state that fosters progress must have power to do its work. The liberty must be secure, for a precarious liberty is none at all but the power must be supreme, contingent power is the lack of it. So the two must remain fully unconflicting."[10] One may, however, partly agree with the exaggerated observation of Dreyfus-Brisac that this work "is the book of all books that is most talked of and least read."[11]

An over-all assessment of the political writings of Rousseau has been a matter of great controversy. It is said that the writings of Rousseau "appear at first sight to consist of a mass of contradictions."[12] Another critic says that Rousseau's works "are often abstract and not always clear."[13] An admirer of Rousseau, though he often asserts the point of basic consistency in his writings, feels that the underlying assumptions of one work are contradicted with that of the other in view of the point that the "human beings brought up on the 'individualist' principles of *Emile* would not be able to breathe in a 'collectivist' political society which is often thought to be the only possible outcome of the *Contract Social*."[14] Hearnshaw says that Rousseau "was an unsystematic thinker, untrained in formal logic. He was an omnivorous reader with undeveloped powers of assimilation. He was an emotional enthusiast who spoke without due reflec-

8. E. Barker: 'Introduction' to *Social Contract,* p.xxxviii.
9. Cole, *op. cit.,* p.xi.
10. Wright, *op. cit.,* p.103.
11. See Cole, *op. cit.,* p.vi.
12. Hearnshaw, *op. cit.,* p.183.
13. M. Judd Harmon: *Political Thought from Plato to the Present,* p.297.
14. Broome, *op. cit.,* p.50.

tion. He was an irresponsible writer with a fatal gift for epigram."[15] However, with a view to keep a reader of Rousseau's political philosophy away from the web of confusing contradictions, Watkins offers a very sound advice that the true nature of his works "can be appreciated only if the reader recognises from the beginning that its underlying unity is psychological rather than logical in character."[16]

FIRST DISCOURSE : INDICTMENT OF MODERN MATERIALISTIC CIVILISATION

The publication of a monograph in 1750 on the contradiction between science and morals–known as the *First Discourse*– *"is a notable event, not only because it marks the real beginning of Rousseau's philosophy, but because in later life he tended to look back on it as the source of much personal misery, and as a kind of accident which condemned him to a literary career for which the often felt himself to be unfitted by temperament."*[17] *"The real significance of this small work of Rousseau–a contribution that won the essay writing competition organised by the Academy of Dijon–has been studied "as the expression of an authentic and highly individualistic revolt against an intellectual tradition and a social atmosphere."*[18] *Giving vent to the same view, Vaughan says that it "was and still remains the most complete version of the revolt against human law and human convention–of the craving for a return to simple and free conditions, for a renewal of man's communion with God and Nature–which was to breathe a new life into the thought, the imagination, the social ideals of the civilised world."*[19]

The central idea of Rousseau's *First Discourse* finds place in his strong affirmation that states and civilisations tend to decay as they allow the developments of arts and sciences that provide 'conveniences' and 'luxuries' and thereby create a materialistic outlook undermining virtues and morals. As he says: "As the conveniences of life increase, as the arts are brought to perfection, and luxury spreads, true courage flags, the virtues disappear; and all this is the effect of the sciences and of those arts which are exercised in the privacy of men's dwellings."[20] Like a vehement critic of the model of materialis-

15. Hearnshaw, *op. cit.,* pp.185-186.
16. Watkins, *op. cit.,* p.x.
17. J.H. Broome, *op. cit.,* p.18.
18. *Ibid.*
19. Vaughan cited in Hearnshaw, *op. cit.,* p.180.
20. For text of this *Discourse* See Cole, *op. cit.,* pp. 117-42.

tic civilisation, Rousseau goes on to assert that one should ignore the preachments of the philosophers and rely upon his own conscience, instinct, feeling, faith and emotion. As he further says: "Why should we build our happiness on the opinions of others when we can find it in our own hearts? Let us leave to others the task of instructing mankind in their duty, and confine ourselves to the discharge of our own. We have no occasion for greater knowledge than this. Virtue! sublime science of simple minds, are such industry and preparation needed if we are to know you? Are not your principles graven on every heart: Need we do more to learn your laws, than examine ourselves and listen to the voice of conscience, when the passions are silent?"[21]

The arguments employed by Rousseau to prove that arts and sciences have their origin in human vices and they corrupt the pure life of natural man are thus summed up by Broome: "His (Rousseau's) first argument is that they are tainted in their origins, being born of human vices; and thus with magnificent disregard for the complexities of human activity, he derives astronomy from superstition; eloquence from ambition, hatred, flattery and deceit; mathematics from avarice; physics from vain curiousity; and all of them including moral philosophy itself, from pride. Similarly, their immediate objectives are all concerned in one way or another with some aspect of moral, political or social failing; thus the arts in general are inseparable from luxury; jurisprudence is born of injustice; and history is concerned (exclusively, it would seem) with tyranny, war and conspiracy. Even if it is conceded that the aim of science is the discovery of the truth, Rousseau maintains (and it is a point of fundamental importance in relation to the subsequent tendencies of his philosophy) that truth is but one, whereas error is capable of an infinite number of variations. The chances are, therefore, bearing in mind the probable insincerity of the seeker and the absence of valid criteria, that the truth will never be recognised, or if it were recognised, that it would be abused."[22]

The message of this work of Rousseau is, therefore, a plea 'to return to the faith of the fathers', "to beware of a too great preoccupation with material values, and to reassert the values of faith, patriotism, and good citizenship."[23] As Rousseau says:

21. *Ibid*, p. 142.
22. Broome, *op. cit.*, p.23.
23. Judd Harmon, *op. cit.*, p.299.

"We have physicists, geometricians, chemists, astronomers, poets, musicians, and painters in plenty; but we have no longer a citizen among us; or if there be found a few scattered over our abandoned countryside, they are left to perish there unnoticed and neglected." It implies that the proper standard, according to Rousseau, is the creation of a natural man uncorrupted by the vices and luxuries of a materialistic civilisation. It, however, does not imply that Rousseau rejects the values of a modern civilised life and makes a clarion call for 'return to the nature'. What he really desires is that the modern civilised society must undergo a fundamental change in the direction of creating conditions whereby one may lead a new social life of a 'wise' and 'pure' man."[24]

The *First Discourse* of Rousseau has been dubbed as the 'poorest of his writings', "polemical, highly charged with emotion, and appears to have been hastily written."[25] It is also said that the refutations of Rousseau attempt to lay down upon all arts and sciences 'an unreasonable burden of responsibility for all the ills of civilisation."[26] It is further said that Rousseau's essay of protest 'is too short to allow the proper development of any of the suggestive insights which it contains."[27] As a result, his superficial denunciation of the materialistic civilisation 'takes the place of detailed argument in too many instances. In spite of this, however, a number of elements in the discourse can be, and are, powerfully developed in Rousseau's greater works, and so stand out as the important parts of a defective whole...In conclusion, therefore, the *First Discourse* can be said to keep its place in the literature of protest: but it is not plausible enough to be taken very seriously as a contribution to philosophy."[28]

Such a line of criticism directed against the *First Discourse* of Rousseau loses its plausibility the moment a precocious reader of Western political thought examines it in the light of the total political and social philosophy of the 'great thinker of the eighteenth century'. A subtle degree of unity prevails in the writings of Rousseau in a way that what one work leaves unfinished, the other does it. Hence, the central

24. Masters, *op. cit.*, pp.253-54.
25. Judd Harmon, *op. cit.*, p.298.
26. Broome, *op. cit.*, p.27.
27. *Ibid.*
28. *Ibid.*, pp.27 and 30.

idea of the *First Discourse* should be fully studied by making it connected with the meaning of his *Second Discourse,* that has been treated as a far more impressive contribution. Not only that, the total picture of Rousseau's political philosophy becomes clear after reading his other great works like *Second Discourse, Emile* and *Social Contract.* Thus, a student of Rousseau's political philosophy is struck with the fact that the essential line of the structure of his system remains unbroken that takes its start from the text of the *First Discourse* and culminates in the portions of the *Social Contract.* As Masters comments: "Since a careful reading of the *First Discourse* shows it to contain the key elements of Rousseau's mature thought, his claims concerning the unity of his 'system', his decision to reveal his principles incompletely at first, and the proper order of reading his major writings seem to be justified; there is no reason to assume that Rousseau's fundamental philosophic position changed radically between the publication of the *First Discourse* in 1750 and the appearance of the *Emile* and *Social Contract* in 1762."[29]

SECOND DISCOURSE : HISTORICAL HYPOTHESIS OF THE ORIGIN OF INEQUALITY

The *Second Discourse* of Rousseau, properly called his *Discourse on the Origin and Foundation of Inequality Among Men,* is his "first writing in which he 'completely developed' his philosophical principles."[30] Rousseau himself describes it as 'the work of greatest importance' that comes to us in the form of the result of his deep philosophical pursuits. As he himself says: "To mediate on this great subject I travelled to St. Germain for seven or eight days...Deep in the forest I sought and found image of the first epochs, whose history I proudly traced; revealed the little lies of men, I dared strip their nature nude, follow the progress of time and things, which have disfigured it, and comparing man's man with natural man, show them in man's supposed perfection the true source of his miseries."[31]

What Hobbes puts in his *Leviathan* and Locke in his *Second Treatise of Civil Government* in regard to the supposed nature of the pre-political phase and its termination by means of a social compact is given by Rousseau in his two works–the

---

29. Masters, *op. cit.,* p.248.
30. *Ibid.,* p.106.
31. *Ibid.*

Second Discourse and the *Social Contract*. The *Second Discourse* looks like his attempt to provide an explanation of the origin of inequality among men that, in a real sense, becomes an essay on the origin of civil society necessitating the creation of political authority in due course when the noble conditions of Arcadian bliss and primitive simplicity are perverted by the savage conditions of cut-throat competition and internecine wars. In this way, the *Second Discourse* of Rousseau becomes a prelude to his *Social Contract*. Herein we find his philosophical description of what the social contractualists call the state of nature that is terminated by means of a social compact made by an ideally reasonable people to establish political community.

A study of the *Second Discourse* of Rousseau illustrates the point that, according to him, the creation of political community witnesses three revolutions. In the initial phase, man is neither moral nor immoral but amoral. He leads a life of pristine simplicity and idyllic happiness. He is not a political creature. Though the general pattern of man's life is marked by a form of isolated existence, his life is not at all like that of the man of Hobbes; man in this state of nature has the benefit of 'free' associations in which there "is no calculation for the future, and no reflection of the kind that will produce later a competitive attitude between individuals; since the only kind of pride or vanity conceivable at this point is a vague collective sense of the superiority of men over the other animals."[32]

The first revolution takes place after the institution of family on a permanent basis that may be interpreted as the beginning of civil society. The establishment of permanent family relationship is described by Rousseau as 'reciprocal attachment'. Now 'reason' enters to create a line of difference between 'mine' and 'thine' and it leads to the emergence of the standards of superiority of some over others. Man living in the state of primitive simplicity and idyllic happiness comes to realise that his association with others, and not isolation, is neessary if he desires to advance from an animalistic, furtive and fearful life to that of a moral being. As Rousseau says: "Whoever sang or desired best, whoever was the handsome, the strongest, or the most eloquent came to be of most consideration; and this was the first step towards inequality, and at the same time towards vice. From these first distinctions arose on

32. See Broome, *op. cit.*, p.41.

the one side vanity and contempt and on the other shame and envy: and the fermentation caused by these new leavens ended by producing combinations fatal to innocence and happiness."[33]

As a result of the first revolution, there comes into being the state of inequality which, according to Rousseau, is of two kinds–natural and moral. While the former consists of those differences such as of age, physical strength and the qualities of mind and soul, the latter is established by man after entering into the phase of social existence. As he records: "I conceive of two sorts of inequality in the human species: One which I call natural or physical, because it is established by nature and consists in difference of ages, health, bodily strength and qualities of mind or soul; the other, which may be called moral or political inquality, because it depends upon a sort of convention and is established, at least authorised, by the consent of men."[34]

The second revolution is brought about by the agriculture and the fortuitous discovery of the usefulness of metals leading towards the specialisation of functions and division of labour. Now the institution of private property comes into being to create conditions of inequality in that phase of man's social existence. The noble conditions of primitive simplicity are replaced by the savage conditions of a competitive existence that amounts to a virtual state of war in which everyman's hand is turned against his neighbour and the honourable qualities of human nature are transformed by abuse into a source of shame. As Rousseau further says: "The first man, who having enclosed a piece of ground, bethought himself of saying *This is Mine,* and found people simple enough to believe him, was the real founder of civil society. From how many crimes, wars and murders, from how many horrors and misfortunes might not any one have saved mankind, by pulling up the stakes, or filling up the ditch, and crying to his fellows, 'Beware of listening to this impostor' you are undone if you once forget that the fruits of the earth belong to us all, the earth itself to nobody."[35]

The creation of the institution of private property divided the society into two classes–the rich and the poor– and thereby opened the Pandora's box of a highly competitive existence. While the poor struggled against the rich for the sake of earning the bare means of subsistence, the rich contended for the safety

33. See Judd Harmon, *op. cit.*, p.299.
34. See Masters, *op. cit.*, p.119.
35. See Judd Harmon, *op. cit.*, p.301.

of their possessions. While the rich, as Judd Harmon says, "were aware that they owed what they had to force and usurpation; they also knew that they could easily lose their possessions in the same manner, and they searched for a way to protect themselves."[36] The solution they found "was the creation of civil society with laws to protect private property and the force required to implement them...The rich persuaded the poor to join in the creation of a power which would protect each in what he had, and thus restore peace. The poor succumbed gladly."[37]

It indicates that the formation of civil society is accomplished by the artificial co-operation between the rich and the poor, though the motives of both the parties differ in their own respects. The civil society comes into being as a result of the third revolution effected by the creation of an ad hoc arrangement in which the rich and the poor join hands for the protection of their conflicting interests. As Rousseau goes on to say: "All ran headlong to their chains, in hopes of securing their liberty; for they had just wit enough to perceive the advantages of political institutions without experience enough to enable them to foresee the dangers. Such was or may well have been the origin of society and law, which bound new fetters on the poor, and gave new powers to the rich; which irretriveably destroyed natural liberty, eternally fixed the law of property and inequality, converted clever usurpation into unalterable right, and for the advantage of a few ambitious individuals, subjected all mankind to perpetual labour, slavery and wretchedness."[38]

It is clear that the creation of civil society, according to Rousseau, is effected by the force of inequality that produced conditions necessary for the artificial victory of the rich over the poor. One may say that it is like an ad hoc arrangement between the rulers and the ruled inasmuch as this state of life is not to live for ever. The poor who willy-nilly succumb to the persuasion of the rich do it all not for the sake of throwing themselves into the fry pan after feeling fed up with the life of a competitive social environment, nor do they do it with the motive of getting back to the previous condition in case they ever feel fed up with the tyranny of a new social order, rather

36. *Ibid.*, p.302.
37. *Ibid.*
38. *Ibid.*

they do it with the hope of replacing this 'bogus' arrangement with a better and nobler one by means of a social contract that becomes the central idea of Rousseau's next and most important work. Thus, the idea of the third revolution should not be identified with Rousseau's meaning of the social contract. As Hacker says: "The transition from the state of nature to society in the *Second Discourse* "is political as well as social. And in building a state on top of society, men jumped out of the frying pan of cut-throat competition into the fire of political tyranny. This transition, then, is not, a contract. It is informal and accidential, non-legal and in fact founded on a gigantic swindle. In no sense are rational or informed processes of consent at work, or in no sense are the resultant society and state to be considered legitimate institutions."[39]

SOCIAL CONTRACT: CREATION OF AN IDEAL ORGANIC COMMUNITY

Correctly understood, Rousseau's *Social Contract* is a further extension of what he says in the *Second Discourse.* As already pointed out, here he seeks to complete what he leaves unfinished in his previous writings. Here he contradicts the wrong impression of his readers that free men of the state of nature by making an artificial compact (as given in the *Second Discourse)* jump out of the fry-pan of anarchy into the fire of tyranny. What he really seeks to tell them is that the 'artificial' compact is terminated by another one whose purpose is "to suggest to men a method for the *Discourse.* Men have left the state of nature for good, and there is no way to return. They have, therefore, become accustomed to social life and material well-being. The task, therefore, is to create a political system which will make power legitimate: if power can be made a servant rather than a master then it will be possible to rediscover much of the freedom which men knew in the state of nature. In short, Rousseau, acting as both a political philosopher and a political scientist, is seeking ways to organise political life so that men can rise out of the slough of social and psychological despond and use power as a means to achieve freedom."[40]

In this way, the *Social Contract* of Rousseau should be studied as a complementary work where he completes the picture of his community in the final form of an ideal and organic political society. The only reason as to why he chooses the

39. Hacker: *Political Theory,* p.301
40. *Ibid.,* p.408.

framework of social contract theory is his awareness of the fact that "all the world was thinking and talking about it."[41] As a matter of fact, in the view of Rousseau, social contract is not a historical truth whereby the first society was ever created, it may be an ideal course for ideally reasonable men in future to establish a perfect society that will substitute 'justice for mere instinct' and that will give man's action that moral character which they lacked before and thereby change man 'from a stupid and limited animal' into 'an intelligent citizen.' It is rightly observed that Rousseau's social compact "is not, as commonly supposed, a thing that we all signed long ago to start the first society; it is what we must sign now if we are to have the right one. It is not history, but may some day be history."[42]

It is for this reason that Rousseau is said to use the doctrine of social contract just as a mere formal framework of the lucid expression of his political theory with a resolve to offer an ideal answer to the fundamental problem of political obligation. His fundamental quest is to bring about an ideal organic political order having harmonious reconciliation of liberty and authority. For this basic reason, he is out to find out a legitimate basis of political society or a universal principle of right authority on the basis of which a political order may claim legitimate obedience of its individuals without involving a loss of their fundamental freedoms. The real problem is, as he says, "to find a form of association which defends and protects the person and property of each member with the whole force of community, and where each, while joining with all the rest, still obeys none but himself, and remains as free as before."[43]

Following the usual course of the social contractualists, Rousseau draws a soft picture of the state of nature in which man is neither moral, nor immoral but amoral-'noble savage'-leading 'a life of idyllic happiness and primitive simplicity'. But this state could not have lasted for long. With the rise of civilisation, the institution of private property was established which brought forth 'reason in the man and 'inequality' in the society. The 'noble savage' enjoyed heavenly pleasures but private property entered like the Serpent into the Garden of Eden. It created a sense of jealousy and struggle and substituted the condition of pristine self-sufficiency and happiness by a state of inequality and acknowledged usurpations.

41. Morley: *Rousseau,* Vol. I, p.115.
42. Wright, *op. cit.,* p.71.
43. *Social Contract,* Book I, Ch.VI.

These evils terminated the era of simplicity and happiness and necessitated the formation of some political organisation. A return to the state of nature grew impossible because the world was too thickly populated to admit the roamings of the noble savage. As a result, the institutions of the family, private property, society, law and government had come to stay. It is thus obvious that, in Rousseau's view, state is an evil to arrest the bigger evils. However, his view, as given in the *Emile,* becomes modified in the *Social Contract* when he comes to believe that the advantages of the civil society are greater than those of the state of nature. Hence, the people in that state of nature make a contract according to whose terms A,B,C,E etc. surrender their natural rights to the collective whole created by the union of A+B+C+D+E etc. Like the men of Hobbes, they surrender all but, unlike them, they put their person and powers under the supreme direction of the collective whole which Rousseau calls the General Will. In his own words: "Then each of us put his person and all his powers in common under the supreme direction of the General Will, and in our corporate capacity, we receive each member as an individual part of the whole."[44]

The making of this contract creates a political society and thereby turns individuals into citizens. By the terms of this contract they not only receive as much as they lose but, in addition, they acquire the common force to preserve what they individually had. It creates a moral and collective body with its own unity, common identity, corporate life and rational will. In this way, it terminates the state of nature and wholly transforms the character of the individuals who place themselves under the aegis of a democratic sovereign–general will–an authority of the corporate whole of the community. They take equal membership of the community, submit to it and yet make themselves an integral part of the sovereign authority. In submission to this moral authority, they never feel subjection to an alien body but to some authority of which each is a part placed on an equal footing with others. Since they were both like an individual and a subject, so they remain both a citizen and a sovereign and thus, while obeying the state as a citizen, they come to obey their own will incorporated in the general will along with the wills of the others. Hence, they continue to live as free as before, for obedience to their own wills involved no loss of freedom. According to Wright, 'Independence knew no

44. *Social Contract,* Book I, Ch.VI.

duty, liberty requires every act to be a duty. Independence knew no rights, for there could be no right when all did as they would, nor any power to fix one, in liberty our rights are fixed and all the power of the group is engaged for that security. It is that security in rights that constitutes liberty. What we have lost is therefore the precarious freedom to do as we please, and what we have gained is the assured freedom to do what all consider right."[45]

According to Rousseau, "The passage from the state of nature to the civil state produces a very remarkable change in man, by substituting justice for instinct in his conduct and given his actions the morality they have hitherto lacked. Then only, when the voice of duty takes the place of physical impulse and right of appetite does man, who so far had considered only himself, find that he is forced to act on different principles, and to consult his reason before listening to his inclinations. What man loses by the social contract is his natural liberty and an unlimited right to everything, he tries to get and succeeds in getting: what he gains is his civil liberty...which alone makes him truly master of himself; for the mere impulse of appetite in slavery, while obedience to a law which we prescribe to ourselves is liberty."[46]

Third, a line of basic contradiction in the political philosophy of Rousseau is discovered in his statement of total surrender of their powers, they lose their freedom in favour of a political authority that may be identified with the leviathan of Hobbes with the only difference that the despotism of one is substituted by the despotism of the multitude. Such a contract creates a state where the individuals lose their freedoms and remain in their usual chains despite being the equal partners of their created authority. As a result, Rousseau's man, who is born free, continues to remain in chains despite his being one of the makers of the political authority. As Barker says: "The paradox conceals a syllogism. I surrender all myself–and I surrender it all to 999 others as well as myself: I only receive a fraction of the sovereignty of the community, and ultimately I must reflect that if I am the thousandth part of a tyrant, and I am also the whole of a slave. Leviathan is still Leviathan, even when he is corporate."[47]

---

45. Wright, *op. cit.,* p.28.
46. *Ibid.,* Book I, Ch.VIII.
47. Barker, *op. cit.,* p.xlvi.

Finally, the *Social Contract* of Rousseau contradicts the very basis of the doctrine of the social contract. The traditional theory of social contract not only dismisses the dogma of divine origin of state, it also subscribes to the artificial character of the society and the state. If state is the creation of a contract made by the people, it loses its natural character. Moreover, the state is the product of a social compact, it can claim obedience only when it fulfils the condition of the trust of its people. But the situation is basically different when we find that the state, despite being the product of a social compact, becomes a natural and moral association in the political system of Rousseau. It shows that Rousseau cuts himself totally off from the line of Hobbes and Locke and makes the way clear for his successors like Hegel who is described as the greatest champion of the German Idealist school. This essential point of Rousseau's political philosophy should be discovered in his affirmation that state "is natural and the 'state of nature' is an abstraction. Without this basis of will and natural need, no society could for a moment subsist; the state exists and claims our obedience because it is a natural extension of our personality."[48]

A critical study of the ideas of Rousseau, as contained in the *Social Contract,* leads to these impressions:

1. Though superficially subscribing to the tradition of social contract school, Rousseau is the follower of the idealist tradition in finding out the legitimate basis of a right political order. He is not a disciple of Hobbes and Loke, he is the teacher of Hegel and Green. The central theme of the *Social Contract* is to seek the rationalised redemption of man. In other words, Rousseau, like Plato, desires moral regeneration of man and his society–that ideal phase of human existence in which man is raised from the level of animal existence to that of a perfect man. As such, this work of Rousseau "in particular, is explicitly concerned with the completion of a social evolution, and the arrival of man at a point of political enlightement which while it is intended to provide a similar situation in terms of happiness, it is in other respects as far removed as possible from the animal-like primitive state."[49]
2. A study of Rousseau's social compact, if made from the standpoint discussed in the preceding paragraphs, leaves

48. Cole, *op. cit.,* p.xxxvii.
49. Broome, *op. cit.,* p.52.

an impression that it is no social compact at all. There is nothing else than a mere name of the same device as adopted by Hobbes and Locke. One may add that, in a real sense, Rousseau talks of two contracts–first made by the rich and the poor to establish a civil society that accords recognition to the state of inequality and the second one to create a political order to do away with the shortcomings of the 'unequal' social existence–which are equally 'spurious' in the sense that his fundamental purpose is not at all to involve himself into the web of social compact but to use them as formal frameworks to express his philosophy of political romanticism. No natural rights form the subject-matter of contract, for the social order is itself the basis of all other rights. The contract does not stipulate the powers of government vis-a-vis the people, for the government is merely the instrument of the people and does not possess independent power.[50] It is, therefore, added that this "is not as much a contract as it is the avoidance of one. It is a donation by the individuals to the community which they form. Rousseau could have constructed his theory without bringing in the idea of contract at all."[51]

It is understandable that, like Hobbes and Locke, Rousseau starts from a hypothetical state of nature and formulates his theory of state on a purely imaginary foundation. The framework in which he seeks to answer the fundamental question of political obligation is realy a hypothesis which cannot be proved by historical, philosophical, logical, and legal standards. The result is that the significance of political institutions is under-rated and the theory leaves scope, although very little as compared to Hobbes and Locke, for the disobedience of governmental authority in the name of general good. Hence, like other social contractualists, Rousseau also contributes to a theory of state which has been dubbed as dangerous, 'harmful' and 'pernicious' by the critics.[52] Thus, the refutation of social contractualism at the hands of Burke is applicable, though partly, to Rousseau's social contract theory if we take into ac-

50. Sabine, *op. cit.,* p.587.
51. Judd Harmon, *op. cit,* p.306.
52. J.L. Talmon comments that in *Social Contract* can be discovered the germs of modern mass democracy, the classless society, dictorship and the monolithic state; in marrying the concept of the general will with the principle of popular sovereignty, Rousseau gave rise to totalitarian democracy." The *Origins of Totalitarian Democracy,* p.43.

count the fact that state is not a result of social compact. Burke warns that state ought not to be considered as nothing better than a partnership or agreement in some low concern, rather it should be 'looked on with reverence."[53]

GENERAL WILL: CREATION OF STATE AS A MORAL PERSON

Rousseau's conception of general will as the single and simple volition of the body politic regarded as a living entity represents his distinctive contribution to the philosophy of state. It is the repository of political authority emanated from the social contract and, although it has been a subject of much argument at the hands of the political commentators, its significance stands out as a unique contribution of Rousseau. According to G.D.H. Cole, "His General Will is the most disputed and certainly the most fundamental of all the most valuable parts of his theory. No critic of the social contract has found it easy to say either what precisely its author meant by it, or what is its final value for political philosophy....Of its broad meaning, however, there can be no doubt. The effect of the social contract is the creation of a new individual."[54]

General will is the will of the corporate body called the community and it stands for the common good and general welfare of the society as a whole. It supersedes the respective will of all those people who enter into social contract and agree to surrender all their powers to the community. The chief sanction or the characteristic mark behind it is not the number of persons willing it but the common good or general interest. However, it is not a mere compromise after the cancellation of pluses and minuses, it represents 'a higher type of the will of the society'. It represents common consciousness of the common good after discussion and proper deliberations. The only important thing about it is that it wills general, i.e., common interest and not that what is willed generally, i.e., by majority of the members of the society. Barker well puts: "When he (Rousseau) speaks of this general will, he uses the adjective to indicate the *quality* of the 'object' sought, and not *quality* of the objects or persons by whom it is sought."[55]

With a view to clarify the implications of the general will, later on Prof. Benard Bosanquet explains that each individual

53. See Bohn (ed.): *Works of Edmund Burke,* Vol. II, pp.368-69.
54. Cole, *op. cit.,* p.xxviii.
55. Barker, *op. cit.,* p.xliv.

has two wills–the actual which is transient and conceives of the present only based on self-interest being unrelated to the well-being of the society, hence narrow and self-conflicting, encouraging a man to be selfish, immoral and bad. The second is the real will which informs man to be altruistic, selfless, sincere, pious and moral. It is a rational will that studies his real interest in relation to the general welfare of the society. It considers more of the common good or general interest than the good of a particular individual and thus it promotes harmony and represents true freedom. As the chief characteristic feature behind the general will is common good, naturally it is the sum-total or synthesis of all the real wills of the society. According to Bosanquet, 'General will is the will of the whole society as such or the wills of all individuals insofar as they aim at common good."[56]

An explanation of the general will indicates that it bears the characteristics of being rational or non-self-conflicting, indivisible or non-sectional, right or willing common welfare, inalienable or unrepresentable, permanent, non-impulsive and national. Such an explanation leads to several conclusions. Firstly, the body politic taken as a whole may be regarded as an organised living body resembling that of a man and also being a moral entity possessed of a will. Secondly, the general will always tends to the preservation and welfare of whole and every part. Thirdly, it keeps all people in a particular relationship with all members of the political community. It is the source of law, justice and power. It constitutes popular sovereignty where the people are both the sovereign and the subject. Above all, it is always on the side of general good. According to Prof. F.J.C. Hearnshaw, "It is always on the side which is most favourable to public interest so that it is needful only to act as justly to be certain of following general will."[57]

Moreover, as general will is the will of the corporate body called the community, it may not be identified with the will of one, few, many or even all. Even a unanimous will of all the members of the community may not be identified with it unless the quality of general good is there. Nor can it be identified with the majority opinion until the same sanction is present. It may, or may not be, the will of one, few, many, all or even none at a particular time, since the characteristic mark behind it is not the number of persons willing it but general interest or the

56. Bosanquet: *Philosophical Theory of State,* p.99.
57. Hearnshaw, *op. cit.,* p.102.

common good as the object of wills. In the words of Rousseau: "There is often a great deal of difference between the will of all and the general will, the latter considers only the common interest, while the former takes private interest into account and is no more than a sum of particular wills; but take away from the same wills pluses and minuses that cancel one another and general will remains as the sum of differences."[58]

This 'cancellation theory' of Rousseau has been explained by certain writers with the help of arithmetical method. For instance, Hacker takes a hypothetical case and explains it thus: "The question of pluses and minuses cancelling each other out is a difficult one. What Rousseau seems to object to in the will of all, the pluralist clash of interests, is the process itself. Even when the general will is operative, there will be differences of opinion among individual citizens. But these differences can be cancelled in a straight-forward and equalitarian way, whereas with the group struggle the result is more apt to be the survival of the strongest. Rousseau's cancellation theory may be illustrated by taking a hypothetical community consisting of only ten individuals. In their political capacity they are considering a revision of the minimum wage law, which now stands at 81·25 per hour. Each of the ten first of all asks himself what the new minimum wage should be : ideally he poses this question in terms of what is good for the community as a whole, not with a view of what is good for his own interest. The ten judgements, or votes, come out as follows :

Citizens	*Revision Downwards*	*Revision Upwards*
A		1'35
B		1'30
C	'Minuses'	1'45
D		1'35
E		1'40
F	1'15	
G		1'30
H	1'10	
I	1'15	'Pluses'
J	1'20	

58. *Social Contract,* Book II, Ch.III.

When the ten opinions are combined, the result is a decision to raise the wage from $ 1'25 an hour to $ '27$\frac{1}{2}$."[59]

In this regard, however, Rousseau reaches very close to Locke inasmuch as he not only adheres to the fact of public good but, for practical purposes, believes in the superiority of numerical strength. Laski points out: "The general will, in practical instead of semi-mystic terms, really means the welfare of the community as a whole, and when we inquire how the general will is to be known, we come, after much shuffling, upon the will of the majority in which Locke also puts his trust. Rousseau's general will, indeed, is at bottom no more than an assertion that right and truth should prevail; and for this also Locke was anxious."[60]

The acceptance of the majority-decision as a formal manifestation of the general will is backed by Rousseau's faith in the eventual triumph of good over evil in a public meeting. When the general will eludes citizens, it seems to him that out of the wills of all process of refinement or of social logic would produce a result that would be the same as the general will. There "would be a general element in the vote taken, for without it there could be no consensus. In other words, the matter, in question would be of interest to all the citizens and would therefore fall within the competency of will. The result of their vote would record their assent or dissent to the proposal in question, and if they agreed, even for different reason, the fact of their vote would enact the general will although it would not express it. Or arguing from the somewhat debatable assumption that out of the class of differences a process of cancellation would remove contradictions and votes that had least reference to the common good, Rousseau concluded that the dominant good would emerge. This good, which would be what was left as the will of all become integrated, would be in effect the same as the general will."[61]

---

59. See Hacker, *op. cit.,* pp.332-33. This illustration indicates that Rousseau's general will is a strange mixture of utopian idealism and plain commonsense. W.T. Jones well understands that it depicts a distinction between motive and overt result of man. Thus what he appears to maintain "is that every man always as a matter of fact does aim at what he thinks will be good for the whole group of men of which he is a part, and it is because of this alleged characteristics of men's motives that he calls the general will good." *Masters of Political Thought,* Vol. II, p.272.
60. Laski: *Political Thought in England from Locke to Bentham,* p.52.
61. A.M. Osborn: *Rousseau and Burke: A Study of Idea of Liberty in*

According to E.H. Wright, perfect general will implies four conditions:[62]

1. It must count the vote of everyone, or otherwise some are making law for others.
2. It must obligate all members equally; it cannot be general if it favours or disfavours one or more of them.
3. It must deal only with common cause and not with any private interest. As soon as it touches individual interest, it ceases to be general; for though many members act upon the personal concern of very few, or even all the rest on that of only one, the will must lack the voice of the few or one. It can, therefore, treat the public cause alone, and must be general in its purpose as well as in its compostion.
4. But, above all, it must be voiced by voters bent upon the common weal and willing to forget their own concerns; it will be perfect in proportion, or they vote in pure devotion to the public good and in oblivion to their personal interest.[62]

Finally, general will alone constitutes the legitimate basis of political obligation. It is nothing but the expression of common consciousness of the common good in terms of the human will and the rightful and legitimate form of the state authority rests on its pillars. There is no doubt that social compact demands unanimity and so members must participate actively in the making of the general will. But Rousseau realises that though differences of opinion may exist in a society, yet the basis of political obligation will remain in the factor of common good. According to Wright, "For just as an individual with a single motive would act on it without any exercise of will or any notion that he had one, so a state whose members are always unanimous would act as an automation and know what it owed a will at all."[63]

Eighteenth Century Political Thought, pp.169-70.

62. Wright, *op. cit.,* p.76.

63. Wright, *op. cit.,* p.75. According to J.C. Merquior, "The core of Rousseau's theory of political legitimacy is the idea of participatory democracy. The general will is to be always activities by constant individual participation in the politics of sovereignty (though not necessarily at every level of executive decision-making process...Even his notorious dislike of political representation is but the obverse of his love for maximum participation. Direct democracy is only a means to ensure the highest frequency to the exercise of responsible freedom within universal franchise." *Rousseau and Weber: Two Studies in the Theory of Legitimacy,* pp.57-58.

It is obvious that Rousseau considers community not as a mere collection or aggregate of individuals but an organic unity embodying the collective will of all its members. In this way, he frees himself from the imposed and arbitrary state absolutism of Hobbes and the empty and misleading individualism of Locke and thus in the history of modern political thought he corrects the idea of community making it akin to that of Plato and Aristotle. However, Rousseau's theory of general will may be criticised on the following grounds:

1. The idea of general will is too abstract and mystical. A will that is necessarily unidentifiable with the will of one, few, many, all, or even none, is no will at all. It indicates *a priori* theorisation. Besides, in a situation of conflicting opinions, who has the title to ascertain the characteristics of public good in varying and conflicting judgements of the people. It appears that Rousseau regards it as a sort of arithmetical balance to be arrived at by striking out the opposite judgements of this and that member of the political community representing a particular interest. Truly speaking, the process is dynamic and believes that collective opinion is not in the nature of a balance or average; it is more like the output of several factors. In brief, general will is purely an abstract notion based on the abstract theorisation of the author. Prof. L.T. Hobhouse in his *Metaphysical Theory of State* rejects its premises by saying: "When it is will, it is not general; and when it is general, it is not will." Sabine also puts it thus: "The truth is that general will is abstract. How does this absolute right stand in relation to many and possible conflicting judgements about it? Who is entitled to decide what is right?"[64]

2. Rousseau's sanction that man may be compelled to obey the dictates of general will looks like to contradicting his theory of freedom. Force is the negation of freedom and its use cannot be reconciled with the fact of individual liberty in a way as he believes. It may never be in the interest of public welfare if the authority of the state is exercised tyrannically and, curiously enough, in the name of community's good. Rousseau nowhere provides safeguards for the individual. His surrender is complete and so he keeps no weapon in his hands to resist the abused authority of the general will. The freedom of the individual is thus overridden by the freedom

64. Sabine, *op. cit.*, pp.591-92.

of the state and the state then gets a valid title to become even oppressive and tyrannical. Cole aptly questions: "What guarantee is there that the state, in freeing itself, will not enslave its members?"[65]

Rousseau's identification of the majority-decision with the general will, even for all practical purposes, becomes an act of contradiction in the premises of his political philosophy. If general will cannot be identified with the will of one, or few, or many, or even all, unless the quality of general good is present, how can it be identified with the decision of the majority for all practical purposes unless the very requirement of the public good is fulfilled? Bluhm rightly questions: "Why the majority should have this technical wisdom rather than the minority, Rousseau does not attempt to demonstrate, however."[66] An implication of this interpretation of Rousseau leads to the assertion that he opens the way for the validation of the tyranny of the majority over the minority. Thus, a critic says that Rousseau's qualifications 'are neither logical nor convincing'. The true meaning of Rousseau's theory of the general will is that a properly constituted and functioning majority is infallible, that what it decides is beneficial to everyone, and that a force is moral which compels individuals to do those things which are good for them and which they would do voluntarily if they were not influenced by selfish interest."[67]

SOVEREIGNTY : INFALLIBILITY OF PURE AND PERFECT POPULAR GOVERNMENT

Rousseau's conception of popular sovereignty is, indeed, his great contribution to the subject of political philosophy. According to Maxey: "Whatever crimes may be laid at his door, whatever glories may be claimed as his due, it is beyond dispute that in the sphere of political thought, he performed a service of incalculable importance–that was his formulation of plausible and largely realisable theory of popular sovereignty."[68] Josephson observes that Rousseau "gave im-

65. Cole, *op. cit.,* p.xxv.
66. Bluhm : *Theories of the Political System*, p. 403.
67. Judd Harmon, *op. cit.,* p.309. As Roger d. Master says: "Rousseau seeks a rule which is simultaneously legitimate and valid, because without a legitimate reason for obedience human society only reveals the violence of the powerful men and oppression of the weak; and without a solid reason for obedience the laws of justice are vain among men." *The Political Philosophy of Rousseau,* p.303.
68. Maxey: *Political Philosophies,* p.368.

petus, during the eighteenth and nineteenth centuries, to the tendency of men, in greater number than ever before, to act as members of the sovereignty."[69] In MacIver's view, "the secret of his political philosophy is found in the substitution for a sovereign of the sovereign."[70] Sidgwick comments that the characterstic of Rousseau's revolutionary doctrine of popular sovereignty is that it rests on three very simple principles which are (1) that men are by nature free and equal; (2) that the right of government must be based on some compact freely entered into by these equal and independent individuals; (3) that the only compact at once just to the individuals becomes an indivisible part of a body that retains an inalienable right of determining its own internal constitution and legislation–sovereign people."[71]

Rousseau's sovereign is the product of social contract that terminates the state of nature and ushers in a political society in which the people are transformed from noble savages into intelligent citizens. The sovereign is either one person (not an assembly) like Hobbes's, nor the community like Locke's, it is the general will–a will of the people standing for the good of the people. However, like Hobbes's, it is illimitable, infallible, indivisible, permanent, all-embracing and unrepresentable; and like Locke's it is popular as it resides not in one person but in the community as a whole. Hence, in Rousseau's view, sovereignty is identifiable with the general interest of the community and thus it exhibits a compromise between the absolutism of Hobbes and the constiutionalism of Locke.

Like Hobbes, Rousseau regards sovereignty as absolute, unlimited, permanent and indivisible but he does not vest its authority in a single person or an assembly of few persons and clearly differentiates between state and government and state and society. In his own words: "The social compact gives to the body politic absolute power over all its members. We can see from this that the sovereign power is absolute, sacred and inviolable, as it is, does not and cannot exceed the limits of general conventions and that every man may dispose at will of goods and liberty as these conventions leaves him."[72]

69. Josephson. *Jean Jacques Rousseau,* p.356.
70. MacIver: *The Modern State,* p.482.
71. Sidgwick: *The Development of European Polity,* p.390.
72. *Social Contract,* Book II, Ch.IV.

Although, like Locke, Rousseau has deep love for popular government, he does not keep his people like sleeping partners. While Locke by means of a tacit contract delegates political authority to the government and authorises his people to rise in revolt only when the authority is abused, Rousseau makes the community an active sovereign giving to it the title of exercising its sovereign will actually and perpetually. He makes general will the source of law and vests legislative authority in a corporate body–the sovereign people–and makes the government only an executive body under its direction and control. According to Rousseau, "The body politic, therefore, is also a moral being possessed of a will and this general will, which tends always to the preservation and welfare of the whole and every part, and is the source of the law, constitutes for all the members of the state in their relations to one another and to it, the rule of what is just and unjust."[73]

Whatever be the minute differences of Rousseau with the ideas of Hobbes and Locke, it is obvious that Rousseau's sovereign stands between the absolutism of the *Leviathan* and the popularism of the *Civil Government*. Thus, according to G.D.H. Cole, Rousseau, as a matter of fact, "unites the absolute sovereign of Hobbes and popular consent of Locke in the philosophical doctrine of popular sovereignty which has since then been the established form of political theory."[74] In addition to this, Rousseau's sovereign is a moral person standing for the good of the community and, therefore, its authority can never be exercised in a way detrimental to the welfare of the whole people. In the words of Rousseau: "If sovereign is a moral person whose life is in the union of its members, and if the most important of the cares is for the care of its preservation, it must have a universal and compelling force in order to move to disperse each part as may be advantageous to the whole."[75] Unhesitatingly, Rousseau restricts the role of his sovereign to the performance of those functions that promote common good. Again in his own words: "It is impossible for the sovereign body to hurt its members. The sovereign for its part cannot impose upon its members any fetters that are useless to the community."[76]

73. *Ibid.*
74. Cole, *op. cit.*, p.xxiv.
75. *Ibid.*
76. *Ibid.* McDonald well observes: "It has been said that the sovereign is like quarter-back of a football team. When he calls the signals, every team

Finally, Rousseau moves ahead with a thorough-going collectivist attitude clearly discarding the tinge of individualism that has essentially been a companion of, or a complement to, Hobbes and Locke. As nature gives each man an absolute power over all his parts, so the social contract gives an absolute power to the body politic over all its integral parts. In the words of Cole, "The sovereign of Rousseau in the philosophical sense is neither nominal nor legal nor even political of fact and commonsense; it is the consequence of the fundament bond of union, the restatement of the doctrine of social contract, the fore-shadowing of that General Will."[77]

Rousseau's theory of sovereignty bears certain formidable proportions when we pass on from a theoretical to a practical plane. Rousseau's sanction of force to compel the obedience of general will destroys the whole fabric designed by him to safeguard the liberty of the people. Rousseau clearly suggests: "In order then that the social compact may not be an empty formula, it tacitly includes the undertaking that whoever refuses to obey the general will shall be compelled to do so by the whole body. This means nothing less than that he will be forced to be free...This alone legitimises civil undertakings which, without it, would be absurd, tyrannical, and liable to the most fruitful abuses."[78] Moreover, Rousseau himself recognised the practical difficulty of his thesis and so he sanctions that, for all practical purposes, majority opinion should be taken as indicative of the general will. Hence, he not only commits a sort of self-contradiction, rather he looks like authorising the majority to suppress the minority tyrannically and, curiously enough in the name of public good. The result is that the gates of majority tyranny are opened and the minority has to suffer irrespective of the fact that its will may, in a certain case, pertain to the formation of general will. Rousseau's *Social Contract* thus reaches very close to Hobbes's *Leviathan* with the only difference that the head of the masterless man is chopped off and substituted by the head of the multitude. This point has been very strongly stressed by his critics. For ex-

member carries out the play to the best of his ability, even though other players might have called different signals. They know and accept the fact that the whole team has to follow signals or be ruined and someone has to call them. Thus, every signal represents the operation of the general will for that miniature society." *Op. cit.,* p.210.

77. Cole, op cit., pp.xxiii-xxiv.
78. *Social Contract,* Book I, Ch.VII.

ample, Cook remarks: "It is a thorough-going defence of majority tyranny." Barker says: "In effect and in the last resort, Rousseau is a totalitarian. Imagine him a perfect democrat; his perfect democrat is still a multiple autocrat. He leaves no safeguard against the omnipotence of his sovereign."[79]

GOVERNMENT : EXECUTIVE COMMITTEE OF THE SOVEREIGN PEOPLE

While Hobbes justifies absolute kingship and Locke favours constitutional monarchy, Rousseau's theory of government prefers direct democracy. However, he clearly differentiates between state and government and assigns a subordinate place to the latter. To him, government is simply an agent or a useful tool of the sovereign people. Not being a result of the contract, it has only limited authority derived from the sovereign people. Being devoid of any original power, its authority can be recalled by the sovereign people at any time. The subordinate character of the government is attested by the fact that, through periodic assemblies, the people decide upon the desirability of the existing government and its personnel to continue in office. The sovereignty "belongs to the people in a corporate body, while government is merely an agent having delegated powers which can be withdrawn or modified as the will of the people dictates. Government has no vested right whatever such as Locke's theory of contract had left to it, but it has merely the status of a committee."[80]

Rousseau also makes an account of the various forms of government and their excellence. He believes that their forms vary with the circumstances of time and place and the number of persons holding and exercising executive authority. It is *monarchy* when the executive power is concentrated in the hands of a single person; it is *aristocracy* when it is put in the hands of a small number in which the number of private citizens is still more than the number of the magistrates; finally, it is *democracy* when it is vested in the whole people and exercised by them or by their majority. However, in this regard, two things should be noted. Firstly, Rousseau points out that no form of government is absolutely static and one particular form may yield place to another in a more or less degree. Secondly, he believes that certain maxims may be laid down to

79. Barker, *op. cit.*, p.li.
80. Sabine, *op. cit.*, p.592.

recognise the excellence of a particular form of government in the light of particular time, place and other circumstances. Rousseau prefers aristocracy to monarchy, but he views aristocracy as a government of three types–natural, hereditary and elective. However, his real preference is for direct democracy existing in very small states where people may freely exercise their sovereign power.

In this regard, Rousseau also warns the people against insidious tendency of governmental encroachments. He suggests that in order to retard the decline of political community, the people should meet periodically and maintain the sanctity of social compact. It is essential that government should be no party to the convening of these essemblies, rather they should be spontaneous. Moreover, in these meetings the people should repeatedly study the question of the retention of their particular form of government and the character of administration by the government over them. The free verdict of the people will thus provide the best safeguard; the government shall never be in a position to encroach upon the sovereign rights of the people.

Further, Rousseau believes that the government means executive alone. The legislative business is to be in the hands of the sovereign people who cannot part with their law-making power without curtailing their sovereign authority. The essence of legislation is will which is unrepresentable. It is thus perfectly obvious that Rousseau rejects the idea of representative democracy, for in his own words, the deputies of the people "are not and canot be its representatives." His ultimate choice is in favour of a small state consisting of about ten thousand people where direct democratic system may successfully prevail. In fine, in his view, government is merely an 'agent of the people and not the master' as Hobbes had done. C.E. Merriam thus points out: "With Hobbes, the government swallowed up the state and became the sole representative of its personality. With Rousseau, the people became the government and the government was lost in the state."[81]

Rousseau's theory of government may be criticised from two points of view. Firstly, Rousseau's idea of true democracy insisting upon perpetual town-meeting is in a strict sense, utopian.[82] Secondly, it cannot be admitted that government is merely an executive machinery having no concern with the

81. Merriam: *History of the Theory of Sovereignty Since Rousseau,* pp.37-38.
82. See Hacker, *op. cit.,* p.326.

legislative business. Rousseau's conclusion can hardly be given a practical shape if it is acknowledged that the government is established merely for the sake of carrying out the will of the people. The works of legislation and execution are not so separable and thus the government is not like a policeman to carry out the will of the sovereign legislators, rather it has to keep and utilise its share in the work of law-making. Conversely, the legislators' job is not merely to make laws, they are also concerned with their execution. Hence, it is untenable to point out that while the will of the legislature is general, of the executive it is particular, and so the wills of both are different from each other. Rightly speaking, Rousseau's theory of general will "greatly diminished the importance of government."[83]

LEGISLATION : DOMINANCE OF SUPERIOR INTELLIGENCE

From the foregoing account, it becomes clear that, in Rousseau's view, legislation is a vital function of the community brought into existence by the social contract. Nothing but an act of the general will can become law. Law, as such, deals with the good of the community and the conditions of civil society must be regulated only by it. Its concern is the common cause and its formulation is a result of common endeavour. It, therefore, follows that law has two main characteristics, namely, the facts of common welfare and that of common formulation. That is, the making of law necessarily involves the participation of the members of the community for the cause of general good. Wright thus remarks that, in Rousseau's view, law exists only when all the people "act for all the people."[84]

83. Sabine, *op. cit.,* p.593. According to Dr. Asirvatham, "It is obviously difficult to draw a sharp line between what is general and what is particular. Even if we can say that a matter is general, if it concerns the whole community equally, and is particular if it concerns particular class of persons, our difficulty is not solved by any means. In the modern state, practically every piece of legislation is of a particular kind. There is hardly anything which concerns the whole community equally. Therefore, if Rousseau's distinction between general and particular measures is to be followed strictly, we shall be defeating Rousseau's very purpose in making the sovereign supreme. Instead of making government a subordinate authority, we shall, in practice, make it a supreme body. Moreover, the setting up of a government itself is a particular act and the people have no right to it. Rousseau's distinction is capable of application to small city-states only." *Political Theory,* p.115.

84. Wright, *op. cit.,* p.78. He further says: "Law has four characteristics. (i) It deals only with the common cause. (ii) It is made by all alike. (iii) It is

In this regard, two points require special attention. Firstly, Rousseau's concern is not limited to civil and criminal (ordinary) legislation by which governmental authority maintains the administration, rather he is concerned with the basic (constitutional) legislation that is essential for the foundation of the state. Secondly, he insists that as legislation is a technical work, it should be entrusted to the competent persons. The popular assemblies may discuss their details and adopt them, but the work of drafting should be entrusted to the competent persons who know what the people really need. However, the job of the legislators is limited to draft and advise, it depends upon the sovereign people to give an independent verdict upon the suitability of drafted measures. According to Rousseau, "The people who are subject to a law ought to be its authors; the conditions of association ought to be regulated by those who form the association. To find what rules are best suited to political societies would require an intelligence which would understand all human passions without experience in any of them, which, without having any relation to our nature, nevertheless comprehend it completely...it would take gods to provide men with laws. From every point of view, the legislator is an extraordinary man in a state."[85]

Rousseau's legislator looks like Plato's philosopher-king in the framing of laws for the good of the community. However, there is a point of difference in that while Plato makes his all-wise philosopher free from any over-riding authority in the name of his 'omniscience', Rousseau makes the will of his wise legislator subject to the decision of the popular assembly. It, however, does not take away the superior position of the legislator of Rousseau in view of the fact that he describes him (legislator) as having a superior intelligence which can survey all the passions of mankind, though itself exposed to none; an intelligence having no contact with our nature, yet knowing it to the full; an intelligence the well-being of which is independent of our own, yet willing to be concerned with it."[86] The legislator is called upon by Rousseau, as he himself says, "to change, as it were, the very stuff of human nature; to transform each individual who in isolation is a complete but solitary whole, into

---

binding upon all alike. (iv) It is made for the common good. But insofar as we forget our personal interests in the making of the law, we shall secure the kind of law that has been shown to keep us free." ***Ibid.,*** **pp.97-98.**

85. *Social Contract,* Book II, Ch.VII.
86. *Ibid.*

a part of something greater than himself, from which, in a sense, he drives his life and being; to substitute a communal and moral existence for the purely physical and independent life with which all of us are endowed by nature."[87]

Such a study of Rousseau's views on the superior intelligence of the legislator (s) virtually overriding the average wisdom of the general body of the people appears like contradicting his thesis of the infallible will of the community called the general will. The legislator of Rousseau assumes the place of a superman, even a demi-god, who may use the licence of his absolute authority in the name of his omniscient legislative statemanship. As Bluhm says: "Using the individualist raw material supplied by nature he creates new social beings, according to a pattern of his own invention, and gives them standards, their way of life their institution. Since his work is so radically creative, the legislator of Rousseau is enjoined to use the tricks of Machiavelli's prince and claim divine sanction and inspiration for his work, for it is only to divine agency that men are willing to grant such awesome licence to shape their lives...Thus, in place of an objective order of right, discoverable by the teleological reason, Rousseau's hunger for righteousness in a naturalistic world substitutes a human artifact."[88]

Obviously, the addition of legislators' element cuts much of the ground of Rousseau's theory of popular legislation. Certainly, in this respect, he draws inspiration from old Greek practice when distinguished citizens and foreigners were invited by popular bodies on important occasions. Rousseau was invited by Corsica and Poland on two occasions to serve as a constitution-maker. It is certain that a legislator of this type will act like Solon and Lycurgus and in the name of his genius may coerce the wills of ordinary members of popular assemblies. In political community based on the theory of general will, there is neither reason nor need to characterise the legislator as a 'holy' or 'super' man merely because of his genius or competence, According to W.T. Jones, "Here again, as so often in Rousseau, we have a curious mixture of penetrating insight and fabulous non-sense...It seems that Rousseau is here himself guilty of a curious naivete: he appears to be taking literally and at their face value his own remarks on divine inspiration and sanction, though in the same breath, he himself tells us

87. *Ibid.*
88. Bluhm, *op. cit.*, p.407.

that these expressions have no real validity and are merely designed to appeal to the simplicity of the plain man...A legislator is not a demi-god, descending from Sinai with a ready-made code of laws; being as much a product of his social milieu as are the men and women whom he serves, he is limited in every way by the level of political maturity which they happen to have reached."[89]

FREEDOM : MIXTURE OF POLITICAL ROMANTICISM AND ETHICAL OBLIGATION

Rousseau's deep love for individual liberty becomes obvious from the opening sentence of his work *Social Contract*: "Man is born free, but he is everywhere in chains." In its original sense, it means that man ought to be free, independent and solitary (as this is the best life for him), but that the conventions and customs of society, the various regulations and restrictions which political and economic institutions involve, enslave him and cause his fall from his original and blessed state of freedom.[90] But the subsequent and final meaning of this phrase, according to Rousseau, means that man ought to be free not in the sense of being able to do just that whatever he wants but in the sense of being an element in the general will of whose common life he is an integral part. At the same time, it asserts that man is seldom actually free, because modern states are actually founded on force that is a negation of the real will of the people.

Thus freedom, in Rousseau's sense, is no more a licence and no longer the unrestricted conduct of a separate and independent individual. The freedom of the individual requires a kind of participation in a larger life which all the various physical organs share when they are functioning harmoniously in a healthy body. Obviously, it is not all the physical freedom to do whatever we can as Hobbes asserted, it is not even the moral autonomy of the individual to judge and decide for himself which Locke advocated. Contradistinguished from the natural freedom of Hobbes and moral freedom of Locke, Rousseau substitutes the conception of a freedom not only compatible with, but actually implying, a certain kind of restraint. In his view,

89. Jones, *op. cit.,* pp.593.
90. W.T. Jones admirably observes that such an emphasis "expresses an attitude of mind which we might call romantic primitivism–a nostalgia for a life of genuineness and simplicity, for that Golden Age of which the complexity of modern life has separated us." *Op. cit.,* p.258.

man is really free when, and if, his behaviour conforms to some pattern or model which he has set for himself irrespective of the thing that this conformity involves considerable restraint of impulses and desires tending to lead him in opposite directions.[91]

Rousseau, therefore, succeeds in establishing a happy reconciliation between the liberty of the people and the authority of the state. The social compact terminates the state of nature and converts man from a stupid and limited animal into an intelligent citizen. As a result, the institution of civil society is founded on the general will with which individual's particular will is naturally indentified, because he is nothing else than an integral part of the community. The people are basically dependent upon each other; since they require the society of their fellows for their perfect development. The state is thus a moral entity to exercise force in a moral way and its existence represents the subordination of respective individual wills to the higher and infallible will of the community. In Rousseau's own words; "Force is physical power; I do not see that its effects can ever be moral. To yield to force is an act of necessity, not of will. It is nothing more than an act of prudence."[92]

Remarkable is the fact that Rousseau's individual remains free in spite of the fact that he surrenders his all rights to the community. The reason is that surrender is not in favour of an alien authority but of a corporate body of which he himself is an integral part. Hence the restrictions imposed on his liberty are self-imposed. The freedom of the individual is consonant with the good of the general body. It is no longer the unrestrained conduct of an isolated and independent individual; it is the rational freedom of an individual who leads a common

---

91. It is quite obvious that Rousseau's conception of freedom is quite different from that of Hobbes, Locke and John Stuart Mill; it is more akin to that of Kant, Hegel and Green. Following the tradition of Rousseau, Kant said, "A free will and a will subject to laws are one and the same." T.K. Abbot: *Kant's Theory of Ethics,* pp.65-66.

92. *Social Contract,* Book I, Ch. II. Joad thus explains the above point: "In representing, as it does, the wills of all its citizens who have contracted to live together in society, it causes to come into existence a new entity over and above the sum of the individual wills, which is the general will and a new personality over and above the sum of the individual personalities, which is the personality of the state that the will and personality of each individual are made to transcend themselves." *Modern Political Theory,* p.12.

life in organic relationship with his fellow-citizens and whose welfare is integrally connected with the welfare of the whole community. The social compact thus successfully establishes a new kind of society in which individual loses his precarious freedom "to do as he liked and gains the assured freedom to do what *all consider right*."[93]

As Rousseau's theory of freedom has an ethical connection, he is taken as the precursor of Immanuel Kant. This aspect of Rousseau's theory of freedom leaves a handle in the hands of his critics either to doubt his real meaning or to hit at some point of inconsistency in his political philosophy. For instance, Cassirer says: "Rousseau's ethics is not an ethics of feeling, but the most categorical form of a pure ethics of obligation that was established before Kant."[94] Irving Babbit holds that Rousseau's general readiness to subordinate his ethical self to his sensibility is indubitable."[95] According to Hudson, Rousseau "talked unceasingly of freedom; but freedom for him meant not that liberty which is to be achieved only through careful obedience to the eternal laws of life, but simply absence of obligation and responsibility. He had no will-power and no moral fibre.[96] However, the observation of McDonald is very convincing that Rousseau's ethical position "was, to be sure, relativistic. He appealed to no fixed metaphysical standard; but this look of absolutes merely strengthened the logic of his call for community, rather than the logic of anarchy. For without a metaphysical base from which to challenge the norms of a given society Rousseau's individual found his salvation in community or nowhere."[97]

STATE : AN IDEAL POLITICAL COMMUNITY AS A MODERN VERSION OF ANCIENT GREEK POLIS

Rousseau's stern reaction agaist excessive individualism of the social contractualists like Hobbes and Locke is contained in his theory of state that places before us the picture of an ideal political community looking like a modern version of the ancient Greek polis as conceived by Plato and Aristotle. The social contract of Rousseau, that establishes civil society, is like a

93. Wright, *op. cit.*, p.28.
94. Cassirer: *The Question of Jean Jacques Rousseau*, p.96
95. Babbit: *Rousseau and Romanticism*, p.130.
96. William Henry Hudson: *Rousseau and Naturalism in Life and Thought*, p.111.
97. McDonald, *op. cit.*, p.206.

solemn act of association that produces a moral and collective body involving the total alienation of each associate and all his rights to the whole of the community. What is really formed by means of this pious association "is a 'public person' which took formerly the name of the city and now takes that of the 'republic' or 'body politic'. It is called by its members 'state' when it is passive, 'Sovereign' when in activity."[98] The salient features of Rousseau's state may be enumerated as under:

First, the real purpose of Rousseau is not at all to involve himself into the issues of controversy between the King and Parliament as had been the case with Hobbes and Locke, rather it is to find out a form of association in which each, while uniting himself with all, renders obedience to his own will and remains as free as before. In other words, Rousseau wants to make his man free from chains that are repugnant to the model of his free-born existence. While the *First* and *Second Discourses* highlight the 'faults' of actual societies, the *Social Contract* expresses his concern with the possibility of a natural society. Thus, the fundamental aim of Rousseau "is to justify the change from 'nature to society', although it has left men in chains. He is in search of a true society, which leaves men as free as before."[99]

Second, the state of Rousseau is based on the pure and infalible public spirit what he calls the general will. The social contract signifies the generation of a true public spirit which means the will of all citizens when they "are willing not their own private interest but the general good; it is the voice of all for the good of all."[100] The doctrine of the general will is the key-idea of the *Social Contract* that signifies Rousseau's eternal contribution to the school of modern idealists. As Wright says: "A society of free consent, and not of force; a union of each with all on equal terms or common good; a sovereignty vested in all and voiced by the general will for the maintenance of liberty in law: this is the heart of the *Social Contract.* All else, whether repeated or omitted here, is contingent, variable, precautionary; or since it is derived in reason from the very nature of our species, for the natural society."[101]

98. *Ibid.*, p.207.
99. Cole, *op. cit.*, p.xv.
100. Wayper, *op. cit.*, p.144.
101. Wright, *op. cit.*, p.90.

Third, the general will is the sovereign authority in the political system of Rousseau. As such, sovereignty is absolute, inalienable, unlimited, permanent and infillable. This will cannot be represented in the form of delegation of power by the people. It is unrepresentable. Thus, Rousseau rejects the case of parliamentary democracy. Moreover, general will is national and, in that sense, it places all authority in the hands of the state at the total expense of the place of groups and associations. The verdict of the community, in the words of Rousseau, can never go against the real good of the people and, for this sake, it becomes the true religion of the state. As Wayper says: "So jealous a God is the general will that Rousseau thinks it should even substitute for the old religions of the world a new civic religion which all whom would remain members of the state must accept, deviation from which, once accepted, should be an offence punishable with death."[102]

Fourth, if the general will is always right, it implies that 'man can be forced to be free'. Simply stated, this well-known phrase of Rousseau implies that a correct state has every right to correct its incorrect member. Not the state but the individual is liable to err and, for that very reason, he should always remain willing to accept the verdict of the state after taking it as an appropriate measure adopted by his rulers to rectify his erratic behaviour. If man wants to lead a life of freedom, it is possible for him by living in the state alone and thus what the state does to correct the erratic life of its citizen, the latter is bound to accept it willingly as something that his ideal nature would take as being in consonance with the pattern of his ideal social life. In this way, Rousseau not only rejects Hobbes's claim that men must choose between being free and being ruled, he positively asserts that it "is only through living in a civil society that men can experience their fullest freedom."[103]

Fifth, the political theory of Rousseau makes a clear difference between the government and the sovereign people. The general will is the will of the people who are sovereign and who by means of discussions in their public assemblies lay down laws for the administration of the state. Different from this, government means executive agency varying according to the particular circumstances and need of the people. The government is, therefore, a servant or agent of the people and, for that

102. Wayper, *op. cit.,* p.145.
103. Maurice Cranston: 'Introduction' to *Social Contract,* p.28.

reason, it is a matter of secondary importance. Such a line of Rousseau's approach makes him think in terms of the suitability of any government–hether democratic, or aristocratic, or monarchical–provided the sovereignty lies with the general will. However, he prefers the case of pure democracy where people make use of their power themselves and thereby present a valid proof of the fact that they are sovereign despite being the members of a political community. What makes the meaning of Rousseau inconsistent at this stage is his affirmation that, for all practical purposes, the will of the majority should be taken as the manifestation of the general will in a modern nation-state having the system of indirect democracy as the only best possible form of government. Thus, majority gets the title of ruling with absolute authority. It leads to the controversial issue that both the ideal of popular sovereignty and the ideal of totalitarian uniformity "have been found in the conception of the general will; and no wonder that hard-headed analysts have for generations been suspicious of its vagaries."[104]

Sixth, Rousseau's state accords recognition to the rule of law. As he says: "It is to law alone that men owe justice and liberty; it is this slautary organ of the will of all that makes obligatory the natural equality between men; it is this heavenly voice that dictates to each citizen the precepts of public reason, and teaches him to act in accordance with the maxims of his own judgement, and not to be in contradiction to himself." In the system of Rousseau the work of making laws is confined to the people who are sovereign. However, he attaches importance to the role of a legislator who is a competent person to draft bills before the assembly of the sovereign people adopts them for the administration of the state. The place of the legislator in the system of Rousseau paves the way for another point of controversy and a critic may find material here for making an allegation that Rousseau makes the will of the 'lay' assembly subject to the 'superior' intelligence of the legislator. A correct interpretation of Rousseau's political theory, in this direction, implies that the legislator "must not be regarded either as a sovereign or as a magistrate. He is to be seen merely as the proposer of the law, not compelling but persuading the people to accept them, with God up his sleeve as the ace which will win him the game."[105]

104. McDonald, *op. cit.,* p.211.
105. Wayper, *op. cit.,* p.148.

Last, Rousseau's state is a small community of about ten thousand people who may assemble for the sake of having public discussion of the policy to be followed and the laws to be administered by the government. The people of such a small state are also very conservative who spend little time for making few laws. This is manifest from his pregnant remark: "The greatness of nations, the extent of states; the first and principal source of the misfortunes of the human race." The social protest of Rousseau 'is directed along by the flavour of the riches, the seductions of curiosities and the charm of new thing'. What makes the general will is not the number of citizens concerned but the common interest by which they are united. It is the admirable identity of interests and justices which gives to the common deliberations of the people a complexion of equity. It is all owing to the influence of his Genevan ancestry and his early life in the small city of Switzerland that he appreciates the idea that community of interest "presupposes certain social conditions. The society must be quite small, its members must share a roughly equal social and economic status, and it must be simple in its way of life and simple in its economic organisation."[106]

In fine, Rousseau's state presents a new version of the idealisation of a small state like that of Plato's *Republic* and Aristotle's *Politics* with the underlying point of difference that his real preference is neither for an all-wise philosopher-king nor for the rule of the middle class but for the rule of an assembly of sovereign people who lay down their policy or adopt legislation in accordance with the principle of general welfare. The most abiding influence on Rousseau is that of Plato whose approach to the study of politics is accepted by him to the extent that he is credited with the movement of the revival of Greek idealism. One of Rousseau's great critics like Burke wrongly calls him 'an insane Socrates', while Sabine rightly regards him as the 'rediscoverer of the community.'[107]

CONFLICTING INTERPRETATIONS : ROUSSEAU AS INDIVIDUALIST OR COLLECTIVIST, LIBERAL OR TOTALITARIAN

The most puzzling aspect of Rousseau's political philosophy finds place in the store-house of conflicting interpretations and re-interpretations that bear testimony to the

106. Bluhm, *op. cit.,* p.401.
107. See Sabine, *op. cit.,* Ch.XXVIII.

fact that it "is a grab bag containing something to support almost any theory of the community. The 'rightists' will seize upon Rousseau's organicism to uphold the contention that the individual must be subordinated to the state. He may see in the legislator, with his knowledge, his foresight, and his leadership abilities, an ancestor image of a 'Fuehrer'; Rousseau's thoughts concerning a Censorship and a 'civil religion', he may view as harbingers of a society in which cohesion and discipline are the principal values. And Rousseau's dictum that a man may be 'forced to be free' found sinister fulfilment in the fascist ideology of the twentieth century."[108] The essence of all conflicting interpretations is that while some have taken Rousseau as an individualist, even an extreme individualist having incidental connection with the ideals of a narchism, others have studied him as a philosopher of a collectivist and a totalitarian school.

Apart from certain points of minor contradictions in the political philosophy of Rousseau emanating from his assumptions, as contained in one work compared with another, the most crucial subject of debate is his doctrine of the general will which is taken even by his ardent critics as his best contribution to political theory. The whole idea of generl will postulates an organic theory of state that inevitably leads to a collectivist and even socialist conclusion. As one important writer visualises that it "is, indeed, the source and origin of both the Hegelian system of politics, which culminated in the lectures of Triestchke, the ravings of Bernhardi, and the Great War; and of the Marxian system of economics, which had issued in the dictatorship of the proletariat and Bolshevik communism."[109] Confining the scope of his study to the greatest work of Rousseau, Wright feels that it "is hard to say whether the *Social Contract* has been oftener indicted for an individualism that will run to anarchy or for an absolutism that will bring the final tyranny."[110]

In order to discover truth out of the conflicting statements, let us first examine the case of Rousseau's being a liberal-individualist. It is said that Rousseau's political theory starts

108. M. Judd Harmon, *op. cit.,* p.313. For a very interesting study of this puzzling aspect of Rousseau's political theory see John Chapman: *Rousseau-Totlitarian or Liberal,* New York, 1955. Merquior calls Rousseau "a mind rent by violent contradictions." *Rousseau and Weber,* p.39.

109. Hearnshaw, *op. cit.,* p.192.

110. Wright, *op. cit.,* p.102.

with the individual and ends with the individual as the keynote of his entire political philosophy is contained in the opening sentence of his *Social Contract:* 'Man is born free, he is everywhere in chains'. The individual of Rousseau accepts the terms of the ad hoc contract that sets up the civil society on the basis of inequality just for the sake of saving himself from the horrors of an unregulated life; he accepts the terms of the social contract not merely to do away with the 'faults' of the civil society but to enjoy real freedom in a political community. Thus, the individual of Rousseau has freedom only in the state which he never had in the pre-political stage. Even after the creation of the sovereign authority he remains an essential part of the political power in the hope and with the conviction that the all-powerful community can never harm his interests. "Each man gives his all to the society on terms equal for all men; and if the terms are truly equal, no man can wish to make them tyrannical, for he will be as much afflicted by them as will any one."[111]

Moreover, Rousseau, as Cole understands him, follows the tradition of Locke and Hooker in taking 'socialities' as an alternative phrase for a social contract. His social contract is not at all concerned with an ingenious attempt to justify the stand of either faction of the great conflict going on between the King and the Parliament, it should be regarded as the formal institutionalisation of the bond of 'social ties.'[112] Is is owing to such an understanding of Rousseau that Rene Hubert calls him 'at every inch an individualist'. Supporting the thesis of Rousseau's being an ardent champion of the cause of the individual, Cassirer holds that he "is a true son of enlightenment even when he attacks it and triumphs over it."[113] Likewise, Alfred Cobban says that, despite his nationalist framework, the central thesis of Rousseau remains in a general sense utilitarian and individualistic.[114]

111. Wright, *op. cit.,* p.73. "Rousseau's principle of general will is, therefore, intended to introduce certain elements of rationality into the wills of all citizens. Whether one's purely private interests, in so far as the individual states his self-interest in the form of a general law that applies equally to all members of the society, he cannot justly will certain things, *e.g.,* that others run the risk of death in his defence without reciprocity, or that he may murder others without fear of punishment or retaliation." Masters, *op. cit.,* pp. 321-22.
112. See Cole, *op. cit.,* p.xvi.
113. E. Cassirer: *The Philosophy of Enlightenment,* p.273.
114. Cobban: *Rousseau and the Modern State,* p.71.

While one may not dismiss the contention of Rousseau's being a thinker of liberalism or of the individualist school, he may hardly agree with the view of his reaching the height of anarchism after reading his *First Discourse* wherein he hits at the corrupting influence of modern society and his *Second Discourse* wherein he asserts that civil society is based on an ad hoc arrangement to legitimise the inequality of possessions. The line of anarchist thought is further traceable in Rousseau's political theory in his obsession with the liberty of the individual. Supporting this point of interpretation, Henri See says that the social contract of Rousseau is a means to guaranteeing citizens the maximum amount of liberty. Similarly, Faguet argues that in his early writings Rousseau begins with the premises of anarchism and provide them with anarchist substance and, much to his own surprise, arrives at anarchist conclusions. It may, however, be pointed out that to take Rousseau as a thinker touching the heights of anarchism is altogether unconvincing in view of the fact that he never says anything about the destruction of the state and the substitution of the civil society with a new and future ideal community having no state and no classes that are denounced by the Anarchists as the instruments of coercion and violence. Certainly, it "is a narrow view of Rousseau to conclude that he was an anarchist: he was, in fact, far from it."[115]

The charge that Rousseau is a collectivist and a totalitarian is sustained by his theory of social contract where we find the surrender of all authority by all in favour of all leading to the creation of the general will–an omnipotent and infallible authority that can even force a man to be free. By laying it down that the individual surrenders his all powers in favour of the state, Rousseau reaches very close to the world of Leviathan with its head chopped off. The result is that the autonomous individual thus "disappears altogether and is absorbed wholly in the category of citizen. Rousseau embraces a totalitarian conception of the political order, reminiscent of classical theory. Society is conceived as a single monolithic unity, and the men who form it are required to think of themselves only as parts of the monolith and to divest themselves of all allegiance to their private concerns as individuals and as members of lesser societies within the great society. The only

115. See Z.M. Quraishi: "The Rousseau Controversy" in *Political Science Review,* Jaipur, Vol. 5, No. 2., Oct. 1966, p.268.

legitimate order is the public order, and its value is absolute, because it is the instrument of human perfection and happiness. To give any freedom to the private itself is to invite it to become radically anti-social and vicious, destructive of one's own happiness and that of all with whom one comes in contact. Virtue is identified in all parts with good citizenship, with devotion to collectivity."[116]

It is due to this way of interpreting the meaning of Rousseau that some critics have, in their own ways, described him as the father or advocate of a collectivist, even a totalitarian, school. For instance, Vaughan presents his classical point of view by adding that Rousseau's political philosophy gives an unmistakable impressioin of collectivism. With particular reference to the *Social Contract* of Rousseau, he goes on to say that it "is the porch of collectivism as absolute as the mind of man has ever conceived."[117] Duguit proclaims Rousseau as the father of Jacobin dictatorship, the Caesarian depotism and the inspirer of absolutist doctrine of Kant and Hegel.[118] Talmon uses equally harsh language to say that Rousseau's general will was the 'driving force behind the rise of totalitarian democracy.'[119] The acme of of such an approach is manifest in the view of Russell who denounces Rousseau as the "ideological godfather of Hitler."[120]

It may be pointed out that the critics have a rather exaggerated view in presenting to us the meaning of the political philosophy of Rousseau touching the height of totalitarianism. They have either misunderstood his real meaning or sought to interpret the philosophy of idealism in terms of realism of a fascist state. True that Rousseau's political theory is amenable to diverse interpretations, it is equally true that the thread of liberalism runs throughout the text of his writings. Cobban's view is thus admirable: "Rousseau, the individualist, Rousseau the prohet of state absolutism, neither of which seems a satisfactory interpretation of his whole thought. It may be that no synthesis of his ideas is possible, that they have to be put into one or the other of the two contradictory groups, but on the other hand the confusion may have arisen partly from reading

116. Bluhm, *op. cit.*, p.405.
117. Vaughan: *The Political Writings of Rousseau*, p.39.
118. Cited in Cobban, *op. cit.*, p.28.
119. J.L. Talmon: *The Origins of Totalitarian Democracy*, p.6.
120. Bertrand Russell: *A History of Western Philosophy*, p.685.

back into Rousseau his suppoosed historical influence, partly from an attempt to force his thought into theoretical categories that he never had in mind when he wrote."[121] What is more striking is Cobban's observation that a hatred of despotic government "runs like a bright thread through the complicated tapestry of his writings and outlines the pattern of his thought."[122]

The real meaning of Rousseau should, therefore, be understood not in his being an advocate of the philosophy of collectivism but in studying him as an idealist thinker justifying the absolute character of state–a state of the supermen, for the supermen, and by the super-men. Undoubtedly, Rousseau is a democrat, but his democracy is an ideal possible only for ideally reasonable men who are guided by their real wills and who are also prepared to be forced to be free if the state corrects their erratic behaviour for the sake of their essential freedom. What a fine interpretation is this: "Rousseau does not say that men can be forced to be free in the sense that the whole community may be forced to be free; he says that a man may be forced to be free, and he is thinking here of the occasional individual who as a result of being enslaved by his passions disobeys the voice of the law, or of the general will within him. The general will is something inside each man as well as in society as a whole, so that the man who is coerced by the community for a breach of law, is, in Rouseau's view of things, being brought back to an awareness of his own true will. Thus, in penalising a law-breaker, society is literally correcting him, teaching him a lesson for which when he comes to his senses, the offender should be grateful. Legal penalties are a device for helping the individual in his own struggle against his own passions, as well as a device for protecting society against the anti-social depradations of law-breakers."[123]

In fine, Rousseau is an idealist like Plato who idealises his community in a way that the sovereignty of the state remains in the hands of the architects of true freedom who are pure creatures of God with their unshirkable duty of purifying the occasional individual going against the law of an ideal community's life. Rousseau cannot be classed as a particular thinker of a particular school. However, a synthesised study of

121. Cobban, *op. cit.,* p.31.
122. *Ibid.,* p.33.
123. Maurice Cranston, *op. cit.,* p.34.

his whole political philosophy is well presented in these words: "Rousseau is unique. He belongs to no particular school of thought, though he is indebted to all of them; and yet none of the later streams of thought has escaped his influence. He neither propounds a theory of rights of individual, nor advances a justification of absolute political authority which suffocates human freedom. Nor is he an anarchist, or a socialist. He is simply a democrat and that also in an esoteric sense. He believes in the divine right of the 'people' and distinguishes it, in a subtle way, from natural rights of the individual. He pleads for the recognition of the right of the people to living in community."[124] The real significance of Rousseau's political theory is condensed in these colourful words that his general will "is a rationalisation of paradise regained."[125]

CRITICAL ESTIMATE : ROUSSEAU AS REPLACER OF THE AGE OF REASON WITH THE AGE OF ROMANTICISM

Rousseau occupies a very important place in the history of modern Western political thought. His theories of general will and sovereignty represented a remarkable reconciliation of liberty and authority and a peculiar compromise between the views of Hobbes and Locke. He created a sharp distinction between state and government and also between sovereign law and governmental decrees. His sovereign law is the ancestor of the modern fundamental or constitutionl law. He emphasised that people are the ultimate source of all political authority; the government is merely an agent of the sovereign people; common welfare is the criterion of political existence; social life has got an organic character; liberty and authority are not anti-thetical to each other, and, as Green later said, 'will not force is the basis of state.'

Rousseau, therefore, exercised tremendous influence on both the political thought and action of his contemporaries and successors. His ideas were intensely popular in the heated and surcharged atmosphere of French revolution that broke out about a decade after his death. In America, the Jeffersonian freedom movement drew inspiration frm Rousseau. The idealists like Kant and Hegel in Germany and Green and Bosanquet in England developed their theories on Rousseau's conceptions of freedom and general will. Even the utilitarians like Bentham and Anarchists like Godwin were influenced by

124. Quraishi, *op. cit.,* p.273.
125. Hearnshaw, *op. cit.,* pp.189-90.

his theories of social good and denunciation of private property system. Besides, Rousseau's cult of back to the nature, hatred of arts and science, reaction against reason and intelligence, passionate belief in the essential goodness of men and enshrinment of sentiment at the cost of reason were so effective that they replaced the Age of Reason with the Age of Romanticism. It is thus said that Rousseau "represents the passage from a traditional theory rooted in the Middle Ages to the modern philosophy of the state."[126]

Commentators have, therefore, admired Rousseau in different ways. Doyle says: "Rousseau offered to Europe at a moment of deep perplexity and discontent a justification to break from the old worn out system, and an ideal to be fought for after the work of demolition was over."[127] Osborn remarks that Rousseau "gave a unifying principle which not only could give coherence to the body politic in all its aspects but could also give meaning and directive to the whole life of the State."[128] Lord points out that it is Rousseau who "told that the state, indeed, has no life apart from the lives of its members; but it has, or may have, a longer, broader, and fuller life than that of any individual or any generation of its citizens."[129] Laski comments that he "believed with passion in progress." Besides, while Constant regards him as the "most terrible ally of despotism in all its forms," Duguit treats him as "the father of Jacobin despotism, Caesarian dictatorship, and the inspirer of the absolutist doctrines of Kant and Hegel." Similarly, Vaughan calls him "a stern asserter of the state on the one hand and a fiery champion of the individual on the other." The truth is that Rousseau cannot be ranked as a particular type of political philosopher and if it is easy to shoot at him, it is equally difficult to bring him down. Wayper rightly says: "To the idealist philosopher the idealist in Rousseau is of supreme importance, to the individualist thinker, the individualist in him alone matters."[130] Gray distinguishes Rousseau and Marx for social condemnation.[131] It "is no incident that the first sentence of *Social Contract* should be the final exhortation of the *Communist Manifesto.*"[132]

126. Cole, *op. cit.*, p.vii.
127. Doyle: *A History of Political Thought*, p.218.
128. Osborn, *op. cit.*, p.164.
129. Lord: *Principles of Politics*, p.139.
130. Wayper, *op. cit.*, p.138.
131. Alexander Gray: *The Socialist Tradition*, p.85.
132. Laski: 'Portrait of Jean-Jacques Rousseau' in *Essay on Obedience*, p.181.

19

MONTESQUIEU

Montesquieu was searching for means to limit the crown, to make a constitution, to build equals through which, but not over which, power should stream to create intermediary bodies, to check and balance probable despotism and yet he did not wish to fly to the extreme of democracy.

— **Herman Finer**[1]

In the history of French political thought the place of Montesquieu is second to that of Rousseau. Born in 1675 and died in 1965, his life was singularly uneventful and lacking in adventure and romance. He was the son of a distinguished French lawyer. His Christian name was Charles Louis Secondat, but after he gained the property of his uncle, he assumed the title of Baron de Montesquieu. In 1728 he made a tour of several important European countries and stayed in England for nearly two years. It is in England where he gained a very fine impression about British thinkers like Locke who powerfully defined individual liberty and political institutions, particularly those which maintained freedom and orderliness. On his return from England, he settled down at Law Brede and wrote strongly on the criticism directed against the church, absolute monarchy and other institutions harmful to the liberties of the

1. Finer : *The Theory and Practice of Modern Governments*, p. 98.

people. As a result, he became very popular among the fellow-countrymen who were critical of the autocratic regime. But the beneficiaries of the autocratic Louis regime looked at his writings with alarm for his trenchant wit and wisdom to perceive and criticise the existing evils. He also revealed his feelings when he became the President of the Parliament of Bordeaux, the most important of Parliaments in France except that of Paris. It is owing to this reason that Montesquieu is ranked among those great thinkers of the mid-eighteenth century who fomented the atmosphere of revolution in their country.

WORKS : MIXTURE OF POLITICS AND SOCIOLOGY

The general character of the political philosophy of Montesquieu holds a combined influence of Roman history and contemporary British institution. His political ideas find expression in his several writings. In 1721, he published his *Persian Letters* under fake authorship. These letters, it is supposed, were written by two Persian travellers to their friends indicating their impression of French social, economic and political life. This work soon became very popular because it attacked the autocratic hold of the church and the state. In 1734 he published his more famous work entitled *Reflections on the Causes of the Greatness and Decline of the Romans* which revealed his belief in the use of historical method. But his immortal work *The Spirit of the Laws* was published in 1748 wherein he propounded his well-known doctrines of liberty and separation of powers.[2]

It is generally commented that the arrangement of the *Spirit of the Laws* "is difficult to perceive, if a systematic arrangement can be said to exist at all."[3] Of the various arrange-

2. Catlin says that Montesquieu "derives his political theory as distinct from his large museum of political illustrations from the writings of Locke and the theories of Roman constitution." It is also said that Montesquieu's political philosophy was effected by the spirit of skepticism and the spirit of rational liberty which characterised French thought in his days and which represented a reaction against the absolutism and general conditions prevailing in the days of Louis XIV. Yet it is also true that although he appeared as a great lover of individual liberty, he was not an extreme democrat. He even preferred monarchy if it was of a constitutional type and did not hesitate in accepting it for France provided it was such as it was before it " was changed into despotism by the evil genius of Richlieu and Louvois". See A.J. Grant : "Montesquieu" in Hearnshaw (ed.) : *The Social and Political Ideas of French Thinkers of the Age of Reason*, p. 125.
3. See Franz Neumann's 'Introduction' to his edited work *The Spirit of the*

ments suggested, we may depend upon one proposed by G. Lanson and followed by Neumann[4] that groups XXXI chapters into 5 parts in this manner: part I of Books from I to XIII deals with the *government as such, its essential and general functions.* Under this head we have chapters dealing with the types of government, their nature and structural principles, maintenance of these principles and their corruption. There is the discussion on the functions of the government and the role of the army as the protective force of the state. Subjects relating to war, protection of the individual and the meaning of political liberty, contributions of the English political system, courts, supplies, finances and taxes are discussed. The second part of Books from XIV to XIX is concerned with *concept of space and climate and their influence on government.* Under this head we have the discussion of various interesting subjects like slavery, relationship between the two sexes, political servitude and despotism, modifications of climatic influences, oil an its cultivation, moral and customs of the people. The third part of Books from XX to XXV is concerned with *economics and religion.* Here we find Montesquieu's views on the general theory of the inter-relation between commerce, morals, poverty and the types of the government, commerce, money, population and religion. The fourth part of books from XXVII to XXVIII and then from XXX to XXXI deals with Montesquieu's *fragmentary contributions* to the role of time on political institution, the Roman law of succession, the origin and evolution of French civil laws, the conflict between Roman and Germanic law and the origin of French feudal institutions. Finally, the part of Books XXVI and XXIX deals with the *theory of law and legislative practice.* It deals with his views on positive, natural, canon and civil laws and also on the manner of composing laws. Though this arrangement seems to be more acceptable, Neumann makes it very clear that it "solves no problem of interpretation but may help a student to overcome the initial bewilderment which is the inevitable fate of every reader of the *Spirit of the Laws.*"[5]

While Montesquieu's *Persian Letters* became a source of 'literary sensation', his *Spirit of the Laws* is considered as a work that "exerted a profound influence on historical method

---

Laws, pp. xxx-xxxi.

4. *Ibid.*
5. *Ibid.*

and the study of sociological basis of forms of government."[6] The critics of Montesquieu have differently looked at it as a work of 'apparently formless design' with its 'apparent determinism'. Its 'conservative implications' were detested by the *philosophers*[7] and a great contemporary of Montesquieu like Voltaire made it a point of his literary attack to hit at the 'historical inaccuracies' of this 'enigmatic figure of political theory'. In our times, a critic of political theory may observe that Montesquieu poured years of work into *Spirit of the Laws* "that apparently incoherent and alternately simplistic and obscure masterpiece of profound and benevolent guile."[8] Distinguished from this is the observation that this work "is serious; and it is constructive in its attempt to discover all the rules that govern social action, especially to find out how the cause of liberty may be advanced through the establishment of particular constitutional condition."[9]

The salient contribution of Montesquieu's *Spirit of the Laws* relates to the disciplines of politics and sociology. Its most essential principle is the doctrine of liberty contained within his theory of the separation of powers. Thus, Neumann says that though this "may not be a great book on the level of the works of Plato, Aristotle, Marsilius, Hobbes, Rousseau and Hegel, but it is an extra-ordinarily stimulating book whose riches have remained neglected because of the attention given to one of the most doubtful of his discoveries: the separation of powers as the instrument of securing political liberty."[10] While lauding the real significance of his work, Jones comments that it "is a monument to, if it is not an example of, sound scholarship. Montesquieu realised that political inquiry should have an empirical basis, and he combined his realisation with the development of a technique of investigation suited specifically to his subject, and not borrowed from theology, logic or mathematics. Thus, Montesquieu is not so important for the permanent value of his contributions to political theorising as he is for his impact on the development of methodology in political studies."[11]

6. McDonald : *Western Political Theory* : *The Modern Age*, p. 175.
7. See Kingsley Martin: *The Rise of French Liberal Thought*, pp.137-62.
8. David Lowenthal : "Book, I of Montesquieu's *Spirit of the Laws*" in *American Political Science Review*, Vol. 53 of 1959, p. 487.
9. M. Judd Harmon : *Political Thought from Plato to the Present*, p. 271.
10. Neumann, *op. cit.*, p. xxix.
11. W.T. Jones : *Masters of Political Thought*, Vol. II, p. 218.

METHOD : PRE-EMPTIVE HISTORICISM

The method employed by Montesquieu is not deductive as we find in the cases of Plato, Hobbes, Locke and Rousseau; rather it is inductive as followed by Aristotle, Machiavelli, Bodin and Vico. Hence, instead of starting from a self-evident truth and then coming to the proper conclusion, Montesquieu adopts an empirical approach and frames his impressions after a comparative study of collected facts. He does not believe in the possibility of constructing an ideal scheme of government suitable to all people of all times and places, rather concludes that the most perfect government is that which guides them in a manner most conducive to their natural inclinations and tendencies.

Like his predecessors as well as contemporaries, Montesquieu also believes in the natural source of fundamental principles of law and justice, but his study of and deductions from nature and consequently his conceptions of law and justice depend upon actual observation as attested by historical evidence and not on abstract notions of nature, reason and justice. Hence, he expresses his full awareness of the fact that human customs, laws and institutions are of a very highly complex nature and subject to great variations. It is thus essential that before prescribing a particular form of government or institution as ideally possible to a people living in a particular place at a particular time, the thinker must take into account a comparative study of the temperamental differences of the people and physical circumstances (like soil and climate) that affect their lives.

Montesquieu's emphasis on this method is further corroborated by the fact that he insists on exploring the natural principles by which the shape of things is governed and then their proper utilisation is made so that the institutions of mankind be placed on a plane of importance. In this way, Montesquieu insists on three things–to find out the basic underlying uniformities, the factors which produce actual diversity, and the ways of their co-ordination, control and adjustment in the best interest of the people.

Agreeing with Meinecke's view of treating Montesquieu as one of the founders of historicism, Neumann points out two major principles to highlight his historical method. They are: "The historical laws of change follow from the structured totality of society. Change of one element of the structure produces a change of the structure. It is true, e.g., that a republic is held together by virtue and is most effective in a small territory, then the Roman republic was corrupted by its physical growth. The collapse of Rome is thus due to too rapid a geographical expansion. Thus, there exists strict and mechanistic casuality. Second, the forces of history assert themselves sometimes even against the will of the actors...The reason why the structures become unbalanced and thus produce changes lies in the psychology of men. The more power they have, the more greedy for power they become. But since totally unlimited power is impossible, the striving for it produces the counter-trends which in turn change the structure."[12]

The method adopted by philosophers like Aristotle, Machiavelli, Bodin, Hume and Montesquieu, in its form and spirit, is really scientific. It "seeks an explanation of what institutions are tending to be more in the knowledge of what they have been and now they came to be what they are, than in their analysis of them as they stand."[13] The proper utilisation of this method requires at first a proper collection and arrangement of necessary data before the actual conclusion is derived. But when we study Montesquieu, it appears that at his hands the utilisation could not be proper. His faith in the universal law of reason is and his appeal to it as the final criterion to judge political institutions constitute an indication of his deductive approach. Similarly, his emphasis on the system of separation of powers and at the same time his unequivocal appreciation of the English constitutional system are logically contradictory to each other.

It is clear that Montesquieu failed to utilise this method properly. Sabine thus points out that Montesquieu acted in a hasty manner and so the main outline of his theory "was determined not by empirical consideration but by his preconceptions about what was desirable in France."[14] So says Grant: "He (Montesquieu) has a genuine interest in history; much more genuine than Rousseau's much wider and more sociological than Voltaire's. And yet his knowledge of history–as was inevitable, for modern history is a creation of the eighteenth century–is narrowly limited. Of Greece he knows naturally far

12. Neumann, *op. cit.*, p. xxxv-xxxvi.
13. Pollock : *An Introduction to the History of the Science of Politics*, p. 11.
14. Sabine: *A History of Political Theory*, p. 556.

less. Of the Middle Ages he writes rather as an archaeologist than as a historian. He knows French history intimately in the sixteenth and seventeenth centuries, and of course he knows his own century. He is deeply interested in English history, and seems fascinated by its problems; but his views are often as strange as they are interesting... His interest in history, then, is great, but it would be a mistake to regard his political philosophy as really drawn from or dependent upon his knowledge of history."[15]

LIBERTY : DOCTRINE OF SEPARATION OF POWERS

The most distinctive aspect of Montesquieu's political philosophy finds place in his view of liberty expressed in the doctrine of the separation of powers. So powerful is the defence of individual liberty in his monumental work that he is dissatisfied with mere formal guarantees provided in a bill of rights or in a constitutional document. He places his main reliance on the nature and character of governmental activity. In his view, it is the temper and spirit of the government in action that should be looked for, because mere paper guarantees are no sufficient safeguards of individual liberty.

Montesquieu's definition of liberty exhibits a unique compromise between the will of the individual and the law of the government. On the former side, it consists in the belief that the individual should be free to act according to his will. However, his approach is not only psychological; on the other hand it is also ideal, for he insists that liberty consists only in the power of doing what we ought not to will.[16] Besides, his belief in the innate goodness of the political authority informs him that what an individual ought to will is best indicated by the laws of the state. Montesquieu thus combines the two propositions and implicitly insists that liberty consists in doing accord-

15. A.J. Grant, *op. cit.*, p. 116. Fredrick Pollock comments: "Montesquieu with all his faults and irregularities, is the father of modern historical research. His information was often crude and imperfect, his reference often hasty, and his judgement often misdirected. Yet he held fast to the great truth that serious politics cannot be constructed in the air by playing with imaginary men of no particular race or country, and building them into arbitrary combinations, as a child builds castles with wooden bricks. He applied himself to study political institutions as belonging to societies of definite historical types, and determined by historical conditions". *Op. cit.*, p. 86.
16. Montesquieu: *Spirit of the Laws* (Eng. Trans. by Thomas Nugent and edited by Franz Neumann), Book XI, Ch. III.

ing to law. Obviously, Montesquieu wants that people should follow the dictates of law, otherwise their claims of liberty may harm the liberties of fellow-citizens.

Montesquieu also differentiates between civil and political liberty. According to his version, the former arises from the relation of citizens among themselves, while the latter depends upon the organisation of the government in relation to the citizens. It follows that political liberty is based on the relationship between the individual and state and it exists in doing all what the laws permit. In other words, political liberty is to be gained by conforming to laws. With this standpoint, Montesquieu criticises despotic government where liberty is not secure because of the unreasoned caprice of an individual ruler. In this regard, he also points out that although political liberty is not associated with any particular form of government, yet it is possible only in moderate governments.

Although Montesquieu does not clearly explain the scope of civil liberty, still he makes it an adjunct of political liberty. He believes that civil liberty may be maintained or crushed by the nature and proportion of punishment awarded to the subjects for the violation and disobedience of law. In this regard, he powerfully defends the freedoms of thought, expression and person. He denounces the institution of slavery. In his view, birth, natural faculties and even defeat in war cannot be the legitimate justifications of slavery, because this institution itself constitutes the negation of civil liberty.

Although, Montesquieu does not clearly explain the scope of civil liberty, still he makes it an adjunct of political liberty. He believes that civil liberty may be maintained or crushed by the nature and proportion of punishment awarded to the subjects for the violation and disobedience of law. In this regard, he strongly defends the freedoms of thought, expression and person. He denounces the institution of slavery. In his view, birth, natural faculties and even defeat in war cannot be the legitimate justifications of slavery, because this institution itself constitutes the negation of civil liberty.

Although, Montesquieu's attempt to synthesise individual liberty with governmental laws appears to be incoherent, yet he solves the difficulty by elaborately developing the doctrine of the separation of powers. A happy reconciliation of liberty with law, as Montesquieu desires, is possible only when state activity, which regulates and determines the conduct of the people, really reflects fundamental principles of right and justice and moral convictions of the people. However, he is fully aware of this difficulty and so realising that different governments make different laws at different times, he explains his theory of the separation of powers.

Simply stated, the theory of separation of powers implies that the three organs of government should be kept apart from each other in the interest of individual liberty. In other words, it implies that the functions of government should be differentiated and performed by distinct organs consisting of different bodies of persons so that each department should be limited to its respective sphere of activity and be not able to encroach upon the jurisdiction and independence of another. The theory is based on the maxim that power should b a check to power. That is, a constitution should be so framed that no organ of government be made to do things to which it is not obliged or empowered.[17]

The idea of the separation of powers has a background of its own. Aristotle designated three parts of government–deliberative, executive and judicial. In the Roman period, Polybius and Cicero also emphasised the three organs of government. But this idea became more popular in the modern age. Bodin faintly dwelt upon this subject. It is Locke who gave a clearer explanation when he discussed the forms and organs of government. However, it is none but Montesquieu who, for the first time, expanded and analysed the whole conception in concrete terms and thus gave to it the character of a particular doctrine. It was not Locke but Montesquieu "who first established the executive, legislative, and judicial power as the current classification."[18]

17. This theory had its definite influence upon the founding fathers of the American constitution. James Madison wrote in the *Federalist* thus: "No political truth is certainly of greater intrinsic value, or is stamped with the authority of more enlightened patrons for liberty than that...The accumulation of all powers, legislative, executive and judiciary, in the same hands...may justly be pronounced the very definition of tyranny." Hence, the American constitutional system conferred executive authority on the President, the legislative on the Congress, and the judicial on the Supreme Court. As a result, no feature of the American governmental system "is more characteristic than the separation of powers, combined with precautionary check and balance." Ogg and Ray: *Essentials of American Government*, p. 38.
18. E. Barker: 'Introduction' in *Social Contract*, p. xxvii.

As already pointed out, Montesquieu draws immense influence from the English constitutional system and advocates this doctrine as a device to make government safe for the governed. He says: "When the legislative and executive powers are united in the same person, or in the same body of magistrates, there can be no liberty, because apprehension may arise, lest the same monarch or senate should enact tyrannical laws, and execut them in a tyrannical manner. Again, there is no liberty if the judiciary power be not separate from the legislative and the executive. Were it joined with the legislative, the life and liberty of the subject would be exposed to arbitrary control, for the judge would then be legislator. Were it joined to the executive power, the judge might behave with violence and oppression. There would be an end of everything, were the same man or the same body...to exercise those three powers, that of enacting laws, that of executing the public resolution, and of trying the cases of individuals."[19]

In this way, Montesquieu endeavours to establish that whoever has unrestrained power will abuse it. His chief contention is that individual liberty is certainly endangered when the two organs of government are combined in the same hands. When the legislature and executive are combined, the liberty of the people is jeopardised, because the makers and executors of law are the same. If the legislature and judiciary unite together, again liberty is destroyed inasmuch as law-makers become the interpreters and administrators of law as well. If the organs of executive and judiciary are aligned, the same agency becomes the prosecutor and interpreter of law with the result that the liberty is killed. The sum and substance of the whole analysis is that if the three organs of government are united in the same hands, then there "would be an end of everything."[20]

Montesquieu's theory of individual liberty and separation of governmental powers has been criticised on the following grounds:

---

19. Montesquieu, *op. cit.*, Book, V, pp. 151-52. William Ebenstein is of the view that in the explicit beliefs of Montesquieu, there "is a curious mixture of hatred and clericalism, and despotism, profound concern for individual liberty, and a strong sense of aristocratic privilege, property and the class." *Great Political Thinkers*, p. 410.
20. Montesquieu, *op. cit.*

Firstly, his reconciliation between the liberty of the individual and the law of the state can hardly be given a practical shape. A really very difficult problem arises when a clash occurs between the two. It is hardly possible that state law should invariably conform to moral convictions of the people. The degree and nature of liberty that the individual enjoys varies with the nature and type of law, but, if there is no law whatsoever, he would have neither security nor liberty and drift towards an uncharted sea. In practical terms, it may be safely stressed that man's action conforming to every law of the state will certainly impair his scope of liberty.

Secondly, his doctrine of separation of powers elaborately developed to meet the particular contingency is also defective in various ways. Of course, the three organs of the government perform three different functions, their absolute separation is an impossibility. Montesquieu forgets that the government is an organic whole whose three organs are integrally connected and in the interest of responsibility and efficiency they cannot be separated. In the modern age of specialisation, it is true that the three organs correspond to three different modes of action, even then no organ can live in perfect isolation.[21] The theory also wrongly advocates that all departments are equal, because with he growth of democracy the responsibilities of legislature have become much more than those of the executive and judiciary. The idea of Montesquieu does not apply to the constitutional systems of all democratic states. It is also argued that in modern welfare states, the responsibilities of the executive have much widened. In brief, separation of governmental functions, as so distinctly suggested by Montesquieu, would inevitably create frequent deadlocks, because each department acting in defence of its own powers "would never lend its aid to the other and the consequent loss in efficiency would outweigh all the possible advantages arising from independence."[22] Similarly, Laski says: "Legislatures would not fulfil their task unless they were able both to interfere in the execution of law, and also, on occasion, to overrule by statute the decisions of the judges the results of which are widely felt to be unsatisfactory. As executive is bound in applying the law to clothe the general principle in the garment of detail: and in the modern state, this function covers so wide ambit that it is often difficult to distin-

21. Barker: *Principles of Social and Political Theory*, p. 261.
22. See John Stuart Mill: *Considerations on Representative Government.*

guish it from the work of the legislature. The judiciary, finally, which settles either the competence of the executive (in which case it determines the substance of legislative will) or dispute between two citizens (in which case it extends the legal imperatives of a state to cover new ground or denies that the ground involved comes within the ambit of those imperatives), is, in fact, performing a function which is legislative in character."[23]

Finally, it is said that Montesquieu misunderstands and misevaluates the English constitutional system. He is right in admiring the fact of the liberties of the English people, but he is decidedly wrong in understanding the nature of relationship existing between the legislature and executive. In a country having parliamentary form of government, his doctrine has no application. The English constitutional system reveals concentration of responsibility which contradicts the theory of separation of powers. This criticism becomes more weighty when we find that he had a chance to stay in England for about two years and had personal acquaintance with men like Locke and, more than that, he followed empirical method. Obviously, Montesquieu could not understand the English governmental system properly and thus the alignment of his theory with the English constitutional system becomes an absurdity.[24]

SOCIOLOGICAL RELATIVISM : LAW, GOVERNMENT AND NATIONAL INSTITUTIONS

Montesquieu has widened the scope of political science by introducing the principles of sociology in the study of politics. His notion of sociological relativism insists upon taking into account those common principles and emotions which produce certain results by influencing the life of the people. Hence, the study of political phenomenon cannot be proper, or scientific, until it is made in the context of those principles, emotions and conditions. In other words, Montesquieu seeks to justify that as political phenomenon cannot be studied in isolation, so a political scientist should necessarily ramble into the spheres of economics, history, religion, geography, psychology and anthropology for finding out and properly evaluating those principles and emotions which influence them. It obviously fol-

23. Laski: *An Introduction to Politics*, p. 63.
24. Gilchrist gives a specific example to substantiate this view. He says: "The Lord Chancellor, who is at once a member of the cabinet, of the House of Lords, and the head of the judiciary is a standing refutation of the doctrine of separation of powers." *Principles of Political Science*, p. 254.

lows that Montesquieu does not care for abstract notion of things, because to him all knowledge is a knowledge of relations. Such an approach of Montesquieu, for our purpose, may be visualised in his conceptions of law, forms and excellence of governmental institutions and their transformation.

Law: Overtly, the general principles of Montesquieu's social philosophy start with his conception of law. His definition of law is based on his theory of sociological relativism whereby he sets aside all definitions of law given by his predecessors. In his view, law is not an expression of reason as believed by Plato and Aristotle, nor is it a command of the sovereign as pointed out by Bodin and Hobbes. In his own words: "Laws, in their most general signification, are the necessary relations arising from the nature of things. In this sense, all things have their laws, the Deity His laws, the material world its laws, the intelligence superior to man their laws, the beast their laws, man his laws."[25]

The definition of Montesquieu implies that everything in this world is related to something, if not to everything else. A proper and complete study of politics or law thus requires a proper and complete study of the relationship subsisting between those phenomena. The law by which God creates and

25. Montesquieu, *op. cit.*, Book I, Ch.I. Obviously, law is a sociological phenomenon or part of the warp and woof of the society. It is not a fictitious bond imposed upon the people by some external agency, rather it involves the whole body of multiple and complex relations which come into being, develop and undergo change. According to Jones, "Law, in its totality, is that which gives a society its particular and unique character." *Op. cit.*, p. 230. The key-phrase in the definition of Montesquieu is the 'nature of things' which, according to him, signifies a logical structure of society, perhaps of an ideal society following its own inner logic, that can be grasped only through the medium of facts. A society having any form of government whether monarchy, republic or despotism 'is thus not an addition to or an aggregate of fact, but the expression of a structure. These ideal types are not arrived at by induction, that is why the collection of data and the elimination of irrelevant ones, but by reading into the historical facts a meaning that illuminates them and reveals their structural principles. Consequently each ideal type is held together by one constitutive principle (republic-virtue; monarchy-honour; aristocracy-moderation; despotism-fear). It is these constitutive principles which integrate society. All the phenomena must be interpreted in relation to this principle. Each nation being thus an essential unit, it is folly to isolate phenomena and to attempt to understand them if they are not seen in their interdependence and in their relation to the constitutive principle." See Neumann, *op. cit.*, p. xxxv.

preserves things are fixed, invariable, uniform and constant. These laws are divine and they control nature. As a physical being, man cannot violate or change the working of any of the divine laws. But he is also an intelligent being and thus he becomes able to modify or transgress the pattern of behaviour imposed upon him by the laws of the nature. His finite intelligence also makes him subject to error and ignorance and amenable to be swayed by passions and emotions. The result is that while nature and non-human species are governed by one type of law (divine or natural law), the society of human beings is subject to two types of laws–divine or natural law and positive or man-made law.

In order to arrive at a proper definition of positive law, Montesquieu presupposes the existence of a pre-political society. In that condition of human life, there is neither perpetual warfare (as Hobbes said), nor an enlightened life (as suggested by Locke), nor noble savagery (as given by Rousseau), nor political authority as established by means of social compact. Montesquieu is not at all a social contractualist and his conception of the state of nature with its essential implications is quite different. He simply believes that when there is no political society, man is a timid creature; his intelligence and knowledge develop with the advancement of civilisation. As man is timid, he is aware of his inferiority and so he would prefer to live in peace. Then, this sense would have given him the consciousness of an associational life. Besides, the self-interest would have further strengthened the usefulness of an associational life. Hence, this condition of living together would have brought more and more acquisition of knowledge and thus led to the formation of political authority.

If so, Montesquieu points out that man's conduct cannot be regulated only by the law of nature, another type of law (made by man himself) is required to regulate and control the behaviour of intelligent human beings. Positive law (man-made law) thus comes into being. The man is thus under the control of two laws–divine and positive. However, the latter differs from the former, because it is made by man and it is not universal, fixed and invariable. Since it is made by man to suit a particular condition, it cannot have the same characteristics which exist in the law of nature.

In addition to defining positive law, Montesquieu classifies it into three types taking into account the behaviour of man towards his fellow beings. Firstly, there is international law which regulates the behaviour of citizens living in various nation-states. Secondly, there is political (constitutional) law which regulates the relationship between man and his political organisation. Finally, there is civil law which regulates the relationship between man and his fellow-beings living in the same community. In this direction, Montesquieu also recognises that while international law is common to all nations, the other two types of laws differ from one nation to another. Further, Montesquieu maintains that political law must have relation to the character of the people and, likewise, civil law be related to geography, climate, size of the population, geography, religion and genius of the people and several other physical factors. His assertion is based on the insistence that different ways have arisen from different wants in different climates which have resulted in different kinds of law. In short, Montesquieu's theory of law is tied up with his conception of environmentalism.

Forms of Government: Montesquieu's theory of environmentalism examines the forms of government and their excellence from a different angle of vision. He dismisses the approach of thinkers like Plato, More and Rousseau who supposed the excellence of a particular form for all times, places and peoples. In his view, any idea of best or ideal state is sheer absurdity, because no form of government can be studied in isolation and it is relative to and varies with the physical environment which is different from place to place.

Although Montesquieu accepts the traditional style of classifying governments into three forms, the implications of his argument are quite different. He classifies them on the basis of nature of state into three–forms–republic, monarchy and despotism. According to his version, a republic is one in which supreme power is vested in the body of citizens or a part of them; it is monarchy if it is governed by a single person in accordance with fixed and established laws, and it is despotism if a single person directs everything by his own will and caprice. Besides, a republic may have two forms–democracy and aristocracy. It is democracy if the supreme power of the state is vested in the hands of the whole body of citizens; it is aristocracy if it is possessed only by a part of citizens.

In addition to this, Montesquieu explains the principles of state which ought to be taken into account. The principles include the motives, intents, emotions and passions of the people which influence the mechanism of government. Firstly, he takes the case of republic where principle is *virtue* which includes political probity, patriotism and love for equality. As republic may have the forms of democracy and aristocracy, this principle has a higher operation in the former and a moderate expression in the latter. Secondly, the principle of monarchy is *honour* of the high sense of the rights and privileges enjoyed by a particular class of the state. Finally, the principle of despotism is *fear*, because all rights and privileges are enjoyed by a single despot under whose stern control the masses are kept in control by means of fear.

Therefore, in Montesquieu's view, no particular form of government may be recommended for a particular people living at a particular place as the best one. The various factors should be fully taken into consideration. He urges that education and legislation must correspond in character to the principles of a particular government. In spite of this, it can be found out that Montesquieu's tacit preference is for the republican system and he particularly dislikes the despotic government, for it "exhausts the resources of the people enslaved by it. Property being in continual danger, the springs of industry and of commerce are destroyed."[26]

Transformation of Governments: Like Aristotle and Bodin, Montesquieu also studies the subject of revolutions, although his motive is entirely different from them. Montesquieu believes that no particular form of government can successfully endure, because every form is subject to inevitable change and decline like every other object of nature. The transformation of governments is inevitable, but its cause is general and not accidental. As every form of government has a principle of its own, and when that principle is carried to excess or when pubic good is perverted by selfish gains, certain forces begin to operate which inevitably bring the downfall of that governmental system. Montesquieu thus does not believe in the permanence of particular form of government. Logically, it may be correct that when the structure of the government is harmonious and consonant with the spirit of the people, there can be no possibility of transformation. But Montesquieu disagrees with this logic, because in his view, the excellence of a particular form of government is so relative a matter that permanence in any

26. A.J. Grant, *op. cit.*, p. 125.

form can never be expected. In this connection, it may also be pointed out that Montesquieu does no believe in the inevitability of the cycle of growth ad decay in a regular order suggested by Aristotle and Polybius, rather his approach is based on the notions of sociological relativism. His purpose is to lay down a rule that no type of government is wholly good or bad, its excellence should be examined in relation to its environment and the transformation of every government begins with the corruption of its basic principle.

National Life and Institutions: Montesquieu also takes into account several factors which influence the life and institutions of a people. He holds that there is correlation between the size of a state and the form of its government. The republican system is suited to small states: the monarchical system is appropriate to little-sized states; and, finally, despotism is befitting to very large states. In the view of Montesquieu, small states should adopt federal system if they desire to maintain their independence. He also emphasises that a material change in the size of the state necessarily causes a corresponding change in the form of government.

Montesquieu goes much ahead of Bodin when he establishes relationship of cause and effect between the physical factors (like soil, climate, fertility, natural resources and topography) of a country and the aspects of her national life (like habits, character, social system, economic ideas, laws, morals, manners and religious beliefs). This standpoint leads him to conclude that a cold climate makes the people energetic and active, it is conducive to liberty and democratic government; conversely, as warm climate induces lethargy and passivity, it is conducive to slavery and despotic rule. The topographic analysis shows that mountainous regions are suited to free governments but plains are appropriate for despotism. He also stresses that democracies exist and develop mostly in the areas divided or kept small by natural barriers, while despotic governments thrive and prosper in vast geographical divisions"[27]

The political institutions of a nation are also influenced by social environment. The customs, manners, morals, religious beliefs and practices have their definite influence and so the nature and structure of political institutions must not be

27. Montesquieu, *op. cit.*, Book VIII, Chs. 16-20.

disharmonious to them. Even religion can prosper only in a particular type of people. He holds that Christianity is best suited to free people, while Islam is meant for those who should live under a despotic rule. Not only this, he suggests that Protestantism is suited to a republican system and Catholicism to monarchy. His strong defence of secularism is clear from the fact that he fears ecclesiastical tyranny and desires to make church merely a department of the state.

In this way, Montesquieu adopts an approach which, in certain respects, appears to be like that of Aristotle, Bodin and Rousseau, yet it is much different from all of them. Unlike all his predecessors, Montesquieu lays emphasis on a grandiose scale and with meticulous care examines the factors which have their definite influence upon the political life of a people. It is none but Montesquieu who "dwelt at considerable length upon the influence of physical environment, upon social and political institutions and particularly upon liberty."[28]

Montesquieu's doctrine of sociological relativism may be criticised on the following grounds:

1. Montesquieu places unduly heavy strain on the importance of physical factors. It is true that the physical properties influence the life of the people, but their influence is not so powerful as he contends. His emphasis is really exaggerated. In this regard, Montesquieu really belongs to the class of Plato, Machiavelli, Bentham and Marx who exploited the significance of a single factor. Sabine rightly calls the whole assumption as a fiction and says that this vague formula "covers always an ambiguity which he does nothing to clear up."[29] It is also pointed out that Montesquieu takes a static view of history. He emphasises the fact that the people of different places having different environments and different tendencies would like to have different sorts of political institutions. But he forgets that even the people of same place may like to have different institutions at the various stages of development. Vaughan thus says: "Indeed, if any complaint is to be raised against Montesquieu, it is that he made too little rather than too much of the side of his theme. He was so much engrossed in proving the unity of a nation's life at any one period of its history that he had scant attention to spare for the parallel truth of the unity which

28. Garner: *Political Science and Government*, p. 40.
29. Sabine, *op. cit.*, p. 553.

ends one period to the other...that the whole life of the nation is woven of one piece and, therefore, it is impossible to make sweeping changes in one direction without laying a change for a thousand changes unforeseen and perhaps desired...It is the chief blot on Montesquieu's achievement that he never thought out his question to its final issue that believing the present to be determined by the past, he never clearly recognised that present being different from the past such determination necessarily carries with it the idea of growth; still less that in such matters growth is only another name for development or progress."[30]

2. Montesquieu's classification of law is defective. His distinction between civil and political law is not obvious and his faith in the law of nature is clearly a contradiction of his empirical method.
3. Montesquieu's classification of government is defective. It is wrong to say that democracy and aristocracy are the subdivisions of the republic. His keeping of despotism at par with other governments in matters of excellence is also a wrong conclusion. The classification is a hotchpotch too, because the entire conclusion is not based on a single principle. The difference between a republic and a monarchy is based on the number of persons holding political authority; while the difference between a monarchy and a despotism is based on the way in which power is actually exercised. "Montesquieu's treatment of the republican form is curious. It is almost utopian. There was hardly anything in Europe of his own day what he would regard as republican."[31]

The truth is that while Montesquieu's environmentalism looks like a novel idea, his over-emphasis hardly deserves unquestioned admiration. His notions could not be as consistent and coherent as empirical method required. Yet his profound love for individual liberty and emphasis on environmentalism had a wide appeal and appreciation. Dunning thus comments: "While he stood for history, observation and broad generalisation as the method of approach to political, social and economic truth, they with few exceptions, set up the absolute standard of nature and deduced from their conception of this entity the doctrines which they have to be of universal validity."[32]

30. Vaughan: *Studies in the History of Political Philosophy*, Vol. II, pp. 287-88.
31. Grant, *op. cit.*, p. 123.
32. Dunning, *op. cit.*, p. 433.

Critical Estimate: Commentators and text-book writers have evaluated the contributions of Montesquieu to the subject of political theory in different ways. The commonest point of objection against Montesquieu is that he is not very clear about his word 'spirit' as contained in the very title of his monumental value. It is said that his purpose "is to consider the spirit rather than the substance of the laws."[33] Lowenthal finds a rigorous design deliberately hidden from the 'vulgar reader'. Vaughan sees in the opening chapter of the book a forthright declaration of the 'vital principles which gives unity to the necessarily scattered details, the torch, in the light of which every detail is seen to take its place as part of an order and intelligible whole."[34] According to Albert Sorel, "Thinkers and politicians accepted in Montesquieu what suited their turn but his method escaped them. They may be seen invoking his authority in details while disposing his spirit: and putting into practice reforms that he advocated while violating the rules he prescribed."[35]

Montesquieu is very important for his memorable defence of individual liberty. His treatise ranks among world classics, it was widely read and appreciated. Curiously, it had its influence not only in Europe but also across the Atlantic. His emphasis on individual liberty and critique of autocratic monarchy infused the ideals which had their manifestation in the French revolution. His ideas were so much liked by the American people that they based their constitutional system on his doctrine of separation of powers. Of course, Montesquieu became the spiritual ancestor of Blackstone, Gibbon, Bentham, Washington, Madison, Jefferson and many other American Federalists. Above all, Montesquieu is the celebrated philosopher of individual liberty for the sake of which he so elaborately developed the theory of separation of powers–a theory whose central purpose "is that of securing liberty by preventing the concentration of power and by restraining its arbitrary employments."[36] It is only for the defence of individual liberty and for its sake the doctrine of separation of powers that Montesquieu won immense admiration. However, his emphasis on sociological relativism is no less an important contribution. Regarding these things, Sorel observes: "We have

33. Judd Harmon, *op. cit.*, p. 274.
34. Vaughan, *op. cit.*, p. 457.
35. Sorel: *Montesquieu* (Translated from French into English by M.B. Anderson and E.P. Anderson), p. 170.
36. Pennock and Smith: *Political Science: An Introduction*, p. 264.

had sublimer philosophers, bolder thinkers, more eloquent writers, sadder, more pathetic and more fertile creators of fictitious characters and authors richer in the invention of imagination. We have had no more judicious observer of human societies; no wiser counsellor regarding great public interest, no man who has united so acute a perception of individual passions with such profound penetration into political institutions–no one, in short, who has employed such rare literary talent in the service of such perfect good sense."[37]

37. Sorel, *op. cit.*, pp. 28-29.

20

HUME

In metaphysics, theory of knowledge, economics, ethics and religion, and in politics, so far as it concerned Americans, he deserves rather to be dubbed a radical; he depended not upon authority, but upon his own reasonings, he accepted no scheme of things, because he established and defended by the Fathers: he disintegrated and destroyed many settled notions by an acid logic of his own.

— **J.Y.T. Greig**[1]

David Hume is ranked with Montesquieu as one of the two most enlightened men of the eighteenth century. In 1711, he was born in an aristocratic family of Edinburgh. He got the best type of preparatory education and at the age of ten he did matriculation from the Edinburgh College. For some time, he pursued the standard classical and philosophical courses. At the age of fourteen, he took up the study of law but left it as he found it to be exceedingly distasteful. He then travelled to Europe. In 1714, he brought out a collection of miscellaneous papers entitled *Essays: Moral and Political* which gave him both fame and money. Shortly after, it had its friendly exchange with Montesquieu's *Spirit of the Laws.* However, the French translation of his *Essays* soon gave him the vast reputation of

1. Greig : *David Hume*, p. 376.

a political theorist. Then, he served as Secretary to Gen. St. Clair on the expedition to France in 1746 and to the embassy of Vienna and Turin in 1748. In 1763, he was appointed as Secretary to the British Embassy in Paris. But in 1766, he returned to England as Secretary to General Conway and lived for two years in London. After this, he lived in his native city until his death in 1776 and it was during this last phase of life that he became involved in the 'famous' imbroglio with Rousseau.

WORKS : A CRITICISM AND A LEGACY OF THE ENLIGHTENMENT

The political philosophy of David Hume is contained in his several works like *Treatise of Human Nature, Essays: Moral and Political, History of England, Political Discourses, Of the Original Contract* and *A Natural History of Religion.* Among his works, his *Treatise of Human Nature* is the most important. When Hume found that his *Treatise of Human Nature* failed due more to its form than its matter, he republished it in a popular form under the name *Enquiry Concerning Human Understanding.*[2] However, the general tenor of his style shows that in turning to the writings of history, he, to a large extent, forsook philosophy and political theory, made onslaughts upon religion and brought reactionism in politics. Hence, in his conversation with Adam Smith, he said: "Here am I, who have written on all sorts of subjects that are calculated to excite hostility. But I have no enemies–except all the Whigs, all the Tories, and all the Christians."[3]

The works of Hume reveal his peculiar position of being both a rejecter of the 'reason' and its accepter by assigning it a secondary place in his political theory. Thus, he should be treated both as a child and a critic of the Enlightenment.[4] The

2. It "is now acknowledged to be one of the world's enduring masterpieces of philosophy." Maxey: *Political Philosophies*, p. 329.
3. J.Y.T. Greig, *op. cit.*, p. 42.
4. The scientific rationalism of the seventeenth century came to maturity in the eighteenth when quite a good number of thinkers and writers adopted a rational and practical outlook signifying their disbelief in the life after death and accordingly in the considerations and sacrifices for its sake. It reveals that scientific curiosity that overflowed all bounds and experimentation became an avocation for all who professed any degrees of sophistication. In other words, it expressed man's belief in a new trend that by intelligence he might free the worlds of vice, disease, poverty and injustice if science and reason were given full reign and if church, state

general notion of Hume's being a critic of the Enlightenment draws its sustenance from the anti-rational feature having so weighty a place that the 'secondary' role of reason is hardly visible to a reader of his political theory.[5] The premises of Hume's vehement assault upon the doctrines of natural law and natural rights signify his refutation of the concept of reason. He emphatically rejects the view of natural law theorists that the norms of moral action exist in an *a priori* form, that they can be discovered by reason, and that the passions of men, which would divert them from the way to a proper study of human behaviour. Such a study of Hume's ideas leaves an impression of his being a thinker of the anti-rationalist school. However, a deeper study of his political philosophy shows that he assigns a secondary place to reason by adding that 'reason is the slave of passions'. Though the use of reason is 'limited', it may be employed to show logical relationship even though it cannot demonstrate the existence or values of natural law. "Human values are determined by passion or feeling. Reason may be helpful in directing action towards the attainment of values, but its role is secondary. It is an instrument."[6]

What seems to take Hume very close to the psychological system of Hobbes is his view that 'passions' move men. However, Hume's treatment of the passions is fundamentally different from that of Hobbes. To him passions are of two kinds–instinctive and secondary–and the experience alone can demonstrate how they can be satisfied. Secondary passions such as desires are based upon experience involving pain and pleasure. There are no *a priori* truths; it is the experience that

---

and all social institutions were subjected to rational analysis and criticism with a view to their improvement. Thus, there appeared an intellectual movement known by the name of Enlightenment "concerned with the problem of releasing the creative forces of the period from the restraint of outworn social system'. See Watkins: *The Political Traditions of the West*, p. 125. A better definition of the Enlightenment is thus given by McDonald: "The enlightenment is the name we give to the philosophical movement that puts faith in reason, by putting reason against faith. Despite many antecedents in the sixteenth century, the movement is identified with the eighteenth century because that century produced a self-conscious rejection of religion as the guiding authority in arts, morals, politics, and scholarship. A new spirit of critical inquiry or 'reason' took religion's place". *Western Political Theory: The Modern Age*, pp. 131-32.

5. One may, however, disagree with the magnified view of McDonald that Hume "seems more a child of the Enlightenment than its critic." *Ibid.*, p. 226.
6. M. Judd Harmon: *Political Thought from Plato to the Present*, p. 319.

tells us what is pleasant and painful. Thus, Hume tells us that social scientists should study human behaviour in these terms instead of concerning themselves with the hypothetical laws of nature. A deeper study of Hume's views on passions being the prime mover of human behaviour reveals both his rejection of the reason and the acceptance of its role in a secondary or tacit form. He distinguishes between 'calm' and violent' passions by adding that it is the force of reason that becomes the very source of distinction between the two. Calm passions are directed by reason capable of understanding and enlightened self-interest; violent passions demand immediate gratification. "The practical political significance of this distinction is that the community must be guided by a minority of persons whose reason is improved by education and who possess sufficient wealth not to be tempted to succumb to the desire to serve a selfish and short-range interest. Justice is achieved when the community functions along the lines of enlightened self-interest."[7] Such a turn in the system of Hume indicates both his attack on the rationalist premises of the natural law school and his rudimentary contribution to the school of utilitarianism drawing sustenance from this observation of McDonald that the whole thrust of Hume's social thought "was to find a basis for distinguishing between justified and unjustified institutions."[8]

STATE : REFUTATION OF SOCIAL CONTRACTUALISM

Hume appears as one of the most distinctive critics of his times. He vehemently attacks the theories of divine origin and social contract on the origin and nature of state. In his work *Of the Original Contract,* he firmly points out that both are purely speculative and hypothetical in as much as they are rational, devoid of factual foundations and absurd in their practical consequences. In his view, the divine origin theory is preposterous, since it makes the position of God ridiculous. It makes him as much responsible for bestowing authority upon an unspeakable tyrant as upon a wise and benevolent ruler and further holds that a constable no less than a king "acts by divine commission and possesses an indefeasible right."[9]

More furious is Hume's attack on the theory of social contract. He maintains that this theory is false both historically and philosophically. A thing like social contract could not have

7. *Ibid.*, p. 320.
8. McDonald, *op. cit.*, p. 234.
9. Hume: *Essays-Moral and Political,* p. 444.

taken place among the primitive people, because they did not have enough reason and intelligence to think of a regular contract and stick to it after its creation. History does not furnish any example of an original contract, nor can the consent of the parties perpetually bind their descendents. He argues that there is no evidence of any formal contract between the ruler and the ruled playing any part in the building up of governmental organisations. It is foolish to say that contemporary rulers have no authority save by the consent of their subjects, or that their subjects are freed from the duty of obedience whenever they choose to hold their rulers derelict in their contractual obligations. It is absurd and without foundation to postulate a contractual relationship between the ruler and the ruled in the absence of any specific and recorded agreement to which reference might readily be made.[10]

Hume continues that the social contract theory is wrong from the philosophical point of view as well. In his view, men are born in the state and they obey it habitually. But voluntary consent given at the time of social contract indirectly implies the power to withdraw from the state. In the primitive societies, no compact could be made, because the people were in a state of savagery. They had neither reason nor intelligence enough to understand the terms of a thing like social contract, it is impossible for the savage beings of Hobbes, or the social beings of Locke, or the noble savages of Rousseau to change their nature so radically and then to submit themselves to an authority of which they had no previous experience at all. He thus concluded that virtually all governments were founded without any pretence of open and voluntary consent of the people. Barker thus remarks: "Locke and Rousseau, if in different ways and different degrees, accepted the idea of the social contract, Hume, more historically-minded, and more conservative in his convictions, was its critic."[11]

10. It may be pointed here that Hume does not outrightly reject the element of consent in the gradual evolution of state. He simply means that to interpret it as a single factor (as done by the social contractualists) is thoroughly wrong. He says: "It is vain to say that all governments are or should be founded on popular consent in as much as the necessities of human affairs will admit. I maintain that human affairs will never admit of this consent; seldom of the appearance of it...My intention here is not to exclude the consent of the people from being the just one foundation of government where it has place, it is surely the best and most sacred of any. I only pretend that it has very seldom had to place it in any degree and never almost in its full extent." *Ibid.*, pp. 449-50.

11. Ernest Barker: 'Introduction' to *Social Contract*, p. liv.

Having thus refuted the theories of divine origin and social contract, Hume expounds his own theory which strikingly anticipates the modern historical and sociological schools of political thought. In his view, the state is a growth and not a make and in its growth several factors (including the consent) have played their part. Hence, Hume propounds a theory of societal evolution. He believes that the governmental institutions grew more casually and more imperfectly where the superiority of courage and genius became more visible, where unanimity and concept were more requisite and where the pernicious effects of chaos and anarchy were more seriously felt. It is possible that the first descendents of one man over multitude had begun during a state of war. "The long continuance of that state", he further said, "an incident common among savage tribes, ensured the people into submission, and if the chieftains possessed as much equity as prudence and valour, he became, even during peace, the arbiter of all differences, and could gradually, by a mixture of force and consent, establish his authority."[12]

In this connection, it may, however, be pointed out that although Hume so furiously denounces the social contract theory, he still recognises that consent might have played its part in the societal evolution of state and wishes that it might emerge as a paramount factor in the life of modern state. The people must consent to their authority to obey not by way of a religious duty or a mystic contract but as the only way where society can exist and advance from lower to higher forms of civilisation. He says: "But as human society is in perpetual flux, one man every hour going out of the world, another coming into it, it is necessary, in order to preserve stability in government, that the new breed should conform themselves to the established constitution, and nearly follow the path which their fathers treading in the footsteps of theirs, had marked out to them. Some innovations must necessarily have place in every human institution, and it is happy where the enlightened genius of the age gives these a direction to the side of reason, liberty and justice."[13]

12. Hume, *op. cit.*, pp. 115-116.
13. *Ibid.*, p. 452.

POLITICAL OBLIGATION : EMPHASIS ON BENEVOLENT UTILITARIANISM

Hume's utilitarianism finds a vague expression in his general theory of political obligation. While dismissing the theories of divine origin and social contract, he recognises that people obey the state, because it suits them to do so and not because they ordinarily reason about it. He holds that, in the last analysis, a sense of the advantage to the individual of peace and order in social life becomes the reason for the general submission to established political authority. It follows that, according to him, utility is the ultimate end while duty is the proximate motive of an individual's obedience to government. Ever since the formation of early political societies, he argues, each exertion of authority in the chieftain must have been particular and called forth by the present exigencies of the case. In his own words: "The sensible utility resulting from this interposition, made these exertions become daily more frequent; and their frequency gradually produced a habitual, and if you please to call it so, a voluntary, and therefore precarious, acquiescence in the people."[14]

Hume's theory of utilitarianism becomes more apparent in his vehement criticism directed against the system of natural law–natural or rational religion, rational ethics and the contractual and consensus theory of politics. The fictitious character of a rational religion is apparent from the indemonstrable existence of God. Opposing the rationalistic school and its philosophy based on the conception of law of nature, he insists that morality is based on expediency and, therefore, vitally related to positive law. He believes that utility is the touchstone of institutions and reason is an inert principle, because passions, arising from a sense of pleasure or fear from pain, motivate human actions. However, Hume does not stick to the single factor of human pleasure or pain like his successors as Bentham. Rather, he believes that human nature is not so simple as to have only a single propensity. His view of human nature thus excludes the excessive amount of calculation and foresight that contemporary moralists of all schools were accustomed to impute to it. Hume clearly points out that men are not very calculating in pushing either their self-interest or anything else: they are only foresighted when their feelings and

14. *Ibid.*, pp. 445-46.

impulses are not directly engaged, but impulse interferes with self-interest as often as with benevolence.[15]

Hume denies that there are eternal varieties rooted in human nature that lay down the standards of social life. The needs of people living in a society have generally been fulfilled by social conventions based on common interest and not on anything like promise, faith or rational truth. Naturally, the people have a right to change their social customs and conventions whenever these outlive their usefulness and to mould them to preserve a stable social life in accord with their propensities and interests. If so, the basis of political authority is neither faith in divine origin, nor belief in some primitive contract, but it should be traced in a set of conventional rules that discriminate a legitimate government from an instrument of usurpation or force. The nature of these rules is purely non-rational on account of the fact that they derive their strength from the fact of their utility and not from some rational or natural agency.

GOVERNMENT : PREFERENCE FOR MONARCHY

Hume's preference for monarchy is based on four reasons. Firstly, like James Harrington, he fears the correspondence between wealth and political power and thus detests both the republican and aristocratic governments. Except monarchy, he suggests, all other governments have 'sources of degeneracy' and they are most ruinous to their provinces. Secondly, his peculiar definition of 'liberty' leads him to prefer this form of government. To his way of thinking, the essence of liberty is not so much freedom as order, security and justice and it is only monarchical government where property is safe, arts and culture flourish, trade and industry prosper, and order and justice are firmly grounded. His reasoning is that only this government is more stable, continuous and congenial to steady advancement in the essentials of true liberty. Thirdly, the cause of the origin of government is war with the neighbouring communities,, with its natural sequel of civil strife over the spoils of war within the community itself. As military camps are the true makers of cities, all governments were monarchies in the beginning. Finally, the excellence of monarchical system is supported by the organisation of the family. As in a family the rule

15. Hume holds that "over and above all the human virtue is benevolence, for nothing can bestow more merit on any human creature than the sentiment of benevolence in an eminent degree...." *Ibid.*, p. 179.

of single head prevails and which entails peace and prosperity, so in the society the rule of a single monarch is most preferable.

As a result, Hume appears as the most powerful defender of the merits and excellence of monarchy in the eighteenth century. For this very reason, he admires the constitutional systems of England and France. His great admiration for monarchy is evident from his own statement which says: "Though all kinds of government be improved upon in modern times, yet monarchical government seems to have made the greatest advance to perfection. It may now be affirmed of civilised monarchies, what was formerly said of republics alone, that they are a government of law, not of men. They are found susceptible for order, method and constancy to a surprising degree. Property is there secure; industry is encouraged; the arts flourish; and the prince lives among his subjects like a father among his children."[16]

In certain respects, Hume took to the side of conservatism. Firstly, he deserted the growing trends of representative government. He greatly feared that the new changes taking place after the Glorious Revolution of 1688 were disturbing the delicate balance between the monarchical and republican elements of the English constitution and afflicting the marked differences of interest between the various classes of English society. Secondly, and as a corollary to the above, he criticised the growing party system. The germs of party politics bred national animosity and its evils were often transmit to the posterity. The differences between the people were never bridged and so national unity suffered. Finally, he denied that the people could bring radical innovations or make violent revolutions in their social and political systems. In short, Hume defended the existing social and political system of England and detested any change in it going to the detriment of the powerful class.

Critical Estimate : The writings of Hume show that he was more a destructive critic than a constructive theorist. He launched a massive attack against the principles of religion and natural law and thus incurred the charge of scepticism. Besides, he vacillated from the poles of Whiggism to Toryism. His preference for monarchy and his frank disapproval of republican system made him a defender of conservatism. By

16. Cited in Garner: *Political Science and Government*, pp. 369-70.

criticising the growing role of party system and by ignoring the achievements of democratic trends, he definitely showed his love for old things and this was distinctly due to his theory of utilitarianism. His idea that people should not destroy the old order but conserve it and improve it by means of gradual reforms did not appeal to the people. As a result, no school of political thought or no resplendent body of political doctrine is associated with his name and, like Montesquieu, his own ideas became a factor of ruining what he desired to preserve.

However, Hume commands some influence. His ideas prepared the way for Adam Smith, Burke, Bentham, Spencer, Henry Maine and others. He was destined to exert a great influence in the period of reaction and reconstruction following the French revolution and to prepare the ground for much of the political thought characteristic of the nineteenth century industrialism. Hume certainly corrected much of the political thought of his predecessors and contemporaries, particularly by rejecting the theory of natural rights, natural law and religious superstition. That is why, Gettell calls him as 'one of the most powerful dissolvents of the eighteenth century."[17] Laski rightly says that Hume was always critical and suggestive.[18]

Hume is generally regarded as the thinker of conservatism. But behind the facade of his conservatism we may study his empiricist enthusiasm. It may be said that while he put a brake on the tradition of rationalist enthusiasm, he gave stimulus to the age of empiricist enthusiasm that precursed the utilitarianism of Bentham. "Hume was something more than the Enlightenment incarnates, for his significance is that turned against the Enlightenment of its own weapons. And herein lies his importance as a conservative thinker."[19]

17. Gettell: *History of Political Thought*, p. 249.
18. Laski: *Political Thought in England*, pp. 11-12.
19. Sheldon S. Wolin: "Hume and Conservatism" in *American Political Science Review*, Vol. 48 (1954), p. 1001.

21

BURKE

Burke is perhaps best known for his fulminations against the French Revolution, and the political theories which underlay it, theories which Burke feared, might seriously invade British culture and work a similar political transformation in the British Isles.

— **W.T. Bluhm**[1]

Edmund Burke has been described as one of the greatest English thinkers who ever devoted themselves to the practice of their country's politics. Born in 1729 and expired in 1797, he played the part of a politician engaged in supporting the principles and practices of one political party and criticising those of the other in a spirit of partisanship. He received his early education in Trinity College, Dublin, and then migrated to London for acting as the practitioner of law. But he developed a distaste for the profession and took to writing on politics. This incurred the wrath of his father as a result of which he was deprived of financial assistance. Hence, he embarked on the career of journalism and soon gained repute by publishing some pamphlets. A turning point in his life came when in 1759, he got the association of W.G. Hamilton who became the Secretary for Ireland after some time. In 1765, he became Private

1. Bluhm : *Theories of the Political System*, p. 425.

Secretary to Lord Rockingham who had recently become the Prime Minister of England. These events gave him a practical training in politics and statesmanship and enabled him to serve as a member of the House of Commons for nearly thirty years. From 1766 to 1794, he maintained a dignified parliamentary career and by his important speeches supported the Whig party and trenchantly criticised the Tory party when it came to power. However, he did not give up liberal-mindedness and even criticised his own party on various occasions. As a lover of liberty and a stern protagonist of clean administration, he criticised the colonial policy of his government. The result was that his fiery speeches delivered in the days of King George III over the issue of American War of Independence displeased even his own party colleagues. For this he did not worry, because the cogency and intellectual content of his arguments had already made him popular. He died three years before the close of the eighteenth century

WORKS : GLORIOUS DEFENCE OF LIBERTY AND CONSERVATISM

The political ideas of Burke are not a product of his academic studies, they are his stern reactions to the contemporary problems of social and political life. As such, his ideas are not in the nature of abstract speculations, they are like his reflections and considerations on the major issues of politics created by the King, the movement of the people of Ireland, and the revolutionary struggle of the peoples of America and France. The political ideas of Burke are, therefore, scattered over his numerous speeches delivered in the English Parliament and elsewhere, letters addressed to his friends and acquaintances, addresses delivered to the people of his constituency (Bristol) and the like. The scattered material has now become available to us in the form of his stray works like *Thoughts on the Causes of Present Discontent, Reflections on the Revolution in France, Speech on Conciliation with America* and *An Appeal from the Old Whig to the New Whigs.* However, what is known as the main part of his political ideas is his reaction against the philosophy of French Revolution.

A study of the collected works of Burke edited by Bohn shows that his major interests were the preservation of thc English constitution against the aggressive and obdurate designs of King George III, the struggle of his people of Ireland for the defence of their rights, the freedom movement of the people of America, the tyranny of the English East India Company over the rulers of India and, above all, his attack on the revolutionary ideas of the French Revolution. While commenting on the significance of Burke's *Reflections on the Revolution in France,* Judd Harmon says: "These publications had a considerable effect upon the development of English opinion about Revolution in France; through them Burke compelled protagonists on both sides of the controversy to consider the *principles* of revolution and reform rather than merely the isolated event of the Revolution itself. In doing so Burke established the main lines of his own political thought."[2]

The value of the works of Burke stands on two important points. First, Burke is not a man of speculation, he is a man of action. He had an intensely practical bent of mind with rare qualities of organising and expressing the fundamental facts of political life. In his speeches and writings we find that he "displayed an intellectual power of the highest order–a power of accumulating and digesting vast masses of material, a power of classifying and arranging it with masterly lucidity, a power of presenting it with overwhelming effect in the light of general principles; and that he combined with his splendid mental capacities a keenly sensitive, high-strung, emotional disposition."[3] Second, his defence of liberty touches the verge of conservatism. It is for this reason that Clinton Rossiter calls Burke "the father of all conservatives."[4] While Viereck takes a moderate view in keeping Burke 'on the borderline' between authoritarianism running through conservatism to liberalism,[5] Kirk bluntly designates him as 'the godfather of modern conservatism.'[6] The conservative mind of Burke, ac-

2. M. Judd Harmon: *Political Thought from Plato to the Present,* p. 328. Pollock says: "With Burke the difficulty is yet greater; he is full of ideas more instructive than other men's systems but they are so admirably woven into the discussion of particular and actual questions that they refuse to be torn out as examples of him. They proceed from a settled way of thinking but are nowhere reduced into a collected argument. A light of great wisdom shines in almost everything of Burke's making, but it is diffused light, of which the focus is not revealed but only conjectured". *An Introduction to the History of the Science of Politics,* p. 90.
3. Hearnshaw: "Burke" in *The Social and Political Ideas of Some Great Thinkers of the Revolutionary Era,* p. 88.
4. Clinton Rossiter: *Conservatism in America,* p. 22.
5. See Peter Viereck: *Conservatism from John Adams to Churchill,* Ch.1.
6. See Russell Kirk: *The Conservative Mind from Burke to Santyana,* Ch. 1. For a summarised version of Kirk's analysis, see McDonald: *Western Political Theory: The Modern Age,* Ch. 9 n. 248 .

cording to Kirk, has six attributes: (i) the belief that divine intent rules; (ii) affection for the mastery of tradition; (iii) the belief that civilisation requires orders and classes; (iv) the belief that property and freedom are inseparable; (v) faith in prescription as a check on man's will; and (vi) the view that change and reform are not identical.[7]

The conservatism of Burke is, however, accompanied by his pragmatism and empiricism. His rejection of all speculative philosophy coupled with his distrust for metaphysical and utopian premises reveals his pragmatic and empirical approach. It is discernible in his remark attributed to the thinker of the abstract philosophy to whom he disparagingly dubs 'refining speculatists', "political aeronauts', 'smugglers of adulterated metaphysics' and 'metaphysical knights of the sorrowful countenance.'[8] Burke's definition of civil liberty is an indication of the fact that he is an advocate of positive social liberty that allows no room for 'abstract' premises. As he says: "Civil freedom is not, as may have endeavoured to persuade you, a thing that hidden in the depth of abstruse science." It is thus rightly observed: "As Godwin or Condorcet was the man of principle, Burke was the man of experience."[9] Fredrick A. Dreyer comments: "The student who tries to define Edmund Burke's political theory attempts something that Burke refused to do himself. He never wrote a practical treatise and often affected to be a practical man who disliked speculation and who thought of politics in practical terms. Burke's writings nevertheless are immensely rich in doctrine. And against his assertion that he was a simple, practical man, we can place the equally strong assertion that he was a man of consistent principle."[10]

PREMISES : PRINCIPLES OF CONSERVATIVE STATESMANSHIP

The political theory of Burke has the premises of conservatism, pragmatism and empiricism wherein we find his views on order, liberty, elite culture, preservation of the English constitution, attack on rationalism, political science and 'forms' of social contract in the institutions of property, religion and prejudice. An epitomised version of Burke's political theory is

7. *Ibid.*
8. Cited in MacCunn: *The Political Philosophy of Burke*, p. 1.
9. McDonald, *op. cit.*, p. 249.
10. Dreyer: *Burke's Politics: A Study in Whig Orthodoxy*, p. 1.

manifest from this observation: "The most conspicuous general feature of his political outpourings are, first his avoidance of abstract political speculation and his denunciation of the metaphysical treatment of political affairs; secondly, his insistence on the empirical nature of the art of government; thirdly, his appeal to history and experience as the only satisfactory guides in administrative matters; fourthly, his emphasis on considerations of expediency, rather than on arguments based on rights in all debatable problems of policy and, finally, the essential moderation of all his opinions, even when he expressed those opinions with extreme moderation of language."[11]

Let us begin with 'order' that should be taken as the underlying principle of Burke's political theory. According to him, the universe "is orderly and intelligible and that it operates according to moral law of which God is the author. Society should be governed by this law."[12] The creation and maintenance of the public order is rather the function of the positive law of the state that applies the supreme norms of natural law according to the rules of prudence. For this reason, civil society is not the product of nature alone, nor of abstract reason, still less of mere human will; it is an artifact made by man's practical intellect working after a basic pattern established by nature but to be realised in history. Herein lies the root of Burke's theory of prescriptive institutions. We may take note of the fact that instead of opposing nature to history Burke "saw history as the expression and actualisation of nature."[13]

Liberty is a derivative of order. It is an 'excellent' thing. However, Burke insists that liberty is a social affair and, as such, it cannot be had at the expense of order. Order requires restraint. Either the individual must have capacity to restrain himself for the sake of enjoying liberty within the framework of order, or the state must create 'circumstances' for the sake of 'forging fetters of the passions of mankind'. As he says: "I cannot stand forward, and give praise or blame to anything which relates to human action, and human concerns, on a simple view of the object, as it stands stripped of every relation,

11. Hearnshaw, *op. cit.*, p. 89. So says Barker: "In the temper of this conviction Burke rings the changes on four bells, which we may call by the names of Experience, History (in the more specified sense of the written record of the past), Prescription and Prejudice." *Essays on Government*, p. 221.
12. Judd Harmon, *op. cit.*, p. 329.
13. Francis P. Canavan: *The Political Reason of Edmund Burke*, p. 89.

in all the nakedness and solitude of metaphysical abstraction. Circumstances (which with some gentlemen pass for nothing) give in reality to every political principle its distinguishing colour and discriminating effect. The circumstances are what render every civil and political scheme beneficial or noxious to mankind." So passionate is the emphasis of Burke on his conception of 'civil liberty' that he contemptuously refers to the advocates of abstract liberty as 'literary caballers', 'intriguing philosophers,' 'political theologians' and 'theological politicians'. Burke emphatically declares: "Liberty inheres in some sensible object; and every nation has formed to itself some favourite point which by way of eminence becomes the criterion of their happiness."[14]

The definition of civil liberty assumes the shape of an aristocratic privilege when Burke goes to the length of saying that it cannot be enjoyed equally by all. Liberty is not connected with the law of equality. According to Burke, each man is entitled to that liberty alone that accords with his station in life. Thus, liberty is identifiable with the privileges that differ from man to man and from class to class in social set-up. Obviously, Burke's liberty "becomes Plato's justice–the principle that secures to every member of the community his due rights in due place.[15] Such an affirmation of Burke is known by the name of his doctrine of the elite culture signifying that "the child of a tailor or of a carpenter, a man who himself has worked at such occupations or at any menial task, will not have the education to fit him to be chosen as a governor."[16]

The theory of elite culture raises the issue of the kind of government and social order best suited to achieve the ends of a society. Burke rejects the fundamental notion of the prophets of the school of law of nature claiming equality in respect of every man's capacity to rule and thereby run 'self-government.' Like Aristotle, Burke asserts that in any society only a few enjoy the leisure and manner of living that produces the nobility of mind and spirit characteristic of the aristocrats. He makes no inhibitions when he says that society requires division of functions and in all societies, consisting of various descriptions of citizens, some description must be uppermost."

14. *Ibid.*, p. 8.
15. Alfred Cobban: *Edmund Burke and the Revolt Against the Eighteenth Century*, p. 57.
16. Bluhm, *op. cit.*, p. 439.

He asks how is it possible for a hair-dresser or an ox-driver to get the wisdom of ruling? We thus find a clear-cut defence of the excellence of the aristocratic statesmanship in the works of Burke. Bluhm thus explains the meaning of Burke: "Therefore, we must seek the natural aristocracy among men of high birth and property, the actual aristocracy and the upper middle classes who enjoy social advantages denied to men of lesser position. These advantages cannot be generally distributed to the entire population in Burke's estimation. A nation which loses its aristocracy stands in grave danger of being plunged into barbarism, a condition with which Burke thought France was threatened by her revolution. For the aristocrats are the carriers of the moral, intellectual and aesthetic values of a culture in his opinion. Civilisation emanates from them and filters down through the other ranks of society. They give the lead and tone to a society in all matters. It is through that the principles of a society's institutions are articulated for the society at large, and in their way of life that the whole people find an object of admiration. An aristocracy is, therefore, itself a most vital institution."[17]

Burke's attack on the radicalism of the French revolution drawing inspiration from his recognition of the principles of order and civil liberty culminating in his thorough-going justification of the excellence of the aristocratic statesmanship constitutes the framework of his doctrine of prescriptive constitution. He is the most vehement critic of the advocates of the 'mechanistic theory' as followed by the revolutionary leaders of France who belonged to the middle and lower strata of society and who were determined to seize power from the hands of the 'best' class of the society. Thus, Burke developed his theory of prescriptive constitution as the best manifestation of his conservative political theory. It is, therefore, commented that Burke "opposed the gathering revolutionary deluge by advocating conservative reform. He aimed at preventing small commotions from becoming great maelstroms. He fought against injustice even more than against disorder, but especially he fought against the principles of political imbecility, which are ever the unwilling parents of both disorder and injustice. He strove to save the British constitution from the quack political doctors who administer poison for remedies, and to save the British Empire by eradicating the evils that made it a target

17. *Ibid.*, pp. 439-40.

for fanatics who are unwilling to destroy what they do not know how to reform."[18]

In fine, the keynote of Burke's political theory is conservatism what Bluhm calls 'teleo-naturalism'. In particular, his *Reflections on the Revolution in France* has been said to constitute 'the Bible of conservatism' in spite of the fact that Cobban has lauded it as 'the greatest and most influential and political pamphlet ever written'.[19] In its full aspects, the political theory of Burke finds place in traditional and slowly evolving institutions that embody the imprint of a divinely ordained order for human society, a divine reason immanent in the collective reason of mankind. Burke is a teleo-naturalist who has tried to synthesise the noumenalist conception of divine order with naturalist empiricism by incorporating the order as an almost mechanical regulator in historical development.[20]

CONSERVATISM : HALL-MARK OF BURKE'S POLITICAL THEORY

The dominant theme of Burke's political theory finds place in his abiding reverence for the established order–government, laws, religion, classes, customs and the like that constitute the paraphernalia of a social and political life. This is known by the name of 'conservatism,' though the real definition of this term fails to carry a single set of meanings equally applicable to each follower of the conservative variety of social and political philosophy. In a loose sense, the term 'conservatism' represents a broad spectrum of ideas that may vary from one believer to another. A conservative is one who struggles for the maintenance of the status quo; a conservative is also one who wants gradual change or who adheres to some abstract idea of presenting a model of his good order without allowing any room for the entry of radical innovations. However, when we apply this term to designate the political theory of Burke, we are required to stick to the salient feature of conservatism in taking it as a form of social and political philosophy that "implies the desirability of conserving."[21]

Burke's conservatism is evident from his insistence that any reform in the existing institutions should be made with

18. Ross, J.S. Hoffman and Paul Levack: *Burke's Politics: Selected Writings and Speeches of Edmund Burke on Reform, Revolution and War*, p. xiii.
19. Alfred Cobban, *op. cit.*, p. 129.
20. Bluhm, *op. cit.*, p. 445.
21. M. Judd Harmon, *op. cit.*, p. 338.

equity and consideration of disposition to preserve, while ability to improve upon should guide the statesmen. Any reform or improvement is justified only in the context of reference to the past. Burke thus favours gradual reform and sternly denounces any step that effects a radical innovation. Reform is allowed only when it is made very cautiously with regard to venerable traditions of antiquity. Hence, it is said that he "was always a reformer and never a revolutionary, always a conservative and never a Tory."[22]

Burke's conservatism is visible mainly in his two notions—eulogy of the English constitution and repudiation of the principles of French Revolution.

As Burke, more than any other thinker of the eighteenth century, approaches the political tradition with a sense of religious reverence, he believes that political institutions form a vast and complicated system of prescriptive rights and customary observances. These practices grow out of the past and adapt themselves with the present without any break in the continuity, and that the traditions of the constitution and of society at large ought to be the objects of reverence similar to religion, because it forms the repository of a collective intelligence and wisdom of a particular civilisation. He thus eulogises the English constitutional system in the name of his conviction that the arrangements of a political society are conventions sanctified by use and wont. He affirms that the English constitutional system is a balance of the Crown, the Lords and the Commons, but its present form is a result of very long evolution which should not be disturbed by sudden innovations. To tamper with them is to violate the reflection of a natural order which is founded in the political and social institutions of a nation. He thus warns: "To destroy any power, growing wild from the rank productive force of the human mind, is almost tantamount, in the moral world, to the destruction of the apparently active properties of bodies in the material."[23]

Burke's eulogy of the English constitution is contained in his famous statement: "Our constitution is a prescriptive constitution, it is a constitution whose sole authority is that it has existed time out of mind. Your King, your lords, your judges. your juries, grand and little, all are prescriptive. Prescription

22. Hearnshaw, *op. cit.*, p. 98.
23. Burke: *Reflections on the Revolution in France*, p. 58.

is the most solid of all titles, not only to property, but which is to secure that property, to government. It is a presumption in favour of any settled scheme of government against any untried project, that a nation has long existed and flourished under it. It is a better presumption even of the choice of a nation far better than any sudden and temporary arrangement by actual election. Because the nation is not an idea of local extent, and individual momentary aggregation, but it is an idea of continuity, which extends in time as well as in numbers and in space. And this is a choice not of one day or one set of people, not a tumultuary and giddy choice; it is a deliberate election of the ages and of generations; it is a constitution made by what is ten thousand times better than choice: it is made by the peculiar circumstances, occasions, tempers, dispositions and moral, civil and social habitudes of the people, which disclose themselves only in a long space of time. The individual is foolish: the multitude, for the moment, is foolish when they act without deliberation: but the species is wise, and, when time is given to it as a species, it always acts right."[24]

Burke appears as a fearless critic of the principles of the French Revolution. The leaders of the French Revolution developed mechanistic theory which meant that state was a purely artificial contrivance deliberately created by some formal contract or convention, which operated and functioned like a machine and which could be arbitrarily reformed or reconstructed at the will of its creators in complete disregard to historical laws and established traditions of a people.[25] Burke makes a very powerful attack on this theory by insisting that state is not like a piece of cloth or a kind of building which can be made or unmade as human will informs. It is a product of long evolution and its present structure is based on the wisdom of the past, hence it is fallacious to think in terms of its sudden renovation. Strongly criticising the ideology of the French revolutionaries, Burke says: "The science of construct-

24. Bohn (ed.): *Works of Burke,* Vol. IV, p. 146.
25. According to Garner, this theory regards the state "as somewhat analogous to an edifice and its founders to an architect; and just as an architect with a commission to construct a new edifice clears the ground of old foundations and debris and erects thereupon a new structure, so the people of a community can make *tabula rasa* of old institutions, cut loose from the past, ignore the forces of history and tradition and erect upon the ruins a new state organisation conceived and fashioned according to their own momentary notions and ideas." *Political Science and Government,* p. 212.

ing a commonwealth or renovating it, or reforming it, is like every other experimental science, not to be taught *a priori*."[26]

Burke's attack on the principles of French Revolution is based on five premises. Firstly, he rejects the principle of natural equality. As a champion of aristocracy, he does not believe that all men are born equal. He firmly upholds the principle of inequality in an Aristotelian manner and thus marks out a division of the society between the ruler and the ruled. Secondly, he dismisses the notion of popular sovereignty. He argues that in a well-ordered state the individual will or a number of such wills are not the arbiters of sovereignty. Thirdly, he repudiates the concept of majority government. Contrary to the thesis of Locke, he justifies the cause of aristocracy on the plea that a joint action is to be achieved. Fourthly, he ridicules hasty exercise of the right of revolution. The people may really rise in revolt but only by way of last remedy and not of the first choice. Finally, he scoffs at the efficiency of a written constitution. To him constitution is not made, it grows in response to the growth of wisdom and experience of the people. Every constitution should reflect the indigenous wisdom, otherwise its importation or imposition will naturally cause its failure.

Burke's conservatism thus dwells on the emphasis that institutions are a growth, not a make, and so they should be approached with reverence and touched with caution. Any hasty, sudden or rash attempt to renovate them will destroy the wisdom and experience hidden in them. Their proper and smooth working is a result of long habituation, familiarity and reverence behind them and no radical innovation will work until it has amassed a similar body of habit and sentiment. Owing to this, Burke ridicules the philosophy of the French Revolution. Sabine thus observes: "He had an almost mystical reverence for the embodied wisdom of a people. Always, he assumed, a great political tradition contains the clues for development, not by the slavish following of precedent but by the adaptation of a customary practice to a new situation."[27] Murray thus holds that Burke "gave vivid expression to this basic conviction that the state is not a man-made machine but an immensely complicated organisation which the efforts of individual have certainly helped to shape, but whose evolution and destiny cannot be wholly understood by any individual.

26. Burke: *Reflections on the Revolution in France*, p. 154.
27. Sabine, *op. cit.*, p. 614.

Burke believed that the way in which a state evolves and develops is largely determined by forces which no individual can fully comprehend, and that when men make changes they should do so with restraint and caution, since the consequences of their actions cannot be foreseen and may conflict with the most fundamental interest of the community as a whole."[28]

Burke's conservatism is a clear indication of his both being a reactionary and an aristocrat. His eulogy of the English constitutional system is much exaggerated and seeks to give a synthetic explanation of the Whig politics on the one hand and his own wisdom on the other. His reverence of the past was so deep-seated that he miserably failed to study the present in its proper perspectives. It is surprising that even after the Glorious Revolution of 1688 he did not appreciate the growth of representative institutions as is visible from his repudiation of the principles of natural equality, popular sovereignty and majority rule. It was due to this that the ideas of Utilitarianism appealed more to the people which outplaced the philosophy of conservatism. Laski points out: "It is easy to show that his picture of the British constitution was remote from the facts even when he wrote. Every change that he opposed was essential to the security of the next generation; and there followed none of the disastrous consequences he had foreshadowed."[29]

It may also be pointed out that Burke's theory of prescription has its necessary companion in his doctrine of prejudice. The two (prescription and prejudice) have never received a more consistent and courageous defence than Burke's championship of the wisdom of his ancestors. It is said that Burke "was sincerely convinced that man's power of political reasoning was utterly inadequate to their task that all his life long he urged the English nation to follow prescription, to obey, that is to say, on impulse their habitual political impulses."[30] And yet it may be added that he had very little to say concerning the greatest social quandary of our time; once prescription and prejudice are violated, once the mass of mankind have been cast adrift, with only miscellaneous crops of custom and tradition left to mingle with their private stock of reason, how society is to be kept from disintegration?"[31]

---

28. Murray: *Introduction to Political Philosophy,* p. 140.
29. Laski: *Political Thought in England from Locke to Bentham,* p. 169.
30. Graham Wallas: *Human Nature in Politics,* pp. 182-83.
31. Russell Kirk: "Burke and the Philosophy of Prescription" in Isaac Kramnic

Barker well recognises the fact that after the death of Burke the philosophy of conservatism could not endure. He says: "Men began to feel the need of a more scientific explanation of the facts, and a more scientific attempt to cure the defects of social life. Two revolutions had passed over the world in the last few decades–the political revolution which had started in France in 1789, and the industrial revolution which had begun in England about 1760. The fruits of one had still to be garnered, the unforeseen results of the other had still to be faced. On the one hand, the political demands of the Chartists had to be met with some reasonable answer; and statesmen had to determine how far, and by what means, the French doctrine of the sovereignty of *volonte generale* should be incorporated into the parliamentary system and electoral machinery of England. On the other hand, sterner and more exacting, there loomed the massive problem of the conditions of England. With the eye of a genius Disraeli had already seized and stated the problem in Sybil; with the sympathy of a philanthropist Shaftesbury had already begun to attempt some solution."[32]

STATESMANSHIP : EMPHASIS ON EXPEDIENCY AND PRAGMATISM

Burke's views on statesmanship bear the distinctive stamp of expediency and pragmatism. It means that he discards abstract principles of metaphysics and insists on the practical usefulness of things. With this standpoint, her rejects the doctrine of social contract and the dogma of natural rights and sharply criticises the colonial policy of his government. Coupled with his thesis of conservatism, Burke's counsel of expediency and pragmatism implies that it is essential to preserve what has been gained in the long struggle and experimentation of centuries. But as human affairs develop only at a slow, gradual and orderly pace, and sudden change disintegrates and destroys, it may be necessary at times to make sacrifices of the old and introduce innovation moderately in order to preserve the general pattern. The principle of expediency should be strictly followed by the statesmen in understanding the present and accordingly changing the past.[33]

(ed.); *Essays in the History of Political Thought,* p. 292.

32. Barker: *Political Thought in England, 1848 to 1914,* pp. 1-2.
33. Cook thus explains the application of Burke's argument: "The politician must above all be cautious and must base his reformation on a careful comprehension of the past. He is the temporary custodian of a permanent

Hence, Burke's criticism of the colonial policy of British Government is possessed of remarkable political sagacity and statesmanship. He is not at all a stubborn defender of the *status quo*, he twins the principles of preservation and improvement and thus puts his view: "A disposition to preserve and an ability to improve, taken together, would be my standard of a statesman. Everything else is vulgar in the conception, perilous in execution. A good patriot or a true politician always considers how he shall make the most of the existing materials of his country."[34]

Burke's speech on conciliation with America published in 1775 fully shows that he was not a doctrinaire philosopher but a practical statesman. The issue of American War of Independence became a very acute and menacing problem for the government of Lord North. The British Navigation Act, Stamp Act, Import Duties Act and several other enactments that regulated and controlled American industry and commerce in the interest of British capitalists threw the American colonies to the verge of a rebellion against the oppressive enforcement and mis-rule of British officials. Burke thus insisted that the problem should be studied not in the context of superstition and abstract rights but concrete interests, not on the basis of legality but that of expediency and commonsense. He thus advised the Parliament to give up its sovereign rights of taxation and control and by following the profitable course of prudence and utility should secure the goodwill and co-operation of the American colonies. He forcefully warned that the policy of repression and suppression so obdurately followed by the English government would result in total loss of the colonies to the Empire and thus he urged that the pursuance of a policy of expediency would enhance safety, prosperity and prestige of the Empire. He forcefully said: "The question will be not whether you have a right to render your people miserable, but whether it is not in your interest to make them happy."[35]

Burke's strong insistence on sanity and liberalism in statesmanship is also visible in his criticism of the rule of

treasure, and for a vision of passing pleasure he must not risk its loss in a gamble where victory is uncertain. Yet an unyielding stubbornness may be destructive as utopian hopes, and the tensile strength of enlightened expediency is more valuable than the brittle force of unanchored principles." *History of Political Philosophy from Plato to Burke*, pp. 681-82.

34. Burke: *Reflections on the Revolution in France*, p. 153.
35. See Bohn, *op. cit.*, p. 475.

English East India Company. In very clear terms he condemned the rule of many a Governor-General (chiefly Warren Hastings) who sacrificed the principles of justice, humanity and order for the sake of amassing great wealth. He predicted that the rapacious rule of the Company and the loss of honesty and far-sighted intelligence would result in bitter resentment of the people amounting to the instability of the Empire. In a speech on the debts of the Nabob of Arcot he said: "Fraud, injustice, oppression, speculation engendered in India, are crimes of the same blood, family and caste with those that are born and bred in England. The difference (between peculation in Westminster and in Madras) is in our attention to the one and our total neglect of the other."[36] He further said: "Had this attention and neglect been regulated by the value of several other objects there would be nothing to complain of. But the reverse of that supposition is true. The scene of the Indian abuse is distant indeed, but we must not infer that the value of our interest in it is decreased in proportion as it recedes from our view. In our politics, as in our common conduct, we shall. be more than infants if we do not put our senses under the tuition of our judgment, and effectually cure ourselves of that optical illusion which makes a bier at our nose of greater magnitude than an oak at five hundred yards distance."[37]

ORGANICISM : REVERENCE OF STATE

Burke's theory of state is quite different from that of Hobbes and Locke. He emphasises that state and society are an organic growth an not an artificial creation. He does not rely on abstract reason or on abstract principles of metaphysics, rather he believes in the utilisation of empirical method yielding concrete results. His denunciation of the deductive method makes him a stern disbeliever in the dogma of natural rights. He turns down Lockean thesis and calls natural rights as national wrongs. Men cannot enjoy rights in a pre-civil or a pre-political stage of development. The rights of a pre-social and pre-political condition may be true abstractly or metaphysically, they are false in a political community. Thus, Burke regards the Declaration of the Rights of Man and Citizen as a sort of institute and a digest of anarchy. Rejecting the doctrine of social contract school, Burke says that the metaphysical and alchemi-

36. Cited in Jones : *Masters of Political Thought*, Vol. II, p. 342.
37. *Ibid.*,

cal legislators "have attempted to confound all sorts of citizens as well as they could into one homogeneous mass."[38]

Thus, Burke's theory of state assumes an organic character. Contradistinguished with the erstwhile doctrine of social contract, he holds that civilisation is the possession not of individuals but of communities and that the entire spiritual possessions of a man flow from his membership of an organised political society. A clear distinction between savagery and civilised life lies in the thing that the entire society is the guardian of all that the generations of human race have produced and a man living in it has natural access to its store. Obviously, society is not a sand heap of individuals living like isolated and independent atoms; it "is not a burden but an open door to human liberation."[39]

It becomes fully obvious with the following famous statement of Burke: "Society is indeed a contract. Subordinate contract for objects of more occasional interest may be dissolved at pleasure–but the state ought not to be considered as nothing better than a partnership agreement in a trade of pepper and coffee, calico or tobacco, or some other such low concern, to be taken up for a little temporary interest, and to be dissolved by the fancy of the parties. It is to be looked up with reverence; because it is not a partnership in things subservient only to the gross animal existence of a temporary and a perishable nature. It is a partnership in all sciences, a partnership in all arts, a partnership in every virtue, and in all perfections. As the ends of such a partnership cannot be obtained at all in many generations, it becomes a partnership not only between those who are living, or dead, but are yet to be born. Each contract of each particular state is but a clause in the great primeval contract of eternal society, linking the lower with the higher nature, connecting the visible and invisible world, according to a fixed compact sanctioned by the inviolable oath which holds all physical and all moral natures each in their appointed place."[40]

38. Burke: *Reflections on the Revolution in France*, p. 101.
39. Sabine, *op. cit.*, p. 615.
40. Burke: *Reflections on the Revolution in France*, pp. 93-94.

REPRESENTATIVE GOVERNMENT : PARTY AND REPRESENTATION

Burke gives a classical definition of political party by saying that it "is a body of men united for promoting by their joint endeavours the national interest, upon some particular principle in which they are all agreed."[41] Burke's awareness of the significance of party system becomes obvious with the thing that he stoutly opposed the autocratic policy of King George III and organised Whig party on proper lines. His definition reveals that he adhered to the fact of public good or national interest and thus regarded party not as an end in itself but as a means to a higher end. It may also be pointed out that Burke justified the importance of party politics in the system of representative government.

In this direction, more important in his thesis of parliamentary representation. He frankly rejects the idea of a constituency as a numerical unit based on the territorial division of the country and of parliamentary representation as implying the possession of the ballot by any considerable portion of the population represented. In Burke's view, a parliamentary representative does not sell away his freedom and conscience to the members of his constituency, rather he enjoys full independence, although he is expected to pay high regard to the feelings of his constituents. He asserts that it ought to be the happiness and glory of a representative to live in the closest union, the clearest correspondence , and the most unreserved communication with his constituents, and that their wishes ought to have great weight with him and their opinions high respect. In other words, Burke desires that a parliamentary representative should not sacrifice the feelings of his constituents and, at the same time, he should not follow them blindly, he pleads that the representative should be a pillar of the state, not a weather-cock at the top of the edifice exalted for his levity and versatility and of no use but "to indicate the shiftings of every fashionable gale."[42] In one of his addresses delivered in 1780 to the electors of Bristol, Burke defended the independence of parliamentary representative thus: "The parliament is not a congress of ambassadors from different and hostile interests, which interests each must maintain as an agent and advocate against other agents and advocates. But

41. Cited in Sabine, *op. cit.*, p. 611.
42. Cited in Garner, *op. cit.*, p. 680.

parliament is a deliberative assembly of one nation, with one interest, that of the whole where not local purposes, not local prejudices, ought to guide, but the general good resulting from the general reason of the whole. You choose a member indeed, but when you have chosen him he is not a member of Bristol, but he is a member of parliament."[43]

Though Burke's classical definition of political party has won appreciation, his thesis of parliamentary representation has not been liked by those who present the extreme current of democratic conception. The extremist view in this regard holds that the representative is bound by the restrictions of his constituents and his office is restricted merely to ascertaining and registering their sentiments. In other words, the principles of political ethics require that when he is accredited to the legislature like an ambassador, he cannot act independently according to his own convictions. This argument is supported by the system of recall whereby the constituents may withdraw their elected representative when they find him acting contrary to their sentiments and send another delegate in his place. The appropriate conclusion seems to be that the representative should really pay regard to the wishes of his constituents and give a proof of best representation, no matter he happens to act independently on certain occasions.[44]

43. *Ibid.*

44. Instances are not wanting to show that prior to 1913 the States of USA exercised such right over their representatives sent to the Senate. It is due to this practice that when in 1836 the Senators of Virginia disobeyed the mandate of their State, Benjamin Watking Leigh resigned, while John Lyler retained his seat at the cost of his strength. But this situation changed in 1913 when the election of the Senators became direct. Clarifying this situation, Burgess writes: "The principle is that each Senator and each Representative represents the whole United States, according to his own intelligence and judgment, and that there is no constituency in the United States which can demand a control over its representative in either House of the Congress to require his resignation." *Political Science and Constitutional Law,* Vol. II, p. 50. Lieber also pronounces the doctrine of instruction to be "unwarranted, inconsistent and unconstitutional." *Political Ethics,* Vol. II, p. 351. Garner thus sums up: "With regard to the duty of the representative who is chosen directly by the people, it is widely asserted today that, in order to be what the word implies, namely the mouthpiece of those for whom he speaks, he ought simply to register their will rather than his own wherever it is known to him in unmistakable terms, or he ought to resign and make way for someone who more truly represents their sentiments. Otherwise, how can he be said to be a representative of the people and how can he speak for them as they themselves would speak if they could be in his place?" *Op.*

FORMS OF SOCIAL CONTROL : PROPERTY, RELIGION AND PREJUDICE

Burke looks upon property, religion and prejudice as the forces of social control, for they contribute to the preservation of established institutions. Like Aristotle and Locke, he defends the institution of private property. In his view, this institution is a twofold blessing–it gives a sense of security to its owners, and allows them to develop the habits necessary for the responsible use of power; it enables the government to continue its rule by ensuring proper safeguards. Besides, it also helps in reaching higher standards. He says: "The power of perpetuating our property in our families is one of the most valuable and interesting circumstances belonging to it, and that which tends the most to the perpetuation of society itself. It makes our weakness subservient to our virtue, it grafts benevolence even upon avarice. The possessors of family wealth and so of the distinction which attends hereditary possession, are the natural securities for this transmission."[45]

It is clear that in Burke the institution of private property finds its another strong defender. Burke prefers that, as far as possible, property should be based on the land, for it can set up straightforward lines of authority and control between the employer and the employee. Rejecting the concept of social contract, he argues that private property system be based on historical patterns and not on any hypothetical contract. The property under possession should be fairly substantial so that significant social status and power be enjoyed by those who own it. If it is so, then the owner shall be able to establish personal relationship of authority with his subordinate tenants. Moreover, this system will make the citizens capable of respecting the authority of their masters.

If private property system breeds such advantages, naturally its equalisation is unjustified in the view of Burke. Once again, Burke's conservatism justifies unequalisation of wealth. Not only this, he insists that no such step should be undertaken that attacks the privileged status of the property-owners. The state must protect the legitimate rights of the owners. He warns that if the state takes concerted efforts to diffuse property, its defensive power is thereby weakened. At the same time, he advises the people to respect the property of

cit., p. 672.

45. Burke: *Reflections on the Revolution in France*, p. 49.

others and keep themselves consoled of what they gain by their own labour in the name of eternal justice and bliss available to them in another world. Burke strongly says: "Of this consolation whoever deprives him, deadens their industry and strikes at the root of all conservation."[46]

It is understandable that Burke's defence of private property undermines the principles of democracy and socialism. It is a clear justification of private property system and through it of an aristocratic form of government. His justification is based on the assumption that if the ruling class has substantial private property, it has every right to shoulder and carry out great responsibilities, every opportunity of acting wisely and virtuously and every possibility of understanding properly the requirements and feelings of the people.[47] But Burke forgets that the institution of private property is not only a blessing, it is a curse too. Its holders can degenerate in character and ability and thus miserably fail to act wisely and virtuously. The concerted efforts of the state in maintaining unequalisation of wealth will certainly breed the feelings of class war and drag the people to the brink of a revolution. The obstinacy of the ruling class will still more excite the feeling of envy and rapacity in the common people and thus lead to the germination of those factors which destroy social peace and harmony. People will no longer tolerate the obstinacy of their rulers and create such problems which can be solved by nothing short of a revolution. In the beginning the problems will appear to be surmountable, but their accumulated form will speak of their insurmountability. Laski is right when he foresees the possibility of every such danger and says: "It remains historically obvious that a community divided between rich and poor i.e., when the latter are numerous, is built upon the foundations of sand. For the basis of the state is envy, and envy is the nurse

---

46. *Ibid.*, p. 241. As Burke says: "Everybody is satisfied that conservation and a secure enjoyment of our natural rights is the great and ultimate purpose of civil society, and that therefore all forms whatsoever of government are only good as they are subservient to that purpose to which they are entirely subordinate." *Works*, Vol. 6, p. 333.

47. Peter Stanlis is of the view that "Burke was essentially a Thomist in his political philosophy." *Edmund Burke and the Natural Law*, p. 249. Leo Strauss holds that Burke "integrated his notions of natural right into a classical Thomistic framework." *Natural Right and History*, p. 296. Likewise, Francis Canavan says: "The basic premises of Burke's mature political thought strongly resemble those of medieval Christian Aristotelianism." *The Political Reason of Edmund Burke*, p. 205.

of factions...Yet the state remains divided into rich and poor, and men, after a period, refuse to suffer quietly. The revolution supervenes to alter the balance in the state."[48]

The intensely religious bias of Burke is responsible for uniting religion with politics. Burke argues that religion is not an alien or artificial intrusion, rather it "it's the basis of civil society, and the source of all good and comfort."[49] In his view, religious instruction should be given to the people, because it removes gnawing doubts and frustrating uncertainties from their minds and hearts. The teachings of religion also instal a sense of earthly consolation which checks social classification. The religious teaching makes men pious which ennobles their character. At the hands of Burke, religion becomes one of the forces of social control inasmuch as it incalculates public knowledge and belief that inequitable social adjustment is upright. Burke says: "It is the public ornament. It is the public consolation. It nourishes the public hope. The poorest man finds his own importance and dignity in it, while the wealth and pride of individuals of every movement makes the man of humble rank and fortune sensible of his inferiority, and degrades and vilifies his condition."[50]

Once again, it is obvious that Burke's utilisation of religion as a force of social control is nothing but a dexterous attempt to safeguard the interest of the rich class. In the name of eternal bliss and justice, he whishes to keep the 'have-nots' consoled with their petty fortunes. The doctrines of religion are utilised as a means of public control over those in society who might otherwise feel a sense of class consciousness and thus upset the established order to secure a redressal of their sufferings and grievances. The assertion of Burke that religion should be used as a tool takes him very near to Machiavelli.[51]

The third force of social control is the 'prejudice' whose cultivation is necessary for the sake of social order. By prejudice

48. Laski: *A Grammar of Politics*, pp. 176-77.
49. Burke, *op. cit.*, p. 88.
50. *Ibid.*, p. 59.
51. The Communists and the Anarchists thus reject conventional religion on both scientific and spiritual grounds. A great critic of religion as Kropotkin said that it "is either a primitive cosmogony, a rude attempt at explaining nature, or it is an ethical system which through its appeals and ignorance to the superstition of the masses, cultivates among them a tolerance of the injustices they suffer under existing political and economic arrangement." *Anarchist Communism*, p. 35.

Burke means widely held opinions and sentiments that have long existed to bring unity and stability to the community. Though prejudice, Burke makes it clear, may look like something abstract or speculative, it may also contain a wisdom which "is part of higher reason that always conduces to the preservation of established institutions."[52] As Burke says: "Instead of casting away all our old prejudices, we cherish them to a very considerable degree, and to take more shame to ourselves, we cherish them because they are prejudice: and longer they have lasted and the more generally they have prevailed, the more we cherish them. We are afraid to put man to live and trade on his own private stock of reason, because we suspect that this stock in each man is small, and that the individuals would do better to avail themselves of the general bank and capital of nations and of ages. Prejudice is of ready application in the emergency; it previously engages the mind in a steady course of wisdom and virtue, and does not leave the man necessitating in the moment of decision, skeptical, puzzled, and unresolved. Prejudice renders a man's virtue his habit: and not a series of unconnected acts. Through just prejudice, his duty becomes a part of his nature."[53]

Apart from the fact that Burke's invocation of the term 'prejudice' goes against the very spirit of empiricism, what should be noted here is that he makes different implications of the term at different occasions, though all veer round to the theme of his prescription. In its simplest sense, prejudice is nothing but everything having its synonymous interpretation in the respected traditions or opinions of the past. A prejudice becomes a force of social control in the system of Burke for the simple reason that it contributes its share to supporting the established institutions of a civil society. It is, therefore, understandable that despite all anti-rationalist shibboleths, prejudice, not in an ordinary and pejorative but in an approbative sense, is 'closely related to custom and tradition' that, in effect, signifies 'old inveterate opinion.'[54]

52. M. Judd Harmon, *op. cit.*, p. 334.
53. See Bohn, *op. cit.*, Vol. II, p. 359.
54. Canavan, *op. cit.*, p. 74.

EMPIRICISM : ATTACK ON RATIONALIST POLITICAL SCIENCE

So stern is the emphasis of Burke on practical reason that he is said to be a vehement critic of the metaphysical and abstract forms of political theory depending upon the premises of rationalist political science. Herein we find the empiricism of Burke in the sense that he discards the principles of a rationalist science that consists wholly of the propositions about logical relationship between metaphysical or abstract principles and, for this reason, ignores the 'circumstances' or the state of reality verifiable by human experiences that lay down the roots of empirical political theory. However, the most astonishing aspect of Burke's political theory in this regard finds place not in his disdain for the men of abstract and speculative theory but in the tribute given to him by the admirers of Hobbes and Hegel who called him 'the enemy of political philosophy' and chided his method "not only as a useless but as a dangerous pursuit."[55]

The foundations of Burke's empiricism may be discovered in the following respects. First, Burke discards the 'speculative' method of men like Hobbes on the ground that it stands on the foundation of 'speculative reason' that either has no logical relationship with the world of 'circumstances' or, if perforce applied to bring about 'great innovations', it is sure to bring chaos into the world of politics. He accuses men of 'abstract theory' of being the makers of 'an infallible political science' which is altogether impossible. Such an approach leads to dangerous fantasies. He calls deductive method as invalid as well as incapable of laying down universal, eternal and immutable principles of political behaviour. The contention of Burke is that politics, whether descriptive or prescriptive, should have its logical connection with the world of 'circumstances' that are real and verifiable by human experiences. As he says: "There are some fundamental points in which nature never changes, but they are few and obvious, and belong rather to morals than to politics. But so far as regards political matter, the human mind and human affairs are susceptible of infinite modifications, and of combinations wholly new and unlooked for."[56]

It is understandable that actual circumstances become all-important for Burke. Not a principle of geometrical exact-

---

55. See Bluhm, *op. cit.*, p. 326.
56. *Ibid.*

ness, as suggested by Hobbes, but a principle of practical usefulness is needed for 'political' question. The enjoyment of civil liberty, which is real liberty, is integrally associated with the world of circumstances. As Burke says: "It is because liberty in the abstract may be classed amongst the blessings of mankind, that I am seriously to felicitate a mad man who has escaped from the protecting restraint and wholesome darkness of his cell, on his restoration to the enjoyment of light and liberty? Am I to congratulate a highwayman and a murderer, who has broken prison, upon the recovery of his natural rights?" The concept of freedom is, therefore, tied up with the world of actual circumstances that allow no room for the use of speculative or deductive study. We may notice here that Burke goes much ahead of the current liberal thought in laying down that all men are bound by an elaborate network of social obligations and to seek an escape from them is highly immoral. That is, Burke repudiates the concept of 'autonomous individual' as given by the liberal thought and supplements it with his concept of autonomous individual bound by the laws of social obligation and who is required to accept those 'obligation' reverently.

Though Burke discards the metaphysical, abstract and speculative philosophy, he accepts the premises of the law of nature and natural rights in a peculiar way. It may be said that instead of rejecting the doctrine of natural rights in a downright manner like his successor Bentham, he transforms their real meaning. He clearly asserts that possession of the 'scared' natural rights is nothing less than the great purpose of civil society, and whenever any public measure is proved mischievous to effect them, the objection ought to be fatal to that measure. The underlying point of Burke's emphasis is that the idea of man's natural rights must not be mixed up with the 'abstract' philosophy of metaphysics or any speculative logic as done by thinkers like Locke and Paine; rather it must be logically linked up with the considerations of political expediency and social utility. Thus, Burke comes very close to the system of Aristotle who regarded state as a natural association and St. Thomas who held it a divinely sanctified institution. "The true rights of men, therefore, did not derive from a mythical state of life antecedent to the formation of civil society and the institution of property and government, but from the fixed and permanent nature of beings on whom lay an obligation to obey their Maker's ordinances. IIis law alone gave sanction to all good political institutions, and the test of a good one was not how well it corresponded to schemes contrived by the most benevolent doctrinaires, but how well freedom, justice, property, peace and all the conditions requisite to a good human life flourished under it."[57]

It, however, does not mean that Burke is an anti-rationalist, rather he should be regarded as the prophet of political reason. The political reason of Burke is both practical and prescriptive. It should be discovered in the institutions of social and political life that have lasted over long period of time and that have assumed the form of unchanging, though not unchangeable, habits of the society. The political reason of Burke has four characteristics. First, it is *concrete* and thus it is not connected with abstract objects. Second, it is *practicable* and this it is connected with anything that is capable of being realised in a situation in which a statesman has to act. Thirdly, it is *complex* as it is associated with the good of the state that is a network of relationships of a diverse variety. Finally, it is *imperfect* and thus a public-spirited prudence sometimes demands a compliance with the impracticable nature of inveterate evils.[58]

Burke's empiricism is commonly misunderstood in the light of his overshadowing conservatism. It is absurd to call him an enemy of change, rather it will be in all fairness to describe him as an enemy of violent and radical change as was done by the revolutionary leaders of France. Change must be gradual without disturbing the equilibrium of a political system. Political prudence informs to 'support traditions, says Burke. But he also says that when the reason of old establishments "is gone, it is absurd to preserve nothing but the burden of them." It is for this reason that while Burke spoke against the philosophy of French Revolution, he insisted on a policy of conciliation with the leaders of the American revolution. The point of essential consideration here is that some principles should be laid down to know whether the reason of old establishments is gone and, if gone, what should be done to effect the necessary change in a gradual manner. What Burke really desires is that even a gradual change should be brought about in a spirit of practicability, of moderation, and of mutual convenience.

In fine, the empiricism of Burke has much to do with the rule, political judgment and practical conduct of a statesman

57. Ross, Hoffman and Levack, *op. cit.*, pp. xvi-vii.
58. See Canavan, *op. cit.*, pp. 7-10.

in a given situation rather than with the formulation of a theory of the best political order or a taxonomic illustration of different political systems. It is rightly said that against all metaphysical thinking in politics, Burke "offered his conception of political reason operating according to the rules of prudence. Its function was to estimate properly the ends which must be achieved or safeguarded, to evaluate the means for attaining the ends and the situation in which those means must be used, to combine all the elements of the situation into a consistent course of action, and finally to make those decisions which would translate its purpose into reality. Political reasons connoted a mind which was never doctrinaire and yet respected consistency, which consulted history and experience but was not bound by them and which had clear eye both for desirable goals and for the actual world in which they were to be realised. All this was implied in Burke's notion of political reason and the virtue of prudence."[59]

CRITICAL ESTIMATE : BURKE AS CHRYSOSTOM OF ENGLISH POLITICS

Burke has been described as 'one of the greatest men and, Bacon excepted, the greatest thinker who ever devoted himself to the practice of English politics'. However, our study of Burke's political philosophy leaves the most unmistakable impression that he is a prophet of the school of conservatism. It is discernible in his own view of history where a great volume 'is unrolled for our instruction'. To Burke, the instructions of history are not to be taken as the raw materials for an inductive examination of things, it is to be used as an authentic evidence for proving the wisdom of the past that should never be undermined. As Barker says: "God operates and man, under His guidance, co-operates. Holding this view, Burke can believe at one and the same time in the immortality of the state and the experimentalism of politics. He can hold at one and the same time, that he cannot escape from the past, and that we can and must escape from the head of the metaphysical theories of politics which would cast life unalterably and irrevocably in one hard iron mould. The immortal state and the experimentalism of the politics by which the state is guided and governed–this is the paradox, the seeming paradox with which Burke seeks to confront the votaries of revolution...The past is not a dead

59. *Ibid.*, p. 17.

hand, but a moving finger of guidance. If we respect the past, and the present in which the past lives, we are essentially and fundamentally free".[60]

Such a deep and abiding interest of Burke in the world of conservatism militates against his so-called theory of empiricism. One may question as to how conservatism and empiricism may go together. Empiricism has the central theme of innovation in the sense that it is always scientific and, therefore, changing. Contrary to this, Burke uses the forces of religion, property and traditions to strengthen the premises of his theory of prescriptive institutions. For instance, Burke refutes all standards of empiricism when we find him saying: "There is no room on earth, I believe, more willing than I am to lay it down as a fundamental of the Constitution that the Church of England should be united and even identified with it." This point is clearly evident from the interpretation of MacCunn: "Burke's political religion has its deep roots in three convictions. The first is that civil society rests on spiritual foundations, being indeed nothing less than a product of divine will; the second that this is a fact of significance so profound that the recognition of it is of vital moment, both for the corporate life of the state and for the lives of the each and all of its members; and the third, that whilst all forms of religion within the nation may play their part in bearing witness to religion, this is peculiarly the function of the established Church in which the 'conservation' of the 'State' finds its appropriate symbol, expression and support."[61]

A further difficulty in the way of appreciating the empiricism of Burke arises when we find out a line of contradiction in his attack on the basic philosophy of the French revolutionaries and his own basic philosophy of eulogising the principles of his English constitution. If empiricism means refutation of all abstract and speculative doctrines, it should be applied in a way that all abstract and speculative doctrines, like the dogma of divine origin of state and hypothetical rights of man given by nature, are discarded as 'non-sense'. A deeper examination of the political philosophy of Burke, in this direction, brings home a subtle point that while he refutes his predecessors like Locke as well as his contemporaries involved in the revolution of France clamouring for the defence and

60. Barker, *op. cit.*, pp. 231-32.
61. J. MacCunn, *op. cit.*, p. 122.

preservation of their 'natural rights', he, at the same time, struggles for the 'natural rights' of his own people with the shrewd tongue of a parliamentarian. It is thus pointed out by Hearnshaw: "The inherent primeval rights of the individual–the right to life, the right to liberty, the right to property–were in the same case. Burke did not and could not as a good Whig definitely denounce them. Nay he even appealed to them now and again, when it suited to do as, for example, in his defence of the people of India against the tyranny of Warren Hastings. But as a rule he ignored them to be employed as weapons to rebut the claims of the French monarchy. The only rights to be commonly admitted as valid were rights based on the civil laws of the state, provided that civil laws accorded with the precepts of the eternal law of God."[62]

Above all, Burke's empiricism is undermined by his own reverence of the state that reaches very close to divine heights at the cost of social contract theory. Not a rejection of the social contract theory making state an artificial organisation but a justification of the celebrated state reaching the pinnacles of a divine institution is the underlying feature of Burke's political theory. Burke's famous statement that state is not like a partnership in some low concern but a partnership, if partnership at all, in all sciences, arts, virtues and perfections, and among those who are not only dead and living but also among those of the coming generations, personifies the idea of an organic state having a sanctified character. As Hearnshaw once again says: "If one asks what is the meaning of this sonorous passage, the answer is that as it stands it has none. It is a resounding nonsense. In particular, the concluding sentence respecting primeval contracts and 'inviolable oaths' is the emptiest verbiage...The way is made clear for the entry of the new (yet immemorially only) idea of society as an organism; of the state as arising from the will of God rather than from the will of man; of community as an entity claiming priority to each and all of its members."[63]

Finally, Burke's ideas on representative democracy covering the areas of political party are 'hopelessly idealistic' and his consideration on the nature of representation are nothing else than a shrewd version of the excellence of the aristocratic form of government. It is for this reason that Thomas Paine accused

62. Hearnshaw, *op. cit.*, p. 94.
63. *Ibid.*, p. 93.

Burke of making dead men more important than the living ones, of advocating rulers accountable to nobody because they are ruled by prescription, and of treating the mass of men as contemptible fools. It may be pointed out that what Burke really desired went against much what his times demanded and this may be taken as another weakness in the empiricism of Burke. It is thus said: "Burke's ideas on representation are more medieval than modern. To him men are important as members of the class to which they belong; representation should be based on this principle."[64] Similarly, McDonald says: "Burke's conception of representation, or rather his conception of the priority of delegation over representation, rested on the aristocratic premise not only overly idealistic for its own day but largely irrelevant to his own non-aristocratic age."[65]

It is true that, in a strict sense, Burke was not a political philosopher like Plato, Aristotle, Hobbes, Rousseau and Montesquieu. His political ideas were a product of occasion and not of academic speculations. He did not write books on the subject of politics; it is mainly the collection of his speeches, letters and addresses wherein the material of his political theory is available.[66] Still Burke occupies a very important place in the history of modern political thought. The reason for this may be traced in his valuable contributions. For instances, he avoided abstract political speculations and denounced metaphysical treatment of practical affairs; he laid stress on the empirical nature of the art of government; he appealed to history and experience as the only satisfactory guides in administrative matters; he asserted the consideration of expediency rather than arguments based on natural or ideal rights and he advised essential moderation of opinions. His sharp criticism of social contract theory and the philosophy of French Revolution not only gave a majestic complexion to his political philosophy, rather effected a decent burial of all those doctrines and dogmas that considered the state in terms of an artificial creation.

It is due to this that Burke is said to have started a new tradition. Statesmen like Canning and Disraeli, men of letters like Wordsworth, Coleridge and Southey, and philosophers like

64. M. Judd Harmon, *op. cit.*, p. 333.
65. McDonald, *op. cit.*, p. 256.
66. Dr. Margaret Sapher thus observes: "Despite an approach that suggests later historical school, Burke wrote not as a scientific historian but as the inspired and indignant prophet of conservatism and aristocracy.' *Readings in Recent Political Philosophy*, p. 46.

Paine and Mackintosh followed the ideas of Burke in different directions. It is rightly said that the reaction which he led against the French Revolution was the beginning of a shift which carried the prevailing social philosophy from attack to defence and therefore to a new emphasis on the value of stability and the power of custom on which stability depends. Laski well concludes that it "is easy to praise Burke and easier to miss the greatness of his effort" and that there "is hardly a greater figure in the history of political thought in England."[67] Fredrick A Dreyer observes: "If the question we ask is whether Burke made a major contribution to the development of political theory, the answer must be that he did not. He wrote and speculated within the framework of natural rights individualism: there is nothing in the text of his writings to suggest that he rebelled against the orthodoxies of his time or that he anticipated the novelties of the nineteenth century speculation. To picture Burke as a profound and original thinker is to misread the principles that he actually asserted. It is, moreover, to thrust upon him a status which he laid no claim to."[68]

In fine, Burke is a representative thinker of the conservative school having his sympathy with the interest of the rising capitalist class. It is well observed: "Everyone sees that Burke had always been a defender of a tradition, inherited social order of subordination of ranks. What has not generally been seen is that the traditional order which he cherished was not simply an hierarchical order but a capitalist one. His case against the French principles was the same as his case against the Speenhamland principle: both would destroy traditional society by destroying the prerequisite condition of a capitalist accumulation, that is, a submissive wage-earning class."[69] Likewise, Andrew Hacker comments: "Burke's political theory uses as its model a society which is old and established. A nation which has but recently come into existence, or one in the process of accelerated social change, poorly suited to follow the precepts Burke lays down. Except for a few sheltered corners of the

---

67. Laski: *Political Thought in England,* p. 182. Coker admires Burke thus: "He upheld the values of rank and social privilege in insuring the preservation of good manners, heroic enterprise, orderly living, respectful subservience of the humble to their betters and generous guardianship of the common by the noble." *Recent Political Thought,* p. 8.
68. Dreyer, *op. cit.,* p. 83.
69. C.B. Macpherson: *Burke,* p. 61.

globe, hardly any societies have experienced–or will in the future experience–the luxury of gradual and cautious development. Burke's prescriptions are not meant for a recently emancipated colony in Africa or an Asian nation undergoing the tremors of sudden industrialisation. The importance of his theory, then, lies in its values: the principles of tradition and authority, class and civility, are enduring and of wide application. Even in an age characterised by democracy and industrialisation Burke's ideas are recurrent. While old ruling classes may be replaced by new elites, it is interesting to note that these elites strive to achieve the qualities of the class they have supplanted. Even the commissars of a Soviet state eventually begin to talk of history, stability and tradition; and they seek to perpetuate the social order through their property and children."[70]

70. Hacker: *Political Theory, Philosophy, Ideology, Science*, p. 381.

22

RECENT POLITICAL THOUGHT

Indeed, all schools of political thought-authoritarian or liberal, collectivistic or intellectualistic, conservative or reformist–agree that there is room somewhere for the fruitful use of human reason in choosing wise and avoiding unwise course of political action; all assume that man, by taking thought, can in some manner play an effective part in the mighty movement of human history.

— Francis W. Coker[1]

After Burke, we pass on to the political thought of the nineteenth century in which different schools find their conspicuous place. In a sense, the political thought of the nineteenth century or recent political thought, as it is generally called, should be taken as an extension of the early modern political thought that covered the period of previous three centuries. However, a study of the Western political thought covering its modern and recent phases should be made with this impression in mind that while the political thought of the early modern period witnessed the emergence of great issues and concepts relating to the sovereign, secular and popular character of the nation-state, the political thought in the later modern phase found its channelisation into different directions all

1. Coker : *Recent Political Thought*, p. 30.

hinging upon the basic issue of, what Herbert Spencer epitomised, 'man versus the state'. The trend of liberalism underwent a shift from a negative to a positive dimension so much so that the State was identified with the 'march of God on earth' by the idealists, while it was denounced as the 'instrument of exploitation and oppression by one class over another' by the Anarchists as well as the Marxists, though in different perspectives. Thus, recent political thought looks like a set of divergent ideas presenting the spectacle of a veritable 'Babel of promiscuous and largely unrelated concepts and doctrines'.[2]

REVISION OF LIBERALISM : OUTSTANDING CHARACTERISTICS OF RECENT POLITICAL THOUGHT

A study of recent political thought is struck with this fact that throughout the nineteenth century the notion of liberalism found its modification and reinterpretation, even mutilation, at the hands of eminent thinkers who sought to make it in tune with the fast changing social and economic conditions. As in the early phase of modern period, so now the impact of Industrial Revolution continued to have its sway in the domains of sociology and economics as a result of which several schools arose that studied the question of individual liberty *vis-a-vis* political authority from different, even opposite, standpoints. For instance, while the individualists looked at the state as a necessary evil and on that basis justified the doctrine of the minimum possible area of state activity, the Collectivists dubbed the state as an agency of public welfare and on that ground defended the increasing area of its activity in the name of public welfare. However the common point is that both discarded abstract notions like those of law of nature or other assumptions of the age of reason.

In this direction, the school of the English utilitarians finds its first important place. Jeremy Bentham, the founder of the English utilitarian tradition, ridiculed the notion of 'natural rights' as 'rhetorical nonsense upon stilts' and justified the action of the individual as well as of the state on the maxim of 'utility'. Accordingly, utility was substituted for conscience as the link between objective order and subjective will. Freedom was conceived less and less as a natural right and more and more as a social utility. Happiness in the sense of pleasurable sensation was conveniently discovered to coincide with moral

2. Maxey: *Political Philosophies*, p. 450.

duty and the moral problem was solved by denying its abstract existence. Thus the state was now justified less and less in moral but more and more in hedonistic terms; its function "was no longer conceived as the protection of man's natural rights but as the promotion of the greatest happiness of the greatest number."[3]

The revision of liberalism at the hands of Bentham is traceable in the fact that, in the place of absolute standards of good and evil, which were supposed to be rooted in the abstract conception of natural law, he substituted a relative ethical standard rooted in the principle of 'utility' that meant nothing else than the worldly satisfaction of the individual.[4] It is for this reason that he advocated a number of reforms in the spheres of law, justice, prison houses, educational curriculum, electoral system and the like. Keeping this salient fact in view, it is commented that 'first, last and always Bentham is a reformer. But we must remember that he is a curious kind of reformer. Most reformers are perhaps too practical, too shortsighted; they cannot see the woods for the trees. But Bentham was so much pre-occupied with his own definition of 'forest', and with various deductions from it that he did not see how little real woods are like his conception of them."[5]

Such a shift in the philosophy of liberalism from a negative to a positive side is very much evident in the changing notions of John Stuart Mill. Mill who had advanced the doctrine of individual's sovereignty over himself, his own body and mind, and thereby shunned the case of state intervention until one were a nuisance to the freedom of others, sanctioned the case of heavy taxation on 'unearned increments' accruing from 'socially- created values'. Moreover, towards the last phase of his life, he went to the extent of defending the case of nationalisation of very important industries. He desired the state to overstep its sphere in this direction so as to enforce compulsory education to remove the ignorance of the citizens, release persons from the obligations of the contracts in perpetuity where the parties could not be competent judges of the effects of such obligations, make subject to public control all monopolies, limit working hours and regulate conditions of work, encourage scientific works, increase wages, levy taxes on economic rent,

3. Hallowell: *Main Currents in Modern Political Thought,* p. 198.
4. M.J. Rendall : *An Introduction to Political Thought*, p. 330.
5. W.T. Jones: *Masters of Political Thought,* Vol. II, p. 368.

protect public health, introduce factory legislation, and launch insurance against illness, industrial accidents and indigence in old age. To a student of political thought such a shift in the stand of Mill looks quite puzzling. He may hold the view that reconciliation of the principle of *laissez faire* with that of socialism is an impossible task. However, the reason for this should be traced in his "strong defence of competition and his equally strong disdain for the economic growth and expansion."[6]

It may, however, be conceded that the reinterpretation of liberalism at the hands of Mill was a result of his conscious as well as unconscious thinking. While he condemned governmental interference in the name alike of economic and political liberty, he also took to condemning the same in the name of social oppression. He came to realise that liberty for the manufacturing class did not imply the same thing for those belonging to the class of workers and toilers and thus a modification of the old philosophy of human action, if not an entirely new philosophy, was an urgent necessity if social progress was not to be checked by a social creed.[7] However, this fact has a better realisation at the hands of T.H. Green who gave a distinctly positive turn to the notion of liberty. It is evident from his own version of liberty that it is power 'to do or enjoy something', the element of worthiness to be determined by man's life in common with others. As Barker says: 'Liberty is, therefore, no negative absence of restraint, any more than beauty is the opposite of ugliness. It is a positive power of doing or enjoying something worth doing or enjoying."[8]

As a matter of fact, Green could well visualise the new social trend that had overtaken England in the later part of the last century. The first Reform Act of 1832 and the second one of 1867 had democratised the character of the House of Commons and after the Chartist agitation of 1848 the legislation, as Prof. A.V. Dicey says, was passing from an individualist to a collectivist trend.[9] Thus, Green in stead of feeling satisfied with mere emphasis on the negative area of state activity (contained in the dictum that 'the function of the state is to hinder hindrances to good life') frankly advocated the case of a welfare state

6. R.J. Halliday: *John Stuart Mill*, p. 108.
7. E. Barker: *Political Thought in England, (1848-1914)*, p. 3.
8. *Ibid.*, p. 24.
9. *Ibid.*, p. 22.

determined to eradicate three gigantic social ills–ignorance, intemperance and pauperism.[10] Obviously, according to Green, the "state's characteristic function is that of removing external hindrances to the voluntary performance of good acts. In executing this task it has much more to do than defend the community from foreign attack and check traditional crimes and torts."[11]

The individualistic line of argument found its reiteration in the leading lights of the scientific school as well of which Herbert Spencer is the best exponent. Though he sought to discover and formulate the laws that determine or reveal the upward course of social evolution, the thrust of his argument relating to the province of government went to the justification of the concept of *laissez faire*. He subscribed mainly to the doctrine of individualism while contributing his part to the organic theory of state–something that makes his political philosophy incoherent in so many important respects. His argument was that uninterrupted evolution takes place in the world of nature, so should happen in the sphere of social development. In this way, the laws of biology and sociology confirm the fact of evolution. Naturally, it is no function of the state to create obstruction in the way of social evolution. In other words, he sought to justify the least possible scope of state activity on the basis of the biological laws of 'struggle for existence' and 'survival of the fittest'. It informed him to propound that "an individualistic policy for modern government could be proved to be right by the laws of both universal and organic evolution."[12]

It is, therefore, obvious that the case of liberalism underwent a basic revision in the nineteenth century. What was once negative in character gradually became a positive one. As a result of this, the concept of *laissez faire* as so strongly advocated by the individualists like John S. Mill, Adam Smith and Herbert Spencer found its gradual erosion by a new trend that paved the way for the emergence of socialism. Bentham made an improvement upon earlier liberals like Locke; Mill revised Benthanism and, finally, Green "gave Englishmen something more satisfying than Benthamism at a price they were prepared to pay, that he left liberalism as a faith in stead of an

10. Green: *Lectures on the Principles of Political Obligation*, p. 208.
11. Coker, *op. cit.*, p. 424.
12. *Ibid.*, p. 392.

interest, that he made individualism moral and social and idealism civilised and safe."[13]

LOCATION OF SOVEREIGNTY : TRIUMPH OF THE CASE FOR REPRESENTATIVE GOVERNMENT

Allied with it is the case of representative government that finally settled the problem of the location of sovereignty. Preference for popular rule had its germination in the seventeenth and eighteenth centuries, its proper revision dominated the period of the nineteenth century. Keeping it in view, the terms like classical and neo-classical democratic theories may be made use of on the assumption that the group of theorists who followed the classical democratic line differed from their successors in a number of ways, though they had much in common with them as well. However, the line of distinction between the two may be traced in the fact that while the classical democrats like Locke and Burke were trying to justify a political system whose successful results had been visualised by them with optimism, the neo-classical democrats like Bentham, Mill and Green contemplated in terms of designing governmental scheme in an environment that had already become democratic and needed reform so as to make the best practicable system of democracy in tune with the new social and economic conditions.[14]

The political thought of Locke and Burke was a shrewd attempt to justify the rule of the privileged class that could not retain its acceptability in the nineteenth century. Thus, Bentham repudiated the notion of Burke that rulership could be given only to the aristocratic class. In stead, he advanced the dictum that 'each one is to be counted for one and none for more than one.' He also enunciated the principle of one-person one-vote'. Bentham mixed up the case of the excellence of the popular rule with that of the principle of utility and, in this way, justified the excellence of democracy on the basis of his utilitarian doctrine. It is the only system of government in which the principle of the 'greatest good of the greatest number' may find its best realisation. Thus, freedom and happiness must go together.

The defence of Bentham is, for this reason, based on the assumption that men "have a natural right to self-government

---

13. C.L. Wayper: *Political Thought*, p. 193.
14. L.P. Baradat: *Political Ideologies: Their Origins and Impact*, p. 72.

only in the sense that experience and common reason show that freedom is an essential element of happiness and that natural self-interest is the best security against oppressive or negligent political action. Democracy is government by those who have a greater awareness of and a greater concern for the interest of all the members of the community. It has, therefore, been adopted to serve both freedom and happiness. Where government is controlled by the general body of citizens, it is least likely to establish unreasonable restraints upon individual conduct and most likely to be impartial in the determination and enforcement of whatever restrictions experience shows it is necessary to impose."[15]

The defence of democracy or representative government found its most outspoken form at the hands of John Stuart Mill. He not only appreciated the reform movement of democracy, but also made some important suggestions for the better operation of the same. Democracy is the best form of government, because it casts best effect upon the character of the people. It alone promotes a better and higher form of national character than any other polity whatsoever. However, even this best possible system (as it obtained then) needed certain reforms. Thus, he laid emphasis on the introduction of proportional representation system, plural voting, public ballot, minimum educational qualifications for franchise, property qualification, independence of the chosen delegates, weightage in favour of the minorities, female voting and the like. Obviously, Mill goes much ahead of Bentham and thus studies the case of democracy not only in the light of the principle of 'utility' or worldly happiness but also in the light of his own notion of 'liberty' that is the dearest possession of man. The whole treatment is based on the conviction that the representative government "is the only type that is conducive to the freedom and development of the moral and intellectual faculties in the individual, which a free society alone encourages."[16]

The defence of democracy at the hands of Green witnessed the same thing from a largely idealistic orientation. As already stated, he studied the case of individual liberty in terms of what is 'worth doing and enjoying in common with others' and faintly advocated the case of a social welfare state. He suggested that individual freedom comes not from the people being able to con-

15. Coker, *op. cit.*, p. 11.
16. Frank Thakurdas: *The English Utilitarians and the Idealists*, p. 189.

tribute to their own welfare, it comes from the people being able to contribute to the society as a whole. The role of the government was not merely confined to that of an arbiter of disputes between the individuals, instead it should take definite steps to increase the freedom of the citizens. He found that one of the elements in the society that restricted liberty of the individual was private property. This was undemocratic and, for this reason, he encouraged the state to pursue policies that would end such abuses and protect the welfare of the citizen.[17]

Apart from taking note of the justification of the system of democracy along with need for some important reforms in it as done by the neo-classical thinkers, it should also be borne in mind at this stage that it was this very system that went to the positive advantage of the 'bourgeois' class. Liberalism thus appeared like a bold defence of the interests of the class of the 'haves' that naturally found its reaction in the school of socialism of one sort or another. It is a different matter that the entire socio-economic system looked like squeezing ownership into the hands of a fewer people who paid low wages to the workers, enhanced their working hours and exploited them for the sake of earning more and more profits. It all made it clear that the people could be controlled by economic forces the way they had been controlled by the government in the past. Capitalism which had long been supported by the liberals, because it tended to increase individual freedom and equality, became suspect of its ability to exploit people. "Gradually those on the left of the political spectrum began to wonder why if the government is supposed to be democratic and if the economic forces in the society are exploiting the people, the people do not use their control of government to regulate the economy? This new emphasis revolutionised liberal democracy, making it more socially oriented and less individualistic."[18]

MOVEMENT FOR SOCIO-ECONOMIC JUSTICE : EMERGENCE OF DIFFERENT VARIETIES OF SOCIALISM

Shift in the trend of liberalism toward socialism of different sorts, as pointed out above, made the political thought of the nineteenth century perplexing as well as interesting–perplexing because it created a sort of veritable Babel of largely varying concepts about the nature and form of a new and just

17. Baradat, *op. cit.*, p. 98.
18. *Ibid.*, p. 96.

social and economic order, and interesting because it gave a message of hope for the exploited and oppressed sections of the community. Whether it was the mild socialism of some French and English socialists like Charles Fourier, St. Simon, William Thompson etc. (also known by the nicknames of 'Christian' and 'Utopian' socialists) or extreme socialism of Marx and Engels, the triumphant pace "meant a truceless war"; it also signified that "every society was divided into two armies engaged in that war, with the object on the one side of fastening and, on the other, of defeating the revolution which should inaugurate the final day."[19]

Although socialism in its present-day comprehensive and systematic forms has its definite origin mainly in the works of Karl Marx, many of his fundamental assumptions may be discovered in the writings of those whom he denounced as 'utopians'. Prior to him some thinkers like William Thompson, Thomas Hodgskin, John Gray and John Francis Bray had set forth fully the doctrine that wage workers serving in the fields or factories were the real producers of wealth, most of which was taken away in a quite unjust manner by the community of the capitalists, traders and employers.[20] Moreover, as a solution to this problem they suggested certain collectivistic schemes like state monopoly of the services of marketing and banking, a currency system based on time units of labour, voluntary co-operative societies in order either to ensure an exchange of goods on the basis of the quantities of labour employed in producing them or to secure generally an equitable distribution of wealth among those who create it.[21]

The central theme of the arguments advanced by the Christian or Utopian socialists was to find fault with the system of private property and unrestrained economic competition. However, they avoided the course of a violent struggle or a revolution and in stead believed that changes, as desired by them, could be achieved through appeals to the reason and good sense of the influential members of the community. They preferred the course of ushering in the new era of socialism by means of implementing the experiment of co-operative societies of communes in which the norms of justice, equality, brotherhood, benevolence and free association would replace the bad

19. Barker, *op. cit.*, p. 185.
20. See Max Beer: *History of British Socialism*, Vol. I, Part II, Ch. VII.
21. Coker, *op. cit.*, pp. 17-18.

features of competition, coercion and class disharmony. Thus, a new form of society would come into existence. It may, however, be added here that while the scheme of co-operative societies, as desired by them, could not be implemented successfully, wherever it was done, their basic doctrine received wide acceptability that if co-operation were substituted for competition as the mainspring of economic activity, most of the social evils would disappear.[22]

The English Fabians proved themselves as the best exponent of this variety of socialism. The English intellectuals like George Bernard Shaw, Sidney Webb, Beatrice Webb, Harold Pease, William Clarke and some others took inspiration from the writings of Mill and thereby frankly repudiated what was said by Marx and Engels. Other leading English writers like David Ricardo and William Morris also influenced their thought. The Fabian Society founded in 1884 brought out a collection of articles (*Fabian Essays*) in 1889 in which a distinctly anti-Marxian socialism was advocated. It highlighted that the goal of the English Fabians was 'the socialisation of the means of production, exchange and distribution, the whole to be controlled by a democratically organised state in the interest of the entire community.' They also frankly repudiated the idea of a bloody revolution and in stead laid emphasis on the use of constitutional and democratic means. Keeping it in view, it is well observed that if the Marxists think in terms of the class war, the Fabians do the same in terms of the solidarity of classes.[23]

However, the most clear-cut and consistent form of socialism found its place in the works of Marx and Engels. It became a 'scientific' doctrine meaning thereby that they not only set forth its premises elaborately but also laid down the principles of social and economic change. Marx discovered the principles of social change and on that basis predicted the emergence of a new society that would entail the end of the era of exploitation. The basis of Marxism is the doctrine of class war which signifies that every society is ridden with the antagonism of two classes and, as a result of the struggle between the two, new social order takes place. Economics is the maker of history. That is, it is the means of production, exchange and distribution of goods that determine the character of a social stage and also define relations between the owners of these means and those

22. *Ibid.*, p. 18.
23. See R.C.K. Ensor: *Modern Socialism*, pp. xxxiii ff.

who are dependent upon them for the sake of their existence. It is on the basis of such an economic interpretation of history and the application of the law of dialectical materialism that Marx could predict that the future society would signify the liquidation of the capitalist system in which class antagonism would go and the toilers become the real masters in a classless society that would eventually convert into a stateless condition of life. For this reason, Marx is considered to be the first socialist writer whose work "can be termed scientific. He not only sketched the kind of society which he desired but spoke in detail about the stages through which it must evolve."[24]

It is, therefore, clear that the political thought of the nineteenth century demonstrates an amalgam of various schools of socialist thought ranging from the visionary image of the utopians to the 'scientific' presentation of Marx and Engels. The story of such a thought hovers between the poles of Fabianism and Revisionism with their insistence on gradual development of society towards a new social order through democratic means as well as the need for reaching non-proletarian forces with the socialist appeal on the one side and Marxism with its emphasis on the importance of the economic factor in the progress of society and the part played by the class struggle in the fight to abolish class struggle on the other. However, some points common to both are like attainment of an economic order whose aim is service rather than profit, public in preference to private ownership of the principal means of production and distribution, elimination of waste, removal of gross inequalities of wealth, eradication of the insecurity of livelihood and establishment of the conditions of social justice.[25]

POLITICS AND ETHICS : SEARCH FOR AN IDEAL POLITICAL ORDER

However, the most baffling characteristic of the recent political thought should be traced in the school of Idealism where the thinkers have tried to take state to mystical heights. What is quite puzzling at this stage is that simple and easily intelligible affairs relating to philosophical study of state have been muffled up in the cloak of metaphysics. The result is that state, an association of mortal creatures, is deified and the in-

24. C.E.M. Joad: *Modern Political Theory*, p. 41.
25. H.W. Laidler: *Social-Economic Movements*, p. 751.

dividual, instead of being treated as an end, becomes a means particularly at the hands of the extremist advocates of this highly philosophical theory of state. The outstanding fact remains that the state becomes a sacred, divine, mystical or metaphysical entity and the people are taught to exalt, glorify and adulate it, because it represents the realisation of the best and perfect condition of life. The result is that political theory reaches very close to the world of ethics and metaphysics.[26]

The idealist trend is quite old. It had its earlier reflections in the ideas of Plato and Aristotle who treated state as a moral organisation and lauded it as 'a partnership in virtue'. Plato created a 'grand utopia' based on the principle of justice ruled by an all-wise philosopher-king and Aristotle treated man as a political creature meaning thereby that in the state alone he could have the best possible development of his personality. This line of thought disappeared after the death of Aristotle and witnessed its resurgence in the works of Rousseau in the modern period. He sanctioned that every person was bound to follow the dictates of general will–a will of the community for the good of the community. Thus, Rousseau proved himself not as the last important apostle of the social contract school but as first great thinker of the idealist school, not a follower and disciple of Hobbes and Locke but a teacher and precursor of Kant and Hegel.[27]

From Rousseau, idealism passed over to its strong adherents like Kant, Fitchte and Hegel of Germany. Kant is regarded as the 'father of modern idealism'. He laid down the doctrine of 'self-imposed categorical imperative of duty' and interpreted freedom as the right to will it. Thus, he insisted that every man possessing by virtue of his reason such a will existed and ought to be treated always as an end in himself and never as merely a means. However, it is Hegel in whom the trend of idealism found its most formidable manifestation. He laid down the principle that 'what is real is rational and *vice versa*'. Thus he could say that the 'state represents the highest morality in which man finds his outward self raised to the level of inward

26. In appreciation of this, Prof. J.W. Garner says: "Like ethics, political theory is concerned with what ought to be as well as with what actually is; the real nature of a thing is what the thing is when its growth is fully developed; the political philosophers, therefore, may very properly idealise the state and deal with it in its imaginary splendour and perfection." *Political Science and Government*, p. 238.
27. See Barker: *Greek Political Theory: Plato and His Predecessors*, p. 454.

self of thought'. 'Nothing short of the state is the actualisation of freedom'. If so, the state becomes 'the march of God on earth' and, as Trietschke said, 'we should fall down and worship the state'. Obviously, the state becomes infallible that 'cannot act unrepresentatively.'[28]

From Germany the idealist tradition went over to England and found its prominent advocates in Green, Bradley and Bosanquet. However, what engages our attention here is that the English idealists could not ignore the influence of liberalism as a result of which Green followed Kant, while Bosanquet could not prove himself a true Hegelian. Green gave an idealistic touch to the line of liberalism coming from Hobbes, Locke, Burke, Bentham and Mill and thus raised the level of thought about man's participation in the affairs of the state. He frankly rejected the utterly mundane principle of Bentham's utility and also a thoroughly negative view of liberty as taken by Mill. In stead, he gave a positive connotation to the concept of liberty and desired constructive role of state in the eradication of gigantic social evils. In this way, the most important contribution of Green lies in synthesising the principles of liberalism with those of idealism that made the former refreshing as well as humane. For this reason, he won the appreciation of his people. Keeping this in view, Barker says: 'Not a modification of the old Benthamite premises but a new philosophy was needed, and that philosophy was provided by the idealist school of which Green is the greatest representative."[29]

While Green, as a liberal idealist, repudiated the idea of state absolutism, and thereby moved closer to Kant, Bosanquet draws closer to Hegel by affirming that the state is the sole judge in calling upon its citizens to place their lives at its disposal. In this way, he goes to the extent of denying right to resist the authority of the state and even sanctions the case of war. If Hegel treated state under the head of objective mind, Bosanquet speaks of the state as a self-consciousness, a self-knowing and self-actualising individual. He urges that the actual reality of the institutions lies in the fact that certain living minds are connected with it in a living way. The state, as such, is limited to the office of maintaining the external conditions of a good life; but the conditions cannot be conceived without reference to the life for which they exist, and it is true, therefore, to say

28. Joad, *op. cit.*, p. 13.
29. Barker: *Political Thought in England*, p. 4.

that the conception of nation-state "involves at least an outline of the life to which as a power it is instrumental."[30]

The idealist tradition, in short, is based on the assumption that man is a social and political creature by nature as well as necessity. As such, the life of an individual isolated from the life of his fellow beings is a life against nature and the real nature of the individuals can in consequence be developed only in society. It is only by living in society that a man can realise all that he has in him to be; only by intercourse with his fellows by the realisation of social duties and the fulfilment of social obligations he can develop his full self. In addition, therefore, to the obvious benefits of security against violence and redress against injustice that the individual receives from the state, he owes it a debt of gratitude for its bestowal upon him of his own individuality in all its riches and with all its potentialities.[31] In this way, idealism maintains a close connection between ethics and politics and rightly holds that no political progress is possible apart from the application of the highest moral principles to our individual and social lives."[32]

IMPORTANCE AND CONTRIBUTIONS OF RECENT POLITICAL THOUGHT

A bird's eye view of the recent political thought shows that different trends like those of liberalism, socialism, and idealism prevailed in the nineteenth century which not only demonstrated need for new thinking in the light of changing social and economic conditions of the people but also directed attention towards a plausible solution to the key issue of individual liberty vis-a-vis political authority. Various momentous issues revolved around the problems relating to the province of government, location of sovereignty, area of individual liberty, man's relationship with the society and the state and the like and answers to them, as given by a host of eminent thinkers of England, Germany and France, contributed to the enrichment of the stock of political theory in various important ways.

The trends which developed and prevailed in the nineteenth century witnessed their continuance in the present century also. As a result of this, the socio-economic problems

30. *Ibid.*, p. 59.
31. Joad, *op. cit.*, p. 11
32. E. Asirvatham: *Political Theory*, VI ed., p. 47.

that the thinkers studied and the solution they could find out in the last century continue to be relevant even in the present one. For this reason, contemporary political thought should be studied not as basically different from but a continuation of the recent political thought. If some important line of difference between the two is yet to be discovered at all, it should be traced in the use of new techniques devised by the political theorists of the advanced western countries so as to present contemporary political theory and more in empirical terms with an inter-disciplinary approach.

In brief, the recent political thought has an importance of its own. Though it is full of diverse trends that make it perplexing, they also make it interesting inasmuch as they provide material for the political thought of the present century. In particular, it is Marxism of the last century that has now become the focal point. Whether accept it, or refute it, or modify it, it all constitutes the essential feature of contemporary political thought. Thus, we may appreciate the view: "In our political discussions today, when we seek some basic theoretical position to support or attack a proposed arrangement in governmental structure of policy, we still make use of criteria that were familiar in the writings of early nineteenth century. We argue variously as to the natural rights or the happiness of individual men. We deduce conclusion from conceptions of the nature of human society in general or the history of a particular political community. We consider the nature of man in terms now of his 'primitive' characteristic and now of his potentialities for development towards an 'ideal' to be attained in the future."[33]

33. Coker, *op. cit.*, p. 29.

23

BENTHAM

From the beginning until the end of his life, Bentham was, above all, a reformer. Even his more erudite speculations such as those on language and mathematics, were typically intended to contribute to change in the moral and political life of society. But, unlike many reformers, Bentham sought to be comprehensive in his suggestions and to ground his proposals firmly on science of morals and legislation.

— **James Steintrager**[1]

Jeremy Bentham (1748-1832) passed a very long but uneventful life of eighty four years. As his father (Jermiad Bentham) was a man of law, he also studied law at the Lincoln's Inn and was called to the bar in 1772. However, his natural aptitude forced him to take to the study of legal philosophy and jurisprudence. It made him very popular so much so that he was consulted by the Portuguese Constitutional Party and offered a diamond ring by the Prussian czar as a token of appreciation for his desire to supply a code of law. He enjoyed the association of several distinguished persons like James Stuart Mill, Sir Samuel Romily, David Ricardo, Lord Brougham, Joseph Hume and Lord Shelburne. In particular, his association with James Stuart Mill made him a philosophical radical,

1. Steintrager: *Bentham*, p. 117.

while the opposition of the Tory government made him a democrat. Thus, with a view to propagate his views as a radical and also as a democrat, he founded the illustrious *Westminster Review* in 1823 and thereby threw himself more and more in matters concerning the political life of the country. And yet his deep love for the study of legal philosophy remained paramount and his legal publications revealed that he was a legal reformer in the first place and a philosopher after. At the ripe age of eighty four, he left this world as 'a patriarch, a spiritual leader, almost a god, with James Mill as his St. Paul."[2]

WORKS : LITERATURE ON ENLIGHTENED HEDONISM AND PHILOSOPHICAL RADICALISM

The political philosophy of Bentham comes to us from his several works showing reconstruction of the legal system in the main, though they represent his multi-sided interest. For instance, his writings on the *Principles of International Law* rank him among the teachers of international jurisprudence; his *Catechism of Parliamentary Reform* (1809) entitles him for being an ardent advocate of parliamentary reforms. His monograph entitled *A Table of the Springs of Action* indicates his reflections on social psychology. However, for our purpose, his two works *Fragment on Government* and *An Introduction to the Principles of Morals and Legislation,* published in 1776 and 1789 respectively, are important that lay down his contribution to the doctrines of utilitarianism and philosophical radicalism in recent English political thought.

In the *Fragment,* Bentham introduces the concept of utility as a criterion for morals and jurisprudence indicating the scope of its application to both fields and thereby exposes the inadequacy of the prevailing abstract notions of natural law and natural rights and a host of other fictions which were frequently invoked to criticise and defend the *status quo* in a social order. Here the point of his emphasis is that in the principle of utility alone we have a simple and adequate test by which differences of opinions regarding law and institutions can be made with less passion and with a greater possibility of reconcilement. In other words, it is a valid test for judging the worthwhileness or otherwise of existing social and political institutions without reference to the prestige and prejudices acquired from tradition and antiquity."[3]

2. Phyllis Doyle: *A History of Political Thought,* p. 229.
3. Frank Thakurdas: *The English Utilitarians and the Idealists,* p. 66. As

The same idea finds its elaboration in his work on the *Principles of Morals and Legislation.* As he himself says, his purpose is to work out a system the object of which is to rear the fabric of felicity by the hand of reason and law. Here his whole idea is to show how legal and moral questions can be handled objectively. In other, words, in the legal science which he conceives as a branch of the possible logic of will, he is concerned with the introduction of order into legal thinking so that improvement of legal techniques can be undertaken as such a science would emanate from a body of proposed laws accompanied by a commentary of reasons. However, what attracts our attention here is that Bentham unites psychology, ethics, jurisprudence and politics in such a way that he supersedes Helvetius, Hutcheson, Hume, Shaftesbury and Adam Smith.[4]

Apart from this, the *Commentaries* of Bentham show a direct attack on the contributions of Blackstone. Blackstone in his commentaries on the English legal system defended the constitution of his country in the name of representing a combination of the three different virtues of monarchy, aristocracy and democracy. The burden of his argument was that the English constitution represented a combination as well as a continuation of these three forms of government. Bentham did not appreciate it at all and argued that the forms of government could not be classified so easily, nor could the virtues of strength, wisdom and goodness be attributed to them in the like manner. Thus, he ridiculed Blackstone's sycophantic eulogies and asserted that the constitution of his country did not represent a happy blending of the three forms of polities through the King, the Lords and the Commons or of their virtues without assimilating their vices.[5]

N.C. Rosenblaum observes: "If a single ideological stance can aid in understanding Bentham's work, it is that he was a self-conscious modern. More than any of his contemporaries who shared emphasis on progress, Bentham rejected everything in the classical tradition of political philosophy. He diverged not only from classical metaphysics, but from classicism in all matters of subject and style. He abandoned Aristotle's classification of regimes (including mixed government) and the peculiar imperatives that govern each. He abandoned the notion of the best regime. He concentrated in stead on individualism as the ethical basis of every modern political order and on the single rationality that is its accompaniment." *Bentham's Theory of the Modern State*,. p. 8.

4. Frank Thakurdas, *op. cit.*, p. 67.
5. *Ibid.*, p. 62.

A study of these important works of Bentham shows that he freely borrowed ideas from Locke, Hume, Hartley, Voltaire, Barington, Helvetius, Montesquieu, Beccaria and Priestley in varying measures and thus made his own contribution to the school of utilitarian radicalism. It is, however, a different matter that his contributions have been differently evaluated by his critics. For instance, John Plamenatz is of the view that Bentham is "quite unwittingly trying to reconcile two couples of irreconciliable doctrines—egoistic hedonism with utilitarianism on the one hand and a psychological system with an objective theory of morals on the other."[6] The charge of E. Halevy is that Bentham did not invent the moral arithmetic the elements of which are found in Beccaria, Hartley, even Hobbes : he did not invent the principle of utility the formula of which was to be found in Hume ; he did not invent the formula of the greatest happiness of the greatest number that occurs in the writings of Hutcheson, Beccaria and Priestley.[7] Different from both, C.L. Wayper holds: "This is the greatest contribution of Bentham to political theory that he sees every question in terms of the men and women whose lives it will effect and never in terms of abstraction."[8]

UTILITARIANISM : JUSTIFICATION OF THE PRINCIPLE OF THE GREATEST GOOD OF THE GREATEST NUMBER

The political philosophy of Bentham centres round the principle of 'utility' in which he discovers a practical commandment as well as scientific law, a proposition which is at one and the same time what *is* and what *ought to* be. He admires the psychological system of Richard Cumberland who refuted innate moral ideas of a rationalist doctrine and accepted the theory of general welfare. He also admires the views of Francis Hutcheson who in his work *Moral Philosophy* urged that moral evil of an action "is as to the degree of imagery and the number of sufferers so that action is best which accomplishes the greatest happiness of the greatest number." He also draws much inspiration from Priestley's *Essay on Government* in which it was said that the greatest happiness of the greatest number "is the great standard by which philosophy relating to that state must finally be determined." Then, from Hume, he

6. Plamenatz: *The English Utilitarians*, p. 72.
7. Halevy: *The Growth of Philosophical Radicalism* (Translated from French into English by Mary Morris), p. 34.
8. Wayper: *Political Thought*, p. 106.

gets the instruction of introducing the experimental method of reasoning into moral objects. Thus, he rejects the *a priori* and abstract notions of natural rights, social contract, and metaphysical convictions and insists on the logic of usefulness, good and expediency.[9] Naturally the conclusions of Bentham become quite different from those of the social contractualists and the rationalists of the earlier centuries.

Bentham's principle of utility bears the following important characteristics :

1. Bentham gives a peculiar meaning of the term 'utility'. To him utility means, positively speaking, all that is good, pleasant, useful, agreeable, advantageous and beneficial; or negatively speaking, all that is the reverse of painful, useless, disadvantageous, bad and disagreeable. The characteristic mark of utility is, in simple terms, pleasure. Like an economist, Bentham does not define utility as a want-satisfying power of a commodity, rather it is something synonymous with what is pleasant. In his own word : "An adherent to the principle of utility holds virtue to be a good thing by reason only of the pleasures which result from the practice of it : he esteems vice to be a bad thing by reason only of the pains which follows in its train."[10]
2. Another important point is that, according to Bentham, utility possesses the power of motivation. That is, human actions are motivated by the consideration of pleasure and pain. Like the early Epicureans of Greece and the modern Hedonists of France and England, he believes that man by nature desires to do what seems pleasant to him and refrains from doing wherefrom he fears pain. He writes : "Nature has placed mankind under the governance of two sovereign masters, pain and pleasure. It is for them alone to point out what we ought to do as well as to determine what

9. Prof. A. Albee in his work *History of the English Utilitarianism* holds the view that the background of this tendency can be seen in John Gray's *Concerning the Fundamental Principles or Virtue of Morality* and Selby Bigg's *British Moralists*, Vol. II.
10. Hence, W.L. Davidson says that utility "means what is best for the elements of his nature and what can most effectively promote his full and ultimate good, and the full and ultimate good of his fellows." *Political Thought in England : The Utilitarians*, p. 48. According to this writer, utility, then, is welfare; and welfare covers every conceivable element that goes to determine and constitute man's happiness." See John MacCunn : *Six Radical Thinkers*, p. 15.

we shall do. On the one hand, the standard of right and wrong; on the other, the chain of causes and effects are fastened to their throne. They govern us in all we do, in all we say, in all we think : every effort to throw of subjection will but serve to demonstrate and confirm it. In words a man may pick to abjure their empire, but in reality be will remain subject to it all the while."[11]

3. It follows that Bentham finds in utility an incontrovertible fact of human psychology that whatever human beings think, feel, or do they are actually swayed by the happy and painful consequences. Not only psychologically, even ethically, they desire to do what gives them pleasure or avoids their pain. Bentham explains : "By principle of utility is meant that principle which approves or disapproves every action, whatsoever according to the tendency it appears to have to augment or to diminish the happiness of the party whose interest is in question, or what is the same thing, in other words, to promote or oppose happiness. I say of every action whatsoever; and therefore not only of every action of private individual, but of every measure of government."[12]

4. The peculiar thing about Bentham is that he suggests a felicific calculus of pleasures and pains and emphasises the possibility of their mathematical computation. He views that by balancing pains against pleasures, the work of computation is a possibility. Mere guess work would be unnecessary when both the pains and pleasures are dimensional. Their characteristics are reducible to the shape of units which can be mathematically measured. But in the case of a single individual or a group of persons, it would be possible to give a mathematical value of the sum of pleasures and pains. But, for this work of computation, two conditions are required. Firstly, each individual should be counted for one and no one for more than one. Secondly, it should be taken for granted that the pleasures and pains have no qualitative but quantitative difference.

5. For the sake of mathematical computation, Bentham's second assumption is very important. Bentham believes that there is no qualitative difference between various pleasures, for all pleasures are pleasures and pains are

11. Bentham : *An Introduction to the Principles of Morals and Legislation*, p.2.
12. *Ibid.*, p. 3.

pains. However, there is a quantitative difference between one pleasure and another. Reading poetry is as good as playing pushpin, so the result may differ on the basis of quantity alone. And this quantitative difference is created by seven factors, namely, *intensity* (more or less efficaciousness), *duration* (longer or shorter life), *certainty* (consideration of definiteness or indefiniteness), *propinquity* (consideration of nearness or remoteness of time), *purity* (accompaniment of all pleasure or pain), *fecundity* (capacity of being productive or barren), and *extensiveness* (the number of persons fallen under influence). In short, Bentham means to say that the role of these factors makes one pleasure bigger or smaller as compared to other and creates dimensions whereby their units may be made for their mathematical computation.[13]

6. This enables Bentham to suggest that a felicific calculus may be established. He thus puts : "Sum up all the values of all pleasures on the one side, and those of all the pains on the other. The balance, if it be on the side of the pleasure, will give the good tendency of the act upon the whole, with respect to the interests of that individual person; if on the side of pain, the bad tendency of it upon the whole. Take an account of the number of persons whose interests appear to be conceived, and repeat the above process with respect to each. Sum up the numbers expressive of the degrees of good tendency which the act has, with respect to each individual, in regard to whom the tendency of it is good upon the whole: do this again with respect to each individual in regard to whom the tendency of it is bad upon the whole. Take the balance, which, if on the side of pleasure, will give the general good tendency of the act with respect to the total number of community of individuals concerned; if on the

13. However, it should be taken into view that Bentham was not blind to the qualitative difference between the pleasures and pains. Rather, he had a different purpose. He apprehended that if it was suggested that there existed a qualitative difference as well, *i.e.*, if it was admitted that certain pleasures were no pleasure at all in the real sense, the government then would act tyrannically and allow only those pleasures to the individual which it preferred. Ivor Brown thus clarifies Bentham's view by remarking that it "has an immense value, because it denies the infallibility of the superior person who endeavours to foist his own morality or his own type of happiness upon others whom he believes to be the pitiful dupes of ignorance." *English Political Theory*, p. 102.

side of pain, the general evil tendency with respect to same community."[14]

7. Bentham also takes the care of proving that the work of mathematical computation is accurate and objective and for this he describes pleasures of two kinds--simple or those which can not be resolved into others (as the pleasures of senses, wealth, skill, amity, good name, power, piety, benevolence, malevolence, memory, imagination, expectation, assistance and relief); and complex or those which can be resolved into various simple ones. He suggests that simple pains are those of privation, awkwardness, enmity, ill-repute, benevolence, malevolence, memory, imagination, expectation and association. Their compound forms makes complex pleasures and pains. Besides, Bentham also suggests that other factors (health, strength, hardiness, physical imperfection, quantity of knowledge, power of mind, moral sensibility, natural aptitude, sanity, habit, financial status, sex, religious view, age, climate and government) should also be considered.

Bentham is of the view that by means of computation the formula of the greatest good of the greatest number can be established. What gives maximum possible pleasure to the maximum number of persons should prevail. However, by doing this Bentham makes his utilitarianism universalistic and thus differentiates it from the egoistic hedonism of the Greeks. He realises that the happiness of one individual on the one side and that of the many on the other, the formula of the greatest hapiness of the greatest number is the right answer. Thus, at the hands of Bentham utilitarianism takes a benevolent and universalistic shape.[15]

Apart from clarifying the dimensions of the principle of utility and the possibilities of its measurability so as to work out the formula of the greatest good of the greatest number. Bentham also envisages four sanctions that would act as a deterrent for the potential offenders of the rules of conduct. As

14. Bentham, *op. cit.*, p. 31.
15. Compare it with that of the Greek Epicureans who held that so far as human beings "are concerned nature means self-interest, the desire of every man for his individual happiness." See Sabine : *A History of Political Theory*, p. 133. According to Bentham, every human action should be judged by the standard of social usefulness. Hobhouse points out that it "contemplates the complete subordination of the individual to social claims." *Liberalism*, p. 67.

he says: "Regarding pains and pleasures in the character of punishment and reward attached to certain rules of conduct, we may, therefore, distinguish four sanctions :

1. The *physical* or natural sanction comprises the pains and pleasures which we may experience or expect, in the ordinary course of nature, not purposely modified by any human interposition.
2. The *moral* sanction comprises such pains and pleasures as we experience or expect at the hands of our fellows, prompted by the feeling of hatred or goodwill, or contempt or regard; in a word, according to the spontaneous disposition of each individual. The sanction may also be styled popular; the sanction of public opinion or of honour, or the sanction of the pains and pleasures of sympathy.
3. The *political* sanction comprises such pains and pleasures as may experience or expect, at the hands of the magistracy, acting under law. This might, with equal propriety, be termed the legal sanction.
4. The *religious* sanction comprises such pains and pleasure as we may experience or expect, in virtue of the forebodings and promises of religion."[16]

Bentham also makes it clear that the application of these sanctions is never uniform; it is subject to the conditions and circumstances that obtain in view of the fact that these "do not, of course, act upon all men in the same way with same effect; and, indeed, the four sanctions are sometimes found as allies, at other times as rivals, or even as open enemies. When they act together, they operate with irresistible force; when they are in direct conflict, they mutually enfeeble each other; while even if they be rivals, they can hardly fail to lead man into hesitating confusing actions."[17]

Bentham's utilitarianism may be subjected to the following lines of criticism :

1. Benthamite utilitarianism stands on the ethical and psychological foundations of hedonism which cannot be regarded as a sound moral philosophy. It certainly debases the character of human personality by regarding man as a 'creature of feelings' and not of 'thought'. It is true that man

16. Bentham, *op. cit.*, Ch. III.
17. *Ibid.*

loves pleasure and hates pain, but it is the pain that ultimately gives pleasure. 'Sweet are the days of adversity.' It is also believed that 'our sweetest songs are those that tell of the saddest thoughts.' Obviously, Bentham takes too simple and superficial a view of human nature and his philosophy "purchases the simplicity and lucidity of life at the expense of depth and comprehensiveness of view."[18]

2. Like Aristotle and Hobbes, Bentham also takes into view a single factor and builds upon it the whole theory of state. To him utility is the only factor that motivates human action and impels the need for a legal and political system. Utility is one of the factors but not the only factor. Human beings are motivated by the consideration of other factors as well like love of motherland, and culture, religion etc. W.T. Jones thus very aptly comments: "The fact seems to be that men are not moved by one motive but by many diverse ones, that there is not one satisfaction, pleasure present in varying amounts but many qualitatively different satisfactions."[19]

3. Bentham's assumption that pleasures differ in quantity and not in quality is also wrong. The pains and pleasures of one person are certainly different from the pleasures and pains of another. What is one man's food is another's poison and

---

18. J. Seth : *Ethical Principles*, p. 115. Murray says that if we take away conscience as Bentham does, there "is no such thing as a moral or an immoral action, though there may remain acts that are generally useful or the reverse. And there is no individual conscience, so there is no collective conscience. The culprit does not feel the censure of the community." *History of Political Science from Plato to the Present*, p. 314. Bentham's psychology "is a generalisation from his own barren experience; it is equally arid and so are the ethical and political theories he built upon it. Men are moved by many things besides pleasures and pains taken narrowly. Taken broadly, his hedonism is a truism. Leslie Stephen agreed with Mill that Bentham "overlooked the moral part of man's nature in the strict sense of the term." *History of English Thought in the Eighteenth Century*, Vol. II., p. 126.

19. Jones : *Masters of Political Thought*, Vol. II, p. 374. So shrewd and usually sympathetic a man as Schumpeter denounced Bentham's boisterous and vulgar utilitarianism and described it as 'the shallowest of all conceivable philosophies of life." *History of Economic Analysis*, p. 66. Stendhal deplored the fashion and cult of the greatest good of the greatest number after which the nineteenth century has run mad." See Mary P. Mack : *Jeremy Bentham : An Odyssey of Ideas*, p. 2. Marx raged against the arch-philistine, Jeremy Bentham, the insipid pedantic leather-tongued oracle of the commonplace bourgeois intelligence of the nineteenth century. I should call Mr. Jeremy a genius in the way of bourgeois stupidity." *Capital*, Vol. II, p. 671.

what is pleasant to a wise is painful to a fool. In this regard, John Stuart Mill was right when he said : "It is better to be a human being dissatisfied than a pig satisfied; better to be a Socrates dissatisfied than a fool satisfied. And if the fool and the pig are of a different opinion, it is because they know only their own side of question. The other party to the comparison knows both sides."[20]

4. Bentham's felicific calculus is an absurdity. The pleasures and pains are not concrete units which may be arithmetically counted. They are subjective and not objective things. Any such idea that they may be arithmetically computed and a formula may be established on that basis is nothing short of a mockery. Bentham quite wrongly assumes that the standard of right and wrong worked out on the basis of the greatest good of the greatest number could be related to tangible and objectively measurable values. The truth, however, is that Bentham did not offer a systematic theory of ethics based on exact calculation, but a series of prudential rules addressed to legislators and judges based on a new vocabulary and a new logic."[21] The comment of John Plamenatz is that "such a calculus is impossible not merely in practice but also in theory."[22]

5. And it follows from above that Bentham confuses the sphere of state activity. On the one hand, he sanctions that the rulers should act according to the formula of the greatest good of the greatest number, while, on the other, the formula cannot be realised in practice and thus implicitly authorises them to do as they deem proper and expedient. It may thus be apprehended that if the rulers act in their discretion, there would be a despotic government; and if they leave all to the census of respective pleasures and pains, there might be no government activity at all. Maxey thus rightly says : "Either the state must impose upon all the pain-pleasure

20. Mill : *Utilitarianism*, p. 18.
21. Mack, *op. cit.*, p. 18.
22. Plamenatz : *The English Utilitarians*, p. 76. Elsewhere he says : "The truth is that it is not possible to make sense of what Bentham is saying." *Ibid.*, p. 72. More vehement is the remark of J.W. Allen : "To read it all would be a waste of time : I have not attempted the task." Refer to his paper "Jeremy Bentham" in F.J.C. Hearnshaw (ed.) : *The Social and Political Ideas of Some Representative Thinkers of the Revolutionary Era*, p. 181. A little later, he says that Benthamite ethics "are rubbish". *Ibid.*, p. 198.

reckoning of the majority, or it must resign authority and give way to the arithmetic of anarchic individualism."[23]

6. It is clear that Bentham believes in the atomistic conception of society, for in his view the society is nothing but a collection of individuals and social pleasure is nothing but a bundle of the pleasure of the majority of its members. He considers community as a fictitious body composed of the individual persons. In his view, the interest of the community is the interest of its members. Hence, he suggests that it is vain to talk of the interest of the individual. He thus adds : "A thing is said to promote the interest, or to be for the interest of an individual, when it tends to add to the sum of all of his pleasures or what comes to the same thing to diminish the sum total of his pain." This atomistic conception was soon replaced when the idealistic theory penetrated the English soil and Green rediscovered the meaning of Plato, Aristotle, Rousseau and Hegel.
7. Bentham's attempt to reconcile egoism with altruism also creates a difficulty. It does not appear invariably probable to a man seeking his own pleasure that he will like to sacrifice himself for the greatest pleasure of the greatest number. How is it possible that a man devoid of rational elements and saturated with the standards of hedonistic psychology would like to ignore his happiness and contribute to the promotion of happiness of others? Since man is a bundle of pleasures; it would not be expected that his egoism will ever have a benevolent, universalistic and altruistic character.

The weaknesses of Bentham's utilitarianism became evident shortly after his death. No other thinker could sustain the vigour of Benthamite philosophy and, curiously enough, a great utilitarian like John Stuart Mill undertook the work of its modification. The result was that Mill's modification altered the fundamental character of Benthamism and when Green preached his idealism, Benthamite utilitarianism lost its place. In spite of these shortcomings and inconsistencies, however, Bentham's political philosophy gained immense fame. The people appreciated the new approach and thus relieved themselves of many social ills. They examined their social institutions from a practical standpoint. By way of admiration, it is thus said that Bentham put a very definite ideal before the

23. Maxey, *op. cit.*, p. 468.

statesmen, politicians and legislators. Doyle says that Bentham "did not wander into the labyrinth of abstract speculation."[24] Rightly speaking, Benthamism brought political theory back from the abstractions of the Age of Reason to the level of concrete realities. Hence, it has been said that Bentham's political philosophy was intensely humane and intensely practical being directly in touch with the living movements and interest of men."[25]

STATE : AN INSTRUMENT SUBSERVING HAPPINESS OF THE INDIVIDUALS

Like social contractualists, Bentham is not concerned with offering a plausible explanation of the origin of state, though he takes up the issues of its nature. He examines the nature of state from utilitarian point of view and comes to hold that a political society is distinguished from a natural society in which a number of persons or subjects "are suffered to be in the habit of paying obedience to a person or an assembly of persons of a known and certain description (whom we may call governors). Such persons altogether (subjects and governors) are said to be in a state of political society."[26] Thus, natural society and political society are distinguishable on the ground that while, in the former, the subjects are not in the habit of obedience, they are so in the latter the reason for which should be traced in their realisation that state is an instrument to realise the principle of the greatest good of the greatest number.

The principal features of Bentham's theory of state may be put as under :

1. Like Plato and Aristotle, Bentham does not consider state as a natural association and, for this reason, prior to the individual. To him, the individual is prior to the state. State is not an instrument that promotes the personality of the individual, rather it is a contrivance to ensure his happiness. Since man is endowed with rational faculty, he lives in the state so as to seek pleasure and avoid pain. Obviously, state

24. Doyle, *op. cit.*, p. 229.
25. Davidson, *op. cit*, p. 29. Though an uncompromising critic of Bentham, Schumpeter admits that "the essential point to grasp is that Utilitarianism was nothing but another natural law system. The programme of deriving, by the light of reason, 'laws' about man in society from a very stable and highly simplified human nature fits the Utilitarians no less well than the scholastics." *History of Economic Analysis*, pp. 132-33.
26. Bentham : *Fragment on Government* (edited by W. Harrison), p. 28.

is the means to promote happiness of the individual. It has no integral relation with the moral life of the citizen. It seeks to change his behaviour; it cannot change him. It cannot help him to develop his character, to bring out the best that is in him. For it is not the state that moulds the citizens, it is the citizens that mould the state."[27]

2. Bentham regards state as a law-making agency. The state is a group of persons organised for the promotion and maintenance of happiness; but for this end, it acts through law. By means of law, the state rewards or punishes so that the happiness is increased and the pain decreased. He urges that the law should take cognisance of bad actions and inflict punishment on the people so that the net balance of pleasure is increased and that of pain decreased. Mere morality is not sufficient and unless law comes into operation, bad things cannot be out of place. Only law being the command of the sovereign can secure habitual obedience of the people. So Bentham lays stress on the existence of a legal sovereign in the state.
3. Bentham's emphasis on law accompanies his repudiation of the phrase of natural law. He calls natural law simply as a phrase and natural rights as 'simple nonsense natural and imprescriptible rights, rhetorical nonsense, upon stilts'.[28] For the abstract phrases of natural law and natural right he substitutes the practical norms of utility. Denouncing the abstract notion of natural law and rights, he says : "Absolute equality is absolutely impossible. Absolute liberty is directly repugnant to the existence of every kind of government."
4. Although Bentham repudiates theory of natural law and rights, yet he recognises that all men are born free and equal. But, in this regard, his approach is neither rational nor metaphysical. He insists that all men are equal in the eye of law; all have equal rights as regards the promotion of happiness; and it is the duty of the state to ensure a greater equalisation of property. If absolute equality is not possible, the state may do away with gross inequalities, for too great inequality is an insuperable obstacle on the road to the greatest good of the greatest number.

---

27. Wayper, *op. cit.*, p. 98-99.
28. See David Baumgardt : *Bentham and Ethics of Today*, p. 405.

5. In this connection, Bentham also distinguishes between natural liberty and social liberty. He calls natural liberty as freedom to do whatever one wishes and civil liberty to do only that is conducive to the formula of the greatest happiness of the greatest number. Natural liberty prevails in the forest, while civil liberty is a matter of social life and thus Bentham wants that the state should create laws whereby natural liberty is minimised and civil liberty is protected and promoted.
6. Bentham also recognises right to resistance against the state. If the opposition produces less pain and thereby adds to the store of happiness, it is justified. If the individuals find it essential to resist political authority, *i.e.*, if it is in their interest, they may adopt measures of resistance against the state.
7. Bentham assigns a democratic character to the state by holding it as a trustee for the happiness of the individual. The particular character assigned to the state centres around the function of the realisation of the principle of utility. Obviously, Bentham's explanation of the state is a complete statement in terms of his principle of utility, that is, greatest good of the greatest number, not confined to the vague generalities but demanding specific services. In short, to Bentham, the state is not a natural institution or a moralising agency as conceived by the Idealists or an instrument of public welfare as suggested by the Collectivists, or an instrument of exploitation and oppression as denounced by the anti-authoritarians; it is an instrument to realise the principle of the greatest good of the greatest number. Moreover, as a legal reformer, he interprets security as the essential function of the state and for this he recognises the usefulness of the system of law.[29]
8. Bentham accepts the usual classification of governments into three forms, namely, monarchy, aristocracy and democracy. But he prefers a democratic government where the realisation of the formula of the greatest good of the

29. Prof. Sorely thus points out : "The chief case of law is security; and the principle of security extends to the maintenance of all those expeditions with which law itself was credited. Security, one may say, is a necessity for social life and for any moderate degree of human happiness; equality is rather of the nature of a luxury, which legislation would promote when it does not interfere with security." *History of English Philosophy.*

greatest number has the maximum possible chances. Only in a democratic government there is an identity between the interests of the governors and those of the governed. Here public virtue or goodness of intention is more likely to be found, for the right of law-making resides in the people. Besides, democracy also breeds patriotism. A monarchy is, indeed, more powerful than all other kinds of government where all sinews are knit together in the hands of a single ruler, but there are imminent dangers of his employing that strength to improvident or oppressive purpose. So, in an aristocracy, there is less strength and honesty. Bentham puts: "In general, all mankind will agree that government should be reposed in such persons in whom those qualities are most likely to be found the perfection of which are among the attributes of him who is emphatically styled the Supreme Being; the three grand requisites, I mean of wisdom, of goodness, and of power: wisdom to discern the real interests of the community, goodness to endeavour always to pursue that real interest, and strength of powers to carry this knowledge and intention into action. These are the natural foundations of sovereignty, and these are the requisites that ought to be found in every constituted frame of government."

A study of Bentham's political theory in this regard leaves this strong impression that he ultimately prefers a democratic system for realising the principle of the greatest good of the greatest number. Obviously, such an affirmation becomes consistent with his moral theory. A problem arises as to how we may get the principle of utility realised by the political authority when the members of the government are naturally and primarily concerned with their own happiness. Bentham well studies this problem and he convincingly observes that only under a system of self-government, the interests of the governors and those of the governed would coincide. And if there is any problem in this regard, its only possible solution is to have a fully representative body.[30]

---

30. M.J. Rendall : *An Introduction to Political Thought*, p. 322. It may, however, be pointed out that Bentham's outright preference for a democratic system was not so clear in his early writings. For instance, in his *Principles of Morals and Legislation*, he felt satisfied with any political system that realised the principle of the greatest happiness of the greatest number. It appears that he could prefer any system of government that protected liberty of the individual and, at the same time did not expand

RADICALISM : A VIGOROUS CAMPAIGN FOR REFORMS

As already pointed out, Bentham was not a political thinker in the first instance. His main interest was law and his coming into the field of politics and launching a vigorous movement for reforming legal and political institutions was a definite result of his frustration and disillusionment. The rejection of his plan of 'Panopticon' by the government as well his friendship with James Stuart Mill are the two important events to which the cause of changes in his thought should be attributed. As a matter of fact, he wanted to bring about drastic reforms in the legal, political and administrative institutions of his country and nothing but a grand failure in this regard pushed him towards a world of deep disillusionment and bewilderment. Thus, he took to the course of fighting for reforms with passion. He sharpened the trend of radicalism in contemporary English political thought keeping which in view it is said that he "gave to English radicalism of the 18th and 19th centuries its theoretical formulation."[31]

The reforms suggested by Bentham cover different fields like politics, education, legal system, administration, religion and the like. They may be summed up in the following manner:

1. In the sphere of politics, Bentham suggested universal manhood franchise to all tax payers, annual general election, unicameral legislature implying abolition of the House of Lords, republican system desiring end of monarchy, annual session of the Parliament, vote by secret ballot, equalisation of electoral districts, freedom of the press so as to publish parliamentary debates, competitive examination for the recruitment of public servants, freedom of representative from the hold of the constituents, recall of public officials, existence of a code to limit the powers of the government etc.
2. In the sphere of law and justice, Bentham emphasised need for civil and criminal code without unnecessary technicalities, redundancies and obsolete phraseology, keeping provisions of law in a simple and easily intelligible language, availability of legal texts to a common man easily and on a cheap price, quick and fair disposal of cases by the courts, constitution of single-judge benches for expeditious adjudication of disputes and the like. We may also refer to

its area of activity. It made Bentham liable to lay down the 'principle of the carrot and the stick'. See M. Judd Harmon : *Political Thought from Plato to the Present, p. 375.*

31. Halevy, *op. cit.*, p. 418.

his proposals like institution of frugality banks, code of merchant shipping, abrogation of usury loans, reform of the poor law etc. Not only in the case of national law, he also laid emphasis on the codification of international law.

3. Bentham paid much attention to the problem of proper punishment. The execution of justice should be exhibited to the people as far as possible so that the prospective wrong-doer may be frightened. The main purpose behind giving punishment to the wrong-doer should be to reform the person so as to protect the happiness of the society. For this sake, he advanced the plan of 'Panopticon' or a semi-circular building of the prison house having barracks of the criminals on the periphery and the seat of the superintending staff at the centre so that all the activities of the prisoners could be watched by the jailor. The criminals should be given such training that they become good people and when they are released, they should be given some useful employment.
4. Bentham touched the sphere of education also. Here he suggested that the education should be such that goes to the advantage of the man as well as of the society. The imparting of education should be governed by the considerations of natural aptitude, age and capacity of the student. In particular, he laid stress on the education of the poor children. He desired suitable changes in the poor law of the country so that state may give financial assistance to the education of poor children. His national education scheme is important in this connection.
5. Finally, the reform proposals of Bentham touched the sphere of religion. He criticised the sinecure and extravagant offices of the church. He also denounced the system of ecclesiastical peers in the House of Lords. In his view, the religious leaders hindered the intellectual progress by supporting belief contrary to the implications of the principle of utility.

A brief review of the proposals advanced by Bentham amply illustrates that he was by all means a vigorous campaigner of reforms in all walks of life so that the principle of utility could be applied for the regeneration of the whole people. Keeping this in view, Dunning likened Bentham with a "veritable bull that entered the China shop."[32]

32. See W.A. Dunning : *A History of Political Theories*, Vol. III, Ch. 6.

CRITICAL APPRECIATION : BENTHAM AS THE 'NEW MOSES' OF LEGISLATION AND POLITICS

The political thought of Bentham has been widely appreciated for making a major shift in the prevailing current of liberalism, though some commentators have also found fault with his approach in debasing the level of human life and thought. It is said that he made the principle of utility so commonplace that political philosophy looked like reduced to the level of bare commonsense. Thus, J.W. Allen could say that Bentham " is the philosopher of commonsense...masquerading as philosophy, with much tiresome and really useless apparatus and a dogmatic self-satisfaction that is apt to irritate."[33] A study of the trend of utilitarianism, as started by Bentham and further developed by John Stuart Mill, also reveals the weakness that he committed by ignoring the aspect of qualitative distinction between pleasures and pains. Thus, John Stuart Mill could diagnose the weakness and criticise Bentham for contributing a "one-eyed thought and also accused him of narrowness, want of experience and rigidity."[34]

However, the weak aspects of Bentham's philosophy should not be taken to the length of ignoring his real contributions. He definitely gave a constructive turn to the trend of liberalism in English political theory. While Hobbes committed the wrong of establishing an all–powerful authority of the despot, and Locke simply defended the case of constitutional monarchy, Bentham gave the message of discarding the useless and accepting the beneficial. His formula of the greatest happiness of the greatest number "is made a hook to put in the nostrils of Leviathan that he may be tamed and harnessed to the chariot of utility. Indeed, if Leviathan will haul the chariot, it matters little whether he has one head or many."[35]

What has really immortalised the name of Bentham is his doctrine of enlightened hedonism and a vigorous campaign for reforms. Perhaps John Stuart Mill is not wrong when he says: "A place, therefore, must be assigned to Bentham among the masters of wisdom, the great teachers and permanent intellec-

33. Allen : "Bentham" in Hearnshaw (ed.) : *Sociai and Political Idεas of Some Great Thinkers of the Revolutionary Era.*, p. 191.
34. Mill : "On Bentham" in his *Utilitarianism, On Liberty and Essay on Bentham* edited by Mary Warnock, pp. 78-125.
35. Sir Fredrick Pollock : *An Introduction to the History of the Science of Politics*, p. 107.

tual ornaments of the human race. He is among those who have enriched mankind with imperishable gifts."[36] It is true that some of the important suggestions advocated by Bentham, particularly those relating to prison reform, were not accepted by the government and a frustration flowing therefrom forced him to fight for reforms in almost all walks of social, economic and political life, it is equally true that several of his ideas found favour with the government after his death. Keeping this important fact in view, E.M. Young says that it "would be hard to find any corner of our public life where the spirit of Bentham is not working today."[37] In defence of Bentham, MacCunn says: "But, then, it was not Bentham's mission to do justice to what was old, nor even to attempt to hold the balance between the old and the new. His task was to prepare the way for whole truths by enforcing partial one; and, in particular, to subject the law of England to the task of a unity stripped of the last shred of reverence for participation."[38]

36. Cited in William Ebenstein : *Political Thought in Perspective*, p. 408.
37. See Wayper, *op. cit.*, p. 83. Wilfred Harrison says : "Any difficulties that arise in understanding Bentham are of a different order from those which arise in understanding Plato, Rousseau or Hegel : there are few great puzzles of interpretation, his ides are not intrinsically complicated and his ambiguities of expression are not impenetrable." Refer to his 'Introduction' in his (ed.) : *A Fragment on Government and Introduction to the Principles of Morals and Legislation by Jeremy Bentham*, p. 11.
38. MacCunn : *Six Radical Thinkers*, p. 11.

24

MILL

...while Spencer and Comte, Paine and Buckle, even Carlyle and Ruskin–figures who loomed very large in their generations–are fast receding into the shadows of the past, Mill himself remains real. One of the symptoms of this kind of three-dimensional, rounded, authentic quality is that we feel sure that we can tell where he would have stood on the issue of our own day.

— **Isaiah Berlin**[1]

If Jeremy Bentham gave his friend James Stuart Mill 'a doctrine' and received in turn by the latter ' a school',[2] James's son (John Stuart Mill) made it all in tune with the needs and aspirations of the contemporary age and thereby won the credit of giving a positive turn to the prevailing thought of English liberalism. Thus, in the history of recent English political thought not the father (James Stuart Mill) but the son (John Stuart Mill) has a very important place who covered a quite long span of the last century (1806-72) and who, while subscribing to the tradition of philosophical radicalism, "sharpened the future political speculation by bringing to the fore the external

1. Berlin : *Four Essays on Liberty*, p. 31.
2. E. Halevy : *Growth of Philosophical Radicalism* (Translated from French into English by Mary Morris and with an 'Introduction' by A.D. Lindsay), p. 251.

problem of human freedom in an organised society."[3] It is for this reason that while he followed the utilitarian tradition laid down by Bentham and strengthened by his father, he also altered its course; he not only subscribed tot he doctrine of *laissez faire* as preached by David Ricardo and Adam Smith but also reformulated it. In this way, he managed to give a fresh interpretation to the fundamental problem of political theory—relationship between individual liberty and political authority. It all demonstrated that while Mill "completed one epoch, he inaugurated another."[4]

WORKS : TRANSFORMATION OF ENGLISH LIBERALISM FROM A NEGATIVE TO A POSITIVE SIDE

As already pointed out, John Stuart Mill carefully took note of the fast changing social and economic conditions of his times and thereby sought to reinterpret the premises of English liberalism.[5] It is because of this that his political ideas look like shifting from the plane of individualism to that of collectivism. The earlier writings of Mill frankly show his firm faith in the principle of *laissez faire* that is evident from his *Principles of Political Economy* published in 1848 and that finds its most powerful defence in his *Essay on Liberty* that appeared in 1859. The life of individualism finds its reiteration in his *Utilitarianism* too published in 1861, though here Benthamite premises are revised so much so that the work of modification amounts to that of its destruction. However, what makes him a great democrat as well as a philosophical radical is his *Considerations on Representative Government* (1861) wherein the excellence of popular government is justified mainly on a moral ground and some concrete suggestions are also advanced for its better operation. Mention should be made of his *Subjection of Women* published in 1869–a monograph in defence of female suffrage and role of women in politics that perhaps attracted

3. Frank Thakurdas : *The English Utilitarians and the Idealists*, p. 120.
4. See F.J.C. Hearnshaw : *Social and Political Ideas of Some Representative Thinkers of the Age of Reason and Reconstruction*, p. 114.
5. In the words of McCallum, "The state, the old-fashioned state which had been overthrown or shaken by the French Revolution, by the American Revolution, and the great radical reform movement in England, was something aged, obstinate and blind. Bound in straiter limits, confronted and in the end controlled, by the growing democratic power of free, individual men, it would never again cast its sway so far over the spirit of enlightenment." *On Liberty and Considerations on Representative Government by J.S. Mill*, p. xiii.

Mrs. Harriet Taylor (the leader of the movement) so much so that he entered into a wedlock with her. His *Autobiography* published in 1872 has its own importance for the reason of recording his views in favour of collectivism.

Mill is generally regarded as the leading light of the old individualist school the reason for which should be traced in his strong affirmations contained in *Essay on Liberty* wherein he says that 'over himself, his own body and mind, the individual is sovereign'. As classical individualism stood for the minimum possible state interference, the same line finds place in his *Utilitarianism* with the result that Mill remains a strong advocate of the *laissez faire* school. However, a change in his thought appears in 1865 when he is elected to the House of Commons and thereby comes to have closer connection with the social and economic realities of his times. Thus, in the fourth edition of the *Principles of Political Economy* (1867), we find him pleading the case of taxation over 'unearned increments' and 'socially created values'. This trend has its more powerful reiteration in his *Autobiography* (1872) wherein he goes to the extent of advocating the case of public ownership of the natural resources of the country and nationalisation of very important industries.[6]

The merit of the works of Mill lies in the fact that he not only shifted from one plane to another, he cautiously watched the changing conditions and thereby sought to assimilate different trends into the revised form of English liberalism. He drew inspiration from several distinguished figures like Bentham, James Mill, Coleridge, Carlyle, Wordsworth, Comte, St. Simon, Ricardo and Adam Smith and managed to bring about a curious reconciliation of divergent trends of thought. One is really amazed to see that Mill could synthesise Bentham's experimental, infidel, abstract, matter of fact and essentially prosaic philosophy with Coleridge's conservative, religious, concrete, historical and poetic doctrine.[7] The reason for this lies nowhere else than in the fact that he was conscious of the necessity of reconciling these opposed views of life and believed that whoever "could master the premises and combine the methods

6. To a student of philosophy and logic, Mill's another work *System of Logic* (1843) is quite important in which he moves away from the deductive method of Bentham as well as of his father and attempts to connect empiricism with historical growth.
7. R. Metz : *A Hundred Years of British Philosophy*, p. 65.

of both would possess the entire English philosophy of the age."[8]

UTILITARIANISM : MODIFICATION OF THE BENTHAMITE PREMISES

A study of the political philosophy of John Stuart Mill begins with his work of altering the basic premises of Benthamite utilitarianism. As pointed out above, the most important exponent of English utilitarianism after Bentham is not the father James Stuart Mill but the son John Stuart Mill who did the excellent work of modification of the premises of Benthamism. At the hands of John Mill, Benthamite utilitarianism witnessed a penetrating revision so much so that even its foundations were changed. In doing as a modificator and a reformer, Mill acted as a most errant follower. The various points of modification incorporated by Mill coupled with shift in his own political thinking took Benthamite utilitarianism to the extent that it lost its original character. Hence, John Mill has been regarded as the most penetrating revisionist of the Benthamite utilitarianism.[9]

Mill's restatement of utilitarianism finds expression in his *Utilitarianism*. By heart Mill was not a defender of Bentham, but whatever contact he could have with the utilitarianism of Bentham, was a result of stern training and uncompromising control of his father who was a staunch supporter of the principle of Bentham. The paternal control was so strong that the son could not make himself a declared revisionist until the father died in 1836. The death of the father proved like the declaration of independence to the son, for he "was subject to his father by the most thorough indoctrination ever suffered by a man who afterwards raised himself to a plane of intellectual independence."[10]

8. *Ibid.*
9. As a matter of fact, Benthamite utilitarianism took a peculiar swing at the hands of two Mills–the father and the son–while the father supported and saved, the son modified and destroyed. Dunning very aptly says : "The century covered by these two lives fixed very clearly the chronological bounds within which the Benthamite utilitarianism rose, flourished and passed away by absorption into later philosophical growths." *A History of Political Theories*, Vol. III, p. 235.
10. C.H. Sabine : *A History of Political Theory*, p. 665. Bertrand Russell observes : "Firstly he (James) fashioned his son John Stuart Mill as Hamican fashioned his son Hannibal. Secondly, his capacity for discipleship combines a number of separate eminent men into a single

A study of Mill's utilitarianism shows that he is not an anti-utilitarian but a reformer of the creed of the founder. He accepts the principle of utility but reinterprets it in a way that the conclusions become different from, even antagonistic to, the basic premises of Benthamite utilitarianism. For instance, while defining the principle of utility, he says : "The creed which accepts as the foundations of morals, Utility or the Greatest Happiness Principle, holds that actions are right in proportion as they tend to promote happiness, wrong as they tend to produce the reverse of happiness. By happiness is intended pleasure and the absence of pain : by unhappiness pain and the privation of pleasure."[11] Obviously, like Bentham, Mill also identifies his notion of utility with the principle of pleasure and pain. To him utility "means the property or tendency of any particular thing to shield from some evil or to secure some good. The principle of utility accordingly consists in taking as our starting point, in every process of ordered reasoning, the calculus of comparative estimates of pains and pleasures and in not allowing any other idea to intervene."[12]

Mill's restatement of utilitarianism bears the following main characteristics :

1. Mill repudiates the view that the pleasures and the pains differ in quantity and not in quality. He finds out its testimony in the thing that the pleasure of a wise man is different from the pleasure of a fool. To him the experience of human life indicates that pleasures and pains differ both qualitatively and quantitatively. He argues that it "is better to be a human being dissatisfied than a pig satisfied; better to be a Socrates dissatisfied than a fool satisfied."[13] He fully rejects the Benthamite dictum that quality of pleasures being equal, pushpin is as good as poetry and holds that poetry as a source of pleasure is higher than the playing of an ordinary game. Naturally, Mill desires that man as a nobler and superior creature should pursue higher and real pleasures and avoid those that give happiness to a beast or a foolish person.

---

school, and thereby increased their collective influence." *Freedom and Organisation*, p. 121.

11. Mill : *Utilitarianism*, p. 13.
12. Jones : *Masters of Political Thought*, Vol. II, p. 369.
13. Mill, *op. cit.*, p. 18.

2. Mill refutes the view of Bentham that the pains and pleasures can be computed mathematically. In his view, the pleasures of a man are not objective or external units and thus the thesis of the felicific calculus is a sheer absurdity. When the pleasures and pains differ both in quality and quantity, the necessary standards of computing cannot be operative and thus no question of their counting arises. He says : "There is no other tribunal to be referred to even on the question of quantity. What means there are of determining which is the acutest of two pains or the interest of two pleasurable sanctions except the general suffrage of those who are familiar with both?"[14]

3. Mill's utilitarianism is more benevolent and humanistic, for he narrows down the gulf between individual interest and general happiness. If there is a question of individual's happiness and that of the others, Mill's utilitarianism "requires him to be strictly impartial as a disinterested and benevolent spectator."[15] Mill writes : "To do as you would be done by, and to love your neighbour as yourself, constitute the ideal perfection of utilitarian morality."[16] Quite unlike Bentham, Mill recognises that not only external, but internal sanctions also constrain the individual to promote general happiness, because every individual possesses a feeling for the happiness of mankind.[17]

---

14. Cf Wayper: Political Thought, p. 111.
15. Asirvatham : *Political Theory*, p. 491.
16. Mill, *op. cit.*, p. 32.
17. Mill continues : "In the golden rule of Jesus of Nazareth we read the complete spirit of the ethics of utility.... As the means of making the nearest approach to this ideal; utility would enjoin first that laws and social arrangements should place the happiness, or (as speaking practically it may be called) the interests of every individuals as nearly as possible in harmony with the interests of the whole; and secondly that education and opinion, which have so vast a power over human character, should so use that power as to establish in the mind of every individual an indissoluble association between his own happiness and the good of the whole; especially between his own happiness and the practice of such modes of conduct, negative and positive as regards the universal happiness prescribes; so that not only he may be unable to conceive the possibility of happiness to himself consistently with conduct opposed to the general good but also that a direct impulse to promote the general good may be in every individual one of the habitual motives of action, and the sentiments connected therewith may fill a larger and prominent place in every human being's sentient existence." *Ibid.*, pp. 32-33.

4. Unlike Bentham, Mill pays regard to the intrinsic worth of human existence. Not self-realisation but the achievement of pleasure and the avoidance of pain is the object of human life according to Bentham, but by desiring that man should pursue a real and higher pleasure, Mill introduces the sense of dignity in man. He thus introduces a conception of the good life as something more than a life devoted to mere pleasures. This is to place moral ends above happiness which becomes not indeed a state of pleasures but a state of mind that ensues when one pursues some moral end. Maxey very finely puts it thus : "Bentham's principle of utility, in a society of wolves, would exalt wolfishness; in a society of saints it would exalt saintliness. Mill was determined that saintliness should be the criterion of utility in any society whatsoever."[18]

5. One more point of retreat from Benthamite utilitarianism in Mill is visible in his defence of liberty. By seeing that all men are born in subjection, Bentham puts individual happiness under the stern subordination of the greatest good of the greatest number so much so that he empowers the majority to crush the happiness of the minority. On the contrary, Mill is a strong defender of individual liberty and is never prepared to see that it is crushed by the political authority. Particularly, in the self-regarding sphere, Mill wants no state intervention and sanctions such interference only when one man's freedom becomes a nuisance to he freedom of his fellow-beings. Mill says : "The only part of the conduct of anyone, for which he is amenable to society, is that which concerns others. In the part which merely concerns himself, his independence is, of right, absolute."[19]

6. Mill does not accept Benthamite view that democracy is the best form of government, for it will realises the formula of the greatest good of the greatest number. On the contrary, Mill asserts that no such absolute standard can be set forth. Even despotism is the best type of government for the barbarians and uncivilised peoples. Bentham justifies democracy because of the nature of man, by regarding him so inherently selfish that any other form of government would be a rule in the sinister interest of the governing class; Mill believes that the democratic institutions cannot be

---

18. Maxey: Political Philosophies, *p. 480.*
19. Mill : *Utilitarianism, Liberty and Representative Government*, p. 73.

recommended for a society whose members do not have the requisite quality of character, otherwise despotism is a legitimate mode of government for them. Thus, whereas Bentham "justifies democracy because of the nature of man, Mill justifies it because of the condition of man."[20]

7. Mill does not regard the state as a creation of self-interest as Bentham does, rather he introduces the element of will, and in the last phase of life his appreciation of collectivism impels him to wish that the state should take positive interest in fostering social welfare. Mill thus repudiates the negative role of the state. He desires state control over the institution of private property by holding that it can well impose taxation on the socially-created values. Mill's acceptance of compulsory education, acquisition of private property, general supervision of state over factory administration, regulation of working hours etc. reveals that he wants expansion of the sphere of state activity to an extent that Bentham could never contemplate.

8. Unlike Bentham, Mill is very keen for the introduction of the criterion of self-development. He does not define liberty in a rigid way, rather justifies its being within necessary checks. For instance, he accepts that a man may be prevented if he insists upon crossing a damaged bridge. Nor does he accept the shape of democracy as such as Bentham does; he suggests certain proposals of reform like open ballot, plural voting, female franchise, minority representation etc. We find that Mill wants to secure the development of man, for he is convinced that 'all wise and noble things come and must come from him.' Hence, he believes that there can be no self-development without liberty and it is this connection between liberty and self-development which interests him most, and even though he goes on to argue that liberty is also necessary for social happiness, it is clear that liberty is not to be expressed in terms of utility, but the former is yet more fundamental than the latter."[21]

---

20. Wayper, *op. cit.*, p. 115.
21. R.P. Anschutz thus comments : "In asserting the reality of individuality, Mill denies its reducibility to pleasures and pains or to anything else; in asserting the absolute importance of self-development he identifies the well-being of the individual with a sort of well-being very different from the passive happiness of Bentham." *The Philosophy of John Stuart Mill*, p.20.

The restatement of utilitarianism, as seen above, shows in a real sense that Mill "made it at once more humane and less consistent."[22] Of course, by making alterations, Mill made the premises of Benthamite utilitarianism soft and humane, yet the critics point out that it all meant confusion and abandonment of the basic premises. In stead of playing the role of a moderator and a reformer, Mill did the work of a destroyer. He introduced certain criterions which were quite opposed to the basic premises of utilitarianism and thus he passed on making one standard after another. Sabine thus observes : "Unfortunately, the modification of early utilitarianism which was undertaken by John Stuart Mill did nothing to effect a clarification. On nearly every subject his general position was a highly abstract statement of the older utilitarian theory, but having stated the principle, he proceeded to make concessions and restatements until in the end of the original theory was explained away without any new principle being put in its place."[23] It all made vital breaches in the stronghold of the theory of utilitarianism. As a result, the reformed or modified utilitarianism became non-utilitarianism. The alterations assumed a revolutionary character–a character which set aside what Bentham and James Mill had taken as a matter of conviction. Wayper very rightly says : "In all these alterations that he makes in Benthamism, Mill may think that he is defending it, but in fact he is destroyingit."[24]

INDIVIDUALISM : POWERFUL DEFENCE OF INDIVIDUAL LIBERTY

Mill's ardent individualism finds its best exposition in his *Essay on Liberty*.[25] Here he touches the problem of individual liberty and the relationship between individual freedom and social obligations. However, it should be remembered that in enunciating his theory of liberty, the views of Mill have much been influenced by the contemporary conditions of his age. The First Parliamentary Reform Act of 1832 had widened parliamentary representation and social legislation and had multiplied the scope of governmental concern so much so that even

22. Ivor Brown : *English Political Theory*, p. 11.
23. Sabine, *op. cit.*, p. 665.
24. Wayper, *op. cit.*, p. 116.
25. **Joad says that Mill's essay on liberty "is perhaps the most famous vindication of freedom of thought, and the most powerful plea for the toleration of opinions we fail to understand in the whole of literature".** *Modern Political Theory*, p. 27.

the affairs of daily life were covered by the interference of state. The campaign of reforms advocated by Bentham had also stimulated the concern of the government in the direction of the greatest good of the greatest number. As a result, the freedom of the people "was at stake."[26]

It is in this background that Mill develops his thesis and with a Miltonian fervour fights for the cause of individual liberty. Following are the implications of Mill's thesis :

1. Mill emphasises the necessity and desirability of diversity and originality which lead to the free play of individuality. In the presence of liberty, monotony and mediocrity diminish. Every individual keeps liberty to enrich his personality, but for this variety is essential. In his own words : "Such are the differences among human beings in their sources of pleasure, their susceptibilities of pain and the operation of their different physical and moral agencies, that unless there is corresponding diversity in their modes of life, they neither obtain their fair share of happiness, nor grow up to the mental, moral and aesthetic level of which they are capable."
2. A very important feature of Mill's justification of liberty lies in his division of human activity into two parts. To him the actions of an individual are of two types–self-regarding, *i.e.*, concerning none but himself alone and others–regarding, *i.e.*, affecting or likely to affect the life of others. The self-regarding sphere includes the freedom of conscience, thought, opinion and expression. On the basis of this division, Mill insists that in self-regarding sphere no external intervention is justified; but the state may interfere in the liberty of the individual only when his behaviour becomes a nuisance to the liberty of his fellow-beings. He thus puts : "The sole end for which mankind are warranted individually or collectively in interfering with the liberty of action of any of their member is self-protection. The only purpose for which power can be rightfully exercised over any member of a civilised community against his will, is to prevent harm to others. Over himself, his own body and mind, the individual is sovereign."[27]
3. The rationale of individualistic attitude of Mill still retains the touch of utilitarianism, for he asserts that it is the busi-

26. Doyle, *op. cit.*, p. 260.
27. Mill : *Utilitarianism, Liberty and Representative Government*, pp. 72-73.

ness of the government to promote actively the happiness of individuals and if it fails, it must give way to some other form of social organisation. This approach impels Mill to accept that individual liberty can be interfered with only when it is painful to the liberty of his fellow-citizens. Mill argues: "I regard utility as the ultimate appeal on all ethical questions; but it must be the utility in the largest sense, grounded upon the permanent interests of man as a progressive being. Those interests, I contend, authorise the subjection of individual spontaneity to external control, only in respect to those actions of each which concern the interest of the people."[28]

4. One thing that Mill greatly apprehends is the force of majority tyranny or the oppressive weight of public opinion and passionately revolts against the pressure of public opinion and convention. In his view, it is the tendency of society to usually impose, by means other than civil penalties, its own ideas and practices as rules of conduct on those who dissent from time to time. The social tendency usually does much to fetter the development and prevent the formation of any individuality not in harmony with its ways and compel all characters to fashion themselves upon the models of its own. The government is not justified in infringing the happiness of minorities by suppressing their views even when it is backed by the compact majority of men holding the contrary views. At one place, Mill asserts : "Mankind are greater gainers by suffering each other to live as seems good to themselves, than by compelling each to live as seems good to the rest."[29]

5. Another remarkable thing about Mill's thesis on liberty is that he attaches certain qualifications and exceptions to his doctrine of liberty. To him the comprehensive meaning of liberty may be understood only by a man who has natural faculties, *i.e.*, he is not below a certain age-limit and that he possesses requisite character to enjoy it. In other words, the doctrine of liberty cannot be applicable to those who had the deficiencies of mind body and character. Thus, Mill justifies

---

28. *Ibid*, p. 74. As McCallum says : "Liberty to Mill was no abstract right to be asserted by men as self-justifying activity, a notion of liberty which often covers more arrogance, pride and angularity; liberty had its purpose in human affairs; it was to be judged by utility." *On Liberty and Considerations on Representative Government* by *J.S. Mill*, pp. xix-xx.
29. Cf. Joad, *op. cit.*, p. 28.

despotism to the barbarian and backward peoples as a legitimate mode of government. According to Mill, it is the best form of government "in dealing with the barbarians provided the end be their improvement, and the means justified by actually effecting that end. Liberty, as a principle, has no application to any state of things anterior to time when mankind have become capable of being improved by force and equal discussion."[30]

It follows that Mill's doctrine of liberty is a very comprehensive term designed to develop, expand and enrich individual personality in all possible ways. It stands for the least possible state interference and even that only when the behaviour of one is detrimental to the liberty of another. Mill thus makes the role of state activity negative and recognises liberty as a means to the material interest of the individual. A.D. Lindsay thus observes that Mill's ideal "demands a state whose members are really individuals, proud of their individuality and variety, and respecting personality in themselves and in their neighbours."[31]

Mill's statement of liberty, according to Bowle, "carried on and enriched a most valuable stream of English thought, at once lucid, practical and humane."[32] But the thesis of Mill has been denounced for being negative, pessimistic, atomistic and empty. Three points have been raised in this connection :

1. It is said that Mill's statement does not find congruity with the fact of social harmony. It goes against a very celebrated tradition of political thought that man's existence should not be studied in isolation. Mill wrongly assumes the case of individual liberty apart from his social existence. For a social animal there can be no such thing as a rigid self-regarding sphere. It is due to this inadequacy that Green's affirmation of positive liberty became more popular when he defined it as a positive power of doing or enjoying something that is worth doing or enjoying in common with others.
2. Mill's rigid division of human actions into two parts is thoroughly unconvincing. There can be no water-tight division of individual's actions. The distinction between self-regarding and others- regarding spheres cannot be

30. Mill : *Utilitarianism, Liberty and Representative Government*, p. 73.
31. Lindsay : "Introduction," *Ibid.*, p.xviii.
32. Bowle : *Politics and Opinion in the Ninteenth Century*, p. 195.

worked out in practice, for whatever a man does, that has some direct or indirect bearing on his social behaviour. Obviously, committing suicide is a self-regarding action in Mill's view, but it can never be accepted that the state should do nothing to stop it. It has thus rightly been pointed out that the line between the two types of actions " is one which it is impossible to draw, and that, since we are all members of one society, all our actions must necessarily affect in some degree the other members of that society."[33]

3. Finally, Mill's conception of state activity has been contested. The state is not a necessary evil : it is a welfare agency and its laws don't always curtail the liberty of the individual. Mill wrongly supposes that the state should adopt a policy of minimum possible interference. Now when every democratic state enjoins upon itself the responsibility of rendering welfare services to its people, Mill's hypothesis definitely fails to win recognition. It is universally accepted that the state is the first condition of a civilised life and that all sorts of progress has been achieved with the help of the state. Owing to this, Mill's thesis was before long rejected when the Oxford idealist Green preached that the state "was not a necessary evil, nor a policeman to protect the natural rights of property but an instrument of positive good essential to the lives of its members."[34]

Barker thus says : "Yet when all these allowances are made, it still remains true that Mill was a prophet of an empty liberty and an abstract individual. He had no clear philosophy of rights, through which alone the conception of liberty attains a concrete meaning, he had no clear idea of that social whole in whose realisation the false anti-thesis of 'State' and 'individual' disappears."[35]

---

33. Joad, *op. cit.*, p. 28. On this point, John MacCunn says : "It is only an untenable atomism or a dangerous self-sophistication that can foster the illusion that in the hour of our self-regarding actions we are engaged in what concerns none but ourselves." *Six Radical Thinkers*, p. 83. Likewise, R.B. McCallum comments : "But when the line is to be drawn between self-regarding acts and acts which regard others is and must be a matter of endless dispute. The battle on this question is not where any particular line is to be drawn, but whether the drawing of any line is permissible." *On Liberty and Considerations on Representative Government* by *J.S. Mill*, pp. xxv-xxvi.
34. R.H.S. Crossman : *Government and the Governed*, p. 195.
35. Barker : *Political Thought in England*, p.4.

REPRESENTATIVE GOVERNMENT : EXCELLENCE OF THE POPULAR RULE

Although Mill appears as a qualified admirer of democracy in his *Essay on Liberty*, in his *Representative Government* he is a stern advocate of democracy what he calls by the name of representative government. To him the representative government gives an answer to the question of the best form of government. But Mill is not satisfied with the democratic system as such; he also insists on certain innovations as well and thus representative government, as desired by Mill, holds a type which was not existing in the nineteenth century. It is clear that Mill recognises the excellence of the democratic system but also points out its elements of weaknesses and introduces constitutional reforms for rendering it in an ideal character.

Mill takes up the question of best government and answers in a way quite different from that of Plato, Aristotle and Rousseau. He rejects the view that political institutions are a natural growth and must be taken as they are found, or like biological organisms, they cannot be effectually improved by conscious human innovation. Similarly, he repudiates the notion that the government is wholly an affair of innovation and contrivance. However, taking a middle course of these two points of view, he assumes that political institutions, though a natural growth, don't resemble vegetative phenomena, rather in every stage of existence are given a definite shape by voluntary human agencies. Obviously, to Mill, governments are made good or bad by the judgment and skill of the people and thus political machinery must be adjusted to the capacities and qualities of such men as are available in that stage of existence. No permanent standard can be fixed; Plato's rule of philosopher-king, Aristotle's rule of law, Cicero's mixed system, Hobbes's unlimited monarchy, Lock's constitutional government, Rousseau's direct democracy, all fail to serve the purpose of Mill. Mill rejects the view that any one type of government may be regarded as the universal and eternal panacea. He adds: "To enquire into the best form of government in the abstract (as it is called) is not a chimerical, but a highly practical employment of scientific intellect: and to introduce into any country the best institutions which, in the existing conditions of that country, are capable of, in any tolerable degree, fulfilling the conditions is one of the most rational objects to which practical effort can address itself."[36]

Mill then defines representative government as one in which the political power is exercised by the representatives periodically elected by and ultimately accountable to the people. But this definition embodies an implication which is quite different from the interpretation of other protagonists of democracy. Mill does not agree with the Lincolnian view that it is a government of the people, or by the people. On the contrary, in his view, the proper nomenclature of democracy should be representative government, for modern democracy does not imply the rule of the people as a whole. It is a rule of the representatives of the people and thus in defining democracy, Mill warns, the difference between the nominal residence of sovereignty and real exercise of political power should be kept in mind. The wielding of sovereignty is a thing the people or their elected representatives can do and should do : but the administration of government with all sorts of intricacies and complexities is beyond the capacity of even the most intelligent and virtuous people.

Another important feature in this regard is Mill's qualified approval of the excellence of representative government. As already pointed out, he does not approve of the representative government as a good or the best form of government for all times, of all peoples and of all ages. The essential requisite is the character and capacity of the people and, until the people are fully civilised, the representative government cannot be successfully operative. Representative government recognises liberty and the exercise of liberty is beyond the competence of the barbarians, uncivilised and the backward peoples of Asia and Africa. Mill very forcefully puts that the liberty as a principle "has no application to any state of things anterior to the time when mankind have become capable of being improved by free and equal discussion."[37]

But when Mill sanctions representative government for a people, he also attaches certain requirements with it. Instead of satisfying himself with the medicine, he also prescribes its dosage as well as the introduction of certain new tactics for the health of the patient and usefulness of the medicine itself. He explains the duty of the representative assembly in these

36. Mill, *op. cit.*, p. 181.
37. *Ibid.*, p. 73.

words: "Instead of the function of governing, for which it is radically unfit, the proper office of a representative assembly is to watch and control the government; to throw the light of publicity on its acts; to compel and secure full exposition and justification of all of them which anyone considers questionable; to censure them if found condemnable; and, if men who compose the government abuse their trust, or fulfil in a manner which conflicts with the deliberative sense of the nation, to expel them from office, and either expressly or virtually appoint their successors."[38]

However, Mill admires excellence of representative government from moral and psychological points of view. To him the test of good government lies in the effect that it leaves on its people. The first element of a good government is the virtue and intelligence of human beings composing the community. Hence, the most important "point of excellence which any form of government can possess is to promote the virtue and intelligence of the people themselves. According to Mill, the acid test of governmental machinery is the degree in which it is adopted to take advantage of the amount of good qualities which may at any time exist, and make them instrumental to the right purpose."[39] With this standpoint, Mill examines the case of various forms of governments and gives his verdict in favour of representative government inasmuch as it "promotes a better and higher form of national character than any other polity whatever."

Then, Mill is not merely a protagonist of the representative government under the required conditions, he also sanctions certain qualifications and requirements and introduces reforms, rather innovations. He very strongly hits at the weaknesses of a democratic system and then warns that unless they are removed, the system cannot have an ideal character. To him, general ignorance, incapacity of the people to speak moderately, insufficient mental qualifications, overflow of the interest detrimental to the welfare of the community, are the most vulnerable points of a representative system. Mill thus very frankly detests demagogism, bossism and pressure

38. *Ibid*, p. 239. According to McCallum, "Representative institutions are, therefore, not to Mill what they were to revolutionary socialists, a medium in which to conduct the class war or else an insidious means of distracting attention from it. To Mill representative government was a healing art." *Op. cit.*, p. xi.
39. Mill, *op. cit.*, p. 193.

politics and with a note of caution writes that democracy is not ideally the best form of government unless it "can be so organised that no one class, not even the most numerous, shall be able to reduce all but itself to political insignificance, and direct the course of legislation and administration by its exclusive class interest."[40]

It follows that the representative government can have an ideal character of its own if it is given a reformed shape and, in this direction, Mill insists on the following requirements:

1. Like other distinguished students of democracy, Mill accepts the significance of minority representation and advocates the use of Hare Scheme. He desires that it is an essential part of democracy that minorities should be given proportionate and adequate representation. He regrets that modern democracies lose the character of being a government of the whole people equally represented and rather become a contrivance of the majority rule. Proportionate representation should be given even to the minorities, otherwise there would be a government of inequality and privilege–something opposed to the principle of democracy itself. He puts : "Nothing is more certain than that the virtual blotting out of a minority is not a necessary or natural consequence of freedom, but instead is diametrically opposed to the first principle of democracy : representation in proportion to numbers."[41]
2. Mill very strongly defends the cause of female franchise. For this sake, he wrote a book *The Subjection of Women*. He advocates the case on the ground that it would wield a decisive influence in securing the enactment of advanced social legislation. It is a sin that the women should remain disfranchised or live as dependents just on the bidding of their husbands. The female franchise would open avenues for the good which males cannot impart. It would also enhance the moral position of the women and instead of assigning them the job of a hot-house cultivation, reveal their capabilities not for the benefit of their husbands and masters but for the good for the whole society.
3. Mill favours the system of public voting. Rejecting the notion of secret ballot, he contends that the value and effective-

40. *Ibid*, p. 277.
41. Cf. Garner, *op. cit.*, p. 648.

ness of voting depends on the manner in which the right of voting is exercised. In his view, secret voting encourages selfishness and harms the consciousness of moral responsibilities, while public voting indicates proper performance of duty owing to the fact that it is discharged under the very eye and criticism of the people.

4. Mill sanctions weighted suffrage. While recognising that the vote has a value which should be shared by all, he also contends that in the light of superior knowledge, education and intelligence, weightage should be given to some in comparison to those who are ignorant, stupid or of an indifferent character. On the basis of mental, moral and natural qualities, Mill even goes to the extent of presenting various groups of citizens deserving weighted franchise. As a supporter of plural voting, Mill calls it wise "to allow all graduates of universities, all persons who have passed creditably through the higher schools, all members of the liberal profession, and perhaps some others who registered specifically in those characters, to give their votes as such in any constituency in which they choose to register : retaining in addition their votes as simple citizens in the localities in which they reside."

5. Mill recognises the importance of educational qualifications. Unless a person has the minimum knowledge of reading, writing and elementary arithmetic, he should not be enfranchised. Moreover, he also makes it mandatory for the government to make suitable arrangements for this and deprive only those people of franchise who fail to utilise the benefit of opportunity. And it would be the duty of the Registrar to enrol one as a voter only when he demonstrates his knowledge of reading, writing, and elementary arithmetic at the time of seeking registration. If such a condition is attached, Mill hopes, it would, after a few years, exclude none but those who care so little for the privilege.

6. Mill justifies the imposition of property qualification as well. His contention is that the persons having property behave more responsibly than the propertyless ones and when the representative assembly discusses a taxation measure, only persons having property can make a show of responsibility. The propertyless people are most likely to demonstrate lavishly and irresponsibly and thus vitiate the character of general discussion on financial matters. In his

own words : "The voting of taxes by those who do not themselves contribute is a violation of the fundamental principle of the free government; representation should be coextensive with taxation."

7. Mill insists on the gratuitous services of the representative. He refutes the view that the parliamentarians should be compensated by way of salaries and allowances in view of the heavy expenses incurred by them in their elections and valuable services which they in their daily career perform. Mill's contention is that the practice of paying to the parliamentarians renders to politics the character of a gainful profession, makes seats in the legislature the object of desire, even ambition, on the part of politicians and attracts incompetent persons. The result is that legislative assemblies are captured by those who, instead of regarding service as a public duty, consider their successful performance a big reward.
8. Mill lays emphasis on the independent role of the representative. He does not consider the electorate as the teacher and master of the representative or party rules as iron-chains for him. Like Burke, he desires that the delegate should exercise his own fair judgement and that when his views coincide with the views of his constituents, he may naturally act according to their wishes, otherwise he should not suppress his judgement except when he finds that his views need be changed or moderated in the face of insistence being presented by very able members of his constituency whom he considers abler than himself.
9. Finally, it may be mentioned that Mill disfavours pre-election commitments by the contesting leaders, supports indirect election method on the plea that it acts as an impediment to the full sweep of popular passion; contends for the election of the head of the executive out of the party having majority in the legislature; wants optimum tenure of a legislative assembly being neither so short that the full conduct of the representative may not be judged by the electors, nor so long that the delegate forgets his responsibility and neglects the case of public advantage. He also lends support to the idea of bi-cameralism where the upper chamber is constructed on the principle of political experience and training without reference to the consideration of birth or wealth.

In short, Mill's thesis of representative government is a very thoughtful attempt to being out the excellence of such a particular system as well as offer a corrective of its weaknesses and inherent dangers. Here Mill detests a despotic system; he is also aware of the dangers of a paternalistic state and very seriously suggests certain conditions that may render to it an ideal character. The trend of utilitarianism also survives here, for Mill believes that democracy contributes to the happiness of the individual. However, more important is the fact that his benevolent approach overflows in supporting the cause of democracy from a moral point of view. Wayper thus rightly says: "But Mill is a democrat above all not because he believes that democracy makes men happier, but because he is convinced that it makes them better."[42]

No doubt, Mill's views on representative government are very important and they constitute a classical defence of democracy, yet he has also been criticised for adding certain innovations which frustrate the very purpose he seeks to defend and foster. For instance, in the subsequent decades after his death, several states have given implementation to his suggestions of female voting, minority representation and bicameralism, but his suggestions for public voting, open ballot, weighted franchise, property and educational qualifications, independence of the delegate, non-payment of remuneration to the parliamentarians etc. have been disfavoured. However, a more serious danger may be found in Mill's advocacy of the excellence of representative government. Even if all reforms and innovations, as suggested by Mill, are introduced, still there would remain loopholes to vitiate the excellent character of representative government. Mill nowhere sanctions checks which would be used against the oppressive and arbitrary behaviour of the legislators. The representatives would act independently but do nothing except tempting and hoodwinking their constituents at various intervals so much so that the very fact of consent would disappear. The majority tyranny would still persist and the geographical divisions of the country would not make a parliament expert in professions, honest in commitments and really democratic in character. In the name of the

42. Wayper, *op. cit.*, pp. 117-118. "The problem of character is the determining voice in the question of government. If men could be spoon-fed with happiness, a benevolent despotism would be the ideal system." Hobhouse: *Liberalism*, pp. 112-113.

mandate of the people, the representative assembly would rule in a way "taxing political sagacity to the utmost."[43]

COLLECTIVISM : QUALIFIED SANCTION OF INCREASE IN STATE ACTIVITY

A very peculiar feature of the political philosophy of John Stuart Mill finds place in the fact that, representing the influence of the age, it shifts from one plane to another. Hence, Mill who was a reluctant utilitarian in the beginning, and an ardent individualist in the middle, ends as a qualified collectivist. Now he regards social utility as the goal and emphasises that it is the supreme duty of the individual to sacrifice himself for the sake of social good. He finds it necessary to entrust the state with larger functions of controlling the distribution of national wealth. This trend is quite visible in the later editions of his *Principles of Political Economy* and *Autobiography*. Barker correctly points out that Mill "is a transitional force and in his hands utilitarianism begins to be less individualistic, and assumes more and more a socialistic quality."[44]

In the subsequent editions of his work on political economy, Mill advances a theory of special taxation of unearned increments and socially-created values. The benefits that accrue to the landlord owing to the increase in value created by the advancement of human civilisation constitute 'unearned increment' and because of being in the nature of socially–created values, they should be subject to special taxation by the state. If there is an income which constantly tends to increase without any exertions or sacrifices on the part of the owners, it would be no violation of an individual's liberty if the state appropriates or specially taxes the enhanced portion of his in-

---

43. Maine : *Popular Government*, p. x. Radcliffe correctly questions that when the representative body "advances from the work of accepting or refusing to the work of making and unmaking the laws themselves, displaces the old monarchical power and becomes a sovereign in its own right, does not the theory of consent become a rather individual support for the laws claims to obedience?" *The Problem of Power*, p. 45.

44. Barker, *op. cit.*, p. 12. M. Judd Harmon well observes : "For one thing, it becomes obvious that the mysterious making of the unseen hand of competition did not always have the beneficent result which Adam Smith had predicted. The ghastly conditions of the industrial working classes were eloquent testimonies of the fact that a policy of government restraint with respect to the functioning of the economic system was totally inadequate. Liberal thought turned perceptively and quickly from individualism to collectivism." *Political Thought from Plato to the Present*, p. 379.

come. Mill says that it would not be taking anything from anybody rather be like applying an accession of wealth created by the circumstances to the benefit of society instead of allowing it to become an unearned appendage to the riches of a particular individual or class. Mill thus puts : "The first step should be a valuation of all land in the country. The present value of land should be exempted from the tax, but after an interval had elapsed, during which society had increased in population and capital, rough estimate might be made of the spontaneous increase which had accrued to rent since the valuation was made."

Mill thus authorises the state to overstep its sphere already laid down in his essay on liberty. He is now prepared to make following concessions in the fourth edition of his work on political economy. The state should enforce compulsory education to remove the incompetency of the citizens; release persons from the obligations of contracts in perpetuity in cases where the parties cannot be competent judges of the effect of such obligations; make subject to public regulations all monopolies; limit working hours and conditions of work; encourage scientific research and works of exploration; increase wages; levy tax on economic rent; protect public health; introduce factory legislation; and launch insurance against illness, industrial accidents and indigence in old age.[45] Likewise, in another work, he says: "The social problem of the future was considered to be how to unite the greatest individual liberty of action with a common ownership in the raw materials of the globe, and an equal participation of all in the benefits as combined labour."[46]

It appears that by taking this position, Mill cuts across what he says on earlier occasions. His doctrine of negative liberty is contradicted when he sanctions the idea of state interference in the name of social utility. The very purpose of individualism is thus defeated. The whole position becomes inconsistent as well. But, in spite of this, Mill's inconsistency adds to the strength of his influence that he shed over his successors. The influence takes such a great shape that Mill, not Marx, becomes the intellectual father of the English Fabians who "do not begin, like Marx, by attacking capital as the stolen fruits of labour which have been filched by the capitalist from the workingman : they start along the lines suggested by Mill, with

45. Mill : *Principles of Political Economy*, V ed., pp. 573-693.
46. Mill : *Autobiography*, p. 232.

an attack on rent, as the unearned increment of land, which has been stolen (or at any rate substituted) by the landlord from the society which is its creator, and to which it properly belongs."[47]

CRITICAL APPRECIATION : MILL AS PROPHET OF INDIVIDUAL LIBERTY AND SOCIO-CAPITALISM

We have thus surveyed and uncritically examined the various aspects of Mill's political philosophy. To sum up, two things strike at the end. First, Mill lays a very strong emphasis on the liberty of the individual and for this sake he revolts against the extension of state authority if thereby individual liberty is menaced or harmed. Hence, it is rightly said that Mill's 'abiding and fundamental message to his age was the value of freedom."[48] Secondly, Mill does not speculate and thereby give expression to his ideas from a narrow outlook. He repudiates much what Bentham had preached and his father reiterated and, keeping in view the fact of changing times, he contends for the course of individual liberty. As a result, in the last phase of his life he happens to say much what becomes the anti-thesis of his chosen principle of *laissez faire*. Lancaster thus admirably comments : "Actually Mill had neither the narrowness of outlook nor the dogmatic temper required to build the sort of system put together by his father and Bentham. At bottom he was in this respect a commonsense Englishman not much interested in system. As he grew older, he came more and more to regard unsatisfactory the original utilitarian creed, and to acknowledge that his creed was far too simple to explain the fact of social life."[49]

The political philosophy of John Stuart Mill should be appreciated from one more important standpoint. He not only understands the currents of socio-economic change, but also lays the foundations of, what may be termed, 'socio-capitalism'. His faith in utilitarianism as well as in humanism, as expressed in

47. Barker, *op. cit.*, p. 189.
48. Hearnshaw, *op. cit.*, p. 189.
49. Lancaster: Masters of Political Thought, Vol. III, p. 118. Mill himself recognised it thus : "If I am asked what system of political philosophy I substituted for that which, as a philosophy, I had abandoned, I answer, 'No system'. Only a conviction that the true system was something much more complex and many sided than I previously had any idea of and that its office was to supply, not a set of model institutions, but principles from which the institutions suitable to any given circumstances might be deduced." *Autobiography*, p. 136.

his faint conception of a welfare state, also inspired him profoundly to seek a plausible reconciliation of capitalism and socialism. His sympathy for a socialist movement appeared in his support to several important themes like co-operative societies, policies of public works, birth control enforced by the state, state interference in the maintenance and regulation of the property of the corporations and ecclesiastical bodies, creation of state-controlled peasant proprietorship after abolishing all types of absolute property rights in land, a theory of labour relations with various welfare schemes for the working classes like minimum wages, full employment, profit sharing, fixed working hours, trade unions and a reformed poor law. In this enthusiastic vein, he even goes to the extent of suggesting that a fair trial should be given to the experiment of socialist programme that may solve the problem of the liberty of the individual.[50]

And yet Mill does not break his connection with the basic tenets of a capitalist system. Thus, he continues to argue for the preservation of free trade and free competition. In the name of liberty of the individual, he denounces the system of communism for the loss of initiative, non-payment of higher wages or remuneration to a man of superior skill and industry, regimentation of thought, education and culture and the like. He forcefully asserts that the system of capitalism should not be criticised unless it had a fair trial. It all shows that Mill "is conscious of the danger of Socialism as also of the dangers of Capitalism in their imperfect forms. But he is also aware of the good sides of the ideal forms of both. This explains why he is eager to synthesise the good sides of Socialism with those of Capitalism in his concept of socio-capitalism.[51]

Whether Mill was 'a cautious and uncertain pessimist'[52] or in whom emerged 'a new man with a deep sympathy and wide intellectual outlook' as a keener perception of the needs of human beings and realisation of the 'importance of cultivating the emotions as well as intellect',[53] it is certain that he strengthened the line of Benthamite liberalism that the state exists for the individual and not *vice versa*. For this reason, the legitimate basis of political obligation or the proper justifica-

50. Sobhanlal Mookerjee : *The Political Philosophy of John Stuart Mill*, p.297.
51 *Ibid*, pp. 267 268.
52. R.J. Halliday : *John Stuart Mill*, p. 142.
53. Davidson : *Political Thought in England*, p. 162.

tion of the area of state activity "is to be found in the services which it renders to the individual, whether in satisfying his desire or protecting his rights or realising his ideal."[54] Viewed thus, both Bentham and Mill contributed significantly to the creed of utilitarian radicalism and thus in the nineteenth century "awakened interest in active politics, social reforms and beneficial legislation to an extent that had previously been unthought of. The benefit is being felt today."[55]

54. Murray : *An Introduction to Political Philosophy*, p. 162.
55. Davidson, *op. cit.*, pp. 249-250. Ivor Brown rightly feels that the creed of utilitarianism, though long discredited, "has in it the prospects of immortality." *English Political Theory*, p. 129.

25

COMTE

The Utopias of the eighteenth century had made on idol of the individual : those of the nineteenth sacrificed everything to the community or the State. The earlier Utopias defied history; the latter ones, that of Comte at any rate, have at least sought to build their dreams of the future upon the experience of the past. In all this, the influence of Hegel, indirect though it may be, is unmistakable.

— **C.E. Vaughan**[1]

The representative thinker of the scientific school in France is August Comte (1798-1857) who is known as the creator of Positive Philosophy and the father of modern sociology.[2] In his early days he displayed his love for the study of

---

1. Vaughan : *Studies in the History of Political Philosophy before and after Rousseau*, p. 184.
2. This school has been characterised as 'scientific' for the simple reason that it sought to interpret human life in terms of natural sciences. Its representative thinker, Herbert Spencer, adopted a biological point of view in his study of society and state and thus contributed to what is also known by the name of biological school. To a good number of thinkers in England as well as elsewhere, it appeared that all human problems might be solved by a scientific methodology. Naturally appeal to science represented a new orientation and a new tendency standing for the possibility of mustering natural sciences into the service of social theory. This type of study "became so wide-spread in the last century that political science, for a

mathematics and his expulsion for insubordination from the Echole Polytechnique demonstrated his life-long unwillingness to submit to authority. By temperament he had scorn for academic conventions as well as his egoism increased the number of unsympathetic supporters. But he was much benefited by serving as the secretary to St. Simon. This brief crucial contact cemented his scientific approach which led him to find an amazing contrast between the dynamic character of science and industry and the static nature of politics. Comte thus realised that the governments, in spite of their superficial differences in successive regimes, remained as before in the hands of 'unscientific creatures' (like orators, lawyers, politicians, demagogues, journalists) and thus emphasised that political authority must reside in the hands of those who were well-acquainted with the plain lessons of progress. In other words, it meant Comte's insistence on social control by the men of science. The political ideas of Comte are contained in six large volumes on *Positive Philosophy* which strike as exceedingly detailed and long-winded, but they comprehensively deal with his philosophy of positivism.

POSITIVISM : REJECTION OF THEOLOGICAL AND METAPHYSICAL ASSUMPTIONS

Comte's political philosophy has received the nomenclature of positivism, for he makes a study of the society and the state from a positive point of view (that is to say, positive in the sense of being divorced from the theological and metaphysical assumptions) of 'social physics'–that is to say of natural causes and natural laws of society.[3] However, so strong was his emphasis on the usefulness of positive method that he had no patience with the disinterested search for truth. He viewed that knowledge was valuable only when it could be applied to the practical concerns of life. He thus condemned the knowledge of

---

time, seemed in danger of being swallowed by the natural sciences." See Garner : *Political Science and Government*, p. 215.

3. See Barker : *Political Thought in England*, pp. 136-37. "The positive method rejects all *a priori* arguments; it rejects all abstract ideas : it rejects all absolute standards. It is inductive, concrete and relative. The mark of the positive thinker is to apply the methods and, so far as may be, the results of natural science to the investigation of the higher problems presented by the individual and political life of man. It is to build his conclusions upon the accumulated experience of the past as modified by observation of the changing circumstances of the present." See Vaughan, *op. cit.*, p.200.

theoretical and metaphysical schools and regarded much of the university education as useless. His conviction in the use of positive methodology rendered him hopeful of the fact that one day the 'useless' would be substituted by 'useful' and by the application of the laws of human society (as discovered by him), human affairs would be managed scientifically. He very strongly urged : "The positive philosophy offers the only solid basis for the Social Reorganisation which must succeed the critical conditions in which the most civilised nations are now living."[4]

This approach leads Comte to repudiate the view that 'Ideas' or 'Opinions' govern the world. He condemned all abstract and metaphysical researches as 'intellectual anarchy', for they are not based on 'observed facts'. Only positive study can produce empirical and verifiable results. He contrasted his positive method with what he called 'metaphysics', the basing of knowledge on assumptions that go beyond concrete facts : whereas science to him consisted of positive facts which may be empirically tested. All other political theories and psychological doctrines, in his view, are nothing but statements of what people wished to believe in spite of the absence of any empirical evidence. Naturally, in his view, all political doctrines that lacked positive approach were obsolete and unscientific. In this way, Comte expressed his regret for all intellectual pursuits and was bent on retaining no more of them than was strictly indispensable."[5]

Comte believed that the laws of society can be formulated like the laws of science and it is only through these laws that a proper study of society in its various aspects can be made. However, Comte's search is not for inventing or discovering the 'why' of things, he is merely satisfied with the 'how' of things. That is, Comte wants that the law should be based on observed uniformities. Just as a natural scientist by careful observation finds that the matter invariably behaves in a certain way and he discovers a law in that regard, so a social scientist must establish a law on the basis of the observed uniformities and not bother about the remote cause of things or in any alleged transcendent reality behind observable facts. He advises that by speculating upon causes, we "could solve no difficulty about origin and purpose. Our real business is to analyse accurately

4. See Lancaster : *Masters of Political Thought*, Vol. III, p. 74.
5. John Stuart Mill : *August Comte and Positivism*, p. 176.

the circumstances of phenomena, and to connect them by natural relations of succession and resemblance."[6]

In order to make his point yet more clear and strong, Comte explains the law of three stages which reveals an inevitable progression of the human mind from its infancy to its acceptance of positivism. According to Comte, from the study of the development of human intelligence, in all directions and through all times, the discovery arises of a great fundamental law, to which it is necessarily subject, and which has a solid foundation of proof, both in the facts of our organisation and in our historical experience. The law shows that each of our leading conceptions–each branch of knowledge–passes successively through three different theoretical conditions–Theological or Fictitious, Metaphysical or Abstract, and Scientific or Positive. In the first stage, the human mind seeks the essential nature of things and supposes that all phenomena are produced by the immediate action of super-natural beings. In the second stage, the mind supposes abstract forces inherent in all things and capable of producing all phenomena. In the final stage, mind discards all those notions and applies itself to the study of their laws–that is their invariable relations of successions and resemblance. Here we find a good combination of reason and observation. Thus, Comte lays emphasis on the third stage and rejects all theological, metaphysical and abstract notions. He says : "The first is the necessary point of departure of the human understanding, the third is its fixed and definite state. The second is merely a state of transition."[7]

Comte introduces his positive approach to the study of society and contributes to the subject of sociology. He defines sociology as a science which interprets the facts of human history, apart from those of human individual biology, in terms of general laws, and by studying those laws seeks to discover a scientific technique of regulating human society. Moreover, Comte also takes the help of history. He proposes a careful observation of every known fact and situation in history from the standpoint of all its antecedents. On the basis of this data, he raises a body of empirical generalisation as the laws of social phenomena. These tentative laws would be checked against the laws of human nature as discovered by biology. Then, Comte advocates that sociological generalisations found to be consis-

6. Cf. Lancaster, *op. cit.*, p. 76.
7. *Ibid*, p. 77.

tent with human biology would be recognised as positive laws of society, and those found inconsistent with biological laws would be rejected, for it would be clear that in their case, history had been misinterpreted. He says : "In sociology the correlation assumes this form : Order is the condition of all Progress; Progress is always the object of Order; or to penetrate the question still more deeply; Progress may be regarded simply as development of Order; for the Order of nature contains within itself the germs of all possible progress."[8]

However, Comte's positivism may be criticised on these grounds :

1. Comte, like Aristotle, Hobbes and Bentham, sticks to a particular factor so much so that he ignores the place of other factors. That is, he relies exclusively on the factor of 'science' and thereby overlooks the significance of other factors like religion and metaphysics that have their own place in social life. Even theological and metaphysical, what he terms 'non-positive', factors have a value of their own by means of which human beings secure satisfying explanations of the mysteries of their existence. Certainly, he is wrong in denying the reality of any puzzle insoluble by the methods of science.
2. Comte fails to furnish a complete analysis of human history as an explanation of three stages of development. It is clear that his explanation lacks universality, or its application is limited to the white European peoples only. Undoubtedly, he could have found it hard to fit the social experience of other parts of the world into his science. Modern anthropological findings demonstrate that he knows very little about early society to speak as confidently as he does. Although all sciences have passed through various stages of development, yet the case of only three stages, as given by him, cannot be construed as final truth.
3. It may also be pointed out that Comte has done a wrong by excluding the significance of speculative part in political philosophy. Thus, it is critically observed : "Large as is the place assigned to scientific question in Comte's political theory, he makes no serious attempt to sift the speculative problems which lie at their root, and in the few passages,

8. Comte : *A General View of Positivism* (Translated from French into English by Bridge), p. 114.

where he touches on such matters, he betrays a confusion of mind, an inability to understand what exactly are the points at issue, which contrast decisively with the clear-sightedness and profundity of Hegel."[9]

POLITICS AND SOCIETY : SEARCH FOR AN UTOPIA

Comte studies the state and government from his positive point of view. But here the application of the law of three stages is related to his political philosophy in two ways. Firstly, he believes that the political system of any group reflects the stages of explanation of the universe which the group happens in any age to have accepted. Thus, in the theological stage the rulers were priests. In the middle ages, there was the metaphysical stage when abstract notions of 'natural rights' and 'natural law' were in prevalence, and political authority passed into the hands of politicians, journalists and the lawyers. The second point of contact between the law of three stages and his theory of politics appears in his view on the development of various sciences. According to him, each science passes through three stages and thus master science (Sociology) is no exception. He points out that as yet sociology has not reached the final stage and still has within it the elements of theology and metaphysics. The notable thing about Comte here is that he "conceived it to be his mission to complete the transition to a positive sociology. Once this is done, control in society will inevitably pass to scientists."[10]

Thus, Comte sweeps aside all theological and metaphysical constructions by calling them as mere projections of the mind as irrelevant and clears the way for a completely scientific way of looking at life and organisation of society by reducing all knowledge to the knowledge of the phenomenon. He is convinced that as other subjects like chemistry and physics have reached the positive stage by discarding the abstract principles of God's grace and sin, so the surviving metaphysical modes of thought will also go and even social sciences will gain the character of positivism. With this approach he insists that the social sciences should be perfected by demonstrating the irrelevance of those modes of thought and thereby bringing forth a scientific organisation of society.

---

9. Vaughan, *op. cit.*, p. 186.
10. Cf. Lancaster, *op. cit.*, p. 83.

Comte presents a very untraditional picture of government and then passes on to the formulation of an international political system. At first, he denounces the big size of modern states and wants their decomposition into very small units each having a population from one to three millions. His plan reveals the division of the world into five hundred areas (states) each small enough to allow a real sense of relations of citizenship. If this done, his positivism shall finally have become universal.

However, his attitude towards government takes a bureaucratic shape when he prefers a dictatorship of the bankers whose rule would be moralised by the sufficiency of women and of the priesthood of the new Religion of Humanity intended to replace the traditional beliefs. The priests would in reality be expert sociologists, who have mastered the laws of society and since those laws depend upon the laws of the subsidiary sciences of the latter also. Women would contribute to the softening influence appropriate to their inherent character. Apart from their small priestly class, the entire population would be divided between the patricians (rich) and the proletariat (poor). The principal patricians would be the bankers controlling manufacturing, agricultural and commercial concerns. The families of the aristocracy would be a thirtieth part of the active population. Since, however, the proletarian household would have seven members, while the patrician would have thirteen, the workers would be only sixteen times as numerous as the aristocrats. According to Comte's calculation, each agricultural patrician would direct thirty five proletariats, each manufacturing patrician seventy, and each commercial patrician sixty.

It may, thus, be pointed out that Comte rejects Platonic metaphysics and reconstructs his ideal state in a Platonic manner. He rejects all metaphysical and abstract principles and refuses to accept any but positive principles drawn by induction from the past and the present; he is nevertheless a Platonist owing to the reconstruction of an ideal state, though in the light of his scientific principles. Again, though influenced by the medieval church more than by Plato, somewhat in a Platonic manner, he draws distinction between the temporal and spiritual classes. The result is that his ideal state represents a complex amalgam of Platonic approach and his acceptance of the scientific principles. Barker thus comments : "His ideal state would have been one in which the spiritual class, a combination of *savants*, orthodox in science, expressive of reason and acting by persuasion rather than force, guided the course of affairs in the light of scientific principles."[11]

CRITICAL APPRECIATION : COMTE AS THE APOSTLE OF THE RELIGION OF HUMANITY

A brief look at the political philosophy of Comte shows that he could not save himself from the impact of the French Revolution as well as of Hegelianism, though he certainly tried to react to both in varying degrees. The leading feature of his political and social thought is undoubtedly the idea of humanity implying the subordination of the individual to the community at large. Comte's explanations in this regard ascribed to him the credit of being the "first writer outside of Germany–and, of those who had any popular following, the first writer in Europe–to work out organic principles in politics as a detailed and comprehensive whole; the first writer, that is to gain a general hearing for such principles as are not based on the autonomy of the individual. And what is yet more distinctive, he was the first to free those principles from the trammels of the purely speculative, if not abstract, form in which they were originally proclaimed."[12]

As a matter of fact, Comte made significant contributions to the field of sociology and thereby provided ample material to the 'scientific' study of politics. Taking into view, the importance of his untraditional approach, it is rightly commented : "We are now so accustomed to the scientific way of looking at social and political questions that we are prone, perhaps because of his oddities, to under-rate a man like Comte. If, however, we consider the state of opinion at the time he wrote, we get a more balanced estimate of the significance of his suggestions. It was only the rare thinker at that time who had shaken himself free from what Comte called the theological and metaphysical preconceptions and Comte was only one of those who did so most boldly."[13] Thus, Sabine says : "What Comte contributed was not so much a new discovery as the hope that speculation might be replaced by science, that the concept of society might be analysed and its laws discovered by method that would conform to the canons of empirical verification, and

11. Barker, *op. cit.*, p. 176.
12. Vaughan, *op. cit.*, p. 198.
13. Lancaster, *op. cit.*, p. 84.

that relationship might be traced in detail between social institutions and human natures–Comte's philosophy was not a culmination but the beginning, the mid-point from which might be dated the whole vast effort to bring social studies within the sweep of modern science."[14]

---

14. G.H. Sabine : *A History of Political Theory*, III ed., pp. 600-601.

26

SPENCER

Those who cite him (Spencer) as a champion of our existing scheme should not be allowed to forget that he has formulated a communist land doctrine which he has never taken back.....those who rail at him as a reactionist and an enemy of progress, forget that, as an evolutionist, he has rendered invaluable service to thought in general, and to the cause of socialism in particular.

— **W.C. Owen**[1]

The greatest representative thinker of the Scientific School in the nineteenth century in England is Herbert Spencer (1820-1903) who has also been called 'the Aristotle of the Victorian age" by his admirers. Though the son of a teacher of pronounced individuality, he got very little formal education and was rather a self-educated man. In his boyhood days he took up engineering and experimented with various inventions. But he entered the carrer of a journalist and accepted the editorship of *The Pilot* at the age of twenty four and sub-editorship of *The Economist* at the age of thirty. This career of sub-editorship proved useful, for it brought him in contact with several great persons like Tyndall, Huxley, Newman and Elliot. This contact had a very stimulating effect on his enquiring

1. Owen : *The Economics of Herbert Spencer*, p. 248.

mind. But his resignation from this post in 1853 entailed a bad future in the immediate years unless he could improve his financial circumstances by the sale of his books. Even then his health did not improve and although he often detested botheration and drudgery, he remained a serious patient of insomania, dyspesia and neurasthenia. This physical incapacity did have its adverse impact on the character of his thought and writing. From 1898 onwards, he moved to Breighton where he lived in broken health till he died in 1903.

WORKS : BIOLOGICAL DEFENCE OF THE PRINCIPLE OF LAISSEZ FAIRE

Spencer was a prolific writer and his works filled many shelves. The important thing about him in this regard is that he contributed a lot to different fields of social sciences like politics, economics, ethics, sociology and psychology and used biological method so as to prove his contentions. However, the line of individualism runs through all so as to keep him in the category of the defenders of the creed of liberalism. Besides, as Spencer had seen the rise and growth of the creed of utilitarianism at the hands of Bentham and followed by James Stuart Mill and John Stuart Mill, he could not ignore the basic notion of the happiness of the individual. What makes Spencer different from Mill in the history of nineteenth century liberalism of England however, is that he seeks to give a scientific orientation to social philosophy by bringing it into relationship with biology and sociology and, for this reason, with biological and social evolution.[2]

Spencer's *Social Statics* (1851) is an important work in defence of natural rights and individual freedom. Here he lays down the doctrine of the law of equal freedom whereby each individual desires to attain freedom limited only by the necessity of like freedoms for others so that the maximum amount of happiness may be attained by the maximum exercise of capacity. The theory of organism is also traceable here. He asserts that the development of society may be conceived as a result of he tendency to individuate and then become a thing. However, an elaborate explanation of the same is contained in his *Social Organism* (1860) where he emphasises that society is like an organism, because 'it grows and is not made' and that it should be left to grow under the free play of social influence

2. G.H. Sabine : *A History of Political Theory*, IV Ed., p. 652.

and not made. The state has no right to hinder the process of social development. His paper on *Administrative Nihilism* (1871) contains a partial explanation in favour of the same point.

Almost a similar idea is contained in the *Principles of Sociology* whose first volume appeared in 1876 and where Spencer sought to make use of his labours done for his *Descriptive Sociology* begun in 1867, but that could not be completed. Here he affirms that if we want to comprehend social aggregate, we must understand the units of society. Here his purpose seems to prove that "the characteristics of the associated state must be the consequences of the inherent properties of the associated individuals. The individual may be regarded from two aspects, an outer and inner. In the former aspect, he is a being with a faculty that demands freedom as the condition of that adaptation to function which constitutes perfection; in the latter, he is a consciousness, endowed with an inherent sense of justice which makes him claim for himself, and with a sympathetic affection which makes him respect in others; the freedom his faculty requires."[3]

The line of individualistic argument is also traceable in *Man Versus State*. The engaging point of this work is that the idea of social contract is emphasised in a way different from that of Hobbes and Locke. The justification of the existence of political authority is sought in the protection and promotion of the happiness of the individual by the action of the state. 'If the state tries to give me more, which it can only do by taking more from me, in order to get the means for its gifts, it breaks the tacit agreement we have made.' Once again, this emphasis becomes implicit that natural rights necessarily involve social contract whatever incidental or irrelevant mention of social organism may adorn the process of the argument."[4] Finally, we may make a passing reference to his minor works like an essay on *The Proper Sphere of Government* and a monograph on *The Sins of the Legislators*.

In brief, a look at the works of Spencer shows that he not only covers the vast field of social study and presents a more or less synthetic philosophy, it perplexes a student of political philosophy when he finds that some impressions of the author given at one place are not congruent with others given else-

3. Barker : *Political Thought in England*, p. 83.
4. *Ibid*, p. 87.

where. It all looks like an astonishing system of the nineteenth century 'rationalism' hinging on the fact of 'an indefinite incoherent homogeneity to a definite coherent heterogeneity'.[5] It is, however, a different matter that a critic calls Spencer 'not a scientist but a salesman of ideas and we no longer like his goods'.[6]

EVOLUTION : IDEA OF SOCIAL EQUILIBRIUM AND ADJUSTMENT

One of the important aspects of Spencer's political philosophy is that he studies politics through biology and the great task to which he sets himself is an attempted synthesis of all scientific knowledge. It appears that Spencer plunges into the sphere of metaphysics, ethics, theology, biology, psychology and sociology and claims that he emerges with the supreme law of the universe in his grasp. He also seems confidently asserting to have actually chalked out the boundary line between the knowable and the unknowable and thus correctly divined the basic laws of cosmology. It has been given the name of synthetic philosophy, because he bequeathed to the posterity a larger understanding of the essential inter-relationship of formerly dissociated departments of knowledge. One of the admirers observes that Spencer "abstracted, classified, generalised and moved forward to more and more abstract unifications until he had reached a point from where he could sum up the universe in a single formula."[7]

Spencer thus believes in the theory of evolution. Happily confirming the conclusions of the biologists like Darwin, Huxley and Wallace, he turns eagerly to biology to amplify and sustain his philosophy. But he differs from other biologists as well. For instance, he rejects the thesis of Weismann and believes in the inheritability of acquired characteristics. Likewise, he dis-

---

5. Sabine, *op. cit*, p. 652.
6. Crane Brinton : *English Political Thought in the Nineteenth Century*, p.239.
7. Metz : *A Hundred Years of British Philosophy*, p. 102. Spencer "used to explain the present constitution and condition not only of the starry universe, the planetary system, the face and figure of the earth, the flora and fauna of the world, together with the bodies of men, but also of the minds of the men and the forms of human society. Indeed, the primary aim of the Synthetic Philosophy was precisely the solution on naturalistic and evolutionary lines of the problems of ethics and politics." Hearnshaw: *The Social and Political Ideas of Some Representative Thinkers of the Victorian Age*, p. 80.

cards the Darwinian thesis that selection takes place through accidental variation and substitutes it with the view that variation and adaptation are manifestations of purpose. Yet, he agrees with the Darwinian doctrines of the 'struggle for existence' and the 'survival of the fittest' and always maintains the perfect reasonableness of inferring that structural adaptations are transmissible by heredity.

Spencer's concept of evolution exhibits a process resulting from the perpetual anti-thesis of two great forces of nature, namely, the dynamic tendency towards change and the static tendency towards equilibrium. In the struggle for existence only the fittest survive, for chance variation in their inherited characteristics enables them to adjust themselves to the environment more easily and better. The surviving species pass on the favourable traits to the offspirng. The living species thus constantly tro to adapt and adjust themselves to the environment and thereby develop new functions and traits. As with other living species, so the individual equilibrates himself with his social environment by adaptation, and by inheritance of that adaptation until he attains a perfect equilibrium the blessedness of final anarchy.

Such a reasoning of Spencer tells us that the perfect society will appear only when man has fully adjusted himself to his environment; in other words, when an equilibirium is reached between the individual organism and the social organism. For this Spencer's argument is that the law of adaptation should not be disturbed. He postulates : "All evil results from the non-adaptation of constitution to conditions.....Equally true is it that evil perpetually tends to disappear. In virtue of an essential principle of life, this non-adaptation of an organism to its conditions is ever being rectified, and modification of one or both continues until the adaptation is complete. Whatever possesses vitality from the elementary cell upto the man himself, inclusive, obeys this laws."

A study of Spencer's principle of evolution leads to two main points :

1. Spencer wants that the operation of the law of evolution should not be obstructed by state and government. The state should refrain from placing obstacles in the operation of this law. It is no business of the state to protect the weak and the unfit, for the ultimate result fo shielding fools from folly would be to fill the world with fools. Let the social equi-

librium be set up and for that let there be a struggle for existence entailing survival of the fittest. It is clear that any human species whose constitution is to be moulded into fitness for new condition of existence must be placed under those conditions. He writes : "Only by the process of adaptation itself can be produced that character which makes social equilibrium spontaneous. And hence while his process is going on, an instrumentality must be employed, firstly, to bind men into the social state and secondly to check all conduct endangering the existence of the state. Such an instrumentality, we have in government."[8]

2. It implies that if the law of evolution were allowed to take its natural course, a state of static balance and perfection would come when conditions of anarchy have their sway. The genuine adjustment of the individual with his surroundings would occur when there is such liberty of action as to enable the individuals to learn by experience what is best to pursue. In Spencer's view, the accruing experience transmitted from one generation to another would inevitably and necessarily mould human faculties into complete fitness for social life. This leads Spencer to make a glowing prophecy that when the final stage is reached, political authority would disappear. In the presence of perfect equilibrium or in the absence of any antagonism between the individual and society the state would be unneccessary and superfluous.

It may, however, be pointed out that the defence of *laissez faire* leading to the phase of golden anarchy is inherent with these serious drawbacks :

1. The principle of evolution and the hope for a perfect equilibrium are contradictions in terms. Modern science completely rejects the notion of a final equilibrium where the process of evolution stops. Science believes that the evolution is a never-ending process wherein each adaptation creates new conditions calling for fresh adaptation. The evolution of human conduct can never attain such a static repose. The horizon always recedes and there is never a perfect and final adaptation, rather each new adaptation suggests a new set of problems and leads to a newer sort of adaptation.

8. Spencer : *Social Statics*, pp. 126-127.

2. Spencer's ideal of the future is thoroughly utopian. By denouncing the existing social system he adopts a medieval point of view which sees in all government the producer and author of all evil and violence. It is surprising that in stead of holding fast to the idea that the social conditions of a given time are just and perfectly good, so far as they represent the best possible approximation to the ideal, he is apt to set such social conditions over against his ideal and then to criticise them by his ideal standard as imperfect and unjust. If such a stage of evolution represents a state of equilibrium or adaptation, the present society does the same. But Spencer erroneously looks at the social institutions as unjust and unprofitable. It is clear that his denunciation of the existing social system (including the sphere of state activity) and the hope for a final equilibrium are at war with one another; they cannot be reconciled with each other.
3. Finally, Spencer's defence of *laissez faire* on biological grounds has also been denounced. It is true that human species cannot live by the ethics of the forest. The Darwinian principles of the struggle for existence and the survival of the fittest cannot be operative in a society of human beings. In stead of throwing the weak before the strong, the modern conception of state activity demands protection of the downtrodden against the privileged. Naturally, Spencer's defence of *laissez faire* on biological grounds added to the infamy of individualism. Joad says that it "implied a reversion to the ethics of barbarism, and not only discredited Individualism in the eyes of socially-minded men, but had particularly important consequences in the economic sphere."[9]

SOCIAL ORGANISM : ANALOGY BETWEEN NATURE AND SOCIETY

Spencer is regarded as one of the most powerful advocates of the organismic theory on the nature of state–a theory which goes to the extent of portraying the state as a real person, a living organism possessing organs which perform functions analogous to those of an animal or a plant. Spencer's doctrine of social organism frankly represents an anti-thesis of the juridical theory which conceives the state as a legal fiction or a pure mental concept. His biological conception describes the state in terms of a natural science; he views the individuals who

9. Joad : *Modern Political Theory*, p. 30.

compose it as akin to the cells of a plant or an animal, and postulates a relation of inter-dependence between them and society such as exists between the organs and parts of a biological organism and the whole structure.[10]

Spencer's doctrine of social organism manifests his belief in a parallelism that can be established between the individual (physiological) and the social organisms. The elaborate analogy brought out by Spencer holds the following main features:

1. Both the physiological and social organisms begin as germs, undergo a process of continuous growth and with growth the parts become more and more unlike and exhibit greater complexity of structure. The development happens from simple to complex, from homogeneous to heterogeneous, from indifferentiation to differentiation. As the lowest type of animal is all stomach, respiratory surface limb, so primitive society is all warrior, all hunter, all hut-builder, all tool-maker. As society grows in complexity, division of labour follows, that is, new organs with different functions appear corresponding to the different functions in the animal and in that fundamental trait they become alike.

2. There is a mutual dependence of parts in the case of both the organisms, the full performance of the functions of each member being essential to the health and preservation of the rest. If the iron-maker in the social organism stops works or the miner fails to discharge his natural functions, the whole social organism suffers from failure.

3. The slow but consistent replacement of cell tissues and blood corpuscles in a natural organism, by which it is destroyed and reproduced, is paralleled by the processes in society by which it is permanently maintained, not-

10. Barker very finely defines the term organism thus : "When we speak of an organism we mean (1) a living structure composed of parts different in kind; (2) that those parts, by reason of their difference, are complimentary to one another and mutually dependent; (3) that the health of the whole consequently depends on the healthy discharge of each part of its own proper function. An organism thus possesses the correlative attributes of a high degree of differentiation and a high degree of integration; and 'organic unity' means unity in and through difference. Again, an organism just because it is a living structure and just because it works so subtly through the reciprocal functions of its parts, cannot be changed from without by any mechanical act. It grows; it grows from within by a development which affects all its parts simultaneously; and such growth is what is called organic growth." *Political Thought in England*, pp. 90-91.

withstanding the death of component members. Spencer's analogy shows that just as the up and down lines of the railway furnish the circulation of commodities in the social organism, so there are the veins and arteries in the animal organism, money being the blood corpuscles and the telegraphic wires the nerves.

4. Finally, Spencer attributes to both the animal organism and the social organism a 'sustaining system' consisting of the alimentation in the former and production in the latter; a 'distributing system' consisting of the circulatory apparatus in the human body and a transportation system in the society; and a 'regulatory system' consisting of the nervous system in the animal, and of government and armies in the social organism. Murray explains the meaning of Spencer thus : "The workers, the men who form the soil, work the mines and factories, and workshops are the alimentary organs of a society, the whole-salers, retailers, bankers, railway and steamshipmen correspond to the vascular system of an organism. The professional men–doctors, lawyers, engineers, rulers, priests–the thinkers, in short, perform the functions of the brain and the nervous system."[11]

In fine, Spencer maintains an analogy between the physiological organism made by nature and the social organism made by man. When both start as small aggregates but grow in size; both grow and their initial relative simplicity is replaced by increasing complexity of structure; with increasing differentiation, there comes about an increasingly mutual dependence of the component parts, the life and normal functioning of each becomes dependent on the life of the whole; the life of the whole becomes independent with a far more prolonged nature than the life of the component parts; the parallelism can easily be set. Thus, Spencer concludes that the state is an organism, a social organism.

However, a very important thing in this regard is Spencer's acceptance of certain points of extreme unlikeness between the physiological and social organisms. While the natural organism is concrete in structure as its units are bound together in close contact, the social organism is discrete as its units are free and more dispersed. Then, he admits that the social organism has no nervous sensorium. As in the animal

11. Murray : *Social and Political Thought of the Nineteenth Century*, p. 21.

organism sensorium is concentrated in a small part of the aggregate, so in the social organism it is diffused throughout the aggregate. In other words, it means that there is no social sensorium, each individual member of a social organism is a separate centre of consciousness, and is capable of independent action and even of existence to a certain degree.

Besides, Spencer very subtly points out that although the difference between the two is fundamental; yet upon a close examination it will not put comparisons out of question, for it can be shown that the social aggregate, though discrete, is still a living whole. It is obviously a contradiction in itself. When Spencer advocates the theory of organism, he ought to maintain consistency. But for the sake of defence of his *laissez faire*, he takes a turn by suggesting that the social organism is of discrete character. Garner thus puts : "Spencer's denial of the existence of a nerve sensorium in society was probably the result of his individualistic thinking. After his long argument in support of the organic theory of society, it seemed necessary to reconcile his biological theory with his doctrine of individualism by showing that, after all, there is a difference and that the parts are not dependent on the whole, as they are in the case of animal organism."[12]

Spencer's theory of social organism may be subjected to the following lines of criticism :

1. Spencer exaggerates the points of similarity between the natural and social organisms. Both differ largely from each other and to draw an elaborate analogy between the two to this extent is sheer exaggeration. It is true that there may be discovered some lines of analogy, but their depiction with such a deep and strong fervour is certainly misleading. Barker rightly points out : "The state is not an organism; but it is like an organism. It is not an organism, because it is not a physical structure.....The fact, however, remains that state is not an organism, because it is a self-determining system of minds which are themselves self-determining, and the whole analogy leads to confusion in stead of clearness, unless we are clear about the terms of the comparison, and unless we are also clear that metaphor is not arugment, and that a parallel between the state and the individual is not an explanation of this relation."[13]

12. Garner, *op. cit.*, pp. 217-18.
13. Barker, *op. cit.*, pp. 91-92. A critic like Le Fur observes that if we pass

2. Another difficulty arises when we fail to be convinced with the reconciliation that Spencer wants to establish between the organic character of society and the atomistic character of individual personality. Obviously, Spencer wants to eat and keep his cake at the same time. The more he labours for the parallel, the more he forgest about the nature of proper relationship. The turn he takes for the sake of justifying his defence of *laissez faire* makes his entire analysis inconsistent. If the society is an organic whole, the individual cannot maintain its organic character. And if it is all done for the sake of a definite purpose (that is, defence of *laissez faire*), the theory is not at all a theory of organism, rather it is an essay on expediency for the simple reason that in spite of doing such a great labour, Spencer "bows the social organism out of doors."[14]
3. Finally, Spencer's idea of organism does not coincide with his theory of evolution. Keeping in view his principle of evolution, it may be pointed out that the law demands continual adaptation to continually progressing state of conditions. Naturally, for the sake of coincidence, it is essential that in the study of parallelism between the social and physiological phenomena, the fact of the state of adaptation should not be ignored. But the mistake of Spencer lies in the fact that he is much more careful of the social organism and sometimes he picks up a feature of undifferentiated jelly fish and at others of a higher type of vertebrate. Besides, as a scientific thinker, he ought to have suggested what the future stage of evolution would be and then what type of parallelism would eventually take place. In stead of doing this, he even comes out with a glowing prophesy that in future perfect equilibrium would take place and then he seems to be quite unmindful of the fact of evolution.

---

from comparison to identification and say that the state is a person or a veritable animal because its roads and railways and soon perhaps because its ballons correspond to our arteries and veins, we "shall experience the feeling that it is a defiance of all commonsense." A German writer Treitschke says that, obviously, it is 'misleading to look upon the state as an organism as many theorists do.' Likewise, an English sociologist Hobhouse remarks that to observe society as if it "were a physical organism is a piece of mystification, if indeed it is not quite meaningless." In a very strong way, Garner reacts that at many points the comparison "utterly fails and the resemblance becomes pure fancy." *Op. cit.*, p. 219.

14. Barker, *op. cit.*, p. 118.

NATURAL RIGHTS : AFFIRMATION OF INDIVIDUALISM

Like other representative thinkers of the English liberalism, Spencer reaffirms faith in the dogma of natural rights and asserts that since every individual consciously recognises the rights of others and feels bound to respect them and since natural rights alone ensure both happiness and freedom, the rights have a sacrosanct character and even the state cannot abrogate them. He advocates that the primary function of the state is to find out means of securing these rights for the citizens, otherwise the individual may defy the authority of state for the sake of defending his rights. Obviously, the theory of natural rights constitutes a solid core of Spencer's thought and firmly reiterates his hostile attitude towards the state. As Barker says : "Natural rights are the sand of refuge in which the individual buries his head to escape a pursuing State."[15]

Spencer defines rights as nothing but artificial divisions of the general claim to exercise one's faculties. But he calls them natural, because they are pre-social and are inherent properties of the human constitution as divinely ordained. In his view, the fundamental thing in the world is the free exercise of individual capacity wherein alone lies the happiness ordained for man by nature. Spencer thus justifies the law of equal freedom whereby each individual attains a freedom limited only by the necessity of like freedom for others and whereby alone maximum happiness follows from the maximum exercise of this capacity.

However, while taking the case of natural righs, Spencer studies individual freedom from two sides–internal and external. In the former, he is a being with a faculty which demands freedom as the condition of that adaptation to function which constitutes perfection; in the latter, he is consciousness endowed with an inherent sense of justice which makes him claim for himself, and with a sympathetic affection which fills in him respect for others, the freedom his faculty requires. Besides, in speaking of the external aspect, Spencer expresses his belief in the benevolence of nature and harmony of interests; while his speaking of the internal aspect expresses his belief in the innate instinct of justice and in that sympathetic affection of this instinct termed beneficience which makes everyone spon-

15. *Ibid*, p. 109.

taneously inclined to allow others to claim, and to support others in claiming what he defends himself.

Then, Spencer's defence of natural rights suggests their twofold classification–private and public. The private rights are concerned with individual's life, family and property. The free exercise of faculties is a natural right. Then, property is also one of the elements of our nature, but right to property excludes the case of private ownership of land owing to the fact that it contravenes the law of equal freedom demanding equal access to the land. In regard to family, Spencer's most novel emphasis is on the political freedom of the families. Spencer attacks the subjection of women and children and insists that in an ideal system the family should disappear and the law of equal freedom should be extended to all men, women and children–representing the withering away of coercion at the hands of males over females, and of the parents over their children.

The public rights of the individual are concerned with the state. Here Spencer calls the government a vicious and immoral institution, which in all its action most unnecessarily interferes with the free play of human faculties. The government, though an evil, is a necessity, for it has to maintain conditions ultimately leading to the stage of a perfect equilibrium. Yet being a necessity, it must do to efface itself in the ultimate course and justify its existence by interfering as little as possible. In Spencer's view, it can be done in three ways. Firstly, the state must permit its citizens to abandon the benefits of citizenship by ignoring its burdens. Secondly, it must meet the demands of the law of equal freedom by admitting all the citizens to an equal share in its imposition of all the restraints it imposes. Finally, it must try to delimit its scope of activity and concern itself only with three things–namely, protection, administration of the law of equal freedom, and the maintenance of natural rights.

However, it should be pointed out here that Spencer's defence of natural rights embodies an identification of science with morality. In other words, his natural rights become moral rights, for he argues that if we look at the life of the individual on the assumption that it is worth living, we must conclude that the acts necessary for its maintenance are rights and the claims and liberties necessary to those acts are rights. The argument of Spencer implies that there is a clear difference between the rights of a man and that of a tiger. The presence of other fellow-beings demands that man must not claim any right of action which interferes with the rights of his fellows. Naturally, if man thus abandons some of his claims and liberties the rest of his claims and liberties may be regarded as ethical rights.[16]

Spencer's defence of natural rights may be criticised on these grounds :

1. The statement of Spencer is confused and self-contradictory at various places. For instance, he puts property in the list of natural rights, but he wants that the state must not interfere with the natural rights of the individual. And yet his law of equal freedom postulates public and national ownership of soil. His justification does not cohere with his basic postulate when he recognises that such ownership of soil once granted, there may and must be private property in its products not only because the producer has mixed his labour with the products but because he has hired the soil for a consideration for the community and has obtained a right which is valid because he has secured the consent of society before expending his labour. The phrase of social consent obviously destroys his whole defence. If a right so elementary as that of private property involves social recognition, it is difficult to see how rights can in their nature be pre-social or independent of social recognition.
2. Spencer's defence of natural rights cuts across the earlier premises of his thought. His emphasis on the organic character of society in his theory of evolution and his belief in the natural rights implying an atomistic character of individual's personality are like two opposite poles. The conception of individual's natural rights cannot accord with the organic and evolutionary conception of the state which he attains through the use of natural science. If society has an organic character, individual's rights are subject to the fact of social recognition. But Spencer's stress on the independent position of individual's personality is destructive of any reconciliation that might possibly be established. Barker thus correctly points out that Spencer's philosophy

16. Spencer very clearly says that "to recognise and enforce the rights of the individuals is at the same time to recognise and enforce the conditions to a normal social life : there is one vital requirement for both." Cf. *Ibid*, p.105.

"consequently begins and ends as an incongruous mixture of natural rights and physiological metaphor."[17]

3. Spencer ought to be accused of under-rating the significance of man's social existence by defending the case of natural rights. Bentham was certainly right in calling natural rights 'rhetorical nonsense'. Undoubtedly, there can be no right independent of man's social existence and to say that natural rights are pre-social is to talk like a utopian philosopher. Green rightly visualised that there can be no possibility of rights existing in a pre-social stage. Rights are also co-relative with the duties. Laski thus insists: "He that will not perform functions cannot enjoy rights any more than he who will not work ought to enjoy work."[18] Similarly, Hobhouse asserts : "Rights and duties, then, are conditions of social welfare, or as we define such welfare, of a life of harmony to this welfare, every member of the community stands in a double relation. He has his share in it. That is the sum of his rights. He has to contribute his share. That is, the sum of his duties."[19]

4. Spencer's defence of natural rights confuses the scope of state activity. If the society has been in a stage of evolution and one day the stage of perfect equilibrium would arrive, naturally the stae has to wither away. But Spencer's defence of natural rights wants the state to continue independently with the need to preserve and protect the individual and his rights, ultimately enforcing that free energy of faculty which was the instrument for obtaining complete individuation. The very assertion that men entered into a sort of contract with each other to preserve their natural rights shows that the primary function of the state changed from a gradually slackening adjustment between individuals to the continual enforcement of these contracts. Doyle thus observes : "The conception of the state as a gradually evolving natural organism whose main function was to harmonise the individual parts into a living whole disappeared. In its stead, Spencer envisaged a mechancial contrivance made by men to preserve their individuality."[20]

17. *Ibid*, p. 71.
18. Laski : *A Grammar of Politics*, p. 34.
19. Hobhouse : *The Elements of Social Justice*, p. 34.
20. Doyle : *A History of Political Thought*, p. 226.

SCOPE OF STATE ACTIVITY : ARDENT INDIVIDUALISM TOUCHING THE VERGE OF ANARCHISM

The political ideas of Herbert Spencer present the most powerful defence of *laissez faire*. Like John Stuart Mill, Spencer sets out with a frank denunciation of the ideal character of the state and calls it 'a necessary evil'. Yet his individualistic approach is much more subtle and ardent so much so that in the end individualism is replaced by a state of anarchy. The business of the state is to help the advent of the stage of perfect equilibrium and then to make its necessity outlived. Obviously, while Mill confined the scope of state activity to a minimum possible extent, Spencer seeks to do away with it in the age of final prefection and reaches the point of 'condoning complete anarchy.'[21] Spencer's advocacy of ardent individualism is contained in the following points:

1. Spencer begins with the assertion that the existence of the state is a result of man's inherent perversity and egoism and that in reality it is an aggressor rather than a protector. He very forcefully argues : "Be it or be it not true that man is shapen in iniquity and conceived in sin, it is unquestionably true that government is begotten of aggression and by aggression."[22] Analysing it, Barker thus puts : "There is much aggression on freedom within the state as without the state, for the state is making its small aggressions daily."[23]

2. Spencer's individualism draws much support from the Darwinian principles of the struggle for existence and the survival of the fittest. In the social organism, Spencer warns that those members who are not fit to play their part must be eliminated in the interest of the whole and it is not the business of political authority to perpetuate their weakness by making provisions for them. It follows that each individual should be allowed to stand alone or fall according to his worth unaided by the props and support of the state. He should be left free to work out his own destiny without the guidance and tutelage of the government. Thus, by leav-

21. Refer *ibid*, p. 566. Elliot thus puts : "Spencer was a man of immensely strong individual personality. There can be a little question that this was the basis of his doctrine of social freedom. He could not bear to have his liberty of thought and action curtailed in any kind of way. His personality was everywhere intruded and could suffer no limitations and live under no compulsion." *Herbert Spencer*, p. 54.
22. Spencer : *Man Versus State*, p. 54.
23. Barker, *op. cit.*, p. 87.

ing each individual to do unaided that for which he is best fitted, the strong and fit classes survive, the unfit elements are eliminated and thus the good of society is promoted.

3. The defence of individualism is strengthened by the condemnation of state interference. Emphasising the negatively regulative character of state activity, Spencer inveighs against all legislation for the regulations of trade and commerce, sanitary arrangements, public education, poor relief, post offices, currency, public health and recreation etc. If the state happens to do anything in regard to above, it violates the principle of legitimate intervention. The state has to do nothing beyond the works of protection, administration of law and justice and rigid enforcement of contracts, for the liberty which a citizen "enjoys is to be measured, not by the nature of government machinery he lives under, whether representative or other, but by the relative paucity of the restraints it imposes on him."[24]
4. This approach has its further reiteration in his monograph on *The Sins of Legislators*. Spencer very rabidly denounces the heavy work of legislation. The statue books, in his view, are full of errors, blunders and unhappy guesses. He thus protests against the worship of the legislature and asserts that as the great political superstition of the past was the divine right of kings, that of the present is the divine right of parliaments; and the divine right of parliament means only the divine right of the majority. Spencer argues that the majority has no right to be respected. It follows from his arguments that the laws passed by the parliaments are not sacred in themselves, and they may be challenged by the people over whom they intend to exercise coercion. This monograph also reviews much of the unwise legislation of the past, dwells upon the evils which result from it, and concludes that because most of this type of legislation has been replaced or modified in the past, it ought never to have been enacted.[25]
5. Spencer's defence of natural righs entails the argument further. He specifically warns that the state should not usurp the natural rights of the individual and, if it does, he authorises the individual to rise in revolt. In this connection he propounds the phrase of 'ignoring state'. His argument

24. Spencer : *Man Versus State*, p. 54.
25. *Ibid*, p. 95.

desires the individuals to shake off the burdens of citizenship. The law of equal freedom permits that for the sake of its maintenance the individual can refuse to fulfil his social obligations. Hence, the government must meet the demands of the law of equal freedom by admitting all its citiens to an equal share in the enforcement of all restraints it imposes. The factor of dissent must be generalised by the state. As the state is to disappear in future, in the present it should remain in existence for the sake of protecing natural rights alone and do nothing to overwhelm them, otherwise individual can defy the power of state in defence of his own rights.

6. Finally, the important thing about Spencer's individualism is the turn that it takes towards anarchism. When the state is merely instituted for the purpose of curbing the wicked propensities of the individual and protecting him from the fraud and violence of his fellow-beings, it follows that in the morally perfect conditions of society, government can have no reason of its existence–a doctrine that the state is unjustified in doing whatever tends to produce the greatest happiness or which will subserve the general good. Spencer denounces it and calls it by the name of governmental despotism, since there is no standard or test for determining what is expedient or what is for the general good except the opinions of the governors themselves. Hence, Spencer finds the government not as essential but incidental and existing until the conditions of voluntary outlawry are adopted by the individuals. He says : "As amongst Bushmen we find a state antecedent to government, so may there be one in which it shall have extinct."

The weaknesses and inconsistencies of the political ideas of Herbert Spencer have already been discussed. However, in this regard it will be sufficient to say that Spencer's assumption of *laissez faire* is wrong and untenable. The argument that the state is a necessary evil and that all restraints as such are wrong has not been borne out by the experience of mankind under the regime of political organisation. In fact, history unmistakably shows that the progress of civilisation in the past has been achieved to a very large extent by wisely directed state action. The state is definitely a positive good and a welfare agency. Of course, it is true that at times the end of the state has been perverted to the detriment of the public good, but this is no reason for condemning the state, indiscriminately as an evil than for arguing that railroads are an evil, because their operation sometimes results in accidents. Seeley rightly says that to characterise each restraint as inherently evil in itself is to ignore the fundamental distinction between that which is useful and good and that which is bad.[26] So says Garner : "Spencer's doctrine that the state exists only because crime exists, and that it would subserve no purpose in a society of morally perfect beings, cannot be accepted. The function of the state in the complex civiliation of today is not merely repressive, not simply negatively regulative; it has a higher task than that of restraints and punishment : the task of protecting, encouraging and fostering the common welfare."[27]

Nor can it be accepted that the scope of state activity be limited to a particular minimum, for one day the state has to wither away. On the contrary, all indications tell that with the increasing complexity of modern civilisation the need for state action is growing and its role being more extensive. In comparatively recent years a strong reaction against the principle of *laissez faire* has taken place owing largely to the conditions resulting from the growth of industrialism. Huxley rightly observes : "The higher the state of civilisation, the more completely do the actions of one member of the social body influence all the rest, and the less possible is it for any one man to do a wrong without interfering more or less with the freedom of all his fellow-citizens. So that even on the narrowest view of functions of the state it must be admitted to have wider powers than the advocates of police theory are disposed to admit."[28]

CRITICAL APPRECIATION : SPENCER AS 'THE ARISTOTLE OF VICTORIAN ENGLAND'

We have thus examined the various aspects of Spencer's political philosophy and also studied the points of strength and inconsistencies therein. However, one very peculiar thing about Spencer's political philosophy lies in the fact that he puts discrepant elements together. In stead of starting from a single

---

26. See Garner, *op. cit.*, p. 465.n.
27. *Ibid.*
28. *Ibid.* p. 466. Likewise, Garner observes : "So long as men live in groups, they will have collective want which can be satisfied only through state organisation, and hence there is no reason for believing that necessity for the state will ever disappear, or that the role which it now plays in the life of human societies will ever diminish." *Ibid.* p. 465.

point like a deductive theorist or taking conclusions out of the given material like an empiricist, he draws inspiration from different sources and thus produces their incongruous mixtures in his political theory. For instance, as a member of the family of the Dissenters or Non-Conformists, he had a deep aversion for political authority and his association with uncle Rev. Thomas Spencer made him a radical in politics believing that every institution must continually adapt itself to the changing external conditions. But his contact with Thomas Hodgskin made him a believer in the natural rights of man. It all led him to revolt against bribery in elections, the corn laws and state church. The result was that Spencer distracted from the path of liberalism and accepted what Bentham had floutly repudiated.

Similarly, his natural aptitude for engineering and the study of natural sciences filled in him a love for study of the principles of evolution; and his study of the German Idealism of Schelling and Schlegel (through Coleridge's translation) convinced him with the idea of life. But his hope in the final stage of anarchy and his insistence on the naturalness of rights does not enjoy a natural fitness with his theories of social evolution and social organism. Barker thus points out : "In Spencer this interpretation is confused. He did not really approach politics through science, without preconceptions drawn from other sources, and with the sole idea of eliciting the political lessons which science might teach. On the contrary, he was already charged with political preconceptions when he approached science, and sought to find in science examples or analogies to point out a moral already drawn and adorn a tale whose plot was already sketched. The fundamental confusion which he never surmounts is due to the fact that the *a priori* conceptions of individual rights with which he starts do not and cannot accord with the organic and evolutionary conception of the state which he attains through the use of natural science."[29]

On the whole, Spencer's place in the nineteenth century political thought of England is definitely important. True it is that many of his doctrines have now outlived their usefulness, yet it is also true that to a very great extent he reflected the spirit of his age.[30] Certainly, his various theories are full of

29. Barker, *op. cit.*, p. 71.
30. Ebenstein thus remarks : "Modern individualism was largely the product of the revolt of the individual against obsolete and obstructionist state

inconsistencies and confusion, but it is all due the existence of two different and incompatible systems in his political philosophy. In the field of political thought he ranks as a great champion of individual liberty in an age of growing collectivism. He lived and wrote in an age of political awakening–an age in which the aim of the thinkers was to liberate man's energies from outward restraints and aggressions. The importance of the individual was being proved in the clearest terms and with sound arguments. The idea of society as a unit was fraught with danger. Therefore, an attempt was made to liberalise individual faculties and to limit the functions of the state and to decentralise power. Catlin thus admirably puts that the final political liberties "were not worth sacrificing to subordinate economic securities."[31]

regulation of economic life." *Great Political Thinkers*, p. 600.

31. Catlin : *A History of Philosophers*, p. 411. Barker thus concludes : "On the whole, Spencer suited England; and on the assumption that a nation deserves the political theory which it gets, we may say that England deserved Spencer." *Op. cit.*, p. 54.

27

KANT

Although Kant was no revolutionary, in his autonomy of the individual will, he put forward a revolutionary principle which was to take effect when the middle class attained consciousness of their strength and began to transform the ethical problem of autonomy into the political principle of collaboration in the government. It is in this sense that Marx's assertion is true, that Kant's theory is the German theory of the French Revolution.

— **Reinhold Aris**

Immanuel Kant (1724-1804) is regarded as the Father of German Idealism, though some would wrongly ascribe this title to Hegel.[2] The peculiar thing about Kant is that he passed a very long and principled but uneventful life of a rational creature.[3] The only important phase of his life is traceable in his

1. Aris : *History of Political Thought in Germany*, p. 103.
2. According to G.A. Kelly, the critical philosophy of this age may be called 'idealism' in three respects : (i) it places uncommon emphasis on the productive power of 'Ideas' which are not given through the media of sense; (ii) it alleges that reality of a noumenal or 'ideal' world is unknowable; (iii) it subscribes to the central doctrine of the 'ideality' of time and space. Kant sometimes called his method 'transcendental idealism', and he understood the term generally on the basis of our definition. *Idealism, Politics and History*, pp. 113-114.
3. Kant's biographer Heine thus describes the principled pattern of his life:

career as a university teacher of Konigsberg where he taught logic and metaphysics for more than thirty years. Basically, he was not attracted towards political questions, his main interest was concerned with philosophical and theological problems. However, as a rationalist, he found fault with several scriptural premises of Christianity for which he was admonished by the King of Prussia in 1774. He looked at the French Revolution of 1789 with disfavour, since he did not appreciate the design of encroaching upon the sacred institution of enlightened royalty in the field of political action and yet he lauded the great event in the name of liberty and equality for the middle classes. As a matter of fact, Kant lived in "a loftier world of thought, which had little relation to everyday life."[4]

WORKS : ETHICAL FOUNDATIONS OF POLITICAL PHILOSOPHY

The political ideas of Kant are contained in his several works like *Critique of Pure Reason* (1781) followed by a *Critique of the Pure Practical Reason* that appeared in 1788. These two works are hailed as monumental contributions to the field of philosophy in view of the fact that while the former presented the categories and formulas through which all phases of existence could be known in thought, the latter dealt with the categories and formulas through which existence could be known in experience. In other words, while the former dealt with what is 'thinkable', the latter with what is 'observable' and, for this reason, while the former was concerned with the 'noumenal', the latter with the 'phenomenal'. However, the common feature is that both belonged to the field of speculative philosophy.

"The history of his life is hard to write, in as much as he had neither life nor history, for he lived a mechanically ordered and abstract old bachelor life in a quiet retired street in Konigsberg, an old town on the northeast border of Germany. I do not believe that the great clock of the Cathedral there did its work more dispassionately and regularly than its compatriot Immanuel Kant. Rising, coffee drinking, writing, reading college lectures, eating, walking, all had their fixed time, and the neighbours knew that it was exactly half-past three when Immanuel Kant in his gray coat with Manila cane in his hand, left his house door and went to the Lime Tree avenue. So he promenaded up and down, during all seasons, and when the weather was gloomy, or the grey clouds threatened rain, his old servant Lampe was seen plodding anxiously after, with a large umbrella under his arm, like a symbol of Prudence." Cf. Will Durant : *The Story of Philosophy*, p. 264.

4. Aris, *op. cit.*, p. 75.

In the realm of political philosophy, Kant's important works are *Metaphysical First Principles of the Theory of Law* published in 1796 and his monograph *For Perpetual Peace* published a year earlier. While the former contains his views on different political themes like state, government, freedom, constitution, law, social contract, punishment, property etc., the latter is a very distinctive work on the subject of international peace and co-operation. The influence of Rousseau and Montesquieu is quite evident here that "was destined to promote greatly the influence of liberalism when the Kantian system got a firm hold on intellectual Germany."[5]

A critical study of the works of Kant shows that he lacks originality the type of which we could see in the writings of Hobbes, Locke, Rousseau, Montesquieu and Burke. He could not demonstrate himself as an innovator of ideas and his role " was rather that of the harmoniser and systematiser of familiar but conflicting doctrines. In metaphysics he mediatised between the dogmatists and the intuitionists on the one side and the sceptics and the empiricists on the other who in their reciprocal antagonism had brought philosophy to an *impasse*."[6] However, the important thing about the works of Kant is that here ethics subordinates politics and thus we are once again taken to the world of Platonism. The whole analysis of Kant's political philosophy is based on his doctrine of 'self-imposed categorical imperative of duty' which is nothing but a rational formula to solve the problem of individual liberty and political authority in a highly philosophical manner. What is striking here is that the entire concept of individual freedom is not a political question, but essentially an ethical one. That is to say, Kant "is not so much concerned with the relation of man to one another as with the relation of man to his better self."[7]

HISTORY : A RECORD OF MORAL DEVELOPMENT OF MAN AND HIS UNIVERSE

Kant's philosophy of history is contained in his essay "An Idea for a Universal History from the Cosmopolitan Point of View" that appeared in 1794 as an attempt to improve upon what was given by his student Herder in his monograph on "Idea and Philosophy". It is said that with Herder began the

5. W.A. Dunning : *A History of Political Theories* (*From Rousseau to Spencer*), Vol. III, p. 132.
6. *Ibid*, p. 130.
7. Aris, *op. cit.*, p. 103.

movement of interpreting human history as a single process of development from a beginning in savagery to an end in perfectly rational and civilised society. Thus,. in the epistemology of Kant, we may trace the germs of methodology, i.e., dialectics which he applied for the first time in the history of philosophical speculation to aesthetic and teleological judgment–an instrument which constitutes the essence of Fichtian metaphysics, Hegel's 'Science of Science' or dialectical idealism and thereon the historical materialism of Marx.[8]

In the view of Kant, history signifies a record of the development of individual's personality. If the world is viewed as a natural system, then it has no end. But man, though a part of the same system in whom the spiritual system operates, can be said to have an end. Thus, man's development is nothing but a historical process in time. Man's struggle is two-fold for the sake of developing his personality–against the forces of nature so as to have mastery over them and against his own self–so as to make himself subordinate to the law of reason. That is, the plan of nature in human history is related to the continual realisation by man of his rationality. In this way, history "becomes a voyage of discovery of the human race as a whole."[9]

Besides, Kant's view of history seeks to establish a logical and rational nexus between the development of man's personality and the progress of the whole human race. It is obvious from his explanation that if the whole history is a process towards an end determined by the idea of man, it becomes a record not of a particular individual but of the whole human race for the reason that none can realise the end of his life alone. As he says : "Man's will is for harmony; but nature knows what is good for his species; her will for dissension. He wills that he should be dragged out of idleness and inactive content and plunged into labour and trouble, in order that he may be made to seek his own prudence for the means of again delivering himself from them. The natural impulses which prompt this effort,

8. Frank Thakurdas : *German Political Idealism*, p. 95. However, the main significance of Kant's political writings lay more in the way he related political to moral theory and his emphasis on the necessity of pursuing the former under the guidance offered by the latter." C.E. Vaughan : *Studies in European Political Philosophy*, Vol. II, p. 69.
9. *Ibid*, p. 98. As Kant says : "The history of mankind can be viewed as the performance of a hidden plan of nature to achieve a state which is not only inwardly but also outwardly complete and which is the only condition in which mankind can develop to the full all its qualities in the species." See Aris, *op. cit.*, p. 77.

the causes of unsociableness and mutual conflict out of which so many evils spring are also, in turn, the spurs which drive him to the development of his process."[10]

Simply stated, history is a record of the moral development of man from rudeness to civilisation. The tendencies in man opposed to the canons of morality are the forces that make for his moral progress. Search for mere happiness, as suggested by the utilitarians like Bentham, is no end of man's life. The real purpose of man's life is development of his personality and so one should remain in pursuit of cultivating his powers so as to conquer nature and, at the same time, discipline his passions so as to have a higher level of self-determination, i.e., moral freedom issuing forth in the form of a categorical imperative of duty. Obviously, history "becomes a record of the moral progress of man as well as an education of the human race."[11]

Viewed in a different perspective, history is a record of the struggle of opposite forces as well. Conflict is at the root of the progress whether of a particular individual or of the society of which he is a part. Inequality is like a 'splendid misery' that motivates both the individuals and social classes to fight as a result of which conquest over nature as well as growth of civil society take place. Though man loves freedom, he also realises that his passions make it impossible for him to subsist along with others. Hence, he is forced to set up a civil society through which alone his freedom may be expressed. And if individual is forced to live in a society, the same society desires a community of all civilised people as a result of which history becomes a record of the moral development of the whole mankind. That is, human history and the forces operating in it, all point to the idea of a World History by which alone a perfect equilibrium of man's impulses, desires for unity and freedom will be secured."[12] •

On the whole, in the view of Kant, history is more than a mere enumeration of facts or an unmarshalled succession of events,[13] for he is convinced with the possibility of reducing the welter of historic events "to order and he achieved this over by recognising in history a secret plan of nature which guarantees a regular course."[14] As Aris says : "The clue which runs through

10. See E. Caird : *Critical Philosophy of Kant*, pp. 510-511.
11. R.G. Collingwood : *Idea of History*, p. 97.
12. Frank Thakurdas, *op. cit.*, p. 101.
13. See E.E. Carritt : *Morals and Politics*, p. 96.
14. See T.B. Bury : *The Idea of Progress*, p. 243.

history is the law according to which all natural dispositions of men are designed to be developed completely and appropriately in the future. To make man a perfect being is accordingly the aim of history, but the individualistic 'character' which seems to be assigned thereby to history is counter-balanced by the fact that completion cannot be reached in the individual but only in the species. Nature has endowed man with reason and thus enabled him to attain that completion."[15]

Kant's philosophy of history may be criticised for being too idealistic. Here full reliance has been placed on the factor of reason in man that forces him to fight for the mastery over nature and also for the betterment of his own individuality. Such a line of argument cannot appeal to those who have no faith in the world of idealism. Thus, Marx could find fault with the basic premises of dialectical idealism as developed by Hegel on the foundations of Kant. However, viewed in a different perspective, it may be said that Kant's philosophy of history has a significance of its own. Kant teaches Hegel who passes on the same formula to Marx. Even the father of scientific socialism (Marx) adopts the same framework with the difference that he replaces the Idea by the Matter. In this way, Kant becomes the teacher of Marx through Hegel.

The philosophy of history as enunciated by Kant and passed on to Marx through Hegel, in this way, becomes a very dominant theme of the political philosophy of the nineteenth century. In appreciation of Kant, in this regard, it is said that the philosophy of history in the last century is the history of the variation on the themes of Kant.[16] Likewise, it is commented : "What is most interesting to the modern reader is his obvious relation to dialectical materialism, but Kant and the dialectical materialist resemble one another more closely ... by being mainly interested in social development and by emphasising the paradox that progress towards peace and union is necessitated through conflicts and struggle rather than is dependent on our conscious efforts."[17]

FREEDOM : CATEGORICAL SELF-IMPOSED IMPERATIVE OF DUTY AT WORK

Kant adopts Rousseau's doctrine of moral will as the corner stone of his thought and coins the phrase 'autonomy of

15. Aris, *op. cit.*, p. 76.
16. A.D. Lindsay : *Kant*, p. 291.
17. Carritt : *Ethical and Political Thinking*, p. 104.

the moral will'.[18] He assigns moral content to the concept of freedom and thus argues that man is truly free when he is morally free. However, his concept of freedom is distinctly different from license (unrestrained liberty) or something synoymous with the power of satisfying every desire, whether reasonable or unreasonable. Nor, like Mill, Kant treats freedom as absolute or unqualified in the self-regarding sphere, rather he believes that the only kind of freedom to which a person has a right is freedom qualified by respect for others and controlled by universal laws. Obviously, in Kant's view, the freedom and right are practically coincidental, since one expands into another. Summing up the view of Kant, Vaughan says : "Right expands into freedom and freedom expands into right."[19]

Kant's conception of moral freedom stands for the respect of individual personality. He denies that the individual is a means for the good of another, rather every individual is an end in himself. But he insists that the 'self-imposed categorical imperative of duty' should guide the actions of every rational individual. The individual should act in conformity with that maxim only which he at the same time wills to be a universal law. Like Rousseau, Kant forbids man to follow the dictates of ego or self-interest but urges that he should pursue those ends which are of universal application. The moral will of the individual is free only when it wills rational or universal objects and such a will is the good will and the fulfillment of that will should be the supreme object of a person's endeavour. Kant thus puts : "Nothing can possibly be conceived in the world or out of it which can be called good without qualification except a good will."

To support the above premises, Kant adopts the plea of pure practical reason or moral experience. Since man has a consciousness which tells him about the 'ought' and 'nought', he is required to do something which is universally binding on

18. Both Rousseau and Kant try to find out general will which is to be binding for all. For both freedom is not the possibility of doing everything one likes, but the limitation of the empirical will. As Larenz puts it : "Freedom is not a quality which man has as a natural being, but a task which he sets himself as a reasonable being." There is, however, one remarkable difference in the attitudes of the two thinkers. If Rousseau talks about political freedom he means freedom in a certain political community. Kant talks about freedom as an ethical problem, the solution of which is independent of political circumstances." See Aris, *op. cit.*, p. 70.
19. Vaughan : *Studies in the History of Political Philosophy*, Vol. II, p. 86.

reason to do these things is contrary to the very nature of reason itself; it is self-contradictory, suicidal."[22]

Kant's account of the contents of a categorical imperative of the principles of morality ends up in a paradox. It begins "by subordination of self to the law and ends with the subordination of law to the self."[23] That Kant's categorical imperative is too formal and rigid to be of much use as a guide to action is a charge which has been repeated by all his critics from Hegel to Prof. Teale. Thus, H.H. Rashdall asserts : "That these rules by themselves give us no practical guidance till we know what the good is which ought to be promoted by every rational being ... The test of ethical truth which lays down is at best a negative test, i.e., to maintain that the supreme ethical precepts must contain harmonious and self-consistent system of precept, is no guide as to what rule of action in particular is reasonable."[24]

Then, Kant's defence of individual liberty contributes to the authoritarian tradition by adhering to the supremacy of reason. Kant's emphasis on reason opens the gate of tyranny of the rational few over the less rational many, for he clearly indicates that the wishes and desires of every section of the community could well be ignored. It follows that the government has a perfect right to make and enforce any law it likes as long as it is in accordance with abstract eternal principle, even though it be vigorously opposed to the ninety nine per cent of the population. McGovern thus observes : "With this proposition of Kant the later authoritarians are heartily in approval. They merely add that surely the wise *one* or the unwise *few* are in a better position to judge of what is and what is not in accord with the rational principles of abstract right than is a turbulent and stupid democracy."[25]

---

22. Dewey : *German Philosophy and Politics*, p. 64. The categorical imperative in plain language is the simple ethical principle which forbids man to do something which he does not want somebody to do to him. "This is perhaps the best expression of the bourgeois attitude according to which society is an agglomeration of individuals whose chief interest is to live in peace and to be left in peace. Kant did not realise that by introducing the categorical imperative as the fundamental ethical principle he presupposed the bourgeois society which he purported to explain." Aris, *op. cit.*, p. 83.
23. Lindsay : *Kant*, p. 178.
24. Rashdall : *Theory of Good and Evil*, Vol . II, pp. 111 and 134.
25. McGovern, *op. cit.*, p.142.

POLITICS : A GRUDGING DEFENCE OF INDIVIDUALISM

By giving a negative, limited and subjective meaning to the concept of freedom, Kant adopts a somewhat grudging and individualistic attitude towards the state. Apparently, there is no place for state in the Kantian system for the simple reason that man may realise his true freedom by acting in conformity with the demands of moral law. But the influence of Rousseau entails the necessity of state when Kant speaks of the requirement of the political authority. The state is the only means to protect man from the evil effects of the actions of his fellow-beings and to see that his free moral will may function in a proper and effective manner. Barker thus puts : "The individual who wills the imperative of duty is willing something which, if it applies to the particular occasions, is at the same time universal. When he lays down the rule *Thou shalt not steal*, he is really constituting a general rule and ultimately because he builds a whole system of such rules, he is creating a set of laws which must increasingly be enshrined in and enforced by the state."[26]

In order to provide a better and clearer framework for this approach, Kant adopts the argument of social contract. Again, like Rousseau, Kant discards the historical significance of the social contract but retains the conception of the contract as regards the nature of state. Hence, Kant interprets the contractual nature of the state with the idea of reason. He puts that by contract men "surrender their external freedom in order to receive it immediately back again as members of a commonwealth, they abandon their wild lawless freedom in order to substitute it with a perfect freedom–a freedom undiminished, because it is the creation of their own free legislative will; but a freedom which nevertheless assumes the form of a lawful dependence, because it takes its place in a realm of right or law."[27]

If so, the state, in Kant's view, is a condition for moral life and is required to enforce the universal laws which can be deduced from the categorical imperative of duty. The state is not at all an evil, necessary or unnecessary, or an instrument of exploitation or oppression; it is a good and moralising agency. But Kant makes the sphere of state activity wholly negative by limiting it to the hindrance of hindrances to freedom and good life. Since morality lies in performing functions from the sense of duty and in obeying moral law, the state cannot promote it

26. Barker : *Political Thought in England*, p. 18.
27. *Ibid.*

directly. All that the state can do is to establish external conditions favourable to it by removing obstacles to good life. It is justified in repelling what is opposed to the free play of moral will. Dewey thus puts : "Man in his rational or universal capacity must, therefore, will an outward order of harmony in which it is at least possible for acts dictated by rational freedom to get a footing. Such an outer order is the state. Its province is not to promote moral freedom directly–only the moral will can do that. But its business is to hinder hindrances to freedom : to establish a social condition of outward order in which truly moral acts may gradually evolve a kingdom of humanity."[28]

Kant defines state as a lody of the members of such a society when united by the purpose of law as citizens. And their just attributes inseparable from their nature as citizens are :

(i) Legal Freedom : That a man renders obedience to no other law than that to which he has given his consent;

(ii) Civic Equality : That a man recognises in the people no superior save on the understanding that he has the moral power to bind that superior by legal obligation as truly as a superior can bind him;

(iii) Civic Independence : That a man owes his existence and maintenance not to the arbitrary will of another person but to his own rights and powers as a member of the community;

(iv) Civic Personality : That a man in question of right is to be represented by no one but himself.[29]

Kant frankly rejects the positive view of jurisprudence that law is a command of the sovereign enforced by sanctions. In issuing a command, the sovereign may well be swayed by selfish whims or momentary desires and caprices. Hence, the command itself might well be contrary to the dictates of pure reason. In a like manner, Kant refuses to believe that true law can be based upon customs, traditions or precedents, for at many times the custom has permitted acts which were contrary to the dictates of pure reason. The true law is that which is based upon the dictates laid down by man's rational will in accordance with *a priori* principles. Neither history nor personal experience can give us any sure guidance. Reason informs, Kant argues, that law must be universal in character and be applicable to all persons and at all times. Obviously, it

28. Dewey, *op. cit.*, p. 97.
29. See Caird, *op. cit.*, p. 309.

exists prior to all governments and hence is prior to all statutory legislation.

Kant's true jurisprudence automatically includes the case of punishment. He insists that all laws should be based on reason and punishment should follow whenever the system is broken or deflected. In Kant's view, every action is either good or bad, and if it is bad, eternal and absolute justice demands that it be punished just because it is bad. He rejects the idea of striking terror or bringing reform in the criminal and defends punishment for the sake of the maintenance of rights and to see that the eternal principle of justice is not upset. According to McGovern, "Kant's idea of justice smacks not a little of the old 'eye for an eye, a tooth for a tooth' philosophy, and in view of his notions on the subject, it is not surprising that he was distinctly suspicious of the pardoning power usually granted to public officials and that he was violently opposed to those persons who wished to abolish capital punishment."[30]

If Kant follows Rousseau in regard to the origin and nature of state, he also follows Montesquieu in the subject of forms of government.[31] Kant classifies states into three forms–autocracy, aristocracy and democracy; and puts government into two forms–republican and despotic, accordingly as there "is or is not a separation of the legislative and executive powers."[32] Yet Kant offers a superstitious reverence for monarchy and seeks to justify the absolute character of royal authority. At first he discards any form of government as irrational if it is not representative, but he argues that the function of the representatives may be vested in a king or nobility as well as in elected deputies."[33]

The reason for the superstitious reverence for monarchy should be traced in the influence of the horrors of French Revolution on Kant. Thus, Kant denies the right of resistance and insists that if the constitution is defective, changes should be made by the sovereign and not by the people. The existence of the state is so essential to man for the realisation of his moral

30. McGovern, *op. cit.*, p. 141.
31. Dunning thus puts that Kant's doctrine as to the origin and nature of the state "is merely Rousseau's put into the garb of Kantian terminology and logic; his analysis of government follows Montesquieu in like manner." *op. cit.*, p. 131.
32. *Ibid*, p. 133.
33. *Ibid*.

purpose that there can be no right to revolution. It is the law of reason 'holy and inviolable' which impels man to the institution of the state, not natural sociability, much less consideration of expediency. Naturally, in Kant's view, the overthrow and execution of the sovereign "is an immoral and inexpiable sin like the sin against the Holy Ghost spoken of by the theologians, which can never be forgiven in this world or in the next."[34]

It is clear that Kant's theory of state and government stands on the premises of individualism. He fully adheres to the worth and dignity of the human personality and is never prepared to sacrifice his individual at the altar of state. However, being a Prussian and living under the horrifying influence of the French Revolution, he pays superstitious reverence for the institution of monarchy, denies the right to revolution and supports the cause of internationalism. Barker thus sums up : "Kant, it appears, had little idea of the corporate life of a national state. The free will of the individual is the core of his thought. The state he conceives is in its nature a contractual body; and far from exalting the control of the state over the individual, he emphasises the necessary subordination of the state to the ideal of a permanent peace of Europe, and advocates a federal league of nations each subject to the adjudication of the general collective will."[35]

By way of criticism, it may be commented that Kant's political ideas on state and government reveal a confusing admixture of individualism and idealism. By regarding man as an end in himself and by boldly adhering to his independent worth and personality, Kant becomes an ardent individualist; but by assigning to state the character of a moralising agency and prescribing to it a negative sphere of activity he contributes to the idealist tradition. The individualistic approach cannot be synthesised with that of the idealistic in as much as it denies the organic character of society in which the individual lives and acts. Then, Kant's preference for monarchy and his denial of the right to revolution add to the trend of royal etatism, absolutism and authoritarianism which cuts much across his defence of individual freedom. Obviously, Kant wavers between

34. Dewey, *op. cit.*, p. 98. If Rousseau was the spiritual inspirer of the French Revolution, then Kant may well be described as the evaluator of the intellectual and moral implications that lay buried in that great act." A.D. Lindsay : *Kant*, p. 9.
35. Barker, *op. cit.*, p. 18.

the eighteenth century individualism and later idealism and fails because of hovering between two different conceptions of the state. Vaughan thus puts : "It is clearly a conflict of his mind between the claims of justice and the claims of individual freedom. He does not see his way fully to reconcile the two. He is too honest to sacrifice either."[36]

ECONOMICS : JUSTIFICATION OF THE CAPITALIST SYSTEM

Like the idealists in general, Kant accepts the institution of private property on the ground that it is necessary for the expression of man's will. But he rejects the Lockean conception that right to property is natural, or that a thing with which one mixes his labour becomes his property. Mere will or mixing of labour does not entitle a person for anything, rather in the apportionment of any object, man should take care that he does not, either by his will or act, do any indirect injury to his neighbours. In other words, property requires the express sanction of those who are immediately interested in it. It is a derived right and does not belong to man by nature. Arguing thus, Kant concludes that all such rights "must be derived from the sovereign and overlord and paramount superior of the soil, or, as it may be better put, the Supreme Proprietor of the Land."[37]

But Kant repudiates the idea of natural or social ownership of land, for to deprive a man of the natural ownership of land would reduce him to the status of a serf and hence would be reprehensible. Rather he enjoins upon man to remember that his right to private property is derived from the state by the assignment and that the state retains the right to assess private proprietors, demand taxes, take special services, exact even forced loans. In like manner, the state has a right to interfere, if it so wishes, with private property by abolishing primogeniture. However, in some cases, Kant would sanction outright confiscation of private property, if the property belonged to the feudal lords and nobles, for in modern times their authority has been taken over by the state. The state may also confiscate Church property if public opinion so favours. Similarly, the state has a right to confiscate the property of such endowed institutions as charities, hospitals, schools, churches etc. if and when they cease to perform functions compatible

36. Vaughan, *op. cit.*, p. 286.
37. McGovern, *op. cit.*, p. 286.

with the public will. It also shows Kant's gross dislike of feudal ideas and institutions.

It is obvious that in regard to the question of property, Kant takes a stand different from that of Rousseau. While the latter sought to limit right to property by demanding that nobody may occupy more than he needs to satisfy his wants, and by maintaining that mere occupation without actually working on land is no legitimate title, the former recognises no such limitation. It is evident from Kant's own affirmation : "What I bring into my possession in accordance with law, and what I will to be mine, that becomes my property." Such a categorical statement bears testimony to the fact that this "is, in fact, the economic theory of capitalism. One of the essential traits of modern capitalism is the transformation of all economic-ethical relations into purely economic-legal ones on the analogy of the property relation. One feudal vassal, for instance, owed loyalty to his over-lord, the modern citizen owes to the state his taxes."[38]

However, from a critical standpoint, it may be pointed out that Kant's view of right to property coupled with his defence of the class system are striking examples of the essential dependence of political philosophy on the economic foundations of society. A sort of confusion between economic and philosophical premises becomes obvious here in view of the fact that it "is very difficult to understand what he meant by reason, but it is evident that property is not a postulate of reason but a social institution developed by men in a very definite historical process."[39]

INTERNATIONALISM : SEARCH FOR ETERNAL PEACE

Though Kant is an idealist, he is not an etatist. He supports the case of internationalism that is contained in his denunciation of the global warfare and the establishment of a league of states for the pacific settlement of international disputes. His work *On Perpetual Peace*, as already pointed out, outlines philosophical rules for an international association as the indispensable presupposition for a lasting peace. The great philosopher goes to the extent of suggesting disarmament and abolition of standing armies. Kant's plan of perpetual peace of

38. Reinhold Aris, *op. cit.*, p. 97-98.
39. *Ibid*, p. 98.

1795, undoubtedly, is the 'most celebrated piece of his political writings."[40] It signifies following commandments :

1. No conclusion of peace shall be considered valid as such if it was made with a secret reservation of the material for a future war.
2. No independently existing state, whether it be large or small, may be acquired by another state by inheritance, exchange, purchase or gift.
3. Standing armies will gradually be abolished altogether.
4. No national debt will be contracted in connection with the external affairs of the state.
5. No state shall forcibly interfere in the constitution and government of another state.
6. No state at war with another state shall permit such acts of hostility as would make natural confidence impossible during a future time of peace. Such acts would include the employment of assassins or poisoners, breach of agreements, the instigation of treason within the enemy state etc.[41]

Apart from this, Kant issues three definitive articles on the conditions of perpetual peace. These are :

1. The civil constitution of every state should be republican. A republican system furnishes a powerful lever of control over governments and curbs their aggressive instincts.
2. The law of nations should be founded on a federation of free states. Positive law requires the existence of a sovereign authority to ensure that all illegal acts are justly punished.
3. The ultimate goal of human progress is that man ought to leave his ethical state of nature in order to become a member of an ethical commonwealth. The true church is universal. All members of the human race regardless of colour, race, nation are potentially to be regarded as one of its members.[42]

In other words, Kant's internationalism bears the following important characteristics :

40. Howard Williams : *Kant's Political Philosophy*, p. 245.
41. *Ibid.*
42. *Ibid.*

1. Kant deprecates the case of international warfare. Though he feels compelled to acknowledge that wars may be inevitable, as long as there is nothing like an international sovereign authority, he desires that in all conflicts no state could employ means that isolate the acknowledged principles of humanity. As he says : "No state in war shall avail itself of hostile actions which would make mutual confidence in the future peace impossible, such as abetting, assassination, poisoning, breach of capitulation and treason."[43]
2. There should be a league of states bound by the canons of morality, if there is nothing like the system of legal sanctions. As perpetual warfare is the natural result in a pre-political stage when every man is the enemy of man (as conceived by Hobbes), so every state is an enemy of another in the international state of nature. As such, perpetual peace is not possible until a league of states is set up as a postulate of pure reason. Treaty of peace must be signed by all states with clear and strong conditions to guarantee its continuance. There should be no secret reservations which might furnish the cause of outbreak of hostilities. As he sanctions : "No state shall violently interfere with the constitution and administration of another."[44]
3. Like Plato, Kant suggests that all rulers must consult philosophers and wise persons in matters of state so that they may have the advantage of implementing schemes of international friendship and co-operation.[45]

Three important points engage our attention at this stage. First, Kant's scheme of an international body is not at all a utopia but an ideal which he desires the states of Europe to pursue. The purpose of this philosopher is to lay down that perpetual peace is not only a postulate of reason but also a question of practical politics. Second, Kant holds that only a republic could join the proposed federation of states. Here Kant's use of the term 'republic' signifies any political system in which law prevails and, as such, which is the opposite of

43. Aris, *op. cit.*, p. 80.
44. *Ibid.*
45. Hannah Arendt is of the view that Kant agrees with Aristotle against Plato that the philosophers should not rule, but the rulers should be willing to listen to the philosophers. Refer to her *Lectures on Kant's Political Philosophy*, edited by Ronald Beiner, p. 29.

despotism. Third, Kant himself realises the limitations that stand in the way of establishing a Federal Union and yet he affirms : "In the place of the positive idea of a world republic we must be satisfied with the negative substitute of continually advancing League of States to prevent war and this may be of sufficient avail to resist the pressure of lawless passion, though it cannot secure indecisively against the dangers of their breaking loose."[46]

However, a closer study of Kant's theory of internationalism shows that it is simply an extension of his theory of individual's moral freedom. If freedom is the essential attribute of individual's personality and if it, through law, is the ideal of internal civil peace, then by itself or independently of state's external relations, it can either never be solved, or would remain incomplete until we have solved the problem of regulating the external relations of states by law. Thus, for Kant, the principle of the freedom of mankind already divided into nation-states is a single principle which must be applied within and without if man has to achieve not only freedom but perpetual peace."[47]

Critical Estimate : Undoubtedly, Kant occupies an important place in the history of European political thought. He strengthened a new trend started by Rousseau whose earliest reflections were contained in the idealistic affirmations of Plato and Aristotle. Once again, we find politics and ethics drawn closer so much so that the latter dominates the former and thereby the trend of the ethicisation of politics dominates the scene that by its freshness replaces the dull and sub-standard trends of social contractualism and utilitarianism. Keeping it in view, Prof. C.E. Vaughan says : "By binding Politics to Ethics, Kant gave an entirely fresh turn to the conception both of Right in general and of such subordinate notions as those of Property and of contract in particular. He may take the order of his subject from the hands of the Roman jurists; but his treatment of each link, taken separately, is entirely his own."[48]

---

46. See Caird, *op. cit.*, p. 113.
47. Frank Thakurdas, *op. cit.*, p. 105.
48. Vaughan : *Studies in the History of Political Philosophy Before and After Rousseau*, p. 69. The strength of Kant's theory lies in his expression of the antagonism in the moral life between what is and what applies to be between an end determined for us by the affections of our sensibility and an end determined by our own self-conscious nature. The weakness of this theory lies in the fact that in expressing antagonism, he carries it to a

Indeed, Kant started a new trend–the trend of idealism–in the history of western political thought. The idealistic trend remained dominant throughout the nineteenth century and it enormously influenced the continental philosophers like Fichte, Hegel, Schelling, Schiller, Geothe and Humboldt in Germany and Green, Bradley and Bosanquet in England. In spite of many attacks by the critics, the edifice built by Kant having complex structure of logic, metaphysics, psychology, ethics and politics stands today and the idealistic philosophy of Kant "represents an event of paramount importance in the history of thought."[49] Dewey thus admires : "To scoff at him is fair sacrilege. In a genuine sense, he marks the end of the older age. He is the transition to distinctly modern thought."[50]

point it disappears altogether, where the community necessary even for antagonism disappears." E. Caird : *Critical Philosophy of Kant*, p. 286.

49. Will Durant : *The Story of Philosophy*, p. 286.
50. Dewey, *op. cit.* p. 63.

28

HEGEL

No other philosophical system has exerted such a strong and enduring influence upon political life as the metaphysics of Hegel. Yet Hegelianism has had a rebirth not in the field of logical and metaphysical thought, but in the field of political thought. There has hardly been a single great political system that has resisted its influence.

— **E. Cassirer**[1]

Georg Wilhelm Friedrich Hegel (1770-1831) has the reputation of being the most difficult of philosophers owing to the abstruse nature of his thought and the complexity of the language in which he expressed it.[2] Born in the town of Stuttgart, he acquired the knowledge of theology at Tubingen but left the institution calling it as 'deficient in philosophy'. For several years he served as a teacher in the cities of Bonn and Frankfurt, then as a professor in the Jena University, a newspaper editor and head of a gymnasium department in Nuremberg, till he occupied the important chair in Heidelberg University in 1816. More important than this is his career as

1. Cassirer : *Myth of the State*, p. 248.
2. Prof. Loewenberg remarks : "To reproduce the spirit of Hegel's philosophy without its letter is to sacrifice subtlety; to produce it with its letter is to renounce intelligibility." Cf. Lancaster : *Masters of Political Thought*, Vol. III, p. 20.

a professor in Berlin University since 1818 which in a sense made him the 'official philosopher of his government'. In 1831 he died of cholera epidemic making the 'end of an epoch, the last fine effort of Germany's greatest age.'[3]

WORKS : POLITICS DOMINATED BY LOGIC AND METAPHYSICS

Like Kant, the works of Hegel are of a highly philosophical nature in which politics is dominated by logic and metaphysics. His political ideas are traceable in numerous lectures that he delivered at the university of Jena between 1804-06 in which he touched the issues of ethics, logic and metaphysics and thereby displayed his philosophy of nature and mind. These ideas assumed a form of their own in his *Philosophy of Mind* (1816) and the *Science of Logic* (1812-16). The thought of Hegel found a more precise and expansive formulation in the *Encyclopaedia of the Philosophical Sciences* first published in 1816. However, his *Philosophical Sciences* is specially important wherein he discussed logic and philosophy of nature and spirit.

However, in the field of political thought, his work *Outlines of the Philosophy of Right* (1821) is very important that appeared as an elaboration of his earlier work titled *Philosophy of Spirit* containing his ideas on ethics and theory of state. The Berlin lectures of Hegel (published separately as the *History of Philosophy, Philosophy of History* and *Philosophy of Fine Art and Religion* are an elaboration of third section of the *Encyclopaedia*. It is generally believed that Hegel's methodology and the basic assumptions of philosophy are contained in his *Philosophy of Right*. However, the general tenor of this work is of a highly philosophical order about which Reyburn remarks that it is intended to point out the way in which the principles of right realise mind and give it objectivity; and it is more concerned to show how the infinite self contained the whole mind which intrinsically comes to the light of day than to display the insufficiency of the whole field of right."[4]

What is really perplexing about Hegel is that he puts his ideas in a very difficult language that is not easily intelligible to an average reader. It is also said that different works of Hegel lack consistency. It appears that connecting bonds are missing

3. Will Durant : *The Story of Philosophy*, p. 295.
4. See T.M. Knox (ed.) : *Hegel's Philosophy of Right*, p. 242.

with the result that his political philosophy suffers from lack of intelligibility and flow of expression due to "an isolated study".[5] Prof. J.H. Stirling in his monograph titled *The Secret of Hegel* feels nervous at the confirmation of endless jargons in the philosophical system of Hegel and remarks that there is "a scrutiny of thought so profound that it is for the most part unintelligible".[6] Different from all, however, is the observation that the critics have wrongly interpreted the meaning of Hegel's philosophy and dared say that perhaps Hegel himself would not have understood what he meant by it. But the truth is that when his philosophy "is stripped of its pretentious logical apparatus, Hegel is saying something both very old and very simple".[7]

HISTORY : FORMULA OF DIALECTICAL IDEALISM

The political philosophy of Hegel shows on him a very penetrating influence of Aristotle, Rousseau, Kant and Fichte. But the peculiar thing about Hegel's political philosophy is that the answers to various political questions are given in a methodical manner. The questions are old and so their answers are not incomprehensible. The only novel thing is the use of method adopted by Hegel while discussing them. Hegel himself insists that the method adopted by him to deal with the questions is inseparable from the answers. Hence, it is easy to call Hegel a conscious charlatan or a confused philosopher, but the truth is that he is discussing such persistent issues of politics as consent, freedom, use of force, role of bureaucracy, proper organisation of the government and the state, and giving their answers in a way different from the philosophers who had already contributed much to the field of philosophical knowledge.

It follows that the novel thing about Hegel's political philosophy is the method to which he gives the name of dialectic. The method of dialectics is as old as the Greeks but the peculiar thing with Hegel is its different application. The earlier Greek writers had used the term to describe the process by which in controversy one proposition was set over against another, and out of this confrontation a new proposition emerged, uniting the truth contained in each of the original ones. But what is distinctive in Hegel is the adoption of this term to describe the movement of reason in human affairs as

5. Frank Thakurdas : *German Political Idealism*, p. 212.
6. See Karl R. Popper : *The Open Society and Its Enemies*, Vol. II, p. 27.
7. Lancaster : *Masters of Political Thought*, Vol. III, p. 66.

well as the strictly technical process by which truth is arrived at, although reason being the final reality to him, this is one process.

For the sake of a proper study, the salient features of the theory of Hegelian dialectic may be put as under :

1. Like Fichte, Hegel believes that ultimate reality is 'Reason' or 'Spirit', but not matter.[8] He describes it as 'Absolute Idea' or 'Reason' or 'Spirit' and contrary to the Kantian view, insists that there is nothing in the universe which the human mind can not comprehend.[9] This reason is something dynamic; it is essentially the principle of growth and development. The essence of reason which makes reality is self-consciousness and it has to pervade through several stages in an attempt to attain the highest form of self-consciousness of which it is capable. In other words, the fundamental premise of Hegel is that what is rational is real and what is real is rational. By this he means that everything that exists (including the state) is the embodiment of reason, and that permeating all mere appearance–the show of temporal and transient–is a rational principle giving meaning to political institutions just as it gives harmony· what men call the natural universe. When Hegel maintains that rational is real and *vice versa*, he simply means that the motivating power lies not in inert matter but in self-propelling thought which is independent of matter. By real or actual, he does not mean the 'existing' but the force that really actuates the existing. Hegel says : "What is rational is actual and what is actual is rational. On this conviction, the plain man like the philosopher takes his stand, and from it philosophy starts in its study of the universe of mind as well as the universe of nature. If reflection, feeling, or whatever form subjective consciousness may take, looks upon the present as something vacuous and looks beyond it with the

8. It should be noted here that Hegel uses capital letters in the beginning of various terms and this creates a sort of apprehension in the mind of the readers. Its reason lies in the style of German language. The commentators have copied the style of Hegel, otherwise the terms might have been produced in the English style. Reason, Spirit, Idea Geist, Mind all have identical implications and they may be interchangeably used.
9. In Hegelian philosophy again and again we come across such passages as the distinctive feature of human life is that it "is not swayed by blind impulses only, but is guided and controlled by ideas and it is ideas after all that rule the world." Halder : *Neo-Hegelianism*, p. 333.

eyes of superior wisdom, it finds itself in a vacuum, and because it is actual only in the present, it is itself mere vacuity. If, on the other hand, the Idea passes for only an Idea, for something represented in an opinion, philosophy rejects such a view and shows that nothing is actual except the Idea. Once that is granted, the great thing is to apprehend in the show of the temporal and transient the substance which is immanent and the eternal which is present."[10]

2. If reason motivates the law of dialectic, it becomes a law of logic denying any distinction not only between the thought and things but between the thought of different persons. Like earlier writers of ancient Greece, Hegel does not mean by the dialectic the way in which opposite tendencies are adjusted in political life and history. Hegel does not talk about the 'law of pendulum', nor is it his purpose to say that historical changes proceed with the inter-action of opposite forces; rather in his view, the dialectic constitutes a mechanism by which thought propels itself, or the way in which reason progressively embodies itself in the institutions. Wright thus points out : "The dialectic begins with the most abstract conception of pure logic, that of mere being and terminates with the most concrete phases of thought, the philosophy of the Absolute Mind in its full comprehensiveness and concreteness."[11]

3. According to Hegel, there are three stages involved in the process by which reason moves through history and nature and they may be called the thesis, anti-thesis and synthesis. The thesis passes into its anti-thesis with the result that synthesis takes place. But the synthesis becomes a new thesis and the process is repeated until all contradictions are resolved. Thus, any assertion one can make is never wholly true, and because of this is immediately seen to involve its opposite. Between these two attributes of truth and falseness-which it is to be observed, are aspects of the same assertion-there exists a tension which is resolved or rather resolves itself, the dialectic being self-propelling. But Hegel maintains that each new stage of synthesis represents a higher stage of growth or a still more true stage of evolution

---

10. Hegel : *Philosophy of Right* (Translated from German into English by T.M. Knox), pp. 10-11.
11. Wright : *History of Modern Philosophy*, p. 328.

and this process continues to operate until the stage of final truth is reached.

4. Hegel not only amplifies the above methodology, rather he examines the case of social development on its basis. He is wresting with a real problem. He maintains that the family representing love is the thesis, but the civil society representing competition is its anti-thesis; and their synthesis lies in the nation-state which represents the elements of both love and competition. Hegel's system of triad takes the Family as Unity, the Civil Society as Particularity and the State as Universality. The tension between the unity of the family and the particularity of the civil society is resolved with the appearance of the state as the actuality of the universal order. Both the family and civil society are to some degree rational, since both are of course actual, but only the state which transcends both is perfectly rational and perfectly ethical.

5. It follows from above that the state (nation) represents the synthesis of family and civil society and is a perfect embodiment of reason.[12] The process of dialectic stops here, for the reconciliation has reached the stage of final truth. In the words of Hegel: "The ethical substance, as containing independent self-consciousness united with its concept, is the actual mind of a family and a nation. The concept of this idea has being only as mind, as something knowing itself, and actual because it is the objectification of itself, the movement running through the form of its movements. It is therefore (A) ethical mind in its nature or immediate phase–the Family. This substantiality loses its unity, passes over into divisions and into the phase of relation, i.e., into (B) Civil Society–an association of members as self-subsistence, is only abstract. Their association is brought about by their needs, by the legal system–the means to security of person and property–and by an external organisation for attaining their particular and common interests. This external state (C) is brought back to and welded into unity in the Constitution of the State which is the end and the actuality of both

12. Hobhouse thus says : "Just as in a simple religion the powers that be are ordained of God, so with the metaphysician who starts from the belief that the things are what they should be, the fabric of social life; and in particular the state system, is part of an order which is inherently rational and good, an order to which the lives of individuals are altogether subordinate". *The Metaphysical Theory of State*, p. 17.

the substantial universal order and public life devoted thereto."[13]

If shorn off its crude manifestations and technical phraseology, it appears that Hegel is speaking something both very old and very simple. He has done nothing marvellous but to put the Aristotelian theory of the origin of state clothed with the tapestry of his system of dialectic. The entire analysis may be summed up thus : that reason is the sole motivating factor; that movement takes place in a spiral or zigzag form; that there is nothing like chance or accident in the working of dialectic; that progress lies in the struggle of opposite forces; that the process continues to operate until the final reconciliation takes place. Thus, art is the thesis, religion is its anti-thesis, and philosophy represents their synthesis. So family is the thesis, civil society is its anti-thesis, and the nation-state exhibits their synthesis. The dialectical process begins from family and through civil society culminates in the nation-state.[14]

The law of dialectical idealism not only lays down that idea is original, primary and self-operating, it also confirms the role of some Absolute Spirit in the making of history. In this way, Reason or Idea becomes inter-changeable with God. As Hegel himself says : "The Reason in most concrete form is God: governs the world the actual working of His government–the carrying out of plan is the history of the world. Philosophy strives to comprehend this plan for only that which has been developed as a result of it possesses a *bona fide* reality; that which does not accord with it is negative. Before the pure light

13. Hegel : *Philosophy of Right*, paras 156-157.
14. A good example of the loose and fanciful way in which the conception of opposites is used is thus put by Hegel : "The building of a house is, in the first instance, a subjective aim and design. On the other hand, we have, as means, the several substances required for the work–Iron, Wood, Stones. The elements are made use of in working up this material : fire to melt iron, wind to blow up the fire, water to set wheels in motion, in order to cut the wood, etc. The result is that the wind, which has helped to build the house, is shut by the house; so also are the violence of rains and floods, and the destructive powers of fire, so far as the house is made fireproof. The stones and teams obey the law of gravity, press downward, and so high walls are carried up. Thus, the elements are made use of in accordance with their nature, and yet to co-operate for a product by which their operation is limited. Thus, the passions of men are gratified; they develop themselves and their aims in accordance with their natural tendencies and build up the edifice of human society; thus fortifying a position for Right and Order against themselves." *Philosophy of History*, p. 27.

of this divine idea–which is more than mere ideal–the phantoms of the world whose events are an incoherent concourse of fortuitous circumstances, utterly vanish. Philosophy wishes to discover the substantial purport, the real aspect of the reason in the comprehension of divine work."[15] In fine, history, according to Hegel, is the autobiography of God.[16]

Hegelian system of dialectic has been subjected to seething denunciation by various trends of political philosophy as under :

1. The most important trend is that of Marxism. Although Marx borrowed heavily from Hegel, he put the latter right side up. The system of triad is correct, but, according to Marxism, the motivating force is not reason but matter. Marx insists that matter is self-working and thus it has a motivating force within itself. Contrary to the metaphysics of Hegel, Marx insists that it is not the consciousness of man that motivates matter; on the contrary, it is the material factors that influence human consciousness. Marx thus retained the method but rejected the contention of Hegel. In one of his letters to Dr. Ludwig Kugelmann, Marx wrote in 1868 thus : "Hegel's dialectic is the basic form of my dialectic, but only after it has been stripped of its mystical form, and it is precisely this which distinguishes my method."[17]
2. Hegel's entire analysis is based on the premises of rationalism. Contrary to this, modern school of psychoanalysis is not prepared to admit that the reason is the only or decisively motivating factor. It is true that man is a rational creature, but the elements of irrationality also influence his behaviour. In their point of view, man is less rational and more irrational in as much as the non-rational factors like habit, sentiment, instinct, impulse etc. do play their part in governing the patterns of human behaviour. The non-rational character of human activity is often visible in the actions motivated by fury, zeal and excitement. Thus, Graham Wallas asserts that human mind "acts like a harp,

15. Hegel : *Philosophy of History* (Translated from German into English by J. Siberee), p. 38.
16. Sidney Hook : *From Hegel to Marx*, p. 36.
17. Cf. Carew Hunt : *The Theory and Practice of Communism*, p. 54. It may also be commented that the notion of Absolute Idea "is not a cognitive fact as we are entitled to discard it as a pious wish, for Hegel suggests no method through which its existence can either be proved or disproved." V.R. Mehta : *Hegel and the Modern State*, p. 40.

all of whose strings throb together; so that emotion, impulse, inference, are often simultaneous and inter-mingled aspects of a single mental experience".[18]

3. Finally, it may be pointed out that every kind of development does not take place in the way as the law of Hegelian dialectic tells us. Two serious flaws may be pointed out here. First, Hegel treats social institutions in a process of evolution and interprets their existence as a synthesis arisen out of their opposite elements of thesis and anti-thesis. If the process operates, how can the state (imperfect as it is) be taken as a final synthesis. Hegel ought to have told us about the anti-thesis of the state and about the future mechanism of dialectical process. Second, when the dialectic is examined, the fact that strikes one is its extreme vagueness. It is not clear as to how art's anti-thesis is the religion and how philosophy represents their synthesis. The scheme requires that all change should be explained in terms of the operation of thought in resolving a series of contradictions, so that at each higher stage greater logical consistency may be achieved. But the contradictions discovered by Hegel consist of so many sorts of different and opposite things that the dialectic "frequently loses its plausibility".[19]

"Essentially, Hegel's weakness lay in two realms. He was perhaps unaware of their connection. The first weakness lay in his overt and daring conjugation of history and reason, in the claims he made for his secular providence of the will that had become mind, the mind had become will. Whatever history is, it is obviously not reason, no matter how reasonable the mind that perceives it, even if the mind is a creature of history. History is probably closer to Herder's variety of forms than to any idealist union of life and divinity created or imposed by the conceptual apparatus. The second Hegelian weakness is his continued assertion of the European cultural claim."[20]

---

18. Wallas : *Human Nature in Politics*, p. 99.
19. Lancaster, *op. cit.*, p. 66.
20. Kelly: *Idealism, Political and History*, pp. 356-357. To make the meaning of the second weakness more revealing, Kelly further says : "The religio-political synthesis or Eurocentric destiny within an ever-renewing and deepening system of speculation had been attacked by Strauss, Feuerbach, Bauer, Ruge and Marx. Their criticism exploded the cultural homogeneity of Europe by discovering masters and slaves where Hegel had thought to close the problem. Coercive transcendence, soon to be remitted to other continents, remained." *Ibid.*, p. 357.

FREEDOM : RECONCILEMENT OF MAN'S WILL WITH SOCIAL GOOD

Hegel's conception of freedom is thoroughly different from that of Kant, for while the latter treats it as a subjective and a limited phenomenon, the former considers it to be positive and objective. Drawing inspiration from Rousseau, Hegel treats freedom as the essence of man; the distinctive quality of human life, the renunciation of which is tantamount to the renunciation of humanity itself. He writes : "The notion of freedom must not be taken in the sense of the casual free will of each individual but in the sense of the reasonable will, the will in and for itself."[21] Hegel's approach is quite different from other German idealists also who conceived it to be 'an attribute or faculty of an individual person."[22] To Hegel man's freedom is associated with his life in society : it is no longer his in obeying the dictates of self-imposed categorical imperative of duty. Hegel interprets it as one aspect of pure abstract intelligence : the idea of the will, as a last abstraction, is the free will that wills the free will. In Hegel's own phrase, it "is eternal, universal, self-conscious, self-determining."[23]

The burden of Hegel's argument is that freedom consists in transcending the limitations imposed on us by our material and egoistic self and in realising the social aspects of our personality. In other words, it implies that the more we develop our rationality and spirituality, the more conscious we become of freedom in and around us. Obviously, Hegel does not follow the line of John Stuart Mill in taking freedom as something of a negative character implying absence of restraints. Likewise, to Hegel, freedom does not signify the life of a man who has left this world like an ascetic. It implies two things : (i) it is the positive power of an individual to determine his actions actively, deliberately and consciously and, for this reason, distinguishable with anything like whim or caprice or sentiment and the like. (ii) It is to be realised in relation to others, because

21. Cf. Bosanquet : *The Philosophical Theory of State*, pp. 220-221.
22. Dunning, *op. cit.*, p. 155.
23. *Ibid*, p. 156. As Herbert Marcuse observes : "Since man wishes to be judged in accordance with his own self-determined choices, he is free in relation to himself, whatever the external situation may impose upon him. No one can break in upon this inner conviction of mankind." *Hegel and the Rise of Social Theory*, p. 206.

relation to others is not merely a possibility but the necessity of mind, for it is by means of others and by means of sublation that mind preserves itself.[24] Keeping it in view, Prof. Vaughan says that by freedom "is meant not the mere absence of external restraints : not the liberty of the individual to do what he wills with his own faculties and his own possessions, but the untrammelled development of man's powers, moral, intellectual and spiritual, according to the fundamental laws of our own nature."[25]

When Hegel interprets freedom, he is distinctly under the influence of Aristotle and Rousseau. It is owing to this that he rejects the interpretation of Kant and insists that the freedom of a man cannot be conceived in isolation or in a self-imposed pattern of rational life. When man is a social creature, his freedom is necessarily bound with his life in society. Freedom has a positive and an objective character : it expands itself and consists in the will to make one's outward self adequate to the measure of the fullness of his thinking self. Hence, when the will is free, objective, outwardly expressed, and creative, it manifests itself into three forms–law, inward morality and social ethics or *sittlechkeit* variously translated as social morality, ethical system, moral life and customary morality.[26]

The first manifestation of will is law. Under this head, Hegel discusses the idea of personality, property and contract, and shows that all of them are the manifestations of free will. According to him, a living creature becomes a person only so far as he exercises free will to be a person. Material objects are like property, because they are expression of man's free will and have no will of their own. For instance, a slave is no better than a property, since he lacks the free will to be free. Throughout Hegel judges laws and rights "not by a fixed standard, but with reference to various stages of culture and self-consciousness that history reveals."[27] But the second manifestation of will is the rules of inward morality. Here Hegel "discusses those

24. Mehta, *op. cit.*, p. 32.
25. Vaughan : *Studies in the History of Political Philosophy*, Vol. II, p. 153.
26. Prof. Barker identifies *sittlechkeit* with social righteousness and says that it "is a spirit and habit of life expressed in the social opinion and enforced by the social conscience of a whole people; it is at one and the same time a mind of self-consciousness, because it is a spirit, and a thing of external existence, because it is a visible system of habit and conduct." *op. cit.*, p.49.
27. *Ibid*, p. 157.

aspects of self-determination in which the mere externality of law and the mere inwardness of morality are reconciled."[28]

The final manifestation of will is the whole system of institutions and influences that make for righteousness in the nation-state. This is the sphere where mere externality of law and the mere inwardness of morality are reconciled. It is the sphere of concrete morality or conduct. It includes law, custom, sentiment and moral will. In simple terms, it is the nation-state which represents social morality condensed in itself. In obeying customary morality of the community which is the working of a universal cause, the free will of the individual is fully raised. Hence, it projects itself beyond itself and in so doing reaches the stage of perfection. It is the nation-state where man "has fully raised his outward self to the level of the inward self of thought : his free will has found its broadest expansion which its positive quality demands, and the highest expression which its objective character requires."[29]

With this interpretation of freedom Hegel exalts the nation-state. If state is the final embodiment of will, then no idea of force or contract can apply and the state must be envisaged not in terms of law or inward morality but as a custodian of social ethics–the highest expression of that social ethics at once precipitated in and enforced by social opinion which lies behind the life of the family, the political community itself. Barker thus observes : "That social morality is the product of a free will seeking to realise itself in a positive and objective form : and the state, as the highest expression and organ of social morality, is therefore also the product of that will–a product not in the sense of definite creation, at a given point of time, but in the sense of something gradually evolved, yet implicit all the time".[30]

---

28. *Ibid.* "Hegel's philosophy of law is an immense advance on Kant and just because of that the abstractions of Kantian Ethics are really overcome in Hegel". See A.D. Lindsay : *Kant*, p. 295.
29. Barker, *op. cit.*, p. 19.
30. *Ibid.*, pp. 19-20. It is obvious from the above interpretation of Hegel that his conception of freedom leads to the justification of state absolutism. Dewey thus puts : "Freedom is the consciousness of Freedom. Liberty of action has little to do with it. Obviously, it is only in this German idealistic system–particularly in the system of Hegel himself–that this has fully taken place. Meantime, when citizens of a state, (especially of the state in which this philosophic insight has been achieved), take the laws of their state as their own ends and motives of action, they attain the best possible substitute for a reason which is its own object. They appropriate as their

Hegel's idea of freedom may be criticised on the following grounds :

1. Hegel offers a very confused as well as a perplexing meaning of freedom. It is full of paradoxes. To say that we are free only when we pursue our rational will embodied in the state and its institutions is to say that we have nothing like an independent choice. Choice is the essence of freedom and to deny its place is to deny freedom. Thus, Hegel takes the meaning of freedom to the point of absurdity by holding that freedom is no freedom when it does not coincide with the good will. "Thus may seem a facile reconciliation of the free moral will with the system of the state, achieved at the cost of the suppression of one of the factors and one of the impossible exaltation of the other".[31]
2. Such a meaning of freedom may have some conspicuous implications in the realm of philosophy, logic or metaphysics, but the case is quite different when we examine it in the world of politics. The world of politics is full of diversities and conflicts in which the fact of common good or general will may not be discovered so easily as visualised by Rousseau and Hegel to the extent that the individual may reconcile his will thereby and have the enjoyment of freedom. Naturally, for all practical purposes, individual's freedom would mean subordination to the will of the majority.[32] Prof. Berlin, therefore, accuses Hegel of doing an act of "monstrous impersonation".[33]
3. Above all, Hegel's idea of freedom in the realm of politics signifies nothing else than meek acceptance of the authority of the state. State and society become identifiable with each other and an attempt to ignore the distinction between the two "may lead to unlimited state regulation of life".[34]

In short, the purpose of Hegel is to convince us with the absolute character of political authority. According to him, "The right of individual to become subjectively destined to freedom is fulfilled when they belong to an actual ethical order, because their conviction of their freedom finds its truth in such an ob-

---

own personal reason the objective and absolute reason embodied perforce in law and custom". *op. cit.*, p. 133.

31. Barker, *op. cit.*, p. 52.
32. See Bertrand de Jouvenel : *Sovereignty*.
33. See Isaiah Berlin : *Two Concepts of Liberty*.
34. Barker, *op. cit.*, p. 54.

jective order that they are actually in possession of their own essence or their own inner universality".[35] But the conclusion of Hegel fails to win the admiration of one who traces herein the germs of a totalitarian system. To convince a man with such an interpretation is to crush his reasoning power and thus to convert him into a pawn for the benefit of a clever master. The noted English sociologist thus condemns Hegelian interpretation for setting up the state as "a greater being, a spirit, a super-personal entity, in which individuals with their private consciences or claims of rights, their happiness or their misery, are merely subordinate elements".[36]

STATE : A PHILOSOPHICAL JUSTIFICATION OF TOTALITARIANISM

Hegel's theory of state bears the salient characteristic of absolutism, etatism, authoritarianism. Every argument leads to the same goal and the result is that the imperfect institution of the state is first raised to the level of divinity, a mystic entity, an absolute idea, ethical substance, and then the same creation is identified with the imperfect state of Prussia. It may rightly be visualised that all has been done to justify the glory and majesty of the Prussian state the reason for which should be traced in the historical movements of the nineteenth century. The influence of the ideas of Plato, Aristotle and Rousseau coupled with the events of national reaction against Napoleon Bonaparte after 1812 enthused Hegel to exalt the nation-state to a mystical height. Following points may be summed up in the connection :

The process of dialectic shows that the state is the final synthesis where the contradictions of family and civil society are resolved. In order to justify his fundamental objective, Hegel finds that here the law of dialectic ceases in as much as the state represents a stage of final reconciliation. The civil society represents the anti-thesis of family, but both find their reconciliation in the nation-state. As society is different from family, so state is different from the civil society. The family rests on merely natural feelings of kindness, generosity and affection, but the civil bourgeois society stands for the economic and industrial world in which men appear as bread-earners. For the successful pursuits of their common interests, they

35. Hegel : *Philosophy of Right*, p. 158.
36. Hobhouse, *op. cit.*, p. 27.

demand police functions and administration of justice. At first sight, it seems that a society of this kind does not materially differ from the state, yet Hegel insists on this distinction partly with a view to giving an artistic symmetry to his system by dividing it into three stages and also by giving the highest place to the state. The civil society is not a separate society, but only an appearance within a larger system; it is only within the state proper that such a world as that of the bourgeois society could arise or be conceivable. Bosanquet thus puts : "Its priority to the state is, like that of the family, the priority of comparative narrowness or simplicity, of dealing with fewer factors and representing human nature in a more special, though necessary, aspect".[37]

J.O'Malley makes the meaning of Hegel clear in these words : "Hegel uses the expression 'civil society' to designate that phase of human social life in which the needs and, therefore, the interests of the individual govern his relations with others. Thus understood, civil society is ... the battlefield where everyone's individual private interest meets everyone else's ... This is the sphere of economic life, whose regularities are expressed in the laws of political economy, and whose content is the pursuit of selfish ends."[38] He further says that the unity of social and political life "is effected within the modern state despite the apparent duality of civil and political life by means of an institutional framework whose principal features are (i) a monarch who comes to the throne by birth and thus independently of political factions, (ii) an extensive bureaucracy of salaried civil servants who constitute an estate or class whose aims are identical with those of the state itself, and (iii) an Assembly of States in which representatives of the crown and the executive power meet with representatives of the civil estates to deliberate and determine the way in which the aims of the state and of civil society shall be reconciled, and to translate their decisions into law".[39]

Then, Hegel's conception of freedom very clearly justifies the case of state absolutism. The basis of the state is the free will of the individual and the state sustains it. The objective and positive character of freedom creates law and rules of in-

37. Bosanquet : *The Philosophical Theory of State*, pp. 252-253.
38. J.O'Malley : "Introduction" to *Critique of Hegel's Philosophy of Right by Karl Marx*, p. xlvii-xlviii.
39. *Ibid.*, xlviii.

ward morality and finally manifests itself in the nation-state. Thus, the state maintains individual as a person and promotes his welfare and protects the minor groups of family and social life in which he partially seeks his welfare. The state sustains social personality of the individual by carrying him away from an isolated to a social life. Besides, it teaches personality to transcend itself by giving its devotion to something beyond itself. Obviously, without the state man is nothing but a beast and a stupid and limited creature. Hegel says : "All the worth which the human being possesses–all spiritual reality–he possesses only through the state".[40]

If so, the state is an all-knowing and all-comprehending entity. In a real sense, the purpose of the individual cannot be contrary to or incompatible with that of the state. The individual realises freedom to the extent to which he identifies himself with the reason as manifested in the state and its institutions. The freedom of individual thus lies in willing the purposes of the state as his own. Only in this way, he can be sure that he is willing what is rational. As the reason manifested in man may be imperfect or warped by his impulses and desires, the reason finally manifested in state is always right and thus the only way to secure freedom from bondage to the irrational impulses and desires lies in voluntary submission to more perfect impression of the reason manifested in the state. Analysing the meaning of Hegel, Wayper suggests that the state "is the school-master which brings him knowledge of the Spirit, of Absolute Reason. His real will impels him to identify himself with the Spirit. The spirit is embodied in the state. Therefore, it is the real will to obey the dictates of the state."[41]

It follows from above that the state is an infallible institution. It can do wrong and no plea of morality can frustrate or denounce its purpose. Nor is there any standard of international law or external morality that might bind the jurisdiction of state activity. Hegel thus repudiates the case of internationalism. There can be no ground, in theory or practice, for resisting state's decrees in the internal or external spheres, for those over whom it exercises authority are not different from those who exercise it, and its decrees are inspired by the real wills of those who obey him, even though they obey unwillingly. Rejecting the idea of super-national authority, Hegel writes :

40. Hegel : *Philosophy of History*, p. 39.
41. Wayper: *Political Thought*, p. 168.

"The nation-state is mind in its substantive rationality and is therefore the absolute power on earth. It follows that every state is sovereign and autonomous against its neighbours ... There is no Praetor to judge between states; at least there may be an arbitrator, mediator, and even he exercises his functions contingently, i.e., only in dependence on the particular wills of the disputants. It follows if the states disagree and their particular wills cannot be harmonised, the matter can only be settled by war."[42]

In the same context, Hegel admires war and denounces the idea of world peace. In an emergency the state may do as it pleases and as to what constitutes an emergency the state is to judge for itself. In theory at all times but in practice during war, the state may lawfully exercise complete authority over the lives of its citizens. It is the state of war that reveals nation's distinctive qualities and judges the glory and worth of a people. Hegel again writes : "War has the higher significance that by its agency, the ethical health of peoples is preserved in their indifference to the stabilisation of finite institution; just as the blowing of winds preserves the sea from the foulness which would be the product of a prolonged, let alone, perpetual peace .. Sacrifice on behalf of the individuality of the state is the substantial tie between the state and all its members and so is a universal duty ....."[43]

The above explanation is but a step to the clear-cut doctrine of the absolutism of the state. Whereas the state is a self-conscious ethical substance and a self-knowing and self-actualising individual, three somewhat paradoxical conclusions "follow from this conception. Firstly, the state can never act unrepresentatively. Thus the policeman who arrests the burglar and the magistrate who locks him up, are really expressing burglar's real will to be arrested and locked up, the policeman and the magistrate being the executive officials of a state which necessarily represents and expresses the real will of the burglar who is a member of it. In the second place, the

---

42. Hegel : *Philosophy of Right*, paras, 333-34.
43. *Ibid.*, paras 325-28. Hegel believes that a state may, of course, sign treaties with another state, but because there "is no authority above the states and because the relations between them are governed not by universality but by contingency, these relations are continually shifting, and treatises, even if they purport to be binding in perpetuity, become in fact obsolete when the conditions which produced them change." See Stace : *The Philosophy of Hegel*, p. 437.

relations which bind the individual not only to every other individual in the community, but also to the state as a whole, themselves form an integral part of the individual's personality. He would not be what he is without them, and he only is what he is because of them. Thirdly, the state contains within itself and represents the social morality of all its citizens. Just as the personalities of all the individuals in the state are transcended and merged in the personality of the state, so the moral relations which each citizen has to each other citizen are merged in or transcended by the social morality which is vested in the state."[44]

With this Hegel is led to a belief in the divinity of the nation-state. The state is glorified to the extent that it becomes a mystic entity. At Hegel's hands, the state is a self-certain, absolute mind which acknowledges no abstract rules of good or bad, shameful or mean, crafty or deceptive. An idealised version of the *Rupblic* of Plato and that of *Social Contract* of Rousseau reappears when Hegel says : "In considering freedom, the starting point must not be individuality, the single self-consciousness, but only the essence of self-consciousness; for whether man knows it or not, this essence is extremely realised as a self-subsistent power in which single individuals are only moments. The march of God in the world, that is what the state is."[45] Again, he says : "The state is the Divine Idea as it exists on Earth."[46]

However, one very peculiar aspect of Hegel's theory of state lies in the thing that he identifies his ideal state with his non-ideal or imperfect state of Prusia. Like Machiavelli, Hegel's patriotism plays the part and so he exalts his Prussian state simply to stand well with its rulers. His love for the motherland, his exile from the town of Jena, and his enthusiasm for the French Revolution all combined together to inculcate in him the conviction that only militant success would restore the prestige and self-respect of his nation. He thus says : "The German nation, under the influence of Christianity were the first to attain the consciousness that man, as man, is free; that it is the freedom of Spirit which constitutes the essence. The Eastern nations knew only that *one* is free, the Greek and Roman

44. Joad: *Modern Political Theory*, pp. 13-14.
45. Hegel, *op. cit.*, p. 36.
46. *Ibid.*, p. 279.

world only that *some* are free; while we know that *all* men absolutely (man as man) are free."[47]

The sum and substance of the entire explanation finds place in an attempt to justify the absolute character of state authority. To Hegel the state is not like an association of ordinary human beings; it is a Divine Idea or a mystic entity incapable of doing any wrong. It is infallible, supreme and omnipotent entitled to secure every sacrifice which its interest may require of the individual. In other words, it is an end in itself, while the individual is the means who can be sacrificed at its altar. Among the social institutions that must nominate the mankind, the society is more important and higher than the society. Hegel insists that every account of the nature of state is inadequate until it postulates that the individual "can utilise his potentialities as a man only by participating in the life of a great whole. And this greater whole is for Hegel, as it was for Plato and Aristotle, political society or the state."[48]

Hegel's theory of state may be subjected to three main lines of criticism :

1. Hegelian theory of state is too philosophical, abstract and metaphysical. Not only the phraseology is bombastic, Hegel in very abstract terms attributes to the state a personality of its own distinct from that of the nation and teaches us about its omnipotence, absolutism and divine character. The jargon of philosophical language sacrifices the inde-

47. Hegel : *Philosophy of History*, paras 18-19. Keeping it in view, Dr. Lancaster says : "His views on state absolutism, moreover, reflected German experience–an experience through which he had himself lived–as well as the constitutional history of Germany on which he had a realistic grasp. In that history there had been no revolution to throw into relief the kinds of ideas of individual rights that had been important in both French and English history. In the Germanies there had been cultural nationalism, but this had not been accompanied by the sort of political unity long existent in Britain and France. Such a unity had to be imposed by force upon dozens of provincial populations and rulers." *op. cit.*, p. 46.

48. F.C. Copleston : "Hegel" in Maurice Cranston (ed.) : *Western Political Philosophers*, p. 66. Bringing out the essential implications of this statement, G.A. Kelly remarks : "Formally the state comprehends, enables, satisfies; it is the vessel of the *gemeines Leben*, the materialisation of Volksgeist (world spirit). When Hegel says that a concept is 'divine' or is a concrete 'universal', we must understand him as saying that it is something man cannot do without, if he is to fulfil his humanity, a 'situation' that he cannot be abstracted from. The state is pre-eminently a concept of this kind. Hegel also calls the state 'a temple of human freedom'." *Idealism, Politics and History*. p. 327.

pendence and autonomy of the individual at its all-embracing power, denies to him not only the inalienable right of resistance but even the right to question the legitimacy or moral rightfulness of the authority or conduct of the state. Man is certainly a rational creature, but rationalism should not be over-emphasised. The rationalism on the basis of which Hegel constructs the entire theory of state is definitely beyond the understanding of a common man. Rightly Hegel does not deal with the things as they are and the state of which he conceives, resting on the free consent and co-operation of the moral will of every citizen, "may be laid up in heaven, but it is not established on earth."[49]

2. As a corollary to the above, it may be pointed out that Hegel's repudiation of internationalism cannot be accepted. His idealisation of war and his denunciation of world peace as well as his rejection of international law and world morality all are false and pernicious. Though an idealist, Green did great service by calling the necessity of war as 'cruel'. Both Kant and Green advocated the cause of internationalism. But, in this regard, Hegel's point of view invites nothing but gross denunciation. That is why, Hegel has been worshipped as a prophet by the war-mongers. On the contrary, all peace-loving philosophers and statesmen have despised Hegel's philosophy.[50] Owing to this, Prof. Copleston treats it as 'an unpleasant feature of Hegel's political theory, and admires both Kant and Green for their support to the cause of federation of mankind.[51]

49. Barker, *op. cit.*, p. 91.
50. So strong was the aversion of Prof. Hobhouse towards the political philosophy of Hegel that in one of his letters to his son, he thus wrote : "In the bombing of London I had just witnessed the visible and tangible outcome of a false and wicked doctrine, the foundation of which lay, as I believe in the book before me. To combat this doctrine effectively is to take such part in the fight as the physical disabilities of middle age allow. Hegel himself carried the proof sheet of his first work to the printer through streets crowded with fugitives from the field of Jena. With that work began the most penetrating and subtle of all the intellectual influences which have sapped the rational humanitarianism of the eighteenth and nineteenth centuries, and in the Hegelian theory of the god-state all that I had witnessed lay implicit." *op. cit.*, p. 6.
51. Copleston *op. cit.*, p. 97. A great internationalist like Laski very rightly says : "The notion of an independent sovereign state is on the international side fatal to the well being of humanity. The way in which a state should live its life in relation to other states is clearly not a matter in which the state is entitled to be the sole judge. The common life of states is a matter

top and gradually sinking downwards, rather than rising from the bottom to the top. Or, to put the matter in other words, Hegel, like Carlyle, craved a social and political hierarchy, the many being guided and controlled by the few, and the few in turn being subordinated to one–the supreme head of the state."[56]

In his discussion of the constitution of the state, Hegel recognises three organs of government–legislative, executive and the crown. Two things deserve special mention here. First, Hegel does not believe in the separation of powers, for each organ is not self-subsistent or hostile to the other. Second, the whole is more real than the part, i.e., one organ cannot be entrusted with all the powers. In other words, Hegel does not believe that one organ of government can have an independent character of its own. Rather his dialectical interpretation curiously treats the legislature as the thesis, executive as the anti-thesis, and the crown representing the synthesis of the two.

In regard to legislature, Hegel says that its authority is vested in the Estates Assemblies. But the legislature should not be thoroughly representative of the people. It should consist of only those persons who are capable of and have profound comprehension and insight. Besides, the legislature should be bicameral - one house composed of the land-owners and the other of the representatives chosen by professional and cultural associations. However, Hegel does not assign to the legislature the right of acting as a powerful check upon the executive. The legislature can neither appoint nor dismiss the executive, for it is the sole concern of the monarch. The legislature is to act as an advisory body to the bureaucracy. Even with respect to the legislation itself, the legislature is to confine itself to proposing general rules to be given legal effect by the sovereign and detailed application by the body of civil servants. But the executive function of the legislature is to serve as teachers to the people so that healthy public opinion is formulated and expressed. It appears that Hegel does not want to place legislature on a strong pedestal; he urges that the government should largely be conducted by the decrees of executive with a minimum of oversight by the legislature.

56. McGovern : *From Luther to Hitler*, p. 321.

The executive occupies a very strong position in Hegel's theory of government. In effect, it consists of the permanent civil servants chosen for their demonstrated ability and serving in good behaviour. The executive represents the general will and reason of society. Curiously enough, Hegel admits that there may exist unions, corporations or other units of local administration, but the bureaucracy has the right to direct, control and superintend their activity.[57] The civil service is not responsible to the legislature, rather its organisation lies within the jurisdiction of monarch's authority. In Hegel's view, the highest civil servants necessarily have a deeper and more comprehensive insight into the nature of state's organisation and requirements and that they are also more habituated to the business of government and have greater skill in it, so that even without the legislature they are able to do what is best. It follows that the laws should normally be proposed by the higher civil servants and the legislature should perform the functions of presenting the former such urgent needs of society as might have escaped their notice and calling their attention to public criticism likely to be directed to their administration of affairs. Hegel wants that the law should take the form of general prescriptions, the detailed application of which should be made by the civil servants on their own responsibility subject to royal intervention in cases of abuse of authority.

Finally, there is the place of the crown. The crown represents the synthesis of the legislature being the thesis and the executive being its anti-thesis. As such, the monarch becomes the sovereign in practice holding absolute authority in his hands. The king is the element in the constitution that makes the government coherent. Without king the people are like a formless mass and no longer a state. Hegel very specifically lays down that only during emergencies is the personal will of the ruler to be decisive; under all ordinary circumstances government is to be carried out by the ministers and the bureaucracy. Yet in Hegel's system the king being sovereign stands at the

57. This shows that Hegel is in agreement with the federal character of social organisation and thus admits something which contradicts the case of state absolutism. Its reason should be traced in the influence of French Revolution on him. Lancaster says : "On the contrary, Hegel showed a tenderness for these primary groups in human society which makes it impossible to regard him as a fore- runner of modern totalitarianism. His state is indeed authoritarian, but there were fields of human concern from which he felt compelled to exclude it." *op. cit.*, p. 57.

apex whose authority is unlimited in theory during normal times and in practice during the days of national emergency. Hegel says : "The sovereign is entrusted with the salvation of the state at the sacrifice of these particular authorities whose powers are valid at other times, and it is then that the ideality comes into its proper actuality."[58]

Hegel's theory of government may also be criticised. It does not put the judiciary in a separate position which is now universally recognised as an integral part of the government. Like other French writers, Hegel also builds his theory on the premises of duality theory according to which political organisation has only two organs - the legislature and the executive, judiciary being an adjunct of the latter. Then, it is also clear that Hegel's theory stands for the justification of bourgeois aristocracy. His purpose appears to be to create a substitute for a part of the aristocratic governing class a class recruited by birth and disposed to look upon office as private property. The whole system resembles neither the parliamentary nor the presidential models which have now received universal recognition; rather a philosophical defence of the bourgeois civil service necessitates the entire attempt. Thus, Lancaster observes that Hegel "is pleading for a neutral civil service lifted above the sordid struggles of civil society and given dignity and moral authority by its responsibility to a monarch mystically conceived as the personification of the national culture and the national spirit. It was in many ways a noble conception, if in the end powerless in the face of the harsh realities of bureaucratic power."[59]

CRITICAL APPRECIATION : HEGEL AS THE RECONSTRUCTOR OF MODERN POLITICAL THOUGHT

In the history of political thought Hegel has been both denounced and lauded by the text-book writers and commentators. The greatest charge that is levelled against him is the unintelligible way in which he expressed his ideas. A noted German philosopher and a contemporary of Hegel, Schopenhauer, rejects rationalism and emphasises in its place his intuitionism. His attack on Hegel is highly devastating when he says : "Hegel installed from above, by the powers that be, as the Certified Great Philosopher, was a flat-headed, insipid,

58. Lancaster, *op. cit*, p. 65.
59. Lancaster *op. cit.*, p. 65.

nauseating, illiterate charlatan who reached the pinnacles of audacity in scribbling together and dishing up the craziest mystifying nonsense. This nonsense has been noisily proclaimed as immortal wisdom by mercenary followers and readily accepted as such by all fools, who thus joined into a perfect chorus of denunciation as had never been heard before. The extensive field of spiritual influence with which Hegel was furnished by those in power has enabled him to achieve the intellectual corruption of a whole generation."[60] Another critic thus remarks : "But the height of audacity in serving up pure nonsense, in stringing to other senseless and extravagant mazes of words, such as had previously been known only in mad houses, was finally reached in Hegel, and because the instrument of the most barefaced general mystification that has ever taken place, with a result which will appear fabulous to posterity, and will remain as a monument to German stupidity."[61] An uncompromising critic of Hegel, Prof. Popper thus concludes with a note of warning : "The Hegelian farce has done enough harm. We must stop it. We must speak–even at the price of soiling ourselves by touching this scandalous thing which, unfortunately without success, was so clearly exposed a hundred years ago."[62]

But Hegel has his admirers as well who have ranked him among one of the greatest philosophers of the world. Hegel's dialectical method sought to bridge up the gulf between reason, fact and value (which had completely been sundered by Hume) and it showed the way for Karl Marx. During his tenure of professorship, the university of Berlin became the intellectual centre of Germany. Several well-known thinkers like Marx, Schopenhauer, Nietzsche, Trietschke, Bernhardi, Droysen, Green, Bradley, Bosanquet and Savigny drew inspiration from him in varying degrees. Out of the translations of his works in other languages, several schools developed in various other countries of the world which are still known by the names of Hegelianism and Neo-Hegelianism. Men like Augusto Vera, Benedotto Croce and Gentili popularised Hegelianism in Italy by emphasising the glorification of the nation-state. Even in America the influence of Hegel appeared on Morris, Palmer, Royce and John Dewey.

60. *Ibid.*
61. Caird : *Hegel*, p. 18.
62. Popper, *op. cit.*, p. 273.

John Dewey thus concludes : "For a period Hegelian thought was almost supreme in Germany. Then its rule passed away almost as rapidly as it had been achieved. After various shiftings, the trend of philosophic thought was definitely 'Back to Kant'. Kant's greater sobriety, the sharp distinction he drew between the realm of phenomena and science and the ideal world, commended him after the unbridled pretensions of Hegelian absolutism. For more than a generation Hegel was spoken of with almost universal contempt. Nevertheless, his ideas loosed from the technical apparatus with which he surrounded them, persisted upon the historical disciplines. His influence was peculiarly deep and abiding. He fixed the pieces of Fichte and fastened them together with the pin of evolution. Since his days histories of philosophy or religion or institutions have all been treated as developments through necessary stages of an inner implicit idea or purpose according to an indwelling law. And an idea of a peculiar mission and destiny of German history has lost nothing in the operation. Exasperation which a bewildered world has sought since the beginning of the war to explain through the influence of a Darwinian struggle for existence and survival of the fittest, or through the influence of a Nietzschean philosophy of power, have their roots in the classic idealistic philosophy culminating in Hegel."[63]

Hegel's influence is not limited to theoretical side alone; it took a practical shape as well. His ideas served as an official philosophy and Bismarck carried out in fact what Hegel and his students expressed and demanded. Till the days of Hitler, Hegel's political philosophy lived like a gospel truth in Germany. Leaving aside the charge that Hegel wrote for the sake of absolutism, it cannot be denied that he did great service to political thought by laying stress upon the significance of nation-state without which man cannot realise his true nature and freedom. By idealising the nature and character of political authority, Hegel continued the tradition of Plato, Aristotle and

63. Dewey, *op. cit.*, pp. 136-137. As Hegel says : "Philosophy by its very nature is something esoteric which is not made for the mob, nor is it capable of being prepared for the mob. Philosophy is philosophy to the extent that it is the very opposite of the intellect and even more the opposite of commonsense, the world of philosophy as such is a world turned upside down. For the beginning of philosophy must be lifting oneself up above the kind of truth given by common consciousness, the premonition of a higher truth." See *Hannah Arendt's Lectures on Kant's Political Philosophy* ed. by Ronald Biener, p. 35.

Rousseau. Sabine thus admirably comments : "The philosophy of Hegel aimed at nothing less than a complete and systematic reconstruction of modern thought."[64]

After Hegel the idealist tradition in Germany continued, but no other philosopher could match or supersede his excellence. Certain elements of the Hegelian conception of state found adherents in other German writers and militarists like Nietzsche, Trietschke and Bernhardi who preached the nobility and indispensability of warfare, rejected internationalism and apotheosised the nation-state of Germany. Among them the name of Trietschke is more important who pronounced Hegel as 'the first real political personality among the German political philosophers' and idolised the Machiavellian dictum that the state is power. Trietschke expressed serious contempt for the small and weak states and eulogised imperialistic expansionism by maintaining that the first duty of the state is to make itself strong and powerful. Coupled with these ideas, the other disciples alike laid stress on the self-assertive, aggressive and militant character of the state. These idealists did not stop here : they even enjoined upon a strong and civilised state to impose its ideology upon the weak and backward states. It is owing to this that the intellectual guilt of the first great war is attributed to the teachings of Hegel's disciples. These later intespretations contradicted much what Hegel had said in the nineteenth century and thus defamed the idealistic system in the present century. J.W. Garner rightly says : "It is only fair to Hegel, however, to state that his philosophy was far less brutal and materialistic than that of Trietschke and that many of the latter's conclusions can hardly be said to have had anything in common with the Hegelian philosophy."[65]

64. G.H. Sabine: *A History of Political Theory*, Ch. 31.
65. Garner: *Political Science and Government*, p. 234.

29

GREEN

All through he (Green) is considering what the state can and therefore should do to secure the conditions within which men can act as free moral beings. But the poles of his thought are still the individual and the state. He does not consider how both are affected by the existence of other associations, with the instrumentalities than political law. Had he done so, he would have seen that the problem is not simply what the state should do but also what the state is permitted to do, surrounded as it is by other powers, limited as it is by definite organisation of other kinds, fulfilling functions of their own in ways of their own. Green remains on the verge of the modern problem of sovereignty.

— **R.M. MacIver**[1]

Thomas Hill Green, first tutor at the Balliol College and later Whyte Professor of Moral Philosopher at the University of Oxford, well contributed to the change in the history of English liberalism of the nineteenth century.[2] He was born in

1. MacIver : *The Modern State*, p. 471.
2. It should be noted here that while English political thought was dominated by the trends of liberalism in the nineteenth century, this term had its different implications to different thinkers of different periods. It arose as a reaction against the philosophy of absolute monarchy and thus it stood for freedom and democracy in its essentials. It is correctly stated : "At first

Yorkshire in an Anglican parson's family in 1836. But having spent the first fourteen years of his life in his home town, he moved to Rugby where he stayed for about six years. He finally settled down in Oxford. Besides, being a professor of philosophy, he also took part in the social and political life of his country. Unlike an academic recluse, he served as a member of the Oxford School Board, Oxford Town Council and joined governmental committee on secondary education. He was instrumental in founding the City Oxford School for Boys and opening a coffee shop in Oxford to check the evil practice of drinking alcohol. His political career witnessed his close touch with the liberal school of John Bright. In addition, as a social reformer, he actively participated in the educational and temperance campaigns. He undertook injection work in Birmingham schools. However, by temperament he was a sober rather inarticulate and a slow worker but a possessor of fillipant disregard for contemporary views. His active association with these many-sided activities exercised a moudling effect on his thought. In 1882 he died of scepticaemia at the young age of forty six.

WORKS : A MARKED SHIFT IN THE TREND OF LIBERALISM

From Germany idealism went over to England and became popular in the writings of Green, Bradley and Bosanquet. The English idealism, however, also got the name of Neo-Hegelianism for the simple reason that the English idealists drew heavily from the Hegelian system. The influence of Kant was there, but the influence of Hegel outweighted it. Yet it should be remembered that, in spite of this British idealism was not without the native traditions of its own liberalism. And if it was called Neo-Hegelianism it was not all Hegelianism, though it was much more than semi-Hegelianism or pseudo-Hegelianism. Among the English idealists Bradley and Bosanquet maintained closer affinity with Hegel as compared to Green, but even on them the stamp of English traditions sur-

---

sight the most striking thing about the liberal tradition is its intellectual incoherence. No one would reasonably deny the name of Liberal to any of the men represented in this connection, yet each of them Fox and Bentham, Richard Cobden and Lloyd John Russell, Macaulay and Acton, Herbert Spencer and T.H. Green, Gladstone and Lloyd Geroge, Mill and Keynes held views widely different in some respect from those of programmes - those are more easily explained - but also of principle, for example, on the role of the state, the vcxed question of *laissez faire*." Allan Bullock and Maurice Shock (eds.) : *The Liberal Traditions from Fox to Keynes*, p. xix.

vived as a result of which British idealism exhibited a fundamental continuity with the liberal thought coming from the days of John Locke. Of course, if the English idealists were the followers of German idealism, they were also the suceessors of the Utilitarian tradition. The master of Balliol, Dr. A.D. Lindsay, has correctly held that so far as their social and political theories were concerned, the idealists of England "are all of them, for their Platonism and Hegelianism, in the succession of the Utilitarians."[3]

The political philosophy of Green is contained in his *Prolegomena to Ethics, Lectures on the Principles of Political Obligation* and *Liberal Legislation and the Freedom of Contract*.[4] His political philosophy reveals on him a deep influence of the ancient Greeks, like Plato and Aristotle, yet among the immediate ones it shows his debt to Rousseau of France, Kant and Hegel of Germany, and Benjamin Jowett of England. In the main, it seems that Green brought forth an idealistic revision of the nineteenth century liberal tradition in as much as he rejected the Benthamite liberalism in the name of its materialistic and egotistic connotations and replaced it with a new form wearing an idealistic apparel. However, at bottom, he was a democrat and an individualist like Bentham and John Stuart Mill, and yet in stead of equating human purpose with material happiness and reducing individual to a bundle of earthly pleasure and pains, he, as his biographer says, endeavoured "to awaken a consciousness of what man actually is and does certain functions of his everyday life, this being, as he conceived, true way to awaken the further consciousness of what he ought to be and do."[5]

Two important points engage our attention at this stage. First, a look at the writings of Green shows a peculiar amalgam of metaphysics, ethics and politics all forming a systematic whole. Keeping it in view, Metz observes that of all these parts, "ethics is the critical one ... it bears the weight of his system, is preceded ... by the metaphysics which itself is preceded by a theory of knowledge and issued in a doctrine of the state, of

3. F.J.C. Hearnshaw (ed.) : *The Social and Political Ideas of Some Representative Thinkers of the Victorian Age*, p. 151.
4. Green's political philosophy is almost wholly contained in his *Lectures on the Principles of Political Obligation*, included in Vol. II of *Works*, edited by R.L. Nettleship and also issued as a separate volume with a Preface by Dr. Bernard Bosanquet.
5. See Barker : *Political Thought in England*, p. 22.

moral conditions of social life..."[6] The system of Green "is about the nature of reality. Man is a person of moral being; the state is a multiplicity of such beings, and God is a being from whom all the rest derive their meaning."[7]

Second, Green gives a remarkable turn to the prevailing trend of liberalism. Metz holds that when German idealism "made its way into England, it turned the philosophic rudder in an entirely new direction."[8] However, Dockhorn is one of those critics who allege that British idealism represents a departure from the tradition of idealism. His argument is that when the salient characteristic of English liberalism is the worth and dignity of the independent individual, it cannot be reconciled with the philosophy of idealism where organic theory submerges the individual with the society and exalts the supremacy of the nation-state. Even Rudolph Metz has agreed with the view that English idealism represented a complete break with the native liberal tradition, for it asked the individual to lose himself in a mystic union with the superior unity of the state. However, such observations ignore the fact that British idealists never justified an autocratic political system and preferred their parliamentarianism to continental dictatorship. E.P. Harris in a very strong language thus affirms that the social philosophy of British neo-Idealism "exhibits a fundamental continuity with British liberal thought from the time of Locke. The problem running as a single thread throughout this tradition is that of the status of the individual in the great society of which his opportunities, rights and duties are to be. In the seventeenth century, the battle of Parliament and King having been brought to a decisive issue the attempt was made to determine the political power of the British citizen; and in the eighteenth and early nineteenth centuries the idealists emphasised men as social beings and the problem of their 'perfection'. In each case, an ethical theory was elaborated to make a place for socialised individuality; and in each, changes in practice, in associations and in institutions were insisted upon that would make individualism something more than mere theory."[9]

6. Rudolph Metz : *A Hundred Years of British Philosophy*, p. 275.
7. Frank Thakurdas : *The English Utilitarians and the Idealists*, p. 227.
8. Metz, *op. cit.*, p. 327.
9. Harris : *The Neo-Idealist Political Theory : Its Continuity with British Tradition*, p. 1.

REJECTION OF UTILITARIANISM : RE-INTEGRATION OF INDIVIDUAL AND SOCIETY

The days of Green were distinctly different from those of Jeremy Bentham. We have seen that even John Stuart Mill had visualised that the philosophy of Benthamite utilitarianism could not satisfy the new urges of the people arising out of social progress. The parliamentary reform movement, the rise of Chartism and the newer socio-economic conditions engineered by the Industrial Revolution necessitated the advent of a new political philosophy. It clearly refused to worship the negative liberty of the individual, because it was proving destructive to the real liberty of the common man. A revolution of ideas had actually come to take place that preferred to emphasise the moral well-being and betterment of the whole people. It also conceived in terms of social, instead of individual, well-being and instead of starting a central individual to whom the social system was suposed to be adjusted according to Benthamite liberalism, it proceeded from a central social system in which the individual was supposed to find his appointed orbit of duty.

Naturally, Green drew inspiration from Rousseau and Hegel and thus rejected Bentham and Mill. He was convinced that Benthamite utilitarianism had grown barren as a political creed and its doctrines of reform and liberty were merely bulwarks of reaction and privilege. He insisted that the ideals of Benthamism were inadequate and that no further progress could be made in an understanding of politics till a new philosophic basis was found for liberalism. This new basis was the basis of emerging 'collectivistic' trends which demanded that the state should no longer confine itself to the rigid idea of *laissez faire*, rather address itself to the more positive function of public good. Since Green adhered to this new tendency and since he reaffirmed the notion of organic relationship between the individual and the community, his ideas dominated the English political thought at the expense of Benthamite liberalism.[10]

Distinctly opposed to Bentham and Mill, Green adopts an ethical point of view. He expresses his dismay and dis-satisfaction over the progress of the society caused by the Industrial Revolution. Hence, he criticises the new social system in which the newly prosperous class enjoyed the benefits and privileges

10. Barker, *op. cit.*, p. 4.

at the cost of others who were still deprived of them. He sternly warns that it is hard to square igonorance, poverty and moral depravity with any kind of real freedom. In the first of his lectures on political obligation, he expresses his uneasiness with eloquence in these words : "To an Athenian slave who might be used to gratify a master's lust, it would have been a mockery to speak of the state as the realisation of freedom; and perhaps it would not be much less so to speak of it as such to an untaught and underfed denizen of a London yard, with gin shops on the right hand and on the left."[11]

Different from the utilitarian standard of the greatest good of the greatest number, Green suggests that the real function of the government is to maintain conditions of life in which morality shall be possible. As morality consisted in the performance of self-imposed duties, "paternalistic government did its best to make it impossible by narrowing the room for the self-imposition of duties and the play of disinterested motives."[12] Yet Green does not wholly reject the central idea of *laissez faire*. He sanctions that the individual should be allowed to make his own choice and concedes that early liberal legislation had been on the whole directed to that end. But the change which he wants to bring forth is to reorientate liberalism to suit the new conditions of society. He advances the notion of positive liberty and thus his criticism amounts to the charge that *laissez faire* "is only the defence of class interests, and as such ignores the general welfare."[13]

In short, the purpose of Green is to reintegrate the individual with those socially created values which the unhistorical Benthamites had ignored. Giving an idealistic version to the school of liberalism, he strongly holds that as the individual is the source of all spiritual values, he should be considered in his universality. Like Plato, Aristotle, Rousseau and Hegel, he adopts an organic point of view and thus studies the case of individual in terms of his social existence. Hence, he rejects the thesis of Bentham that the community is a fictitious multitude of people and in its place outlines a new sphere of individual liberty reconciled with political authority. He disfavours both unfettered individualism as well as unrestrained paternalism and yet he feels that a point of compromise can possibly be

11. Green : *Political Obligation*, Sec. 18, p. 40.
12. *Ibid.*
13. Lancaster : *Masters of Political Thought*, Vol. III, p. 213.

established between the two. This standpoint is clearly visible in his theory of liberty when he says : "If the ideal of true freedom is the maximum of power for all members of a human society alike to make the best of themselves, we are rightful in refusing to ascribe the glory of freedom to a state in which the apparent elevation of the few is founded upon the degration of the many, and in ranking modern society, founded as it is on free industry with all its confusion and ignorant license and waste of effort above the most splendid of ancient republics."[14]

Throwing light upon the same fact, Dr. A.D. Lindsay says: "The individual in Benthamite philosophy was reduced to a bundle of pleasures or desires, and the state to a collection of independent atoms. When the progress of the industrial revolution disappointed the facile optimism of the early Utilitarians, their individualistic creed, which had in the early part of the century been a doctrine of reform and liberty, became largely a bulwark of reaction and privilege. It demanded reform in the early days on the ground that if unwise state restrictions and interference were not removed, the natural harmony of economic interests would ensure that all would be well. When these restrictions had been removed and *laissez faire* largely realised, the doctrine was used to oppose any attempt to deal with the disharmonies of economic interests. Utilitarianism had done all that it could, but democracy, more alive than ever, was faced with any number of new and unexpected problems. If democracy was to grapple with these new problems with any success, some way had to be found for reconciling true individualism with any new functions which were being thrust upon the state."[15]

POLITICAL OBLIGATION : WILL, NOT FORCE, AS THE BASIS OF STATE

Green's theory of state has been influenced by four main sources - Greek, French, German and English. The first inspiration is that of the Greeks, Plato and Aristotle, and its reason finds place in his career at the Oxford. The lessons of the Greek classics that man is a social, political and rational creature, that state is a moralising agency, that law is an expression of pure and passionless reason, and that justice

14. Cited *Ibid.*, p. 214.
15. Refer to his 'Introduction' in Dr. Bosanquet (ed.) : *Political Obligation*, pp.vii-viii.

demands each to perform his duty honestly by staying at the appointed place in the community and the like have had a peculiarly deep influence there. The second influence on Green is that of Rousseau of France who rediscovered the teachings of the Greek classics and, once again, reaffirmed that man is a rational being and the basis of political authority lies not in force or divine sanction but in the will of the people. The third great influence is that of the German idealists who built their political philosophy on the foundations of rationalism and metaphysics. From Kant, Green borrowed the ideas of individual freedom, the worth and dignity of the individual person, and of internationalism; but from Hegel he learnt that there 'is one spiritual self-conscious being of which all that is real is the activity or expression; that we are related to this being not merely as parts of the world which is its expression, but as partakers in some inchoate measure of the self-consciousness through which it at once constitutes and distinguishes itself from the world; and that this participation is the source of morality and religion'. Finally, Green was influenced by the doctrines of English Non-Conformists who taught the lessons of freedom and advocated reforms in the social and religious life of the people.

As a result, Green's theory of state contains much of what he draws from these sources. At the same time, Green does not borrow from them copiously, he leaves much of them as well. The peculiar thing about his theory of state is that it exhibits a fusion of all these influences in such a way that English liberalism undergoes a serious transformation. Starting from a metaphysical foundation, Green comes to the conclusion that the basis of political authority lies in human consciousness. The state is rooted in the will but it cannot be autocratic or misrepresentative, otherwise resistance to its authority is justified. This is very beautifully summed up by Barker in these words : "Human consciousness postulates liberty : liberty involves rights : rights demand the state."[16] Each phrase is meaningful and for this an explanation may be thus furnished:

(i) Human Consciousness : Green starts with a metaphysical point that consciousness is the distinctive characteristic of human beings. This quality makes the humankind different from other species. It makes man conscious of other things as well as aware of his ownself. It follows that man is some-

16. Barker, *op. cit.*, p. 23.

thing more than merely a part of nature - he is endowed with a free intelligence, a self-realising and self-distinguishing consciousness. Hence, his personality cannot be explained merely in naturalistic terms, nor can he be treated as a bundle of earthly peasures and satisfactions. The true good of man lies in the full realisation of the divine element which is the special trait of his personality. Obviously, Green rejects the ethics of Epicureanism, Hedonism and Utilitarianism. According to Metz, "The individual consciousness is said to be the medium of instrument of the universal consciousness, and to have some sort of participation in the latter, but of the manner of this participion we are told nothing more than the eternal consciousness is communicated to us under the limitations imposed by our bodies."[17]

Green's metaphysical approach takes something from Kant and blends it with the postulates of Hegel. He starts with the Kantian thesis that the nature of the ultimate reality can be comprehended with the aid of pure reason with occasional flashes of intuition and not by the empirical or inductive method. However, Green does not accept the Kantian view of things-in-themselves as the source of the material side of knowledge. Agreeing with Fichte and Hegel, he holds that the world around us which we know must be of the same stuff as the knowing-self, it must be spiritual in character. Just as the eternal self reproducing itself in men, unites sensations with knowledge, so the permanent moral self-consciousness - theoretical and practical - one makes knowledge possible and the other gives purpose and direction to human motivation. Harris thus points out : "Green's metaphysics of knowledge and his theory of the moral will are simply one way of expressing the significant fact of man's having unique capacities and of their attempting to exploit them."[18]

17. Metz, *op. cit.*, pp. 276-277. Similarly, Harris says : "In his ethics as in his theory of knowledge Green reacted against the atomistic interpretation that he found represented in empiricism and, above all, in utilitarianism. A theory of ethics could not be based upon a set of pleasure and pains, particularly when that amounted a reduction of all motives for conduct to a mere group of isolated sanctions." *Op. cit.*, p. 19.

18. *Ibid.*, p. 20. In this conviction of Green lay the roots of his struggle with the materialistic implications of evolutionary science and naturalistic ethics. Green's theory of moral self-consciousness need have been no more than his way of showing that men "are motivated by an idea of personal

(ii) Freedom : Green's conception of freedom bears upon him the influence of Rousseau and Hegel. As a corollary to the above, Green argues that human consciousness postulates freedom as the necessary condition of its very growth and expression. However, Green takes a positive view of freedom and in this respect his approach is distinctly different from that of Mill, the individualist and Kant, the idealist. In one of his lectures delivered at Leicester in 1881, he defines freedom thus : "When we speak of freedom as something to be so highly prized, we mean a positive power or capacity of doing or enjoying something worth doing or enjoying, and that too something that we do or enjoy in common with others. We mean by it a power which each man exercises through the help or security given to him by his fellowmen, and which he, in turn, helps to secure for them."[19]

In Green's view, freedom has got two qualities - it is positive and implies title to do something and not a title for having something done to one; it is determinate, i.e., a freedom to do something of a definite character or something which possesses the quality of being worth doing. Obviously, like Hegel, Green believes that freedom being positive can be realised only in and through participation in the life of the state. Green maintains that freedom does not lie in merely obeying the dictates of self-imposed imperative of duty, rather it depends upon the nature of the object which the individual makes his own and upon his ability to identify himself with it. In other words, it means that the individual is free only when he sets his ownself against those impulses which do not tend to his true good. In short, freedom signifies the liberation of the powers of man for promoting the social good. Sabine thus points out that freedom means an actual possibility, and a view of existing circumstances, about developing human capacities and a genuinely increased power on the part of an individual to share in the goods which the society has produced and an enlarged ability "to contribute to the common good."[20]

(iii) Rights : Then, liberty involves rights. From here Green proceeds to enunciate his theory of rights. The self-con-

---

good which they seek to realise in action." *Ibid*.

19. Green : "Liberal Legislation and the Freedom of Contract" in Bullock and Shock, *op. cit.*, p. 181.
20. Sabine : *A History of Political Theory*, p. 674.

sciousness of man wills good both in respect of itself as well as of otherselves. It wills the goodness of its relations with others; it wills the goodness of society which is constituted by such relations. Hence, when each recognises his own goodself and at the same time recognises the good self of others, a system of rights comes into being. When an individual makes a claim out of his self-consciousness, he knows that it shall automatically be recognised by others for the very claim stands for the good of hisown as well as for the good of others. Hence, when a claim is recognised by others, it becomes a right. Barker thus puts : "Claims thus recognised are translated into rights, and it is such recognition that constitutes them right. Thus, if we care to make the distinction, we may say that rights have a double aspect. On the one hand, a right is the claim of an individual, arising from the nature of self-consciousness, for permission to will his own ideal objects; on the other hand, it is the recognition of that claim by society and there and thereby, the addition of a new power to pursue these objects."[21]

One important point should be noted here. When Green uses the term recognition, he does not adopt a juristic point of view like that of Hobbes, Bentham and Austin. His concern is with the ideal rights which a society properly organised on the basis of the good will should ideally recognise if it is true to its own basic principles. These rights are relative to morality, for they are the conditions of the attainment of the moral end; and the recognition is given by moral consciousness, because it knows that they are the necessary conditions of its own satisfaction. In short, Green believes in the moral recognition of the community and not in the legal recognition of a legislative body. The rights may, however, take a legal shape if the moral consciousness of the community is translated by the legislature into the form of statutes. On the whole, the rights of which Green speaks are more relative to morality rather than law; they have a moral character, although they may assume a legal character as well. Barker thus clarifies : "On the one hand, the rights of which Green speaks are so far related to law that they can be and ultimately are embodied in law : and they are so far related to morality that their value lies in their service to the moral end, and their source is to be found in the moral con-

21. Barker, *op. cit.*, p. 25.

sciousness of man. On the other hand, they are distinct from law, because the actual rights embodied in the actual law of a community never square with an ideal system; and they are distinct from morality, because they are enforceable (whether or not they are actually enforced) by external sanctions, and morality is not and cannot be thus enforced."[22]

(iv) Need for Political Authority : Like Rousseau, Green admits of the need for political authority. It is true that man actuated by his selfless or real will should move on the right path; he would not like to do or enjoy what is unworthy of doing or enjoying, but even then the selfish or the actual will might operate and then compel him to do or enjoy what is not worth doing or enjoying in common with others. Hence, the rights need security and for this sake, state enters into the system of Green. If a man violates the system of rights, the state is there to use force against him so that the freedom is preserved. However, by using force, the basis of political authority is not changed, it is still the will of the people. The use of force by the state becomes essential in order to maintain the system of rights which the moral consciousness of the community makes up.

With this interpretation Green justifies that will, not force, is the basis of the state. If human consciousness postulates freedom and creates rights, it also sanctions political authority for the maintenance of those rights. Green asserts that the ultimate moving force which inspires and controls political action is the spiritual force of common conviction that alone constitutes the paraphernalia of political authority. It then enjoins upon the sovereign to maintain the system of rights and create conditions favourable for the sustenance of moral consciousness of the community. Barker says : "Conviction or conscience at once creates rights, creates the law or system of rules by which those rights are maintained, and creates the sovereign whose mission it is to enunciate and enforce that law, and to sustain in full vigour and in complete harmony with one another all the living institutions which are the concrete embodiment of rights and law."[23]

It leads to Green's idea of sovereignty. From the above it follows that Green, like Hobbes, does not regard sovereignty as the coercive power of the state distinguishing it from all other

22. *Ibid.*, p. 27.
23. *Ibid.*, p. 29.

associations of society. Nor, like Austin, does he agree with its location in a determinate human superier who receives habitual obedience from the bulk of a given society and is not in the habit of obedience to a like superior. Green locates sovereignty in the general will and while he accepts the Austinian dictum that sovereign should be a determinate person, he rejects the view that the basis of political obligation lies in fear or compulsion. Rather, he asserts that the real determinant of the habitual obedience is the moral conviction of the people. The consciousness informs the people that the laws of the state are meant for their own good and the sovereign embodies and expresses the general will of the community. It is the power which sustains and guarantees the social and political institutions of the society which are the precondition of the existence of rights. It is for this sake that sovereign uses coercive authority. In short, presence of a sovereign is necessary for the existence of a political community; its basis is rooted in the general will, and its supereme coercive authority is necessary for the protection of a common system of rights and obligations.[24]

However, by general will Green means the common consciousness of the common good. Society exists in the consciousness of a common good or interest. If so, the state does not arise out of the social contract; it is the result of the desire of men for a common good and so it is the indispensable condition of its realisation. The desire is present in the mind of every citizen, though in a quite rudimentary form. It is present and operates much in the same way in which the idea of moral obligation is present and operative. Green is very emphatic on the point that

24. Green thus says : "The sovereign should be regarded not in an abstraction as the wielder of coercive force, but in connection with the whole complex of institutions of political society. It is as their sustainer, and thus the agent of the general will, that the sovereign power must be presented to the minds of the people. If it is to command habitual loyal obedience, and obedience will scarcely be habitual unless it is loyal and forced." *Op. cit.*, Sec. 93. Commentators have thus explained the meaning of Green. Catlin says that the freedom for a man lies in being reconciled to the law of his being, which he obeys as being the law of the realisation in himself of the idea of perfection and in the discipline through inheritance and education of natural impulses mitigating against law." *A History of Political Philosophers, p. 513. Bowle says that Green "believed in the integrity, the importance and the goodness of the free personality .. It should encourage and harmonise institutions which embodied a way of life directed to good ends in which self was transcended in a wider freedom."* *Politics and Opinion in the Nineteenth Century*, p. 278.

the individual becomes an outlaw and the state does not endure if instinctive recognition is not given to this elementary conception. Not only this, he also enjoins upon the state to develop and cultivate this rudimentary conception and convert a lazy and stupid individual into an intelligent patriot by giving him a share in the management of public affairs.[25]

Finally, one important thing may be pointed out here. When Green justifies that will not force is the basis of the state, he is not at all concerned with the problems of democracy or dictatorship. His purpose is to explain that whatever be the form of government, the basis of the state is neither force nor divine sanction but the consciousness of the people who are its citizens. He is simply content to analyse and elucidate the thesis implicit in the life of the existing states. Though Green's dictum that will not force is the basis of the state is more easily traceable in a representative government, he is prepared to lay down that every state is based on the foundation of general will and nothing else.

The salient features of Green's theory of state may be summed up thus :

1. Green makes a sort of fusion between idealism and realism and while discussing the case of an ideal state based on the foundations of metaphysics, he even identifies the foundations of an existing state with the same.
2. Green makes a blending of individualism with idealism. He regards state as the maintainer of rights and a protector of moral consciousness of the community, yet he is not prepared to sacrifice the individual at the altar of the state.

---

25. **A proper study of Green's theory shows that he is not antagonistic to the freedom of the individual, for his task "was the analysis of society and the solving of the problem. What is my duty to my neighbour, and why should I pay my attention to the constituted authority ?" Brown : *English Political Theory*, p. 140. Green's definition of freedom is inherent with the meaning of socialised individuality of man. MacCunn rightly says that Green's eye is always on substantial freedom. It is not free institutious alone, nor rights alone, nor immunity from interference alone, that can satisfy him but the fuller and better life into which the citizen comes when all these preliminaries have opened the way." *Six Radical Thinkers*, p. 25. So Brinton says : "The individual is politically free when by an act of imaginative reason, he accepts the whole nexus of social relation as a necessary guide when he realises that his own good must also be the common good." *English Political Thought in the Nineteenth Century*, pp.217-218.**

His conception of freedom is never apt to be identified with the idea of passive obedience as already suggested by Hegel.

3. Green distinguishes between state and society by insisting that the latter makes rights and the former comes after to protect them.
4. Green admits that various permanent groups within the society have their own inner system of rights and that the authority of the state over them is one of making adjustments.

We now turn to the critical evaluation of Green's theory of state. The elements of strength and weakness in Green's theory spring from the central fact of his being a Hegelian in general philosophy and a liberal in English politics. It is unquestionably true that Green gave something more satisfying than Bentham's hollow happiness and Mill's empty liberty and thus made liberalism a faith instead of interest.[26] Indeed, his theory witnesses a remarkable influence on him of the underlying change that was a consequence of the contemporary conditions - a fact that enabled Crane Brinton to say : "No one, not even Mill, who wrote so sympathetically of Socialism in his later years, marks better than Thomas Hill Green the change which came over English liberalism in the later part of the nineteenth century."[27]

In spite of this, Green's theory of state has been subjected to these lines of criticism :

1. It may be pointed out that Green attempts to bring about a unique synthesis between the fundamental postulates of liberalism and idealism. While *laissez faire* was the keynote of the former that shunned the ideal character of state and justified its minimum possible intervention in the interest of individual's pleasures or liberty, conversely the deification of state appeared as the keynote of the latter. In other words, while the former as interpreted by Mill and Spencer wanted the sacrifice of the state at the altar of the individual's liberty, the latter as interpreted by Coleridge and Carlyle appeared to sacrifice the inividual at the altar of state authority. A unique compromise or reconciliation between the two tendencies is really something strange, if not entirely impossible, and if Green does so, he naturally be-

26. Wayper : *Political Thought*, p. 193.
27. Brinton, *op. cit.*, p. 212.

comes responsible for infusing a hopeless confusion. His swinging between the poles of Plato and Aristotle of the ancient age and of Kant and Hegel of the modern remains a distinctive feature of his own and a definite change appears in the English idealism after him particularly in the works of Bosanquet. A general review of his theory bears testimony to the fact that there is a good deal of assimilation of the two incongruous tendencies of German idealism and English liberalism.[28]

2. Like other idealists, Green may be held guilty of over-emphasising the fact of free will - a will that is spontaneous, subjective, internal. The school of modern psycho-analysts is not prepared to accept that individual is a mere creature of his rational will in as much as his life is also governed by irrational forces. The practical manifestation of elections, propaganda, national movement and war all bear ample testimony to the fact that the people are motivated less by their faculty of rational will but more by their habits, emotions, instincts, etc. Barker rightly observes that a full philosophy "should start from a full man, armed with all thoughts, all passions, all delights, whatever fills this mortal frame."[29]
3. Green's recognition of the single factor of free will or pure consciousness has been criticised from another point of view. Wayper finds Green's picture of man as a being of pure consciousness to be as unreal as Benthamite picture of the pleasure-seeking man or Adam Smith's picture of the economic man. This tendency has also been a target of rigorous criticism by the Marxists who deny the fundamental postulates of metaphysics and, in opposition to them, justify the weight of material forces. Similarly, the Pluralists have repudiated the notion of Green. When Laski argues that we live not in a universe but in a multiverse, obviously he means that the forces of external social invironment cannot be ignored. True it is that Green bids departure to Hegel and in a Gierkean fashion regards state as 'a society of societies' and recognises that the associations have their own minor system of rights which arise out of their nature as societies, yet by so affirming he is no pluralist, since he also asserts that when the state "has come and guaranteed those rights, they arise in the state and proceed from it." The

28. Wayper : *Politicaal Thought*, p. 193.
29. Barker, *op. cit.*, p. 68.

supremacy of the state is thus retained and with it the vital importance of external things is ignored. Due to this a pluralist like Barker points out : "Any critical idealism must admit the vital importance of external things; and a political theory based upon it must recognise that if the state has any duty it has the duty of so adjusting external conditions, that the self into whose self-determination they enter shall not necessarily determine itself by evil to evil."[30]

4. Finally, Green confuses the scope of state activity by calling the state as 'a society of societies'. The result is that he now stumbles between the poles of monism and pluralism. In practice, such a state would have a very confused area of activity.

RIGHTS : LEGITIMACY OF RIGHT TO CIVIL DISOBEDIENCE

Green's theory of rights constitutes a very important aspect of his political philosophy. He rejects the Benthamite conception of the rights being the creation of a sovereign with power to inflict penalties in the event of their breach; as well as he repudiates the Hobbesian argument of their having a purely conventional character. In one more respect, his approach is different from that of Bentham; he disagrees with the view that natural rights are 'nonsense'. He retains the nomenclature of natural rights and reinterprets the idea in a way that is totally different from other protagonists of natural rights like Locke and Spencer. The reason for this should be traced in the elaborate expression of his standpoint in the general framework of his mataphysical and idealistic doctrine. The general characteristics of Green's theory of rights may be thus enumerated:.

1. Rights are created by the moral consciousness of the community and enforced by the state. When the claim of an individual arisen out of his self-consciousness receives the recognition of social consciousness, it is translated into a right. The foundation of rights lies in the capacity on the part of an individual of conceiving a good as the same for himself and others, and of being determined to action by that conception. According to Green, "In analysing the nature of any right, we may conveniently look at it from two sides, and consider it on the one hand as a claim of the individual, arising out of his rational nature, of the free ex-

30. *Ibid.*, p. 41.

pression of some faculty; on the other, as a concession of that claim by society, a power given to the individual of putting the claim in force."[31]

2. The rights may be termed natural in the sense that they are necessary and indispensable means to an end which every rational and moral being should pursue for the fulfilment of his vocation in a rationally constituted society. Hence, the rights constitute the conditions under which the realisation of the moral capacity of a man is rendered possible.
3. Technically speaking, such rights are ideal rights in as much as they ought to be recognised by a society that is properly organised on the basis of a good will. In this way, the rights have a normative aspect to which we should look for. Obviously, they are not the privileges that men had enjoyed in the past, rather they are the goals to which we are supposed to move ahead on account of our rational nature.
4. The natural rights are broader than the actual rights, for the actual righs having the sanction of society's law never square with an ideal system. The natural rights are ideal rights and so they are perfect rights whereas actual rights are imperfect rights as they lack the ideal character. Moreover, the natural rights lay down the norm to which actual rights must conform.
5. Natural rights are also different from legal rights in the sense that they are closer to morality rather than law. They are created by the moral consciousness of the community and not by the resolution of a legislative body. Green does not regard it essential that the rights should receive the sanction of a legislative agency. However, he prefers legal sanction for the sake of their better enforcement.
6. Finally, the state does not create rights, it simply enforces and protects them. The rights arise out of the eternal self-consciousness of the individual and thus assuming the shape of claims receive moral recognition of the community as a whole. Hence, the state gives full reality to the rights already in existence. The rights are the product of an ideal society alone and so to call them pre-social is a contradiction in terms.

31. Green, *op. cit.*, p. 144.

On the whole, Green regards righs as natural in the same sense as state is natural to Aristotle. To him right is a certain liberty of action claimed by an individual as necessary for pursuing ideal objects and developing his capacities of reason and will. But it assumes his character only after it receives the moral recognition and force of the society. Viewed thus, rights are nothing but the creation of an individual's social life in an ideal community. Green says : "The capacity on the part of an individual of conceiving the good as the same for himself and others, and of being determined to action by that conception for the foundation of rights; and rights are the conditions of that capacity being realised."[32]

According to Green, the conditions of reststance arise out of the discrepancy between the natural rights of the ideal type and the actual rights recognised by the law of the imperfect state. He cites the case of slavery and questions how far the sympathies with the cause of the slaves could resist master's legal right to property over the slave to be free. However, in an un-Hegelian manner, he sanctions qualified right to civil disobedience. He recognises the right to resistance only when its necessity is warranted by the social consciousness. However, he warns that there should be no breach of political obligation for the sake of disturbing social peace and harmony or spreading chaos and disorder. Yet when the state fails to discharge essential services conforming to the norm of natural rights, resistance to its authority is justified. Dr. Lindsay thus explains: "The doctrine that the justification of state's force depends on the services which the force renders ought to imply that when these services are not rendered, the state's force is not justified and political obligation disappears."[33]

In this connection, Green warns that the whole must not be sacrificed for the sake of the part and the existing system of rights must not be disturbed for the sake of adding a new element to it due to the danger of social disturbance. The implication is that first a healthy public opinion be created and thus when the whole community becomes convinced with the need of civil disobedience for the sake of public good, the resistance will be justified. Green says: "The common good, must suffer from resistance to a law or the ordinance of a legal authority, until its repeal can be obtained. It is thus the social duty of the

32. *Ibid.*, Sec. 29.
33. Lindsay, *op. cit.*, p. xvii.

individual to conform and he can have no right that is against his social duty."[34]

Green, therefore, has been admired for recognising the right to resistance and here he has revealed a clear departure from the premises of German idealism. But the difficulty is that his interpretation is confined to merely theoretical side. The way he recognises right to civil disobedience is purely a matter of academic significance. Hardly that situation might come when the public as a whole would agree to resist the oppressive machinery of the state, for always there would remain a section of the community to support the side of the rulers. Lancaster thus remarks: "In short, he gives us no clear test by which to decide when acts of resistance are for the general good, and it is hard to see in his theory how one could object to their forcible repression by a minority pretending to be the sole reliable agents of the General Will."[35] Likewise, Maxey points out: "Reserving to the individual the right of disobedience only when it would serve to make the state be more nearly its ideal self, as Green has done, leaves the ground for resistance very doubtful."[36]

However, Green's theory of rights has been found both inconsistent and confusing. Two difficulties arise in this regard. First, Green nowhere draws up a list of rights which he would call natural or ideal. For this he may be condoned on the plea that no final list of natural or ideal rights can be prepared owing to the fact that social conditions change and the standards of morality change simultaneously. But the second difficulty stands out. If the society considers something for the moral

34. Green, *op. cit.*, Sec. 100. Barker very clearly puts it thus: "We must not sacrifice what is almost the whole for the sake of a part: we must not risk social chaos, and the disturbance of the existing system of rights for the sake of adding a new element to the system. But when there is already implicit social acknowledgement of the claim to a natural right, we know that there is no possibility of such sacrifice or such risk. The same force of a common social consciousness, which is the ultimate sustainer of legal rights, is here resisting legal rights, for the sake of their greater perfection." *Op. cit.*, p. 32.
35. Lancaster, *op. cit.*, p. 231.
36. Maxey: *Political Philosophies* p. 508. McGovern thus points out: "But who is to decide if rebellion or the forcible seizure of power is or is not for the public good. On Green's principles, might not a militant minority claim to be the true agent of the general will? It is hard to see on what theoretical grounds Green could have objected to the Fascist or Nazi denounements in Italy or Germany." *From Luther to Hitler*, p. 179.

development of the people as necessary, but the people in their individual capacity think otherwise, certainly a state of conflict would take place. The question arises that who is to be the judge of what natural or ideal rights are really necessary at a given time in a given society. Lancaster thus observes: "Green's treatment of the doctrine of natural rights is confused and inconsistent. He tries to draw a distinction between it and what he regards as a correct explanation of the origin of rights, but in reality he accepts something like the usual theory."[37]

STATE ACTIVITY : REVISION OF THE DOCTRINE OF LAISSEZ FAIRE

In this respect, Green's views have been influenced by Kant's emphasis on the negative character of state activity as well as by the conditions of his own age which demanded shift from an individualistic to a collectivistic trend. As a result, when Green insists that the effectual action of the state is necessarily to be confined to the removal of obstacles or to the maintenance of the conditions of life in which morality shall be possible and morality consists in the disinterested performance of self-imposed duties, he also insists that the state should make positive attempts to remove three gigantic evils, namely, ignorance, pauperism and drinking alcohol. In other words, Green's views on the character of state activity have both negative and positive aspects.

Negatively, the state should hinder the hindrances to good life and do nothing to promote morality directly. Such is the nature of moral development that each can achieve it for himself alone; it cannot be forced upon one from outside. All that the state can do is to secure that one's actions should conform to one's duties. Green holds that an act can be truly moral only when it is freely self-determined. According to Green, "Now any direct enforcement, by means of threatened penalties–and a law requiring such conduct necessarily implies penalties for disobedience to it–does interfere with the spontaneous action of those interests, and consequently checks the growth of the capacity which is the condition of the benefical exercise of rights. For this reason, the effectual action of the state, *i.e.*, the community as acting through the law, for the promotion of habits of true citizenship seems necessarily to be confined to the removal of obstacles."[38]

---

37. Lancaster, *op. cit.*, p. 244.
38. Green, *op. cit.*, p. 208. As Coker has said: "The state's characteristic work,

Positively, Green lays special emphasis on the eradication of three gigantic evils by the state, namely, ignorance, pauperism and drinking alcohol. In Green's view, these three evils are so big that unless their eradication takes place by the action of the state, the promotion of morality among the citizens may not be possible. Hence, for this Green emphasies the need for compulsory education, employment opportunities and prohibition. So firmly he was convinced of the pernicious effects of these evils that he took part in social campaigns and opened a coffee shop in Oxford to distract the attention of the drunkards. The state may ask its citizens to educate their children and to limit, even abandon, the use of selling and buying alcohol.

It is clear that herein lies a philosophical justification of the idea of a welfare state. Green's anxiety for removing the gigantic social evils is so penetrating that it pushes him out of the philosophical orbit of idealism. Unlike Carlyle and Ruskin, who simply wrote on the ugliness and evils of industrialism, Green suggests concrete steps and tries to work out a theory of state activity quite consistent with the actual conditions of his own age. Nor like Maine, Lecky and Mill, he is simply satisfied with the question of political democracy, rather he lays stress on the need for economic and social democracy as well. The idea of welfare state which gained currency in the twentieth century is thus precursed here by Green more than half a century earlier. However, it may be pointed out that a theoretical deficiency creeps here. Green forgets that by launching a positive programme of eradicationg these gigantic evils, the state may do much what he denies to it in the name of its negative sphere of activity. So Lancaster says : "If, as one might now argue, a welfare state must necessarily be a very powerful one, the perhaps fatal defect of his philosophy is that, because of his preoccupation with current abuses, he fails to see the authoritarian implications of his basic metaphysics."[39]

according to Green, is that of removing external hindrances to the voluntary performance of good acts. In executing this thask it has much more to do than defend the community from foreign attack and check traditional crimes and torts. It must help to create social traditions in which there will be the fewest possible impediments in the way of each individual making the best of himself." *Recent Political Thougth*, p. 242.

39. Lancaster, *op. cit.*, p. 228.

OTHER ASPECTS : PUNISHMENT, PROPERTY, INTERNATIONALISM AND INDIVIDUALISM

Green's ideas in regard to punishment, at first, dismiss the prevalent theories and, at the same time, present their unison in a peculiar way. According to Green, the punishment should neither be preventive, nor retributive, nor reformatory in an exclusive form; it should be such as to incorporate the essential elements of all. In the first place, punishment should be preventive as it is directed towards the maintenance of the system of rights and obligations. It inculcates fear in the heart of the people and thus prevents them from doing what is lawfully prohibited. Then, it should be retributive, for it is inflicted on the guilty not because of the feeling of any revenge but to make him realise that he has got what he deserved and what was his due in return of the wrong he committed. Finally, it be should reformative as it recovers the person from his criminal habits.

On the whole, the purpose of punishment is moral, since it makes the guilty man capable of realising his true nature and protects the system of rights created by the moral consiousness of the community. The punishment has thus both the negative and the positive effects. In the former, it is a force preventive of a force opposed to freedom; in the latter a corrective of the criminal. Linked with the sphere of state activity, the purpose of punishment is to maintain conditions and remove obstacles from the way of moral life of the people. Like every state action, it has a moral purpose and a moral quality in as much as its ultimate aim is to secure freedom of action for the moral will of every member of the community and to regenerate a good will in the mind of the criminal. In the words of Green: "The state looks not to virtue and vice but to rights and wrongs. It looks back to the wrong done in the crime it punishes; not, however, in order to avenge it but in order to the consideration of the sort of terror which needs to be associated with such wrong-doing in order to the future maintenance of rights."[40]

Like Locke, Green is a strong defender of the institution of private property. He recognises its basis as necessarily the basis of all other rights. Morever, like Aristotle, he considers property as a sum of instruments necessary and useful to the individual for promoting the best life of the community. The

40. Green, *op. cit.*, Sec. 204.

property is the outcome of the appropriation of things by a permanent self-demanding free expression of human personality. In other words, it implies that without property no individual would be able to give effect to his free will and contribute to the best life of community. The salient features of Green's ideas on property may be summed up thus:

1. Property is a condition necessary for the free play of a capacity which can be exerted for the common benefit: it is the means of realising a will which in all possibilities is a will directed to social good.
2. Green urges that property cannot be equalised. The social good requires that different persons fill different positions in the social whole. Different positions require different means and, in this way, differences of property are potentially for the good of the society, and for this reason they may be properly recognised by the social conscience.
3. Finally, representing the tradition of his own age, Green sanctions the idea of state control over private property in land, though private capital remains unaffected by state regulations.

Green has been criticised for idealising the imperfect institution of private property. As Aristotle idealised slavery and Hegel glorified the state of Prussia, so does Green for the sake of private property. The institution of private property cannot be idealised, for it is not without certain inherent weakness. His preference is really a defence of the interest of the capitalist class. Hence, like Locke, Green has also been denounced for safeguarding the interest of the propertied class at the cost of the propertyless multitude. In the days of democracy and socialism no such defence can be appreciated. Laski is right when he strongly affirms: "It remains historically obvious that a community divided between rich and poor is, when the latter are numerous, built upon the foundation of sand. For the basis of the state is envy and envy is the nurse of faction. Yet the state remains divided into rich and poor; and men after a period, refuse to suffer quietly. The revolution supervenes to alter the balance of the state."[41]

However, one important aspect which shows Green's distinct departure from Hegel lies in his advocacy of internationalism. Like Kant, Green denounces the idea of world war

41. Laski : *A Grammar of Politics*, pp. 176-77.

and emphasises the need for a world organisation. Green argues that war can never be an absolute right, for it violates man's right to life. War is a moral wrong and thus it should be avoided at all costs; but if there is no alternative and resort to war becomes a necessity, Green calls it a 'cruel necessity'. War means destruction of human life inflicted on the sufferers intentionally by voluntary human agency. It is a wrong in every case. The destruction of life in war is always wrong-doing whoever be the wrong-doer. The state, so far as it is true to its principle, cannot infringe the right of man as man by conflict with other states. War does not explode national virtues, rather it represents the want of perfect life. In short, war is never absolutely right; at most under unavoidable circumstances it may be relatively right; it manifests the imperfect character of modern statehood.

Green's ideas on internationalism not only embody his stern denunciation of war, they also reveal his emphasis on world peace and international intercourse. He dreams of an international tribunal with authority resting on the consent of independent states. His argument implies that the more the states of the world will move towards perfection, less would be the prospects of war. According to Barker, "The better organised each state, the freer must be the intercourse of its members with those of other states; the freer that intercourse, the greater must be the sense of common interests; the greater this sense, the more real must be the common society which it implies."[42]

CRITICAL APPRECIATION : GREEN MORE OF A KANTIAN THAN A HEGELIAN

Green has been regarded as more of an Aristotelian and a Kantian than that of a Platonist and a Hegelian. The reason for this should be traced in a unique fusion of individualism and idealism which Green presents. Much has already been said in the prceding portions and only a condensed account will be sufficient to justify the above observation. Green lived in that period of modern England when social, economic and political conditions, in stead of crying for a systematic extension of individual's freedom, demanded state intervention even at the cost of his freedom. This transition upset the ethics of utilitarianism and popularised Southey, Arnold and Carlyle

42. Barker, *op. cit.*, p. 35.

who denounced *laissez faire* as 'false, heretical and damnable'. It had its effective impact on the national legislation which, as Dicey says, passed from an individualistic to a collectivistic trend. Green well visualised the transition and thus he rejected the utilitarian interpretation of liberalism and substituted it by a better alternative received from the idealism of Germany. Wayper thus says: "Possessed of too much commonsense to soar to these high altitudes, in which giddiness is no uncommon affliction, and discredited by its close association with *laissez faire* individualism, utilitarianism in the later part of the century was at a temporary disadvantage. Hegelian philosophy, waiting at hand to replace it, had now the opportunity to do so. But before this could be done, those things which made it difficult for Englishmen to adopt it must first be removed from Hegelianism. This was the task of T.H. Green."[43]

Although an idealist, in Green the element of Kantian individualism outweighs the element of Hegelian absolutism. Green does not idealise the majesty of the state and sticks to the worth and dignity of the human person. MacCunn says: "If it be individualism to see in every public movement the fate of human beings and in every controversy over institutions the weal or woe of fellow citizens, then there are few more declared indiividualists in political philosophy than T.H. Green."[44]

Green's being more of a Kantian than that of Hegelian is visible in these respects:

1. Green regards the state not as an end in itself but a means to a higher end–the full moral development of its citizens.
2. Green adheres to the worth and dignity of man and is not prepared to sacrifice him at the altar of the state.
3. Green emphasies the negative character of state activity and sanctions the eradication of three great evils of ignorance, poverty and drinking alcohol medrely for the sake of removing obstacles from the way of moral life of the people.
4. Green recognises general will as will for the state, not of the state, and does not identify it with something in whose name so many crimes are committed by the state.

43. Wayper, *op. cit.*, p. 175.
44. *Ibid*, p. 189.

5. Green recognises the right to resistance against the state in certain circumstances.
6. Green's idea of natural rights once again reiterates the case of individual freedom.
7. Green's ideas on property circumscribe the jurisdiction of the state activity and safeguard the freedom of the individual in one important sphere of economic life.
8. Finally, Green condemns war in the name of individual's right to life and advocates the case of internationalism.

If Green has saved the individual from being a means to the state, it does not mean that he is without Hegelian influence in this regard. It is visible in these respects. Firstly, Green believes in reason and maintains that all institutions, communities and associations are embodiment of the Divine Spirit. Secondly, he conceives of the individual liberty only in the midst of his social life. Thirdly, he emphasises that without the state individual cannot seek the best possible realisation of his personality. Finally, he holds that each community develops its own standards of morality which moulds the moral outlook of its citizens and so he insists that no reform will endure which ignores rational sentiment, character and institutions.

In short, Green has produced a very peculiar synthesis of individualism and idealism by recognising the worth and dignity of the individual and yet not seeing him as an isolated and therefore unrelated atom of the society. The individual, nevertheless, remains the basis of his thought, although his free will is considered to be willing ideal objects alone. Barker's admiration thus runs: "He has seized the philosophy of Greece and of Germany, and interpreted it for Englishmen with a full measure of English caution, and with a full reference to that deep sense of the liberty of the subject and that deep distrust of reason of state which marks the Englishmen. Partly to this, and partly to the influence of Kant, we may ascribe his firm hold on the worth of the individual."[45]

In brief, Green's political philosophy has been criticised for being too abstract and philosophical clothed in the tapestry of metaphysical idealism. Besides, his idealisation of the private property system ranks his place in the realm of conservatism. But, on the whole, it is certain that Green is both a

45. Barker, *op. cit.*, p. 46.

soaring idealist and a sober realist. His firm hold on the worth of person, his deep sense of the liberty of the individual, his conviction that individual is an instrinsic part of the social good, his refusal to raise the state to mystical heights, his recognition of the universal brotherhood and international authority, his eagerness to place limits on the authority of the state so that spontaneity in the performance of moral acts may not be deadened, his emphasis on rights, his denunciation of war, and his admission that people have qualified rights to civil disobedience are the significant ideas of modern political thought. His philosophical justification of the welfare state took roots in his own country and thus reforms in the socio-economic spheres followed. Hence, Maxey admirably comments: "It is not the matter of putting too strongly to say that Green's political philosophy has supplied much of the intellectual groundwork, at least in English speaking countries, for old age pensions, unemployment insurance, workmen's compensation, factory regulation, and a vast amount of other social legislation which has marked the trend away from *laissez faire* since the middle of the nineteenth century. Green's influence was all the greater in that, while acknowledging the correctness of Hegel's view of the inseparability of the individual and the community, he idealised the state without deifying it and identifying it with absolute right."[46]

46. Maxey, *op. cit.*, pp. 509-10.

30

BOSANQUET

Bosanquet believed that the only acts possessing moral significance were those freely chosen in the light of circumstances involved; that if men were ever to educate themselves morally, they should develop the kind of society wherein the government did not attempt to regulate their lives for them; and therefore that a large amount of individualism is a good thing. On this score, Green and Bosanquet were at one with Bentham and Mill.

— **F.P. Harris**[1]

The last great representative thinker of the idealist school in England is Prof. Bernard Bosanquet who was born in 1843 in Northumberland and died in London in 1923. As a member of the Oxford community, he drew inspiration from Benjamin Jowett and T.H. Green. For about eight years, he acted as the Fellow and Tutor of the Universal College but later shifted to London and wrote papers for the Charity Organisation Society. In the early phase of the present century, he served as the professor of philosophy at the St. Andrews. However, the striking feature of Bosanquet's place in the history of recent English political thought is that he gave to British idealism "its com-

1. Harris : *The Neo-Idealist Political Theory : Its Continuity with British Tradition*, p. 38.

pletest statement a la' Hegel. Less original in his thinking than Bradley, he centainly surveyed more extensively the whole field of philosophical speculation, and applied more vigorously the Hegelian notion of the concrete universal to all aspects of human life and speculation."[2]

WORKS : RESTATEMENT OF HEGELIANISM

As we saw in the case of Green so here, we find a curious blending of metaphysics, logic and politics in the writings of Bosanquet. His *Principles of Logic* (1896) was an attempt to attack and expose the traditional formal logic as well as the inductive logic of Mill and Jevons as it enriched idealistic logic based on the assumption that logical thought apprehends reality and becomes one with it, i.e., the reality is ultimate thought, or 'truth lies in the whole' as immanent in the system and not outside of it. Hence, the contents of logic and metaphysics cannot be different. Then, the best form of his metaphysical expressions is contained in his two Gifford Lectures published in the form of *The Principle of Individuality and Value* and *The Value and Destiny of the Individual* (1912-14). However, the most important contribution of Bosanquet is his *Philosophical Theory of State* (1899) in which British political idealism is said to have come to its 'maturity'.[3]

A brief study of the political ideas of Bosanquet contained in his *Philosphical Theory of State* shows that here the author seeks to examine and expose the fallacy of the individualistic political theory as embodied in the writings of Bentham, Mill and Spencer. Besides, the real nature of the human self is studied. However, to a student of political philosophy what is striking here is that the author draws inspiration from Rousseau and sets him in his right place; he tries to examine the nature and end of political authority including limitations on the scope of state activity. The views of the author on other related themes like liberty, property, punishment and internationalism are also available here.

Looking at all this, critics like L.T. Hobhouse and Leighton go to the extent of calling Bosanquet 'the most modern and most faithful exponent of Hegel'. Though one may take this comment as over-emphasised, it is certain that, as compared to Green, Bosanquet follows Hegel more faithfully, particularly in

2. Frank Thakurdas : *The English Utilitarians and the Idealists*, p. 362.
3. *Ibid.*, p. 365.

the direction of merging individuality with the social whole and discarding the norms of inter-nationalism. Prof. Barker makes a balanced comment thus: "In the light of a fuller experience and of fresh data, he (Bosanquet) would sweep away some of the limitations with which Green had hedged about his doctrine of the state as the organ for the realisation of the free will; and he would thus bring Green's philosophy to a point where it approaches close to, if it does not altogether blend with, the full Hegelian conception of the state."[4]

NATION-STATE : EMBODIMENT OF AN ETHICAL IDEA

In constructing his theory of state, Basanquet starts from a vindication of Rousseau and passing through certain postulates of Green ends in Hegel.[5] This may be explained by a study of his theories of will, institutions and nation-state.

(i) **Will :** The starting point of Bosanquet is the conception of the free moral will of man as stressed by Rousseau. But Bosanquet uses two technical terms–actual will and real will. The actual will is impulsive, unreflective, recalcitrant, while the real will is constant, true and rational. A man is said to be influenced by his actual will when he acts from moment to moment as a conscious individual, and as this will is created and amended by what he wants at all other moments and is adjusted to the will of others, it becomes real. But the real will on account of being rational does not stand alone; it is bound up with the real wills of other individuals living in the society and thus becomes the general will. It implies that the individual can make the best of himself only in society. However, Bosanquet holds that the state is the perfect embodiment of General Will. The common life of society depends upon the law and political order provided by the state.

(ii) **Institutions :** When man's life is social through and through and when even his individual relations are influenced by his common social life, it means that the idea of a common mind or General Will is not a mere fancy but a living reality. Every social group has its own mind and the mind of one member cannot be understood without under-

4. Barker : *Political Thought in England*, pp. 56-57.
5. According to McGovern, "Bosanquet's political ideas are obviously a rehash of Rousseau's theories (minus the social contract) reinterpreted in the light of Hegelian philosophy." *From Luther to Hitler*, p. 302.

standing the mind of the whold association. Institutions are thus embodiments of ethical ideas. Every association is a complicated inter-working of the minds of the individuals; the totality of the group is reflected in the minds of the individual; and every member tends to impose a particular point of view upon other members. According to Bosanquet, "An institution implies a purpose or sentiment of more minds than one, and a more or less permanent embodiment of it...In institutions we have that point of the individual minds which is the social mind. Rather we have here the ideal substance which as a universal structure is the social but in its differentiated cases in the individual mind."[6]

That is, Bosanquet urges that the actual reality of the institution 'lies in the fact that certain living minds are connected in a real way'. Parliament, for instance, is not some six hundred minds sitting in a room; it is fundamentally a connecting idea, which, being concerned with action is a purpose as well as an idea–a purpose common to six hundred minds and uniting six hundred minds in a common experience. Such an idea is backed by a purpose we may call an 'ethical idea'; and so we may speak of the institutions as ethical idea, and we may say that, as such, they are that common substance of individual minds which unites them as a single or common mind. Parliament, in the last resort, is neither bricks nor mortar, not flesh and blood; it is the substance common to six hundred minds; it is, as we say, the 'common mind.'[7]

(iii) **Nation-State :** Although society means a network of institutions, the state stands at the top. The state is a political organisation and by using force it becomes supreme over all social institutions like family, church, neighbourhood group etc. It puts its seal on all those social efforts which are beneficial in their nature. However, in a broader sense, it stands for the general organisation and synthesis of life and is practically synoymous with society. It is the ethical idea, a source of all- pervading adjustments and an operative criticism of institutions. According to Bosanquet, "The state, as thus conceived, is not merely the political fabric. The term state accents indeed the political aspects of the whole, and is opposed to the notion of an anarchical society.

6. Bosanquet : *The Philosophical Theory of State*, p. 277.
7. Barker, *op. cit.*, p. 60.

But it includes the entire hierarchy of institutions by which life is determined from the family to the trade, and from trade to the church and the university. It includes all of them, not as the mere collection of the growths of the country, but as the structure which gives life and meaning to the political whole, while receiving from it mutual adjustments and, through expansion, a more liberal air."[8]

An identification of the society and the state, in this way, occurs in the political thought of Bosanquet. As Barker says: "Society, after all, is within the State, and it has its meaning in the State. It follows that if we take the State, in its fuller sense, not as a political mechanism using force, but as a general organisation and synthesis of life, which includes and correlates all other organisations, we shall see it as a group, a community of communities, embracing and sustaining the whole field of social co-operation. In this sense, we can view the meaning of State from two aspects. We can see it first of all as a source of adjustments, criticising and adjusting in the light of a working conception of life as a whole, the institutions which it contains, and reducing them by such criticism to an ordered and graded system. We can see it again as a driving wheel, giving motive power to the system–as a 'force' invigorating by a constant reminder and suggestion of their duties to every member and every institution, and preventing the lethargy and inertia into which, without such reminder and suggestion, they might too readily fall."[9]

However, the State cannot act in the latter capacity as a force, unless it has presented to itself its first aspect of itself as a working ception of life as a whole. Thus, the argument of Bosanquet runs: "The State, as such, is limited to the office of maintaining the external conditions of a good life; but the conditions cannot be conceived without reference to the life for which they exist, and it is true, therefore, to say that the conception of the Nation-State involves at least an outline of life to which, as a power, it is instrumental."[10]

8. Bosanquet, *op. cit.*, pp. 150-51.
9. Barker, *op. cit.*, p. 58.
10. *Ibid.*, pp. 58-59. Thus, Rudolph Metz observes that, according to Bosanquet, the state "is the general will, or the rational will, a continuous and self-identical being, permeating a multiplicity of particular individuals in and through whom alone it has existence and meaning." *A Hundred Years of British Philosophy*, p. 352.

Bosanquet thus reaches very close to Hegel. To him nation-state is the highest form of social organisation. There is nothing above it, nor is there anything else even inside the society to adjudge the morality of its actions. In this way, like Machiavelli, Bosanquet also contributes to the doctrine of double morality. The standards of private morality cannot be applicable to the state. A man may be held guilty of theft or murder, but the same canons cannot be applied if the state forfeits private property or orders the general slaughter of its ememies. The actions of the state are public and they cannot be made the objects of moral judgement like private acts of an individual. But Bosanquet concedes that certain actions of the state may be criticised only when they are done with the active support of the community. In such a case, the state would be judged before the tribunals of human history.

The above doctrine of double morality shows Bosanquet's debt to Hegel as well as his departure from him at the tail of his argument. But another point which reiterates his debt to Hegel is his denial of the dictates of international morality. When the need arises, the state may call upon its citizens to place their lives at its disposal, for through constitutional methods it is the sole judge of its actions. The state is the guardian of the whole moral world and not of a factor within the organised moral world. Thus, Bosanquet refuses to agree with the idea of universal brotherhood and international morality. In his own words: "Moral relations presuppose an organised life; but such a life is only within the state, not in relations between the states and other communities."[11]

In short, Bosanquet idealises the nation-state in a way which is more of a Hegelian than that of a Kantian type. However, two points may be furnished to reveal weaknesses in his theory of state:

1. It is rightly remarked that the technical distinction between actual and real wills, as pointed out by Bosanquet, is altogether false. The actual is the real and vice versa. Since our experience is continuous and most of us make steady

11. *Ibid.*, p. 303. To Bosanquet the state is a sort of church, the Church of Humanity, and membership of it is nothing else than a great spiritual experience. In short, for him as for Hegel, the state is the ultimate moral authority for the citizen, the keeper of his civic conscience." Murray: *Studies in the English Social and Political Thinkers of the Nineteenth Century*, pp. 311-12.

progress all the time, it is a mistake to split up our acts as if they have no touch with each other. The average man's life is a mixture of the actual and real wills. Moroever, by linking his theory of will with his theory of institutions, Bosanquet finally justifies the case of state absolutism. Hence, Ivor Brown comments that the conception of state as a social organism transcending all the individual organisms that compose it is fundamentally undemocratic. He continues that Bosanquet puts into the hands of the governing class and of those who can worm their way into that charmed circle a weapon of infinite menace, for if the concept of the social organism "is rigorously applied, the result is state slavery on an unparalleled scale."[12]

2. Likewise, Bosanquet's denunciation of internationalism cannot be accepted. The state is certainly responsible for the actions of its agents and is nothing but a part within an organised moral world. The actions of the state are in no way different from the actions of its accredited representatives. As on the national so on the international plane, a body of public opinion is steadily growing to make the moral responsibility of the states a real enough phenomenon. Barker rightly questions that if a citizen "can treat his own state as legally responsible for damages, it is difficult to see why a state, which can undergo legal responsibility, should not also undergo moral responsibility if there is any body of opinion to affix responsibility."[13]

OTHER ASPECTS : RESISTANCE, STATE ACTIVITY AND PUNISHMENT

In regard to right to resistance, Bosanquet's approach is more conservative than that of Green. Apparently, Bosanquet does not recognise the right to civil disobedience on the plea that the state represents the will of the community, it has the sole right to judge when the expressions of individual conscience are dangerous to the welfare of the people as a whole. The orderly processes of the state as sole organiser of rights and as guardian of moral values are always important in the presence of which individual should have no right to revolution. But, in a deeper sense, Bosanquet shows a sneaking acceptance of the right to resistance exercisable only on the basis of social

---

12. **Brown : *English Political Theory*, p. 148.**
13. **Barker, *op. cit.*, pp. 78-79.**

conscience. The private conscience cannot be a judge of the need for revolution. However, Bosanquet urges the individual not to exercise this right, for he "is more liable to be mistaken and that the petty gain in practical value may be more than offset by the injury alone done to the stability of the social organisation itselt."[14]

Like Green, Bosanquet accepts the negative character of state activity, for the state as such can do nothing for the best life but hinder hindrances to it. On account of the nature of the means it has at its disposal for the achievement of its end or purpose and also because of the nature of morality, the function of the state is limited to the removal of obstacles to good life. Again, like Green, Bosanquet insists upon the performance of certain positive acts like the removal of illiteracy and intemperance. Although positive in content, the purpose of such acts is moral being the liberation of the resources of character and intelligence greater beyond all questions than the encroachment which they involve. The only essential thing is that the state should refrain from enforcing acts whose value lies in their being determined by free will. On the whole, the function of the state is to secure the external conditions necessary for the free action of the good will by repelling forces opposed to it and that it should not attempt to direct and control the free exercise of man's real will.

In regard to punishment, Bosanquet calls it futile to draw any distinction between the theories of retributive, preventive and reformatory punishments. He examines the case of punishment from a psychological standpoint. Punishment is a reaction against an aggression. Hence, when aggression takes place, punishment follows. But as punishment is a retaliation against an injury, it is retributive; then, as punishment is a bulwark against a menace, it is preventive; finally, as punishment affects the character of the guilty, it is reformative. The purpose of Bosanquet is to justify that punishment is the means of securing rights and when rights are invaded, it follows. However, the primary motive is neither retributive, nor preventive, nor reformative; all are inseparable and each expands so as to include others. Besides, Bosanquet takes the help of psychology as well. In his view, man commits wrong by his lower nature, but punishment awakens his higher nature which was pre-

14. N. Wilde : *The Ethical Basis of the State*, p. 68.

viously lying in a sub-conscious state. The punishment thus pulls man back to himself as his real self.

Estimate : Like Green, Bosanquet also occupies an important place in the history of English idealism. J.A. Leighton has called him 'the greatest of the English idealists'. A.B. Ulam considers that Bosanquet "analysed acutely theories and institutions rather than life".[15] The above account shows that Bosanquet, being an Oxford idealist and a student of Green, gave way to a sterner Hegelianism. Bosanquet himself admits that he desired to lay aside the scrupulous caution of Green in estimating the role of the state. Yet Bosanquet does not depart from the English tradition in toto and holds that the basis of progress lies in the moral striving of the individual will. Harris thus concludes: "It was Bosanquet and the idealists who found it necessary to emphasise that individuals in their striving are not isolated. Bosanquet calls repeated attention to the impact of social system upon its members. Beneath the details of his political theory it is the habits and beliefs evoked by institutionalised behaviour, the whole atmosphere of ideas and attitudes and activities in which one is immersed and which clearly forces and moulds him, that engage Bosanquet's attention. The merit of Bosanquet's Hegelianism was to put men back into the social context from which Hobbes and Spencer had abstracted them."[16]

As a last word, it may again be pointed out that the Oxford Idealism as represented by Green and Bosanquet continued the tradition of English liberalism. True it is that the English idealists drew heavily from Kant and Hegel, although more from the latter in a cumulative sense, they were interested in politics as a means to moral excellence; they were, first and foremost, concerned with the fulfilment of man's vocation as a moral being. This fulfilment means that the individual must be left free to develop himself and governmental interference is tolerable only so far as it maintains the conditions of free action. According to Harris, "Bosanquet believed that the only acts possessing moral significance were those freely chosen in the light of circumstances involved; that if men were ever to educate themselves morally, they should develop the kind of society wherein the government did not attempt to regulate their lives for them; and therefore that a large amount of individualism is

15. Ulam : *Philosophical Foundations of English Socialism*, p. 50.
16. Harris, *op. cit.*, p. 422.

a good thing. On this score, Green and Bosanquet were at one with Bentham and Mill."[17] Coker points out: "All the Oxford idealists have emphasised the influence of a man's social contacts. Each individual is the sort of man he is not primarily because of his native endowment or the physical environment in which he lives but because of the sort of conventional and institutional relationships in which he finds himself. The standards of conduct and opinion which these conventions and institutions express and to which he habitually conforms go far towards determining her character and success. If he is removed from the pressure of law, custom, and social opinion, then his character becomes that of a hermit–on a low plane, culturally, intellectually and spiritually, and lacking the essential attributes of what we understand as human personality."[18] Prof. C.C. Maxey is of the view that Bosanquet contributed to the philosophy of nationalism by treating the state as "the sublimation of all virtue and authority, arguing that the state may legitimately do whatever is required for the preservation and improvement of the organised life fo the community, and the sole judge of what is so required."[19]

17. *Ibid.*, p. 38.
18. Coker, *op. cit.*, p. 422.
19. Maxey : *Political Philosophies*, p. 599.

31

MARX

Karl Marx put forward a philosophy which claimed to show how the present order had come about, and how it would be changed in due time into a better one; and he succeeded because he created a belief that the ultimate salvation of man was guaranteed by science. His system brought into being the largest mass movement since the rise of Christianity; and it is the greatest subversive force in the modern world, though it took a revolution in Russia for the West to become aware of this.

— **R.N. Carew Hunt**[1]

Among the various schools of political thought that developed in the nineteenth century none but socialism created a stir on an unprecedented scale. But the stir whose shock has persisted even to this day is the scientific socialism whose architect is Karl H. Marx.[2] Marx was born in 1818 at Treves in

1. R.N. Carew Hunt : *Theory and Practice of Communism*, pp. 25- 26.
2. The socialism of Marx has been termed 'scientific' in opposition to the 'utopian' socialism of his predecessors as well as contemporaries. The word 'utopian' has been used to designate their schemes of social reconstruction as purely dreamy or visionary, and although the utopian socialists criticised the evils inherent in the system of *laissez faire* and, in oppposition to the prevailing stress on the claims of the individual, laid emphasis on the social element in human relations as well as preached

Rhineland in a Jewish family which in 1824 adopted the Protestant creed of Christianity. But he abandoned faith in religion as such and developed interest in the study of philosophy which was very popular at that time. Later on, he came under the influence of Hegel who preached that the evolution 'takes place through a process of dialectics' and of Ludwig Feuerbach who maintained that man becomes estranged from himself by projecting into a supernatural being the qualities which belonged to his nature and would be realised one day in the religion of humanity. In 1842 he joined the staff of a German newspaper *Neue Rheinischo Zeitung* as editor. Then, he had to leave for Paris when the Prussian government suppressed this paper. Now his meeting with French labour leader Proudhon proved much useful. In 1844 the came into contact with another great leader Bakunin. But the most important event took place in 1845. It was his association with Dr. Fredrick Engels which lasted till the end of his life. Engels informed Marx about the conditions of workingmen in England and this had such a great impact on him that he desisted from remaining like a mere academic recluse. In 1845 Marx had to leave Paris and then he stayed in Brussels. From 1849 onwards Marx lived in England where Engels gave him literary cooperation and financial assistance till he died in 1883.[3]

---

that no improvement could be possible so long as the existing social order based on free competition continued to exist, they failed to impart a revolutionary and optimistic character to their doctrines. Joad says: "Marx, then, is first socialist writer whose work can be termed scientific. He not only sketched the kind of society which he desired, but spoke in detail of the stages through which it must evolve." *Modern Political Theory*, p. 41.

3. In the life of Marx, his partnership with Engels is very important. Not only that Engels rendered financial assistance, he also added clarifications and explanations to the ideas of Marx. Marx once said: "Engels is always one step ahead of me." When Marx died in 1883, Engels pronounced over his grave an oration in which he declared that his work in the field of social science "was equal to that of Darwin in the natural science." Carew Hunt, *op. cit.*, pp. 34-35. Isaiah Berlin thus points out that in Engels, Marx "found a devoted friend and an intellectual ally, whose very pedestrianism restored his sense of perspective and his belief in himself and his purpose. Throughout the great part of his life, his actions were performed in the knowledge that his massive and dependable man was always at hand to support the burden in every contingency. For this he paid him with an affection, and a sense of pride in his qualities, which he gave to none else besides his wife and children." *Karl Marx: His Life and Environment*, p.102.

WORKS : LITERATURE ON SCIENTIFIC SOCIALISM

Marx was a prolific writer on whom the influence of philosophers like Hegel and Feuerbach and political economists like David Ricardo, Adam Smith and William Thompson is quite visible. It is, however, a different matter that while he drew from different sources, he could give his idea a shape of their own. Likewise, it is a different matter that while he took something from his socialist predecessors, he refuted their thought by giving to it the bad name of 'utopian socialism'. Keeping it in view, a critic has gone to the length of saying: "The important thing about the work of Marx was not its originality, but its synthetic power. He seized upon philosophic materials which had been lying about loose and largely unused for many years and fused them into a systematic whole that supplied the proletarian movement with a dynamic theory and a tremendous impulse to action."[4]

The political ideas of Marx are contained in his several important works like *Eleven Theses on Feuerbach* (1845), *The German Ideology* (1846), *The Poverty of Philosophy* (1847), *The Communist Manifesto* (1848), *The Class Struggle in France* (1850) and *A Contribution to the Critique of Political Economy* (1859). Besides, reference should be made to his numerous monographs, addresses, articles etc. that he contributed from time to time the important ones of which are *Inaugural Address of the International Workingmen's Association* (1864), *Value, Price and Profit* (1865), *Civil War in France* (1870), *Criticism of the Gotha Programme* (1871) etc. Of all these works, *The Capital* (1867) and *The Communist Manifesto* deserve a special place of their own in the literature on Marxian political philosophy.

The *Communist Manifesto* constitutes the Bible of the Marxian thought. Written in collaboration with Fredrick Engels, it deals with the history of social evolution based on the doctrine of the class war, the principles of the Communist Party and their jurisdiction and also with their programme of action for the proletariat and the means of their realisation, an attack on different varieties of prevailing thought that is debunked as 'utopian' and, finally, a summary of the position of the Communists and their strategies and tactics in the face of the opposition. Keeping all this in view, it is observed that the

4. Maxey : *Political Philosophies*, p. 569.

Communist Manifesto "was at once an interpretation of the role of the working class in past and future history and a clarion call for labour to unite for the purpose of securing its emancipation and, through that emancipation, freedom of all mankind. It marked the definite decline in the leadership of the utopian school of thought among the advocates of a new social order. It marked at the same time the advent of Marxian or scientific socialism, a social philosophy which has exerted such a powerful influence on the political, social, economic and cultural thought of the last half century and which seems destined to play a still larger role in future historical developments."[5]

Equally important is *A Contribution to the Critique of Political Economy* in which Marx embodies his fundamental thesis. The whole thought of Marx is contained in his own affirmation here that reads: "In the social production which the men carry on, they enter into definite relations that are indispensable and independent of their will; these relations of production correspond to a definite stage of development of their material powers of production. The sum-total of these relations of production constitutes the economic structure of society—the real foundation on which rise legal and political super-structures and to which correspond definite forms of social consciousness. The mode of production in material life determines the general character of the social, political and spiritual processess of life...At a certain state of their development the material forces of production in society come into conflict with the existing relations of production,or—what is but a legal expression for the same thing—with the property relations within which they had been at work before. From forms of development of the forces of production, these relations turn into their fetters. Then, comes the period of social revolution. With change of the economic foundation, the entire immense superstructure is more or less rapidly transformed."[6]

---

5. H.W. Laider : *Social-Economic Movements*, p. 121. However, a critic like G.D.H. Cole holds that this work "can by no means be taken as a balanced formulation of Marx's ideas. He put into it more of his fundamental philosophy than he thought could be digested by the members, actual and prospective, of the body under whose auspices it appeared, or that it would be endorsed by the delegates whose approval it required." *A History of Socialist Thought*, Vol. I, p. 261.
6. See Marx : *A Contribution to the Critique of Political Economy* (Translated from German into English by N.I. Stone), pp. 11-12.

Commentators are of the view that most of the ideas we find in Marx were anticipated by German, French and English social theorists and which may be said to have provided him with the necessary material to build up not only a theory of socialism what he terms 'scientific' but also a programme of international socialist movement embodied in the call of the *Communist Manifesto* : 'Workers of all countires unite.' The contribution of Marx is that he could build up a momentous theory of social development in his own way. So Alexander Gray says: "It is doubtless true that the component parts of Marxian thought can be traced to a multitude of sources. He collected his bricks from many masons and yards but he used them to construct a building which was very much according to his own design."[7] However, it may be further observed that by making such an observation one should not try to belittle the significance of the contributions of Marx. Let us appreciate the view of Prof. H.J. Laski that Marx found communism like a chaos and left it as a movement.[8]

DIALECTICAL MATERIALISM : A LOGICAL DOCTRINE OF SOCIAL DEVELOPMENT

The term dialectic was developed by the ancient Greeks to denote a method of disputation according to which a speaker was tipped up by revealing that the implications of his statement were self- refuting. It was not a method of demonstrating known truths or discovering new truths. Sometimes, this method was used even in public assemblies and court rooms and at the philosophical exhibitions of a low order. It simply revolved around ambiguities of terms and geometrical abstractions as a method of twisting a meaning from words and expressions which was quite different from the intention of the person who uttered them. Plato meant by dialectic a process of thinking by which the dramatic conflict of ideas was resolved by convincing explanations. However, the Greeks used the method purely to reveal meanings and essences without any reference to existence.

In metaphysics dialectic appears as a distinctive contribution of Hegel. Hegel realised that the world was not static but essentially dynamic and so the problem of philosophy was to comprehend reason working behind nature and the entire

7. Gray : *The Socialist Tradition*, p. 229.
8. See Laski : *Communism*.

world of experience. He viewed that the progress of human civilisation happened in a spiral or zigzag form like a ship tacking against an unfavourable wind. Unlike the Greeks, Hegel applied a new method for the purpose of seeking to explain change and development through contract and contradiction and called it dialectic and, therefore, while the Greeks had thought of balancing the opposites, he though of it as leading rather to an equilibrium. Hegel found that contradiction was the very moving principle of the world and this took place through a formula of thesis, anti-thesis and synthesis, or affirmation, contradiction and solution, or being, not being and becoming, or negation of the negation. Hence, dialectic is not a law of pendulum but a law of logic or mechanism by which thought propels itself or the way in which Reason progressively embodies itself in institutions.[9]

Although both Marx and Hegel are monists and alike point out that contradiction works in a peculiar way and the changes take place gradually and imperceptibly until a certain point is reached beyond which it becomes sudden so that each synthesis is brought about very abruptly, yet the two sharply differ on the point of motivating force working behind this contradiction. For Hegel the universal substance of thesis or affirmation breeds its anti- thesis or contradiction, and the tension brings about a sythesis or solution. But Marx holds that it is matter which operates the law of dialectic. In his own words: "My dialectical method is not only different from the Hegelian, but it is its direct opposite. To Hegel the life process of thinking....and the real world is only the external, phenomenal form of the idea. With me, on the contrary, the ideal is nothing else than the material world reflected by the human mind and translated into form of thought."[10]

The distintive contention of Marx is that while he stands on the Hegelian foundation, he calls the Hegelian dialectic as 'standing on its head'. Obviously, contradistinguished with the Hegelian idealism, Marx justifies the case of materialism. Con-

9. Hegel saw the universe as the expression of a Divine Logic "working itself out by a process of perpetual contradiction and conflict. All human history spreads itself out before him as a long process of ideal conflict leading irresistibly towards the final exclusion of contradiction in the perfect realisation of the Universal Idea. This evolution of societies on the physical plane of existence was for him but the derivative expression of his ideal process." Cole : *Meaning of Marxism*, p. 270.

10. Marx : *Capital*, Vol. I, p. 25.

trary to Hegel, Marx argues: "It is not the consciousness of men that determines their being, but, on the contrary, it is their social being that determines their consciousness."[11] Yet the Hegelian foundation cannot be repudiated, for Marx accepts the formula of thesis, anti-thesis and synthesis.[12] According to Hacker, "Marx and Engels are willing to use the dialectic so long as it is stripped of its idealist foundation. Their strategies to stand on Hegel's theory which they believe to be standing head-downward, back on its feet. This must be done if the dialectic is to do service with a materialist base."[13] Consciousness is thus the product of evolution of matter. But having arisen on the basis of matter, it actively influences the latter's development...Dialectical materialism, however, does not in the least underestimate the role of consciousness in the development of matter, of being. As a product of matter and its reflection, consciousness does not remain passive, but actively influences the world. It is in this sense that Lenin wrote in his 'Philosophical Notebooks' that man's consciousness not only reflects the objective world but creates it.[14]

But Marx is a materialist owing to the fact that, unlike a metaphysical idealist (whose enquiry informs that only ideas are a fundamental reality), he advocates that matter is a reality. It is not a thing like Reason that motivates the law of dialectic, rather it is the Matter that plays decisive part in the drama of social progress. So Marx says: "In direct contrast to the German philosophy which descends from heaven to earth, that is to say, we donot set out from what men say, imagine, conceive, nor from men as narrated, thought of, imagined, conceived, in order to arrive at men in the flesh. We set out from real active men, and, on the basis of their real life process, we demonstrate the development of ideological reflexes and echoes of this life process. The phantoms formed in the human brain are also necessarily sublimates of their material life process

11. *Ibid.* Marx syas that the ideal "is nothing else than the material world reflected by the human mind, and translated into forms of thought." *Ibid.*, p. 29.
12. Lenin was right in saying how impossible it is to underst and Marx without having studied Hegel. The only important difference between them is that Marx "applied the dialectic to the future and indulged in much pseudo-scientific fortune-telling which Hegel would have been the first to condemn, and that, of course, he completely rejected Hegel's philosophical idealism." Cf. Wayper: *Political Thought*, pp. 200-1.
13. Hacker : *Political Theory, Philosophy, Ideology, Science*, p. 519.
14. Marx-Engels : *Collected Works*, Vol. 38, p. 212.

which is empirically verifiable and bound to material premises."[15]

Thus, contrary to metaphysical idealism that stands for the ultimate reality of thought and ideas, or mechanical materialism that regards evolution being a path taken by material things under the pressure of their enviornment, Marx propounds dialectical materialism signifying that evolution is the development of matter from within, enviornment helping or hindering, but neither originating the evolutionary process nor capable of preventing it from reaching its inevitable. To Marx matter is active not passive and it moves by an inner ncessity of its nature. Naturally the dialectical materialism of Marx is more interested in motion than in matter, in a vital energy within the matter inevitably driving it towards a perfect form. As Engels says: "The dialectial method grasps things and their images and ideas essentially in their sequence, their movement, their birth and death."[16]

Stalin has thus summed up the essential features of dialectical materialism :

1. The phenomena are generally conected with, dependent on, and limited by each other.
2. The phenomena should be considered from the standpoint of their movement, change and development.
3. Change is no more quantitative but as a result of gradual accumulation becomes qualitiative as well at a certain stage of development.
4. The internal contradictions are inherent in all things and phenomena, for all things have a past and a future, something dying away and something developing. The struggle between these opposite forces constitutes the internal content of the process of development and of the transformation of quantitative changes into qualitative ones.
5. Finally, the laws of evolution and change are discoverable. Hence, it is quite evident that the Hegelian and Marxian systems of dialectic stand distinctly opposed to each other on the point of motivating force that plays a decisive part.

In short, the dialectical materialism of Karl Marx contends the inevitable play of the formula of thesis, anti-thesis

15. Marx and Engels : *The German Ideology*, pp. 13-14.
16. Cf. Wayper, *op. cit.*, p. 200.

and synthesis behind which the force of matter plays the decisive part. "Morality, religion, metaphysics, all the rest of ideology and the corresponding forms of consciousness have thus no longer the semblance of independence. They have no history, no development: but men developing their material production and their material intercourse, alter along with their real existence, their thinking, and the products of their thinking. Life is not determined by consciousness but consciousness by life."[17]

The study of the general picture of world's development is an important task of materalistic dialectic. Engels says that dialectic "is the science of the general laws of motion and development of nature, human society and thought."[18] It regards development as movement from the lower to the higher, from the simple to the complex, as a leap-like revolutionary process. Morever, this movement proceeds not along a closed circuit, but in the form of a spiral, each spire being deeper, richer and more diverse than the preceding one. Dialectic sees the sources of development in the intrinsic contradictions of objects and phenomena. Only Marxist dialectics furnishes the correct, truly scientific understanding of the process of development. The basic laws of materialist dialectic give a general picture of the development of the world, its congnition and transformation. The law of the unity and the conflict of opposites reveals the sources, the driving force of development. The law of *the passage of quantitative into qualitative changes* indicates the leap-like revolutionary change of the world, the continuous transformation of the intrinsic quantitative changes of objects into fundamental qualitative changes. The l*aw of the negation of the negation* characterises the progressive spiral-like character of development.[19]

---

17. Marx and Engels, *op cit.*, pp. 13-14. The philosophy of Marxism is *dialectical materialism*. It is materialist because in solving the fundamental question of philosophy it proceeds from the premise that matter, or being is primary and consciousness is secondary. It recognises the materiality and knowability of the world, and examines the world as it really is. Marxist philosophy is dialectical because it examines the material world in constant motion, development and regeneration. V.G. Afanasyev: *Marxist Philosophy*, p. 21. Consequently dialectical materialism is a science which on the basis of a materialist solution of the fundamental question of philosophy discloses the more general, dialectical laws of the development of the material world and the ways for its cognition and revolutionary transformation. *Ibid.*, p. 22.
18. Engels : *Anti-Duhring*, p. 172.
19. Afan asyev, *op. cit.*, pp. 72-74. Drawing on scientific achievements and

However, the Marxist dialectic does not regard every new phenomenon, or everything that claims to be new, as truly new. It implies following important points :

1. The new is that which is progressive, improved and viable, which constantly grows and develops.
2. The new is invincible above all because it stems from the very course of development of reality and best of all corresponds to the objective conditions.
3. The invincibility of the new is particularly apparent in social development. The new in society triumphs because it corresponds to the requirements of economic life, of material production.
4. The new meets the interest of the advanced, progressive classes of society and that is why they fight vigorously for its victory.
5. The new in social development is also invincible, because its social base is constantly growing, expanding. The new, as it emerges, rallies round itself the most progressive forces of society.[20]

Marx's theory of dialectical materialism has been subjected to various lines of criticism :

1. It canot be conceded that dialectical materialism of which Marx and Engels so proudly claimed was an original and scientific contribution. Its foundations may well be traced in the works of Marx's predecessors and contemporaries. Keeping it in view, an American critic says that the *Communist Manifesto* of Marx and Engles "is, in fact, an extract from the thoughts of Helvetus, Rousseau, Morelly, Pierre Leroux Produhon, Bazard, Enfantin, Buret, Cabet, Dezamy and Considerant on the French side and from those of Hegel, Heine, Boerne, Gutzkow, Froebel, Feuerbach, Brouno, Bauer, Hess and Weitling on the German side. Marx is as lit-

---

society's practical exprience, at different stages of history, dialectic maintains that the world is an endless process of movement, regeneration the demise of the old and the birth of the new. Says Engels: "For it (dialectical philosophy) nothing is absolute.....It reveals the transitory character of everything and in everything; nothing can endure before it except the uninterrupted process of becoming and passing away, of endless ascendancy from the lower to the higher." Refer to his paper "Ludwig Feuerbach and the End of Classical German Philosophy" in Marx and Engels: *Selected Works*, Vol. III, p. 339.

20. Afanasyev, *op. cit.*, pp. 73-74.

tle original of Socialism and Communism as the Chairman of General Motors Corporation is the inventor of the automobile."[21]

2. It appears that Marx and Engels utilised the law of dialectic purely as a measure of expediency, i.e., to meet their purpose. Not the least of the difficulties that confront a student of dialectical materialism is that Marx and Engels never thoroughly worked out their ideas about it. It is pointed out that nowhere "do they treat it in detail, though it is, of course, assumed in all their writings."[22] After the death of Marx, Engels overstated the extent to which economic causes could be found for legal and political institutions. In a letter written to Blonch in 1890 (a letter which he found so satisfactory that he repeated the gist of it to Starkenburg four years after), Engels said: "Marx and I are partly responsible for the fact that at times our disciples have laid more weight upon the economic factor than belongs to it. We were compelled to emphasise its central character in opposition to our opponents, who denied it, and there was not always time, place and occasion to do justice to the other factors in the new reciprocal interactions of the historical process."[23] As a matter of fact, Marx was not interested in dialectical materialism as a philosophical system, rather wanted it as a basis for his programme of action. He was mainly impressed with the revolutionary use to which the method of dialectic could be utilised.[24]

3. Finally, although the dialectic may give us a valuable insight into the history of human development, the Marxists' claim that it constituted the only scientific approach to reality cannot be appreciated.[25] From the metaphysical

21. Stefan T. Possony (ed.): *The Communist Manifesto*, p. xiv.
22. Wayper, *op. cit.*, p. 201.
23. *Ibid*. p. 202.
24. J.L. Grey puts it in these words: "The fallacy into which Marx fell proceeds from two causes. As a perfectibilitarian communist he believed that a classless society, being inherently desirable on ethical grounds, must therefore be the next stage in social evolution. As an agitator and revolutionary he sees in the working class movement the only available instrument for the achievement of his aim in the immediate future, and consequently was tempted to regard it as the final negation of the negation." Refer to his essay" Karl Marx and Social Philosophy" in Hearnshaw (ed.): *The Social and Political Ideas of Some Representative Thinkers of the Victorian Age*, pp. 145-46.
25. Carew Hunt, *op. cit.*, p. 29.

point of view, it cannot be accepted that a dead thing like matter can be active and thus motivating. Only the force of spirit can motivate things and the lifeless, dead or inert matter undergoes development or change only owing to the existence of that invisible and incomprehensible force. The force of matter cannot be given the significance of being decisive as other non-material forces do serve the shape of society. Hacker thus asserts that even non- material forces can also motivate the process of dialectic. He adds: "Only a blind man would focus on a society's technology and ignore everything else...However, there are periods, perhaps when the invention and exploitation of new machines are not proceeding at a rapid rate, when non-economic forces can make their weight felt. And at these times, political, religious and other developments may seem to shape society."[26]

HISTORICAL MATERIALISM : ECONOMIC INTERPRETATION OF HISTORY

The doctrine of historical materialism (also designated as the materialistic or economic interpretation of history) is the application of the principles of dialectical materialism to the development of society. Naturally, it presents a materialistic interpretation of history. In other words, it offers an interpretation of history on the lines of dialectical materialism. For its purpose, it utilises the contention of materialism–a doctrine which denies the independent existence of mind and regards it as a derivative product of matter and takes consciousness as the result of motion of grey matter in the brain. Bu-Marxism, in this regard, contends that material things are 'powers of production' which include three things-(i) natural resources including land, climate, fertility of soil, mineral resources like coal and iron, water power etc., (ii) machinery, tools and technique inherited from the past, (iii) mental and moral qualities of the men of the time. The powers of production are the active determinants of historical development.

Thus, historical materialism designates the economic forces as the sole and ultimate determinants of historical development. Men may accelerate or change the direction of economic movement, but ultimately the character of life is really determined by the economic system, since the final cause of all social

26. Hacker, *op. cit.*, p. 522.

and political changes lies in the modes of production and exchange. According to Engels, historical materialism "designates that view of the course of history, which seeks the ultimate cause and the great moving power of all important historical events in the production and exchange, in the subsequent division of society into distinct classes, and the struggle of these classes against one another."[27]

According to this doctrine, the transition in history from one form of social organisation to another is not effected by the emergence of new conceptions of truth or justice or some new rational principles, but it is the product of new inventions which radically change the character of material things or the factors which influence the production and distribution of wealth. Legal and political institutions, cultural manifestations, religious and moral beliefs, art and literature etc. are the creations of the factors of production. In all stages of human life the forms or conditions of production determine the structure of society and the structure of society in turn makes attitudes, beliefs, actions, theoretical outlooks and the standards of civilisation. "The hand mill gives you society with the feudal lord, the steam mill a society with the industrial capitalist."[28] Marx says: "The mode of production and the material means of existence condition the whole process of social, political and intellectual life."[29]

So, history is the interplay of economic forces. In terms of social history, these economic forces imply two things-forces of production and relations of production. While the forces of production or technological and scientific knowhow include the available natural resources, the tools and machinery inherited from the past and the mental and moral habits of the people; the relations of production create social, economic and political institutions for the sake of making a most effective use of these forces of production. A change in the forces of production causes a corresponding change in the relations of production and the history of society is an interplay of these forces and relations of production. Engels says: "In every historical epoch the prevailing economic mode of production and exchange and the social organisation necessarily following from it, form the basis upon

27. Cf. Lancaster : *Masters of Political Thought*, Vol. III, p. 196.
28. Cf. Wayper, *op. cit.*, p. 203.
29. Marx : *Capital*, Vol. I, p. 25.

which it is built up, and from which alone can be explained the political and intellectual life of that epoch."[30]

However, it is obvious that the historical materialism of Marx is quite different from Hegel's interpretation of history in as much as he contends that the spiritual is fashioned by the material and not *vice versa*. While Hegel sticks to metaphysics, Marx relies on economics. It is economics that substituted primitive society by the slave society, the slave society by the feudal society, and then feudal society by the modern capitalist society. Besides, Marx predicted that the capitalist society would be replaced by the socialist society owing to the invitable role of the law of dialectial materialism.

In short, the doctrine of historical materialism regards economics as the decisive factor in the making of the social history. The history of every age and of every society must, therefore, be studied in the context of economics alone. Marx says: "The materialist conception of history starts from the principle that production, and with production the exchange of its production, is the basis of every social order; that in every society which has appeared in history, the distribution of the products, and with it the division of society into classes or estates, is determined by what is produced, and how the product is exchanged. According to this conception, the ultimate causes of all social changes and political revolutions are to be sought, not in the minds of men, in their increasing insight, into eternal truth and justice, but in changes in the mode of production and exchange; they are to be sought not in the philosophy but in the economics of the period concerned."[31]

The doctrine of historical materialism has been regarded by the Marxists as the most unique and distinctive contribution of the father of scientific socialism. According to Lenin, it "is the central point around which the entire network of ideas, expressed and discussed, turns. But the critics have discovered serious flaws inherent in this doctrine. It is pointed out that this doctrine lacks a proper nomenclature. Alexander Gray feels that it "is not too happy in its baptismal name."[32] A better designation would have been a 'Realist Conception of History' as suggested by Cole. Really speaking, it is an economic interpretation of history on account of the fact that in its view all

30. Cf. Seligman : *The Economic Interpretation of History*, p. 142.
31. Cf. Lancaster, *op. cit.*, p. 169.
32. Gray, *op. cit.*, p. 301.

the mass phenomena of history are determined by economic conditions alone. Hence, it has been widely commented by the critics that although philosophers right from Aristotle upto David Ricardo and Adam Smith have emphasised the significance of economics, but in the historical materialism of Marx, the importance of economic factor has been exaggerated. All events of social history, great and small, can never be interpreted only in terms of economics. The force of non-economic factors like religion, philosophy, culture, nationalism etc. cannot be thoroughly ignored and so the doctrine of Marx is too lop sided to explain all the facts of experience. The possession of wisdom, courage and other forms of talents, in different forms of social organisation, also bring about changes in the character of political and economic institutions of the society. The economic factor may undoubtedly exert a very effective influence. But the lure of personal glory, ambitions of the monarchs, adventurous spirits of the people, reciprocal rivalries and jealousies also play their part often times. The truth is that social events are influenced not only by the economic conditions but also by several other non-economic factors. The English philosopher Bretrand Russell rightly holds that larger events in our political life "are determined by the interaction of material conditions and human passions."[33]

CLASS STRUGGLE : ROLE OF ANTAGONISTIC SOCIAL SEGMENTS

The doctrine of class struggle is a corollary to the doctrine of historical materialism. It is true that St. Simon and Guizot had made use of this idea even earlier, but the original feature with Marx "is the union of this idea with Hegel's dialectic."[34] The doctrine, in simple words, emphasises that each dominant

---

33. This point has been reiterated by several noted writers. Laski says: "The impulses of men, in fact, are never referable to any single source. The love of power, herd instince, rivalry, the desire of display, all these are hardly less vital than the acquisitiveness which explains the strength of material environment." *Karl Marx : An Essay., Likewise, Carew Hunt says: "If it be true that the way in which men think and the various institutional and other forms to which their ideas give rise are influenced by the manner in which they make their living, the converse is equally true. Marx is a good servant but a bad master. He was quite right in drawing attention to the importance of the economic factor, which had been seriously neglected, but he gave it an undue prominence and thus over- simplified the complexity of the social situation as his followers have continued to this day." Op. cit.*, pp. 78-79.
34. Wayper, *op. cit.*, p. 597.

class necessarily develops its opposite class and, out of the clashes between the two a new ruling class emerges indicating the growth of society from one stage of development to another. Once more, the Hegelian line is apparent in the working of dialectic. However, the difference remains that while in Hegel the Spirit tends towards its goal, in Marx economics plays the part. In the present society, the class war "at least reaches its simplest phase when the capitalist class is faced with the proletariat."[35]

As the doctrine of class war is a corollary to the doctrine of historical materialism, it may be pointed out that while the latter embodies the theory of social change, the former describes its mechanism. It tells that all social movements which make history are class movements. Hence, every major historical epoch is characterised by the dominance of one economic class but yielding place to another rival class in the succeeding epoch which was exploited in the preceding era. The great movements of history are a consequence of the struggle between the two classes for economic and political power. In the words of the *Communist Manifesto*: "The history of all hitherto existing society is the history of class struggle. Freeman and slave, Patrician and Plebian, lord and serf, guild-master and journey-man, in a word, oppressor and the oppressed, stood in constant opposition to one another, carried on an uninterrupted, now hidden, now open, fight, a fight that each time ended either in a revolutionary reconstruction of society at large or in the common ruin of the contending classes."[36]

When social movements are class movements, the term 'class' occupies a different connotation for Marx. By the term 'class', Marx means a collection of people who feel a sense of solidarity created by their consciousness of their very position in the economic order of the day.[37] It implies that the persons in a class will entertain sentiments, illusions, forms of thought and views of life not as individuals but as members of the class. Taking the case of the present capitalist society, Marx insists that the lines are rigidly drawn between two classes –the bourgeoisie and the proletariat. The bourgeoisie is the owner of

35. Wayper says : "The Capitalism, the thesis, calls into being its anti-thesis, organised labour, and from the resultant class the final synthesis of the classless society will result when pre-history ends and history begins." *Ibid*.
36. Cf. Lancaster, *op. cit.*, pp. 172-73.
37. *Ibid.*, p. 177.

property and prospers on the illicit profits (surplus profits) from the labour of the proletariat. However, Marxism, being more emphatic on the side of the proletariat, defines it as a class whose existence depends upon the sale of its labour power. So Engels says: "The proletariat is that class of society whose means of livelihood entirely depend on the sale of its labour and not on the profits derived from capital: whose weal and woe, whose life and death, whose existence depends upon the demand for labour, depend upon the alternations of good time and bad, upon the fluctuations which are the outcome of unbridled competition. The proletariat, or the class of proletarians, in a word, is the working class of the nineteenth century."[38]

According to this doctrine, the development of society has witnessed following stages. First, there was the society of primitive communism knowing no class contradictions as such due to the communistic pattern of social life. Second, it was replaced by the slave society having freemen and slaves, the two classes contending for their respective mastery over one another. Third, the inexorable law of history worked and so this society was substituted by the feudal society. As agriculture became the force of production, the landlords ruled over the landless class of the serfs. Fourth, when the industrial revolution threw agriculture into the background, there emerged a new society called the capitalist society having capitalist and the proletariat as the two contending classes. Finally, Marx predicted that the same progress would lead to the emergence of a socialist society on the debris of the existing capitalist society.[39]

However, Marxism is particularly emphatic on the fact of class war going on in the present capitalist society. It is even prepared to admit that while, in the earlier epochs of history, there existed a complicated arrangement of society into manifold gradations, in the present bourgeois society it has simplified class antagonisms. It has brought forth new contending classes called the bourgeoisie and the proletariat: it has

38. Engels : "Principles of Communism" in *The Communist Manifesto* edited by D. Ryazanoff, p. 319. *The Communist Manifesto* says: " By bourgeoisie is meant the class of modern capitalists, owners of the means of social production and the employers of the wage labour. By proletariat is meant the class of modern wage labourers who having no means of production of their own are reduced to selling their labour power in order to live."

39. Marx and Engels : *The Communist Manifesto*, p. 49.

established new conditions of oppression and new forms of struggle. Marx is so optimistic that similar developments of bourgeoisie will invite its downfall, for the capitalist class digs its own grave. The *Communist Manifesto* says: *"The weapons with which the bourgeoisie felled feudalism to the ground are now turned against the bourgeoisie itself."*[40]

Curiously enough, Marx finds that the socialist society will reveal a new type of social development hitherto unseen. The Communist Manifesto says: "All previous historical movements were movements of minorities, or in the interest of minorities. The proletarian movement is the self-conscious, independent movement of the immense majority, in the interest of the immense majority." As it will be a classless society, the fact of class antagonism will disappear and with it the law of dialectic also lose its operation. Naturally, the socialist society will represent the climax of social development.

The doctrine of class struggle has been criticised in these important ways :

1. It is pointed out that Marxian interpretation of the term 'class' is not scientific, rather it is arbitrary. The society never lives in a condition of water-tight division between the two hostile classes. Obviously, Marx and Engels had primarily the case of France in their mind and hence they assumed that the proletariat largely consisted of urban factory workers and the bourgeoisie of the owners of industrial property. Indeed, the lines drawn by Marx are extremely vague and tenuous, since the various gradations in modern society are as manifold as in these past epochs before. As the world has persistently refused to divide itself rigidly into two hostile classes, the Marxian argument amounts to creating classes simply by arbitrary definition for a particular purpose. Sorel says: "According to Marx, a fully developed class is a collection of families united by tradition, interests and political views, and exhibiting such a degree of solidarity that one can attribute to it a personality and consider it a reasoning being which acts in accordance with its reasoning. It is clear that observation never shows us the perfect class; consequently, the Marxian theory of classes is an abstraction. As to the middle class, there is an incessant upward and downward movement of individuals; groupings

40. *Ibid.*
41. *Ibid*, p. 69.

are almost always temporary, very unstable currents agitate the mass; its influence is extremely variable and thence arises the chief source of the contingencies which are found in contemporary history. In the hope of reasoning more scientifically about the future, the social democrats proceed by abstractions; by ignoring the influence of chance they get rid of the middle classes."[42]

2. This doctrine is extremely pernicious in the sense that, according to it, all workers ought to regard themselves as proletarians and feeling convinced with the hopelessness of their situation, should hate their employers. It creates the feelings of hostile antagonism between the two classes and informs proletariat that it is now war to the death with victory assured to them. It thoroughly ignores the forces of love, co-operation and sacrifice. Murray comments that Marx "was a Mahdi preaching a holy war, a Peter, the Hermit preaching a crusade for the recovery of the holy city from the infidels who had impiously taken possession of it. Only the name of the holy city is Wealth, the infidels are the Capitalists, and the motives appealed to are somewhat different."[43] Marxism seems to identify every social force with a class having an economic condition and this equates its struggle between the classes of the exploiters and the exploited. On so many occasions, there have been a series of fights even among the ruling classes. According to Popper, "Indeed, so far the divergence of interests with the ruling and ruled classes goes, Marx's theory of classes must be considered as a dangerous over-simplification, even if we admit that the issue between the rich and the poor is always of fundamental importance."[44]

3. Finally, the prophecy made by Marx has also been disproved by the real conditions of the twentieth century. The com-

---

42. Lancaster, *op. cit.*, p. 179. Keeping the above interpretation in view, Lancaster says; "As propaganda this is excellent, if for no other reason than that it puts the worker on the side that, it informs him, is sure to win. As science it is considerably less satifactory, since there are grave diffculties about the term 'class' and therefore about the reality of the class struggle. In view of the fundamental importance of the conception of class, it is curious to see how little attention the Marxists give to defining it. It seems almost to be taken for granted that everyone knows what 'proletariat' and 'bougeoisie' mean." *Ibid.*, pp. 179-80.
43. Murray : *History of Political Science from Plato to the Present*, pp. 383-84.
44. Karl Popper : *The Open Society and Its Enemies*, Vol. II, Ch. 16.

binations of petty bourgeoisie in the shape of cartels and joint stock companies have saved the middle class from extinction and its eventual assimilation either with the bourgeoisie or with the proletariat. Likewise, it is not essential that the capitalist system would be substituted only by a rule of the proletariat. History shows that after the successful overthrow of the bourgeoisie, dictatorships have arisen and even they have again strengthened themselves on the support of the capitalist class.[45] Laski rightly observes: "The breakdown of capitalism might result not in communism but in anarchy from which there might emerge some dictatorship unrelated in principle to communist ideals."[46] In developing the doctrine of class war, Marx has certainly concerned himself with the labour conditions of England which "had all the symptoms of a hunger revolt based on acute misery."[47] To quote Carew Hunt: "Yet nowhere Marx seeks to prove that the worker is, in fact, fitted for the role assigned to him, nor does it occur to him that the negation of capitalism may lead to the emergence of a wholly new class which is, strictly speaking, neither capitalist nor proletarian. The belief in human perfectibility that he had inherited from the eighteenth century led him to believe that a classless society inherently desirable on ethical grounds, must be the next stage in evolution, which as a revolutionary and an agitator he saw in the working class movement the only available instrument for the achievement of this aim in the immediate future and was thus induced to regard it as the final 'negation'.[48]

ECONOMIC ANALYSIS : INEVITABLE DISINTEGRATION OF THE CAPITALIST SYSTEM

Marx took from the earlier economists like Smith, Ricardo and Lassalle the idea of labour power as creating value in the commodities and on this basis propounded his own theory of value which is almost an exact anti-thesis of his predecessors. This theory has got two aspects known as the labour theory of value and the theory of surplus value. The labour theory of value regards labour as the sole creator of value in a commodity

45. See Westmayer: *Modern Economic and Social System*; and E.F.M. Durbin: *The Politics of Democratic Socialism*.
46. Laski : *Communism*, pp. 87-88.
47. Cole : *Socialist Thought*, pp. 253-54.
48. Carew Hunt, *op. cit.*, p. 66.

and insists that the value of a commodity is determined by the amount of labour power spent over the production of that commodity. Marx uses the term 'exchange value' to denote the worth of an article in terms of its relation to other articles. This exchange value, commonly represented by price, may fluctuate according to the market conditions, but these fluctuations are accidental and donot eliminate or even obscure the real influence which determines both the value and ultimately the exchange value of a commodity. Thus, the labour time which is socially necessary for the production of commodities asserts itself like an over- riding law of nature in spite of superficial variations in exchange value, as the real standard or measure of exchange value.

The same interpretation further leads to Marx's theory of surplus value. As a result of inventions in science and technology, the instruments of production (like machinery, steam power, factories, electricity etc. enormously increased both in number and efficiency) are owned by a relatively small class of the capitalists. The capitalist buys the labour power of the destitute workman, applies it to the machinery and raw materials which he owns and as a result produces a commodity having exchange value. The commodity is sold at a price which is greater than the amount expended on the amount of the workmen's wages and the upkeep of the factory. This difference between the exchange value of the manufactured commodity and the price paid to the workmen who produced it is called the surplus value. Marx contends that in each factory or enterprise the wages paid to the workers "are not equivalent of the full value they produce but only equal to about half of this value or even less. The rest of the value produced by the worker during hs working day is taken outright by his employer."[49]

Marx tells us that this appropriation of surplus value by the capitalist class constitutes the fundamental injustice which socialism seeks to remove. In fact, the capitalist industrial system is different only in form from a slave society. The slave worked perforce and created value, the modern workman creates surplus value under a free contract into which he voluntarily enters. But in as much as the workman is unprovided with the means of production, he has, in fact, no alternative but to sell the one commodity he possesses (labour power) to the capitalist who after paying him a bare subsistence wage pock-

49. Emile Burns : *What is Marxism*?, p. 21.

ets the proceeds. From this theory of surplus value, Marx deduces three laws :

1. There is the law of capitalist accumulation. Competition forces the capitalist to accumulate capital, i.e., to install more and more labour saving machinery in his factory in order to produce more goods. Yet in so doing he acts to his own hindrance, because any increase in the production of constant or variable capital is liable to resist in a fall of his profits.
2. Then, there is the law of the concentration of capital. Under competition the number of the capitalists will contract, for the weaker elements will be driven out of the field and swell the rank of wage earners.
3. Finally, there is the law of increasing misery. As a result, the misery of the workingmen will continue to increase. With the increase of machinery production will go higher, but it will also entail unemployment and consequent fall in wages. Meanwhile, the unemployed worker will be pushed to the state of increasing misery and degradation and join the 'industrial reserve army' to overthrow the rule of the bourgeoisie.

Marx says : "Along with the constantly diminishing numbers of the magnates of capital, who usurp and monopolise all advantages of this process of transformation grow the mass of misery, oppression, slavery, degradation, exploitation; but with this too grows the revolt of the working class, a class always increasing in numbers and disciplined, united, organised by the very mechanism of the process of capitalist production itself. The monopoly of capital becomes a fetter upon the mode of production, which has sprung up and flourished along with and under it. Centralisation of the means of production and socialisation of labour at least reach a point where they become incompatible with their capitalist integument. This integument is burst asunder. The knell of capitalist private property sounds. The expropriators are expropriated."[50]

Marx's theory of value has been denounced. Although he is right in pointing out the injustices of the capitalist society done to the labour class, his assumption that labour is the only source of value connot be accepted. When labour is only one of the agents of production, its reward may also be nothing more

50. See Carew Hunt, *op. cit.*, p. 89.

than a part of the total dividend. Nor does the prophecy of Marx hold true that with the growth of capitalism the conditions of revolution will draw more and more near. Besides, with the help of new inventions the middle class has survived its entity and the proletariat not reached the stage of misery and degradation. A great economist like Keynes has thus described Marx's *Capital* as "an obsolete text book on economics...not only scientifically erroneous, but without interest of application for the modern world."[51] Popper calls the whole theory as 'redundant.'[52] Likewise, Carew Hunt finds that it "introduces an element of confusion."[53] He further says: "It is, in fact, a theory of exploitation, designed to show that the propertied class has always lived on the labour of the non-propertied class...Labour without capital is equally unproductive. The capitalist system is open to abuses like any other. Yet those who desire to abolish it would do well to reflect that the only alternative to the profit and loss motive that has so far shown any indication of being equally effective is the fear of punishment imposed by a totalitarian state."[54]

STATE : AN INSTRUMENT OF EXPLOITATION AND OPPRESSION BY ONE CLASS OVER ANOTHER

The Marxian theory of state finds place in the principal tenets of his political philosophy already discussed in the preceding sections. However, under this head, a synthesised study of all of them will reveal the attitude of Marx towards the state. It may be discussed under these heads:

(i) State as a Class Institution : Various doctrines of political theory deal with the nature, origin and scope of state activity, but behind their divergent conclusions, a general recognition exists on the point that the state exists to promote the welfare of its citizens and that with the development of civilisation it has become more conscious of its very mission or ultimate end. But Marx repudiates all such doctrines and characterises the state as a class institution. According to Marx, the state is nothing more than a machine for the exploitation and oppression of one class by another. It follows that the edifice of state is rooted in the class war. Engels maintains that it is not a natural institution and that

51. Keynes : *Essays in Persuasion*, p. 300.
52. Popper, *op. cit.*, Vol. II, p. 165.
53. Carew Hunt, *op. cit.*, p. 90.
54. *Ibid.*

it comes into being when society is cleft into irreconciliable and antagonistic groups. Taking the case of the present capitalist society, the *Communist Manifesto* declares that the state is the 'executive committee of the bourgeoisie'. Since the capitalist class is in power, it uses the state as an instrument to exploit and oppress the proletariat. The whole paraphernalia of the state is so devised as to consolidate the hold of the bourgeoisie itself over the class of the proletariat. As Laski says: The capitalists identify social good with their own preservation. Attacks upon them they will punish as sedition. Education, justice, religious teaching are tempered to serve their interests. This is not, it should be insisted, a conscious effort on their part to exclude members of the non-possessing class from a share in social benefit, it is simply the natural reaction to the material environment. But the class excluded from the privileges of possession naturally also desires a share in them. Hence arises, in every society, a struggle between the classes for control."[55]

(ii) State as an Institution of Violence : If so, the state stands not on the will of the people but on violence. It uses violence. The dominant class utilses every instrument to exploit and suppress the dependent class. The military, police, courts, law, breaucracy etc. all are employed to use violence and force for the good of the dominant class. Naturally, when these things are in the hands of the bourgeoisie in capitalist society and are being used against the proletariat, in a socialist society the position will be reversed. Then, the working class will take hold of them and the same apparatus will be used against the bourgeois class. Every society undergoes a change by means of a revolution. In the view of Marx, revolution is the midwife of progress, it 'delivers the child but can do not more for it'. The bourgeoisie prepares the ground for revolution. The accumulation of capital into fewer and fewer hands, the network of the means of transport and communication established for the good of the bourgeoisie, and the concentration of surplus profits create conditons necessary for the outbreak of a revolution.

The *Communist Manifesto* says : "The modern worker, on the contrary, in stead of rising with the progress of industry, sinks ever deeper beneath the social conditions of his own class.

55. Laski : *Communism*, p. 63.

The labourer becomes the pauper, and pauperism increases ever more rapidly than population or wealth." Coker thus sums up: "Thus, the capitalist system enlarges the number of workers, brings them together into compact groups, makes them class conscious, supplies them with means of inter-communication on a world-wide scale, reduces their purchasing power, and by increasingly exploiting them arouses them to organised resistance. Capitalists acting persistently in pursuit of their natural needs and in vindiction of a system dependent upon the maintenance of profits, are all the time creating conditions which stimulate and strengthen the natural efforts of workers in preparing for a system that will fit the needs of a workingmen's society."[56]

Marxism predicts that as the bourgeoisie has to dig its own grave, the society of proletariat will arise when the time of revolution is ripe. According to Marx, "A social system never perishes before all the productive forces have developed for which it is wide enough: and new, higher productive relationships never come into being before material condition for their existence have been brought to maturity within the womb of the old society."[57] In the bourgeois society the dominant class necessarily produces the conditions when the stage of revolution inevitably arises, for the proletariat reaches that stage of misery and degradation which nothing short of a revoluton can emancipate."[58]

But what type of means should be adopted to make the revolution successful. In this regard, Marx visualises that only revolutionary and violent means are useful. The *Communist Manifesto* declares at the end: "They Communists disdain to hide their views and aims. The openly declare that their ends can be achieved only by the forcible overthrow of all existing social conditons. Let the ruling classes tremble at a communist revolution." However, the influence of the English traditions wrought upon a change and so in 1872 Marx told the Amsterdam section of the first International that he did not deny that there were countries such as England and the United States

56. Coker : *Recent Political Thought*, p. 152.
57. Carew Hunt, *op. cit.*, p. 102.
58. Carew Hunt comments that the role of bourgeois democracy "was thus to act as the foster mother of the proletariat during the stage of pre-emancipation." *Ibid.*, p. 99.

where the workers could be able to achieve their aims by peaceful means.[59]

(iii) State as a Temporary Institution : Finally, Marx regards the state as a temporary institution. After the successful overthrow of the bourgeoisie, the state will merely have a 'quasi' character. It will be like an instrument in the hands of the proletariat to be used against the bourgeoisie and the reactionary and counter-revolutionary forces. Engels strongly asserts that the party which "has triumphed in the revolution is necessarily compelled to maintain its rule by means of that fear with which its arms inspire the reactionaries. Now the proletariat will set up its own centralised apparatus of forces in order to complete the defeat of the capitalist class and defend the new order against attacks from enemies both within and without. A staunch Marxist like Trotsky says that a revolutionary class which has conquered power with arms in hand, is bound to and will suppress rifle in hand, all attemps to tear power out of its hands. Where it has against a hostile army, it will oppose it by its won army. When it is confronted with armed conspiracy, attempt at murder or killing, it will hurl at the heads of its enemies an unsparing penalty."[60]

This interim period has been called the Dictatorship of the Proletariat. But in encompassing the downfall of the bourgeoisie and other reactionary and counter-revolutionary forces, the state will effectuate its own downfall in order to ultimately wither away. The classless society will change into a stateless society. Marx says that in order to breakdown the resistance of the bourgeoisie, the workers invest the state with a revolutionary and temporary form. At another place, he says: "Between capitalist society and communist society lies the period of the revolutionary transformation of the one into another. There corresponds to this also a particular transitional period in which the state can be nothing but the revolutionary dictatorship of the proletariat."

In the *Communist Manifesto*, Marx and Engels outline a series of steps that should be taken by state during this transitional period. These are :

1. Property in land should be abolished and rents used for public purposes.

---

59. G.M. Stekloff : *History of the First International*, pp. 240- 41.
60. Laski, *op. cit.*, p. 140.

2. A progressive income tax should be levied.
3. Rights of inheritance should be abolished.
4. The property of emigrants and rebels should be confiscated.
5. There should be state control, centralisation and monopoly of credit.
6. The state must control and centralise transportation and communication.
7. There should be expansion of state control of production and state improvement of agriculture.
8. There should be enforcement of obligation of all persons to work and the formation of industrial armies to be used specially in agriculture.
9. Agricultural and manufacturing industries ought to be combined, together with a population re-settlement with a view to the elimination of the urban-rural division.
10. Child labour should be abolished and a system of free public education established.

In the phase of the dictatorship of the proletariat, the primary object of the state will be to destroy the capitalist system, transfer the control of the means of production from private to public hands, and set up a centralised planned economy. This will imply the establishment of a classless society and will prepare ground for the eventual advent of a stateless soceity in which regular military and police will be substituted by the people's militia, the bureaucracy by the representatives chosen by and responsible to the people, and the assemblies and councils by the free and voluntary groups or associations of the people. But the law of dialectic will now be out of operation, since the society will have no class contending for the mastery over or against another. That will be the stage of communism and the state 'will wither away to find its place in the museum with bronze axe and spinning wheel.'

Marx thus describes : "In the higher phase of communist society after the enslaving subordination of individuals under division of labour, and therewith the anti-thesis between mental and physical labour, have vanished after labour has become not a means to live, but has become itself the primary necessity of life: after the productive forces have also increased with the all-round development of the individual, and all the springs of the co-operative wealth flow more abundantly - only then can the narrow horizon of bourgeois right be fully left behind, and society inscribe on its banners: 'From each according to his ability, to each according to his needs.' Likewise, Engels says: "Since the state is only a temporary institution which is to be made use of in the revolution in order forcibly to suppress the opponents, it is perfectly absurd to talk about a free, popular state. So long as the proletariat needs the state, it needs it not in the interest of freedom, but in order to suppress its opponents: and when it becomes possible to speak of freedom, the state as such ceases to exist."[61]

The Marxain theory of state has been a subject of denunciation on certain grounds :

1. It is pointed out that Marx has studied the origin of state from a wrong point of view and in this direction the conditions of civil war in France have left a deep and abiding influence on his mind. To call the state as an institution of violence or class coercion is never justifiable if its worth is objectively adjudged. The state is the first condition of civilised life and its termination is bound to call back that horrible state of nature as portrayed by Hobbes. True it is that at times the state has done exploitation of and oppression over the people, it does not depict the real nature and significance of political authority. Right from the days of Plato and Aristotle, it has been believed by a good number of thinkers that the state is an ideal institution, a moralising agency and an instrument of public welfare. Laski very rightly says that the state strives by its policy to effect such an adjustment of the relationship between citizens as will enable each of them to realise, if he so desires, the fullest implictions of human personality."[62] William Ebenstein thus points out: "If Marx had accorded the political factor its due weight, if he had fully grasped the importance of Reform Act in England and of the Jacksonian revolution in the United States, he might have realised that Socialism too might be accomplished without violence in countries that possessed the democratic traditions strong enough to absorb far-reaching social and economic changes without resorting to civil war."[63]

---

61. See Carew Hunt, *op. cit.*, p. 106.
62. Laski : *Communism*, p. 174.
63. Ebenstein : *Today's Isms*, p. 11.

2. It is pointed out that the existing form of dictatorship of the proletariat frustrates the purpose of Marx. Recent history reveals that the dictatorship of the proletariat is, indeed dictatorship over the proletariat and the ruling class is so ambitious that it does not look like relinquishing its political power in a form eventually leading to the withering away of the state. It may well be argued that wherever a revolution of the Marxist type occurs, it leads to much the same form of government seeing which it is impossible to introduce communism without resorting to violent conditions. Carew Hunt remarks: "For the essence of the dictatorship of the proletariat is that it is the rule of a single section of society whose mission is to eliminate all other sections as counter-revolutionary."[64]
3. Finally, the Marxian theory of state denounces the democratic character of authority and wants to substitute it by a new type of democracy called the 'people's democracy'. The democracy of the other type is labelled as 'bourgeois democracy' which, according to Marx, stands for the government of the dominant class alone. On the other hand, people's democracy is pure or genuine in as much as there is no class antagonism and no powerful class to exploit or oppress the powerless. But the truth is that even this proletarian democracy established under the dictatorship of the proletariat is no democracy at all. Carew Hunt again observes: "Yet this is the negation of democracy, which is the rule of the people, the term people in this context transcending that of class, so the merchant, farmer and small shopkeeper belong to it with as good a right as do the industrial worker and agricultural labourer. Democracy, if it has any liberal content, accepts that in any society there will be conflicts of interests, and, thus, provide the necessary machinery for reconciling them. Marx's position is altogether different."[65]

SOCIOLOGY OF ALIENATION : CONTROVERSY OF YOUNG MARX AND OLD MARX

Marxism, as given in the writings and utterances of Karl Marx and Fredrick Engels, is said to have started from 1848 when the world saw the *Communist Manifesto* as the Bible of

64. Carew Hunt, *op. cit.*, p. 107.
65. *Ibid.*

Scientific Socialism. Some recent studies on Marxism have, however, thrown light on the early writings of Marx that he produced in the premature stage of his thought. These were written by him in the German language while living mostly in France. These papers, however, remained unpublished for some reason. Marx died in 1883 and Engels in 1895. Then, an anxiety to discover the unpublished papers of Marx developed. In 1902 Mehring published some of the literary remains of Marx and Engels. In 1911 Plenge brought out a book depicting pre-1848 Marx as a genuine pupil of Hegel. Interest in this direction developed more and more. In 1920 Mayer published the first volume of the definitive biography of Engels that led to the renewal of interest in Hegel and the impact of his philosophy on early Marxism. In 1923 Karl Korsch wrote his *Marxism and Philosophy* in which he discussed the abiding impact of Hegel on 'young' Marx. In the same year *History and Class Consciousness* written by George Lukacs (with its subtitle *Studies in Marxist Dialectic*) elaborated the same theme.

Researches in this important direction took a concrete shape of their own in 1927 when a complete edition of the early writings of Marx was produced first in Frankfurt and then in Berlin (under the editiorship of D. Rajaznov) under the auspices of the Marx- Engels Institute in Moscow. As a result of this, the early writings of Marx saw the light of the day with the titles of *Early Works* (EW), *Paris Manuscripts* (PM) and *Economic and Philosophic Manuscripts* (EPM). These works appeared in the German language, but their English version could be available as late as in 1961. These portions are in the form of unrefined, unrevised and unfinished documents, but herein contemporary sociologists have been able to find out Marx's theory of 'alienation'. It not only shows his intense debt to the philosophy of Hegel, it also puts him as a social theorist different from what he appeared after the publication of his *Communist Manifesto*. Thus, Marx of the days of 1844-46 is described as 'Young Marx' in contrast to Marx of the subsequent period described as 'Old' or 'Mature' Marx. Owing to this, a sort of controvery has come into being hinging on the point that the latter stands for the detriment of the former.[66]

The EW, or the PM, or the EPM of young Marx is a rough collection of four parts. In the first part we find his study of the wages, capital and rent. Here he critically examines the

66. David McLellan : *Marx before Marxism*, p. 210.

economics of Adam Smith and, at the same time, lays down his theory of alienation. Here he notes that the bitter struggle between the capitalist and the worker not only determines the wages but also reduces the workers to the status of a commodity. Borrowing from a German economist Wilhelm Schulz, he also hits at the facts of pauperisation and dehumanising effects of industry on the life of the labour class. The result is that the interest an individual has in society is in exactly inverse proportion to the interest which society has in him. The only wheels which political economy puts in motion are greed and competition or war among the greedy capitalists. This realisation of labour appears as dimunition of the worker, the objectification of the loss of and the subservience to the object and the appropriation as alienation, as externalisation.[67]

The fact that the worker is related to the product of his labour as to an alien object means that the more the worker produces, the more he approaches loss of work and starvation. The sense of dis-possession leads to the fact of alienation. The state of alienation reaches a point where a worker feels alienated not only from what he produces but also from his society, his own class, even his ownself.[68] This argument is continued in the second part of the EPM where Marx says that the worker is only a worker when he exists as capital for himself and he only exists as capital when capital is there for him. The existence of capital is his existence, his life, since it determines the content of his life independent of him. This tragic condition of life can find its end only in the state of 'democratic' communism. Thus, Ruge calls the transition in the thought of Marx relating to the period of 1843- 44 as transition to 'crass socialism.[69]

The last part of these writings consists of a rather uncharacteristic digression on the question of whether the world was created or not. One of the key ideas in Marx's picture of man is that man is his own creator; any being that lives on the favour of another is a dependent being. If man has created

67. *Ibid.*, p. 169.
68. Schlomo Avineri puts the meaning of Marx in these words: "We arrive at the result that man (the worker) feels himself to be freely active only in his animal function eating, drinking and procreating, or at most also in his dwelling and in personal adornment, while in human functions he is reduced to an animal". *The Social and Political Thought of Karl Marx*, p.106.
69. McLellan, *op. cit.*, p. 184.

society, he may also change it. The law of social change cannot be retarded. In a state of communism the evil of alienation having its from in the fact of reifiction or objectification of labour will go. As he says: "The position of communism is the negation of the negation and hence for the next stage of historical development, the necessary actual phase of man's emancipation and rehabilitation."[70]

A study of the ideas of Marx as contained in the EPM leaves this definite impression that it is like a collection of incomplete papers with its matter in a quite disjointed form. If we keep our study of Marxism confined to this period of the last century, we may definitely come to this conclusion that his use of the terms like 'alienation' and 'realisation of the human essence' shows that his analysis is not scientific. Nor is it empirical or devoid of any value judgement; "it is full of dramatically over-simplified pronouncements that border on the epigrammatic."[71] McLellan concludes: "Marx himself supplied conclusion to the *Paris Manuscripts* and it is impossible to draw one from such a disjointed work; economics, social criticism, philosophy, history, music, dialectics and metaphysics are all present. Although each section is dominated by a different subject matter, there is a certain amount of mutual influence. Here for the first time occur what Engels described as three constituent elements in Marx's thought–German idealist philosophy, French socialism and English economy–appear together, if not united."[72]

The defenders of Marx, however, have their own strong points to counteract the propaganda of two Marxes,the old one to the detriment of the young one. It is said that there is continuity in the thought of Marx with this line of distinction that while in the EPM he looks like a mild critic of the bourgeois system, in the later writings he is the most ardent champion of the socialist system. In no way, the young Marx can be taken as the friend, philosopher and guide of the capitalist class in his early writings. Marx is far away from the influence of a liberal Hegelian like Arnold Ruge and a pseudo-materialist like Feuerbach. "If his political standpoint in 1844-46 is still democratic, his critique of society increasingly sounds the socialist theme. And it is precisely this critique which causes

70. *Ibid.*, p. 191.
71. *Ibid.*, p. 179.
72. *Ibid.*, p. 206.

him to see society as a whole, i.e., to develop a theory of how it functions. Feuerbach had sought the secret of alienation in anthropology; Marx sees it in sociology or rather, he is obliged to sketch out a rudimentary sociology in order to account for phenomena–religion, class division, the state–which had remained incomprehensible as long as radical thinkers failed to grasp their historical and social character."[73]

CRITICAL APPRECIATION : MARX AS THE PROPHET OF A NEW AND JUST ERA

Although the principal tenets of Marxian political philosophy have been subjected to scathing criticism, the magnitude of his achievements cannot be denied even by his most unsympathetic critics. His ideas struck the world like a flaming religion. As a result, conversion to his creed appeared like conversion to a religion and to the acceptance of an entirely working class philosophy utterly uncompromising in its hostility to capitalism. His doctrines were looked as 'scientific', for they were based not upon moral or ethical consideration but upon the demonstrable laws of economics and politics borne out by the overwhelming testimony of history. His pointed emphasis on the significance of economic factors rendered great service to social studies and his recognition of the close interdependence between the legal and political institutions and the prevailing economic system makes him the most important social philosopher of the last century. His ideas inculcated a sense of class consciousness among the labour class and thus saved the toiling millions from the oppressions and exploitation of the small section of the bourgeoisie. It is owing to this fact that for the advocates of scientific socialism, Marx is an incarnate personality. In 1883 Engels thus said: "We are what we are because of him: without him we should still be sunk in slough of confusion."[74]

73. George Lichteim: *Marxism : An Historical and Critical Study*, p. 45.
74. Cf. Berlin, *op. cit.*, p. 219. Berlin thus concludes : "All those whose work rests on social observation are necessarily affected. Not only the conflicting classes and their leaders in every country but historians and sociologists, psychologists and political scientists, writers and creative artists; so far as they try to analyse the changing duality of the life of their society, owe the form of their ideas in part to the works of Karl Marx." *Op. cit.*, p. 274. Alexander Gray thus observes : "Yet despite his prosy and interminable dullness the confusions and inherent contradictions of his theories, despite his manifold defects in temperament and disposition render in him the least fitted of men to be a hero of the people, the indubitable fact remains

Various colourful expressions have been made to appreciate the contributions of Karl Marx. For instance, Liebnecht declared that Marx "has raised social democracy from a sect, from a school to a party which now already fights unconquered, and in the end will win the victory."[75] His great friend and collaborator (Engels) offered his tribute thus: "Just as Darwin discovered the law of the evolution of organic nature, so Marx discovered the evolutionary law of human history, the simplest fact hitherto hidden under ideological overgrowths, that above all things, men must eat, drink, dress and find shelter before they can give themselves to politics, science, art, religion, or anything and the corresponding stage of the economic evolution of a people or a period provides a foundation upon which the national institutions, legal systems, art and even the religious ideas of the people in question have been built and upon which, therefore, their explanation must be based."[76]

The most outstanding contribution of Marx, however, should be seen not only in his examination and enunciation of the laws of social development on which the entire structure of political, economic and cultural pattern of human existence depends, it also lies in his message given to the oppressed and exploited humanity. Thus, an English socialist like Prof. Laski observes: "Marx put in the forefront of social discussion the ultimate question of the condition of the people. And he performed the incalculable service of bringing to it a message of hope in an epoch where men seemed to themselves to have become the helpless victims of a misery from which there was no release. In every country of the world where men have set themselves to the social improvement, Marx has always been the source of inspiration and prophecy. Where he was also irresistibly right, was his prophecy that the civilisation of his epoch was built upon sand. And even the faults of his prophecy may be pardoned to an agitator in exile to whom the cause of the oppressed was dearer than his own welfare."[77]

---

that Marx has proved the most influential figure of the nineteenth century." *The Socialist Tradition*, pp. 333-34.

75. Cited in Laidler, *op. cit.*, p. 158.
76. *Ibid.*
77. Laski : *Karl Marx : An Essay*, pp. 47-48.

32

LENIN

This means that no state, however democratic its form, not even the reddiest political republic.....is capable of giving the people what they need; the free organisation of their own interests from below upward, without any interference, tutelage, or coercion from above. That is because no state... in essence represents anything but government of the masses from above downward, by an educated and thereby privileged minority which supposedly understands the real interests of the people better than the people themselves.

— Michael Bukharin

The greatest leader and theoretician of the Marxist school in the twentieth century was V.I. Lenin (1870-1924) of Russia described as a 'Genius theorectician'[2] and 'a rare combination of a theorist and a man of action'.[3] The thing that strikes our attention at the very outset is that since Lenin made some necessary revisions in the theory of classical Marxism in order to apply it to his country, his interpretations have been taken as an updated version of classical Marxism by his protagonists, but as shrewd deviations by his critics. However, before coming to this point of debate, it shall be better first to have a brief study of the views of Lenin on some important themes like state, Communist Party, revolution and imperialism as the final stage of capitalism.

Lenin's political ideas are contained in a number of pamphlets and monographs that he wrote from time to time.

---

2. Bukharin: *Lenin as a Marxist*, p.5
3. Hallowell : *Main Currents in Modern Political Thought*, p.490.

His ***What is to be Done?*** is a major work on the organisation and role of the Communist Party. His ***State and Revolution*** elarifies the nature and operation of the transitional state formed after the successful socialist revolution what was termed 'dictatorship of the proletariat' by Marx and Engels. Then, his ***Imperialism - The Final Stage of Capitalism*** presents a reinterpretation of Marxism in the phase of the growth of monopoly capitalism in the twentieth century.

STATE : A TRANSITIONAL INSTITUTION EVENTUALLY TO WITHER AWAY

Like Marx and Engels, Lenin regards state as an instrument of exploitation and oppression by one class over another. But the main contribution of Lenin should be seen in his exposition of the nature of the state after the successful socialist revolution and its eventual 'withering away' to signify the life of a totally emancipated man kind. In his view, after the overthrow of the bourgeoisie, a 'quasi-state' of the workers would be established in place of the existing bourgeois state. This new state of necessity would be a classless organisation, but it would function as representative of the revolutionary working class. Thus, the state would ruthlessly suppress all reactionary and counter-revolutionary forces. In January, 1918 Lenin declared that the Bolsheviks "must break the old, savage, despicable and disgusting prejudices that only the rich can administer the state, since every rank and file worker who is able to read and write can do organisational work. There are masses of the people like that."[4]

The destruction of the capitalist state would lead to the construction of a new state (a socialist state) in the form of a 'quasi' or a transitional state. Power would be in the hands of the working class and the state would be used as an instrument to liquidate all reactionary and counter-revolutionary forces. It would be the 'dictatorship of the proletariat'. In declaring like this, Lenin is a dogmatic follower of Marx and Engels who repudiate the line of anarchism that state

4. Alexander Gray : *The Socialist Tradition*, p.468.

would be abolished just after the successful revolution of the working class.[5] The new transitional state of the dictatorship of the proletariat has clearly nothing to learn from the old in the essential feature of being a class organisation and an instrument of suppression. "But indeed from the moment the dictatorship of the proletariat is acknowledged to be a kind of state, freedom is excluded: While the state exists, there is no freedom. When freedom exists, there will be no state."[6]

The dictatorship of the proletariat is not the end of class war, it is rather a continuation of the same in a different form and with a different goal. Now the class in power is at war against its enemy and is determined to crush and bury the enemy for ever so that it may never arise in the form of its anti-thesis. And the aim is to see the end of state itself. The state would perform certain functions like defence, security, communications, banking etc. At the same time, it would be a proletarian democracy in fact. It would ensure participation of the workers through their free and voluntary association at all levels of administration. It would prohibit exploitation of any kind. It would remove all social and economic evils that prevail in a bourgeois state. All power of the working class would be in the hands of their only party (Communist Party) and the constitution would declare the state as 'the state of the workers and toilers'. Thus, Lenin could say that the Soviet democracy was million times more democratic than any bourgeois democracy of the world. "This was the first open assertion of the doctrine of parliamentary democracy."[7]

But the most striking feature of such a state is to act for its own end. It has to 'wither away' in the end so that the era

---

5. Lenin says that the error of the anarchists lies not in favouring the abolition of the state (for on this point he is at one with them), but in preaching that the state can be abolished overnight. *State and Revolution,* p.46. Elsewhere he repeats that the mistake of the anarchists should not be defended. The state must be preserved during the period of transition. *The Task of the Proletariat in Our Revolution,* p. 16.
6. Gray, *op, cit.* p. 470.
7. R.N. Carew Hunt : *The Theory and Practice of Communism,* p. 182.

of communism is ushered in with this principle 'from each according to his ability, to each according to his needs'. As Gray puts: "The establishment of the dictatorship of the proletariat on the debris of the bourgeois state represents the point as from which the state should, in theory, begin to wither away. From that moment classes begin to disappear, and with the progressive disappearance of classes, the state and indeed, the party itself, suffer atrophy *pari passu*."[8] In short, in Lenin's view, the state in the form of dictatorship of the proletariat "is not communism; it is the period of transition in which the state is withering away."[9]

The implications of Lenin's theory of state may be thus enumerated:

1. The state is a special organisation of force; it is an organisation of violence for the suppression of the enemy class.
2. The state is the armed and the ruling proletariat. Hence, it would exist in the transitional stage. To proilaim the withering away of the state prematurely would distort the historical process.
3. After the successful revolution, the party and the state would be inextricably interlinked. Class relationships would be exercised under the leadership of the Communist Party.
4. At the same time, the state would create conditions of its own decomposition. It would establish a classless society that would find its culmination in a stateless society.
5. The retention of the state during the transitional phase would be necessitated by the new conditions created by imperialism—the final stage of capitalism.

However, keeping in view the political development of Russia after the first World War, a critic may say that Lenin played fast and loose with what he preached and what he did. Crick says : "Fundamentally Lenin had rejected politics as a practical, natural, compromising and humane activity

8. Gray, *op, cit.* p. 475.
9. G.H. Sabine: *A History of Political Theory,* p. 740.

for the belief that history had created a single true ideology, immediately accessible only to the heightened consciousness of the vanguard of the working class and their leaders, and that it was in the future interest of the whole working class that this must be instituted by whatever means were needed. Human history was a history of violent class oppression, so that violence which hastened on the coming of a classless society and the famous 'withering away of the state' was not only justifiable in terms of the eventual lessening of human suffering, but was an 'historical necessity'. The present always had to be sacrificed for the future, and they were sure of the future. But the actual history of the Russan Revolution and the Soviet State disapproves any notion of predictable historical necessity."[10]

COMMUNIST PARTY : VANGUARD OF THE PROLETARIAT

One important point where Lenin takes a line neither so boldly conceived nor so strongly appreciated by Marx and Engles is the role of the party of the workers (Communist Party). He lays special stress on the role of the Communist Party as 'vanguard of the working class'. It is the party that would indoctrinate the working class, organise the workers and prepare a plan of revolution. It would be 'a small and compact core of the reliable, experienced and hardened workers with responsible agents in the principal districts'. It would absorb all the best elements of the working class, their experience, their revolutionary spirit, and their unbounded devotion to the cause of the proletariat. "But in order that it may be really the vanguard, the Party must be armed with a revolutionary theory, with a consciousness of laws of the movement, with a knowledge of the laws of the revolution....The Party must take its stand at the head of the working class, it must see ahead of the working class, lead the proletariat and trail behind the spontaneous

10. Bernard Crick : *Socialism,* pp. 60-61.

movement."[11]

As a competent strategist and tactician, Lenin intoduces these positive proposals in his view about the organisation and role of the Communist Party :

1. Given the Party's task of assuming he role of leading all exploited classes in the democratic revolution, it must have an all-Russian organisation.
2. The organisation should be composed of professional revolutionaries or such people who would devote themselves fully to party work and they would be fully trained.
3. The leadership would have to be chosen through the oligarchical principle of co-option. There would be election to all offices of the Party and full publicity of its activities would be made.
4. The principle of centralism would also work. It means that the highest unit of the Party under its supreme leader would take all decisions and issue directions that must be followed by all lower units of the organisation.
5. Since the Bolshevik Party had stagnated while remaining underground, he urged his followers to extend their bases, rally all organisations of the workers, and make the nucleus of the workers party broader and broader. And yet the idea of a 'clandestine party,' could not be fully abandoned.[12]

But the Communist Party becomes the state after the successful socialist revolution. It assumes all power in its

11. See Stalin: *Foundations of Leninism,* pp. 105-06. A resolution adopted at the 20th Congress of the Communist International in 1920 said: "The Communist Party is a party of the working class: its most progressive, most class conscious and, therefore, most revolutionary part. The Communist Party is created by means of selection of the best, most class-conscious, most self-sacrificing, and far-sighted workers. The Communist Party is the lever of political organisation, with the help of which the more progressive part of the working class directs on the right path the whole masses of the proletariat and the semi-proletariat." See W.H. Chamberlain: *The Russian Revolution,* Vol. II, p. 361.
12. Stalin, *op. cit,* p.35.

hands in the name of the state of the workers and the toilers. Its size is constantly reduced so as to keep it as a body of the most faithful and most active members in the form of the 'rallying centre of the finest elements in the working class'. It would provide inspiration and leadership to the dictatorship of the proletariat. As Stalin affirms: "Not a single important political or organisational question is decided by the Soviets and other mass organisations without guiding directions from the Party."[13] Apparently the dictatorship of the proletariat is the dictatorship of the communist party, but Lenin says that its real implication is 'leadership of the communist party' in spite of the fact that the party runs the administration of the country with the help and cooperation of the Soviets, the trade unions and other mass organisations as 'transmission belts'.[14] In the words of A.G. Meyer: "Perhaps Lenin's most conspicuous contribution to twentieth century politics is his conception of the Communist Party as a creative history-making force and as the general stuff of the world revolution. In the Bolshevik movement he created the model on which many other modern totalitarian parties have been built. Lenin must, therefore, be considered a pioneer of the tota-litarianism of our age."[15]

REVOLUTION : FROM FEUDALISM AND CAPITALISM TO SOCIALISM

How can a revolution be brought about? On this question, as we have already seen, Marxism is both revolutionary and evolutionary. But Lenin sticks only to the side of a violent revolution. Taking lessons from the Paris Commune of 1871 and his abortive attempt of 1905, he very confidently asserts that the aim of a revolution can be achieved only by violent means. All tactics of a revolution are justified if they help in achieving the goal. The communists "should prepare a secret programme of insurrection and carry it out with the help of theirmost

13. David McLellan: *Marxism after Marx,* p. 89.
14. *Ibid,.* pp. 134-35.
15. Meyer: *Leninism* (London: Westview Press, 1986), p. 19.

faithful and most committed followers."[16] In this connection, following important points emerge from what he asserts:

1. No revolutionary movement can be durable without a stable organisation of the leaders which preserves continuity.
2. The broader the mass which is spontaneously drawn into the struggle, which forms the basis of the movement and participates in it, the more urgent is the necessity for such an organisation, and the more durable this organisation must be because broader in mass, the easier it is for any demagogue to attract the backward sections of the mass.
3: Such an organisation must consist mainly of the people who are professionally engaged in revolutionary activities.

Lenin's ideas on revolution started from the orthodox tradition which he inherited from Plekhanov and more specifically from his examination of Russia's economic development. If deeply examined, his views are not different from those of Trotsky who insisted on the idea of a 'permanent revolution'. It is evident from Lenin's own statement: "From the democratic revolution we shall at once and precisely in accordance with the measure of our strength, the strenght of a class-conscious and organised proletariat, begin to pass to the socialist revolution. We stand for uninterrupted revolution. We shall not stop half-way."[17]

The significant feature of Lenin's theory of revolution is that it takes into account the possibility of creating a revolution in any country of the world, if the leadership is capable of doing it. The role of the party as the 'vanguard of the proletariat' is very important. Though a party of the working class, it may include all revolutionary sections of the people who have full faith in or revolutionary devotion to the eventual triumph of socialism. In this way, Lenin "removed Marxian revolution as a possibility only in

---

16. While clarifying the view of Lenin, Laski says: "There is no other way of breaking the class will of the enemy except by the systematic and energetic use of violence." *Communism,* p. 139.
17. David McLellan, *op. cit,.* p. 93.

advanced capitalist societies and placed it within the realm of possibility for virtually any country, provided a revolutionary situation existed there and a revolutionary party was present that could guide the society on the road to socialism. By particularising Marxian analysis to Russia. Lenin taught that the Marxian model was useful in any society. It was a lesson that other revolutionaries, including the Chinese, were to learn well."[18]

IMPERIALISM : FINAL STAGE OF CAPITALISM

Lenin calls imperialism as the 'final stage of capitalism'. As he says: "Imperialism is capitalism in that stage of development in which the domination of monopoly capital and finance capital has taken shape; in which the export of capital has acquired preponderating influence, in which the division of the world by international trusts has begun; in which the partition of all the territory of the earth by the greatest capitalist countries has been completed."[19] With this point of view, Lenin called the first World War 'not a people's war' but an imperialist war and discovered its cause in the world of economics. It was a result of the clash among the capitalist countries of the world that had their vested interest in keeping their hold over as big a part of the world as possible for the sake of collecting raw materials therefrom and then flooding the markets with their finished goods so as to reap as much profit as possible. What Lenin really desired to emphasise was that the meaning of Marxism should be reinterpreted in the light of such development of capitalism in the twentieth century.

Following important implications may be drawn from this interpretation :

1. Capital has become international and monpolistic in its dominance.
2. Uneven economic and political development is absolute law of capitalism.
3. The export of capital has a preponderating influence.

---

18. A. S. Cohan: *Theories of Revolution,* p. 93
19. Lenin: *Selected Works,* Vol.II, p. 709.

4. There is the beginning of the division of the world by international trusts and cartels.
5. After the war, begins the partition of the world among victorious capitalist countries.

With such an interpretation of the growth of capitalism in its final form, Lenin could put his finger at the plight of the colonial countries of the world. He insists that the problem of a socialist revolution should be related to the problem of liberation from colonialism. Since the theatre of class struggle has shifted from the capitalist to the poor and backward countries of Asia and Africa, the possibilities of revolution may be explored there. Second, the system of imperialism has made the capitalist countries so rich that even the proletariat of these places has seen its 'bour-geoisification', a point that was taken by Engels. It has its adverse effect on the pace of a socialist revolution. "The solidarity of the working class is thus undermined, since a privileged upper stratum of the workers is enabled to live at the expense of the oppressed nations."[20]

LENIN AS A MARXIST : CONTROVERSY OVER HIS BEING A TRUE OR A SHREWD FOLLOWER OF HIS TEACHER

Now we may be in a position to examine the case of Lenin as a Marxist. In this direction, we have two different views. According to one view. Lenin is regarded as a true and dogmatic Marxist who interpreted and followed his teacher like a faithful disciple. On one occasion Lenin himself asserted: "You cannot eliminate even one basic assumption, one substantial part of the philosophy of Marxism (it is as it were a solid block of steel) without abandoning objective truth, without falling into the arms of

20. Gray, *op. cit.,* p. 464.

the bourgeois reactionary falsehood."[21] So Stalin could assert that Lenin neither repudiated any principle of Marxism, nor did he add any new one to the stock of Marxism. In his view, Leninism signifies three important points."[22]

1. Leninism is the updated version of Marxism. What Marx and Engels said in the nineteenth century, Lenin could reinterpret it in the light of the astonishing developments of the twentieth century.
2. Leninism is the applied form of Marxism. What Marx and Engels wrote and said, Lenin put it into practice.
3. Leninism is the application of Marxism to the peculiar conditions of Russia.

But these contentions are not convincing to the critics who take Lenin as a shrewd leader and a theoretician who followed his master where he liked and freely changed his master's ideas where he felt so necessary for his purpose. Hallowell makes three important points in this direction:[23]

1. According to Marxism, a successful socialist revolution would take place only in a very advanced capitalist country, but Lenin could make it possible in a backward country like Russia with the use of the power of the peasantry. Marx had contended that following a revolution, the land should be immediately collectivised. On the other hand, Lenin argued that the discontent of the peasantry could be successfully utilised to bring about a socialist revolution and, as a

21. Lenin: *Collected Works,* Vol XIII, p. 281. Leninism is, however, that school of Marxism in the age of imperalism which did not let this conclusion remain the final word. Instead of resigning themselves to the failure of the original Marxian prognosis, or even taking pleasure in the changed prospects, the Leninists are in a continual search for forces not recognised by Marx as a revolutionary force that will carry on the fight for the socialist revolution in lieu of the Western proletariat. In this sense, Leninism is the last refuge of that optimum which characterised the doctrine of Marx and that it maintains the spirit of the *Communist Manifesto."* A.G. Meyer, *op. cit.,* pp. 247-47.
22. Stalin, *op. cit.,* p. 13.
23. Hallowell, *Main Currents in Modern Political Thought.,* pp. 490-92.

matter of tactic, he encouraged the peasants to believe that following the revolution, they would become individual land-owners and for a time, following the Revolution, sustained them in that belief.

2. For the most part Marx favoured imperialism, since he believed that it would hasten the advent of socialism by extending capitalism to backward areas of the world and since socialism could only come into existence after capitalism had been established. On the other hand, Lenin believed that national revolts should be encouraged whether socialist in character or not, since any allies against the capitalists were useful whether strictly proletarian or not. Uppermost in Lenin's mind was the desire to bring about a successful revolution in Russia, and if Marxian theory had to be sacrificed or modified to that end, then he was willing to sacrifice or modify it.

3. The most significant way, however, in which Lenin differed from Marx was his interpretation of the role of the proletariat. According to Marx, the proletariat would become increasingly class conscious and militant as the contradictions in capitalism would become more and more apparent and acute. According to Lenin, the proletariat, if left alone, would develop only a trade union mentality. The working class is unable to develop a socialist consciousness of the irreconcilable nature of the class struggle unless it is impregnated with this consciousness from outside. This would appear to be a direct refutation of the Marxian thesis. Mistake or not, it was Lenin's belief that the proletariat had to be impregnated with the socialist consciousness, organised and led into revolution and the instrument for this purpose was the Communist Party.

No doubt, the revision of Marxism at the hands of Lenin looks like both an updated version of the ideas of the teacher as well as a shrewd modification of his preceptor's teachings for a certain purpose. The charge of 'careful opportunism' on Lenin cannot be entirely washed off. We may endorse the view of Sabine that. "Lenin's Marxism presents the anomaly of being at once the most dogmatic assertion of orthodox adherence to the principle of the master and at the same time the freest rendering of it on points where circumstances required its modification."[24]

CRITICAL APPRECIATION : LENIN AS A SHREWD STRATEGIST AND TACTICIAN

The contributions of Lenin have been differently evaluated. His ideas contained in his *State and Revolution* are described as his greatest contribution to political theory.[25] Crick comments that 'the greatest innovation made by Lenin, hardly present in Marx, was the concept and reality of the party rather than movement.'[26] At the same time, it is commented that Lenin distorted the foundations of classical Marxism and laid the foundations for its replacement by new and contradictory interpretations. "By claiming to know better the true interests of the working class than the working class itself, Leninism represented the intellectual marginalisation of the class, a process that after 1917 resulted in its political expropriation. Communism became whatever Lenin or Stalin said it was. It is out of ambiguities like these that post-communism was born."[27]

Lenin was a worthy successor to and a continuator of the cause and teaching of Marx and Engels in the new historical epoch, the epoch of imperialism and proletarian revolutions. Leninism—Lenin's views making a system and a doctrine—is the creative elaboration of the views and doctrines of Marx and Engels on the basis of fresh scientific and practical data. Leninism is the Marxism of the twentieth century and it is, therefore, right and proper that the revolutionary world outlook of the working class and its communist parties is called Marxism-Leninism today. Without Leninism there could be today no Marxism as a living guide to understand-

---

24. Sabine, *op. cit.,* p. 741.
25. L. Colletti: *From Rousseau to Lenin,* p. 224.
26. Bernard Crick: *Socialism,* p. 61.
27. Richard Sakwa: *Post-Communism,* p.9.

ing reality and to revolutionary aition. Marxism-Leninism is an integral international doctrine which has become the theoretical asset and guide of the Communists and revolutionaries of the world.

In the light of what we have said above, main contributions of Lenin may be pinpointed as under :

1. In Lenin the Russian and the international working class movement acquired a great thinker, a brilliant strategist and a technician who made a creative study of new economic, political and ideological phenomena in the light of the Marxist doctrine.
2. Lenin enriched Marxist economic science with his study of imperialism as the highest and last stage of capitalism.
3. Relying on the ideas of Marx and Engels, Lenin created a coherent doctrine of socialist revolution and advanced the key propositions on the revolutionary situation, the objective and subjective factors of revolution, the growth of the bourgeois-democratic revolution into a socialist revolution initially winning out in one individual country.
4. Lenin interpreted the nature and the characteristic features of the dictatorship of the proletariat as the truly popular power consistently expressing the interests of all the working people, clarified the substance of the socialist state and socialist democracy, brought out the principal regularities of socialist society and formulated a concrete programme for its construction.
5. Lenin profoundly developed Marxist theory of the colonial and national question and of the principles of proletarian inter-nationalism.

Of course, Lenin gave to the world something new by putting the fundamental postulates of Marx and Engels, whom he reverently addressed as 'twin stars', into practice. No doubt, he was a great tactician and a competent strategist apart from being an excellent theorist. And it is for this reason that he had to make modificatory inter-pretations of

Leninism. It is well observed: "Marx's statement that a socialist society can be established only in a highly civilised and industrialised country remains unrefuted in spite of Lenin's adaptation of Marxism to Russia. Yet, even if his is bastard Marxism, no one will minimise the significance of what he bequeathed to Russia and to the world."[28]

---

28. Wayper: *Political Thought,* p.230. In the words of M.A. Kaplan: "Under Lenin's leadership, the Bolsheviks were the inheritors of that strand of the tradition that believed that the revolution would inevitably result from the self-conscious activities of the revolutionary vanguard, that is the leadership of the Communist Party, the legitimacy of which rested on its ability correctly to interpret history and to act effectively upon this understanding. This vanguard would recognise the correct historical moment and would seize it to introduce a new scientific regime in which, in Lenin's phrase, administration would be replaced by accountancy meaning that politics of discretion would be replaced by addition or logic. It would bring to pass scientifically first socialism and then communism. History, in effect was God and the party its pope, or at least its authorised accountant." Refer to his "Introduction: What is Communism?" in his (ed): *Many Faces of Communism,* p. 2.

33

MAO

Once our party has seized state power, it should immediately expropriate the big landowners and the factory owners. Whether this expropriation requires the use of buying out, it is a matter primarily to be determined not by us, but by the conditions prevailing when we attain political power and is even more determined by the actions of the landowners themselves. We should not state that ransom is impermissible under all conditions.

— Fredrick Engels[1]

A further reinterpretation of classical Marxism may be seen at the hands of Mao Tse-tung of China who occupies the same position in his country what was enjoyed by Lenin in Soviet Russia. As such, the same point of debate comes up: whether Mao is a true Marxist or not. We shall see that as Lenin had made certain modifications in the tenets of classical Marxism so as to apply it to the peculiar conditions of Russia, Mao had done the same so as to apply it to the peculiar conditions of China. That is why, Maoism may be defined as the Sinified version of Marxism-Leninism. A new feature of Maoism should, however, be traced in the fact that he showed extra zeal in implementing the 'utopian' element of Marxism through the system of 'communes' so as to establish his claim that China was the only country in which the rudiments of final stage of socialism (communism) could be seen. So Hans Granqvist says: "What today is called Maoism is in part a theoretical complex of communist idea representing a further development of Marxism-Leninism

1. Marx - Engels : *Collected Works,* Vol. II, p. 438.

but by and large remaining within its framework and in part the practical application of those ideas. It is in the latter area that Mao has contributed something original: first he has dared to try to apply the utopian element of Marxism in a much more fundamental way than have other communist leaders (at any rate, he goes much farther than the present leaders of the Soviet Union) : second, he has attempted to harmonise Marxian utopianism with China's unique conditions and traditions."[2]

ON CONTRADICTION : SYNDROME OF ANTAGONISTIC AND NON-ANTAGONISTIC DIFFERENCES

According to the law of dialectical materialism, progress is caused by the role of opposite forces subsisting within a phenomenon. Marx, Engels and Lenin call them thesis versus anti-thesis having their reconciliation in a synthesis. Mao puts the same idea in his theory of contradictions. In his paper 'On Contradiction' of 1937, he contends that the total reality of this world teems with contradictions as life and death, plus and minus, action and reaction, positive and negative, combination and dissociation, class struggle, offence and defence, and war and peace. In other words, he contends that the law of unity of opposites is the most fundamental thing in materialist dialectic. It demands that everything should be observed from two angles—the whole and the parts—if one wants to settle a dispute, answer a question, perform a task, or even direct a military operation.

While referring to the two-world outlooks, Mao contends that in the history of human knowledge, there have always been two views concerning the laws of development—the metaphysical and the materialist-dialectical. The former view of 'vulgar evolutionism' consists in looking at the world from an isolated, static and one-sided angle and thereby it regards all things of this world as for ever isolated from one another and for ever changeless. Contrary to this, the latter view advocates the study of development of things from inside, from the relationship of one thing to others. As the

2. Granqvist: *The Red Guard: A Report of Mao's Revolution* (Eng. Trans. by E.J. Farisi). p. 12.

basic cause of development of things does not lie outside but inside and in their contradictions, social development is chiefly owing to the development of inherent contradictions in man's social life, namely, the contradiction between the productive forces and the relations of production, the clash between the classes, the struggle between the old and the new order. In a word, the basic cause of the development of a thing is not external but internal, contradictions taking to two basic forms 'relative rest and conspicuous change.[3]

However, a novel feature of Mao's theory of contradictions is that he classifies all contradictions into two kinds—non-antagonistic and antagonistic. Non-antagonistic contradictions are those differences that may be resolved by discussion, negotiations and other peaceful ways as differences among the members of the Communist Party. But antagonistic contradictions are those which can be resolved only by means of a revolution or a war as differences between capitalist and working classes or between socialist and capitalist states. As he says: "Qualitatively different contradictions can only be solved by qualitatively different methods. For example, the contradiction between the proletariat and the bourgeoisie is resolved by the method of socialist revolution; the contradiction between the great masses of the people and the feudal system is resolved by the methods of democratic revolution; the contradiction between colonies and imperialism is resolved by the methods of national revolutionary war; the contradiction between the working class and the peasantry in a socialist society is resolved by the methods of collectivisation and mechanisation of agriculture; the contradiction within the communist party is resolved by the methods of criticism and self-criticism; the contradiction between the society and nature is resolved by the method of developing the productive forces. Processes change, old processes and old contradictions disappear, new processes and new contradictions emerge and the methods of resolving contradictions differ accordingly."[4]

3. Mao: *On Contradiction*, p. 9.
4. See Stuart R. Schram: *The Political Thought of Mao Tse-tung*, pp. 130-31.

Further, Mao distinguishes between principal contradiction and principal aspect of a contradiction. In the development process of a complex thing, there are many contradictions among them one is necessarily the principal one whose existence and development determine or influence the existence and development of other contradictions. In any contradiction the development of the contradictory aspect is uneven and of the two contradictory aspects—primary and secondary. For instance, in the feudal epoch, capitalist forces had a subordinate position, but in the new period of social development, the subordinate became the dominant. Mao also takes into account the identity and struggle of the aspects of contradictions. In his view identity, utility, coincidence, interpermeation, interpenetration, interdependence, interconnection all mean same things and refer to two conditions. First, each of the two aspects of every contradiction in the developmental process of a thing finds the presupposition of its existence in the other aspect and both aspects coexist in an entity. Second, eachof the two contradictory aspects in the given conditions tends to transform itself into the other which is called identity. The dialectical materialism advocates that a contradictory aspect cannot exist in isolation as each loses the very condition of its existence in the absence of another.

The law of contradictions is the law of ceaseless development of the society according to the tenet of dialectical materialism. Struggle within the contradictions is ceaseless, it exists both when the opposites coexist and when they are transforming themselves into each other and the struggle is especially manifest in the latter case. Mao frankly admits the prospects of contradictions even when the classless society is transformed into the stateless condition of life. Contradictions may take place within the Communist Party as well which may be resolved by means of criticism and self-criticism. It is required that a line of action correctly devised for a given stage will, or should, remain valid until the advent of conspicuous change, when contradiction within that process is resolved. The important thing is that a contradictory aspect has a special quality of transforming itself into an extremely antagonistic position what Mao calls 'dialectical reversal'. But in 1957 Mao came to hold the view that all contradictions of a socialist society are non-antagonistic and, as such, may be resolved peacefully without undergoing a dialectical reversal.

What we have said earlier about Hegel and Marx should be repeated now that the formula of dialectical process of development is adopted for a particular purpose and when it is served, it is abandoned. With Mao the case is a little different. Unlike Marx, Engels and Lenin, he frankly talks about the possibilities of contradictions in a socialist society, but the end is the same. In Mao's strong affirmation, all such contradictions are of a non-antagonistic variety and hence they may be resolved by peaceful means like discussion and negotiation. So in reality there is no difference between Marxism and Maoism on this point except this that Mao clarifies an eventual situation. Contradiction can be synonymised with dissimilarity, opposition, conflict and antagonism. Since the leader in power is always confronted with some hostile opposition and since he lives vigilant to crush such a force, the thesis of contradiction imparts a theoretical justification for his acts of commission and omission. The doctrine of contradictions serves the purpose of a shrewd leader who herein gets a ready-made framework adaptable to any situation of his choice. As a matter of fact, any serious discussion on this subject looks like 'a tepid and tiresome verbal game.'[5]

JOINT OR DEMOCRATIC DICTATORSHIP OF THE PROLETARIAT: THESES OF NEW DEMOCRACY AND NEW ECONOMY

A striking feature of Maoism should be seen in Mao's view of a section of the 'left wing' of the feudal lords and the capitalists as a 'revolutionary force' particularly in a country under colonial dispensation. Not merely the peasantry and the urban industrial working class but the landlords and the capitalists also may make a united front to fight against the imperial power and thereby win national emancipation. It follows that the hall-mark of a revolutionary class lies in playing a distinctly and strictly an anti-imperialist role.

5. Benjamin Cohen: *The Communism of Mao Tse-tung, p. 140*

Naturally, if the various classes joining the revolutionary ranks adopt a rigidly anti-imperialist attitude, the prime basis of the determination of the 'quality' is available and their revolution, irrespective of their class character, becomes a part of the proletarian socialist world revolution. In this way, Mao asserts that the Chinese national bourgeoisie in the era of imperialism retains to a certain degree a revolutionary quality which enables it "to ally with the proletariat and petty bourgeoisie to oppose the enemies it sets itself against."[6] It well implies that feudal and capitalist elements may survive in a socialist state provided they support the Communist Party and happily work under its supreme leadership. Mao frankly states that all the classes in the 'interim socialist state' "will be under the leadership of the working class and the Chinese Communist Party and we have the people's democratic dictatorship led by the working class through the Party :"[7]

In 1957 Mao issued six principles for distinguishing 'poisonous weeds' from fragrant flowers' :[8]

1. Words and deeds should help unite, and not divide, the people of all our nationalities.
2. They should be beneficial, and not harmful, to socialist transformation and socialist construction.
3. They should help to consolidate, and not undermine or weaken, the people's democratic dictatorship.
4. They should help to consolidate, and not undermine or weaken, democratic centralism.
5. They should help to strengthen, and not shake off or weaken, the leadership of the Communist Party.
6. They should be benificial, and not harmful, to international socialist unity and the unity of the peace-loving people of the world.

Thus, what is called 'dictatorship of the proletariat' by

---

6. Mao: *Selected Works,* Vol. II, p. 634.
7. Mao: *Selected Works,* Vol. IV, p. 1480. A noted Chinese writer Hu Chiaomu in 1954 says: "In the present historical period the People's Republic of China still permits the national bourgeoisie to exist. Herein lies the difference between people's democracy in China and people's democracy in the countries of South-East Europe." *Thirty Years of Chinese Communist Party,* p. 76.
8. Mao: *Selected Works,* Vol. V, p. 412.

Marx, Engels, Lenin and Stalin, becomes joint or democratic dictatorship of the proletariat' at the hands of Mao. The word 'democratic' has a special significance here that creates a line of basic difference between the model of 'people's democracy' as established in Poland and the 'new democracy' as introduced by Mao in China. In the former model there is no place for feudal and capitalist elements at all; in the latter model, feudalism and capitalism of small and medium scales are allowed if these elements are prepared to live under the direction and control of the Communist Party. Mao has made this innovation so as to harmonise his socialism with the political and economic culture of his countrymen. It may also be named 'joint dictatorship of several revolutionary classes'. In 1939 he had said: "Politically, it means the joint dictatorship of several revolutionary classes.... Economically it means nationalisation of all big enterprises.... distribution of the land of the landlords among the peasants and at the same time the general preservation of private capitalist enterprises."[9]

The new democracy of Mao has its complementary part in his thesis of 'new economy'. In simple words, it means the system of 'mixed economy'. In his Report to the Seventh Congress of the Chinese Communist Party held in April, 1945 Mao explained that the task of New Economy "is to assure the Chinese people of the possibility of freely develo-ping a private capitalist economy which, however, must not hold its grasp over the livelihood of the people.[10] In 1947 he further clarified that private capitalism would not be wiped out and the new democratic revolution "will eliminate feudalism and monopoly capitalism. It will eliminate the landlord class and the bureaucratic bourgeoisie (enriched by the Government offices under the Nationalists); but it will not eliminate capitalism in general, nor the petty and middle bourgeoisie. On account of the backwardness of the Chinese economy, it will be necessary to permit the existence, for a long time, even after national victory, of the capitalist economy represented by the broad petty bourgeoisie and middle bourgeoisie."[11]

9. Mao: *Selected Works,* Vol. II, p. 642.
10. See B. Cohen, *op. cit.,* pp. 115-16.
11. See Peter S. Tang: *Communist China Today,* p. 253.

The implementation of the systems of 'new democracy' and 'new economy' should be done according to the law of, what Mao calls, 'bloodless change'. In stead of dismantling the entire bourgeois system in a single hasty jolt and thereby upsetting the entire economic stability pregnant with many insurmountable difficulties and then reverting to the old line in pursuance of a new economic policy, Mao believes in following a correct line of creating basic conditions for transition to socialism by peaceful means as far as possible. The line taken by Mao, though looking like a radical departure from the line of orthodox Marxism, is in consonance with Engels' theory of'buying out rather than violent acquisition of capitalism'. The private sector is allowed a limited place, it is put under restraints imposed by the government of the Communist Party, and then it is hoped to be reformed and transformed in a way that its corrupt and backward face is ultimately dispensed with the state economic sector.[12]

It shows that Mao's analysis of classes in the Chinese society is different from that of Marx and Lenin. He lays less emphasis on the role of industrial proletariat, but more on that of the rural peasantry. Not only this, he finds his friends in the semi-proletariat and petty bourgeoisie provided such segments are prepared to live under the control of the Communist Party. As he says : "To sum up, it can be seen that our enemies are all those in league with imperialism, the warlords, the bureaucrats, the comprador class, the big landlord class, and the reactionary section of the intelligentsia attached to them. The leading force in our revolution is the industrial proletariat. Our closest friends are the entire semi-proletariat and petty bourgeoisie. As for the vacillating middle bourgeoisie, their right wing may become our enemy and their left wing become our friend ---

12. A theorectician of the Chinese Communist Party, Shu Wel-kuang says: "In a state where the proletariat has seized political power, under definite social and historical conditions, establishment of the principle that capitalists can be basically transformed under socialist guidance is another brilliant contribution of Comrade Mao Tse-tung to the treasure-house of Marxism-Leninism." Cohen, *op. cit.,* p. 127.

but we must be constantly on our guard and not let them create confusion within our ranks."[13]

REVOLUTION : EMPHASIS ON THE MEANS OF VIOLENCE AND GUERILLA WARFARE

Marxism is a revolutionary doctrine. We have seen Lenin's views on this question where he suggests as to how the socialism of Marx can be implemented. But Mao makes an improvement upon it in the light of the typical conditions prevailing in poor and backward countries of the Third World. He believes in the strategy of two-pronged revolution—first a bourgeois-democratic revolution that would yield place to the 'democratic dictatorship of the proletariat'. The subsidiary revolution displaces social, economic and political institutions of the medieval period; the 'main revolution' brings socialism after the successful overthrow of the bourgeois order. But Mao's stress is on three main points. First, the cooperation of the left-wing feudal and bourgeois elements may be enlisted in a revolution if such elements are willing to support the cause of a socialist revolution. Second, the leadership of the revolution must remain in the hands of the Communist Party and all elements of the joint front must follow its command. Last, more emphasis is to be given to the role of the peasantry living in the rural areas and not to the urban industrial class. As Mao said in 1927: "The leadership of the poor peasants is absolutely necessary. Without the poor peasants there can be no revolution. To attack them is to attack the revolution. The general direction they have taken in the revolution has never been wrong."[14]

---

13. Mao; *Selected Works,* Vol, I, p. 19.
14. As Mao further says: "Every Communist must grasp the truth: 'Political power grows out of the barrel of a gun.' Our principle is that the Party commands the gun, and the gun must never be allowed to command the Party. Yet, having guns, we can create Party organisations, as witness the powerful party organisations which the Eighth Route Army has created in northern China. We can also create cadres, create schools, create mass movements. Everything in Yunan has been created by having guns. All things grow out of the barrel of a gun." Mao : *Selected Works,* Vol. II, p. 224.

The main features of Mao's theory of revolution may be summed up as under:[15]

1. The whole theory of Marxism-Leninism should be revised in the light of the local conditions existing in the poor and backward countries of the Third World like China. Here a large peasantry combined with other revolutionary elements fighting against the colonial power may form a united front under the leadership of the Communist Party. Thus, a revolution may occur in a pre-capitalist society, if it is properly guided by the Communist Party that has the potentiality to lead the society through different stages of social development.
2. It follows that in a country where the working class is not available in sufficient strength, or it is unable to participate in the revolutionary movement, other classes constituting 'semi-proletariat', which may be in a similar relationship with the dominant class as the proletariat is with the bourgeoisie, may have class consciousness and, therefore, revolutionary potential.
3. Since the under-developed countries of the Third World are predominantly agricultural, much reliance should be laid on the role of peasantry, though petty-bourgeoisie may also join hands with the peasant forces. Moreover, the real centres of struggle would be in the rural areas. Thus, a socialist revolution would primarily be anti-feudal and secondarily anti-bourgeois in character. The slogan should be 'from villages to the cities'.
4. All means of violence and extremism, including guerilla warfare, should be adopted by the revolutionaries.
5. The concept of the 'mass line' must also be understood. It signifies that there is a continual movement towards communism. It is based on the principle that one stage gives way to another new stage. But the new stage already exists in the minds of the masses. It is,

15. A.S. Cohan, *Theories of Revolution,* pp. 107-08.

however, scattered and fragmented; therefore, the party leadership must bring the ideas together and return them to the masses. The method of the mass line includes four progressive stages—perception, summarisation, authorisation and implementation.

6. Revolutionary fervour must be maintained even after the successful results of a socialist revolution. Revolution must go on so that the revolutionary era does not become part of a dimmer past.

This impression may easily be gathered that Mao's theory of revolution is an improvement upon the line of Lenin we have seen earlier. As Cohen says: "It can reasonably be argued that Lenin had opened the door and Mao stepped through it. That is, Mao's strategy for waging the revolutionary struggle in China constituted a practical advance over Lenin's general idea of establishing peasant soviets in backward countries.'[16]

MAO AS A MARXIST : CONTROVERSY OVER HIS BEING A TRUE OR A SHREWD FOLLOWER OF MARX AND LENIN

The Chinese revolution of 1949 is indisputably one of the most important events of the mid-twentieth century and its doctrine, known as Maoism, has accordingly been one of the chief elements in the contemporary war of ideas irrespective of its intellectual value. Measured by European standards, the ideological documents of Maoism and especially the theoretical writings of Mao himself appeared in fact extremely primitive and clumsy, sometimes even childish in comparison with what is given by the purposeful theorists of the Soviet Union.[17] "Maoism in its full shape, is a radical peasant utopia in which Marxist phraseology is much in evidence but whose dominant values seem completely alien to Marxism. Not surprisingly, this utopia owes little to European experience and ideas. Again, "Maoism may be seen as a naive interpretation of few

16. B. Cohen, *op. cit.,* p. 54.
17. Kolakowski: *Main Currents in Marxism,* Vol. III, p. 495.

commonplaces of Leninist-Stalinist Marxism. Mao's originality, however, lay in his revision of Lenin's strategic precepts. This and the peasant orientation of Chinese communism were the essential causes of its victory."[18]

What Mao actually did after being in power further testifies to what a critic like Kolakowski has said above. For instance, under the organic law (constitution) of 1954, the petty-feudal and petty-bourgeois elements were not deprived of political rights as could be feared in a socialist state committed to the principles of Marxism-Leninism, The 'great leap' programme of Mao inaugurated in early 1958 reflected the development of the new Maoist tenet that the peasant masses could do anything by the power of ideology that there must be no 'individualism' or 'economism' (i.e., material incentive to production) and that the enthusiasm could take the place of the bourgeois knowledge and skills.[19] The modifications, rather deviations, of Mao may be noted in these directions:

1. Mao seems to have believed that stabilisation always leads inevitably to the privilege and the emergence of a new class; this calls for periodical shock treatment in which the revolutionary masses destroy the germs of bureaucracy. Thus, apparently there can never be a definitive social order without classes or conflicts. Mao often repeated that contradictions were eternal and must eternally be surmounted; one of his charges against the Soviet revisionists was that they did not speak of contradictions between the leaders and the masses. Mao's disbelief in a harmonious communist social order is clearly at variance with the traditional Marxist utopia. He went further still, however, in his speculations about the distant future; as everything changed and must perish in the long run, communism was not eternal and neither was humanity itself.[20]
2. Another essential departure from orthodox Marxism is the cult of peasantry as the mainstay of communism,

18. *Ibid.*, p. 499.
19. *Ibid.*, p. 503.
20. *Ibid.*, p. 511.

whereas to European communists they are a mere auxiliary force in the revolutionary struggle and are otherwise despised.[21]

3. It may also be seen in Mao's views on democracy and freedom. He enumerated 6 criteria for distinguishing right from wrong. Views and actions are right if (i) they unite the people in stead of dividing them; (ii) they are beneficial not harmful to socialist construction; (iii) help to consolidate not weaken people's democratic dictatorship; (iv) help to strengthen democratic centralism; (v) help to support the leading role of the Communist Party; and (vi) are beneficial to international socialist unity of all peace-loving peoples of the world.[22]

One may say that in all these precepts concerning democracy, freedom, centralism and the leading role of the Communist Party, there is nothing contrary to Leninist-Stalinist orthodoxy. There does, however, seem to be a difference in practice; not in the sense imagined by many Western enthusiasts for Maoism, that in China the 'masses' rule, but in the sense that the government has a more consultative air because the party has more methods of ideological manipulation at its command than have the social leaders. On the whole, it may be affirmed that Mao's interpretations contribute to the further modification of classical Marxism so as to make it adaptable to the peculiar conditions of the Third World countries. As Kolakowski critically sums up: "From the point of view of the history of Marxism, Maoist ideology is noteworthy not because Mao developed anything but because it illustrated the unlimited flexibility of a doctrine once it becomes historically influential.... But one thing is beyond doubt: Communism, as Marx understood it, was an ideal for highly developed industrial societies, not a method of organising peasants to create the rudiments of industrialisation. Yet it has turned out that the aim can be achieved by means of an ideology in which vestiges of Marxism are blended with a peasant

21. *Ibid.*, p. 512.
22. *Ibid.*, p. 518.

utopia and the traditions of oriental despotism—a mixture that describes itself Marxism par excellence and works with certain efficiency."[23]

CRITICAL APPRECIATION : MAO AS THE MAKER OF THE CHINESE VERSION OF MARXISM

In the history of Marxist political thought, Mao occupies a unique place. Like Lenin, he makes many modifications in the basic premises of classical Marxism and justifies his stand in the light of the peculiar conditions of the twentieth century as well as typical conditions of his own country. Some important contributions of Mao may be thus pointed out :

1. Mao reinterprets Marxian principles in the light of the Chinese conditions and thereby presents a sinified version of Marxism. If Lenin reinterprets the principles of Marx so as to make them suitable to the peculiar conditions of Russia, Mao does the same for the sake of his own country. On one occasion he said : "For the Chinese Communists who are part of the great Chinese nation, flesh of its flesh and blood of its blood, any talk about Marxism in isolation from China's characteristic is merely Marxism in the abstract, Marxism in a vacuum. Hence, to apply Marxism concretely in China so that its every manifestation has an indubitably Chinese character, i.e., to apply Marxism in the light of China's specific characteristics, becomes a problem which it is urgent for the whole Party to understand and solve. Foreign stereotypes must be abolished, there must be less singing of empty abstract tunes and dogmatism must be laid to rest; they must be replaced by the fresh lively Chinese style and spirit which the common people of China love."[24]

2. Mao sets aside talk of the law of dialeitic and puts the notion of contradiction into the centre of his view of the world. He declares that the contradiction is universal and it exists in the development of all things. In the process of development of each thing a

23. *Ibid.*, p. 521.
24. Mao: *Selected Works,* Vol, II, p. 209.

movement of opposites exists from beginning to end. "This comes very near to establishing an ontological principle."[25]

3. Mao contends that guerilla forces should be so organised that through rapid concentration, they may mount local offensives with superior forces, despite an over-all inferiority. As soon as possible, they should operate in conjunction with regular troops, working behind the enemy's lines, disturbing his communications etc. Thus, McLellan says: "In many ways, the most original contribution of Mao to the theory and practice of contemporary Marxism are his views on guerilla tactics and the strategy to be adopted in a lengthy struggle against a militarily superior opponent."[26]

4. As a Leninist, Mao places the 'masses' under the iron hold of the Communist Party. If viewed deeply, we find that he bifurcates the masses into the categories of the passive and active segments. The masses are the proletariat and they include the peasants, the workers, the toilers, the small landlords and the petty borgeiosie. It constitutes the 'absent' segment of the masses. But the Communist Party constitutes its active segment and thereby becomes entitled to establish its authoritarian nature. McLellan calls it 'the phenomenon of substitutism'.[27]

5. Mao's idea of 'permanent revolution' may sound akin to that of Trotsky, but it is, in fact, very different. Perforce he has to allot a much more important role to the peasantry in the revolutionary movement than Trotsky who was even more pessimistic about the potential role of the peasantry than was Lenin. He refuses to adopt emphasis on heavy industrialisation at the expense of the agricultural development of the country.[28]

---

25. MoLellan, *op. cit.*, p. 210.
26. *Ibid.*, p. 208.
27. *Ibid.*, p. 223.
28. *Ibid.*, p. 222.

It may be concluded that, like Lenin, Mao is a shrewd follower of Marx. He has modified certain principles of classical Marxism so as to apply them to the peculiar conditions of his country. It may be stressed that Mao is more of a Leninist than a Marxist. It may also be noted that his modifications had a better impact on the Marxists of the poor, backward and predominantly agricultural countries of the Third World. As early as in 1939, he had stated: "A Communist is an international Marxist, but Marxism must take a national form before it can be applied." It is well said: "Maoism is a synthesis of Leninism and Chinese economic backwardness with the addition of certain traditional Chinese ideas."[29]

29. David McLellan: *Marxism after Marx,* p. 238.

34

LASKI

Laski was a scholar and a political philosopher; he was a politician, author, and journalist; he was above all, a teacher and a friend. All these aspects of his personality were closely knit together by his conception of the task of an intellectual in society.

— Kingsley Martin

Prof. H.J. Laski holds the reputation of being the greatest teacher of Political Science of his age. Born in 1893 and died in 1950, he represented within himself the unique capability of being an excellent political scientist as well as a politician. The two great wars had their definite impact on his life as a result of which his political ideas shifted form one position to another. Luckily, his contact with eminent persons like Justice Holmes and President Roosevelt of America and with Sir E. Barker and Prime Minister Attlee of England also imparted much to his practical approach. Besides, his career at the Harvard University and at the London School of Economics and Political Science enabled him to acquire a first-hand knowledge of the American and English institutions. It all made him a great teacher and a scholar as well as a politician. For some time he served as a member of the Fabian Society,but the last years of his life passed in very close association with the Labour Party. The political ideas of Laski come to us from a good number of his books, pamphlets, articles, reviews, editorial comments, prefaces added to the works of others etc. and they may be

1. Kingsley Martin : *Harold Laski : A Biographical Memoir*, pp. 256-57.

discussed as under.

PLURALISM : FEDERAL NATURE OF AUTHORITY

Among the galaxy of political thinkers, Laski is ranked as a pluralist in as much as his main quest seems to be like that of a stern critic of the monistic doctrine of sovereignty.[2] Hence, the ideas of Laski represent a constant polemic against the mystic monism of sovereignty and they reveal an attempt to destroy the conception that the state in political theory is what the 'Absolute' is to metaphysics. In other words, he repudiates the view that the state is mysteriously one above all other human groupings and thus on account of its superior position and higher purpose it is entitled to the undivided allegiance of its people. Like J.N. Figgis, he contends that the state has developed out of the final break up of feudalism and thus the view cannot be magnified that the citizens must bow their heads before the supreme authority of the state. He, therefore, "attempts to destroy the monistic view by concentrating his critical fire on the concept of sovereignty."[3]

Laski's attack on sovereignty has two dimensions.[4] In the first place, he considers the existence of a legal sovereign nothing more than a fiction of logic.[5] In his view, men do not merely obey the commands of their sovereign, they also pay allegiance to the rules and regulations of their various social groupings and associations. Even a sovereign law-making body like the English Parliament cannot do all

---

2. Pluralism is a recent political theory which sternly reacts against the monistic conception of sovereignty developed in the writings of thinkers like Bodin, Hobbes, Hegel and Austin. Its main contention is to deprive the state of its exclusive sovereign character. In part, it is a rationalisation of recent practical movements that "look in various ways towards a decentralised application of social control." See Coker: *Recent Political Thought,* p. 508. According to K.C. Hsiao, "Pluralism undertakes to transform the state. It criticises it, it discredits it, and seeks to reduce it from its place of honour to a place of servitude." *Political Pluralism,* p.1.
3. Laski: *Studies in the Problems of Sovereignty,* p. 208.
4. H.A. Deane: *The Political Ideas of Laski,* p. 13.
5. Deane says that Laski's attack of the concept of sovereignty "is double barrelled."

what it wants or may want to do. Laski considers the concept of sovereignty both absurd and useless as a working hypothesis in any adequate political theory. He insists that it is unwise to dwell on the legal aspect of the state sovereignty too much at the cost of its social and political aspects. Secondly, he argues that the monistic theory of sovereignty is absurd from an ethical point of view. He emphasises that the repeated surrender of the judgment of the conscience of the individuals necessarily implies an unqnestioning obedience to the dictates of the state in as much individual's personality an surrender of the judgment of the conscience of the individuals necessarily implies an unquestioning obedience to the dictates of the state in as much as it stunts the development of individual's personality and his moral stature.

The salient features of Laski's theory of state sovereignty in this regard may be summed up as under:

1. Firstly, as a Pluralist, Laski attacks the validity of the doctrine that ascribes sovereign power only to the state. He appeals to the claims of individual conscience. He strongly urges that the state has no right to command allegiance of the individual unless his conscience so permits.[6] He says: "The claim of authority upon myself is...legitimate proportionately to the moral urgency of the appeal.[7] Again, he says: "The only state to which I owe allegiance is the state in which I discover moral adequacy....Our first duty is to be true to our conscience."[8]
2. Secondly, to Laski the state is not the only association but one of the associations of society. The state does not exhaust the associative impulses of men. When society is federal, the authority should also be federal. If the state is a reality, the associations are no less real than that. The state must compete with church, trade unions, employers' associations, clubs, friendly societies, political parties etc., but if there happens to

6. Laski: *The Foundations of Sovereignty and Other Essays,* p. 236.
7. Laski: *A Grammar of Politics,* p. 249.
8. *Ibid.,* p. 289.

be any conflict, the pre-eminence of state over other social institutions is justified only upon the superiority of its moral appeal in that case, otherwise the state is not all-in-all, since no association "can legislate the whole of myself." In one of his articles, Laski specifically says: "We give to this particular group (State) no peculiar merit."[9]

3. Thirdly, in order to prove that the doctrine of sovereign state is practically untenable, Laski refers to actual instances of state importance in the face of determined resistance by groups within the State itself. According to him, during the first World War, the British Parliament lost heart to enforce anti-strike provisions of the Munitions Act against the defiant Welsh miners, or to put into operation the Irish Home Rule Act against the rebellious masses of Ulster. Similarly, in 1916, the association of railway employees forced the Congress in U.S.A. on a threat of strike to pass a law prohibiting more than eight hours' work. It indicates that the associations and groups of the society have got a strength and personality of their own which cannot be ignored or undermined by the sovereign state as conceived by the protagonists of monism.'[10]

4. Fourthly, at a later stage, Laski shows a curious deviation when he explicitly modifies his stern pluralistic attitude by insisting that the sovereignty of the state is essential for the maintenance of class relations and the performance of civil and political responsibilities. Apparently, he indicates his shift to the school of Marxism. In the fourth edition of his great work, he even stresses that the greatest weakness of

9. Laski: "The Personality of Associations" in *Harvard Law Review*, Vol XXXIX (1915-16), p. 426.

10. Coker says that the common feature of all these discussions of the essential functions of the smaller groups "is the idea that the state is confronted not merely by unassociated individuals but also by other associations evolving independently, eliciting individual loyalties, better adapted than the state—because of their select membership, the special forms of organisation and action—for serving various social needs." *op. cit.*, p. 508.

the doctrine of pluralism lies in the thing that it does not sufficiently realise the nature of the state as an expression of class relations."11 In a distinctly Marxian way, he adds that the state "is simply the executiv instrument of the class in society which owns the means of production."12

5. Then, Laski's attitude towards the state has got a pragmatic character as well. Like Professors James and John Dewey of the United States, he evaluates the importance of the state in terms of the services it renders to its people. The state is not only one of the associations of the society, rather, according to Laski, as Duguit once said, it is 'a public service corporation'. Its value is to be judged by the adequacy of the services that it renders from time to time to the satisfaction and betterment of its people. Laski writes: "Political group refuses the swaddling clothes of finality and becomes a shifting conception. It cannot be Hegelianised into a permanent compromise. It asks the validation of men and actions in terms of historical experience."13

6. Finally, in the case of Laski, the state neither withers away as Marxian socialism predicts; nor does it happen to co-exist with other social groups

11. Laski: *A Grammar of Politics* (1938), pp. xi-xii.

12. *Ibid.*, p. vii. The Marxist leanings of Laski grow more sharply clear when he adds a new chapter titled. "The Crisis in the Theory of State" in his book and emphasises therein that only with the attainment of classless society the need of state's sovereignty and coercive power will disappear. He argues that only when the conflicts based upon property have been eliminated, we can conceive of a social organisation in which the truly federal nature of society "receives institutional expression. And in such a social organisation, authority can be pluralistic both in form and expression."

13. Laski: *Authority in the Modern State,* p. 166. So Deane points out: " In the pluralistic and pragmatic philosophies of James and Dewey he found a point of view that was extremely congenial to his own opposition to idealism and monism and to his conviction, which marks him as to the utilitarian tradition of Bentham and Mills; that the state is to be judged in the light of its actual contributions to the well-being of its citizens." *op. cit.,* p. 21.

and associations as Cole's guild socialism desires. The state, though one of the social groupings, exists on a higher and superior pedestal, because its membership is natural, compulsory and useful. It is natural, because man "finds himself in the modern world living under the authority of governments and the objective to obey their orders arises from the facts of his nature."[14] Then, it is compulsory, because it "is the keystone of social arch. It moulds the form and substance of the myriad human lives with whose destinies it is charged."[15] Finally, it is useful, because it "becomes an organisation for enabling the mass of men to realise social good on the largest possible scale."[16]

LIBERTY : MAINTENANCE OF AN ATMOSPHERE FOR THE DEVELOPMENT OF HUMAN PERSONALITY

Laski bases his idea of liberty upon a broad and idealistic theory of the purpose for which the state exists in as much as he means by it the eager maintenance of that atmosphere in which men have the opportunity to be at their best selves. As such, liberty is a product of rights and is built upon the conditions essential for the full development of human faculties. It has the power to release their individuality and thus enable them to contribute their peculiar and intimate experience to the common stock of the society. In addition to this, according to Laski, the liberty wields the capacity to know whether the decisions

14. Laski: *A Grammar of Politics,* p. 17.
15. *Ibid.,* p. 21.
16. *Ibid.,* p. 25. Laski thus admits: "Thus state is thus a fellowship of men aiming at the enrichment of the common life. It is an association like others, churches, trade unions and the rest. It differs from them in that its membership is compulsory upon all that live within its territorial ambit, and that it can, in the last resort, enforce its obligations upon its subjects. But its moral character is not different from all other associations. It exacts loyalty upon the same given condition that a man exacts loyalty from his friends. It is judged by what it offers to its members in terms of the things they deem to be good." *Ibid.,* p. 37.

of the government are built upon the widest possible knowledge open to its members and prevent that frustration of creative impulse which destroys the special character of men. Laski holds: "Without rights there can be no liberty, because without rights men are the subjects of law unrelated to the needs of personality."[17]

According to Laski, liberty has three main characteristics. First, it is a positive thing involving positive restraints. That is, it is not a thing of the woods, it lives within restraints. Second, it is a social and not an individual phenomenon. It should be studied taking the case of the society as a whole. Individual has no liberty independent of his social life. Third, liberty has a normative aspect and thus lays standard for the character of political authority. Moreover, liberty has three aspects-(a) private, (b) political and (c) economic. Private liberty means the opportunity to exercise freedom of choice in those areas of life where the actions of the individual affect him alone. For instance, religion is a private affair and the state should not interfere in its domain. Political liberty means the power to be active in the affairs of the state. Education and a free press are the two essential conditions for it. Economic liberty means an opportunity to find reasonable security in the earning of one's daily bread. The people should be free from the constant fear of unemployment and insufficiency. It also implies democracy in the economic sphere.

In this regard, Laski also discusses the safeguards of liberty. The achievement of freedom by the people wants two special guarantees. First, there should be no special privileges creating an atmosphere of contingent frustration in society. It is immaterial that a particular individual has no desire to take full advantage of that access. However, its denial would mean sheer acceptance of that allotted station as a permanent condition of his life and that, in turn, it is fatal to the spontaneity that is the essence of freedom. The habituated endurance of oppression in an atmosphere of frustrated impulse retards the growth of

---

17. *Ibid.*, p. 142.

initiative and kills the habit of creativeness thus incapacitating the individual to take advantage of his opportunities. The unprivileged life, over a period of decades and centuries, causes the loss of will and power of activity and in its place fills the element of fatalism or superstitions. Beside, the privileged position creates whim that those who possess it are themselves capable of freely moulding it. Laski rejects this argument by holding that such freedom is apt to be misutilised for personal gains, since the restraints may be manipulated for the sake of their own advantages. In an Aristotelian fashion, these privileged people will defend their security or, in the Macaulayan fashion will like to console the unprivileged in the name of their fortune. Hence, the enjoyment of liberty demands the absence of special privileges. In the words of Laski, "special privilege is incompatible with freedom because the latter quality belongs to all alike in their character as human beings."[18]

The second safeguard is that the rights of some should not depend upon the pleasure of others. There should be equality in regard to the exercise of power and no group, or section of the society should be allowed to encroach upon the liberty of others. The political authority should plan certain principles of social action entailing the absence of those uncertainties which result in social loss and are deliberately planned to the individuals. Natural uncertainties are, of course, an exception but the human uncertainties are definitely controllable and thus they demand their regulation by the state. However, in this direction, it is presupposed that the exercise of political authority should be unbiased and for this a system of rights is the best possible guarantee. Again, this guarantee implies the exercise of eternal vigilance.

The relationship between the liberty of the individual and the authority of the state is a very sensitive matter. To a negativist, the two are opposed to each other and so restraints, in view of their unavoidability, should be as little as possible. To a positivist, the two are not antitheti-

18. *Ibid.*, p. 130.

cal and so there may be as many restraints as are necessary in the interest of the society as a whole. The stand of Laski on this point is not consistent. He wavers between the two poles. When we see his views in the first edition of *A Grammar of Politics* (1925), he is a positivist, for he defines liberty as eager maintenance of that atmosphere in which an individual may seek the best possible development of his personality. But in his Clover Brown lectures delivered in 1929, his stand is changed when he says that liberty implies absence of restraints and there should be no checks on the freedom of the press even in times of war or national calamity. Now he defines liberty as "the absence of restraint upon the existence of those social conditions which in modern civilisations are necessary guarantees of individual happiness."[19]

In other words, Laski takes up the paradox of liberty and self-government. Certain restraints on freedom add to man's happiness. The idea of liberty has to be understood in the context of social life. For once it is admitted that no man is sufficient unto himself, there must be rules to govern the habits of his intercourse. His freedom is largely borne from the maintenance of those rules. An individual abstracted from the society and his title to freedom outside the environment is devoid of any meaning. The need to give way to others, to accept, that is restraints upon our rights to unfettered activity is inherent in the nature of things. It is evident that Laski hovers between the poles set by a negativist like Mill on the one side and a positivist like Green on the other. Bay comments that "if Laski had considered the idea that there may be psychological as well as social restraints operating on the individual, he might have avoided both the dilemma and the conversion."[20]

---

19. Laski: *Liberty in the Modern State,* p. 49. In this book, Laski affirrms: "Uncontrolled power is invariably poisonous to those who possess it. They are always tempted to impose their canon of good upon others, and in the end they assume that the good of the community depends on the continuance of their power. Liberty always demands a limitation of political authority."
20. Christian Bay: *Structure of Freedom,* p. 58.

EQUALITY : A PROCESS OF REASONABLE LEVELLING

According to Laski, no idea is more difficult to define in Political Science than the concept of equality. He insists that equality does not mean identity of treatment, since there can be no such thing as long as people are different in matters of want, capacity and need. Nor does equality imply an identity of rewards. It, however, means a certain levelling process commanding that no man shall be so placed in society that he can overreach his neighbours to the extent which constitutes a denial of the latter's citizenship. Each individual should have equal prospects for the achievement of the best self. There is inequality if the voice of some is more weighty than that of others or is answered unequally by those who control political authority and who make the fulfilment of certain private desires in the name of public good.[21]

Laski's concept of equality bears the following salient characteristics: First, it wants the absence of special privileges. Each individual should be on an equal footing in the society. Particularly in the political sphere, it implies that the will of one should be equal to the will of another. It also signifies that there should be no discri-minated selection in the conferment of publi offices and that the authority of one employee should not be qualitatively different from that of another. Hence, Laski finds no justification in the retention of a hereditary second chamber like the House of Lords. Second, equality wants equal opportunities open to all. However, it does not mean the identity of original chance, since the native endowments of every individual are not equal. What is needed is that at least all are given such training which seems in the light of experience more likely to develop their faculties to the full. Those circumstances should be created in which the training of mind becomes successful and which guarantee the fact that the talent does not persist for want of encouragement.[22]

---

21. Laski: *A Grammar of Politics,* p. 150.
22. *Ibid.*

PROPERTY : DEFENCE OF THE FABIAN ARGUMENT

Laski's concept of property is both a critique of the existing economic order and a justification of the existing institution of property largely on the Fabian lines of argument. To him, it is the institution of private property which guards man's root instincts of self-preservation. It emancipates him from the care of the morrow, the ghost of starvation, the dread of want, the yoke of involuntary work, the drudgery of undesired activity and the web of a grim routine. Positively speaking, it is a measure of security enabling the possessor to lead a comfortable life and seek intellectual attainments. However, Laski makes it clear that the number of such people in every society is always very small and the fortune of this type is a legacy not of some virtue or excellence of work but of a lucky descension or an outrageous extortion.

At the same time, Laski undermines the significance of private property system in view of the fact that greater disparities of wealth are incompatible with social cohesion and that the domination of wealth leads to plutocracy. And although the power of combination has enabled the labourers to protect their rights against the encroachments of the capitalist class, they have not been very useful in mitigating these unhappy circumstances on account of developing industrialism. Laski criticises the present capitalisti system in the name of its wasteful and unplanned production entirely ignoring the facts of social utility. Essential services relating to health and education are not provided, while ample amounts are squandered on making picture halls, battleships and beautiful garments. Under capitalism, Laski says, the motivating consideration is not social good but private profit and for the sake of its realisation several malpractices vigorously flow.

Laski further points out that the evils of private property system weaken the foundations of society in an incessant manner. The arguments of the capitalists are entirely untenable and egoistic in as much as they are nothing but clever tricks to hide the facts of cruelty, exploitation and damage suffered by the community at their hands. Their activities destroy the good character of political life, pervert educational system and religious institutions and certainly add to the insecurity of the well-ordered state. Hence, Laski says: "It remains historically obvious that a community divided into rich and poor is, when the latter are numerous, built upon the foundation of sands."[23]

Furthermore, Laski warns that the capitalist hold is always pregnant with the germs of a revolution.[24] When the capitalist class unbendingly adheres to its own policies and actions quite detrimental to social utility and wants to keep the propertyless class fully ignorant of its own prowess and even lives well prepared to stifle the protests of workingmen, it prepares in turn very risky grounds for the germination of a revolution. Again, he asserts; "For the basis of the state is envy, and envy is the nurse of faction. Yet the state remains divided between rich and poor and men after a period refuse to suffer quietly. Then revolution supervenes to alter the balance in the state."[25]

In addition to criticising the system of private property, Laski also gives justification of private property in some ways. In a Platonic manner, he rejects the apparent implications of various justifications employed by the lords of private property and then injects new implications in them according to his own standpoint in the following manner. In the first place, he adopts the psychological line of defence. It is said by the capitalists that the love of private property infuses an incentive to work. But he warns that the use of labour power and the exercise of such incentive must always be governed by the idea of social good. Thus, according to him, the present method is not a solution but a problem finding its appropriate solution not in the capricious inter-pretations of the capitalists as such but in the wider interests of the society.

Secondly, Laski takes up the ethical line of defence. It

---

23. *Ibid.*, p. 176.
24. *Ibid.*, p. 176-77.
25. *Ibid.*, p. 183.

is said by the capitalists that the property is a return made to the individual for his efforts. It is ethically sound to duly reward the labours of a railway builder, radio inventor, island discoverer or a machine-maker. But he insists that there is definitely a flaw in this assumption in as much as when everybody makes efforts in various directions, the rewards appear to be unequal. To defend their position still more, the capitalists argue that this difference is due to natural variation in the ability and capacity of abstinence of the persons. But he rejects this assumption on the ground that the factor of abstinence is an obsolete and shameless argument and the factor of ability lies behind the mischievous capacity of reaping profits.

Thirdly, Laski takes up the philosophical line of defence. It is said by the capitalists that the property is essentially a nurse of social virtues like generosity, inventiveness and energy. But he once again very easily dismisses this defence by holding that such virtues have been present only in the persons having no property.

Fourthly, Laski takes up the historical line of defence. It is said by the capitalists that all progressive societies have been constructed on the basis of private property. He at first agrees with this line of defence, but refutes it in the name of its being fallacious. In his view, this argument does not stand valid today as it was in the past. In the modern age, the conception of private property is necessarily bound to undergo change and its idealisation is thoroughly anachronistic like that of the practice of slavery. Today the right to private property cannot be treated as sacrosanct as it was possible in the days of Locke, since the modern state is under an obligation to mitigate the glaring inequalities of wealth.

The above explanation shows that Lsski wants to give a new meaning to the celebrated concept of private property. He wants to see the retention of this institution but within the limits of greater social interest. He insists that the essential thing in this regard is to keep a happy balance between the private property and social service. Thus he puts: "The wider, moreover, the right of property, the less equal is the incidence of legislative benefit, and the less close is the relation between property and service."[26]

RIGHTS : AN INSTRUMENT FOR THE RECOGNITION OF A STATE

Laski defines rights as those conditions of social life without which no man, in general, can seek to be himself at his best. But, in this regard, he rejects the notion of any right that came into being in the pre-social stage; nor does he agree with the natural and immutable character of rights; nor does he support the view that rights imply power to seek a satisfaction of desires. However, he reinterprets the old theories pointing out that rights are pre-political in the sense that whether they are recognised or not, they are there; they are historical in the sense ·that at some given period or place, they are demanded by the character of its civilisation; they are also natural in the sense that under certain limitations the facts demand their recognition. The rights have a content which changes with the times and places. In fine, he contributes to the social utility theory of rights. In his view, rights are rights, because they are useful to the people living in the society and the state. As such, rights are built upon the utility to the individual and the community. According to him, "I can not have rights against the public welfare, for that, ultimately is to give me right against a welfare which is intimately and inseparably associated with my own."[27]

Laski's theory of rights has certain other aspects too. He calls certain rights as particular rights. These are:

1. Every citizen has a right to work which means the right to be occupied in producing a share of those goods and commodities which are useful for the society.
2. Every citizen has a right to adequate wages which means that all those who work must be given sufficient wages to maintain themselves.

---

26. *Ibid.*, p. 93.
27. *Ibid.*,

3. Every citizen has a right to reasonable hours of work which means that he should be asked to put in that amount of work which does not exhaust him completely and thereby makes him unfit to fulfil his duties as a citizen.
4. Every citizen has a right to education which means that he should be given that minimum of education which is essential for the performance of his duties.
5. Every citizen has a right to political power which means that he should have the right to vote, to be elected, and also the right to assume governmental office and run the administrative machinery.
6. Every citizen should have the freedom of speech which means that he should have the right to ventilate his grievances and organise public opinion in his support.
7. Every citizen should be guaranteed the freedom of association and public meeting and be provided with judicial safeguards so that justice may be secured without fear or favour.
8. Every citizen has the right to private property limited only to that extent which is necessary for the growth of his personality and does not prove detrimental to the interest of the society.

Laski also deals with the right to resistance against the state. However, in this regard, he suggests four points. First, rights also imply duties in as much as they are real only to the extent they have been accepted by others as an obligation. Second, rights are co-relative with functions as the number of rights possessed by an individual must correspond to the contributions which he makes in person to the society. Third, rights are identical with necessity at a minimum level and it is the duty of the state to guarantee a certain minimum of rights without which it is impossible for the individuals to lead a creative life. Finally, he holds that a state is known by the rights it maintains. It is the duty of the state to provide the individuals with those outward environments which are essential for the development of their character. The citizen has claims upon the state and the latter must maintain his rights and guarantee him those conditions without which he cannot attain his best self. Hence, if the state violates them, the resistance by the people against its authority would be justified.

Finally, Laski deals with the question of safeguards. He dismisses the view that a bill of fundamental rights embodied in the national constitution is a sufficient safeguard, for although musty parchments do attach great sanctity, they cannot ensure their realisation. He also rejects the idea of separation of powers as a sufficient weapon of safeguarding the rights. But he puts three conditions by which rights of the individual can be safeguarded.

1. The state should decentralise its authority and when the people manage their own affairs, and have the functioning of authority before their own eyes, they will develop the capacity of resisting any abuse of authority that happens to arise.
2. The national government should work with the help of consultative bodies. To every department there should be attached a group of experts to the line whose duty is to advise on the problems facing it.
3. The state should not interfere in the internal affairs of various associations unless any group becomes a menace to its own existence.

INTERNATIONALISM : RESTRAINTS ON THE EXTERNAL ASPECT OF SOVEREIGNTY

Laski is a powerful advocate of international peace and goodwill. He is dissatisfied with the traditional doctrine of sovereignty which has made every state a master of its own activity even in those spheres which affect the life of the entire mankind. In this direction, he says: "The notion of an independent sovereign state is on the international side fatal to the well-being of humanity. The way in which the state should live its life in relation to other states is clearly not a matter in which the state is entitled to be the sole judge. The common life of states is a matter for common agreement between states. England ought not to settle what armaments she will erect and the immigrants she will permit to enter. These matters erect the common life of people; and they imply a united world organised to administer them. If men are to live in the great society, they must learn the habits of co-operative inter-course. In a world state, however, if built, and whatever the measure of decentralisation that obtains, there is no room for separate sovereignty."[28]

Laski's views on internationalism may be seen in his attack on the external aspect of sovereignty. Science and economics have changed the shape of the world. Modern science means a world market; world market means world interdependence; and, finally, world inter-dependence means world government. To act upon the consequence of tremendous syllogism is the only pathway to our security. As he says: "We are being rapidly driven to the point where, once we assume the sovereignty of the state, we have to infer the impossibility of those international institutions which the facts themselves are compelling us to establish."[29] Again: "Just as we spent the nineteenth century in thinking nationally, and in completing the pattern of the institutions of national self-government, so we must spend the twentieth century in learning to think in international terms, in building as best as we may, the organs of that international community every year of whose delay in coming brings us so much nearer to disaster."[30]

STATE : QUEST FOR A SOCIAL WELFARE DEMOCRATIC ORDER

Man is a social and political creature and so a social and political thinker gives his views on the theme of man in relation to his social and political existence. State is a natural association for the idealists like Plato, Aristotle,

---

28. *Ibid.*, pp. 55-6.
29. Laski: *Power Politics*, pp. 91-92.
30. Laski: *The State in Theory and Practice*, p. 223.

Rousseau, Hegel and Green; it is a conventional association for others like Hobbes, Locke, Mill, Spencer and Marx. Laski belongs to neither side. He recognises that state is a universal phenomenon in view of the salient fact that obligation to obey the dictates of state arises from the facts of human nature. Robinson Crusoe on his desert island, or. Simon Stylites upon his pillar may defy the normal impulses which make them men, but for the vast majority to live with others is the condition of a rational existence.[31] It implies that, in the view of Laski, state is neither a natural nor a moral but a an essential association in which a man may realise his best self.

Laski's views on state may be clarified with the help of these significant points:

1. State is a part of society and its membership is also co-extensive with it, but it has its autonomous place. It may set the key-note of the social order, but it is not identical with it. In personal composition the legal association (state) and the social organisation (society) are one, for they include the same body of persons. But in purpose, they are different, Society exists for a number of purposes, the state exists for a single purpose—enforcement of law. State is an association having coercive authority.
2. So the state is different from the government despite the fact that a theory of state is, at the same time. a theory of government. The state in practice is a body of men issuing orders and enforcing obedience to them. Its will is the decision arrived at by a small number of men to whom is confided the legal power of making decisions. The membership of the state is shared by all citizens, while government is a part of the state whose membership is available to those who work in some administrative capacity. Sovereignty is an attribute of the state, not of the government.
3. As a pluralist, Laski says that sovereignty should be shared by those social groups and associations

31. Laski: *A Grammar of Politics,* p. 17.

which meet requirements of the people, but he does not appreciate the liquidation of the state as desired by the anarchists, the syndicalists or the communists. Like MacIver, he asserts that state is superior to but not supreme over other social associations. Social groups are real in the same sense as the state is real. That is, it has an interest to promote and a function to perform.

4. Then, as a Fabian, Laski frankly abandons the case of a laissez-faire state. He treats state as a public welfare agency and for this reason favours the model of a functional state. That is, his principle of state action admirably balances the claims of the individual and society; his principle of individuality is uncompromising in its refusal to surrender the core of individuality expressed in the mind and conscience of the individual. So he says that state should increase its area of activity and thereby narrow the gap between the rich and the poor sections of the community. In his view, Marxism is mistaken in its inevitability of a violent revolution.[32] So, fascism constitutes the case of a counter-revolution.[33]

5. Laski is an internationalist and, as such, he desires to put the sovereignty of the state under the control of some international organisation. No state has the right to make as many atom bombs as it likes and then to drop them whenever it so desires. It is dangerous to combine nationalism with sovereignty in a blind and aggressive form. We must contemplate

32. The main weight of Laski's atack on Marxism is directed against the insistence on the inevitability of a violent revolution in the transition to socialism and the corollary, the belief in the necessity of an iron dictatorship during the period of consolidation... Security and freedom will vanish from the earth if profound liberty in any cause is held to be a justification for a resort to revolutionary violence." Deane, *op. cit.*, p. 71.

33. Deane says : "In essence, fascism is a counter-revolution whose purpose is to adapt capitalist society to the conditions of modern technology, of a world market, of a division of labour which has made the collectivistic organisation of social relationship inevitable." *Ibid.*, p. 235.

nothing less than the establishment of a world legislature, directly responsible to the peoples of the world, a world police, a world judiciary. To this the experience of two World Wars and the incredible speed of scientific inventions have left us no alternative.

6. The state is never infallible and the people may resist if they find that its authority lacks moral adequacy. The state ought to secure and maintain the conditions of self-realisation to the citizens. In case they find that their rights are not secured and that the state is acting contrary to the proper purpose of serving the community, the people have every right to resist it. The social conscience of the citizens is the surest guide to the conduct that the people should display in the face of events.

7. Last, the rejection of the general will of Rousseau or the 'social ethics' of Hegel is an important point in Laski's theory of state. The ideas of Rousseau and Hegel are quite abstract and so related to an abstract individual. That all men desire the 'good' of the society and the state must invariably act in the 'public interest' are vague expressions and so entirely useless for any practicable theory of state.

In short, Laski is both a pluralist and a democratic socialist. As such, he thinks about the state of concrete individuals "who realise that their good is involved in common good which their actual state is establishing."[34]

A critic may, however, comment that what is interesting in the thought of Laski is that his views regarding the position of state change with the change of topic under consideration. In regard to the right or freedom of expression, the claims of society receive greater attention and the state becomes more prominent as the guardian or promoter of social welfare; inequalities of property lead to the frustration of personality and to rectify them, state sction would be necessary. Then, in regard to the right to resist, there is a generous statement of the claims of the individual to start with, but all circumspection is urged upon the individual in

34. Laski: *State in Theory and Practice,* p. 61.

the exercise of the right lest social peace be disturbed. It is rare that the balance of the claims of the individual and the state is kept in view in considering each particular right. "Laski resembles Mill in this respect; Mill is at once an individualist and a socialist. The two elements stand unreconciled and unintegrated both in Mill and Laski."[35]

CRITICAL APPRECIATION : LASKI AS A GREAT FABIAN LEADER AND AN INTELLECTUAL

In spite of the great influence that Laski exercised on contemporary political philosophy, it is beyond dispute that at various stages he has assumed a shifty, self-contradictory, even utopian, stand. It appears that his ideas have undergone a serious change with the passage of time, and whatever be the reasons for it, they make his whole approach towards the state philosophically inconsistent. The difficulty increases as we find him shifting from the plane of hard pluralism to that of soft absolutism of state. Deane thus remarks: "At successive stages of his career, he was an ardent proponent of Pluralism, Fabianism and, finally, Marxist socialism."[36]

As regards the case of sovereignty, Laski plays fast and loose with it. His hard attack on the sovereign character of the state is not justified.[37] He forgets the fundamental fact

35. G.N. Sarma: *Political Thought of H.J. Laski,* p. 116.
36. Deane, *op. cit.,* p.3, Likewise, W.E. Sandelius says: "Harold Laski, who in his earlier writings became a chief contender for this point of view, shows in his later production a decided shift in the direction of increased emphasis upon the coercive aspect of political process." Refer to his article "The Question of Sovereignty and the Recent Trends of Juristic Thought" In J.C. Roucek (ed): *Twentieth Century Political Thought,* p. 164.
37. It shows Laski's pluralistic approach and so his ideas are to be criticised from the point of view directed against the idea of the divisible character of sovereignty. Zimmern has correctly hinted that those who "talk of state absolutism, are ignoring the simple truth there is no tyranny like the tyranny of near neighbour. The smaller the group, the tighter their stranglehold over your life and activities." Refer to his essay "Political Thought" in R.W. Livingstone (ed) : *The Legacy of Greece,* p. 348. Coker also points out that many who "raise the loudest outcry aginst state encroachment upon the individual or group freedom are the most ardent supporters, or the most complacently tolerant of other forms of social coercion." *Op. cit.,* p. 517.

that sovereignty, as Calhoun rightly says, is a whole thing and that to divide it is to destroy it. Like Miss Follet, he contributes to the doctrine of competing loyalties. Not only this, in the later years of his life, he negatives much what he had said about sovereignty at earlier stages. It appears that while he wants to drive sovereignty out of the front door of this new society, he quietly smuggles it again through the backdoor more or less disguised, but nevertheless it is sovereignty. Deane observes that even if we "agree that this is what Laski means by sovereignty, we may conclude that he should have abandoned the term altogether in its own expositions; he succeeds only in bewildering his reader of both attacking the concept and seeking to retain it with an altered meaning."[38]

Likewise, it is alleged that Laski's theories of liberty, equality, property and rights donot fully cohere with his approach to the state. While dealing with all these themes he has dwelt on the utility of the state and adopted it as an instrument of social welfare. But when we notice the general tenor of his argument, it appears that he wants to keep the hands of the state off by warning against an usurpation of the jurisdiction of other groups and association of the society. In other words, the pluralistic approach of Laski does not naturally fit in when he renders normative version to his concepts of liberty, equality, property and rights. Again, Deane remarks that Laski bases his entire discussion "upon a broad and idealistic theory of the purpose for which the state exists, which is hardly compatible with his anti-statism and anti-idealism."[39]

Yet, Laski's ideas exercised such a tremendous influence that the days of his eminence became known by the name of the 'Age of Laski'. His books now find place in the shelf of every lover of learning and knowledge. It cannot be forgotten that he was not a mere academic recluse: he was a theorist as well as a man of action. He was a teacher as well as a leader of the Labour Party. It is

38. Deane, *op. cit.*, p. 16.
39. *Ibid*, p. 43.

notable that so many diverse aspects formed a synthetic fusion in his personality. This combination of roles — political philosopher, teacher, publicist, party leader, public speaker and confidential adviser to statesmen and politicians gave Laski unmatched opportunities to achieve political insight and understanding."[40]

40. Deane, *op. cit.*, p. 4

35

GANDHI

I heartily accept the motto — 'That government is best which governs the least'; and I should like to see it acted up to more rapidly and more systematically. Carried out, it finally amounts to this, which also I believe — That government is best which governs not at all; and when men are prepared for it, that will be the kind of government which they will have. Government is at best but an expedient; but most governments are usually, and all governments are sometimes, inexpedient....Law never made men a whit more just; and by means of their respect for it, even the well disposed are daily made the agents of injustice.[1]

— Henry David Thoreau

Mahatma Gandhi(1869-1948) occupies a unique place in the history of political thought. Two viewpoints, sharply opposed to each other, may be studied in this regard. If the subject of political philosophy is rigidly confined to a study of the explicitly and formally political propositions, concepts, categories and entities, Gandhiji is not at all a political philosopher. But if it is a wider thing and includes a study of the philosophical, ethical, sociological and economic foundations and the implications of political propositions, then he should by all means be regarded as a political philosopher. Of course, Gandhi is not a political philosopher like those who wrote monumental treatises on politics or delivered fiery speeches on the desirable character of political authority; he is a political philosopher in the sense that even in his accidental touch with poli-

1. Thoreau : *Walden and Civil Disobedience,* pp. 224-25.

tics, he contributed much to this field as well.[2] Instead of living as an academic recluse, Gandhi practised what he preached and during the course of long struggle against falsehood and injustice, first in South Africa and then in India, he stressed some fundamental ideas for the regeneration of man and the reconstruction of society. Thus, if Gandhi failed to be a systematic philosopher or a theorist, he certainly triumphed in proving himself an inspired leader, a teacher, a prophet, and, above all, a man of action. Naturally, the political ideas of Mahatma Gancihi do not find place in a particular source, they are available to us in the form of a huge material lying in his voluminous writings supported by the accounts of his contemporaries and the actual practices of his life. Some important ideas of Mahatma Gandhi may be discussed below.

RELIGIOUS APPROACH : INTEGRATION OF POLITICS WITH DHARMA

Contrary to the Western ideals of dry and barren secularism, Gandhi adopts a religious approach and tries to penetrate it even into the domain of politics. Yet his approach is not purely theocratic; it is due to his search for the spiritualisation of politics. Like his political teacher Gokhale, he lays stress on the incorporation of moral values in politics with a view to make it free from the barren and profaned spheres of materialism. The approach of the Mahatma is so enlightened that he treats religion not as a mode of worshipping God; rather in his view, religion is a very liberal and comprehensive thing whose external and universal values are applicable to the entire human-

2. Gandhi visualised that his touch with politics was not deliberate. On one occasion, he said that if he seemed to take part in politics, it "is only because politics encircles us today like the coil of a snake from which one cannot get out, no matter how much one tries." See V.P. Varma: *The Political Philosophy of Mahatma Gandhi and Sarvodaya,* p. 73. A critic thus points out: "Gandhian political philosophy is, indeed, elusive. To the scholar who sees internally consistent and systematised bodies of thought, the study of Gandhi is unrewarding. I shall try to show that the most serious efforts to classify Gandhi in terms of exclusive schools of political theory have failed." J.B von Bondurant: *Conquest of Violence,* p. 147.

kind.[3] So deep and unbending is his faith in religion that he is never prepared to abandon it at any cost and hence it is religion which "forces him to take part in politics."[4]

It follows that Gandhi imparts a very comprehensive meaning to the term 'religion'. He grossly detests the dogmatic approach adopted in the name of religion and interprets it as a means to tame our savage nature and suppress the elements of bestiality. Obviously, in his view, a religious life does not consist in offering prayers to God in a particular way, it lies in leading a chastened and purified life that is bound to cast immense social and political impact. If so, religion cannot be separated from any kind of social system—political, economic, cultural or any one else. Gandhi strongly asserts that the advocates of rigid secularism do not understand the real meaning of religion. When religion pervades every human action and when the whole gamut of human activity constitutes an indivisible whole, one cannot divide the religious and non-religious aspects into water-tight compartments. Religion provides a moral basis to all other activities which they would otherwise lack reducing life to 'a maze of sound and fury signifying nothing'.[5]

Hence, Gandhi contributes to the religious basis of politics by asserting that 'politics bereft of religion is a death-trap that kills the soul'. However, distinctly contrary to the notions of medievalism and communalism, he incorporates religion into politics as a progressive movement towards justice and truth. Instead of considering politics as a pastime or anything concerned with nothing more than the conduct of state activity, Gandhi considers it as one of the ways to the service of God through the service of humanity. It is owing to this particular attitude that while taking part in politics, Gandhi maintains his unbroken and unbreakable touch with religion. In his own words: "I could not be leading a religious life unless I identify myself with the

3. According to Gandhi, "Religions are not for separating man from one another, they are means to bind them." *Harijan,* 8 June, 1940.
4. B.S. Sharma: *Gandhi as a Political Thinker,* p.4.
5. D.G. Tendulkar: *Mahatma,* Vol. IV, p. 387-88.

whole of mankind and this I could not do unless I took part in politics."[6]

The political domain existing as such, according to Gandhi, is unspiritualised and unmoralised. He wants that a radical moral orientation should be provided to political action. He frankly repudiates sectarianism and the love for narrow group self-interest. By the religious basis of politics he means the concept of moral 'right' in place of divine right of rulers, princes and other antecedent groups. Instead of referring to the supremacy of the ecclesiastical heads, he stresses the sanctity of the purified inner light which should prevent men from doing in collective life which, they would not do to themselves or their family. With this outlook; he never ascribes a religious foundation to political governance and contends that religious attitude is a vindication of truth and never a command to suffer exploitation and oppression. Thus, he warns that to try to root out religion itself from society "is a wild goose chase and were such an attempt to succeed, it would mean the destruction of society."[7]

Finally, the religious approach of Gandhi is a clear contradiction of the notion of a theocratic state. He never supports the idea of state religion, or any discrimination in the name of religion made by the political authority. The state should maintain its secular character by guaranteeing religious freedom to its people. As the state cannot implement a religious policy in a honest way, he is opposed to the idea of giving religious training in state controlled institutions. It will be good if religious education is imparted by voluntary agencies. However, he realises that it is a different thing if the educational institutions impart such elementary training in ethics or morals that is conducive to the fundamental principles of every religion. According to him, "We have suffered state-aided religion and a state church. A society or a group which depends partly or wholly on state aid for the existence of its religion does not deserve, or better still, does not have any religion worth the name."[8]

6. See Varma, *op. cit.*, p. 73.
7. *Ibid.*, p. 77.
8. Gandhi: *Harijan*, 25 March, 1947.

The religious approach of Gandhi, as discussed above, has been denounced by those who have failed to understand the meaning which the Mahatma has so elaborately given to the term 'religion'. It may be alleged that since the days of Machiavelli, secularism has been a dominant characteristic of modern state. The modern nation-state has arisen out of the great conflict with the church. As a result, the political philosophers have sought to take politics away from the shackles of religion. Besides, much harm has been done to humanity in the name of religion. Under the opiumatic influence of religion the tyrannical rulers have suppressed and exploited their masses. Hence, the modern state holds secularism as one of its important characteristics and thus ·to reintroduce the element of religion in politics, as Gandhi has done, is to contradict the sanctity of this great political truth. The social and political power of today cannot and should not be made an adjunct of religion. But any objection of this type does not hold water if the comprehensive meaning of religion, as given by Gandhi, is taken into full consideration.[9]

PHILOSOPHICAL ANARCHISM : CULMINATION OF SWARAJ INTO RAM RAJ

It is difficult to put Gandhi into any school of contemporary western political philosophy for the simple reason that he left no sect after him, nor did he ever claim to have originated any new principle or doctrine relating to the origin, nature or end of state activity. He simply tried in his own way to apply central truths to the problems of his daily life and the opinions he formed and the conclusions he arrived at were free from the claim of finality. As a man of open mind and a gross detester of extremes, he never wanted his friends, colleagues or disciples to follow his precepts blindly and simply indicated any direction without trying to

9. G.N. Dhawan says: "Gandhi believes that the spiritual law does not work on a field of its own, but expresses itself only through the ordinary activities of life. Thus, religion provides a moral basis to all activities. Gandhi does not know religion apart from human activity; nor does he consider religion as one of the many activities of mankind." *The Political Philosophy of Mahatma Gandhi*. p. 39.

fill in the details for all times to come. Hence, the principles which he preached and the modes he practised could never have the character of rigidity or inelasticity. It is owing to this that Gandhi ever despised the pretentious suffix of 'ism' and insisted that all he had done was to try experiments with truth on as vast a scale as he could.[10]

Nevertheless, a synthesised study of the ideas of Mahatma Gandhi shows that although he does not belong to any school of contemporary western political philosophy as such, yet he is very close to the school of philosophical anarchism. The reason for this lies in his denunciation of the existing state with its total paraphernalia of governance in the name of its having a coercive, exploitative and violent character and its substitution by a future society in which the state either withers away, or transforms itself into a nonviolent organisation. A distinguished authority so observes: "Gandhi is a philosophical anarchist, because he believes that his end can be realised only in a classless and stateless democracy of autonomous village communities based on non-violence instead of coercion, on service instead of exploitation, on renunciation instead of acquisitiveness, and in the largest measure on local and individual initiative instead of centralisation."[11]

---

10. Acharya J.B. Kripalani puts his impression thus: "I believe there is yet nothing like Gandhism. All 'isms' come into existence, not at the initiative of those in whose names they are preached and promulgated, but as a result of the limitations imposed upon the original ideas by the followers. Lacking the creative genius, the followers try to systematise and organise. In so doing, they make the original doctrines rigid, inelasitc, often dogmatic and fanatical; they deprive them of their primal freshness and flexibility, which are the signs of vigorous youth. Further, Gandhi is no philosopher. He has created no system. He has from the beginning been a practical reformer. As such he deals with and writes upon problems as they arise." See his *Gandhian Thought.,* pp. 111-12.
11. Dhawan, *op. cit.,* p. 3. The ancharchists consider state in any form as unnecessary and undesirable. While the revolutionary anarchists advocate its total destruction, the peaceful or philosophical anarchists are satisfied if its violent character disappears no matter the state survives. In the view of Bertrand Russell, the theory of Anarchism "is opposed to the state as the embodiment of force employed in the government of the community." *Roads to Freedom,* p. 49.

Obviously, the Gandhian theory of state has two aspects—a denunciation of the state as it exists today and an analysis of the non-violent state which should come as its substitute in time to come. Both these aspects may be discussed thus:

(i) Denunciation of the State : Gandhi views the modern state as an engine of violence and exploitation that kills the sentiments of service and sacrifice. He repudiates the usefulness of state on every ground—philosophical, ethical, historical, economic, political. The argument of Gandhi is based on the point that the compulsive nature of political authority mutilates the moral value of human actions. In other words, the state damages what otherwise comes from the force of conscience or consciousness. He very clearly says: "The state represents violence in a concen-trated and organised form. The individual has a soul, but the state is a soulless machine; it can never be weaned from violence to which it owes its very existence." At another place he asserts: "I look upon an increase in the power of state with the greatest fear, because while although apparently doing good by minimising exploitation, it does the greatest harm to mankind by destroying the individuality which lies at the root of all progress."[12]

As a corollary to the above contention, we find Gandhi as a most uncompromising critic of the institutions of western democracy. In his view, all such institutions are misrepresentative of the people in as much as they, instead of having real servants of the society, consist of intriguers, mischief-mongers and social cheats. Even the British Parliament is like a 'sterile woman' to Gandhi, for it has out of its own accord done not a single good thing. In very forceful terms, Gandhi characterises every parliamentary body as a 'talking shop' or an institution consisting of the hypocrites and self-seekers, or an organisation suffering from fickle-mindedeness and uncertainty, or something mercurial and unsteady in its fiedlity to the people. Taking the case of British Parliament, Gandhi once said: "Today,

12. Refer to N.K. Bose: *Studies in Gandhism,* pp. 202 and 204.

it is under Mr. Asquith, tomorrow it may be under Mr. Balfour....what is done today may be undone tomorrow. It is not possible to recall single instance in which finality can be predicted for its work."[13]

Then, Gandhi is thoroughly opposed to the Hegelian and Austinian interpretations of sovereignty. In his view, positive law being the command of the sovereign and the entire political structure built on violence, authoritarian dictates and compulsive commands do not help the genuine realisation of the system of individual rights. Speaking for the moral sovereignty of the people, Gandhi visualises that the glorification of state power is a challenge to the moral fibre of the civilisation. He condemns any concept of the exaltation of the absolute implying uncontrolled and illimitable power of the state and insists that the purified and the regenerated will of the community can alone be the sovereign. In this regard, Gandhi raises three points. First, while catalysing the superior authority of the soul force over temporal authority, he holds that no ruler can be above God. Second, while relying on the unprofaned force of *satyagraha,* he sanctions that the individual can resist sovereign authority if it is repugnant to his conscience. Third, while preaching the ideal of spiritual force, he stands as the prophet of moral authority against the organised power of legal sovereignty."[14]

Thus, Gandhi refuses to see in the state the manifestation of any superior reason or any inscrutable national purpose. He regards state as the organisation of force and does not conceive of it as the self-actualisation of conscious reason as emphasised by the Idealists. The alternative to it thus lies in the establishment of an ideal state of enlightened anarchy. In his own words: "Political power means capacity to regulate national life through national representatives. If national life becomes

---

13. Gandhi: *Hind Swaraj,* pp. 15-16.
14. According to Dhawan, "To Gandhi also the question of political obligation is essentially moral and disobedience to the law of the state becomes a pre-emptory duty when it comes in conflict with the law of God." *Op. cit.,* p. 258.

so perfect as to become self-regulated, no representation becomes necessary. There is then a state of enlightened anarchy. In such a state, every one is his own ruler. He rules himself in such a manner that he is never a hindrance to his neighbour. In the ideal state, therefore, there is no political power, because there is no state."[15]

(ii) Non-Violent State : The religious anarchism of Gandhi does not find expression merely in the denunciation of the state as such, it also envisages the case of non-violent state based on the willing allegiance of an intelligent body of citizens. The government in such a state will represent the will and ideals of the overwhelming majority of the people. In such a society the scope of state activity would be reduced to the minimum possible extent so that there is no room for coercion and exploitation. By the condition of enlightened anarchy, Gandhi means the elimination of coercive political power based on the automatic operation of dominance. According to him, "The state is perfect and non-violent where the people are governed the least. The nearest approach to purest anarchy would be a democracy based on non-violence."[16]

However, two important points should be noted in this regard. First, Gandhi does not contemplate deliberate destruction of the state machinery root and branch, for he is satisfied with the final withering away of the coercive state by increasing observance of non-violence in political action. He finds the ideal of *swaraj* realisable when only five institutions of army and police, laws and courts, heavy transport and industry, big hospitals, and production by gigantic machinery would continue to function not for any purpose of suppression of individuality but for the sake of common good. By *swaraj* he means an interim period between the destruction of the violent state and the advent of the future non-violent society. He is hopeful of the realisation of the period and would not mind if the above-mentioned five institutions would be used for defensive

15. Gandhi: *Young India,* 22 July, 1931.
16. Gandhi: *Harijan,* 21 July, 1940.

and protective purpose."[17]

But the second point is more important. Gandhi calls his ideal state by the name of Rama Raj and although he himself is doubtful of the ideal, he has no difficulty in accepting it as the goal. He postulates that in the ideal state of the kingdom of God upon earth, there will be the sovereignty of the moral authority of the people and the state as a structure of violence will be extinct. This ideal state will mean the kingdom of love, justice and righteousness and stand on the basis of non-violence and self-discipline. In Ram Raj full justice will be done even to the dog. In this period there will be the fructification of moral spirit and the abolition of tensions, conflicts and egoistic interests. Sympathetic accommodation, non-coercive organisation and spontaneous co-operation will be the cardinal characteristics of this ideal society. Everybody will earn his honest living by the sweat of his brow and there will be no distinction between intellectual and manual workers.

The ideal state of Rama Raj will be classless and stateless and consist of a number of self-contained and self-regulated village communities. Every village will have a *panchayat* having full powers of administration and capable of meeting all its essential needs even to the extent of defending itself. The self-sufficing villages will be bound voluntarily in a federation having no military, police, laws, courts, jails, heavy industries, big transport etc. The pattern of life will be simple and civilisation have a rural character. Moreover, there will be complete decentralisation of authority. Voluntary co-operation will inform the institutions of social life and it will appear that men have acquired complete personal *swaraj* and grown accustomed spontaneously to observe their social obligations without the operation of the state.

On the whole, while realising that the ideal society will always remain an unrealised and unrealisable ideal in its entirely, Gandhi "indicates the direction rather than the destination, the process rather than the consummation. The

17. Refer to Varma, *op. cit.*, p. 211.

structure of the state that will emerge as a result of the non-violent revolution will be a compromise, a *via media*, between the ideal non-violent society and the facts of human nature."[18] In the words of V.P. Varma, "Rama Raj means the realisation of universal peace and humanitarian ethics. There is no place in it for pugnacity, barbarity and war. The realisation of the Kingdom of God would depend, however, on a sincere faith in the Supreme Spirit by millions. It is evident that this Ram Raj will be more a society than the state and its social bonds will be more cohesive than the formal bonds of legal organisations. It may be regarded as a realisation of the synthesis of the Thomistic conception of the natural law and the Rousseauic conception of general will."[19]

Gandhi's approach to the state may be criticised on three main grounds. In the first place, his approach is thoroughly wrong and unwarranted. The state is not the destroyer of liberty or individuality of the people, it is a necessary condition for their existence. History bears so many instances to prove that progress of mainkind has been under the aegis of a political authority. Bertrand Russell rightly points out that whatever may be said against the character of political authority, it is certain that it is and always will be an absolute necessity among the civilised people. Secondly, Gandhi places too much reliance on the innate goodness of human nature. If man by his nature is social, rational and co-operative, he is also a self-seeker. The

18. Dhawan, *op. cit.*, p. 291.
19. Varma, *op. cit.*, p. 218. According to B.S. Sharma, "The state is justified in so far as it helps the realisation of the ethical ideal. But the state through legal enforcement cannot directly promote morality; it can only create conditions necessary for making morality possible. The primary requirement for a moral life is individual initiative and freedom. The structure of the state should thus be such as to facilitate the requirement. The necessity for legal enforcement arises because of human imperfection. The more the individuals have imbibed the ethical virtues of non-violence, the less the necessity of the state. Ultimately, therefore, in the ideal state compulsion should give place to individual initiative and voluntary organisation. This would mean the repudiation of state in any form whatsoever." *Op. cit.*, pp. 89-90.

competitive instincts in man are as strong and powerful as the instincts of love. Obviously, Gandhi expects too much like an idealist who sees only one side of the picture. Finally, the case of an ideal society as envisaged by him is wholly utopian. The form of a social organisation sketched by him as an ideal would be wholly inadequate to deal with the complex problems of the modern world. Hence, the view of Joad given in the case of western anarchism is equally applicable to the case of Gandhi that his whole indictment of the state and the scheme of future society "is necessarily vague because the theory, though simple in outline, exists in outline only."[20]

AHIMSA : POSITIVE IMPLICATIONS OF THE TECHNIQUE OF NON-VIOLENCE

One of the distinctive contributions of Gandhi lies in giving a comprehensive meaning to the concept of *ahimsa* cr non-violence. Instead of regarding it as a tenet of personal motivation and action like that of Buddha and Mahavira, he transformed it into a successful technique of direct mass action. That is, in Gandhi we find that the individualistic message of non-violence is transformed into a two-fold phenomena-personal as well as institutional. Since violence can be manifested both at the personal and social levels, naturally, in Gandhi's view, non-violence should be com-prehended from two sides. Evil thoughts, sentiments of revenge, brutality, verbal pugnacity, accumulation of unnecessary things, falsehood, trickery, intrigues, chicanery, deceitfulness, economic exploitation and stranglehold of others, excess of emulation and competition etc., may be cited as the examples of violence on a personal level, so physical punishment, conscriptions, compulsory recruit-ments in armed forces, wars etc. are the great instances of violence at the institutional level, ie., violence committed by the state. The salient characteristics of Gandhi's concept of non-

20. C.E.M. Joad : *Modern Political Theory*, p.111. Likewise, Lancaster sys that the anarchists "are so unrealistic that it is not possible to take them quite seriously. They make assumptions about people not justified, to put it mildly, by the conduct of any but a few saints."

violence may be summed up thus:

First, non-violence literally means doing no injury to others, but, in a wider sense, it implies a positive quality of doing good to others instead of refraining from doing bad. That is, it is not merely a negative act of refraining from doing harm to others, really it represents the ancient law of positive self-sacrifice and constructive suffering. Its aim is to love the enemy or opponent and to win him over by the force of heart. It is thus equivalent to positive boundless compassion and love. As the quality of non-violence is latent implicitly in all human beings as they all are sharers in the divine spiritual reality, so the supreme vocation of man is its purposive evolution. In Gandhi's own words, "Non-violence is, therefore, in its active form goodwill towards all life."[21]

Second, non-violence does not rule out the taking of life in every case. Gandhi sanctions the idea of killing a living creature in four conditions, viz, if the disease of the patient is incurable; if all concerned have despaired of his life: if the case is beyond the help of service; if there is no possible way to know the wish of the patient. Hence, on one occasion, Gandhi had a calf in his ashram poisoned, because its intense unbearable agony was beyond remedy. However, Gandhi does not merely stress on the element of intention. In doing so a reference to deed is equally necessary. In his own words: "To kill any living being or thing save for his or its own interest is violence, however noble the motive may otherwise be......A reference to both intent and deed is thus necessary in order finally to decide whether a particular act or abstention can be classed as non-violence."[22]

Third, Gandhi realises that normally a man should abstain from committing an act of violence, but there may arise a situation when resort to violence even by arms is a necessity. Thus, he appreciated the decision of the Government of India when Indian forces fought against the aggressors in Kashmir. In Gandhi's view, one has to destroy some life not only for sustaining one's own body but

21. Gandhi: *Young India,* Vol. II, p. 286.
22. Gandhi: *Young India,* Vol. III, p. 883.

also for protecting those under one's care. He says: "Even man's slaughter may be necessary in certain cases. Suppose a man runs amuck and goes furiously about with sword in hand and killing any one that comes in his way, and no one dares to capture him alive. Anyone who despatches this lunatic will earn the gratitude of the community and be regarded as a benevolent man."[23]

Fourth. non-violence is not a defence of the weak but a weapon of the strong. In the view of Gandhi, the sword is not the sign of strength but the symbol of fear and weakness. Fear generates suspicion and arrogance and its accumulation results in the formation of complexes and aggressiveness. Hence, non-violence yields no place to cowardice. It is the summit of bravery. Once Gandhi said that he could no more preach non-violence to a cowardly man than he could tempt a blind man to enjoy healthy scenes. In his own words: "A coward never risks his life. A man who would kill often risks it. A non-violent person's life is always at the disposal of him who would take it. For he knows that the soul within never dies. The encasing body is ever perishing. The more a man gives his life, the more he saves it. Thus non-violence requires more than the courage of the soldier of war."[24]

The comprehensive meaning of non-violence as given by Gandhi has five simple axioms: (i) that it implies as complete self-purification as is humanly possible: (ii) for man its strength is in exact proportion to the ability, not the will, of the non-violent person to inflict violence; (iii) without exception it is superior to violence in as much as the power at the disposal of the non-violent person is always greater and higher than he would have if he was violent; (iv) its force is always invincible; and (v) its ultimate end is surest victory.[25]

Besides, Gandhi not only lays down the simple axioms, he also summarises the implications and conditions of the success of the stupendous force of non-violence. These are:

---

23. Gandhi: *The Story of My Experiments with Truth,* pp. 291-92.
24. Gandhi: Young *India,* 18 Dec., 1924.
25. Gandhi: *Harijan,* 12 Oct., 1935.

(i) It is the law of human race and as such it is superior to the brute force; (ii) it lives in permanence with those who cultivate a living, true and unshakable faith in the force of love and God; (iii) it affords fullest protection to one's self-respect and is of no assistance in the defence of ill-gotten gains and immoral acts: (iv) its practice requires readiness to sacrifice all but self-respect; (v) it is a power which can be shared by all who have an unbending faith in the power of God; (vi) as it is good in the individual cases, so it is a boon for the collective masses.[26]

Finally, non-violence is an effort to abandon violence that is inevitable in man's life. The quality of non-violence that is calculated to take us on the onward path, must be spontaneous, must be the lowest minimum, must be rooted in compassion, must have discrimination, restraint, detachment at its back, and must lead us every moment on the path of good. So Gandhi says: "The religion of *ahimsa* consists in allowing others the maximum of convenience at the maximum of inconvenience to us, even at the risk of life. Everyone has to determine for himself the amount of inconvenience he is capable of putting up with. No third party can determine it for him."[27]

Finally, Gandhi's non-violence is not confined to the national sphere. It is applicable to the problems of internationalism as well. By national freedom Gandhi never means absolute independence which is inconsistent with progressive internationalism. On one occasion he said: "My notion of Purna Swaraj is not isolated independence but healthy and dignified interdependence."[28] In his view, interdependence is as much the ideal of man as self sufficiency, for man is a social being and his social interdependence enables him to suppress his egoism and to realise his oneness with the universe. The international organisation should be freely established and maintained by non-violence which can solve all problems of the world. A non-violent world organisation requires the abandonment

26. Gandhi: *Harijan,* 5 Sept., 1936.
27. Gandhi: *Young India,* Vol. II, p. 984.
28. Gnadhi: *Young India,* 26 March, 1931.

of armaments and of the use of force to defend people's rights. So strong is Gandhi's emphasis on the use of non-violence that he rabidly denounces the feasibility of war and hopes that even the furious aggressors can be checked by the force of non-violence. That is why, he advised the Jews of Germany to offer a non-violent resistance against the Nazi oppressors. In 1947 he advised the Jews in Palestine to offer *satyagraha* in front of the Arabs and offer themselves to be shot or thrown into the Dead Sea without raising a little finger against them. Thus, as a technique of defence against national or international aggressions, the need of non-violent resistance "is most pressing and its efficacy seems to be certain."[29]

Gandhi's doctrine of non-violence has been criticised on certain grounds. It has been called a doctrine of negation and exclusion. Lord Chelmsford characterised it as "the most foolish of all schemes."[30] Not only the foreigners but the Indian leaders as well, including the contemporaries of the Mahatma, have found fault with the implications of this doctrine so elaborately brought forth by him. In the first place, it is pointed out that the idea of non-violence did not originate with Gandhi and although he claimed himself to be an authentic interpreter of the tenets of Hinduism, his contention was always exaggerated. The Vedic tradition coming down from the epics of the *Ramayana* and the *Mahabharata* have justified the use of violence and discriminated between the righteous and unrighteous wars. "The conception of absolute *ahimsa* is a contribution of the creeds of Buddhism and Jainism and thus Gandhi seems to follow the creeds of Gautama and Mahavira and not that of Hinduism as a whole."[31]

Secondly, the theory of non-violence is too spiritual to be successful in politics in as much as it is contrary to normal human behaviour. No doubt, it is good to practise

29. Dhawan, *op. cit.*, p. 335.
30. Cf. Romain Rolland: *Mahatma Gandhi, The Man Who Became One with the Universal Being,* (Eng. Trans, by C.D. Groth), p. 81.
31. V.P. Varma says that in Hinduism there "is place both for violence and non-violence." *Op. cit.*, p. 103.

non-violence, but the use of violence cannot be ruled out to the extent Gandhi desires. History bears so many examples when the practice of non-violence ultimately implied the disintegration of the well-established empire and the consequent slavery of the people. Hence, during the days of second World War so many sober leaders like Patel, Rajaji and Maulana Azad detested the Gandhian insistence on the use of spiritual force against the forces of Germany and Japan. K.M. Munshi thus said: "The utmost that a man can do is to accept non-violence only to the extent to which he is able to translate it honestly into practice."[32]

Thirdly, even if it is admitted that the doctrine of non-violence has very comprehensive connotations and a practical idealist like Gandhi proved them with the practices of his own life, it may be alleged that there was a great contradiction in his own preachings and practices. Instances are not wanting to reveal that he unhesitatingly helped the British imperialism in armed resistance against its enemies. In 1899 when the British Empire was threatened by the Boer challenge, he raised a volunteer ambulance corps and served in several ways for the relief of Lady Smith. In 1906 he raised a stretcher bearer party during the Zulu revolt. In 1914-15 he raised an ambulance corps in London consisting chiefly of the Indian students. Not only this, for these great services he received decorations and his name was mentioned in the official papers. At a later stage, Gandhi himself realised the weakness of his actions and sought to justify them in the name of his want of experience and maturity. But the charge cannot be denied that a votary of non-violent resistance should thus "have

32. K.M. Munshi: *Akhand Hindustan,* p. 220. Even Mrs. Sarojini Naidu, who had nothing to do with violence, insisted on including a complete course of military training as an integral part of national education. She asked, "Is it not the saddest of all shameful ironies that our children whose favourite lullabies are the battle songs of Kurukshetra and whose little feet march gaily to the stirring music of Rajput ballads should be condemned to depend for the safety of their homes, the protection of their sanctuaries, the security of their mountains and ocean frontiers on fidelity and strength of foreign arms?"

co-operated actively with violent activities. It smacks of utter inconsistency in his conduct."[33]

Fourthly, another difficulty arises when the doctrine of non-violence comes face to face with a man who has no faith in the existence of God. Hence, when the doctrine is comprehensive enough to cover so many directions. it is also narrow enough to exclude the unbelievers in God and the non-followers of any religion. Certainly the doctrine of non-violence rooted in an unbending faith in the existence of God fails to find any favour with the school of atheists, particularly the communists.

Finally, it is pointed out that the doctrine of non-violence cannot solve problems at the international level. Certain it is that the problem of national defence can-not be solved by the Gandhian principle of non-violence in a world full of military activities. It is owing to this that his suggestions during the second World War were considered to be unsafe and hazardous. The British Government dismissed his idea of materialising the spiritual force against the Nazi menace and even his own colleagues scoffed at the idea of offering *satyagraha* to the Japanese soldiers. Keeping this in his view, even an admirer of Gandhi thus observes: "Some of the suggestions of Gandhi for the use of *Ahimsa* in world diplomacy appear unrealistic and unconvincing to me."[34]

SATYAGRAHA : A TRUTHFUL TECHNIQUE OF CIVIL RESISTANCE

Like the doctrine of non-violence, the theory of *satyagraha* has very comprehensive connotations. It is moral pressure for the sake of truth. If truth is the ultimate reality, then it is imperative for its votary to resist all encroachments

---

33. Lal Bahadur: "Gandhian Non-Violence and Non-Violent Non-co-operation: A Critical Analysis" in *Agra University Journal of Research* (Jan. 1962), p. 27. A well-known Congress leader K.N. Katju said in 1942 that the sphere of non-violence was limited to the region of private and personal affairs and that in public life, they were honoured only in the breach by the Congressmen themselves." See Gandhi: *Non-Violence in Peace and War,* p. 489.
34. Varma, *op., cit.,* p. 104.

on it. According to Gandhi, it is the imperative duty of the *satyagrahi* to make endless endeavours for the realisation of trulth through non-violence. Obviously, the Gandhian philosophy of *satyagraha* is a natural outcome of the supreme concept of truth. According to V.P. Varma, "It signifies a genuine, intense and sincere quest for truth which is God. It means an assertion of the power of the human soul against political and economic domination. *Satyagraha* is the vindication of the glory of the human conscience. Conscience does not stand for abstract inwardness or withdrawal from the world. Conscience reinforces the battle for the victory of social good. *Satyagraha* is based on an invincible belief in the ultimate triumph of divine justice and right."[35]

Saryagraha denotes the operation of soul force against all forms of injustices and oppressions. It is inconsistent with jealousy or hatred towards the opponent, for the opponent has to be converted and not coerced. The active non-violent resistance of the'heroic meek' makes an immediate appeal to the heart, for it constitutes the gentle process of conversion by love. As such, it is the inherent birth right of a person. However, its practice requires self-discipline and a readiness to bear all kinds of suffering. Gandhi postulates: "It is impossible to do away with the law of suffering which is the one indispensable condition of our being. Progress is to be measured by the amount of suffering undergone.....the purer the suffering; the greater the progress."[36]

Hence, the operation of *satyagraha* is a twofold blessing. It is like a double-edged sword which blesses both the killer and the killed. If it elevates the character of the practitioner, it also brings a change of heart in the opponent. If it purifies the sufferer, it also intensifies favourable public opinion. It makes a direct appeal to the soul of the oppressor. The deliberate acceptance of suffering for a greater cause not only purifies and ennobles the sufferer, but it creates a favourable situation of invincible potency whose dynamic

35. *Ibid.*, pp. 145-46.
36. *Ibid.*, p. 151.

effect almost physically compels the oppressor to yield to the demands of truth and justice. According to the conviction of Gandhi, the voluntary acceptance of suffering does make an appeal to the implicit moral sense of the oppressor and its intensity shows the hollowness of the moral foundations of the opponent's position.

Satyagraha is a weapon of the strong. To be a passive onlooker to tyranny and to allow untruth to prevail over truth is the negation of the sanctity of *satyagraha*. It has no room for timidity and if there is a choice between cowardice and violence, Gandhi prefers violence to the latter, because the use of violence shuns the situation of timidity. He is prepared to risk violence a thousand times rather than to have the emasculation of the race. Thus, the courage involved in *satyagraha* is the courage of dying without killing and is far superior to that involved in violence. In his own words: "For he who runs away commits mental violence: he runs away, because he has not the courage to be killed while he kills."[37]

Then, Gandhi's theory of *satyagraha* should not be confused with the tactic of passive resistance as practised by the Quakers. Passive resistance is a weapon to face enemy, but it does not rule the essentiality of having a pure and clean heart, nor can it be contemplated at a level other than political. But *satyagraha* pre-supposes the existence of a pure heart and its use can be contemplated at any level—domestic, social and political. Gandhi says: "Satyagraha differs from passive resistance as North Pole from the South. The latter has been conceived as a weapon of the weak and does not exclude the use of physical force or violence for the purpose of gaining one's end, whereas the former has been conceived as the weapon of the strong and excludes the use of violence in any shape or form."[38] Similarly, the *satyagraha* of Gandhi is different from the passive resistance of the Swadeshi period as professed by Tilak and Aurobindo. The salient mark of difference lies in the fact that while Gandhi accepts the absolutism of *ahimsa*

37. Gandhi: *Young India,* 20 Oct., 1921.
38. Cf. Varma, *op. cit.,* p. 150.

and presupposes strong faith in the existence of God and purity of heart, the leaders of the Swadeshi period used it as a political technique of limited application without denying the exercise of violence on moral grounds."[39]

According to Gandhi, the operation of *satyagraha* may take five forms. First is non-co-operation. Gandhi believes that oppression and exploitation are possible only on account of co-operation of the people. Non-co-operation with the evil-doer is a mild form, but it can be immensely potent when undertaken on a mass scale. The practice of non-cooperation may manifest itself in the forms of surrender of titles and honorary offices, refusal to attend the government offices and official functions, boycott of the state educational institutions, withdrawal of litigation from the courts, boycott of foreign goods etc. The second form is voluntary exile or *hijrat* from the place of tyranny. In Gandhi's view tyranny is a kind of plague and when it is likely to become oppressive, it is wisdom to leave the scene of such temptation. The third form is civil disobedience. It signifies the resister's outlawry in a civil or non-violent manner. Statutory enactments must be challenged if they are unjust and oppressive, but the manner of resistance must be sincere, respectful and based upon the spiritual conviction of the leader. The fourth form is fasting. In the view of Gandhi, it can be taken for penance and self-purification or for the purpose of resisting injustice and converting the evil-doer. But the practice of fasting requires purity of mind, discipline, humility and faith.The last form is strike. To Gandhi strike does not merely imply the closure of work, rather it is a voluntary and purificatory suffering to convert the erring opponent. Hence, the strikes must throughout be non-violent and peaceful and during the course of strike they should do some other work to feed themselves. They are also required to present their demands in very clear and honest terms.

In addition to this, Gandhi has also laid down certain important rules for the *satyagrahi*. These are: (i) harbouring no anger, (ii) suffering the anger of the opponent, (iii) neither retaliating nor submitting to a given order out of

39. *Ibid.*, pp. 150-51.

fear or physical punishment, (iv) happily conceding arrest and forfeiture of property, (v) defending the property under trust with all means even at the cost of life, (vi) abstaining from swearing and cursing, and (vii) not participating in any activity that insults or harms the feelings of the opponent. The purpose of Gandhi is to give a dynamic meaning to the theory and practice of *satyagraha* by laying stress on three things, namely, that the *satyagrahi* should not harbour ill-will or hatred towards his enemy; that the issue for which *satyagraha* is launched should be true and substantial; and that he must be prepared to undergo all kinds of humiliations, persecutions and sufferings."[40]

The theory and practice of *satyagraha*, as presented by Gandhi, may be criticised for being too rational, spiritual and metaphysical.[41] lt may be possible to understand the various implications of his *satyagraha*, it is certainly quite difficult, even impossible, to realise them in practice without being inconsistent at some stage. At different occasions Gandhi has himself used the phrases which create difficulty in presenting his thesis in a consistent form. For instance, he says: "In my humble opinion, the ordinary method of agitating by way of petitions, deputations, and the like is no remedy for moving to repentance a government so hopelessly indifferent to the welfare of its charge as the Government of India has proved to be."[42] It is inferrable from the above statement that Gandhi does admit the case of physical coercion, which he so stoutly denies at other places. Thus, a critic like Niebuhr says: "Beginning with the idea

---

40. Gandhi: *Young India,* 27 Feb., 1930. Truly, *satyagraha* is a moral force which exerts no power but influence and may be defined in the words of Joad as "the effect produced by one human being upon the mind and actions of another, not through fear of punishment or hope of reward, but by virtue of the latter's intuitive acknowledgement of intrinisic superiority." S. Radhakrishnan (ed.) : *Mahatma Gandhi—Essays and Reflections on His Life and Work,* p. 158.
41. C.M. Case points out that *satyagraha* may be a superior method theoretically, but in practice it is too idealistic as it "demands a stronger self-control, a more enduring solidarity of purpose, a greater capacity for passive suffering, a higher ethical development than most human beings have thus far attained." *Non-Violent Coercion,* pp. 406-7.
42. See C.F. Andrews: *Mahatma Gandhi's Ideas,* p. 337.

that social injustice could be resisted by purely ethical, rational and emotional forces (truth force and soul force in the narrower sense of the term), he (Gandhi) came finally to realise the necessity of some type of physical coercion upon the foes of his people's freedom as every political leader must."[43]

Then, Gandhian *satyagraha* may be criticised from another angle of vision. Gandhi very strongly defends the force of spirit or soul. If anything is repugnant to one's conscience, he insists, one should not submit and resist by the means outlined above. But a curious situation may arise when the decision of one *satyagrahi* is contrary to the decision of another. In such a case what would happen and how a compromise would occur to take place. Thus, C.M. Case regards the various means of *satyagraha* as the instances of coercion, because in them suffering, though self-inflicted, "aims at producing a dilemma in the mind of the opponent. Neither of the alternatives appeals to his desires or his judgement, yet he is compelled by the situation to choose between them. No violence or threat of violence is used against him, on the one hand, nor is he persuaded of the excellence of either alternative, on the other. Whichever he accepts of the alternatives, he remains unconvinced, either by the assent of his judgement to facts and reasons given in argument, or by a reversal of his moral outlook through the contemplation of suffering passively endured. He is coerced, non-violently coerced it is true, but coerced nevertheless."[44]

TRUSTEESHIP : EMPHASIS ON PSYCHOLOGICAL TRANSFORMATION OF THE PROPERTIED CLASS

Gandhian views on the private property system have a

43. R. Niebuhr: *Moral Man and Immoral Society,* p. 242.
44. C.M. Case, *op. cit.,* p. 402. The critics have sought the elements of mental and physical coercion in the *satyagraha* of Gandhi. Arthur Moore says: "I have criticised the high spiritual claim made for the theory of non-violent non-co-operation, because it drew a spiritual distinction between physical and mental violence. It is a method of fighting which is open to unarmed people, and is one at par with boycott and the strike, which are indeed parts of its technique....it is not a distinctly spiritual weapon any more than is armed rebellion or war." See Radhakrishnan, *op. cit.,* p. 192.

two-fold character. In the first place, these constitute a critique of the existing capitalist system, on the other, they speak of a new system which he calls by the name of trusteeship. In this regard Gandhi is critical of the modern capitalist system for reasons quite different from those of the modern communists, anarchists and socialists. Apart from condemning the evils of *laissez faire*, Gandhi is obviously unreconciled to the modern capitalist system of production and technological growth. He denounces the system of private ownership over the means of production because of its being iniquitious and rooted in violence. In very clear terms he says that the concentration and accumulation of capital into few hands is immoral and a kind of theft encompassing lack of faith in the encompassing goodness of the supreme divine being.

Hence, Gandhi desires to substitute the modern capitalist system with his novel concept of trusteeship. It should be noted here that although his conclusions bear some likeness with the doctrine of English liberalism, in the main there is the influence of Hindu scriptures. It is mostly based on the ideals of non-possession (*aparigriha*) as developed in the *Isopanishada*. It also conforms to the ideal of the *Bhagwat* which holds that we have a claim only to so much as would satisfy our hunger, otherwise desiring more than that is like theft deserving punishment.[45] Acknowledging his debt to the *Bhagwad Gita*, Gandhi once said: "I understand the *Gita* teaching of non-possession to mean that those who desire salvation should act like the trustees who, though having control over great possessions, regard not an iota of them as their own."[46]

The implications of Gandhi's theory of trusteeship may be summed up thus: In the first place, It applies with regard

45. See S. Radhakrishnan: "The Individual and the Social Order" in E.R. Hughes (ed.). *The Individual in East and West,* p. 127.
46. Gandhi: *The Story of My Experiments with Truth,* pp. 221-22. Gandhi is much influenced by the teaching of Christ who said: "Persons, then being God's one real concern, and their welfare being the end for which every thing can become human property exists and is held in trust from God, all life becomes a proving of loyalty and love to Him through loyal love to one's brother man."

to accumulated wealth and earnings beyond one's need. It insists that any superfluous wealth should be held in trust. It also implies an ideal of economic equality in the ideal state. Gandhi postulates that in the days of Rama Raj both "the barristers and the *bhangis* (sweepers) will be given equal remuneration,"[47] though in the existing society equitable distribution of national wealth should be justified.[48] To some extent like Marx, Gandhi desires 'from each according to his capacity and to each according to his needs'. In his own words: "Even as the individual members of a body are equal, so are the members of the society. That is socialism."[49]

Secondly, Gandhi insists on the equality of rights, not rewards. Like Aristotle, he is fully conscious of the differences in intellectual capacity of the people and so he sanctions the idea that more talented people have a justification for keeping a greater amount of wealth. Thus, he does not like to cramp the intellectual attainments of the people and allows them to make a full use of their talent in the interest of the community. He wants that the people, apart from making their earnings, should use their talents for the good of the community. In this way, Gandhi stands for the "socialisation of property as well as talents."[50]

Then, with this view, Gandhi detests the case of expropriating the wealthy class. Like Green, he recognises that property is a necesary condition for the free play of a capacity which can be exerted for the common benefit. What is required is the change of heart and thus the property holders should act not as the proprietors but as the trustees utilising the property for the benefit of the whole community. That is, the talented people should create wealth and property by their superior capability and retain and utilise it like that of a true trustee. The trustees should act not in their own right but in the right of the community and should be given a fair honorarium by the state commensurate with

47. Gandhi: *Harijan,* 10 Aug., 1947.
48. Cf. N. K. Bose (ed.), *Selections from Gandhi,* p. 77.
49. Gandhi, *Harijan,* 13 July, 1947.
50. Dhawan, *op. cit.,* p. 85.

the value of services rendered by them to the community. Hence, he warns that by abolishing capitalism, the society "will be poorer, for it will lose the gifts of a man who knows how to accumulate wealth."[51]

But Gandhi does not justify the modern capitalist system. He introduces the idea of trusteeship to retain the capitalist system, if its inherent evils are removed. The holder of the property is not the owner but a trustee devoted to the consideration of social good having the right to nominate his successor. But he admits that the choice of a trustee or his successor should be subject to final approval by the community or state. Thus, he is against inherited riches and unearned incomes. The misuse of the trust property should be set right by the state confiscating it with minimum use of violence.

Finally, it should also be noted that towards the end of his life Gandhi is more trenchant in his criticism of capitalism. Now he is not against the state resorting to confiscation of private property with the minimum use of violence and coercion when so necessary. If voluntary non-violent action fails, Gandhi sanctions state action as the last resort. In his own words: "What I would personally prefer would be not a centralisation of power in the hand of the state, but an extension of the sense of trusteeship, as in my opinion the violence of private ownership is less injurious than the violence of the state. However, if it is unavoidable, I would support a minimum of state ownership. Every vested interest must be subjected to scrutiny, and confiscation ordered where necessary with or without compensation as the case demanded."[52]

It is clear that, like Aristotle and Green, Gandhi has idealised the institution of private property though on different lines and in a different context. Obviously, the whole idea of trusteeship is either hypothetical or too spiritual meant for the 'enlightened few' and, if put into practice, it will furnish a very good ground to enjoy the benefits of private property. Man cannot forsake the charm

---

51. Gandhi : *Harijan,* 25 Sept., 1940.
52. Cf. Sharma, *op. cit.,* p. 138.

of his wealth. There is a good deal of practical truth in the comment of Machiavelli that a man may forget the assassination of his father, but he can never forget the usurpation of his property. So strong is the love for wealth and private property that one may hardly think of doing as Gandhi has suggested. In practice, Gandhian system of trusteeship will give a free hand to the Iords of private property.[53]

END AND MEANS : INTEGRAL RELATIONSHIP BETWEEN SEED AND FRUIT

Another great contribution of Mahatma Gandhi lies in the great significance that he attaches to the case of end and means. For him the end and means are closely related so much so that the former grows out of the latter. When an action in the full sense includes the motives as well as the effects, any separation of the two is a falsehood according to Gandhi. He wholly dismisses the contention that 'end justifies the means' and in its place propounds the view 'as the means, so the end.' In his own words: "The means may be likened to a seed, the end to a tree, and there is just the same inviolable connection between the means and the end as there is between the seed and the tree."[54]

Thus Gandhi attaches paramount importance to the

---

53. Even Nehru, who always professed to be a staunch follower of the Mahatma, expressed his frank disagreement on the case of trusteeship. He asked, "Is it reasonable to believe in the theory of trusteeship to give unchecked power and wealth to an individual and to expect him to use it entirely for the public good ? Are the best of us so perfect as to be entrusted in this way ? Even Plato's Philosopher-Kings would hardly have borne this burden worthily. And is it good for others to have even these benevolent supermen over them ? But there are no supermen or Philosopher-Kings, there are only frail human beings who cannot help thinking that their own personal good or the advancement of their own ideas is identical with the public good. The snobbery of birth, position and economic power is perpetuated, and the consequences in many ways are disastrous." *An Autobiography,* p. 258. Nehru cites Brailsford who observed that Indian usurers and landlords "are the most rapacious parasites to be found in any contemporary social system." *Ibid.,* p.535.

54. Gandhi: *Hind Swaraj,* p. 39.

application of means in every sphere. The state cannot attain its ideal character as long as the means are tainted with violence. In his own words: "For me *ahmisa* comes before *swaraj.*" Even in the political sphere full sanctity should be attached to the side of means, otherwise the end will not be consonant with the means. So close and inseparable is the connection between the two that, according to Gandhi. if one 'takes care of the means, the end will take care of itself' and that realisation of the goal is in exact proportion to that of the means. Hence, he asserts that "the attempt made to win *swaraj* is *swaraj* itself."[55]

SWADESHI AND COSMOPOLITANISM : IDEA OF OCEAN CIRCLES

Gandhi is an intense nationalist, he is also an internationalist. The spirit of sacrifice underlying his idea of *swadeshi* should go beyond a man's own community and embrace the whole mankind. The logical conclusion of self-sacrifice is that the individual should sacrifice himself for the community, the community for the district, the district for the province, the province for the nation, and the nation for the world. Thus, a man can serve his neighbours and humanity at the same time, the condition being that the service of the neighbours is in no way selfish or exclusive. This spirit of self-sacrifice implies that a nation is bound to help others in distress.

To Gandhi the state is not an end in itself but one of the means of enabling people to better their condition in every sphere of life. Thus, he frankly repudiates the view of Hobbes and Hegel that the state is the final goal of human civilisation. He does not consider the state in terms of exclusiveness, rather to him state is one of the means to secure the greatest good of all mankind. Obviously, Gandhi dismisses the Mussolinian dictum that there is nothing above or beyond the state. He adopts a humanitarian and constructive outlook and thus studies the state as nothing else than an instrument to further world unity and

55. *Ibid.*, p. 40.

prosperity. Naturally, he admires internationalism in these words: "It is not nationalism that is evil, it is the narrowness, selfishness, exclusiveness, which is the bane of modern nations, that is evil."[56]

It is in this context that Gandhi visualised the future role of India in world affairs. He said: "I want the freedom of my country so that the resources of my country might be utilised for the benefit of mankind. Just as the cult of patriotism teaches us today that the individual has to die for the family, the family has to die for the village, the village for the district, the district for the province, and the province for the country, even so a country has to be free in order that it may die, if necessary, for the benefit of the world."[57]

Then, Gandhi is not satisfied with mere peace in the world. He is quite insistent on the prevalence of international co-operation. He imparts a dynamic meaning to the idea of internationalism. His ideal is not isolated independence of a particular nation but a healthy and dignified interdependence in the international sphere. It is desired that the representatives of the component states unite under one central governing power. It must be a non-violent world organisation. Gandhi also wants an international non-violent police force to prevent sporadic outbreaks or conflicts. The non-violent international organisation will recognise the principle of equality and treat every state as a sister. It will work for the elimination of imperialism, destruction of war material, removal of racial segregation, and, positively, do much for the good of the entire human race. Finally, Gandhi realises that the new world order will take time to come and yet he is hopeful of the triumph of inter-nationalism over blind and aggressive nationalism of the present time. Indeed, his internationa-lism becomes

---

56. Gandhi: *Young India,* Vol. II, p. 1292.
57. Cf. Mahadev Desai: *Gandhi in Indian Villages,* p. 170. Gandhi identifies this situation with circles within circles formed by the waves of an ocean. So it is known as his theory of oceanic circles as contained in his *Hind Swaraj.*

cosmopolitanism.[58]

CRITICAL APPRECIATION : GANDHI AS THE MAKER OF SPIRITUALISED POLITICS

Though too rational, spiritual and metaphysical, Gandhi was a great personality of creative and constructive powers. His place in the history of political thought is definitely unique. The value of his philosophy does not lie in proposing institutional devices which might help to reduce individual and national conflicts. The value of his ideal consists in providing clear moral goals and rules for those individuals and nations who are willing to strive for them. His political philosophy is inseparably associated with his saintly life and thus it may be said that Gandhi is a politician among saints and a saint among politicians. M.S. Buch thus admires him: "Gandhism, like Hinduism, is a spirit, not dogma, it is and not a hidebound organisation. Gandhi himself is an erring follower of Gandhism, a devoted worshipper of the eternally valid, and yet eternally elusive ideals of the love of God and love of truth. Gandhism is not, therefore, a formula; it is an age-long passion for God directing Gandhi in ways peculiar to him, to realise Him in his service of humanity and of India."[59]

Gandhi was neither an academic recluse nor a power-hungry politician. He was a practical idealist who first thought, then preached and then experimented with it. He did not theorise in any historical vacuum or for any temporal audience. He and his addresses experienced the

---

58. It should be remembered that interdependence, according to Gandhi, is as much the ideal of man as self-sufficiency, for man is a social being and his social interdependence enables him to suppress egoism and to realise his oneness with the universe. In very strong terms he puts: "The better mind of the world desires today not absolutely independent states warring one against another but a federation of friendly interdependent states." *Young India,* 26 March, 1931.
59. Buch: *Rise and Growth of Indian Nationalism, Non-Violent Nationalism, Gandhi and His Schools,* pp. 4-5. According to Dhawan, the political philosophy of Mahatma Gandhi is very important, because it "is the most original contribution of India to political thought and political practice." *Op. cit.,* p. 4.

initial impact of the modern, technocratic, over-organised paradigm of politics. His audience was not confined to the East; it included the people of the West as well. What was needed for human emancipation was not any revised edition of the same technocratic paradigm of government (such as the fascist and Leninist-Stalinist systems), but an alternative, non-violent, educative, mass-based approach to democratisation."[60]

60. Thomas Pantham: "Beyond Liberal Democracy: Thinking with Mahatma Gandhi" in Thomas Pantham and K.L. Deutsch (ed.s): *Political Thought in Modern India,* p.345.

36

SARVODAYA

Real socialism has been handed down to us by our ancestors who taught : All land belongs to Gopal, where then is the boundary line? Man is the maker of that line and he can therefore unmake it. Gopal literally means shepherd; it also means God. In modern language, it means the state, i.e., the people. That the land today does not belong to the people is too true. But the fault is not in the teaching. It is in us who have not lived upto it.

— **Mahatma Gandhi**[1]

Socialism with its many varieties emerged as the most important principle of state activity as well as a way of life in the nineteenth and twentieth centuries. It had numerous adherents all over the world and their divergent and discordant interpretations created such a puzzling situation that C.E.M. Joad compared it with 'a hat that has lost its shape, because everybody wears it'. However, socialism with all its forms or manifestations, as developed in the West, had a thoroughly materialistic nature that was apprehensively looked at by those who lauded its essential features but denounced its means or methods to accomplish the goal. Mahatma Gandhi preferred to call it 'Sarvodaya' and sought to reinforce its essential tenets with the touch of spiritualism. Hence, Sarvodaya may be regarded as the spiritualised form of

1. *Harijan,* 2 January, 1937, p. 375.

socialism with its stern emphasis on the eternal values of liberty, equality, justice and fratenity having their source of inspiration in the sacrosanct character of the human spirit. It has its goal in the establishment of an ideal social, economic and political order based on the moral sovereignty of the people dedicated to the ways of non-violence (*Ahimsa*) and Truth (*Satya*) or God.

MEANING AND ESSENTIAL TENETS

Sarvodaya, literally meaning 'upliftment of all' is the most appropriate name of Gandhian socialism. It is the principle of a new philosophical, social, ethical, economic and political order whose aim, in the words of Gandhiji's spiritual disciple, Vinoba Bhave, is that all may be happy. It may be described as an extension of Gandhism at the hands of his faithful disciples and followers like Vinoba Bhave, Jayaprakash Narayan, Dada Dharmadhikari, Siddharaj Dhadha, Dhirendra Mazumdar, Shankerrao Deo, K.G. Mashruwala, etc. However, it would be wrong to call it mere 'socialism' in view of the fact that this term, as understood in the West, excludes what Gandhiji and his disciples have sought to infuse in it—the ethical and philosophical dimension of Indian spiritualism and culture. As Sampurnanand says : "I would like to begin by admitting that Indian socialism is not a very happy choice as a name .... Sarvodaya is another name which I might perhaps have used. It is the name chosen by Mahatmaji for what he considered to be the goal of all efforts in the field of public work. It means the *udaya* (upliftment) of all, *udaya* standing not only for material prosperity but also for spiritual good."[2]

The meaning of 'Sarvodaya' is very well explained in an official publication of the Akhil-Bharatiya Sarva-Seva Sangh as : "The objective of the Sarvodaya plan is the establishment of a Sarvodaya social order. Sarvodaya

2. Sampurnanand : *Indian Socialism,* p. 1.

is not content with the utilitarian doctrine of achieving the greatest good of the greatest number, nor does it believe that an inevitable historical process is polarising society into classes with nothing about conflicting interests, and producing forces that have only to be accelerated by the scientific application of violence to come to power and establish a classless society through a dictatorship. It is not a philosophy that regards the maximisation of material well-being as man's only measure of social progress. Sarvodaya, as the word implies, stands for the all-round well-being of all. It believes that institutions and relationships should be fashioned on the twin principles of Truth and Non-violence. It believes that the only enduring cohesive forms, that can weld men together in a society of the free and equal, are love and cooperation and not constraint and coercion. These forces can neither be generated nor strengthened by giving free play to the competitive and combative strains in man."[3]

The main tenets of the Sarvodaya philosophy as propounded by Gandhiji and subsequently reiterated and explained by the pioneers of this movement are:[4]

1. It reiterates belief in God and, what is really important, it identifies that belief with faith in the goodness of man and with service of humanity.
2. It accepts Gandhiji's ethical principles but lays greater emphasis on their social and positive aspects.
3. It provides a further clarification of the principle of trusteeship as implying the abolition of private ownership and the application of the principle of non-possession to public institutions is more pronounced in it.

---

3. *Ibid.*, p. 2.
4. V.N. Tandon : *The Social and Political Philosophy of Sarvodaya after Gandhi*, pp. 200-1

4. The philosophy of work and the principle of equality of all religions find better elucidation in some of these thinkers.
5. By their advocacy of the principle of consensus of opinion to arrive at decisions, they attempt to minimize the danger of majority tyranny over minority.
6. They are more vocal in their denunciation of political parties, and their idea of partyless democracy, though consistent with the ideas of Gandhiji, is quite a new development.
7. They develop Gandhiji's technique and organisation of constructive work, and his ideas on planning and satyagraha.

As we shall see, the philosophical, economic and political implications of Sarvodaya movement "is an attempt at the discovery and enshrinement of the soul of India and its fulfilment at the social and economic levels."[5]

PHILOSOPHICAL AND ETHICAL IMPLICATIONS

Sarvodaya aims at the spiritualisation of politics. It stands for integrating the principles of religion (*Dharma*) with politics. It thoroughly rejects the way of crass materialism and, for that reason, repudiates the Marxian tenets of dialectical and historical materialism and class struggle. As Jayaprakash Narayan says : "I feel convinced, therefore, that man must go beyond the material to find the incentive to goodness. As a corollary, I feel further that the task of social reconstruction cannot succeed under the inspiration of a materialist philosophy."[6]

5. V.P. Varma, *The Political Philosophy of Mahatma Gandhi* and *Sarvodaya*, p.6.
6. J.P. Narayan : *A Picture of Sarvodaya Social Order*, p. 6.

Vinobaji claims that the spiritual gnosis and compassion for human beings are the two cardinal concepts of Hinduism. This quest for the Vedantic foundation of Sarvodaya is in line with the devotion that Gandhi had for the *Isopanishada* and the *Bhagawad Gita.*[7]

In this way, Sarvodaya philosophy is in tune with the tenets of Indian culture. All great saints and seers have laid stress on the importance of moral values. Not only that, Indian spiritualists have also shown the way of action. Thus, Sarvodaya is not merely a philosophy of the ascetics and the hermits, it is a way of life of the practical social reformers and constructive workers. It manifests *karmayoga* of Gandhiji. As Prof. Varma says : "Our political, social and economic life has been seized with a malady. The malady of our times—perhaps of all times, is the mad quest for power. Sovereignty is preferred to cooperative activity and sufferings. Service is being given up in quest of personal aggrandisement. Humanity is thus undergoing almost a phase of moral collapse and ethical nihilism. In an era of the mad rush for power, the significance of Sarvodaya lies in stressing the permanent value of self-abnegation. It wants to replace party strifes, jealousies and competition by the sacred law of cooperative mutuality and dominant altruism. Party struggles have corrupted and perverted our political life. In its stress on the replacement of majority voting by unanimity in the village Panchayats, Sarvodaya is giving an expression to moral principle of cardinal importance, because it wants to enshrine the primacy of goodness and character in place of the skill of manipulation and self-assertion."[8]

---

7. Vinoba Bhave : *Bhoodan Ganga,* (Hindi) Vol. II, pp. 155-56.

8. V.P. Varma. *op. cit.,* p. 361. Society based on *Dharma* according to Gandhiji, is free from all evils : Gandhiji says : "I claim that human mind or human society is not divided into water-tight compartments called social, political and religious. All act and react upon one another". *Young India,* 2 March, 1929.

ECONOMIC IMPLICATIONS

Sarvodaya pleads for villagisation, decentralisation and gifts as those of labour(*shramdan*), of land (*bhoodan*), of wealth (*sampattidan*), and of big shares in village property (*gramdan*). It frankly discards the principle of 'nationalisation' of property by the action of the state with reasonable compensation (as advocated by collectivism or democratic socialism), or by means of force and without any compensation (as advocated by Marxian socialism); instead it appreciates the way of 'trusteeship' as given by Gandhiji. It desires the establishment of small village communities in the form of self-sufficing autonomous republics under the administration of Panchayats. Vinobaji puts forward divine theory of land ownership by reiterating that 'all land belongs to Gopal (God)'. In this way, it pleads for three things—repudiation of the proprietory possession of the non-producers, establishment of the proprietory possession of the producers, and neutralisation or negation of ownership.[9]

What is needed is that a man should be deprived of his right to property in the social interest by means of non-violence and Satyagraha so that there is a real change of heart. Thus, man should render voluntary labour for the good of the community in the form of his labour gift (*shramdan*), or should forgo one-sixth of his wealth for the good of the society (*sampattidan*). This should be the first step towards 'full trusteeship' system under which all commercial and industrial enterprises would belong to the community and there would be no employer and employee. As J.P. says :"Then the management and labour would have joint responsibility

9. Dharamadhikarti : *Sarvodaya Darshan*, p. 223. The four principles of Sarvodaya economy are — simplicity of life or a high standard of living, decentralisation, self-sufficiency and self-reliance, and cooperation and cooperative economy. According to Vinobaji, politics + science = annihilation; spirituality + science = Sarvodaya.

to run them not for themselves but for the good of the society as a whole."[10] Obviously, this is a new way of social revolution without imitating the ways of Western socialism of any variety. In the words of Prof. Varma : "If the *bhoodan* and *gramdan* are technics of agrarian revolution based on moral force, *sampattidan* is a significant path in the transformation of capitalism into the Sarvodaya society."[11]

The main features of the economic philosophy of Sarvodaya, as emphasised by Vinobaji, are :[12]

1. Elimination of poverty;
2. Awakening the feeling of affection and love in the hearts of the land-owners thus improving the moral atmosphere in the country;
3. Strengthening the society by forging bonds of mutual help and fellow-feeling, thus avoiding what is as a rule witnessed elsewhere in the form of class hatred between big landholder on the one side and uprooted landless people on the other.
4. Revival of furtherance of Indian culture based on our unique philosophy of *yagna, dana,* and *tapas*, thus strengthening the faith of man in true religion.
5. Building a new social order on the basis of voluntary bodily labour, non-possession, cooperation and self-reliance,
6. Giving an opportunity to all political parties in the country to come together on a common platform and work unitedly,
7. Helping world peace.

It is, therefore, clear that the Sarvodaya movement "seeks to build up a society with a bias towards rural

---

10. J.P. Narayan, *op. cit.*, p. 17.
11. Varma, *op. cit.*, p. 374.
12. Shrinivas Tilak : *The Myth of Sarvodaya : A Study of Vinoba's Concept*, pp. 265-66.

civilisation, in which industries would be decentralised and villages would be as self-sufficient as possible. The desire for a high but simple life would replace the recent craze for multiplicity of goods, cooperation would take the place of competition and community spirit would animate society."[13]

POLITICAL IMPLICATIONS

The Sarvodaya movement desires to put forward a new kind of politics what it calls 'lokniti'. The Western concept of *rajniti* (politics) signifies power, authority, control, administration, coercion, competition for power, role of self-seeking parties and groups and the like, but the concept of *lokniti* signifies self-restraint, self-abnegation, selfless service to the people, moral freedom, discipline, faith in God and performance of duties with a selfless thought.[14] Thus, it not only discards the ways of class struggle and use of violence for the seizure of power, it also condemns the system of majoritarianism and the role of political parties and groups in it. As J.P. says, the principle of consensus should prevail from bottom to the top in the selection of *lok sevaks* (people's servants) from village panchayats at the base to the above units of a pyramidal non-violent political organization. In the words of Vinobaji : "Rule of the majority is the law of the day; whether the majority has or has no scruples and character, it does not matter at all. Is not rule of the majority mere brute force?"[15]

According to the Sarvodayists, the principal demerits of party-democracy are rampant corruption and

13. Tandon, *op. cit.*, p. 117.
14. According to Vinobaji, the task of a Sarvodaya worker must revolve around six things—*vichar* (high thought), *acara* (correct moral conduct), *caritra* (life span), *caritrye* (morally principled way of life), *prachar* (dissemination), and *samchar* (wandering). In 1957 he was moved to say " "I am a reckless *fakir* (mendicant) who serves this world knowing well that it is a *mithya* (delusion)."
15. *Harijan*, 17 January, 1953.

violence emanating out of the mad scramble for power, creation of social and economic inequality and suppression of the will of the majority by the minority of the self-seeking politicians. It is all the more poignant in the case of our country which has an 'imported' system of democracy and, for this reason, has not been able to draw the natural affection and loyalty of the people. This system paves the way for party oligarchy and cabinet dictatorship. Instead, a new kind of democracy is needed having these salient features:

1. A person who has dedicated himself to this movement would not seek any elective post and his choice at the time of consensus formation should be reinforced by the force of his conscience.
2. Only genuine *lok sevaks* would come into the field to be picked up from local panchayats at the base to the national panchayat at the top with thana panchayats, district panchayats, and regional or provincial panchayats in the middle.
3. Different parties of today may join hands and take part in constructive social work; there should be no whip system so as to compel a member to act in a particular way even against his conscience; all should work in a spirit of complete harmony and sincere cooperation.

The anarchistic touch in the philosophy of Sarvodaya may be traced in its advocacy of a new or ideal social, economic and political order. In the view of Vinobaji, such an ideal edifice should stand on the pillars of the instinct of social service, self-reliance, equality of wages, and non-violent protection. The aim of Sarvodaya politics "is to see that all centres of power are abolished. The more this politics grows, the more the old politics shrinks. A real withering away of the state."[16]

16. Narayan : *From Socialism to Sarvodaya,* p. 48. The meaning of J.P. has thus been well brought out by an English writer. "The defect which J.P. sees in conventional democracy is that it is

The features of such an ideal society, as conceived by Vinobaji, are as under [17] :

1. International fraternity
2. Conscious, spontaneous (as far as possible) and hearty cooperation of all the inhabitants of the country.
3. Identity of the good of the capable minority and the general majority.
4. Orientation towards universal and equal development of all,
5. Widest possible dispersal of political sovereignty,
6. Easiest availability of *tantra* (justice),
7. Least possible expenditure,
8. Least amount of government,
9. Lowest degree of external protection, and
10. Universal, uninterrupted and neutral or objective spread of knowledge..

It shows that Sarvodaya as a political doctrine "is mildly anarchist. It regards the emergence of the 'state'

---

still government by a few over the many. It is based, he says, on an atomistic view of society which leaves the individual helplessly at the mercy of power imposed from above. Instead, all legitimate power comes from below and as little as possible should be delegated upwards. The two key objectives which he uses to describe this kind of democracy are 'communitarian' and 'participating'. A genuine pyramid of politics based on village communities must be created; the 'higher' organs of state power will be derived electorally from the lower bodies and will have only residual coordinating functions. In this way, all will participate in the making of the decisions. Not only that, by reviving local communities party politics will be slain and the divisive character of party democracy will be overcome; in the real community that is possible in smaller units, consensus is natural and a general will emerges without impediment from the competition for power." W.H. Morris-Jones : *The Government and Politics of India*, pp. 257-58.

17. Vinoba Bhave : *Swarajya-Shastra* (Hindi), p. 25.

as a form of social organisation as an improvement upon the earlier condition of violent anarchy. It marks a stage in the evolution of society from the condition of violence to that of non-violence. But it is no more than an intermediary stage, and the social fulfilment lies in rising to the higher condition when men would need no coercive authority at all to regulate their conduct".[18]

CRITICISM

What we have seen above may be described by the critics as the Indian version of 'utopian socialism'. It is a disputable point whether a modern democratic system would be able to work without the role of political parties. No matter there is a strong case for decentralisation, it is doubtful if it would be possible to have such a society when the whole trend is against it. Proposals regarding trusteeship system and complete decentralisation of all economic and political set up are nothing more than academic exercises. The Marxists would scoff at the whole school of Sarvodaya as one belonging to the world of Owenites and St. Simonians; the collectivists would not endorse the suggestion of a very little government in view of 'a man's life of minimum wants' and the liberals would have every reason to doubt the feasibility of an ideal society as conceived by the Sarvodayists.

But the leaders of the Sarvodaya movement have their strong convictions. Jayaprakash Narayan claims it as 'a distinct improvement upon the existing social philosophies and systems'. It cannot be lost sight of that the philosophy of Sarvodaya is so synthetic that it seeks to assimilate the best of the philosophies of the West and the East. It takes much from the spirit of Western liberalism and socialism and integrates it with the best of the spiritualism and humanism of the East. It assimilates all that is good and valuable in others so

18. Tandon, *op. cit.*, p. 123. Vinoba says : "Swaraj connotes a condition when none would exercise authority over anybody else." *Lokniti*, (Hindi), p. 176.

long as it is consonant with the ethos and spirit of the Indian culture and philosophy. Moreover, it preserves all that is of value in the culture of the past and seeks to assimilate it with what is valuable in the modern thought and practice. "And yet it represents no patch-work or even 'an intelligent combination of the principles somewhat divergent'. There is an organic unity in the whole of this philosophy."[19]

All critics of modern civilisation have come to realise the significance of envisaging a new pattern of life based on decentralisation of economic and political power ensuring moral freedom of man. As Erich Fromm says: "The aim of humanistic socialism can be attained only by the introduction of a maximum of decentralisation compatible with a minimum of centralisation necessary for the functioning of an industrial society. The function of a centralised state must be reduced to a minimum, while the voluntary activity of freely cooperating citizens constitutes the central mechanism of social life".[20]

19. Tandon, *op. cit.*, p. 199.

20. *Bhoodan*, 20 August 1960, p. 142.

37

ROY

M.M. Roy's general position in the history of socialist thought is that of an Ethical Revisionist. He began his academic pursuits as a Marxist but gradually almost completely restated all the propositions of Marx. But the basic point, nevertheless, in his 'Integral Radical Humanism" is not an absolutely novel construction but a moral restatement of Marxism. I think that his general theoretical position is comparable to that of the left-wing German revisionists. I regard Roy as the Indian Edward Bernstein.

—Prof. V.P. Varma[1]

Among the modern Indian political thinkers, M.N. Roy (1887-1954) may be admired for having a place of his own. Once a nationalist-anarchist, then a staunch Marxist (Communist), then a critical Marxist, and finally a radical humanist, his political ideas undergo a transformation after almost every decade. The remarkable point about him is that he becomes exclusively a man of ideas after renouncing all what he had experimented as a result of his association with the Communist Party of Lenin and Stalin, the Congress Party of Gandhi and Nehru and his own Radical Democratic Party formed in 1945. In the last phase of his life, he contributed a lot in the form of ideas

1. V.P. Varma : "Marxism and M.N. Roy" in *Indian Journal of Political Science*, Vol. XII, No. 4, 1961, p. 279.

which in the words of S.N. Ray, "convert him from a 'revolutionary philosopher' to a 'philosopher revolutionary".

SCIENTIFIC POLITICS

Roy's theory of a new model of politics, what he termed 'scientific politics', finds place in the post-Marxist phase of his intellectual career when he was in search of seeing something 'beyond communism'. The ideas of scientific politics had a 'germinal form' when he started thinking in terms of revising Marxism in the light of peculiarly Indian conditions after 1940. These, however, could come to have a concrete form after 1946 when he abandoned the path of even that revised Marxism and switched over to the world of integral or a scientific humanism. Roy's theory of scientific politics is, therefore, contained in his three important works, namely, *Scientific Politics, New Orientation* and *Beyond Communism to Humanism.* The keynote of all is to suggest that politics should be guided by a scientific philosophy of life. The stress of Roy "is on the social foundations of scientific propositions. He means by scientific politics, a system of political propositions based on the recognition of the class character of the upholders of divergent ideologies."[2]

Simply stated, Roy's theory of scientific politics aims at the rejection of spiritualism, nationalism, communism and even socialism as such and stands for the acceptance of materialism alone. He calls all other philosophies as 'heresies' or 'antiquated creeds' and declares materialism as the only 'possible philosophy', since it "represents the knowledge of nature as it really exists—knowledge acquired through the contemplation, observation and investigation of the phenomena of nature itself."[3] In

2. V.P. Varma : *Modern Indian Political Thought,* II Ed., p. 451.
3. K.C. Jena : *Contributions of M.N. Roy to Political Philosophy,* p. 104.

order to understand the theory of Roy's scientific politics, it shall be in the natural fitness of things if we first study his attack on all contemporary philosophies what he terms the 'heresies of the twentieth century'.

Roy's scientific politics means his relentless attack on the premises of religion and metaphysical philosophy what he calls 'the embodiment of human ignorance'. The main reason for the spread of religion was the ignorance of the people who could not have a rational study of the relationship between a concrete man and an abstract God. It was on account of the lack of education, and also because of the miseducation, that the people remained incapable of understanding the works of a refined order that had their first manifestation in the days of pagan antiquity and their resurgence in the early modern ages. It was due to this unscientific education and training of the human mind that the individual who wanted to escape from the field of rationalism found consolation in the sphere of supernaturalism. The peculiar thing about all this is that the tendency of religious consolation "was not imposed on man by any external agency—it was imposed on man by man himself. It was a creation of the human mind."[4]

Religion made man a spiritual slave. Man was given to understand about the existence of a life after death, about the possibility of a life in the heaven for those who obeyed the commands of the religious leaders, about the need for passive obedience to the decrees of the king who was the vicar of God on earth. Thus, religion entailed the era of spiritual bondage. The unfortunate state of affairs continued till the Renaissance and Reformation movements took place that delivered reason from the shackles of spiritual bondage. As against spiritual dogmas, the enlightened men started to offer natural and rational explanations for different natural phenomena. Man, for this reason, must have a scientific

4. *Ibid.*, p. 96.

philosophy of life which means that he should condemn religion as an instrument of exploitation and degradation. Even to talk in terms of reforming the religion would be an absurdity. "Once human mind has outgrown its infancy, when spiritual needs could be satisfied by the native nationalism of primitive religion, faith in the supernatural conceived either as many gods or one God or an impersonal Providence, places fetters on the possibility of human development. For the sake of further spiritual development— growth, moral uplift and cultural progress— they must burst."[5]

Freedom of the individual is one of the central themes of Roy's scientific politics. He would call any theory reactionary and antiquated which "attempts to sacrifice the individual at the altar of a collective ego."[6] All theories like those of Liberalism, Socialism and Fascism have refuted the fact of the sovereignty of man and, as such, they should be discarded. Says he : "In the modern world since the middle of the nineteenth century, the individual has completely disappeared not only from the frankly reactionary political thought but also from the so-called progressive and liberating political ideologies."[7] Nationalism also stands in the same row, since it emphasises that nation "is a metaphysical concept and yet human beings of flesh and blood must sacrifice everything to make the nation great and glorious"[8] He questions the logic of sacrificing man, a concrete reality, at the altar of a fiction—nation. "The nationalist psychosis is antagonistic to our philosophy. Nationalism cannot be reconciled with radicalism. A conscious nationalist will reject radicalism and be an honest counter-revolutionary, a conscious Fascist."[9]

5. Roy : *Reason, Romanticism and Revolution*, Vol. I, p. 114.
6. V.N. Ojha : *M.N. Roy and His Philosophical Ideas*, p. 205.
7. Roy and Philip Spratt : *Beyond Communism*, p. 132.
8. *Ibid.*
9. Roy : *New Orientation*, p. 42.

Roy's scientific politics calls for getting over the nationalist as well as communist psychosis. Thus, he is not merely a ruthless critic of spiritualism, he is no less a vehement critic of nationalism and communism. It should, however, be added here that Roy differentiates between Marxism as a doctrine and communism as practised in the former Soviet Union. And, while he rejects communism in its entirety, he tries to make necessary revision in Marxism in the light of his hard experiments, no matter the very attempt of modification amounts to its destruction. It is a different thing that Roy's attack on communism covers within its fold much that may be treated as his attack on Marxism as such. The result is that all tenets of Marxism coupled with their interpreted form at the hands of the Russian leaders has its thorough repudiation at the hands of Roy. While rejecting the theory of economic determinism of Marx, Roy says : "Man is greater than any means of production which are his creation."[10] He also refutes the theory of class war by adding that "no class is ever destroyed owing to its antagonism to any other class. Its abolition becomes necessary only when its interests become antagonistic to the welfare of society as a whole"[11] Moreover, there is a cohesive force in society or "some social interest which binds classes together."[12]

As an uncompromising critic of communism, Roy dismisses the theory of surplus value as well by adding that for the development of society it is necessary that everyone must produce something more than what is just enough for himself. Further, "a classless society will be stagnant.... In a classless society the dialectic will of history will cease to operate, progress will come to a standstill, humanity will die."[13] The attack of Roy

10. Roy and Spratt, *op. cit.*, pp. 103-04.

11. Roy : *Scientific Politics*, p. 66.

12. *Ibid.*, p. 83.

13. Roy : *New Humanism*.

on the theory of communism is much ruthless when he denounces the doctrine of the dictatorship of the proletariat as practised in the then Soviet Russia. As he says : "A political system and an economic experiment which subordinates the man of flesh and blood to an imaginary collective ego, be it a nation or a class, cannot possibly be the suitable means for the attainment of the goal of freedom."[14] Finally, the state can never disappear unless human society "will revert to the state of savagery."[15]

Following the tradition of a great Greek materialist thinker like Protagoras, Roy reiterates the old maxim that 'man is the measure of all things.' "What is perceived by man really exists, and that which cannot be perceived by him does not exist. Not only the existence of the inscrutable, supernatural force, is doubted, but the dogma of absolute truth and perfect knowledge is also refuted."[16] In order to add weight to his argument, Roy dwells on the researches of great materialists like Helvetius, Condillac, Lorenz, Oken, Lamarck, Darwin and a number of others who sought to defeat religion by the force of knowledge. He borrows extensively from Marx and Engels, but what he peculiarly adds to the stock of the philosophy of materialism is his integration of the role of ideas in the development of human society. As he says : "If we want to put man in the centre of the stage and measure all social progress by the degree of progress and freedom enjoyed by the individual in society, we shall have to discard this vulgar concept of the economic man and replace it by the concept of a moral man, a man who can be moral, because he is rational. This can be done consistent with materialist philosophy."[17]

---

14. *Ibid.,* Thesis No. 8.
15. *Ibid.,* p. 150.
16. Roy : *Materialism,* p. 57.
17. Roy : *Politics, Power and Parties,* p. 30.

Though Roy's materialism has a character of its own that may be construed as the very negation of what he so enthusiastically claims to profess, it would be sufficient to say at this stage that his scientific politics aims at having a kind of philosophy that embraces every aspect of human life. It is, correctly stated, the philosophy of radicalism that is much different from materialism and that, as Roy himself does, should be designated as 'physical realism'. This new philosophy "is a synthesis between the history of material progress and the dynamics of ideas."[18] It desires a new society, a free society based on the principle of universal brotherhood and the sovereignty of individual.[19] This is the voice of New Humanism, or Scientific or Integral Humanism.

In brief, the scientific politics of Roy is another name for his humanist politics. It desires the building up of a new social order based on the sovereignty of individual, having no collective ego like nation, class or party as an altar at which human freedom should be sacrificed, and working on the lines of a co-operative system so that the ideal of man's being the measure of all things is fully realised. This is the only solution to the crisis of the present times. It alone constitutes a new philosophical orientation.

One may say in defence of Roy's highly intellectual exercise in the form of his scientific politics that he, by virtue of being fully acquainted with the inadequacies of the various current 'isms', wanted to place before the tormented humanity a new outlook." Nevertheless, it cannot be lost sight of that the solution offered by Roy to the crises of the present times is highly utopian. It looks like the voice of a frustrated leader who, after getting nothing to materialise his long cherished ambitions, took to the path of an academic recluse and

18. Roy : *Politics, Power and Parties,* p. 30

19. Roy and Spratt : *Beyond Communism,* p. 164.

came to offer that is nothing else than the model of a highly alienated life decorated with the colourful philosophy of a rank hermit thinking and living in a world far off from reality and practical action. The result is that, like other great idealists, Roy instead of giving anything of practical value, finishes himself as an academic recluse. He ends neither as a Marxist, nor as an Idealist, nor even as a Materialist. "Renouncing Marxian dialectics was his first sin which is responsible for the chain reactions of his subsequent sorrows."[20]

PARTYLESS DEMOCRACY

The unanimous decision of Roy's Radical Democratic Party (formed on 21 Dec., 1943 to effect the 'crystallisation of the progressive urge' underlying the movement represented by the Congress during the twenty years) taken on 29 Dec., 1948 to dissolve itself and to form a comprehensive cultural political movement—described by the Royists as the Radical Humanist Movement—"may be regarded as the culmination of the long and arduous journey of a seeker after truth."[21] It shows that Roy now completely gives up the path of those who believe in creating a revolution by the use of party politics. Instead he becomes a convert to the last testament of Gandhi who had desired conversion of the Indian National Congress into a social service league to usher in a social revolution in the country.

Henceforth, Roy lived like a vehement critic of party politics and desired its substitution by the ideal of a partyless democracy. What the Founding Fathers of the American nation like George Washington, Thomas Jefferson and James Madison had said about the evils of party politics and what was realised by Gandhiji a little after the advent of independence and a little before his assassination was given an elaborate form by Roy in

20. R.K. Awasthi : *Scientific Humanism,* p. 74.
21. V.N. Ojha, *op. cit.,* p. 222.

his theory of partyless democracy. Roy shifted his stand from that of a party to a movement. A vehement attack on the evils of party system and its substitution by a new humanist order giving no place for the scramble of power now became the plank of his social and political philosophy.

Roy's thesis of partyless democracy has two faces—his denunciation of the party system and his design of a new social order in which there is no room for the scramble of power. His indictment of party politics is based on these points :

1. Roy rejects the view that democracy cannot be run without the mechanism of political parties. In order to prove that the parties are not co-existent with democracy, he argues that they have a recent origin. What is needed at the very outset is to dispel the wrong assumption that no political activity is possible without a political party. In order to give more weight to this argument, Roy says that there is no political party in a totalitarian state though every claim is made to establish this fact. In his view, a totalitarian Government is a partyless Government. Thus, democracy can run without the existence of political parties as it used to be before the coming of the party system.
2. The political parties stand for the scramble of power. They work on this assumption that no change in society can be brought about without a particular group of people coming to power. The basic aim of a political party is to gain power. What is really needed is not to jump into the scramble for power but to have the enlightenment of the people. 'Parties fight elections for the purpose of coming to power. Struggle for power results from the existence of parties. A party not in power or out of office may promise anything. But how can the people be sure

that in power it will also be corrupted?"[22] It is here that the violence of the mob, as pointed out by George Washington some two hundred years ago, takes place. Roy insists that power "is not the primary object of party politics; it is a means and there are other means;" and that party politics "leads to concentration of power and hence carries in it the germs of the destruction of democracy."[23]

3. The party rule means misrepresentation of the people. The party system destroys democracy by denying the individuals any significant opportunity for effective political action. Man as a voter has lost his sovereignty because of the role of political parties. In elections fight takes place not between man and man but between one party and another. Moreover, the party control takes away the freedom of the member and thus kills the individuality of man. He says : "As soon as, on one pretext or another, power is taken away from the people by delegation, even for the shortest period of time, democracy is killed. Power must always remain vested in the people; that is the only guarantee for democracy."[24]

4. The party rule signifies rule of the minority. It never amounts to the rule of the people as is so often claimed. Roy rejects the doctrine of implied representation as laid down by John Stuart Mill in his *Considerations on Representative Government*. Party system thus acts against the principle of the diffusion of power. In fact, a representative Government represents only the party which controls it and the membership of even the largest party is only a small fraction of the people.[25] Even

22. Roy : *Politics, Power and Parties*, p. 63.

23. *Ibid.*

24. *Ibid.*, p.84.

25. *Ibid.*, p. 67.

the members of the ruling party in parliament are not free to run the government, because they remain under the leading string of the party whip.

5. The political parties work for the good of the leaders in the name of the good of the people. It leads to dishonesty and corruption in public life. There is no harmonious relationship between the authority of the state and the liberty of the individual in such a situation. The net effect of the party system is destruction of the freedom of the individual that automatically entails the doom of democracy.

Roy is not merely critical of the party system, he also suggests a scheme of his new social order in which rule of the self-seeking opportunist party politicians is replaced by the role of the educated people. There will be a thoroughly decentralised order in which most of the functions of the present state will be performed by free and voluntary associations (co-operative societies) of the enlightened people. In such a new social order the state "will become no more than a clearing house of information, an advisory and administrative machinery to coordinate and supervise policies framed directly by the people as a whole operating through local people's committees. That is how the state will become identical with society, its function confined to an overall co-ordination and harmonisation of social life in a country as a whole."[26]

One may say with due emphasis that while the first part of this study dealing with Roy's denunciation of party politics is very clear and also very sound, the second one dealing with his design of a new social order is not. Like Anarchists and Guild Socialists, Roy leaves nothing more than a very dim and hazy picture of a new social order in which politics of power would be replaced by the politics of humanism.

Roy's theory of partyless democracy may be subjected to three lines of criticism.

26. *Ibid.*, p. 84.

1. He is unduly harsh and bitter in his attack on the system of representative government.[27] Keeping all the achievements of representative Government in view, it may be contended with a good degree of confidence that the system is not as bad as Roy pointed out. True, it has its own blemishes, it does not mean that it is destitute of all possible benefits. From practical experience, we may say that such system has succeeded in a country like Britain so much so that most of the countries of the world have not only appreciated it, they have tried to import it to the greatest possible extent.

2. The alternative suggested by Roy, though so hopefully, is not to be taken as a quite plausible one. It may be admitted that, for the first time, "a party was transformed into a movement through the voluntary will of the members of the party for the lofty ideal of pursuing politics on a higher level."[28] And yet it cannot be lost sight of that the alternative suggested by Roy is not as clear and workable as his attack on the present system. Carlyle ridiculed the legislators as 'talking asses' and Aldous Huxley said that the "political merchandisers appeal only to the weakness of voters, never to their political strength. They make no attempt to educate the masses into becoming fit for self-government; they are content merely to manipulate and exploit them."[29] Likewise, Roy scoffs at the role of modern parliamentarians as an 'empty ritual' in view of the fact that the executive, bureaucracy, committees of experts and the like decide most of the important issues.[30]

27. G.P. Bhattacharjee : *Evolution of the Political Philosophy of M.N. Roy*, p. 194.
28. V.N. Ojha, *op. cit.*, p. 230.
29. Cited in V.N.Tandon : *The Social and Political Philosophy of Sarvodaya after Gandhi*. p. 135.
30. *Radical Humanist*, March 4, 1955.

3. Above all, it may be pointed out that the contribution of Roy has been sparked by the failures and frustrations of his life. The tragic experience of the Russian Revolution "was possibly a potent factor leading to the rise of his concept of politics without party."[31] It is a fact that Roy left the Congress after he felt frustrated in his attempt to radicalise it in a way he so ardently desired and then he founded his Radical Democratic Party that was completely routed in the elections of 1945.

COOPERATIVE ECONOMY

Roy's economic philosophy shows his disagreements with all the existing schools like capitalism, socialism, communism, Fascism and democratic socialism; it also represents his reinterpretation of classical liberalism in a way that the essential points of economic development are reconciled with the values of human freedom. The tenets of co-operative farming, and co-operative economic decentralisation are welded together in a peculiar way that the economic order, as desired by Roy, represents the reconstruction of Indian economy *vis-a-vis* the reconstruction of Indian polity. Economic democracy is thus integrated with political democracy in a way that competition is replaced by co-operation, planning is reconciled with freedom and, above all, co-operative socialism "is offered as a substitute to Communism on one side and to capitalism on the other."[32]

Before coming to the subject of Roy's economic philosophy of co-operative socialism, we may look at the points of his attack on the prevailing doctrines in this regard. First, we refer to his critique of the capitalist economy. According to him, capitalism lays too much stress on the concept of 'economic man'. Its emphasis on

---

31. Bhattacharjee, *op. cit.*, p. 198.

32. K.C. Jena, *op. cit.*, p. 115.

the factor of 'free enterprise' falsifies the ideal of human freedom. It is wrong to say that man is motivated by his economic interests. If this is so, he is bound to be a slave or a slave-holder. The school of capitalist economy justifies the case of free competition that leads to gross economic inequalities and exploitation of man by man. He very strongly asserts that the practice of the *laissez faire* economy has reduced the individual to a helpless position.[33] It is this unfortunate state of helplessness that "has killed the spirit of a democracy and created an atmosphere favourable for the rise of collectivism."[34]

Roy's critique of socialist economy is equally relentless. His criticism of the doctrine of socialism is contained in his frank affirmation that 'that government is the best which governs the least'. He hits at the inadequacies of the doctrine of state control as so ardently desired by the socialists. Instead of entrusting the state with the duties of having superintendence, direction, control, regulation, interference and ownership in economic matters, it should be deprived of all of them. The extension of state control necessarily leads to concentration of power in the hands of the political organisation that results in the diminution of individual freedom. Roy asserts that there is no guarantee that the vast powers enjoyed by the state in the name of economic betterment of the people would be used for the eradication of gross inequalities of wealth or elimination of exploitation of the many poor by the few rich.

Allied with this is Roy's attack on the communist system. His practical experiments with the system of the Soviet Russia drove him home the fact that the model of communist economy was more pernicious than the model of socialist economy. Concentration of political power signifies the accumulation of economic power as

---

33. Roy : *Reason, Romanticism and Revolution,* Vol. II, p. 255.
34. G.P. Bhattacharjee : *Evolution of Political Philosophy of M.N. Roy*, p. 216.

well. The liberty of the individual is mercilessly crushed by the all-powerful state determined to bring about a new social order by means of centralised planning. There is no room for initiative, there is no place for willing co-operation.

In addition, Roy disproves the case of mixed economy that is described by its ardent protagonists as a judicious mixture of the doctrines of capitalism and socialism culminating in the concept of welfare state. Roy admits that mixed economy is a distinct departure from the *laissez faire* economy in as much as it accepts active interference in the economic affairs by the state and, at the same time, it does not go to the extent of rejecting free enterprise and its supposed benefits. It, however, is not a real alternative either to capitalism or to socialism. The state should not act like an entrepreneur, planner, adjudicator and public benefactor. Human exploitation goes on even in a welfare state for the obvious reason that there is no room for co-operation when planning is imposed from the top and public sector dominates private sector in the name of general good. Curiously, mixed economy is essentially 'a modus vivendi' that combines within itself the evils of both—capitalism and socialism—and, more than that, gives place for additional evil resulting from the adjustment between the two artificial sectors.

Centralised planning whether on the Soviet model or of any other totalitarian state like that of Fascists and the Nazis is thoroughly rejected by Roy for the obvious reason that it signifies ruthless suppression of human initiative. Roy "does not permit the individual freedom to be jeopardised by considerations of technical efficiency. If modern technological trends preclude such reconciliation, Roy would like to curb and make them amenable to human welfare."[35]

35. D.C. Grover, *M.N. Roy : A Study of Reason and Revolution in Indian Politics*, p. 63.

Whereas Roy attacks the systems of capitalist and socialist economies or a peculiar combination of them in the name of democratic socialism for the reason of suppression of individual freedom, he rejects the system of Gandhian economy in the name of its being absolutely reactionary and a demonstration of economic ignorance. He ridicules '*charkha*' (spinning wheel) as wasteful employment of labour and a model of the 'god of economic ignorance'. According to him, Gandhian economics can not solve the gigantic economic problems of India like those relating to poverty and exploitation. Instead of returning to the ideal of primitive economy as desired by Gandhi, Roy lays emphasis on the need for industrialisation of the country on the lines of modern economic development.

Roy is not merely a vehement critic of the prevailing economic systems, he also offers his own scheme of a new economic order where co-operation, decentralisation and planned development are the three hallmarks. It may be said that Roy's economic philosophy could not have a clear cut form until he evolved the concept of co-operative economy in 1951. Prior to this, he looks like wandering in search of a panacea for the evils of the Indian economic system. His criticism of the Planning Commission established by the Government of India in 1950 and of the First Five Year Plan framed by it in 1951 manifested a clear change in the direction of his frank approval of a system of co-operative economy.

Roy's economic philosophy has three essential characteristics :

1. He stands for, what he himself calls, 'co-operative economy'. The element of co-operation forms an integral part of human nature. As such, this element should be emphasised as the key factor in the sphere of economic reconstruction. Co-operation is not an innocuous supplement to socialism or capitalism but a powerful rival to both. The entire economic activity shall be

conducted by the multi-purpose co-operative societies at all levels—local, regional, provincial and national. Thus there shall be a pyramidal structure at the district, regional, provincial and national levels. This work of consumers and producers co-operatives built up from the bottom will be assisted by the government as the state will administer public finance. When the agriculture and allied industries have been developed, large-scale industries that cannot be developed locally, will be developed with the help of the surplus pooled by these co-operative societies.

2. Roy's scheme of co-operative economy desires not a rigid but a highly flexible system of planning. He terms centralised planning or any scheme of economic development designed and implemented by the state as 'rigid'. In order to be flexible, planning should be from the bottom and that too through the network of co-operative societies. As per the requirement of an essentially democratic system, the work of planning should be sufficiently restricted to permit all the residents falling within the jurisdiction of the co-operative society to participate actively in the formulation and implementation of the scheme of economic development. What is basically needed is that the work of planning should remain integrally connected with the ideal of freedom.

3. Roy tries to establish a workable balance between his emphasis on the role of co-operative societies and the need for economic development on modern, scientific and technological lines. The state is authorised to establish some control over large industrial establishments alongwith performing the role of a supervisor and co-ordinator of the economic activities of the country. According to Roy, some such form of co-operative economy is needed in which production is carried on in units which are not too large, but large enough to allow the application of power and modern machines and which avoids all unnecessary centralisation. However, he does

admit that for certain basic industries like power, production, steel, coal and transport, a degree of centralisation cannot be avoided. It is this unavoidable centralisation that he "wants to counterbalance by the political structure, which will deprive the state of overriding power, except of co-operating all social needs and activities."

The economic philosophy of Roy looks like an attempt to reconcile the problem of economic development with human urge for freedom. Though we may find out some serious efforts made by him in this direction, the fact remains that his economic philosophy is not free from certain weaknesses and contradictions. We may appreciate his emphasis on decentralisation and dispersal of industries throughout the country, instead of localising them in a few selected areas and his stress on the medium sized mechanical industries rather than on the large-scale enterprises that would go a long way to solve the problems of a mass society ridden with the conditions of feudalism and under-development, it may still be pointed out that the scheme of co-operative economy, as envisaged by him, is quite hazy. A complete picture of the desired system is missing and many important questions remain unanswered. For instance, it is not clear as to how the state will be capable of performing functions of supervision and co-ordination without taking recourse to the action of interference in the sphere of co-operative societies. Who will run industrial units and by what standards the profits be shared? Even the successors of Roy have not been able to present a unanimously accepted plan of economic reconstruction that may be described as the model of a co-operative economy.[36]

The greatest difficulty with Roy is that his solution leads us to nowhere. Whatever contribution he tries to render provokes us to make further enquiry that

36. B.S. Sharma, *The Political Philosophy of M.N. Roy*, pp. 96-97.

irresistibly leads to a critical study of his economic philosophy. The reason is that Roy "stops at a most inopportune bend." The criticism of a learned authority on the social and economic ideas of Roy is thus justified when he adds : "In theory, he (Roy) presents a praiseworthy utopia, where man is the maker of his destiny, planning combined with democracy and individual freedom, where man has the responsibility for his choice of relief and conduct, his inventiveness and initiative, his varied resourcefulness and personality are not swamped. But when faced with brass facts of reality, where one has to go to details, there arise "confusions and disagreements to which his theory gives rise."[37]

CULTURAL REVOLUTION

As in other directions so here, we find that although starting with the Marxian definition of 'revolution', Roy "so completely changes its content as to deprive it of all its original meaning, and emerges as an advocate of liberal philosophy."[38] What, above all, remains Marxian in him at this stage is his conviction that revolution is a determined process of nature. However, his distinctly un-Marxian explanation finds place in his forceful reiteration that revolution is a change brought about through the agency of human will. Freedom once again remains the passion with him to indicate that, to him, the end is not revolution but freedom. "Any theory of revolution that restricts freedom is to be rejected. Roy claims to have given a theory of revolution which secures maximum freedom. Man has an innate urge for freedom. Potentially and by nature he is rational and moral. Theory of revolution should be based on this concept of human nature. In order to bring about a revolution, what is to be done is not violence or insurrection or capture of State power by any other means. That will

37. Awasthi, *op. cit.*, p. 247.

38. B.S. Sharma : *Radical Humanism of M.N. Roy*, p. 104.

not bring about the desired end. Only man's urge to freedom is to be awakened."[39]

The main features of Roy's theory of revolution may be summed up in the following manner :

1. The emphasis of Roy is on social dynamism caused by, what he calls, undying human spirit. "Once a man creates an intellectual value of any abiding significance, nothing can destroy it, and that is the only spring of human progress, everything else is merely instrumental and subsidiary."[40] Thus, Roy rejects the premises of dialectical materialism of Marx in as much as he lays stress on the role of ideas. As he says : "Revolutions are heralded by inconcolastic ideas conceived by gifted individuals. A brotherhood of men attracted by the adventure of ideas, keenly conscious of the urge for freedom, fired with the vision of a free society of free men and motivated by the will to remake the world.... will show the way out of the contemporary crisis...."[41]

2. Second, and it follows from the above, the harbingers of a revolution are 'gifted individuals' banking upon the sincere support of the people who have no vested interest in maintaining the *status quo.* The leadership must be in the hands of the middle class intelligentsia who have outgrown their class interests and, by virtue of this, they think in terms of the good of the human society as a whole, and are moved to action by that sentiment.

3. A revolution as such should be preceded by a philosophical revolution. If man is the maker of history, man must first be made. Not the institutions but the philosophy will change man. The job of Roy's philosopher-revolutionaries is thus to

39. R.K. Awasthi, *op. cit.,* p. 261.

40. *Ibid.,* p. 251.

41. Roy : *Reason, Romanticism and Revolution,* Vol. II. p. 310.

revolutionise the outlook of the people and bring about a philosophical regeneration. While referring to the record of spiritual revolts, he asserts that these events have always preceded great social changes throughout the course of history. In other words, Roy suggests a theory of education to act as the motivating force behind the occurrence of a revolution. The ideal of revolution becomes the education of man. A social structure should be kept untouched until a philosophical revolution has taken place.

4. It is obvious that the lever of social progress or revolution is not class war but philosophy. The crucial issue is not to eulogise or denounce a bourgeois or a proletarian revolution; it is to bring about a philosophical revolution. Moreover, it is not necessary that change must be total *i.e.,* the old order be destroyed for the sake of revolutionary construction. Once again, Roy becomes anti-Marxist. There is a revolution when we find that even in the most adverse circumstances, it is possible to create something new if we go on creating something good in the midst of established order. Revolution implies a long-term change, no matter he has, at several stages, endorsed that it signifies 'sudden change'. The meaning of revolution thus identifies itself with the implications of reform. And yet the spirit of a revolution remains when we find Roy insisting on the idea of ever change. He is against the idea of *status quo.* Every revolution ultimately establishes a new *status quo* and human progress demands that every *status quo* must be subverted, otherwise history would come to a stop.

5. Roy's theory of revolution has a moral sanction. It has nothing to do with the factor of violence or the role of a political party working as the vanguard of a class conscious proletariat. There is nothing like scramble for power. As he says, morality in public

life "presupposes a political theory which does not make capture of power the precondition for any necessary social change; and new political theory must be deduced from a social philosophy which restores man in the place of primacy and sovereignty."[42] What is, therefore, to be done concretely, "is to replace the economic man by moral man by harmonising planned economy with individual freedom."[43]

6. Roy's theory of revolution has a scientific character. There is no place for mysticism or supernatural forces to play their part in effecting social progress. Revolution presupposes the existence of a scientific knowledge. Change can be brought about by man alone when he knows his inherent potentialities as the maker of history. A revolutionary is not an academic recluse or a cloistered hermit believing in the existence of some divine agency that alone brings about social change. On the contrary, a revolutionary is one who is convinced that this world can be made and remade by man and not by any mystical or metaphysical agency.

7. Roy's theory of revolution shows that the dynamics of ideas run parallel to the social evolution, the two influencing each other mutually. One may say that Roy, though a well-known monist, becomes a dualist here, since he lays emphasis on two things—the movement of ideas and the pace of social evolution. Such a statement is, however, misleading. Roy is a monist though his monism may be designated as 'pluralistic monism."[44] What he really desires to tell us is that the movement of ideas and the pace of social evolution should be treated as 'two currents in the integral process of human evolution; the two together constitute human evolution.'

42. Roy : *Reason, Romanticism and Revolution,* Vol. II. p. 253.

43. Grover, *op. cit.*, p. 171.

44. See V.N. Ojha : *M.N. Roy and his Philosophical Ideas*, p. 302.

What is really needed is that there should be no nation-states so that the entire world can be taken as a united human family. The very term 'internationalism' presupposes the existence of nation-states. Roy, like Tagore, believes in universalism, though he moves much ahead of him in saying that his humanist world order stands for the unification of the entire human race without any distinction of religion, colour or place of birth and the like and that great intellectuals alone can bring about such a new order in which the whole mankind "is united as a single family."[48]

It is understandable that Roy is a vehement critic of the doctrine of nationalism. While Tagore called it a 'menace', Roy calls it an 'antiquated cult'. The reason behind it is that he designates every theory as reactionary and antiquated that attempts to sacrifice individual at the altar of some collective ego. Nationalism thus becomes synonymous with other pernicious doctrines like Fascism, Nazism, Socialism and Communism which deny the sovereignty of the individual. As he is says : "Nation is a metaphysical concept, yet human beings of flesh and blood must sacrifice everything to make the nation great and glorious..... That is to sacrifice a reality at the altar of a fiction, of an illusion."[49] Again: "The nationalist psychosis is antagonistic to our philosophy. Nationalism cannot be reconciled with Radicalism. A conscious nationalist will reject Radicalism, and be an honest counter-revolutionary, a conscious Fascist."[50]

Cosmopolitan humanists of the European Renaissance or other spiritual successors like Voltaire, Diderot, Geothe and Heine can be actualised..... A cosmopolitan commonwealth of free men and women is a possibility. It will be a spiritual community not limited by the boundaries of national states, capitalists, fascists or of any other kind, which will gradually disappear under the impact of cosmopolitan humanism." *Ibid.*, p. 195.

48. K.C. Jena : *Contributions of M.N. Roy to Political Philosophy*, p. 95.

49. Roy and Spratt : *Beyond Communism*. p. 132.

50. Roy : *New Orientation*, p. 42.

What strengthened the convictions of Roy in this direction was the emergence of a new kind of tension at the international level. It was the cold war between the two giants—the United States and the Soviet Union. It, indeed, presented a very distressing situation for him and resulted in carrying his criticism of nationalism to the sphere of internationalism. As such, he appeared as a vehement critic of bipolar diplomacy played by the two super-powers of the world each having the destructive potentialities of a modern nuclear war. However, what is noticeable here is that he became more a critic of the Communist than that of the American bloc the reason of which should be traced in his fears of the communist infiltration in the regions of South-East Asia. The rise of Communism in China in 1949 cemented his conviction in this regard.

It should, however, be made clear at this stage that while Roy can be found condemning the designs of the Communist bloc, he is not at all an admirer of the American foreign policy. He desired that the people of a country should have the freedom to determine their political destiny and as any foreign intervention, whether in the form of economic assistance like Marshall Plan or Truman Doctrine or in the form of an armed infiltration as done by the United States in Korea, was uncalled for. For this reason, he dubbed the American foreign policy as essentially aggressive. It all signified a new form of colonialism as the countries of Europe and Asia by accepting economic or military aid would be subjected to American political pressures.

What is the way out? Like Nehru, Roy emphasised the idea of a Third Force. Only a strong force neither pertaining to American democracy nor to Russian communism could prevent clash between two contenders for world domination. It may, however, be made clear that Roy's design of neutrality is fundamentally different from what Nehru termed non-alignment. Though Roy's concept of the Third Force has nothing to do with any partisan alignment like Nehru's non-alignment, it does signify studying each issue on its own merit irrespective of the consideration of national interest. Nothing but the interest of the entire human race should count.

Roy desired a new world based on the premises of economic freedom and democracy. A truly neutral policy would be that presupposes a national economy not depending on foreign assistance. In other words, Roy emphasised that foreign economic assistance was the shrewd way of spreading the tentacles of colonialism or communism. It was obviously the best defence against the onward march of communism. However, as communism also stood for the economic emancipation of man, it was simultaneously needed that the system of democracy should prevail. Moreover, classical democracy would not serve the purpose; liberalism and representative democracy had their days; what is needed now is the democracy of a new type—Radical Democracy—that would serve as an alternative to communism. Further progress of human civilisation calls for neither the return to the good old days of liberalism, nor adoption of the existing parliamentary capitalist democracy, the third alternative calls for the elimination of both for a new one.

Going ahead in this direction Roy emerges as an advocate of World Government. It should not be composed of the governments of the nation-states, because these (nation-states) should be dissolved in the new humanist order. Nation-States cannot serve as the genuine units of a new world order. The League of Nations failed as its constituent members being nation-states pulled in different directions. Likewise, the United Nations is suffering from the tragedy of national antagonisms. For this reasons, he named the United Nations as 'Dis-United Nations' and added with full confidence that a world composed of nation-states could never have peace as, even during normal times, they carried on war through diplomacy and political commit-

CRITICAL APPRECIATION

Roy left for us a philosophy having academic significance along with a small group of his sincere protagonists who hopefully look forward to a day when people will remember him and forget Marx. He was rigorously scientific and analytical and, that is why, he was able to make predictions which often came to be true. Roy had intense passion for freedom and his search for truth led him to seek new ways and to reject the old ones which he found inadequate to achieve freedom and truth. One may or may not agree with Roy, but through sheer force of logic and scientific study he compels one to take note of what he propounds. His concept of grass-roots democracy and decentralisation, his optimistic faith in the so-called illiterate common man's ability to change society are a few examples.

However, it may be commented that Roy ultimately offers us a utopia or something against which he stood throughout his life. By no means he can be ranked in the category of great Indian leaders like Narendra Deva, Rammanohar Lohia and Jayaprakash Narayan who identified themselves with the masses and their downtrodden conditions and thus they could be able to understand what practical statesmen and social thinkers like Gandhi and Nehru called the political reality of this poor and backward country. The message of freedom can be understood only by those who have something to eat. Roy, instead of solving the gigantic problem of bread and butter, dabbles himself into the problem of freedom. Here lies his greatest weakness. It, therefore, leads to the issue of relevance of his social and political philosophy. We may conclude with this observation of one who has shown a proof of his understanding Roy and then critically examining his philosophy of reason and revolution in Indian politics. "It may be reasonable to conclude that if liberalism survives in India, Roy should be remembered periodically as its most disinterested champion."[54]

54. Grover, *op. cit.*, p. 175.